THE ORIGIN OF TYRANNY

BY

P. N. URE, M.A.

GONVILLE AND CAIUS COLLEGE, CAMBRIDGE
PROFESSOR OF CLASSICS, UNIVERSITY COLLEGE, READING

CAMBRIDGE
AT THE UNIVERSITY PRESS
1922

In the interest of creating a more extensive selection of rare historical book reprints, we have chosen to reproduce this title even though it may possibly have occasional imperfections such as missing and blurred pages, missing text, poor pictures, markings, dark backgrounds and other reproduction issues beyond our control. Because this work is culturally important, we have made it available as a part of our commitment to protecting, preserving and promoting the world's literature. Thank you for your understanding.

PREFACE

THE views expressed in the following chapters were first published in the *Journal of Hellenic Studies* for 1906 in a short paper which gave a few pages each to Samos and Athens and a few sentences each to Lydia, Miletus, Ephesus, Argos, Corinth, and Megara. The chapters on Argos, Corinth, and Rome are based on papers read to the Oxford Philological Society in 1913 and to the Bristol branch of the Classical Association in 1914.

As regards the presentation of my material here, it has been my endeavour to make the argument intelligible to readers who are not classical scholars and archaeologists. The classics have ceased to be a water-tight compartment in the general scheme of study and research, and my subject forms a chapter in general economic history which might interest students of that subject who are not classical scholars. On the other hand classical studies have become so specialised and the literature in each department has multiplied so enormously that unless monographs can be made more or less complete in themselves and capable of being read without referring to a large number of large and inaccessible books, it will become impossible for classical scholars to follow the work that is being done even in their own subject beyond the limits of their own particular branch. For these reasons ancient authorities have been mainly given in literal English translations, and when, as happens in almost every chapter, information has to be sought from vases, coins, or inscriptions, I have tried to elucidate my point by means of explanatory descriptions and illustrations.

The work has involved me in numerous obligations which I gladly take this opportunity of acknowledging. In 1907 I received grants from the Worts travelling bachelors' fund of Cambridge University and from Gonville and Caius College to visit Greece for the purpose of collecting archaeological evidence upon the history of the early tyranny. This purpose was partially diverted because shortly after reaching Greece I became associated with the late Dr R. M. Burrows in the excavation of the Greek cemetery at Rhitsona in Boeotia and in the study and publication of the pottery found there. This pottery dates mainly from the age of the tyrants, and the results of my work at it appear in several of the succeeding chapters. To Dr Burrows I owe also the encouragement that led me to start working on the early tyranny: my main idea on the subject first occurred to me when I was lecturing on Greek history as his assistant at University College, Cardiff.

I have also received much assistance at various times and in various ways from Professor G. A. T. Davies, another former colleague of mine at Cardiff, and from several of my Reading colleagues, particularly Professor W. G. de Burgh, Mr D. Atkinson, and my wife. Many other debts are recorded in the body of the book: but considering how many and various they have been, I can scarcely hope that none has been passed over without acknowledgement.

But of all my obligations the earliest and chiefest is to Sir William Ridgeway. It is to the unique quality of his teaching at Cambridge that I owe the stimulus that suggested to me the explanation here offered of the origin of tyranny.

P. N. URE.

UNIVERSITY COLLEGE,
   READING.
      October 1920.

CONTENTS

CHAP.		PAGE
I	INTRODUCTION	1
II	ATHENS	33
III	SAMOS	68
IV	EGYPT	86
V	LYDIA	127
VI	ARGOS	154
VII	CORINTH	184
VIII	ROME	215
IX	SICYON, MEGARA, MILETUS, EPHESUS, LEONTINI, AGRIGENTUM, CUMAE	257
X	CAPITALIST DESPOTS OF THE AGE OF ARISTOTLE, THE MONEY POWER OF THE RULERS OF PERGAMUM, PROTOGENES OF OLBIA	280
XI	CONCLUSION	290
	APPENDICES	307
	INDEX	339

ILLUSTRATIONS

FIG.		PAGE
1	Lophos Loutrou from Daskalio station	42
2	On the road from Daskalio station to Plaka	42
3	Kamaresa	43
4	Kitsovouno from Kamaresa	43
	(Figs. 1-4 from photographs by the author)	
5	Corinthian terra cotta tablet depicting a miner at work	46
	(*Antike Denkmäler*, I)	
6	Coin of Athens with Athena and owl	53
	(Macdonald, *Evolution of Coinage*)	
7	Athenian coins: the wreath on the head of Athena	56
	(*Bulletin de Correspondance hellénique*, xxx)	
8	Persian "archer"	57
9	Samian coin with Samaina and Messanian coin with hare	75
	(Hill, *Historical Greek Coins*)	
10	Aiakes, father of Polycrates	82
	(*Athenische Mitteilungen*, 1906)	
11	Psamtek I	86
	(Petrie, *Hist. Egypt*, III)	
12	Vase with cartouche of Bocchoris found at Tarquinii	94
	(*Monumenti Antichi della R. Acc. dei Lincei*, VIII)	
13	Rhodian or (?) Milesian vase found at Naukratis	111
	(Gardner, *Naukratis II*. By permission of the Egypt Exploration Fund)	
14	Fikellura or (?) Samian vase found at Daphnae	113
	(Petrie, *Tanis II*. By permission of the Egypt Exploration Fund)	
15	Naukratite vase found at Rhitsona in Boeotia	115
	(*Journ. Hellenic Studies*, 1909)	
16	Perfume vase found at Naukratis	119
	(Gardner, *Naukratis II*. By permission of the Egypt Exploration Fund)	
17	Greek wine jar found at Naukratis	120
	(Petrie, *Naukratis I*. By permission of the Egypt Exploration Fund)	

THE
ORIGIN OF TYRANNY

τοῖσι ἐμφανέσι τὰ μὴ γιγνωσκόμενα τεκμαιρόμενος.
Hdt. ii. 33.

Chapter I. *Introduction*

Δόξαιεν γὰρ ⟨ἂν⟩ οὐδὲν λέγειν δίκαιον οἱ διὰ τὸν πλοῦτον ἀξιοῦντες ἄρχειν.
ARISTOT. *Pol.* III. 1283 *b*.

Φαῦλον τὸ τὰς μεγίστας ὠνητὰς εἶναι τῶν ἀρχῶν. ARISTOT. *Pol.* II. 1273 *a*.

The seventh century B.C. is the age

THE seventh and sixth centuries B.C. constitute from many points of view one of the most momentous periods in the whole of the world's history. No doubt the greatest final achievements of the Greek race belong to the two centuries that followed. But practically all that is meant by the Greek spirit and the Greek genius had its birth in the earlier period. Literature and art, philosophy and science are at this present day largely following the lines that were then laid down for them, and this is equally the case with commerce. It was at the opening of

(*a*) of the first known metal coins,

this epoch that the Greeks or their half hellenized neighbours the Lydians brought about perhaps the most epoch-making revolution in the whole history of commerce by the invention of a metal coinage like those that are still in circulation throughout the civilized world.

It was no accident that the invention was made precisely at this time. Industry and commerce were simultaneously making enormous strides. About the beginning of the seventh century the new Lydian dynasty of the Mermnadae made Sardis one of the most important trading centres that have arisen in the world's history. The Lydian merchants became middlemen between Greece and the Far East. Egypt recovered its prosperity and began rapidly to develop commercial and other relations with its neighbours, including the Greeks. Greek traders were pushing their goods by sea in all directions from Spain to the Crimea. Concrete evidence of this activity is still to be seen in the Corinthian and Milesian pottery of the period that has been so abundantly unearthed as far afield as Northern Italy and Southern Russia. It was a time of extraordinary intellectual alertness. Thales and the numerous other philosophers of the Ionian School were in close touch with the merchants and manufacturers of their age. They were in fact men of science rather than philosophers in the narrow modern sense of the latter word, and most of them were ready to apply their science to practical and commercial ends, as for example Thales, who is said to have made a fortune by buying up all the oil presses in advance when his agricultural observations had led him to expect a particularly plentiful harvest[1]. A corner in oil sounds very modern, and in fact the whole of the evidence shows that in many ways this ancient epoch curiously anticipated the present age.

Politically these two centuries are generally known as the age of tyrants. The view that the prevalence of tyranny was in some way connected with the invention of coinage has been occasionally expressed[2]. Radet has even gone so far as to suggest that the first tyrant was also the first coiner[3]. He does not however go further than to suggest that the tyrant started a mint and coinage when already on the throne.

and (b) of the first rulers to be called tyrants.

The evidence appears to me to point to conclusions of a more wide-reaching character. Briefly stated they are these: that the seventh and sixth century Greek tyrants were the first men in their various cities to realize the political possibilities of the new conditions created by the introduction of the new coinage, and that to a large extent they owed their position as tyrants to a financial or commercial supremacy which they had already established before they attained to supreme political power in their several states.

The new form of government was, I believe, based on the new form of capital.

In other words their position as I understand it has considerable resemblances to that built up in the fourteenth and fifteenth centuries A.D. by the rich bankers and merchants who made themselves despots in so many of the city states of Italy. The most famous of these are the Medici, the family who gave a new power to the currency by their development of the banking business, and mainly as a result of this became tyrants of Florence. Santo Bentivoglio of Bologna passed from a wool factory to the throne. Another despot of Bologna was the rich usurer Roméo Pepoli. At Pisa the supreme power was grasped by the Gambacorti with an old merchant named Pietro at their head. At Lodi it was seized by the millionaire

---

[1] Aristot. *Pol.* I. 1259a. The authenticity of the story may be questioned, but the fact of its being attached to Thales is in itself significant.

[2] *E.g.* Busolt, *Gr. G.* I.² pp. 626–7.

[3] *La Lydie*, p. 163; cp. *ibid.* p. 274, "wealth acquires an importance it had never had."

Giovanni Vignate. The above instances are taken from Symonds' sixth class of despots of whom he says that "in most cases great wealth was the original source of despotic ascendancy[1]."

Still closer analogies lie at our very door. It is a commonplace that we are in the midst of an industrial revolution. This modern movement was already beginning a century ago, when Byron pleaded the cause of the frameworkers before the House of Lords. There are of course obvious differences between the two revolutions. That of the seventh and sixth centuries B.C. was mainly financial, that of the present time is mainly industrial. But the difference is not so great as it at first sight appears[2]. The invention of a metal coinage was accompanied by great industrial changes[3], and we can no more divide sharply the financial and industrial activities of the great houses of archaic Greece than we can separate the banking and the mercantile enterprises of the great families of the cities of Italy at the time of the renaissance, such as the wealthy Panciatighi of Florence, who lent money to the emperor Sigismund and exported cloths to London, Avignon and North Africa[4]. On the other hand the modern industrial movement, with its development of machinery and its organization of masters and men into trusts and trade unions, has been accompanied by a revolution in the nature of the currency. The modern financial revolution began at the same time as the industrial. Its earliest phases are described and discussed in William Cobbett's *Paper against Gold*[5]. Since Cobbett's days the paper currency which so distressed him has developed enormously. Even before 1914 we were told that "Gold already acts in England only as change for notes[6]."

This view deserves examination in the light of the modern financial revolution,

which has replaced metal coins by paper,

[1] J. A. Symonds, *Renaissance in Italy, Age of the Despots*², pp. 103-4; cp. *ibid.* pp. 65 n. 1, 66, 73, 76, 77-78.

[2] Some lecturers at Oxford are inclined to minimize the analogies offered by the seventh and sixth centuries B.C. to modern industrial conditions. In so doing they appear to me to be falling into the commonest of modern fallacies, that of overestimating the importance of size and numbers. For a better appreciation of the analogies see *e.g.* Ciccotti, *Tramonto d. Schiavitù n. Mondo ant.* p. 45.

[3] E. Meyer, *Jahrb. f. Nationalök.* IX. (1895), p. 713 and below *passim*.

[4] Sieveking, *Viert. f. Soc. u. Wirts.* VII. p. 87.

[5] Cobbett, *Paper against Gold*, pp. 5, 6 (Aug. 30th, 1810).

[6] Jevons, *Money*²³, p. 203; cp. *ibid.* p. 285: "It is surprising to find to what an extent paper documents have replaced coin as a medium of exchange in some of the principal centres of business."

It is not necessary here to examine in detail the various forms taken by this new paper currency. It is enough to point out that it enables property to be transferred and manipulated far more rapidly and on far larger a scale than was previously possible[1]. Only one other point in the history of the new currency needs to be here mentioned. It cannot be better expressed than in the words used by the Chancellor of the Exchequer in the House of Commons on November 28th, 1914:

> I have been much struck since I have been dealing with these transactions (bills of exchange) with how little even traders who form a part of this great machinery know about the mechanism of which they form an essential part ...I do not think that the general public—and I am putting myself among them—ever realized the extent to which the business not merely of this country, but of the whole world, depended upon this very delicate and complicated paper machinery.

Apparently it needed a European war to bring home to the modern world of commerce the nature of its currency. This fact should warn us against expecting to find in early Greece any very clear recognition of the revolution in the currency that then took place. When gold and silver coins were first circulated they had a corresponding effect to the modern issues of paper. They enabled property to be transferred with greater ease and rapidity. We may be sure however that the character and possibilities of the new currency did not at once receive universal recognition[2]. The merchants in the bazaars of Lydia and Ionia who best understood how to make use of it must have profited enormously.

and led many people to fear a new tyranny of wealth.

The experts in the new finance of the last two generations have been exercising a profound influence upon politics and government. There are many people, particularly in America, who believe that there is a possibility of this influence becoming supreme. It is worth while quoting a few of these opinions:

> This era is but a passing phase in the evolution of industrial Caesars, and these Caesars will be of a new type—corporate Caesars[3].

> The flames of a new economic evolution run around us, and we turn to find that competition has killed competition, that corporations are grown greater than the state and have bred individuals greater than themselves,

---

[1] Cp. Thos. W. Lawson, *Frenzied Finance* (published 1906), pp. 33, 35.

[2] Cp. Poehlmann, *Sozialismus i. d. ant. Welt*², 1. p. 170.

[3] Hy. D. Lloyd, *Wealth against Commonwealth* (1894), p. 2.

and that the naked issue of our time is with property becoming master instead of servant[1].

For some months past the sugar trust has been the Government of the United States[2].

In 1884 there seems even to have been an idea of running a Standard Oil senator for the United States presidency. "Henry B. Payne is looming up grandly in the character of a possible and not altogether improbable successor to Mr Tilden as the Democratic candidate for the presidency[3]."

The danger of supreme power in America passing into the hands of a few capitalists has even been publicly acknowledged by a President of the United States during his period of office. "Mr Wilson also discussed the division between capital and labour. He dwelt for the greater part of the speech on the effort of 'small bodies of privileged men to resume control of the Government,' and added: 'We must again convince these gentlemen that the government of this country belongs to us, not to them[4].'"

Similar views are expressed by French, German and Italian writers. According to the most brilliant of modern Frenchmen the government of France has in some recent periods been in the hands of three or four groups of financiers[5]. Salvioli in his *Capitalism in the Ancient World* speaks of the "kings of finance who exercise in our states a secret but pervading sway[6]." Even the warlike von Bernhardi fears an impending "tyranny of capital[7]."

These quotations might be multiplied[8], but enough have been given to show that the opinion which they express is widely held.

---

[1] Hy. D. Lloyd, *op. cit.* p. 494; see also pp. 297–8, 311; ch. XXVIII. (on a Standard Oil secretary of U.S.A. treasury), 434, 511.

[2] *New York Daily Commercial Bull.* June 4th, 1894, *ap.* Hy. D. Lloyd, *op. cit.* p. 450.

[3] New York *Sun*, May 27th, 1884, *ap.* Hy. D. Lloyd, p. 387.

[4] *Times*, Nov. 4th, 1916.

[5] Anatole France, *L'Île des Pingouins*, pp. 242 f., 309.

[6] Salvioli, *Capitalisme dans le Monde Antique* (traduit A. Bonnet), p. 267.

[7] von Bernhardi, *Germany and the Next War*, p. 65.

[8] See *e.g.* Thos. W. Lawson, *Frenzied Finance*, pp. 6, 35; Hy. D. Lloyd, *Wealth against Commonwealth*, pp. 341, 353, 386 (quoting the *National Baptist of Philadelphia*, the Cincinnati *Commercial Gazette*, and Senator Hoar); J. Ramsay MacDonald, *Unemployment and the Wage Fund*; I. M. Tarbell, *Hist. Standard Oil Co.* II. pp. 114, 116, 137 (quoting the *Butler County Democrat*, Senator Frye, N.Y. State Investigation Report, 1888), 124, 126–7, 290, 291; Truth's Investigator, *The Great Oil Octopus*, p. 227.

There is no need to discuss the honesty of particular expressions of it. If any of them could be shown to have been insincere, it would be only additional evidence of the plausibility of the opinion. Nor is this the place to discuss from a more general point of view the extent to which that opinion has been or seems likely to be verified. To have indicated how widely prevalent is the fear of an impending "new tyranny of wealth[1]" or "tyranny of capital[2]" is by itself enough to show that the relation between the tyranny and the new form of wealth that arose in the seventh and sixth centuries before our era is a subject that deserves investigation, and to show also that the particular view as to those relations that is maintained in these pages has *a priori* plausibility[3].

It should however be said at once that my view appears to have been held by no one who has published opinions on the subject from the fourth century B.C. onwards. This however is not fatal. Later in this chapter reasons will be suggested for holding that the true character of the early tyranny was lost sight of in the days of Plato and Aristotle. Why truer views on this particular subject should be recovered precisely at the present period may be sufficiently explained by the modern financial revolution, which makes it possible to approach the question from a point which has scarcely been accessible during the last two thousand years. With this warning we may proceed to state the nature of the evidence in favour of this view that the earliest tyrannies were founded and based on wealth.

The evidence:

(1) The greater part of it is drawn from anecdotes and incidental statements of fact about particular seventh or sixth century tyrants preserved in Herodotus and later Greek and Latin writers. The various tyrants are dealt with individually in the remaining chapters of the book.

(2) Glimpses into the economic and political life of the seventh and sixth centuries are occasionally to be got from the scanty remains of the poets of the period, supplemented by cautious references to later writers. It will be convenient to examine at once this more general evidence.

---

[1] Hy. D. Lloyd, *op. cit.* p. 493.

[2] von Bernhardi, *loc. cit.*

[3] Karl Marx objected to applying the words Capital and Capitalism to the condition of things in antiquity. But see E. Meyer, *Gesch. d. Alt.* III. p. 550.

(a) statements from the extant writings of the sixth century (Solon and Theognis),

The only two writers of the age of the tyrants of whom more than the merest scraps have come down to us are Solon[1] and Theognis[2]. Both deal professedly with the social and political problems of their day. But both address audiences who are familiar with those problems. Even if their whole works had been preserved instead of a few hundred lines in either case, we should not expect to have the fundamental problems explicitly stated. It would be possible to read a large selection of articles and speeches by quite the best journalists and politicians on many recent political measures and at the end of it to be left in uncertainty as to the content and purport of the measure in question. We must expect the same difficulty in reading Solon and Theognis. And it must be confessed that we find it. But there is nothing in the extant fragments of either writer which discredits the theory. More than that there are passages in both of them that become of the utmost significance if the early tyrants owed their power to their previous wealth but are rather pointless on any other hypothesis.

Solon's position in relation to the tyranny is explained in the chapter dealing with Athens. But a few lines may be quoted here:

> But of themselves in their folly the men of the city are willing
>   Our great city to wreck, being won over by wealth.
> False are the hearts of the people's leaders[3].

By the wreck of the city the poet means the establishment of a tyranny, as is indicated by another couplet:

> Great men ruin a city: for lack of understanding
>   Under a despot's[4] yoke lieth the people enslaved[5].

These last two lines were presumably written after Peisistratus had made himself tyrant of Athens. Solon's fears had been realized. The citizens had been "won over by wealth" to "wreck their great city." Is not the best sense made out of these lines by assuming that what Solon feared and what actually happened was that the popular leader had made use of his wealth to establish himself as tyrant? Neither the "people's leaders" of the first quotation nor the "great men" of the second are specifically stated to have

---

[1] Extant some 300 lines in 35 fragments.
[2] Extant 1389 lines of continuous verse.
[3] Fr. 2 (13), 5–7.
[4] μονάρχου.
[5] Fr. 7 (17), 3–4.

been extremely rich, but to quote again the words of Solon, both may be plausibly identified with the foremost of

> Those who had power and made men to marvel because of their riches[1].

The political aim of Theognis was to prevent a recurrence of tyranny in Megara[2]. What does the poet bid his townsmen beware of? Not of eloquence, not of violence, not of rashly appointing a lawgiver or αἰσυμνήτης. All his warnings are directed against wealth. The whole town of Megara had become commercial[3]. Birth had lost its prestige, and wealth acquired unprecedented power. He complains how

> Tradesmen reign supreme: the bad lord it over their betters[4].
> This is the lesson that each and all must thoroughly master:
>   How that in all the world wealth has the might and the power[5].
> Many a bad man is rich, and many a good man needy[6].
> Not without cause, O wealth, do men honour thee above all things[7].
> Most men reckon the only virtue the making of money[8].
> Everyone honours those that are rich, and despises the needy[9].

When he explicitly alludes to the dangers of the establishment of a tyranny, his references to wealth are no less prominent:

> Neither exalt thou in hope, *by yielding to gain*, any tyrant[10].
> Cyrnus, this city is pregnant. I fear lest a man it may bear us
>   Swollen with insolent pride[11], leader in stern civil strife[12].

The couplet last quoted almost certainly refers to a possible tyrant. Insolent pride (ὕβρις) is one of the tyrant's stock characteristics[13]. There is no reference to wealth in this particular context. But there can be little doubt that this same character is also referred to earlier in the poem. Who, the poet asks, can preserve his reverence for the Gods:

> When that a man unjust and presumptuous, one that regardeth
>   Neither the wrath of a man, no, nor the wrath of a God,
> *Glutted with wealth* waxes proud and insolent[14]?

---

[1] Fr. 3 (14), 3.　　[2] For his hatred of tyranny see *e.g.* 1181-2, 1203-4.

[3] Cp. of the Greeks in general, Theognis' contemporary Cyrus (*ap.* Hdt. I. 153), "these taunts Cyrus flung at the Greeks, because they secure market-places and engage in buying and selling."

[4] 679, φορτηγοὶ δ' ἄρχουσι κ.τ.λ., the "bad" is the regular term in aristocratic writers for their political opponents.

[5] 717-8.　　[6] 315.　　[7] 523.　　[8] 699.　　[9] 621.
[10] 823; cp. Solon quoted above.　　[11] ὑβριστήν.　　[12] 1081-2.
[13] Cp. *e.g.* Hdt. III. 80, ὕβρι κεκορημένος.　　[14] ὑβρίζῃ, 749-751.

CH. I   INTRODUCTION   9

In this last passage the pride and insolence are directly attributed to enormous wealth.

Or again:

Be thou sure that not long will that city remain unshaken,
  Even though now it may lie wrapped in the deepest repose,
Soon as soever to those that are bad these things become pleasing—
  Gains that, whenever they come, bring with them ill for the state.
For from these arise factions, murders of men by their kindred,
  Despots withal[1].

What are the gains that lead up to tyranny? Is it not most probable that they are some form of payment received by the commons ("those that are bad") from the would-be tyrant[2]?

Solon and Theognis wrote with the examples of Gyges, Pheidon, Orthagoras, Cypselus, Theagenes and the rest of the seventh century tyrants before them[3]. If they constantly feared that some wealthy tradesman[4] would make himself tyrant, it must surely have been because the tyrants had sprung from or been allied with this new class of wealthy traders and financiers.

The view here set forth as to the basis of the tyrant's power finds nothing to contradict it in the fifth century references to the early tyranny. On the contrary such few references as are explicitly made to the origin of the tyranny by writers of the fifth century bear it out. "Is it not folly," says Oedipus to Kreon in the *Oedipus Tyrannus* of Sophocles, "this attempt of yours, without a host of followers and friends to seek a tyranny, a thing that's gained only with hosts of followers and money[5]?" "When Greece," says Thucydides, in his introductory sketch of early Greek history, "had grown more powerful, and was still more than before engaged in the acquisition of wealth, tyrannies were established in the cities[6]." Herodotus gives no account of the rise of tyranny, but a large proportion of the evidence as to the careers of individual tyrants is derived from his work. Perhaps the fifth century writer who might be expected to throw most light on the question is Pindar, who visited the courts

(b) the fifth century writers (Thucydides, Herodotus, Pindar),

---

[1] 47–52.

[2] Other interpretations would be possible if in line 51 we read "from this" (ἐκ τοῦ) instead of "from these" (ἐκ τῶν), but the MSS. all support ἐκ τῶν.

[3] Is it possible to see in Solon, 12 (4). 29–32, a reference to the fates of the various tyrant families of the seventh century?

[4] φορτηγός, Theognis, 679.

[5] Soph. *O.T.* 540–542.   [6] I. 13.

of the Sicilian tyrants and wrote odes in their honour. His poems contain many references to the supreme importance of wealth:

> Wealth adorned with virtues
> Brings opportunity for this and that[1].
> Ever in the quest of noble achievements
> Toil and outlay strive after the issue[2].

So elsewhere[3] in a similar spirit he describes Hiero's great victory over the Etruscans as "the crown of his lordly wealth." The Syracusan monarchs of the early fifth century seem to have had fewer affinities with the commercial tyrants of the two preceding centuries than with the military despots of a later age. It is therefore all the more significant that wealth is so frequently regarded by Pindar, who more than any other writer represents the transition from the sixth century to the fifth, rather as a means to power than as one of its rewards. Later documents, as has been said already, give a different account of the early tyrants' antecedents. But here and there statements are to be found in them that, though perhaps reconcilable with other views, only become fully significant on the commercial theory.

Isocrates for instance speaks of the "huge wage bills and expenditures of money by which all modern dynasts maintain their power[4]." He wrote these words between 342 and 339 B.C.[5], but as his modern times are contrasted with those of Agamemnon and he himself was nearly thirty years old at the close of the fifth century, his modern dynasts may well include sixth century tyrants like Peisistratus and Polycrates, the more so as "dynasts" arose so seldom in fifth century Greece.

(c) some statements of fourth century writers,

Aristotle preserves the tradition that the early tyrants were good business men. He speaks of "rendering account of their receipts and expenditure, as has been done already by certain of the tyrants. For by this kind of administration he would give the impression of being a manager (οἰκονόμος) and not a tyrant[6]."

---

[1] *Olymp.* II. 58–9 (to Thero, tyrant of Acragas).

[2] *Olymp.* v. 15–16 (to Psaumis of Camarina). The poem ends with a warning to Psaumis not to emulate the tyrants (μὴ ματεύσῃ θεὸς γενέσθαι).

[3] *Pyth.* I. 48.

[4] ἀλλ' ὅμως τὸ τοιοῦτον ἔτη δέκα κατέσχεν ('Αγαμέμνων), οὐ μισθοφοραῖς μεγάλαις οὐδὲ χρημάτων δαπάναις, οἷς νῦν ἅπαντες δυναστεύουσιν, Isocr. *Panath.* 82 (249). [5] Jebb, *Attic Orators*[2], II. p. 110.

[6] *Pol.* VII. (v.), 1314 b. Endt, *Wien. Stud.* XXIV. (1901), p. 47, sees here a

That the early tyrants had previously been men of wealth is also perhaps to be inferred from certain remarks of Aristotle about the "lawgivers" of the same period. The general character of these "lawgivers" is a matter of some dispute; but they appear to have differed from the tyrants in at least two points. They governed by general consent and they marked an earlier stage in the economic evolution of the city state[1]. They are perhaps to be compared with the "arbitrators" between employers and employed who in recent times have sometimes enjoyed considerable influence[2]. When Aristotle[3] emphasizes the fact that the best "lawgivers" were all drawn from the citizens of moderate means (ἐκ τῶν μέσων πολιτῶν) he is making a fairly pointless remark unless the same could not be said of the tyrants of the period. That Aristotle did actually recognize the connexion between tyranny and extremes of wealth and poverty is shown by another passage of the *Politics*[4]:

> For this reason it is very fortunate when those engaged in politics have moderate but sufficient means, for where some have very great possessions and others none, the result is either extreme democracy or unmitigated oligarchy or tyranny, which is caused by both extremes. For unbridled democracy and oligarchy lead to tyranny, the intermediate and more closely allied forms of government do so far less.

The philosopher himself may have pictured some of the early tyrants as having risen from being penniless demagogues. The difficulties in the way of accepting the view that a poor man ever became a tyrant before the democratic development of the fifth century will be set forth later in this chapter. If there is any basis of fact for Aristotle's statement, the early tyrants must have come from among the wealthiest of the citizens.

reference to Gelo of Syracuse and quotes Diod. XI. 26; Ael. *V.H.* VI. 11; Polyaen. I. 27, which tell how Gelo appeared naked before the Syracusans and gave an account of his government and offered to resign. But the only reference to the Exchequer is in Polyaenus; and there it is only incidental (εὐθύνας δοὺς τῆς αὐτοκράτορος ἀρχῆς, τῆς δαπάνης, τῶν καιρῶν, τῶν ὅπλων, τῶν ἵππων, τῶν τριήρων).

[1] See below on Solon, pp. 34–5, and chapter XI. p. 301, and cp. Aristot. *Pol.* II. 1267; III. 1285 a–b.

[2] *E.g.* Lord James of Hereford, Sir D. Dale, Mr Watson and Mr Mundella, quoted by W. T. Layton, *Capital and Labour*, p. 198. In a simpler and smaller state than the modern kingdom or republic, during an epoch of industrial war between evenly matched parties, it is easy to imagine individuals in a similar position acquiring or even having thrust upon them almost autocratic powers.

[3] *Pol.* VI. (IV.), 1296 a.   [4] VI. (IV.), 1295–6.

There is nothing surprising in this conclusion. In the age that saw merchants like Solon made practical dictators in their native cities[1], and philosophers like Thales anticipating the Rockefellers by making a corner in oil[2], there must have been individuals with something of the abilities of these great men, but little of their disinterestedness, who would be quick to grasp the possibility of reaching through the corner to the crown.

(d) evidence as to industrial conditions during and after the age of the tyrants.

At a later date cornering became less easy. In fifth century Athens there were statutes and magistrates ($\sigma\iota\tau o\phi\acute{v}\lambda\alpha\kappa\epsilon\varsigma$) to prevent corners in corn, and we still have a speech of Lysias directed against some speculators who had bought beyond the legal limit. The context of a passage in this speech suggests that the general controllers of the market ($\mathring{a}\gamma o\rho\alpha\nu\acute{o}\mu o\iota$) were expected to be on their guard against corners in other articles[3].

The detailed evidence in favour of this view is given in the chapters that follow. It will be found however that these men who made themselves tyrants through their riches were not all of them mere speculators. Some at least had acquired their wealth from trade or industry. This means that they were large employers of labour. There are reasons for thinking that from this point of view they would be politically far more influential than their successors in business in the days of the Athenian democracy.

The big merchants and manufacturers of the fifth and fourth centuries relied largely, and more and more as time went on, on servile labour. The thousand miners whose services Nikias commanded were all slaves. Six hundred slave miners were owned by his contemporary Hipponikos and three hundred by Philemonides[4]. The hundred and twenty hands in the shield factory of the orator Lysias were all slaves[5]. So too were the fifty-two in the knife and bedstead factories inherited by Demosthenes[6], and the nine or ten in the boot-making establishment of Timarchus[7], as also those in the flute-making establishment from which the father of Isocrates

---

[1] Plut. *Sol.* 2, 14.

[2] Aristot. *Pol.* 1. 1259a.

[3] Lysias, *c. Frument.* 16 (165). For an oil ring in the Rome of Plautus see *Captivi*, 489, "omnes conpecto rem agunt quasi in Velabro olearii."

[4] Xen. *de Vect.* 4. 14–15; cp. Plut. *Nikias*, 4.

[5] Lysias, *c. Eratosth.* 19 (121).

[6] Dem. *c. Aphob.* A. 9–11 (816, 817); cp. Plut. *Demosth.* 4.

[7] Aeschines, *c. Timarch.* 97 (13–14).

made his living[1], and the sail-makers and drug-pounders who appear in Demosthenes *contra Olympiodorum*[2]. These instances might be multiplied[3]. Slaves were of course only a form of wealth[4]. As human beings they were entirely without influence on politics. It would have been another matter if Nikias had had a big constituency of miner citizens at his entire disposal. That I believe was one of the great differences between Nikias and Peisistratus and generally speaking between the captains of industry in the fifth and fourth centuries and their predecessors in the seventh and sixth. The evidence is not decisive, but as far as it goes it all points in this direction.

At Athens in the generation that preceded the tyranny it is reported of Solon that "he encouraged the citizens to take up manual trades[5]," a policy perhaps to be connected with his release from debt and semi-slavery of the "pelatai" and the "hektemoroi[6]," since fresh employment had possibly to be found for many of these liberated serfs. It is further reported of Solon that he offered the citizenship to any who "transplanted themselves to Athens with their whole family for the sake of exercising some manual trade[7]." Aeschines quotes Solon, laws attributed to whom were still in force when the orator flourished, to the effect that "he does not drive a man from the platform" (*i.e.* he allows him to speak in the assembly of citizens) "even if he is practising some handicraft, but

---

[1] Dion. Hal. *Isocr.* 1, θεράποντας αὐλοποιούς. For θεράπων = slave, cp. Aristoph. *Plut.* 518–521.

[2] *c. Olymp.* 12 (1170).

[3] *E.g.* Xen. *Mem.* II. 7. 3, 6. The contract for building the long walls of Athens in the days of Pericles is said to have been given to a single individual, by name Kallikrates (Plut. *Per.* 13): of his employees we know nothing except that according to the contemporary comic poet Cratinus they were very slow about their work.

[4] Athen. VI. 272e actually speaks of Nikias as a millionaire (ζάπλουτος) owning slaves as capital (ἐπὶ προσόδοις).

[5] Plut. *Sol.* XXII. πρὸς τὰς τέχνας (cp. χειροτέχνης = artizan) ἔτρεψε τοὺς πολίτας. Note too, *ibid.* (cp. Galen, *Protrept.* 8 init.; Vitruv. VI. praef.) the law that a son was not obliged to support his father if the father had not taught him a trade, and further Poll. VIII. 42 (in the days of Solon a person thrice convicted of unemployment lost his vote).

[6] Aristot. *Ath. Pol.* 2. In ch. 12 the *Ath. Pol.* alludes to the difficulties (ἀπορία) of the poor and of those previously slaves who were liberated as a result of the σεισάχθεια (Solon's measure for dealing with slavery and debt), and proceeds to quote Solon himself.

[7] Plut. *Sol.* XXIV.

welcomes that class most of all[1]." Solon himself, describing the various paths by which men pursue riches, declares that

> Another learns the works of Athena and Hephaestus of the many crafts, and with his hands gathers a livelihood[2].

The tyrants themselves are repeatedly found making it part of their policy to keep their subjects employed on big industrial concerns. In more than one case we shall see their power collapsing just when this policy becomes financially impossible[3]. This part of the tyrants' policy is noticed by Aristotle, who quotes the dedications (buildings and works of art) of the Cypselids at Corinth, the building of the temple of Olympian Zeus at Athens by the Peisistratids, and the works of Polycrates round Samos[4]. To these names we may add Theagenes of Megara, Phalaris of Agrigentum, Aristodemus of Cumae, and the Tarquins of Rome, all of whom are associated with works of this kind[5]. Aristotle says that the object of these works was to keep the people busy and poor. This explanation is more than doubtful, as has been already recognized[6]. It is not employment that leads to poverty. More probably the tyrants pursued this industrial policy because, to quote an expression used in another context by Plutarch, "stimulating every craft and busying every hand it made practically the whole city wage earners (ἔμμισθον)," employed, as in the case Plutarch is describing, by the government of the state. In other words may not the tyrants have been building up an industrial state of employee subjects who in their turn involved an army of "customer subjects[7]"? The words just quoted come from the life of Pericles[8] and refer to the way that he employed the poorer citizens (τὸν θητικὸν ὄχλον) in the rebuilding and adornment of Athens. Among the people so employed he mentions carpenters, sculptors, coppersmiths, stone masons, dyers, moulders of gold and ivory, painters, embroiderers, engravers, merchants, sailors, wheelwrights, waggoners, drivers, rope-makers, flax workers, leather cutters, road-makers, miners. We still possess fragments of the accounts of payments made to these workmen or their successors some years after Pericles' death[9]. The Alcmaeonids, the family to

---

[1] Aesch. *c. Timarch.* 27 (4). [2] *Anth. Lyr.* Solon, 12 (4), 49–50.
[3] Notably at Athens and Rome.
[4] Aristot. *Pol.* VII. (v.), 1313*b*. [5] Below, pp. 267, 274 f., 279, 223 f.
[6] E.g. by Endt, *Wien. Stud.* XXIV. (1901), p. 55.
[7] Hy. D. Lloyd, *Wealth against Commonwealth*, p. 364.
[8] Plut. *Per.* 12. [9] Building of the Erechtheum, 408 B.C. *C.I.A.* I. 321, 324

which Pericles belonged, had been opponents of the house of Peisistratus for ages, and had consistently fought it with its own weapons. Pericles himself was commonly called the new Peisistratus[1]. His public works were a continuation of those of Peisistratus[2]. The whole situation as well as our scanty information about industrial conditions in the age of the tyrants alike suggest that in this use of public works to convert the industrial classes into an army of his own employees, which is what they very nearly were[3], Pericles was in a very particular sense a new Peisistratus.

To judge too from the purely industrial evidence Pericles seems to have been continuing the traditions of an earlier age. It is true that free labour was largely employed on the restoration of the great sanctuary at Eleusis some eighty years after the operations just referred to. An inscription relating to the wages paid during this later undertaking shows that the employees included 36 citizens, 39 resident aliens, 12 strangers, 2 slaves, besides 57 persons of uncertain status[4]. But this evidence only tends to show that building was always a free man's trade[5]. We must beware of arguing from one trade to another or from one particular trade to trade in general. There were doubtless many subtle shades of status depending on the nature of either the work or the profits[6]. As servile industry develops, it drives free labour from work thought to be particularly damaging to body or mind such as employment underground in mines. Speaking generally, however, there are signs that in Athens at least between the days of the tyranny and those of the Periclean democracy the conditions of free labour had been radically changed. This is most obvious as regards the status of the citizen artizan[7].

[1] Plut. *Per.* 16, τὴν δύναμιν αὐτοῦ...κακοήθως παρεμφαίνουσιν οἱ κωμικοί, Πεισιστρατίδας μὲν νέους τοὺς ἀμφὶ αὐτὸν ἑταίρους καλοῦντες, αὐτὸν δ' ἀπομόσαι μὴ τυραννήσειν κελεύοντες.   [2] Cp. Mauri, *Cittadini Lavoratori dell' Attica*, p. 56.

[3] Cp. Thuc. II. 65; of Athens under Pericles, "nominally it was a democracy, but in fact it was government by the foremost man."

[4] *Arch. Eph.* 1883, pp. 109 f. =*C.I.A.* II. ii. 834*b* (329-8 B.C.).

[5] Zimmern, *Sociological Review*, 1909, p. 166.

[6] Cp. Cic. *de Off.* I. 42. 151, mercatura, si tenuis est, sordida putanda est, sin magna et copiosa....non est admodum uituperanda; atque etiam si...ex portu in agros se possessionesque contulerit, uidetur iure optimo posse laudari: a view that was doubtless as firmly held in Greece as it has been since in Rome and England.

[7] A fairly complete collection of the authorities for ancient Greek views on manual labour is to be found in Frohberger, *De Opificum apud vet. Graec. condit.* chap. II.

Solon refers to him without a trace of contempt and is careful to maintain his political dignity. In so doing he appears to have been conservative and simply following the tradition of the Homeric age, when a prince was proud to make his own bedstead or build his own house and a princess took pleasure in acting as palace laundress[1]. In Attica at any rate manual labour appears to have enjoyed an equally honourable reputation from the heroic age onwards till the end of the age of the tyrants[2]. In the good old days, so Plato declares in the *Critias*[3], "the other classes of citizens were engaged in handicrafts (δημιουργίαι) and agriculture." The earliest division of the free population, ascribed to the half historical Theseus, comprised three classes—nobles, farmers, and artizans (δημιουργοί)[4]. When Solon, who was himself a merchant[5], reorganized the population he divided it (or perhaps simply preserved an existent division) into four classes, of which the lowest were θῆτες or day labourers[6]. The names of the others (pentekosiomedimnoi, hippeis, zeugitai) show that this class must have included all the artizans, the men who, in the lawgiver's own words, "learn the works of Athena and Hephaestus of the many crafts." This description of the ancient Athenian craftsmen as sons of Pallas and Hephaestus recurs in Plato[7]. A class that is described in this way plainly rests under no stigma. As Wallon puts it, "le travail, loin d'être un titre d'exclusion, était un moyen d'arriver au pouvoir[8]." Some five years after Solon's legislation the old classification of the free population as nobles, farmers and artizans (δημιουργοί) reappears and the artizans secure two out of ten seats on the board of chief magistrates[9].

---

[1] Hom. *Od.* XXIII. 189; *Il.* VI. 313–5; *Od.* VI. 52 f.; cp. also *Il.* V. 59 f.; XXI. 37: *Od.* V. 241 f.

[2] In Megara the aristocratic Theognis has contempt enough for the working classes, but he wrote after the overthrow of tyranny in his city.

[3] Plato, *Critias*, 110c.   [4] Plut. *Thes.* 25.
[5] Plut. *Sol.* 2.   [6] Aristot. *Ath. Pol.* 7.

[7] *Laws*, XI. 920d. For the character of Athens' patron deities cp. Proclus ad Plat. *Timae.* 52b, Athena Ergane (so called) as patroness of the works of craftsmen (δημιουργικῶν ἔργων); cp. Soph. fr. 844 (Jebb and Pearson); Plato, *Protag.* 321e, the common abode in which they (Athena and Hephaestus) practised their crafts (ἐφιλοτεχνείτην); Harpocrat. and Suid. s.v. χαλκεῖα, "A feast common to artizans (χειρώναξι) and especially to smiths": Suid. adds that it was originally a public feast, not till later observed only by artizans (τεχνιτῶν): A. Mommsen, *Heortologie*, p. 313, thinks that the change may be due to Peisistratus.   [8] Wallon, *Histoire de l'Esclavage*, I. 142.

[9] Aristot. *Ath. Pol.* 13.

But in the fifth century this has changed. Contrast the tone of Solon with that of Xenophon[1], who states that some citizens "actually" live by handicrafts, and that mechanical occupations are rightly held in contempt by civilized communities. When Socrates has demonstrated to Alcibiades that the Athenian ecclesia is made up of working men (cobblers, criers, tent-makers and the like), he proceeds to this inference: "if you have a contempt for them individually, then you must have a contempt for them as a body[2]." This contempt for manual work appears in Aristophanes, as for instance in his constant contemptuous references to Euripides' mother, who had been a greengrocer[3]. It is recognized and discussed by Herodotus, who regards it as of comparatively recent growth: as he puts it, "most of the Greeks have learned to despise artizans[4]." His view is supported by Isocrates, who when describing the state of things that prevailed in the Athens of Solon and Cleisthenes, declares that "the propertied classes, so far from despising those who were not so well off, ... relieved their necessities, giving some of them farms at moderate rents, sending out others to travel as merchants, supplying others with capital for their various employments (ἐργασίας)[5]." The passage just quoted is no doubt tendencious. But, as maintained by Mauri[6], it does indicate that labour was not despised in archaic Athens. More than that it suggests that in the days of Solon and Cleisthenes there was a good deal of free labour under the patronage, if not in the actual employment, of rich individuals. The transformation that began in the fifth century seems to have occurred gradually. It had not been completed when Herodotus wrote. Among the Athenian citizens who just at that time were being employed by Pericles on the Athenian acropolis we have seen from Plutarch that there were included carpenters, smiths, and leather workers. In the next generation we find Xenophon declaring that most of those who understand these crafts are servile. The words are put into the mouth of Socrates,

[1] Xen. *de Rep. Lac.* 7; *Mem.* IV. 2. 22; *Oecon.* IV. 2.
[2] Ael. *V.H.* II. 1; so Xen. *Mem.* III. 7. 6.
[3] Aristoph. *Ach.* 478; *Thes.* 387; *Frogs*, 840; cp. Plin. *N.H.* XXII. 38; Aul. Gell. XV. 20; Val. Max. III. 4, ext. 2.
[4] Hdt. II. 167.) Mauri therefore, *Cittadini Lavoratori dell' Attica*, p. 65, rather postdates when he says that our authorities for Athenian contempt of manual work are fourth century and later.
[5] Isocrat. *Areop.* 32 (146).
[6] Mauri, *Cittadini Lavoratori dell' Attica*, p. 69.

who was the younger contemporary of Herodotus by some fifteen years[1]. Socrates and Xenophon however sometimes voice the earlier view. In the *Apology* for instance artizans are compared favourably with politicians, poets, and the like[2]. Similarly in the *de Vectigalibus* of Xenophon, in which the writer expresses some of his own personal views, artizans are placed with no suggestion of inferiority in the company of sophists, philosophers, poets, and sight-seers[3]. In Plato, except for the passage just quoted from the *Apology*, manual labour is consistently condemned as unworthy of a free man in a free city[4]. He would have no member of a state or even the slave of a citizen among those engaged in manual trades[5]. He admits that there is nothing inherently ignoble in trade, but explains at length how all trading has in fact become so[6]. Trade has come to imply money-making and to mean that the city where it flourishes is "infected with money of silver and gold, than which, speaking generally, no greater evil could arise for a city that aimed at producing just and noble characters[7]." When Plato is building up his ideal state wage earning is left to those citizens who are mentally deficient[8]. Plato is above all things an independent thinker with no great respect for the masses and less still for popular opinion. But in this particular point his views do not seem to be unusual. He is echoed again and again by Aristotle: "Citizens ought not to live the life of an artizan or tradesman[9]." "Farmers and artizans and all the working-class element must exist in cities: but the real constituents of the city are the military class and the parliamentarians[10]." "The best city will not make the artizan a citizen[11]." "The city where the artizans are numerous and men at arms are

[1] Xen. *Mem.* IV. 2. 22.

[2] Plato, *Apol.* 22 c–e; cp. Xen. *Mem.* II. 7, where Socrates strongly deprecates the prejudice against manual labour.

[3] Xen. *de Vect.* v. 4.

[4] Plato, *Rep.* VII. 522 b, IX. 590 c; *Laws*, V. 741 e; *Gorg.* 517 d–518 a; *Alcib.* I. 131 b; *Amator*, 136 b, 137 b.

[5] Plato, *Laws*, VIII. 846 d.   [6] *Ibid.* XI. 918.

[7] *Ibid.* IV. 705 b.

[8] *Rep.* II. 371 e.

[9] οὔτε βάναυσον βίον οὔτ' ἀγοραῖον, Aristot. *Pol.* IV. (VII.), 1328 b; cp. *Rhet.* I. 9. 27.

[10] γεωργοὶ μὲν γὰρ καὶ τεχνῖται καὶ πᾶν τὸ θητικὸν ἀναγκαῖον ὑπάρχειν ταῖς πόλεσιν, μέρη δὲ τῆς πόλεως τό τε ὁπλιτικὸν καὶ βουλευτικόν, Aristot. *Pol.* IV. (VII.), 1329 a; cp. VII. (V.), 1317 a.

[11] *Pol.* III. 1278 a.

few cannot attain to greatness[1]." The speech of Demosthenes against Euboulides makes it plain that in the fourth century a doubtful claim to Athenian citizenship might be damaged by pointing out that the claimant was a small tradesman. "It is your duty," the orator makes his client say to the jury, "to uphold the laws and not to regard as outlanders people who work for their living (τοὺς ἐργαζομένους)[2]." Aristotle and Euboulides would have agreed with Pollux[3], our earliest lexicographer (second century A.D.), that thetes is a name for free men who out of poverty do slave's work for money (ἐπ' ἀργυρίῳ δουλευόντων).

The Greeks despised the artizan largely because of his lack of leisure and impaired physique which to their minds necessarily implied a lack of culture and a weakened intelligence[4]. This being the ground of their contempt, the feeling must plainly have grown up when the claims of culture and of industry had become exacting. This means that it was probably subsequent to and a result of the industrial developments of the age of the tyrants; and this dating is confirmed by other considerations.

The growth of contempt for labour has been explained by Drumann[5] as due in part at least to the Persian wars and the resultant plunder, which must have made a good many citizens financially independent. The payment of the huge panels of jurymen, which at Athens did so much to release the poorer citizens from the necessity to work, was an ultimate outcome of the Persian wars. The Peloponnesian war may have completed the process. It lasted through nearly thirty campaigns (431–404 B.C.) and must have deeply disorganized the labour market. Slaves must in all

---

[1] *Pol.* IV. (VII.), 1326a. The *Politics* was based on a series of studies of particular constitutions one of which, the *Constitution of Athens*, was recovered from an Egyptian rubbish heap some thirty years ago. When Aristotle says that a city of artizans cannot attain to greatness we may feel fairly sure that artizans had played no prominent part in any of the Greek cities since the Persian wars. For the period before that his information must have been less reliable.

[2] *c. Eubulidem*, 32 (1308).

[3] Pollux, III. 82; cp. Photius s.v. "θητεία· δουλεία."

[4] See *e.g.* Xen. *Oecon.* IV. 2–3, and cp. the unusually sympathetic account of the working classes in the sophist Prodicus, a contemporary of Socrates: "let us proceed to the artizans and mechanics (χειρωνακτικοὺς καὶ βαναύσους), toiling from night to night and with difficulty providing themselves with the necessities of life and bewailing themselves and filling all their sleepless hours with lamentation and tears." Mullach, *Frag. Phil. Gr.* II. 139.

[5] *Arbeit. u. Comm.* p. 46.

directions have supplanted the free men who were wanted for military service, just as women took men's places in the modern counterpart of the Greek disaster[1]. The continued campaigning is sure to have left many of the fighting men with a distaste for the dull routine of industry[2]. In the *Plutus* of Aristophanes, brought out in 388 B.C., Poverty argues against an even distribution of wealth on the ground that it would destroy the slave trade and drive free men to manual labour as smiths, shipbuilders, tailors, wheelwrights, shoemakers, brickmakers, laundrymen, tanners and ploughmen[3]. Rather than return to their trades they preferred active service in distant lands. When early in the fourth century Agesilaus of Sparta was campaigning in Asia Minor against the King of Persia we are told that most of his troops except his own Spartans were potters, smiths, carpenters and the like[4]. Mechanical occupations are said by Aristotle to have been in his own days in some Greek cities mainly in the hands of slaves and outlanders: "in ancient times in some cities the artizan element (τὸ βάναυσον) was servile or alien, for which reason most of them are such now[5]." This growing contempt and dislike for manual labour as such, combined with the passion for freedom and independence, would make free citizens particularly unwilling to become factory hands or miners or anything that meant working under a master for a daily wage, the receipt of which tended to be regarded as a degradation[6]. Ciccotti[7] observes that piece work becomes much commoner at this

[1] Women were of course involved in the consequences of the Peloponnesian war. "I am told that many women citizens (ἀσταὶ γυναῖκες) became wet nurses and day labourers and grape pickers (τίτθαι καὶ ἔριθοι καὶ τρυγήτριαι) as a result of the misfortunes of the city in those times." Dem. *c. Eubul.* 45 (1313); cp. Xen. *Mem.* II. 7 f.

[2] Cp. the trouble that the Romans were always having with their disbanded troops.

[3] Aristoph. *Plut.* 510–525.

[4] Plut. *Ages.* 26; Polyaen. II. 1. 7; cp. Xen. *Hell.* VI. 1. 5.

[5] Aristot. *Pol.* III. 1278 a. Aristotle is of course a more valuable authority for his own days than for his "ancient times."

[6] Plato, *Rep.* II. 371 e. So Cic. *de Off.* I. 42, "est ipsa merces auctoramentum seruitutis." Cp. Zimmern, *Sociological Review*, 1909, p. 174, who however, when he says that "the Greeks never took kindly to wage earning" is thinking mainly of the fifth and fourth centuries B.C. and rather disregarding the evidence for conditions at that period being of comparatively recent growth.

[7] Ciccotti, *Tramonto d. Schiavitù*, pp. 124 f. In the extant fragments of the Erechtheum accounts for 409 B.C. the payments are partly by the piece, partly by the day.

period. He explains the tendency in abstract Marxian principles. The change may be due to much more human causes, such as the workman's growing desire to work his own hours at his own pace. The work that the free man refused to do was undertaken by the growing population of slaves. There was at this time a glut in the slave market, as is sufficiently proved by the single fact that while the prices of all other commodities went up in the fifth and fourth centuries, that of slaves went down[1]. Among the unpleasant occupations that fell more and more completely into servile hands were mining and quarrying[2], two of the occupations with which we shall find that the early tyrants were most frequently concerned.

If therefore in the fifth and fourth centuries citizen craftsmen appear to have worked mainly in small individual concerns[3], it by no means follows that the same was the case in the seventh and sixth centuries. The conditions during the later period were due to causes that only began to operate during that period. On the other hand industry must have begun to organize itself into considerable concerns somewhere about the beginning of the earlier period, at the time of the developments that are admittedly associated with the beginnings of tyranny. What was the status of the employees in these earlier enterprises such as the potteries of Corinth, the sixth century mines at Laurium, or the metal and woollen works at Samos? Almost our only piece of direct evidence on this subject is a statement of Alexis[4] that Polycrates the tyrant of Samos, whose connexion with Samian industry is established in Chapter III, "used to send for skilled artizans at very high wages ($\mu\epsilon\tau\epsilon\sigma\tau\epsilon\lambda\lambda\epsilon\tau o$ $\tau\epsilon\chi\nu\iota\tau\alpha\varsigma$ $\epsilon\pi\iota$ $\mu\iota\sigma\theta o\hat{\iota}\varsigma$ $\mu\epsilon\gamma\iota\sigma\tau o\iota\varsigma$)." These highly paid artizans may have been foreigners—Athenians, Milesians, or the like[5]—but they can scarcely have been slaves. Indirect evidence in the same direction is more abundant. Periander for example, the second tyrant of Corinth (about 620–580 B.C.), is said to have forbidden the purchase of slaves[6]. This regulation looks like an attempt towards

[1] Cavaignac, *Études Financ.* p. 173. For the large growth of the servile population in fourth century Attica see Beloch, *Rhein. Mus.* 1890, pp. 555 f.

[2] Cavaignac, *Études Financ.* p. 172; E. Meyer, *Kleinschrift.* p. 198.

[3] See Brants, *Rev. de l'Instruct. Publ. Belg.* XXVI. p. 106.

[4] Athen. XII. 540 d.

[5] Cp. on fifth century Athens Xen. (?) *Ath. Pol.* I. 12, "the city needs resident aliens owing to the number of its handicrafts ($\delta\epsilon\hat{\iota}\tau\alpha\iota$ $\mu\epsilon\tau o\iota\kappa\omega\nu$ $\delta\iota\grave{\alpha}$ $\tau\grave{o}$ $\pi\lambda\hat{\eta}\theta o\varsigma$ $\tau\hat{\omega}\nu$ $\tau\epsilon\chi\nu\hat{\omega}\nu$)."

[6] Below, p. 192.

the end of the period of tyranny at Corinth to stem an influx of servile labour.

It is doubtful whether slave owning on a large scale existed at this period[1]. The Greeks of the fifth and fourth centuries regarded slavery as they knew it as a modern development[2]. Timaeus says[3] that till recently the Locrians had a law and likewise the Phocians against possessing either maid servants or slaves (οὔτε θεραπαίνας οὔτε οἰκέτας) and that Mnason the friend of Aristotle having acquired a thousand slaves was ill-spoken of (διαβληθῆναι) among the Phocians as having deprived that number of the citizens of their daily bread. There is much therefore to be said for the view expressed by Clerc[4] that free labour flourished afresh in the seventh and sixth centuries B.C. with the overthrow of aristocracies, or in other words in the age of the early tyrants. Ciccotti has recently well observed that in all the literature from the hymn of Demeter to the writings of Plutarch slaves occupy no place in the picture of social conditions at this period[5].

It was long ago recognized by Buechsenschuetz[6] that in preclassical Greece the manual trades were in the hands of free men, but each man was his own master, there being no factories or division of labour. In classical times there was considerable division of labour and there were businesses employing a large number of hands, but citizens seldom worked in them. The age of the tyrants falls between the two epochs just formulated. It is the one short epoch in Greek history when there were probably considerable industrial enterprises employing citizen labour. Thus it is the age in Greek history when apart from all details of evidence there would be the greatest *a priori* possibility of an individual having secured the political power which may fall to the employer of organized free labour on a large scale[7].

It is difficult in these days to realize how unique a situation is here

---

[1] Cp. Phaleas, Aristot. *Pol.* II. 1267.
[2] Hdt. VI. 137, οὐ γὰρ εἶναι τοῦτον τὸν χρόνον σφίσι κω οἰκέτας.
[3] Timaeus, *ap.* Athen. VI. 264 c. [4] Clerc, *Métèques Athén.* pp. 324 f.
[5] Ciccotti, *Tramonto d. Schiavitù*, p. 47.
[6] Buechsenschuetz, *Besitz u. Erwerb.* pp. 321, 341, 193; cp. Waltz, *Rev. Hist.* 117 (1914), pp. 5-41.
[7] In the oriental Greek states of the Hellenistic period, as also in the Roman East, the government seems sometimes to have run big industrial concerns whose employees have been held to have been free men. Beloch, *Zeits. f. Socialwiss.* II. pp. 24-25. But these establishments belong to a quite different political order from that with which we are now concerned.

implied. We are apt to forget how completely slaves were excluded from any part whatsoever in the life of the state. Politically they were non-existent, and the whole free population was vitally concerned in keeping them so. The slave was an essential form of property. To question the institution of slavery in ancient Greece was like questioning the fundamental claims of property in modern Europe. It was a proclamation of war to the knife against the whole established order of things. Individual slaves might win freedom and political rights, but any organized effort at emancipation on the part of the slaves themselves was put down with merciless severity. When in 71 B.C. Pompey and Crassus had crushed the slave rebellion of Spartacus, the moderate and statesmanlike revolutionary whose name has come again to such prominence in recent days, six thousand of his followers were crucified along the road from Rome to Naples. The distance is about 150 miles. At the time therefore of this exemplary punishment if anyone had occasion to pass along the road in question, one of the most frequented in the whole Roman state, he would see some forty of these victims writhing in agony or hanging dead upon the cross for every mile of his journey. No piece of frightfulness quite so thorough and methodical is to be found in all the frightful history of the present century. The punishment of 71 B.C. is typical of the whole attitude of the ancient republics of Greece and Rome towards rebellious slaves. No wonder then if in their history servile labour played no active part[1].

(e) the history of the states where there was never a tyrant,
Some parts of Greece never passed under a tyrant. The most conspicuous of these is Sparta[2]. The Spartans never struck real coins. The iron pieces "heavy and hard to carry[3]" that formed the classical Spartan currency seem to be a survival of a premonetary medium of

[1] For slave revolts in Greece see Diod. xxxiv. 2. 19 and Athen. vi. 272 f. (Laurium, probably latter part of second century B.C.); Athen. vi. 265c (Chios, apparently later still, *pace* Boeckh, *Public Econ. of Athens*, ii. pp. 470–471); cp. Wallon, *l'Esclavage*[2], i. pp. 318 f., 483–484. The movements at Laurium and Chios in the Peloponnesian war, Thuc. vii. 27, viii. 40, seem to have been not so much revolts against slavery as desertions from one set of masters to another. When Holm, *Hist. Greece* (English trans.), i. p. 263, says that the essence of tyranny was that it rested on force he makes a statement which, so far as it is true, differentiates tyranny from no other ancient form of government.

[2] ἀεὶ ἀτυράννευτος ἦν, Thuc. i. 18.

[3] Plut. *Lysander*, 17.

exchange[1]. Sparta was also practically without any urban population[2]. It may be more than an accidental coincidence that the most anti-tyrannical state in Greece was without a real coinage, and backward in trade and industry.

Another region where nothing is heard of early tyrants is Thessaly. Thessaly had a large serf population called πενέσται, whose position much resembled that of the Spartan helots[3]. Both were mainly agricultural labourers, *asscripti glebae*. Such a population might serve the purpose of a would-be military despot. Pausanias, the Spartan generalissimo against the Persians, had dealings with the helots when he was trying to make himself tyrant of all Greece[4]. But for a commercial tyrant they would not be very useful material. The other important district that seems to have been immune from tyrants is Boeotia. It is natural to associate this immunity with the dominantly agricultural character of the district where Hesiod wrote his *Works and Days*[5].

(*f*) steps taken to prevent a recurrence of tyranny.

When the tyrants had been suppressed or expelled, or their families became extinct, the government in most cases either reverted to an oligarchy or developed into a democracy. Oligarchs and democrats (or at least democratic governments) seem to have been equally inspired with a hatred of the tyranny. The steps that they took and the fears that they displayed under that influence may be expected to throw light on the source of the tyrant's power. Once more however it is necessary to limit ourselves to the fifth century, when the conception of the tyrant had not yet undergone the great change that came over it in the days of Dionysius of Syracuse[6].

---

[1] Hill, *Handbook of Greek and Roman Coins*, p. 17, quoting Lenormant. Hill himself inclines to think that the Spartan coinage may have resembled the iron pieces of Aeginetan weight attributed to Tegea and Argos. But these latter are not "heavy and hard to carry."

[2] οὐ ξυνοικισθείσης πόλεως...κατὰ κώμας δὲ...οἰκισθείσης, Thuc. I. 10.

[3] Aristot. *Pol.* II. 1269a. [4] Thuc. I. 132.

[5] In the days of Plato Thebes contained one citizen of extraordinary wealth in Ismenias, "the man who had just recently received the wealth of Polycrates." Ismenias is classed with Periander, Perdiccas, and Xerxes as a wealthy man who thought he possessed great power; but he is not called a tyrant. He had become rich not through his own wisdom and care, but suddenly as the result of a bequest, so that his wealth would apparently fall under a different category from that of the seventh and sixth century tyrants, and he is in fact placed by Plato in a very miscellaneous company. Plato, *Meno*, 90a; *Rep.* I. 336a.

[6] See below, pp. 30 f.

Of the oligarchic Greek states our knowledge is comparatively slight. History has preserved for us no oligarchic counterpart to the picture that we still possess of democratic Athens. But thanks to the *Politics* of Aristotle, that precious storehouse of incidental statements and remarks, the fact has come down to us that[1] "in many oligarchies it is not allowed to engage in business (χρηματίζεσθαι, perhaps better construed 'money-making'), but there are laws forbidding it."

Of the anti-tyrannical measures of democratic Athens during the century that followed the expulsion of the Peisistratids we are better informed. So are we also as to the measures taken in the early days of republican Rome to prevent a re-establishment of the kingship. The evidence supports the view that in both cases what the established government mainly feared was the rich man becoming politically powerful by means of his riches.

Only, if that view is right, why is it nowhere specifically formulated in extant records?

One set of causes has already been incidentally indicated. The state of things that could lead to a tyranny of the early type was passing away at the time of the Persian wars. The payment of jurymen rendered a recurrence of it in Athens finally impossible. Sparta had always been equally averse from making either coins or tyrants. What Athens and Sparta both disapproved of had little chance of finding a home in fifth century Greece. It was during this period that Herodotus and Thucydides, our earliest Greek historians, composed their works. Each wrote the history of a great war. But even if their themes had been more peaceful, it would be a mistake to imagine that their enquiries into economic causes would have been any more searching. Cornford in his illuminating study of Thucydides[2] complains of the general blindness of the Greeks in this direction. This is hardly fair on the Greeks. Thucydides and his successors are not unusually blind. It is the moderns who are unusual in the way they fix their eyes upon this particular aspect of history. Only in times of financial and industrial revolution does the world at large become distinctly conscious of the financial and industrial basis of its social and political organization. The revolution now proceeding

The evidence is not conclusive; but contemporary documents are meagre and no Greek writers say much about economic causes.

[1] Aristot. *Pol.* VIII. (VI.), 1316b.
[2] *Thucydides Mythistoricus*, p. 32.

has produced this effect. It has led modern historians to concentrate, perhaps unduly, upon the investigation of economic causes and conditions. From this modern point of view the Bank of England or the Standard Oil Company is as fruitful and important a subject of historical research as the policy of a prime minister or the strategy of a general. But this attitude is unusual. The financial revolution associated with the realms of Gyges and Pheidon had been accepted by the whole Greek world before the outbreak of the Persian wars. For writers of the new epoch that began with Salamis and Plataea economic conditions must have appeared a changeless and somewhat boring factor. If the early tyrants had previously been kings of finance or industry, we must not expect many statements or illustrations of the fact in the *Persian Wars* of Herodotus, or the *Peloponnesian War* of Thucydides. It should satisfy us if, as is the case, their allusions to the tyranny are all in complete harmony with that hypothesis.

The writers of the fourth century offer a more serious difficulty. Both Plato and Aristotle deal at some length with the origin of tyranny, and both give explanations quite different from the one that is here offered. As their accounts have been the basis of all subsequent views, it is necessary to state briefly what they are.

The view is at variance with statements of Plato, Aristotle, and subsequent writers:

According to Plato[1] "it is fairly plain that tyranny develops out of democracy."

When a tyrant comes into being, the root he springs from is the people's champion, and no other....What then is the beginning of the change from protector to tyrant?...The people's champion finding a multitude very ready to follow him...enslaves and slaughters, and hints at the abolition of debts and the partition of land. When such a man so behaves, is he not subsequently bound and doomed either to be destroyed by his enemies or to become tyrant and be changed from a man into a wolf? This is what becomes of the leader of the rebellion against the owners of property[2].

[1] *Rep.* VIII. 562a; cp. 564a, 565d.

[2] On tyrants as plunderers cp. Hdt. v. 92: "(Cypselus) deprived many people of their property." So Ephorus, *F.H.G.* III. p. 392, "He banished the Bacchiads and confiscated their possessions." Cp. Plato, *Phaedo*, 82a; *Rep.* VIII. end. The spoils of victory however are quite a different thing from the litigious confiscations of fifth and fourth century demagogues. The way the early tyrants used their wealth is sufficient proof that it was not mainly plunder. There is nothing of the condottiere about the typical early tyrant. Cp. H. Sieveking, *Kapitalist. Entwick. i. d. ital. Städt. d. Mittelalt.* in *Viertelj. f. Soc. u. Wirts.* VII. pp. 64 f.

CH. I   INTRODUCTION   27

Plato goes on to describe how the tyrant either gets banished and effects his return by force or avoids exile only by the famous expedient of demanding a bodyguard.

Aristotle's account is similar, but less rigid, and emphasizes the military element. "In ancient times, whenever the same individual became both demagogue and general, the result was a tyranny. It is fairly true to say that the majority of the early tyrants have developed out of demagogues[1]." Other tyrants he describes as establishing themselves as such after having previously either reigned as kings or held for a long period some important office[2]. In ancient times Aristotle includes the fifth century (and perhaps the beginning of the fourth), as is shown by his quoting Dionysius of Syracuse[3]. Plato's treatment is less historical, but as he specifically excludes the possibility of any other sort of tyrant pedigree than that he gives, his account is plainly meant to hold good for all periods[4].

In short both Plato and Aristotle regard their accounts of the tyrant's origin as being of general application. As such they have always been accepted, and not at first sight without reason. The Platonic-Aristotelian pedigree (with an alternative) is already ascribed to the tyrant by Herodotus: "under a democracy it is impossible for corruption not to prevail...., until some individual, championing the people ($\pi\rho\sigma\tau\grave{\alpha}\varsigma$ $\tau o\hat{v}$ $\delta\acute{\eta}\mu ov$), blossoms out into a monarch ($\mu o\acute{v}\nu\alpha\rho\chi o\varsigma$ = tyrant)[5]." But what are the

but their picture of the rise of tyranny clashes with known facts about the period,

---

[1] *Pol.* VII. (v.), 1305 a; cp. VII. (v.), 1310 b, ὁ δὲ τύραννος (καθίσταται) ἐκ τοῦ δήμου καὶ τοῦ πλήθους.

[2] "Pheidon and others became tyrants with a kingship to start from...those in the parts about Ionia, and Phalaris, from their offices," *Pol.* VII. (v.), 1310 b; cp. *ibid.*, "through starting with power, some that of kingly office," and *ibid.*, "other (tyrannies) from kings overstepping their inherited positions"; VII. (v.), 1308 a, "attempts at tyranny are made in some places by demagogues, in other places by dynasts, or those who hold the highest offices when they hold them for a long time."

[3] Cp. also *Pol.* VII. (v.), 1305 a, where "modern times" means since rhetoric developed and demagogues ceased to be soldiers.

[4] Or else for no historical period at all. As pointed out to me by my colleague Professor W. G. de Burgh, Plato's order is confessedly an order of ascending injustice (*Rep.* VIII. 545 a; cp. 344 a), in introducing which he invokes the muses of Homer and asks them not to be too serious (545 e). Plato's evidence on this point need not be taken so literally as that of the historically minded Aristotle.

[5] Hdt. III. 82. See also Xen. *Hell.* VII. I. 44–46; and cp. Porzio, *Cipselidi*, p. 207, n. 1.

facts? The process just described makes the early tyrant develop out of a demagogue who is usually also a general. Demagogues may have existed in Greece before tyrannies began to be established; but the evidence for their having done so is extraordinarily meagre[1], and it is highly doubtful whether Aristotle adds to it. He does not attempt a picture of a seventh or sixth century demagogue. Those of his own day secured their influence by confiscations effected through the popular courts[2]. They are essentially the product of a full-blown democracy, and pretyrannical democracies are extremely doubtful. Athens is a special and only partial case, and even there, in spite of Solon, Herodotus[3] can speak of Cleisthenes, who overthrew the tyranny, as "the man who established the democracy." The demagogues from whom Aristotle derives his early tyrants are mainly military demagogues: "the tyrant," he says, "is also prone to make war[4]."

This statement is hardly borne out by the facts. As a body, in spite of the times they lived in, the early tyrants were remarkable for their works not of war but of peace[5]. Some of them indeed, as for instance Orthagoras and Peisistratus, are reported to have distinguished themselves as soldiers before they became tyrants. The warlike exploits of the youthful Orthagoras are discussed below[6]. He cannot have been really prone to militarism, since Aristotle declares that a successor of his altered the character of the Sicyonian tyranny by becoming warlike[7]. Peisistratus' early feats of war are

[1] Neither the Homeric Thersites nor the "leaders of the people" of Solon show any of the essential features of the demagogue as known to Herodotus, Plato, and Aristotle. Individual early tyrants are often said to have been demagogues, but only by the writers of the fourth century or later, whose evidence on this point is valueless; cp. below, pp. 30 f.

[2] "The demagogues of the present day win favour with the democracies by securing many confiscations through the law courts." Aristotle, *Pol.* VIII. (VI.), 1320 a.

[3] Hdt. VI. 131.

[4] πολεμοποιός, Aristot. *Pol.* VII. (V.), 1313 b; cp. 1305 a (οἱ προστάται τοῦ δήμου, ὅτε πολεμικοὶ γένοιντο, τυραννίδι ἐπετίθεντο) and Plato, *Rep.* VIII. 566 e (πολέμους ἀεὶ κινεῖ).

[5] Cp. Thuc. I. 17, δι' ἀσφαλείας ὅσον ἐδύναντο μάλιστα τὰς πόλεις ᾤκουν. Hermann, *Staatsaltertümer*[5] p. 253, n. 5, notices that this passage contradicts Plato, *Rep.* VIII. 566 e and Aristot. *Pol.* VII. (V.), 1313 b, 1305 a, which make the typical tyrant warlike. He does not realize that Thucydides is describing the tyrants of an earlier age.

[6] Below, pp. 257 f.

[7] Aristot. *Pol.* VII. (V.), 1315 b. The same change is recorded in the tyranny at

well attested. Naturally enough he made political capital out of them. "He asked of the people that he should receive from them a bodyguard, having previously distinguished himself in the expedition against Megara, when he captured Nisaea and performed other great deeds[1]." But earlier in the same chapter Herodotus has made it perfectly plain that Peisistratus was not a military despot. "Having formed designs on the tyranny he raised a third faction, and having collected partizans, and posing as a champion of the Hillmen, he devised as follows." It was the faction of the Hillmen and not[2] the Megarean expedition, that was the stepping-stone to the tyranny. Who the Hillmen were is discussed in the chapter on Athens. It has never been suggested that they were military[3].

A military demagogue who makes himself tyrant is essentially the product of an advanced democracy threatened by invasion from without. When the tyrants of the seventh and sixth centuries secured their positions there was no foreign invader without the gates and no democracy within. Aristotle[4] calls democracy "the last word in tyranny" ($\dot{\eta}$ τελευταία τυραννίς). From the point of view of historical development the converse comes much nearer to the truth, and tyranny is the first word in democracy. The evolution of the tyrant as described in Aristotle and Plato cannot have taken place until after the reforms of Cleisthenes or precisely the period when the last of the early tyrants was finally banished from Greece. The two philosophers, and likewise Herodotus in the passage just quoted[5], must be reading into more ancient times a state of things that only became prevalent shortly before their own[6]. The words of Herodotus are put into the mouth of Darius. This means that they

and is due to false generalizations from the conditions of their own days,

Corinth: there Cypselus the first tyrant is said to have been a demagogue, possibly because he became tyrant and was not stated in Aristotle's sources to have previously waged any war.

[1] Hdt. I. 59; according to the *Ath. Pol.* 17, "it is obvious nonsense to say that Peisistratus was general in the war for Salamis against the Megareans." But this statement based on chronological arguments can only call in question the date and character of Peisistratus' warlike achievements, not their whole historicity.

[2] *Pace* E. Meyer, *G. d. A.* II. p. 666, following Justin II. 8 (quasi sibi non patriae uicisset, tyrannidem per dolum occupat).

[3] On the essentially peaceful character of the Athenian tyranny, see Ciccotti, *Tramonto d. Schiavitù*, p. 49.

[4] *Pol.* VII. (v.), 1312*b*.   [5] III. 82.

[6] Mixed of course with earlier features. *E.g.* in Plato (*Rep.* VIII. 566*a–b*) the banishment and forcible return and the bodyguard are all genuine Peisistratus.

really hang loose and may be influenced by the careers of contemporary demagogues like Cleon.

<small>and particularly from the career of Dionysius of Syracuse.</small>

But the main source of error lies in Plato and Aristotle, and is still more obvious. The most distinguished figure in the political history of the early part of the fourth century was Dionysius of Syracuse. Dionysius is, like Plato's tyrant in the *Republic*, the product of democracy: like Aristotle's in the *Politics* he begins his career as a military demagogue. The resemblances are not accidental. Dionysius made himself tyrant when Plato was just reaching manhood. Plato visited his court and few political experiments have become more famous than Plato's attempt to turn the tyrant's son into the ideal philosopher king[1]. Aristotle naturally shared his master's interest in the famous Syracusan. His *Politics* bears frequent witness to the fact. It contains only eight references each to the tyrant houses of Corinth and Athens as against twenty to those of Syracuse (eleven to the Dionysii and Dion, nine to the Deinomenidae). Of the three individuals, Theagenes, Peisistratus, Dionysius, chosen to illustrate the way a tyrant may be produced out of a military demagogue, Dionysius is the only one whose career the process fits.

Other philosophers of the period wrote under the same dominant influence, notably Aeschines the Socratic, and Aristippus, both of whom had stayed with the tyrant[2]. Similarly with the fourth century historians: their notion of a tyrant was Dionysius as described by that potentate's own historian, his fellow-citizen Philistus.

Everything tended to confirm this view. The greatness of Dionysius naturally drew attention to that of Gelo and Hiero, his predecessors at Syracuse. Gelo and Hiero were, like Dionysius, military despots. To later generations they were the great soldiers who had saved Sicily from the Carthaginians and Etruscans. Their contemporary Pausanias had tried to raise himself from generalissimo of the Greek army to tyrant of all Greece[3]. These events were still in

---

[1] Plato, *Letters* 1, 2, 3, 4, 7, 8, 13. On the genuineness of the Platonic letters see Burnet, *Thales to Plato*, pp. 206, 207 and note.

[2] Diog. Laert. II. 7. 63; 8. 67 f.

[3] Aristotle, *Pol.* VII. (V.), 1307 a, where Hanno of Carthage, Aristotle's contemporary, is also quoted. Both these would-be tyrants tampered with the slave population (see Thucydides, I. 132 (Pausanias), Orosius, IV. 6 (Hanno)), and may thus have further helped to obliterate the picture of the peace-loving early tyrant and his relationship to free labour.

men's minds. Of the earlier tyrants they had only hazy notions[1]. The best remembered were probably the Peisistratids, both from their late date and from the fact that they were Athenians. Peisistratus, as has been already noticed, chanced early in his career to have distinguished himself as a soldier. It so happened that Polycrates, the other great tyrant of the latter half of the sixth century, also engaged in war. It was forced upon him by the Persians. The evidence is all against the view that it was the basis of his power. But the warlike achievements of these two rulers, the last and perhaps the greatest of the earlier tyrants, lent colour to Aristotle's hasty generalizations[2].

Aristotle himself, speaking of the ways of maintaining a tyranny, says that "the traditional method, in accordance with which most tyrants conduct their government, is said to have been mainly instituted by Periander of Corinth[3]?" Only a few pages later in the same work[4] we are told that Periander abandoned the policy of his father Cypselus and that he did so by becoming warlike or in other words by approximating more to Dionysius of Syracuse. Once more then the typical tyrant of Aristotle is a ruler who departs from the policy of a typical founder of an early tyranny.

For an example of the victory of the Aristotelian view over the truth we may compare Herodotus, I. 59, which states that Peisistratus, who had fought against Megara, made himself tyrant by means of the faction of the Hillmen, with Justin, II. 8, according to whom "Peisistratus, as though he had conquered (the Megareans) for himself, not for his country, seized by craft the tyranny." Justin is a perversion of a passage in Chapter 14 of the Aristotelian *Constitution of Athens*, which states that Peisistratus, "having the reputation of being a great friend of the people, and having greatly distinguished himself in the war against Megara," secured his bodyguard and the tyranny. Aristotle misinterprets the Hillmen and exaggerates the importance of the Megarean expedition. Justin omits the former

---

[1] Cp. Thuc. I. 20; VI. 54 on the inaccurate accounts of the Peisistratids prevalent in Athens in the historian's own days.

[2] On the way that Aristotle's ideas often colour the facts he quotes see Muretus, *Var. Lect.* I. 14; Koehler, *Sitzungsb. Preuss. Akad.* 1892, p. 505; Endt, *Wien. Stud.* XXIV. (1901), pp. 50–51, quoted Porzio, *Cipselidi*, p. 244.

On the general dubiousness of fifth and fourth century explanations of seventh and sixth century motives, see Macan on the *Athenaion Politeia* in *J.H.S.* XII. pp. 34 f.

[3] Aristot. *Pol.* VII. (v.) 1313 a.   [4] Aristot. *Pol.* VII. (v.) 1315 b.

altogether and makes the latter the sole cause of Peisistratus obtaining the tyranny.

Aristotle's conception of the tyrant class as drawn mainly from that of the military demagogue was taken over by the Romans. In the chapter on Rome it will be shown how little this conception fits in with the Romans' own early history. But the times before the great wars at Rome (Samnite, Pyrrhic, Punic) are like those before the Persian wars in Greece. They belong to a different epoch from those that follow. The later history of the Roman republic harmonizes with Aristotle's view. The Gracchi may be represented as demagogues who failed to make themselves supreme for lack of military power[1]. Marius, Pompey, and Caesar succeeded in proportion as they realized the Aristotelian combination. The fourth century conception was therefore unchallenged by Roman writers, the more so since Dionysius appears for a while to have dominated the Roman conception of a Greek tyrant[2]. Fortunately however, owing to the careless way the Roman historians worked over their material, they have left us glimpses of the different conditions that had once existed.

The view that was thus disseminated in classical Greece and Rome was naturally accepted by the scholars of the renaissance and has prevailed ever since.

[1] Mommsen, *Hist. Rome* (Eng. trans.), III. p. 333.
[2] Cp. Dion. Hal. VII. 1, on the statement in his oldest authorities that Dionysius sent corn to Rome in the time of Spurius Cassius (492 B.C.). The name Dionysius appears here a good half century before his birth, doubtless as the Sicilian tyrant *par excellence*.

Chapter II. *Athens*

Exceptional position of Athens.
Of all the tyrants of the seventh and sixth centuries none are so well known to us as those who reigned at Athens. No other city has left us so clear a picture of the state of things not only during the tyranny but also immediately before and after it. Solon lived to see Peisistratus make himself supreme. Herodotus, born a Persian subject about 484 B.C., must have had opportunities of questioning first-hand authorities on the later years of the Athenian tyranny, while his younger contemporary Thucydides was in a particularly favoured position for getting information on this subject through his relationship with the Philaidae, of whose rivalry with the Peisistratidae there will be occasion to speak later in this chapter[1].

This comparative abundance of information is the reason why Athens has been made the starting-point of this enquiry. But even so our knowledge is meagre enough. And there is a special reason for using it with caution. So far in the history of the world there has been only one Athens. The developments that took place in the city during the first two centuries of the democracy are without parallel. Can we be certain that Athens was not already unique in the period immediately preceding? One point in which the
Athens before the establishment of the tyranny.
Athenian tyranny was exceptional meets us at the first glance. With the single exception of Samos, all the other famous tyrannies of the earlier type, at least in the Aegean area, arose in the seventh century. But apart from this fact it will be found that the tyranny at Athens in the sixth century followed the same course as it appears to have done at places like Corinth and Argos, Sardis and Miletus in the seventh. The more highly developed an organism is, the longer it

---

[1] Beloch, *Gr. G.*² i. ii. p. 295, is surely underestimating the value of Thucydides' express statements about the Peisistratids when he calls them "merely oral traditions about the relations of a family that had been expelled from Athens 100 years before." This way of putting it hardly suggests that less than 20 years may have separated the death of Hippias from the birth of Thucydides, and that the tyrant's family was still sufficiently flourishing at the end of the Peloponnesian war to be excluded from the amnesty that restored Thucydides to Athens (Didymus *ap.* Marcellin. *Vit. Thuc.* 32).

takes to reach maturity. This is perhaps the reason why Athens in the sixth century appears in some respects to be a hundred years behind some of the cities whom she was destined so completely to eclipse.

Athens was not exclusively commercial. Her large territory made her partly agricultural. To this fact may be due her failure to compete commercially in the seventh century with cities like Aegina and Corinth[1]. Hence too the late rise of the tyranny. It appears only when the commercial and industrial element had got the upper hand. There was indeed the attempt of Cylon, who conspired to make himself tyrant within a generation of the first appearance of tyranny on the mainland of Greece[2]. But Cylon failed because, though wealthy ($\dot{o}\lambda\upsilon\mu\pi\iota o\nu\iota\kappa\eta s$) and influential ($\delta\upsilon\nu\alpha\tau \acute{o}s$), he could not possibly, in the Athens of his day, be the leader of any dominant organized commercial activity. He was merely an ambitious member of the aristocracy ($\tau\hat{\omega}\nu$ $\pi\acute{\alpha}\lambda\alpha\iota$ $\epsilon\dot{\upsilon}\gamma\epsilon\nu\acute{\eta}s$), connected with the great band of merchant princes only by marriage[3]. The attempt and its result are both what might have been expected from the position of Athens at the time.

Soon after Cylon's attempt Athens began to rival Corinth in the pottery trade, and the influence of the rich city merchants and exporters doubtless increased. But even in pottery the great vogue of Attic ware was still to come, and Solon's measures for encouraging the growth of olives and the export of olive oil also belong to this period[4]: the importance of the landed aristocracy who owned the olive yards must have increased almost equally. No merchant therefore attempted by means of the wealth that he had amassed or the labour that he employed to seize the tyranny. The landed aristocracy were also wealthy and they too employed much labour, and it so happened that the best part of the Attic plain, where lay their estates, was situated round the city, as Cylon discovered to his cost when he seized the Acropolis. Tyranny was almost impossible.

[1] See also chapter III, p. 69.
[2] Beloch, *Rhein. Mus.* L. (1895), p. 252, n. 1, puts Cylon's attempt into the time between Solon and Peisistratus, De Sanctis, *Atthis²*, pp. 280 f., into the time of Peisistratus' exile; O. Seeck, *Klio*, IV. pp. 318 f., puts it at earliest early in the career of Peisistratus; Costanzi, *Riv. d. Stor. Ant.* v. pp. 518-19, about 570 B.C.; so also Lenschau *ap.* Bursian, *Jahresbericht* 176 (1918), p. 190. But see *e.g.* Ledl, *Stud. z. d. ält. ath. Verfassungsges.* pp. 77 f.
[3] Thuc. I. 126.   [4] Plut. *Solon*, 24.

The leading man at Athens was not a mere millionaire, as in the more exclusively trading states. Solon had indeed some experience of trade[1], but he was essentially a politician with a gift for finance, not a financier or merchant with political ambitions. He became, not a tyrant but a lawgiver.

Solon tried to provide for the difficulties that he saw resulting from the existence of two evenly matched parties, the landowners of the plain and the traders of the coast. The tyranny arose from the political organization of a new interest by Peisistratus, who, to quote the exact words of Herodotus:

Peisistratus makes himself tyrant by organizing a new party.

While the coast men of Athens and those of the plain were at strife...having formed designs on ($καταφρονήσας$) the tyranny, proceeded to raise ($ἤγειρε$) a third faction[2].

Some ancient writers represent Peisistratus as owing his tyranny to his gifts as an orator or demagogue[3]. Reasons are given in Chapter I for not accepting this view, and also for not believing that it was mainly as a successful soldier that Peisistratus secured the throne[4]. It was as founder and leader of the "third faction" of Herodotus that Peisistratus made himself tyrant, and he seems largely to have built up his influence with them by rendering them aid, doubtless financial[5].

To understand the position of Peisistratus and to ascertain the basis of his power it is obviously of the first importance that we should know who precisely were the men who made up this third faction. Unfortunately this question cannot be answered directly

---

[1] Plut. *Solon*, 2; cp. Aristot. *Ath. Pol.* 6, where Solon's enemies accuse him of (dishonest) financial speculations. Aristotle dismisses the charge.

[2] Hdt. I. 59; Plut., *Solon*, 13, *Amat.* 18, *Praecept.* 10 (*Moral.* 763, 805), imagines this third party as existing at the time of Solon's reforms: but his account is inconsistent in itself and contradicts Hdt. See Sandys, *Ath. Pol.*² p. 55, Busolt, *Gr. G.*² (1895), II. p. 302, n. 2, following Diels, *Abh. Berl. Akad.* 1885, p. 20, and Landwehr, *Philol.* Suppl. v. (1889), p. 155.

[3] So Isocr. *Panath.* 148 (263); Aristot. *Pol.* VII. (v.), 1310b; cp. Cic. *de Orat.* III. 34; *Brutus*, 27, 41; Val. Max. VIII. 9; Dio Chrys. XXII.

[4] *Pace* Aristot. *Ath. Pol.* 22 ($ὅτι\ Πεισίστρατος\ δημαγωγὸς\ καὶ\ στρατηγὸς\ ὢν\ τύραννος\ κατέστη$).

[5] Cp. Plut. *Solon*, 29, "helping the needy" of Peisistratus when first suspected by Solon of aiming at tyranny: cp. also Aristot. *Pol.* VII. (v.), 1305a (tr. Welldon), "the ground of this confidence being their detestation of the wealthy classes. This was the case at Athens with Peisistratus in consequence of his feud with the (wealthy landed) proprietors of the plain."

from the information that has come down to us. So before sifting the evidence that bears on it, it will be well to examine some later and better known phases of the tyrant's career.

After the tyrant had first established himself he is reported to have been twice banished and twice restored. After his second restoration "he proceeded to root his tyranny with many mercenaries, and with revenues of money, of which part was gathered from the home country, part from the river Strymon[1]."

How Peisistratus "rooted" his power.

The Strymon (Struma) flows through the famous mining district which was afterwards annexed by Philip of Macedon, and brought him his enormous wealth. It is scarcely conceivable that Peisistratus' revenues from this region came from any other source than the mines[2]. Hence Guiraud, in his interesting but sober account of ancient Greek industry, has already been led to suggest that Peisistratus' Attic revenues were derived from a similar source, and that he worked the mines of Laurium[3].

Peisistratus was not using revenues from mines for the first time in his career, when he proceeded to "root his tyranny" in the manner just described. He had already used the same means to compass his second restoration. When driven from Athens for the second time he had "proceeded to the parts round Pangaion, where he made money, and having hired soldiers he went back to Eretria, and in the eleventh year made his first attempt to recover his position by force[4]." Herodotus appears to think that all the period of exile was spent at Eretria; but he too states it to have been spent in collecting money (ἕως...τὰ χρήματα ἤγειρε). The result was that "he now held the tyranny securely[5]." Mt Pangaion is the name of the great

How he secured his second restoration.

---

[1] Hdt. I. 64. Grote's translation, III. (ed. 1888), p. 329, n. 4, which makes the money come from Athens and the mercenaries from Thrace, is highly improbable. Amphipolis, the chief fifth century city on the lower Strymon, is described by Thucydides, IV. 108, as useful to Athens "from its revenues of money." Grote's objections to making Peisistratus a Thracian mining magnate are met below.

[2] So Perdrizet, *Klio*, x. (1910), p. 5.

[3] Guiraud, *La Main-d'Œuvre dans l'ancienne Grèce*, pp. 30, 31; cp. von Fritze, *Zeits. f. Num.* xx. (1897), p. 154, who notes that Maronea, the name of the place in the Laurium district mined in the time of Peisistratus, is also the name of a town in Thrace opposite Thasos (said by Philochorus, *F.H.G.*, I. p. 404, to have been alluded to by Archilochus; cp. Hom. *Od.* IX. 197). E. Curtius (quoted *ibid.*) regards the Attic Maronea as having been named after the Thracian.

[4] Aristot. *Ath. Pol.* 15. [5] Hdt. I. 62, 64.

mining district to the East of the lower Strymon. The mention of it confirms the view that Peisistratus had a personal connexion with the Thracian mines. Eretria, on the West coast of Euboea, is an obvious place from which to swoop down on East Attica, but on the other hand in Euboea too there were mining districts[1], and Eretria had a settlement just to the East of Mount Pangaion, if Svoronos is right in his very plausible identification of the modern Kavalla with the "Skabala: a place of the Eretrians" of Stephanus Byzantinus[2].

About the tyrant's first restoration there is only a story in Herodotus which the historian himself describes as a "very silly business." Its consideration is best left over till we have dealt with his original seizure of the throne. If for this earlier stage of his career the evidence is less specific, we must not be surprised. Like Augustus, Peisistratus was careful, especially at first, to observe the outward forms of the constitution which he overthrew, so that the realities of the situation would not be patent to everybody[3].

The "Hill-men" through whom Peisistratus made himself tyrant

The party through which Peisistratus made himself tyrant is called by Herodotus the Ὑπεράκριοι[4]. The Aristotelian *Constitution of Athens* calls them the Διάκριοι[5], Plutarch sometimes Διακριεῖς sometimes Ἔπακροι[6]. The English terminology is equally fluctuating. Hill, Mountain, and Upland have all been used.

Modern historians have mostly explained the party as made up of small farmers, agricultural labourers, herdsmen and the like, and have generally assigned them to one special district, the mountainous region of North and North-east Attica[7]. But this view, as shown below in detail in an appendix[8], is based on a misunderstanding of the texts that are quoted in its support, and is at variance with all the ancient evidence, whether as regards the political propensities

---

[1] Of iron and copper, Steph. Byz. s.v. Αἰδηψός, Χαλκίς, Eustath. *ad Dion. Periegat.* 764.

[2] Svoronos, *Journ. Int. d'Arch. Num.* xv. (1913), pp. 233-4.

[3] Cp. Muenzer u. Strack, *Münz. Nord-Griech.* ii. i. p. 8, n. 1.

[4] Hdt. 1. 59; so Dion. Hal. 1. 13.

[5] Aristot. *Ath. Pol.* 13.

[6] Plut. *Solon*, 13; *Praecept.* 10 (*Moral.* 805); *Amat.* 18 (*Moral.* 763).

[7] See *e.g.* Poehlmann, *Grundriss*[4] p. 85; E. Meyer, *G. d. A.* ii. p. 663; Sandys, *Ath. Pol.*[2] p. 55; Mauri, *Cittadini Lavoratori dell' Attica*, p. 29; Grundy, *Thucydides and Hist. of his Age*, p. 116; Haase, *Abhand. Hist. Phil. Gesell. Breslau*, i. p. 105.

[8] Below, Appendix A.

of agricultural labourers or the state of cultivation of the Attic mountains. It takes no account of the facts just brought forward as to how the tyrant regained and maintained his power.

In a paper that I published in 1906[1] these facts were made the basis of a new explanation of the Hillmen of Peisistratus. According to the view there put forward the most important section of Peisistratus' followers were the miners who worked the famous silver mines of South Attica, and it was as leader of this mining population that Peisistratus raised himself to the tyranny. At the time this view was little more than a conjecture, topographically dubious. Of the only two places, Plotheia and Semachidai, known to have been situated in the Hill Country, Plotheia had been shown by tombstones to lie somewhere between Marathon and Kephisia[2], and as this fact seemed to confirm the theory of an exclusively Northern Hill Country, Semachidai, for the site of which as within the limits of the three trittyes of its tribe no evidence was available, was placed up in the North in the inland trittys. But that this location was wrong is made practically certain by the discovery of an inscription, published in 1910 by the Greek scholar Oikonomos, that bears directly on the point. It dates from 349–8 B.C. and defines the position of various mining concessions. One of them is described as near Laurium and bordered on the South by the road leading past Rhagon to Laurium and the Semacheion[3].

were probably the miners of the Laurium district

which was certainly part of the Hill Country

The Semacheion is convincingly explained by Oikonomos as the shrine of Semachos, who gave his name to the deme Semachidai[4]. From this fact he proceeds quite logically to argue that we must decide on a more Southerly position for that deme than those proposed by Milchhoefer and Loeper[5], "since the mine to the South of which Semachidai lay, was situated in the neighbourhood

---

[1] *J.H.S.* XXVI. pp. 136–8.

[2] *A.J.A.* 1889, p. 426; cp. Haase, *Abhand. Hist. Phil. Gesell. Breslau*, I. p. 69, n. 16.

[3] *Ath. Mitt.* XXXV. (1910), p. 286, ll. 18–21, μέταλλον ἀνασάξιμον ἐπὶ Λαυρέωι...ὧι γε[ιτνιᾷ...πρὸς] νότο[ν] ἡ ὁδὸς ἡ ἔξω τοῦ Ῥάγωνος ἐπὶ Λαύρειον φέρουσα καὶ τὸ Σημάχειον.

[4] Steph. Byz. s.v.

[5] *Abh. Berl. Akad.* 1892, p. 37; cp. *ibid.* 47; *Ath. Mitt.* XVII. pp. 422, 424.

of Laurium¹." Semachidai belonged to the tribe Antiochis². In the electoral organization of Cleisthenes the coast trittys of the tribe Antiochis occupied the Western part of the mining district, including the villages of Amphitrope (Metropisi), Besa, and Anaphlystus. Thus Oikonomos' conclusions are confirmed by the fact that his Semacheion falls within the borders of Antiochis. But whereas technically this mining district formed the coast trittys of the tribe, we have the evidence of Philochorus, writing early in the third century B.C., that it was spoken of as part of the Epakria or hill country³.

How suitable this name was may be illustrated from the Semacheion inscription itself, in which the sites of mining claims are three times defined by reference to a ridge or hill crest (λόφος)⁴.

As seen from *C.I.A.* II. 570, the Epakria of 400 B.C. was a religious organization⁵, apparently with only a local political significance. This fact makes it probable that the name was already ancient, and that Plutarch and the *Lexicon Seguerianum* were right in equating it with Diakria and Hyperakria⁶. There is indeed the possibility of a con-

and probably the Hill Country par excellence.

---

¹ *Ath. Mitt.* 1910, p. 309. The single tombstone of "Aeschines of Semachidai, the son of Pamphilus" (*C.I.A.* II. 2534), found at Brahami, three and a half kilometres South of the Acropolis, is probably to be classed with *ibid.* 2535–9 as belonging to a Semachid who died at Athens. So too with the fragment ΙΑΧΙΔΟΥ *C.I.A.* III. 3897, found at Alopeke, the modern Ampelokipi, one of the Eastern terminuses of the Athenian tramways. Demesmen seem to have been generally buried either in Athens or in the deme to which they belonged. The ordinary Attic word for travel, ἀποδημεῖν (lit. "to quit one's deme"), seems to have been still appropriate even in the fourth century.

² *F.H.G.* I. p. 396.

³ *F.H.G.* I. p. 396.

⁴ *Ath. Mitt.* XXXV. (1910), p. 277, l. 25; 278, l. 42; 281, l. 46; the word may have been semi-technical. Appian, *Bell. Civ.* IV. 106, speaks of a λόφος not far from Philippi, "in which are the gold mines called the Asyla."

⁵ Cp. Hesych. Ἐπάκριος· Ζεὺς ὁ ἐπὶ τῶν ἄκρων τῶν ὀρῶν ἱδρυμένος. ἐπὶ γὰρ τῶν ὀρῶν τοὺς βωμοὺς αὐτῷ ἵδρυον ὡς ἐπιπολύ.

⁶ *I.e.* with the hill country of the Cleisthenic Interior. Inscriptions (*C.I.A.* II. 602, 603), of the fourth century or later, mention men of the Interior (Mesogeioi) who formed a similar organization to the Epakrioi of *C.I.A.* II. 570, and were possibly composed of lowlanders of the Cleisthenic Interior (Mesogeia). The name Mesogeia is now applied to the "undulating district of hill and plain stretching to the spurs of Pentelicon on the North, to Hymettus on the West, to the vicinity of Marcopoulo on the South, and to the coast hills on the East," Baedeker, *Greece*, 1905, p. 117.

fusion of names. But on the other hand the names suggest a common origin. They are all compounds of ἄκρον. It is curious that nobody in recent times seems to have asked what was the ordinary connotation of ἄκρον to the Athenian of antiquity[1]. There seems little doubt as to what it was.

In Attica the *ἄκρον par excellence* was Sunium. Already in the *Odyssey* Sunium is the ἄκρον Ἀθηνῶν[2]. The same phrase reappears in Aristophanes[3]. Strabo refers to Sunium as τὸ τῆς Ἀττικῆς ἄκρον[4]. Some early scholars recognized this fact. Palmerius explained the Diakrioi as the people living between the two capes, Sunium and Cynosura, and the Hyperakrioi as those who dwelt beyond Sunium, "beyond" being used presumably from the point of view of those coming by sea from Athens[5]. Albertus held that the Diakrioi were so called because they lived "in promontoriis Atticae[6]."

Plato indeed in the *Critias*[7] speaks of Πάρνηθος τῶν ἄκρων; but for the Athenians the peaks of Parnes are ἄκρα with a local qualification, not simply τὸ ἄκρον or τὰ ἄκρα; just as we in England speak of the peaks of Snowdon or Skiddaw, but apply the word unqualified to the heights of Derbyshire. The unqualified expression applied to the Northern heights of Attica was "the land of the mountain (ἡ ὀρεινή)[8]," not "the land of the ἄκρον." The name Diakria appears therefore to be derived geographically not from Mount Parnes but from Cape Sunium[9].

[1] See *e.g.* J. A. R. Munro's note *J.H.S.* XIX. (1899), p. 187.
[2] *Odyss.* III. 278; cp. Steph. Byz. Σούνιον· δῆμος Λεοντίδος φυλῆς. Ὅμηρος δὲ ἄκρον καλεῖ.
[3] Aristoph. *Clouds*, 401.   [4] Strabo, IX. 390.
[5] Palmerius (Le Paulmier), *Exerc.* p. 4, quoted Schoemann, *de Comit. Ath.* p. 343, n. 4.
[6] Albertus, *Hesych.* s.v. Alii aliter; *e.g.* Casaubon *ad Diog. Laert.*, Solon, 58 appears to locate the Diakrioi on the Acropolis.
[7] Plato, *Critias*, 110 d.
[8] Strabo, IX. 391; cp. XIV. 632 f. on the Milesian district where Hdt., VI. 20, mentions the existence of a Hyperakria: Strabo distinguishes clearly the ἄκραι on the coast from the ὄρη of the interior.
[9] No mines are marked actually at Sunium in the map attached to Ardaillon's careful study of the mines of Laurium, but a mine at Sunium (μέταλλον ἐπὶ Σουνίῳ) is mentioned in the inscription published by Oikonomos, *Ath. Mitt.* XXXV. (1910), p. 277, l. 9; so also *C.I.A.* II. 781: cp. also Eurip. *Cycl.* 293-4, "aery Sunium's silver-veined crag (ὑπάργυρος πέτρα)," tr. Shelley. Sunium and Thoricus, also in the mining district ("at Thoricus and Laurium are mines of silver," schol. Aesch. *Pers.* 238), are coupled together by Pliny, *N.H.* IV. 11 (7), as "promontoria."

Herodotus, as already noticed, gives the Sunium district another name. He calls the country between Sunium, Thoricus, and Anaphlystus, *i.e.* the Laurium mining district, by the name of the γουνὸς Σουνιακός[1]. But as in the same sentence he speaks of the ἄκρη of this district, his allusion is less of a difficulty to regarding this district as the original Diakria than it is to the orthodox view, which identifies it with the Paralia (Coast). Especially is this so if we assume that by his days the name Diakria had spread Northward beyond the mining region, so that a new name was wanted for the Southern apex of the peninsula. This assumption is of course only a reversal of the current view, that extends the name indefinitely Southwards from Parnes.

It has sometimes been forgotten in the discussion of these names that we are dealing with common nouns that were used by the Greeks with different connotations at different places and periods like the English downs or forest[2]. Epakria appears to have been used in more than one sense even within the limits of Attica[3]. Possibly the name was applied at large to any region of ἄκρα. If we prefer to assume that it spread from a single district the balance of probabilities points to the name having spread Northwards from the district round Sunium.

From yet another point of view the words Diakria, Hyperakria, Epakria favour the mining interpretation. The inhabitants of El Dorado of Greek legend, the land of the Golden Fleece, are said to have occupied the ἄκρα of the Caucasus[4].

---

[1] Hdt. IV. 99.

[2] There were Diakrioi in Rhodes (Cavaignac, *Étud. Financ.* pp. xl, xli) and Euboea (Hesych. s.v.) as well as Attica. Miletus had its Hyperakrioi (Hdt. VI. 20).

[3] Besides its connexion with (*a*) Semachidai and (*b*) the party of Peisistratus, we find it as (*c*) one of twelve cities founded by Cecrops (Strabo, IX. 397, Steph. Byz. s.v.), (*d*) one of three groups of cities founded by Cecrops (Suid. and *Et. Mag.* s.v.), (*e*) a country near Tetrapolis (Bekker, *Lex. Seguer.* p. 259), (*f*) a trittys (trittys of the Epakrians: *C.I.A.* II. 1053 and (?) I. 517*b*; cp. Loeper, *Ath. Mitt.* XVII. p. 355, n. 3), and (*g*) the recipient of payments from Plotheia (*C.I.A.* II. 570, about 420 B.C.). It is recognized by Milchhoefer that the word is used in a broader and a more restricted sense (*ap.* Pauly Wissowa s.v. Epakria). Though note *à propos* of the Epakrian trittys of the inscriptions that trittyes are generally named after not the district but the chief place in the district, *e.g.* trittys of the Eleusinians, of the Peiraeans, *C.I.A.* I. 517. Semachidai and Plotheia belong to different tribes (Antiochis and Aegeis), and consequently to different trittyes.

[4] Strabo, XI. 499.

Fig. 2. On the road from Daskalio station to Plaka.

Fig. 1. Lophos Loutrou from Daskalio station.

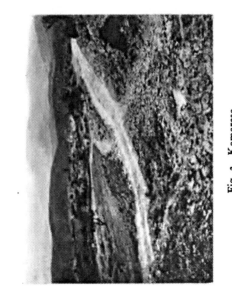

Fig. 3. Kamaresa.

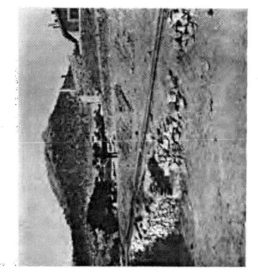

Fig. 4. Kitsovouno from Kamaresa.

Views in the Laurium mining district.

The ἄκρα of the Caucasus are of course not capes but peaks. Trinakria on the other hand is the land of the three capes. It is important to remember that the word ἄκρον has no equivalent in English. It means peak or height as well as cape or headland. To attempt to keep these two meanings separate is to commit a mental mistranslation. Though Sunium is the ἄκρον *par excellence*, the whole Σουνιακὸς γουνός abounds in ἄκρα, or as the inscriptions call them, λόφοι (crests, ridges)[1]. Bursian describes the hills of Laurium (Lauriongebirge) as a continuous mountain chain, and includes it with Parnes, Brilessos, and Hymettos among the main ridges (grössere Gebirgszüge) of Attica[2]. The writer has spent some days walking in the mining district. The sea is always near, and glimpses of it may be had frequently. But it is the hills that dominate the landscape, not the sea. More particularly is this the case in the district that was most mined in the sixth century, where the ground varies in height from 170 m. to 370 m. (550–1200 feet), and lies well inland[3].

In the light of this probability that the Diakrioi occupied the mining district of Attica, and of the fact that their name means hill men, it is interesting to note that the Idaean Dactyls, who "are said to have been the first miners," are stated also to have been men of the mountains[4], and that in German and Welsh the words for miners (Bergleuten, gwyr y mynyddau) mean literally "hill men."

The Greek word Diakrioi would have a peculiar appropriateness for miners. The ἄκρον is precisely the part of a hill that the farmer has least use for. Miners on the other hand preferred to carry on their smelting operations on the hill tops, because a better draught is thus secured[5].

---

[1] *E.g.* Oikonomos, *Ath. Mitt.* xxxv. (1910), pp. 277, l. 25; 278, l. 42; 281, l. 46; cp. Xen. *de Vect.* iv. 2, τῶν ὑπαργύρων λόφων; Pliny, *N.H.* iv. 11 (7), Thoricus promontorium.

[2] Bursian, *Gr. Geog.* I. pp. 254–5. Boeckh, *Pub. Econ.* II. p. 416, n. 6, quotes Λαύριον ὄρος, but gives no reference.

[3] A site between Kamaresa (Maronea?) and Sunium, which Loeper identifies with Potamos, is described by him as "im Inneren liegend," *Ath. Mitt.* XVII. pp. 333–4.

[4] Schol. Ap. Rhod. *Argon.* I. 1129, quoting the *Phoronid*,

ἄνδρες ὀρέστεροι,
οἱ πρῶτοι τέχνην πολυμήτιος Ἡφαίστοιο
εὗρον ἐν οὐρείῃσι νάπαις, ἰόεντα σίδηρον,
ἐς πῦρ τ' ἤνεγκον καὶ ἀρίπρεπες ἔργον ἔδειξαν.

[5] Binder, *Laurion*, p. 25 (cp. de Launay in Saglio, *Dict. d. Ant.* s.v. ferrum,

It has been pointed out by Milchhoefer[1] that the mining district is considerably broken up by the Cleisthenic division of Attica into trittyes. Milchhoefer's arrangement of the trittyes in the mining district has been convincingly simplified by Loeper[2], but Loeper himself leaves the mines divided between three trittyes of three different tribes. We may therefore still follow Milchhoefer in thinking that Cleisthenes took special precautions to break up this district. The same fact is noticed by Milchhoefer about the district round Plotheia, the Northern deme already noticed as belonging to the Epakria. Here too the Russian scholar has simplified, but here too only to a limited extent. "In a breaking up like this of the old hill country of the Peisistratids" Milchhoefer sees unmistakable signs of "measures directed against the Peisistratids." Now that we have as good reason for seeing Peisistratan hill country round Laurium as round Plotheia, we must either reject Milchhoefer altogether, or, more probably, see in both districts centres of Peisistratan influence, of which the Southernmost was the more important. Mining operations in antiquity were conducted on a large scale. Forty thousand workers were employed in mines near Carthagena[3].

Athenaeus[4] speaks of tens of thousands of chained slaves as working in the Laurium mines and losing their lives in an unsuccessful revolt at the time of the second slave war in Sicily (103–99 B.C.). Of the 20,000 who deserted to Decelea when it was occupied by the Spartans in 413 B.C. it is not unlikely that large numbers were miners from Laurium[5].

But what was the state of the Laurium district in the days of Peisistratus?

p. 1087), who says this is still the practice in Peru. Smelting was carried on close by the mines, see Ardaillon in Saglio, *Dict. d. Ant.* s.v. metalla. The sites of the ancient Siphnian mines are to this day called Kaminia (furnaces) and Kapsala (slag?), Bent, *J.H.S.* VI. pp. 196–7.

Note too that at a still earlier epoch gold from mines, as distinguished from alluvial gold, was known in Egypt as "gold of the mountain," Breasted, *Records Anc. Egypt*, IV. 30: so *ibid.* 28, "electrum of the mountains," temp. Ramses III.

[1] *Abh. Berl. Akad.* 1892, p. 47.
[2] *Ath. Mitt.* XVII.
[3] Polyb. XXXIV. 9.
[4] Athen. VI. 272*e*; cp. Oros. V. 9, who dates what is apparently the same revolt in the time of the first Sicilian slave war (139–132 B.C.).
[5] Thuc. VII. 27; cp. Bury, *Hist. Greece*, p. 485.

The mines of Laurium do not appear in history till 484 B.C.[1],
when Themistocles persuaded the Athenians to devote the profits from them to the building of a navy. The *Constitution of Athens* speaks of a discovery of mines in that year. This however is probably rather loose language. The writer's words are "on the discovery of the mines at Maronea." The "discovery" of 484 B.C. was of the mines in this particular part of the Laurium district, or rather, in all probability, of an extraordinarily rich vein in this particular part. "The disposition of the strata" (at Maronea) "is such that the richest are not those that could be first reached.... Some centuries of search and effort were therefore necessary in order to suspect their existence and to reach their level" (*i.e.* of the rich veins "discovered" in 484)[2].

The mines were almost certainly in full work at this period,

Plutarch says that before this time the Athenians were in the habit of distributing the Laurium revenues among themselves, and that Themistocles had the courage to persuade them to give the habit up[3]. This agrees with Xenophon where he declares that "no one even attempts to say from what period people have tried to work them[4]." The mines of Lydia, Cyprus, and Spain all appear to have been developed in the seventh century B.C.[5] The Siphnian mines were at full work about 525 B.C.[6] Mining operations are depicted on several Corinthian clay tablets, that cannot be later than the early part of the sixth century[7]. One of them is here reproduced (fig. 5).

Fig. 5. Corinthian terra cotta tablet depicting a miner at work:

[1] Hdt. VII. 144; Plut. *Themist.* 4; Aristot. *Ath. Pol.* 22.

[2] Ardaillon, *Les Mines de Laurium* (the best book on the subject), pp. 132, 133; where see also a technical explanation of the veins.   [3] Plut. *Themist.* 4.

[4] Xen. *de Vect.* IV. 2.   [5] F. Cauer, *Parteien in Megara und Athen*, p. 17.

[6] Hdt. III. 57; they appear to have been exhausted before 490 B.C. (Perdrizet, *Klio*, x. (1910), p. 7, quoting Hdt. III. 57 and Paus. x. 11. 2), a fact that suggests an early discovery.

[7] Furtwaengler, *Berl. Vas.* 871 B, 639, 831 A: Wilisch, *Jahresb. Gym. Zittau*, 1901, figs. 19 (Saglio, *Dict. d. Ant.* fig. 4987), 20 and p. 20.

Herodotus says nothing about the date of discovery of the Attic mines in his account of the proceedings of 484 B.C.[1]. It would not be like him to keep silence about an epoch-making discovery, or even a phenomenal "rush," if any had occurred just at this time. Elsewhere he tells us that the Siphnians were already distributing among themselves the money from their mines about the year 525 B.C.[2].

Modern writers have been inclined to talk of the great "rush" of 484[3]. But against the silence of Herodotus they can set only the reference in the *Constitution of Athens* to the "discovery" at Maronea, which has been discussed already. What made the great impression at this time was probably not so much the output as the employment of the output on the building of a fleet. That surely is the point of the contemporary allusion in the *Persae* of Aeschylus. The chorus of Persian elders tells the Persian queen about the Athenians'

> Fount of silver, treasure of the land[4]

just after mentioning the prowess of the Athenian troops, and just before explaining the weapons that they use.

The idea proposed in 484 by Themistocles was not original. Seven years earlier the Thasians had used the revenues from their mines to build a fleet against the Persians[5]. It was doubtless the success of the Athenian fleet in a supreme crisis that caused the Athenians to remember with such pride this triumph of the voluntary system.

There can therefore be no question that the mines were worked in the sixth century[6]. But if we are to understand the position of the leader of the mining interests at that period, we must learn something about the conditions and position of the miners.

and the miners free men, good material for a political faction.
The leaders of the Plain and Coast had a powerful body of citizens behind their backs. The mines on the other hand, at least from the time of Xenophon, were worked almost exclusively by slaves[7].

In the fourth century very occasionally poor citizens

---

[1] Hdt. VII. 144.
[2] Hdt. III. 57; cp. E. Meyer, *Ges. d. Alt.* II. p. 610, on Theognis, 667 f.
[3] *E.g.* Perdrizet, *Klio*, x. (1910), p. 2.   [4] Aeschyl. *Persae*, 240 (238).
[5] Hdt. VI. 46.   [6] *Pace* Cavaignac, *Viertelj. f. Soc. u. Wirts. Ges.* IX. p. 7.
[7] Xen., *de Vect.* IV. 17, advised the Athenian state to buy slaves to the number of three for each citizen and let them out to work the mines. The number of

worked their own allotments[1]. Skilled work like smelting seems always to have been done by free men. The tombstone of "Atotes the miner," carved in letters of the second half of the fourth century, declares that he was a Paphlagonian "of the root of Pylaimenes, who fell slain by the hand of Achilles," and boasts of his unrivalled skill[2]. But there is no recorded instance of a citizen working in a mine for wages[3]. This however does not prove that they did not do so in the days of Peisistratus, when, as pointed out in the introductory chapter, the conditions of labour must have been very different from what they became in the fifth and fourth centuries, and industrial slavery had scarcely yet begun. A fragment of Solon suggests that it was quite usual in his days for citizens to work with their own hands, though whether for pay or on their own account is not stated and no particular occupations are specified[4].

About ten years after Solon's legislation the Athenians are found resolving "on account of their factions to elect ten archons, five from the nobility (Eupatridai), three from the farmers (agroikoi), two from the craftsmen (demiourgoi)[5]." The equation of these three groups of archons with the three factions of the Plain, Coast, and Hill is more than doubtful[6]. The farmers *par excellence* are

---

Athenian citizens at the time was about 20,000 (cp. Wallon, *l'Esclavage*[2], I. pp. 222 f.), which makes the proposed number of slave miners about 60,000. This was admittedly many more than the number actually employed at the time of the proposal, and Xenophon suggests starting with 10,000, which Wallon, *ibid*. p. 230, thinks to have been probably the existing number of privately owned mining slaves. But even so these numbers show how influential a free mining population might well have been. See also *de Vect*. IV. 14, 15 and *passim*; Andoc. *de Myst*. 38 (6); Hyp. frag. 33 (Blass); and above, p. 45.

[1] Dem. *c. Phaenipp*. 20 (1044–5).
[2] Bérard, *B.C.H.* XII. (1888), p. 246, τέχνῃ δ' οὔτις ἔριζε.
[3] Ardaillon, *Les Mines de Laurium*, p. 91.
[4] Solon, Bergk, frag. 12 (4), 49–50,
ἄλλος Ἀθηναίης τε καὶ Ἡφαίστου πολυτέχνεω
ἔργα δαεὶς χειροῖν ξυλλέγεται βίοτον.
[5] Aristot. *Ath. Pol*. 13.
[6] A means of equation would be to accept the reading of the Berlin papyrus ἀποίκων for ἀγροίκων and then, *pace* Busolt, *Gr. G.* II.[2] p. 96, n. 1, identify the ἄποικοι (men away from home; cp. the Milesian ἀειναῦται, men always at sea) with the πάραλοι (men of the coast). The demiourgoi would then be identified with the Diakrioi, and it would have to be assumed that the youthful Peisistratus was already leading his faction. Laurentius Lydus, *de Magistr*. I. 47, makes Solon import from Egypt a triple division into philosopher nobles, warrior farmers, and mechanics (τὴν βάναυσον καὶ τεχνουργόν). The statement appears

naturally located in the plain: also it is doubtful whether Peisistratus had already "raised the third faction" twenty years before he became tyrant, and over fifty before his death. The two different sets of names point in themselves to two different groupings of the population. Solon's quadruple division into pentekosiomedimnoi, hippeis, zeugitai, and thetes proves a certain fluidity and tendency to cross grouping. But in any case the two craftsman magistrates prove that craftsmen or artizans were already an important element in the free population.

In this matter of free labour in an industry such as mining, fifth century Phrygia is perhaps a better guide than the Attica of Nikias or Demosthenes as to the state of things in Attica during the sixth century. In Phrygia a generation after the Samian tyrant Polycrates, who died about 522 B.C., Pythes was working mines with citizen labour[1]. Even in Athens in the early days of Pericles the earlier conditions seem still to have prevailed. "Each trade ($\tau \acute{\epsilon} \chi \nu \eta$) had its body of (free) labourers organized ($\tau \grave{o} \nu \ \theta \eta \tau \iota \kappa \grave{o} \nu \ \check{o} \chi \lambda o \nu \ \sigma \upsilon \nu \tau \epsilon \tau \alpha \gamma$-$\mu \acute{\epsilon} \nu o \nu$)" to carry out the great public works that were financed from the Delian treasury. A long list of the trades thus organized ends with miners[2].

Considering the evidence already adduced for equating the sixth century miners at Laurium with the presumably free Diakrioi, may we not use the notices already quoted about the latter as being of impure race and a mob of hirelings[3], and infer that in the sixth century the mines of Laurium were worked by free men, partly of foreign extraction and mainly working for hire?

This is of course conjecture. But it produces for the first time a picture of the Diakrioi that harmonizes with the notices in question. Alien shepherds and alien small farmers are most unlikely in autochthonous Attica.

Outlander miners on the other hand have always been familiar, wherever there have been mines to work. When mining operations were resumed at Laurium some thirty years ago, the immediate result was a very mixed population, the local supply of labour being

among the fragments of Diodorus ix. in Dindorf's text; but the attribution is disputed, *e.g.* by Landwehr, *Philol.* Suppl. v. (1889), p. 141. The reading ἄγροικοι rather than ἄποικοι is supported by Dion. Hal. II. 9; see further Gilliard, *Réformes de Solon*, p. 105, n. 2.

[1] Plut. *de Mul. Virt.* 27 (*Moral.* 262).
[2] Plut. *Pericl.* 12.   [3] Aristot. *Ath. Pol.* 13; Plut. *Sol.* 29.

supplemented from France, Italy, and Turkey. One of the ancient gold mines near Philippi bore the significant name of the asylum[1]. In the Laurium district itself in ancient times the people of at least one deme, Potamioi, were famous for their readiness to admit foreigners to citizenship[2]. Potamioi is placed by Loeper right in the centre of the mining district, well away from the sea[3], and very near the probable site of Maronea[4]. A member of the deme Semachidai is found sharing a tombstone with two strangers from Sinope[5]. We have just had occasion to notice a Paphlagonian miner, though of a later date, and we shall see in a moment that in the sixth century the mines of Laurium were worked in close connexion with those of Thrace. There are no records of specific Thracians employed in the Attic mines during the sixth century. We only know that just after the Persians conquered Thrace, at the close of the reign of Hippias, there was a large Greek element in the mining population near the Strymon[6]. But in the fifth century we have a famous case of a Thracian mineowner settling in Athens in the person of Thucydides, whose father was a Thracian, and whose Thracian mines probably lost him his command in the Athenian navy, and turned a second-rate admiral into the greatest of historians[7].

[1] Perdrizet, *Klio*, x. (1910), p. 22, quoting Appian, *Bell. Civ.* IV. 106. Cp. above, p. 39, n. 4.

[2] Harpocrat. s.v. Ποταμός· "they were lampooned as readily admitting illegal claims to citizenship (ὡς ῥᾳδίως δεχόμενοι τοὺς παρεγγράπτους), as others proclaim and particularly Menander in *The Twins*"; *Potamioi* was the name of a comedy by Strattis; Athen. VII. 299b; Suid. s.v. Ποταμοί.

[3] *Ath. Mitt.* XVII. (1892), pl. xii. Inscriptions mention three Potamioi, see *Ath. Mitt.* XVII. pp. 390-1, Π. καθύπερθεν, Π. ὑπένερθεν, Π. Δειραδιῶται. The first two are grouped together apart from the third, and Loeper is probably right, as against Koehler, *Ath. Mitt.* x. (1885), pp. 105 f.; cp. IV. (1879), p. 102, in assigning them to the city trittys of Leontis and making P. Deiradiotai the mining village. καθύπερθεν is therefore no evidence for an inland mining Potamioi. But "Deiradiotai" means "on the ridge," and supports Loeper's location of Potamioi Deiradiotai, no matter whether the adjective means "P. on the ridge," or "P. near Deiradiotai" (a separate deme, see *C.I.A.* II. 864).

[4] Milchhoefer, *Ath. Mitt.* XVIII. (1893), p. 284.   [5] *C.I.A.* II. 3343.

[6] Hdt. v. 23, "by the river Strymon...a city...where are mines of silver; and a large Greek population dwells around, and a large barbarian."

[7] Thuc. IV. 105, "Brasidas,...learning that Thucydides owned workings in the gold mines in that part of Thrace, and as a result was one of the most influential men on the mainland"; Marcellinus, *Vit. Thuc.* 19, "(Thucydides) married a wife from Skapte Hyle in Thrace, who was very wealthy and owned mines in Thrace"; Plut. *Cimon*, 4.

Nikias hired out a thousand hands whom he owned in the mines to Sosias the Thracian[1].

This ends our examination of the various steps by which Peisistratus made himself tyrant, effected his second restoration, and finally rooted his power. In all three cases the evidence points to the conclusion that the secret of the tyrant's power was his control of mines either in Attica or Thrace. To complete the enquiry it is necessary now to examine the accounts of his first restoration. As observed already, this event is recorded only in anecdotal form. As independent evidence it would hardly be worth considering. All that is here claimed for it is that it can be so interpreted as to corroborate the conclusions already reached.

According to the story Peisistratus persuaded the Athenians to take him back by dressing up a stately woman named Phye to personate Athena and order his recall[2]. It is generally agreed that this story will not do as it stands. Various attempts have been made to explain it away[3], but all of them are equally unconvincing. Perhaps the reason is that all alike are based on some single unessential detail of the story. None of them interprets it in the light of the better known parts of the tyrant's career, and more particularly of the matter of fact accounts of his second restoration. Beloch indeed, like the Russian Hirschensohn, believes that there was only one restoration, with which the Phye story and the account of Peisistratus' return from the Thracian mining district are both to be connected[4]. He notes that the cause of banishment is the same

The strange story of Peisistratus' first restoration

---

[1] Xen. *de Vect.* IV. 14.

[2] Hdt. I. 60; Aristot. *Ath. Pol.* 14; Athen. 609 c; Polyaen. I. 21. 1; Val. Max. I. 2. 2 (ext.); Hermog. περὶ εὑρεσ. I. 3. 21 (ed. Spengel); cp. schol. *ibid. ap.* Walzium, *Rhet. Gr.* v. p. 378. In schol. Aristoph. *Eq.* 447 Phye appears to be confused with Myrrina who appears to have been either wife (*ibid.*) or daughter (schol. Dem. *Aristoc.*) of Peisistratus or more probably wife of Hippias (Thuc., and Hesych. s.v. Βυρσίνης). Athenaeus marries Phye to Hipparchus. The confusion may possibly be due to the fact that myrrina, as a common noun, sometimes means garland (*e.g.* Pherecr. *Metall.* I. 25; Aristoph. *Vesp.* 861; *Nub.* 1364, etc.), while Phye is described as a garland seller (*Ath. Pol.* and Athen.).

[3] See *e.g.* Thirlwall, *Hist.*² II. pp. 67–8; Babelon, *Journ. Int. d'Arch. Num.* VIII. (1905), pp. 17, 18; Stein, Hdt. I. 60; Beloch, *Gr. G.*² I. i. p. 370; cp. also Beloch, *Gr. G.*² I. ii. p. 299.

[4] Hirschensohn, *Philolog. Obozrenie*, x. (1896), Moscow, pp. 119 f.; Beloch, *Gr. G.*² I. ii. pp. 290 f., *Rhein. Mus.* XLV. (1890), p. 469; so De Sanctis, *Atthis*², p. 278, n. 5; Costanzi, *Riv. d. Stor. Ant.* v. pp. 516 f., *Boll. Fil. Class.* IX. pp. 84 f., 107 f.

52 · ATHENS · CH. II

in both cases; that the chronology is suspiciously symmetrical; that Polyaenus combines incidents from the two restorations; and that Eusebius[1] and Jerome[2] both make Peisistratus begin his second reign about the time that Herodotus begins his third, while neither of them mentions a third reign at all. Note too that corresponding to Phye in the first restoration we have in the second a "sacred procession" from the temple of Athena Pallenis conducted by an Acarnanian soothsayer[3].

These points are not convincing. Similar improbabilities, and repetitions and chronological symmetries can often be discovered in narratives of the most unquestionable authenticity[4]. The fact that Polyaenus combines the two accounts proves nothing, unless we assume him to be incapable of confusing two similar events. Further, Beloch is forced to make the marriage of Peisistratus with Megacles' daughter precede his first exile, since he sees that the childlessness of the marriage led to the breach with the Coast[5]. In this he goes dead against the tradition on a point where there is no reason to suspect it.

What Beloch's arguments do emphasize is the fact that the situations during Peisistratus' two periods of exile were in some ways very similar. The sameness of the two situations may in fact be the reason why so little has been remembered about the earlier. It raises the question whether the tyrant mined and coined during his first exile. There is no certainty that he did either, but the probability is that he did both. As regards Thrace we know that Miltiades, probably with Peisistratus' permission and approval[6], had settled in the Gallipoli peninsula soon after the tyranny was first established at Athens[7]. Thrace is the one region that we can be sure that the tyrant must have considered as a possible place of exile. As regards

is connected by Babelon with the Athena-head coins of Athens the coinage it has been suggested on the high authority of Babelon[8], that the famous series with the owl on one side, and the head of Athena on the other (fig. 6), which remained for centuries the coin

---

[1] Euseb. *Chron.* Armenian vers. 544/3 B.C., Pisistratus Atheniensibus iterum imperauit.

[2] Jerome, *Chron.* 539 B.C., Pisistratus secunda uice Athenis regnat.

[3] Hdt. I. 62.   [4] Cp. below, chap. VIII. pp. 237–9.

[5] Beloch, *Gr. G.*² I. ii. pp. 292–3, 297.

[6] Hdt. VI. 35, "Peisistratus held supreme power, but Miltiades also had influence (ἐδυνάστευε)" suggests some sort of co-operation (cp. Hdt. VI. 39, below, p. 63), though Hdt. VI. 35, "annoyed with the government of Peisistratus," shows that it was not cordial.

[7] Busolt, *Gr. G.*² II. p. 316, n. 3.   [8] *Journ. Int. d'Arch. Num.* VIII. (1905), p. 19.

ATHENS

types of the city, was actually started to commemorate the help that the tyrant claimed to have received from his patron goddess at the time of his first restoration.

The evidence is not conclusive. The arguments for and against this date are based on a few literary references that are too vague to be of much use, on points of style and technique from which it is notoriously dangerous to draw conclusions, on a comparison of the coin and pottery statistics from Naukratis which it is no less dangerous to use as evidence, on a hoard found in 1886 among the pre-Persian remains on the Athenian Acropolis which, as far as the circumstances of the find are concerned, may have been lost or deposited there long before the catastrophe, and only establish a *terminus ante quem* that nobody would think of disputing, and on certain alliance coins (Athens-Lampsacus, Athens-Sparta?, Athens and the Thracian Chersonese)[1]. These last look more promising at first sight, but only the Athens-Lampsacus coins can be dated with any certainty, and they, unfortunately, are very small, and may have been struck under difficulties, so that it is not easy to be sure of their chronological position in the Athenian series.

Fig. 6. Coin of Athens with Athena and owl.

We are driven back therefore on to the impressions of experts, most of whom agree with Babelon that the owl-Athena series cannot begin either much before or much after 550 B.C.[2]. That is to say that this double type was certainly in vogue when the tyrant

---

[1] Six, *Num. Chron.* 1895, pl. VII. 8, 7, 1.

[2] *E.g.* P. Gardner, *Earliest Coins of Greece Proper*, p. 28; Hill, *Hist. Gk. Coins*, p. 17; v. Fritze, *Zeits. f. Num.* xx. (1897), pp. 153-5, emphasizing the connexion of Peisistratus with silver as well as with Athena; Lermann, *Athenatypen*, pp. 3 f.

For a somewhat earlier date see Head, *Num. Chron.* 1893, pp. 249, 251; Earle Fox, *Corolla Numismat. B. V. Head*, p. 43; Svoronos, *Journ. Int. d'Arch. Num.* xiv. (1912), p. 3, nos. 1109-1120; Seeck, *Klio*, iv. (1904), p. 176 (Solon or even Draco).

For a date after Peisistratus see Imhoof-Blumer, Howorth, Six, and (*Neue Jahrb.* 1896, pp. 537 f.) Gilbert, all completely answered by Head, *Num. Chron.* 1893, pp. 247 f.; Babelon, *J. I. d'A. N.* 1905, pp. 12-16. Holwerda, *Album Herwerden*, p. 117, who follows Six, only adds some inconclusive comparisons with Greek sculpture.

secured his second restoration by means of his Thracian silver[1], and "rooted his tyranny" in revenues derived "partly from the river Strymon, partly from home."

Pieces with the double type were sometimes colloquially called girls (κόραι), sometimes virgins (παρθένοι), sometimes by the virgin goddess' own name of Pallas (Παλλάδες)[2]. Sometimes they got their nickname from the reverse type, and were called owls[3]. "Virgin" is used by Euripides, "girl" by Hyperides, "Pallas" by Eubulus, "owl" by Aristophanes. "Owl" is said by the Aristophanes Scholiast to have been applied to the tetradrachms; the "girl" of Hyperides is some smaller coin[4]. In the fifth and fourth centuries therefore the bird name, and the virgin goddess names seem to have been used side by side, like our sovereign and crown, to indicate two different denominations. When the names were first used is nowhere stated. The most likely time for a type to give rise to a nickname is when the type itself is still a novelty. If this holds good for the coins of Athens, the nicknames Pallas, virgin, and girl go back to the time of Peisistratus. The owl had already appeared on earlier issues, stamped on the reverse with a simple incuse[5], and would therefore at this time attract less attention than the Athena head.

nicknamed (probably just about this time) girl, virgin, Pallas.

Is it possible that we have here the clue to the Phye story? The details about her being dressed up in full armour and placed in a chariot are not the essence of the story: they all appear in Herodotus in quite a different setting, as part of the ritual of the worship of Athena in North Africa by Lake Tritonis[6]. It can hardly be

---

[1] There is no need to assume with E. Meyer, *Ges. d. Alt.*[1] IV. p. 28, and others, that Peisistratus' Pangaion mines were gold. In the days of Philip and Alexander the Great they were best known for their gold; but silver was also mined abundantly, see Hdt. v. 17; vii. 112; Strabo, 331, 34; Livy, XLV. 29; Justin, VIII. 3; Orosius, III. 12.

[2] Pollux, IX. 74, 75, quoting Euripides (d. 406 B.C.), Hyperides (fl. 350 B.C.), Eubulus Comicus (fl. 350 B.C.); cp. Hesych. s.v. Παλλάδος πρόσωπον, Photius s.v. Παλλάδος πρόσωπον.

[3] Schol. Aristoph. *Birds*, 1106, "the tetradrachm was at that time called an owl."

[4] Cp. Photius s.v. Παλλάδος πρόσωπον, "the staters, from the stamp: for on one side there was a head of Athena." The stater is the didrachm.

[5] Hill, *Hist. Gk. Coins*, p. 16; *Brit. Mus. Coins Central Greece*, pl. XXIV. 18, 19.

[6] Hdt. IV. 180, "They dress up together on each occasion their fairest maiden in a Corinthian helmet and full Greek armour, and, mounting her on a chariot, drive her all round the lake." See further Macan, *Hdt.* IV.–VI. *ad loc.*, who quotes Phye.

doubted that one of these passages is plagiarized from the other, and it is scarcely less certain that Phye is indebted to the ritual of Lake Tritonis and not *vice versa*.

The kernel of the Phye story lies in the tradition that Peisistratus was restored by a woman, "as Herodotus says, from the deme of the Paianians, but as some say, a Thracian flower girl from the deme of Kollytos[1]." In fact Phye, the human goddess four cubits high, said by some to come from Attica, and by others from Thrace, who brought Peisistratus back to Athens for the first time, bears a suspicious likeness to the coins called sometimes girls and sometimes goddesses, derived some from Attica, and some from Thrace, with which Peisistratus secured his second return, and finally established his power.

<small>Was the Athena who restored Peisistratus the lady of the coins?</small>

Assume for the moment that they were indeed identical, and it is easy to see how the Phye story may have arisen. Peisistratus certainly claimed to rule by the grace of Athena. Everyone is agreed in inferring from the Phye story that he attributed his restoration to the intervention of the goddess. After the citizens had fulfilled Solon's prophecy, and "consented to ruin their great city, induced by money[2]," what more natural than that one of the tyrant's opponents should sarcastically agree that it was indeed Athena who had restored Peisistratus: on which another might comment that it was not the virgin goddess of Athens who had restored the tyrant, but an alien being of quite a different order, a Thracian flower girl.

<small>cp. (i) details in the story that suggest a derivation from the coins,</small>

The name of flower girl ($\sigma\tau\epsilon\phi\alpha\nu\dot{o}\pi\omega\lambda\iota\varsigma$) is never applied to Athenian drachmae. If we accepted Head's early dating for the Athena type, and assumed a Peisistratan date for certain Athenian coins[3] where the goddess has had her hair done by a $\kappa\epsilon\rho o\pi\lambda\dot{\alpha}\sigma\tau\eta\varsigma$[4] in corkscrew curls (fig. 7 a) that suggest an early date[5], and wears the garland ($\sigma\tau\dot{\epsilon}\phi\alpha\nu o\varsigma$) of olive leaves (fig. 7 a, b) that appears regularly on coins of the fifth century, we might find in flower girl (lit. garland

---

[1] Aristot. *Ath. Pol.* 14; cp. Athen. XIII. 609 c.
[2] Solon, frag. 2 (13), ll. 5–6
αὐτοὶ δὲ φθείρειν μεγάλην πόλιν ἀφραδίῃσιν
ἀστοὶ βούλονται, χρήμασι πειθόμενοι.
[3] E.g. B.C.H. xxx. (1906), p. 69, fig. 2; Brit. Mus. from Bunbury sale.
[4] Archil. frag. 54 (53), τὸν κεροπλάστην ἄειδε Γλαῦκον.
[5] Bremer, *Haartracht*, p. 64.

seller, στεφανόπωλις) an allusion to this detail. The garland seller may often have advertised her garlands by wearing one herself[1].

Numismatists however are now unanimous in making the earliest στέφανοι on Athenian coins later than Peisistratus[2]. To describe the coins as flower girls would however be natural enough on the simple supposition that Athenian flower girls had no high moral reputation[3], and further perhaps that the business was in the hands of Thracians, just as that of organ-grinding in England is in the hands of Italians. Or conceivably στεφανόπωλις on our present hypothesis is to be explained by reference to the phrase δραχμαὶ (τοῦ) Στεφανηφόρου (drachmae of the garland bearer)[4], applied at Athens to coins fresh from the mint, such as must have been put into circulation in large quantities when Peisistratus returned after his money-making in the districts round Mt Pangaion.

Fig. 7. Athenian coins: the wreath on the head of Athena.

[1] Garlands of flowers worn on the head appear in Attica during the second half of the sixth century; see Pauly Wissowa s.v. Haartracht, p. 2132; cp. Bremer, *Haartracht*, p. 15, vogue begins with red figure vase style.

[2] Time of Hippias, Head, *Hist. Num.*² p. 368 (but cp. *ibid.* n. 3); Seeck, *Klio*, IV. (1904), pp. 173–5; 508 B.C., Holwerda, *Album Herwerden*, p. 119; 500 B.C. or after, v. Fritze, *Zeits. f. Num.* XX. (1897), p. 142: Kampanes, *B.C.H.* XXX. p. 75; 490 B.C., Six, *Num. Chron.* 1895, p. 176: Earle Fox, *Coroll. Num. B. V. Head*, p. 43: Babelon, *Coroll. Num. B. V. Head*, p. 8: *J. I. d'A. N.* VIII. (1905), pp. 44 f.; 480 B.C., Howorth, *Num. Chron.* 1893, p. 245: Lermann, *Athenatyp.* pp. 28 f. As regards a post-Hippias dating, the ungarlanded head of a coin with Hippias' name is not decisive. The coin, which is abnormal, was probably struck by the tyrant in exile, and the absence of garland may indicate either the exile's grief or the local coiner's incompetence. Or was the embarrassed despot casting away the ornaments of sovereignty in the hope of retaining or regaining the reality? "The olive again has been known to lose its leaves and yet produce its fruit; this is said to have happened to Thessalos the son of Peisistratos," Theophrast. *Hist. Plant.* II. 3. 3; cp. Ruehl, *Rhein. Mus.* 1892, p. 460.

[3] Just as was probably the case with the flower girls at Naukratis, the most famous centre of the garland trade, where the Thracian hetaera Rhodopis won such great fame in the days of Sappho and Aesop. See Mallet, *Prem. Étab. Gr. en Égypte*, p. 238, who compares the fioraie of Venice and Florence.

[4] Phot., Harpocrat. s.v. στεφανηφόρος; cp. Boeckh, *Pub. Econ.* I. pp. 193 f. Lenormant, *Monnaies et Médailles*, p. 60; Saglio, *Dict. d. Ant.* s.v. drachmae Stephanephori, p. 403. The inscriptions, however, in which the expression occurs date only from the end of the second century B.C., *C.I.A.* II. i. 466–8, 476.

How readily to the Greek the garland suggested the flower girl is seen from an explanation in the *Lexicon Seguerianum* of a certain "garland-bearing hero (στεφανηφόρος ἥρως)." It runs: "Either because the hero is so called, or by way of nickname, because he had many garlands round him, *or because garlands were sold near him*[1]." The coins themselves, especially when the garland was the new feature, may possibly have been sometimes called garland bearers (στεφανηφόροι), as is shown to be possible by the analogy of such descriptive coin names as "chest bearer (κιστοφόρος)[2]" and "harp bearer (κιθαρηφόρος)[3]."

Such bitter jesting is quite in keeping with the Greek language;

(ii) attested instances of *Jeu de mot* on coin types,

the Greeks were particularly fond of attributing appropriate life and action to types of living things that figured on their coins[4].

The best known instance of a play on such a nickname is that of Agesilaus of Sparta, who complained that he had been driven out of Asia by thirty thousand of the Great King's archers, a colloquial name for the Persian gold stater or Daric (fig. 8), derived from its type[5].

In Athens itself we find Euripides, in a fragment of the *Sciron*, playing on the double meaning of "virgin," as also on that of "pony" (πῶλος), the colloquial name of the Corinthian drachma, that bore on one side the image of the winged steed Pegasus:

Fig. 8. Persian "archer."

> Some you will secure if you offer a pony,
> others with a pair of horses, while others are brought
> on four horses, all of silver; and they love
> the maidens from Athens when you bring plenty of them.

[1] Bekker, *Anecd. Gr.* I. 301, 19.
[2] Livy, XXXVII. 46, 58, 59; XXXIX. 7; Cic. *ad Att.* II. 6, 16; XI. 1.
[3] Diamantaras, *Ath. Mitt.* XIV. (1889), p. 413.
[4] The practice of course is not exclusively Greek; cp., *e.g.*,

il maledetto fiore
ch' ha disviate le pecore e gli agni.
Dante, *Paradiso*, IX. 130.

[5] Plut. *Apophth. Lac.*, *Agesilaus*, 40 (*Moral.* 211); cp. the proverb τὰν ἀρετὰν καὶ τὰν σοφίαν νικᾶντι χελῶναι (virtue and wisdom are vanquished by tortoises), alluding to the famous coins of Aegina; cp. too βοῦς ἐπὶ γλώσσῃ (there's an ox on my tongue), Theognis 815, Aesch. *Agam.* 35, Pollux IX. 61,

The reverse type of the Athenian drachma is punned upon by Aristophanes, who speaks of the owls of Laurium nesting in the purses of the Athenians and hatching small change[1]. In 404 B.C., during the final operations against Athens, Gylippus, the hero of the siege of Syracuse, misappropriated a large amount of Athenian coin, and hid it under the tiles of his roof. The theft was revealed by a servant, who informed the ephors that "there were many owls nesting under the tiles[2]."

These examples are enough to show that there is nothing improbable in the suggestion that the Phye story grew out of a remark made by the tyrant's enemies about his silver drachmae. Our explanation is of course pure conjecture, and even at that it has one weak point. The statement that Phye was a Thracian, so essential to our interpretation, does not appear in Herodotus, according to whom she came from the Paianian deme in Attica[3].

Can this omission be accounted for?

There is an anecdote told by Herodotus in quite another connexion[4] which suggests that it can.

(iii) the story of the dressed-up woman

In the days just after King Darius had made his conquests in Thrace (about 512 B.C.), there lived on the banks of the Strymon two brothers named Pigres and Mantyes, who wished to become tyrants of the land in which they lived. To carry out this aim "they went to Sardis, taking with them their sister, who was tall and handsome." Then waiting till Darius was sitting in state before the city, having dressed up their sister as well as they possibly could, they sent her for water with a pitcher on her head and leading a horse with her hand and spinning flax. She was noticed by the king, but the result was that he sent an expedition to her country, and deported her people to Asia.

which, whether the ox meant is a gold stater, on which the ox was one of the commonest types, or, as P. Gardner suggests, a leather gag, *Num. Chron.* 1881, p. 289, is an instance of a similar *jeu de mot* dating from the actual epoch of Peisistratus.

[1] Aristoph. *Birds*, 1106; cp. Schol. *ad loc.* "the tetradrachm was at that time (*i.e.* of Aristophanes) called an owl"; Suid. s.v. γλαῦκες Λαυρεωτικαί· "of those who have much money," is a misunderstanding of the phrase; cp. his statement that the Laurium mines were gold.

[2] Plut. *Lysander*, 16.

[3] The modern Liopesi, Milchhoefer, *Abh. Berl. Akad.* 1892, p. 17.

[4] Hdt. v. 12.

CH. II ATHENS 59

The Strymon and Pangaion mines are at this period, before the expansion of Macedonia, naturally described as Thracian[1]. But in the days of King Darius, who began his reign about five years after the death of Peisistratus, part of the country round Mt Pangaion[2], and part of the banks of the Strymon[3] were occupied by another race called Paionians. It was to this latter race that Pigres and Mantyes belonged. They failed to secure the tyranny that they sought; but the expedition sent by Darius to deport the Paionians to Asia probably caused Hippias to lose his.

who caused Hippias to lose his throne

It can scarcely be an accident that the tyranny at Athens ended almost immediately after the removal of one of its two roots, the mines of the country of the Thracians and Paionians[4].

as a result of losing his Paionian (Thracian) possessions.

Thus we find the restoration of the tyranny at Athens and its abolition both ascribed to the dressing up of a tall handsome woman[5]. It is hardly conceivable that both these events were brought about by the same "primitive and excessively simple" means. The Paionian dressing up has every appearance of being the original[6].

---

[1] Cp. *e.g.* Hdt. v. 23, 126 (Myrcinus on Strymon called Thracian), vii. 75, 115; Aristoph. *Ach.* 273 ("the Thracian daughter of Strymodorus"); Diod. xii. 68. 1, "this city (Ennea Hodoi on the Strymon) Aristagoras the Milesian had tried previously to settle;...but he had met his death, and the occupants had been driven out by the Thracians" (about 500 B.C.); cp. *ibid.* xi. 70. 5; Plut. *Cimon*, 7, "Eion...a city in Thrace on the Strymon." Cp. Suid. s.v. χρυσὸς Κολοφώνιος; Tzetzes *ad* Lycoph. *Cass.* v. 417 (Hill, *Sources Gk. Hist.* p. 87). For Pangaion see Hdt. vii. 112, "Mt Pangaion, in which are gold and silver mines, which are worked by...most of all the Satrai," with which cp. *ibid.* 110, where the Satrai occur in a list of Thracian tribes.

[2] Hdt. v. 15, 16; Strabo vii. 331.   [3] Hdt. v. 1, 13, 98.

[4] Meyer, *Ges. d. Alt.* iii. p. 297; Macan, *Hdt.* iv.–vi. app. iii., iv. particularly iv. sect. 8; neither of whom sufficiently emphasizes the political importance for Hippias of these Northern mines. Perdrizet, *Klio*, x. (1910), p. 12, denies this removal when he says that the Peisistratid's Thracian possessions had perhaps remained in Athenian hands between 512 and 475.

[5] (*a*) The Paianian (Phye): γυνή...μέγαθος ἀπὸ τεσσάρων πηχέων ἀπολείπουσα τρεῖς δακτύλους καὶ ἄλλως εὐειδής. ταύτην τὴν γυναῖκα σκευάσαντες, Hdt. i. 60; γυναῖκα μεγάλην καὶ καλὴν ἐξευρών...τὴν θεὸν ἀπομιμούμενος τῷ κόσμῳ, Aristot. *Ath. Pol.* 14.

(*b*) The Paionian: ἀδελφεὴν μεγάλην τε καὶ εὐειδέα...σκευάσαντες ὡς εἶχον ἄριστα, Hdt. v. 12.

[6] Nic. Dam. frag. 71, *F.H.G.* iii. p. 413, gives the same story, but calls the

It is possible that the whole Phye story arose at the time of the Paionian incident, just as the good stories about some of the bad Roman emperors must have first had a circulation only after the emperor had ceased to reign. When Hippias had lost his Thracian and Paionian mines, and consequently his throne, it might be said with additional point that the Athena who had restored the father had now deserted the son[1].

If the Paionian story is contemporary, as it well may be without being either true or original, it accounts for the appearance in the Peisistratus story of a dressed-up woman. Further we have brought the story down to a period in the history of Athenian coinage when the garland may already have made its first appearance on the head of Athena[2], in which case "Thracian garland seller" becomes an effective description of the type.

Thus the whole story, as it appears in the Aristotelian *Constitution of Athens*, has been accounted for. In this, as in the account of Peisistratus' second exile, the author of the treatise seems to be following a better authority than Herodotus. Herodotus' deviations appear to be attempts at rationalistic explanation in the best Herodotean style. From Herodotus' account of Peisistratus' second exile it is plain that he knew nothing of the tyrant's connexions with Thrace, of which we are informed in the Aristotelian treatise. According to Herodotus the whole period of the second exile was spent in Euboea. Hence the Thracian reference had to be rationalized away. But a fact mentioned by Herodotus in another connexion[3]

---

woman a Thracian and the king Alyattes. Macan, *ad Hdt.* v. 12 (cp. *ibid.* (*Hdt.* IV.–VI.), app. IV. sect. 7) thinks we probably have a local story transferred to Darius; but the transport of Thracians to Asia, recorded also by Nic. Dam., suggests rather that Hdt. is right in attaching the story to Darius. The Lydian king of the Nic. Dam. version is perhaps due to Sardis being the scene of the story.

[1] Paionian coins, like Athenian, bore the helmeted head of Athena, *e.g. Boston Mus. Rep.* XXII. (1897), p. 40; Svoronos, *J. I. d'A. N.* 1913, p. 197 (fourth century).

[2] The corkscrew hair of the most archaic looking garland coins, above, pp. 55–56, is found on an obol, Babelon, *Corolla Num. B. V. Head*, pp. 1 f., inscribed HIΓ, presumably short for Hippias. Probably it was struck by him in exile, *ibid.* p. 7, but in any case it associates the corkscrew curls with the tyranny. *Num. Chron.* 1908, pp. 278 f. shows the same corkscrew curls, and the inscription III. This has been expanded both as Hippias and as Peisistratus, but cp. Muenzer and Strack, *Münz. Nord-Griech.* II. i. p. 8, n. 1.

[3] Hdt. v. 94.

points to Hippias having maintained some sort of position in the North Aegean till the end of his reign. When in 510 B.C. he was banished, a home was offered him by the king of Macedon.

Thrace and Paionia might be used indifferently in the original account, the latter being the more accurate name, the former the more popular. Herodotus takes Paionian as a corruption of Paianian, and Thracian as a popular version of Paionian. That Herodotus himself was personally responsible for the emendation Paianian is made probable by the words of the *Constitution of Athens*, "as Herodotus says, a Paianian, as some say, a Thracian." The Paionians are made by Herodotus[1] to recognize their own name in the paian or war-cry of their enemies. Only the verb appears in the anecdote, and that in the form $\pi\alpha\iota\omega\nu\iota\zeta\omega$, but Herodotus must have been equally familiar with the forms in -a-, $\pi\alpha\iota\alpha\nu\iota\zeta\omega$, $\pi\alpha\iota\dot{\alpha}\nu$, and the anecdote shows how ready he would be to equate Paionian with Paianian. I am dealing here with pure speculation, but so too has been every one else who has tried to explain away this "extraordinarily silly business[2]." The explanation just offered is at least in harmony with the rest of our knowledge about both Peisistratus and Thrace.

Greeks were certainly capable of misunderstanding a *jeu de mot* based on a coin type. Mention has been made already of Aristophanes' invocation of the "owls of Laurium" to nest in his purse[3]. A Scholiast on the *Knights* has turned these owls of silver into real birds. "The owl," he says, "is the sacred bird of Athena, that haunts Laurium in Attica[4]."

The tyrant Histiaeus and the Thracian mines. Whatever the truth of these speculations there is no doubt that the Greeks of the end of the sixth century were fully alive to the political possibilities of the Thracian mines. Just after the Persian conquest of Thrace and Paionia Histiaeus of Miletus, one of the Persian king's Greek vassals, almost succeeded in securing from the Great King possession of Myrcinus, a mining centre in the very district from which Peisistratus had got so much of his wealth[5]. He was in fact granted the gift by Darius, who however was persuaded by the

---

[1] Hdt. v. 1.
[2] $\pi\rho\hat{\eta}\gamma\mu\alpha$ $\epsilon\dot{\upsilon}\eta\theta\dot{\epsilon}\sigma\tau\alpha\tau\text{ov}$ $\mu\alpha\kappa\rho\hat{\omega}$, Hdt. 1. 60; cp. Aristot. *Ath. Pol.* 14, $\dot{\alpha}\rho\chi\alpha\ddot{\iota}\kappa\hat{\omega}\varsigma$ $\kappa\alpha\dot{\iota}$ $\lambda\dot{\iota}\alpha\nu$ $\dot{\alpha}\pi\lambda\hat{\omega}\varsigma$.
[3] Aristoph. *Birds*, 1106.   [4] Schol. Aristoph. *Knights*, 1092.
[5] Hdt. v. 11.

far-sighted Megabazus to recall it. What alarms the Persian statesman is the prospect of an able Greek like Histiaeus establishing himself in a place where there are silver mines and forests suitable for ship-timber and a large mixed population. He prophecies that this population will quickly become the employees of the new owner and do his bidding day and night[1].

The Myrcinus incident is bound up in the narrative of Herodotus with the story of Pigres and Mantyes and their efforts to become tyrants of the Paionians[2]. Herodotus says definitely that Histiaeus did not aim at establishing a tyranny at Myrcinus[3]. But this statement seems to be simply an inference from the fact that Histiaeus was already tyrant of his own city of Miletus. Even if it is correct, the protests of Megabazus and their effect on Darius, who at once removed Histiaeus to a sort of honourable captivity in Persia, sufficiently show that according to Herodotus himself Myrcinus would have made Histiaeus in the eyes of Darius and Megabazus a different and altogether more dangerous sort of ruler[4].

It was still comparatively recently that Peisistratus had "rooted" his power at Athens partly on revenues from the river Strymon. When Histiaeus' activities near that river so greatly alarmed the Persians, it is hard to believe that they were not thinking largely of the Peisistratids. Thus we have a confirmation of the view that the Peisistratids' Thracian revenues had been derived from the silver mines, and the large mixed population that worked them.

Labour and commerce under the tyranny.

When once established Peisistratus certainly set himself to secure control of a large amount of labour by the public works that he promoted. Kallirrhoe (the Fair Spring), the best source of the Athenian water supply, was improved by him into Enneakrounos (the Nine Fountains)[5]. The building that shelters the actual jets is depicted on a black figure vase[6]. Like Polycrates and the seventh century

---

[1] Hdt. v. 23. Cp. below, p. 271.

[2] Above, p. 58; cp. Svoronos, *Journ. Int. d'Arch. Num.* xv. (1913), p. 277. [3] v. 11.

[4] Cp. also with the Histiaeus incident the intrigues of Aristagoras with the deported Paionians whom Darius had settled in Phrygia (a famous mining country), Hdt. v. 98.   [5] Thuc. II. 15; Paus. I. 14. 1.

[6] *Brit. Mus. Cat. Vas.* II. B 331, where, however, it is called Kallirrhoe (more precisely καλιρεκρενε, perhaps a confusion of Καλλιρρόη and Ἐννεάκρουνος). The aqueduct by which Peisistratus improved and enlarged the supply of water has been discovered by Doerpfeld, *Arch. Eph.* 1894, pp. 3 f.; cp. Theagenes (Paus. I. 40), Polycrates (Hdt. III. 60), and the Corinthian Peirene.

tyrants, he was a great builder; the group of Athena slaying a giant, excavated on the Acropolis in the eighties of the last century[1], probably belongs to the temple that he built to Athena[2]; his temple of the Olympian Zeus was not completed till the time of Hadrian. Like Periander of Corinth, he severely repressed idleness[3]. To Aristophanes, writing just a century after the fall of the tyranny, the Athens of Hippias appeared as a city of labourers[4].

Beloch well insists on the acute commercial instinct of Peisistratus in getting a footing on the coast of the Hellespont by the seizure of Sigeium[5]. Hippias not only kept his hold on the town to the last, and eventually retired there, but actively developed his father's line of policy by forming a close personal connexion with the tyrants of Lampsacus[6], and effecting a reconciliation with the Philaids, his rivals on the European side of the strait[7].

According to the pseudo-Aristotelian *Oeconomica*, Hippias on one occasion called in the Attic coinage at a fixed valuation, and then reissued the same money[8]. Some scholars have tried to explain away this last statement, and assume a change in the type[9]. But if, as

Financial troubles of the tyranny before its overthrow.

[1] E. Gardner, *Gk. Sculp.* fig. 34.

[2] Doerpfeld, *Ath. Mitt.* XXVII. (1902), pp. 379 f.; E. Curtius, *Stadtg. v. Athen*, pp. 73 f.; Michaelis, *Cent. Arch. Discov.* pp. 240-2.

[3] Plut. *Solon*, 31, "the law against idleness was passed, not by Solon but by Peisistratus."

[4] Aristoph. *Lysistr.* 1150 f. "Do you not know that it was the Spartans again, who when you were wearing the labourer's dress (κατωνάκας φοροῦντες), came under arms and slew...many friends and allies of Hippias,...and set you free, and clothed your people like gentlemen instead of labourers once again (ἀντὶ τῆς κατωνάκης τὸν δῆμον ὑμῶν χλαῖναν ἡμπισχον πάλιν)." Cp. the charges made by fifth century Roman republicans against the kings: below, pp. 223-4.

[5] Beloch, *Gr. G.*[2] I. i. 387-8; Hdt. v. 94, "(Peisistratus) having secured it (Sigeium), established as tyrant his illegitimate son"; cp. Periander and Corcyra.

[6] Thuc. VI. 59.

[7] Hdt. VI. 39; cp. above, p. 52. For numismatic evidence of Hippias' ties with both Lampsacus and the Thracian Chersonese see Head, *Hist. Num.*[2] p. 377, Lermann, *Athenatypen*, pp. 17-21, coins of (a) Chersonese, *obv.* Athena head, *rev.* Milesian lion (for Milesian colonies in Chersonese see Strabo, XIV. 635; VII. 331, frag. 52); (b) Lampsacus, *obv.* Athena head, *rev.* type of Lampsacus. This alliance currency points to a broad and far-reaching commercial policy.

[8] Ps.-Aristot. *Oec.* II. 1347a, τό τε νόμισμα τὸ ὂν Ἀθηναίοις ἀδόκιμον ἐποίησε, τάξας δὲ τιμὴν ἐκέλευσε πρὸς αὑτὸν ἀνακομίζειν. συνελθόντων δὲ ἐπὶ τῷ κόψαι ἕτερον χαρακτῆρα, ἐξέδωκε τὸ αὐτὸ ἀργύριον.

[9] Head, *Num. Chron.* 1893, p. 248 (change very slight); Gilbert, *Neue Jahrb.* 1896, pp. 537 f. (Hippias issued fresh coins from the same silver).

is natural to suppose, χαρακτήρ in this passage means type, then the Greek implies that no such change was made. The other actions of Hippias recorded in the same passage are confiscations of property (front doors, projecting top stories of houses, etc.), sold again, with no alteration whatever, to the original owners. Six and Babelon[1] maintain that χαρακτήρ means denomination, and that Hippias proceeded to give the name of didrachm to a piece that had been previously a drachm. They quote with some effect the statement of the Aristotelian *Constitution of Athens*[2], ἦν ὁ ἀρχαῖος χαρακτὴρ δίδραχμον. Their arguments, though plausible, are not decisive: but whatever the explanation of these particular words, the whole passage makes it fairly certain that the step was an attempt to avert a financial crisis by some desperate manipulation of the coinage. It points to a serious threat of approaching insolvency, such as must have been the inevitable result of the loss of the Thracian mines[3].

No aspect of the tyranny at Athens can be adequately examined without some reference to the remarkable family that from first to last with only one brief lapse led the opposition to the tyranny[4], and after its overthrow played the principal part in moulding the destinies of the democracy. In the earlier part of the sixth century the Alcmaeonidae had become extremely rich. That is the fact that emerges from the story of Alcmaeon and the king of Lydia told in Herodotus[5]. They were at the head of the faction of the shore, and Meyer is probably right when he says that their "enormous" wealth was due to trade with Lydia[6]. The fall of Lydia must have meant heavy losses to the family[7]. It is probably no accident that Peisistratus appears to have "rooted" his tyranny only after his rivals had suffered this great financial blow.

The Alcmaeonid opposition to the house of Peisistratus.

Nor is it probably a pure coincidence that as the Peisistratids secured their power by a mixture of commercial enterprise and political intrigue, so it was by a mixture of political intrigue and

---

[1] *Num. Chron.* 1895, p. 178; *J. I. d'A. N.* viii. (1905), pp. 23 f.
[2] *Ath. Pol.* 10.
[3] Cp. Svoronos, *J. I. d'A. N.* v. (1902), p. 32 f. (cp. below, p. 183, n. 6), on a hint that Pheidon may have debased the Aeginetan "tortoises" shortly before his fall.
[4] Cp. Isocr. *de Big.* 25, 26 (351).
[5] Hdt. vi. 125; cp. Isoc. *de Big.* 25 (351).
[6] E. Meyer, *Ges. d. Alt.* ii. p. 637.
[7] Note, however, Hdt. v. 62 (see next note), χρημάτων εὖ ἥκοντες.

commercial enterprise that they were finally driven out, through the Alcmaeonidae undertaking the contract for rebuilding the temple at Delphi[1].

This building operation was regarded by the Athenian informant of Herodotus as an expensive but effective way of purchasing divine favour[2]. But the Aristotelian *Constitution of Athens* says otherwise: "the Alcmaeonidae secured the contract for building the temple at Delphi, and made a fortune as the result[3]." The two versions may not be so contradictory as they at first sight appear. A way of reconciling them is suggested by Philochorus (early third century B.C.), who makes the Alcmaeonids accept the contract, make their money, successfully attack the Peisistratids, and then give rich thank-offerings to the Delphic god[4]. Isocrates and Demosthenes confirm the statement that Cleisthenes organized the expulsion of the Peisistratids with money secured from Delphi, but both regard the money as a loan[5].

But Delphi recalls yet another field of Alcmaeonid activities. According to the official Delphic records not Solon[6], but Alcmaeon, the paternal grandfather of the Athenian Cleisthenes, was the Athenian general in the "sacred" war which early in the sixth century was waged by the Amphictyons, and particularly Athens

---

[1] δεῖ δὲ πρὸς τούτοισι ἔτι ἀναλαβεῖν τὸν κατ' ἀρχὰς ἦια λέξων λόγον, ὡς τυράννων ἐλευθερώθησαν οἱ Ἀθηναῖοι. Ἱππίεω τυραννεύοντος...Ἀλκμαιωνίδαι, ...φεύγοντες Πεισιστρατίδας,...ἐνθαῦτα...πᾶν ἐπὶ τοῖσι Πεισιστρατίδῃσι μηχανώμενοι, παρ' Ἀμφικτυόνων τὸν νηὸν μισθοῦνται τὸν ἐν Δελφοῖσι, τὸν νῦν ἐόντα, τότε δὲ οὔκω, τοῦτον ἐξοικοδομῆσαι, οἷα δὲ χρημάτων εὖ ἥκοντες, καὶ ἐόντες ἄνδρες δόκιμοι ἀνέκαθεν ἔτι, τόν τε νηὸν ἐξεργάσαντο τοῦ παραδείγματος κάλλιον, τά τε ἄλλα καὶ, συγκειμένου σφι πωρίνου λίθου ποιέειν τὸν νηὸν, Παρίο τὰ ἔμπροσθεν αὐτοῦ ἐξεποίησαν. Hdt. v. 62.

[2] Hdt. v. 63, ἀνέπειθον τὴν Πυθίην χρήμασι.

[3] Aristot. *Ath. Pol.* 19. For huge sums made in this way in recent times on classic ground see the *causes célèbres* of the Vittorio Emanuele monument and the Palazzo di Giustizia at Rome.

[4] *F.H.G.* I. p. 395, frag. 70.

[5] Isoc. *Antid.* 232, "Cleisthenes, having been banished from the city by the tyrants, persuaded the Amphictyons to lend him some of the money of the god, and restored the democracy, and banished the tyrants"; Dem. *Meid.* 144 (561), "(the Alcmaeonids), they say...having borrowed money from Delphi, freed the city and expelled the sons of Peisistratus." Themistius, *Orat.* IV. 53a, gives the Alcmaeonidae as the contractors without any mention of means or motives. Hdt. II. 180, Strabo IX. 421, and Paus. x. 5. 13 mention the rebuilding of the temple without referring to the Alcmaeonidae.

[6] Plut. *Sol.* 11.

and Sicyon, against the people of the Delphic port of Krisa. The significance of this war is discussed below in the chapter where Sicyon is dealt with in detail. Here it is enough to notice that Cleisthenes of Athens was, through his mother, the grandson of his namesake the tyrant of Sicyon who took so prominent a part in this "sacred" war. He was probably also his heir[1]. In the days of Hippias Sicyon seems to have been still under a tyrant, but not of the house to which Cleisthenes belonged. His name was Aeschines. Evidence has been adduced by De Gubernatis[2] for believing that this Aeschines was an ally of Hippias of Athens. As we shall see below when dealing with Sicyon, his attitude towards Delphi was a pivotal point in the policy of the Sicyonian Cleisthenes, and in his later years Sicyon and Delphi became deadly rivals. Athens can hardly have kept out of the feud. We know little of the course of events, and the history of recent years shows how idle it would be to assume that internal revolutions are always reflected in foreign politics. But we may be sure that both in Athens and Sicyon an anti-Delphic policy would have its opponents as well as its supporters[3]. It is quite conceivable that the Athenian Cleisthenes had once aimed at a union of central Greece with Athens, Sicyon, and Delphi as the three chief states of the union and Cleisthenes himself as the chief statesman, controlling the immense treasure of the oracle and basing on it a tyranny over the two other cities, with Sicyon controlling the trade of the Peloponnesus and the far West while Athens did the like for the Northern trade and developed with the Persian empire those friendly relations which the Alcmaeonidae were still suspected of favouring at the time of the battle of Marathon. If this is all speculation it at least recalls the fact that the received accounts of Cleisthenes are all centred on what he did in Athens in the few years following the fall of Hippias. That indeed is practically all that is known about the second founder of the Athenian democracy; but considering his varied antecedents and his remarkable ancestry it is well to consider how small a chapter

[1] Grote, *Hist. Greece*, ed. 1888, II. pp. 412–413.

[2] *Atti R. Accad. Torino*, 1916, pp. 303–4, quoting *Cat. Greek Pap. Rylands*, vol. I. p. 31.

[3] That the Peisistratids were unfriendly to Delphi is perhaps to be inferred from the report highly dubious in itself, but prevalent in various quarters, that they had actually caused the fire which destroyed the temple, Philoc. frag. 70, *F.H.G.* I. p. 395.

this must have been in what was probably a long[1] as well as an eventful life. But to return to the short chapter about which something is known we find that the way Cleisthenes secured his position against the banished tyrant was by outbidding him. "He enfranchised many foreigners and slaves and metics[2]." The Peisistratids had ruled Athens as masters. Cleisthenes, by the stroke of genius so excellently epitomized by Herodotus, "took the people into partnership[3]."

It was this memorable partnership that dealt the cause of tyranny at Athens its final blow. Cimon indeed appears to have tried to make himself all-powerful in the state by the lavish outlay of his enormous wealth. But the result was only to cement the partnership between his Alcmaeonid rival and the people. The army, the navy, and the civil service became paid professions, or at least paid occupations, and the state, with Pericles at its head, perhaps the largest and most popular employer of the free population. Individuals of outstanding wealth were more and more kept in their political place by having to perform expensive liturgies. To make a public display of wealth became a perilous thing; anyone who did so was suspected of aiming at the tyranny and dealt with by ostracism or other effective means.

[1] Cleisthenes' parents appear to have married before 570 B.C. Beloch, *Gr. G.*[2] I. ii. p. 286.
[2] Aristot. *Pol.* III. 1275 b.
[3] Hdt. v. 66, τὸν δῆμον προσεταιρίζεται. Cp. *ibid.* 69, ἥν τε τὸν δῆμον προσθέμενος πολλῷ καθύπερθε τῶν ἀντιστασιωτέων.

Chapter III. *Samos*

Samian trade and industry in the seventh and sixth centuries B.C.

THE Samians had from early times been great shipbuilders and sailors. They were among the first of the Greeks to adopt the Corinthian invention of the trireme, somewhere about the year 700 B.C.[1], and in most of the naval warfare of the next two hundred years they are found playing a prominent part[2]. Still more important were the achievements of their merchantmen. It was a Samian ship, commanded by Kolaios, that "sailing towards Egypt, put out for Platea (in Libya)....and hugging the Egyptian coast, continued their voyage, carried along by an east wind: and since the breeze did not drop, they passed the pillars of Herakles and arrived at Tartessus, enjoying divine guidance. That market was at that time unopened (ἀκήρατον)[3]." The opening up of the Spanish silver mines through the port of Tartessus, the biblical Tarshish, was an event of first-class importance. "On their return home these Samians made the greatest profits from the carrying trade (φορτίων) of all the Hellenes of whom we have exact information, excepting only Sostratos the Aeginetan[3]." The date of the Samian voyage to Tarshish appears to have been about 620 B.C.[4].

It was a Samian, Xanthias by name, who about the same time as this brought to Egypt "on business" the famous Greek hetaera Rhodópis[5]. When Amasis, king of Egypt from 569 to 526 B.C., "showing himself a friend of the Greeks...and to those that came to Egypt, gave the city of Naukratis to dwell in[6]," Samos was one of the three Greek states to set up an establishment of its own there[7]. These establishments were of course commercial. "In the old days Naukratis was the only market in Egypt. There was no other[8]."

---

[1] Thuc. I. 13; cp. Pliny, *N.H.* VII. 57 (56). Panofka, *Res Samiorum*, p. 15, quotes Pliny, *ibid.*, for attributing to the Samians the invention of horse-transports, but the reading is doubtful: edd. hippagum Samii (inuenerunt), but for Samii MSS. give Damiam.

[2] Hdt. III. 47 (Messenian war), III. 59 (against Aegina), V. 99 (Lelantine war).

[3] Hdt. IV. 152.

[4] Macan, *Hdt.* IV.–VI. i. p. 106.   [5] Hdt. II. 135.   [6] Hdt. II. 178.

[7] Hdt. II. 178; cp. Steph. Byz. s.v. Ἔφεσος. On the Greek τεμένη at Naukratis see below, Chapter IV. pp. 116–7.   [8] Hdt. II. 179.

Samian trade developed side by side with Samian industry. From early times the islanders had enjoyed a great reputation as workers in metal, especially the fine metals[1]. The beginning of the connexion with Tartessus at the end of the seventh century gives the latest probable date for the beginning of this industry. Samian woollen goods were no less famous[2].

The island was not however exclusively commercial. [Th]ere was a powerful landed aristocracy called γεωμόροι[3], who doubtless owned the rich Samian olive-yards[4]. The late date of the tyranny in Samos is probably to be explained by the power of the γεωμόροι. The result was something very similar to what occurred under similar circumstances at Athens. There may have been attempts like that made at Athens by Cylon[5], but no tyrant appears to have established himself firmly before the rise of Polycrates early in the second half of the sixth century. Till then the geomoroi were sufficiently powerful to make a tyranny impossible. Then, about 545 B.C., the Samian landowners received a fatal blow to their power, when the Greek cities on the coast of Asia Minor were conquered by the Persians. These cities, whether friendly or hostile to Samos, were all equally its commercial rivals, and the disturbances connected

Why no tyranny was established till the middle of the sixth century.

[1] The most famous names connected with this industry are Rhoecus and Theodorus (below, pp. 73, 76, 80, 83) and Mnesarchus, father of the philosopher Pythagoras (see Diog. Laert. VIII. 1. 1; cp. Iambl. *Pyth.* 5, 9).

[2] Theocr. XV. 125–6.

[3] Plut. *Qu. Gr.* 57 (*Moral.* 304–5).

[4] Apul. *Florid.* II. 15; Aesch. *Pers.* 883.

[5] For possible early tyrants in Samos see Meyer, *Ges. d. Alt.* II. pp. 614, 616, who names Amphikrates (Hdt. III. 59), Demoteles (Plut. *Qu. Gr.* 57), and Syloson (Polyaen. VI. 45). All three are extremely doubtful. Amphikrates was probably a legitimate king of the period before the abolition of monarchy: very possibly he was a contemporary of the Argive Pheidon (below, pp. 177–8). Demoteles was, according to our only authority, the monarch whose murder led to the ascendancy of the geomoroi: he is naturally assumed to have been the last sovereign of the legitimate royal house. The Syloson of Polyaenus, VI. 45, is probably a confused recollection of the brother of Polycrates. He helps the Samians during a war with the Aeolians to observe a festival of Hera held outside the city and makes himself tyrant during the celebration. The connexion with Hera points to the family of Polycrates (see below, pp. 76, 81): the Aeolian war may be a disguised version of the struggle waged by Polycrates against the Great King who was in possession of the Aeolian mainland. This struggle went back to the beginning of the reign of Polycrates, when he was associated in his tyranny with his brother Syloson: see also Babelon, *Rev. Num.* 1894, p. 268.

with the Persian conquest, which affected them all while leaving Samos untouched, must have greatly increased the importance of the commercial element on the island[1].

Polycrates becomes tyrant: his tyranny and Samian trade. It was within a few years of these events that Polycrates made himself tyrant of Samos. The exact date is not known, but it was probably after[2] the Persian conquest of the mainland, and may well have been due in part to the increased commercial importance of Samos which resulted from that conquest.

However this may be, Polycrates, when established as tyrant, is found controlling the commercial and industrial activities of his state. All through his reign he was a great sailor and shipowner[3]. He built the famous breakwater in the Samian harbour[4], and was credited with the invention of a new type of boat, called the Samaina[5] (see fig. 9).

The wars and "piracies" of Polycrates and their possible commercial character. The general conception of the Samian tyrant is indeed that he used his ships in naval and piratical operations rather than for peaceful purposes of trade. Thucydides says of him that "having a powerful fleet he made divers of the islands subject to him, and in particular captured Rheneia and dedicated it to the Delian Apollo[6]." But even the capture of Rheneia, which Thucydides seems to regard as the principal warlike achievement of Polycrates' fleet, was one that may have had important commercial consequences. By cap-

---

[1] Meyer, *Ges. d. Alt.* II. p. 777, following Grote III. (ed. 1888), p. 453.

[2] Busolt, *Gr. G.*³ II. pp. 508–9, n. 3, who notes that Lygdamis was already tyrant of Naxos (Polyaen. I. 23, *pace* Plass, *Tyrannis*, p. 236).

[3] Thuc. I. 13; Hdt. III. 39, 122; Strabo, XIV. 637. Max. Tyr. (Teubner), XXIX. 2; Euseb. *Chron.* Armenian vers. "mare obtinuerunt Samii," Lat. vers. "Dicearchiam Samii condiderunt," both just after notice of Polycrates' accession. Cp. S. Reinach's interpretation of the ring which Polycrates cast into the sea (Hdt. III. 41; Strabo, XIV. 638; Paus. VIII. 14. 8; Pliny, *N.H.* XXXVII. 1; Cic. *de Fin.* V. 30. 92; Val. Max. VI. 9. 5 (ext.); Tzetz. *Chil.* VII. 121; Galen, *Protrept.* 4; Eustath. *ad* Dionys. v. 534), with which the French scholar compares the ring with which the doge of Venice annually wedded his mistress the sea (S. Reinach, *Rev. Arch.* ser. IV. vol. VI. (1905), pp. 9 f.), but cp. Marshall, *Brit. Mus. Cat. Rings*, p. xxi, n. 7, who points out that wedding rings seem unknown among the Greeks.

[4] Hdt. III. 60.

[5] Suid. and Phot. Σαμίων ὁ δῆμος; Plut. *Pericles*, 26; Athen. XII. 540 *e*; cp. Hesych. Σαμιακὸς τρόπος; Phot. Σάμαιναι.

[6] Thuc. I. 13, III. 104.

turing Rheneia Polycrates became practically master of Delos. He celebrated the Delian games[1]. Considering the unrivalled situation of Delos it is not unlikely that the festival was even in the sixth century the "commercial affair[2]" that it was in later ages, and such as others also of the great Greek games appear to have been from the days of the tyrants[3]. In that case it is not inconceivable that the repeated purifications of Delos in the sixth and fifth centuries may have had not only a religious signification, but also the purpose of restricting a commercial element that was constantly reasserting itself.

We need not be surprised to find a commercial potentate exerting his power by means of an army or navy. War has so far in the world's history always stood in the immediate background of even the most peaceful political power. There is nothing in the nature of a capitalist government to make it anti-militarist. If, as seems to have been the case, the early tyrants realized how seldom war does anything for commercial prosperity except to ruin it, it only shows them to have been men of unusual insight, as indeed there are many reasons for thinking that they were. If Polycrates was an exception to the generally peaceful character of the early tyranny, the fact may be explained by his antagonism to Persia, with which he appears to have been openly at war during part of his reign[4].

Our records of this war contain obvious mis-statements about the death of Cyrus, and their whole truth has been questioned[5]. But the hostility of Polycrates to Persia is sufficiently shown by his friendship with Egypt. His break with Amasis king of Egypt can scarcely be anything but a desertion to the common enemy Persia. The catholic character of his piracy, which stopped all shipping though it confiscated only hostile craft, is not really explained by his jest when he claimed that by this method he not only injured his enemies whose ships he kept, but also secured the gratitude of his friends, whose ships he released. His proceedings become really comprehensible only if we understand them as one of the earliest instances of a strict blockade, plainly directed against the great

[1] Phot. and Suid. Πύθια καὶ Δήλια. So Zenob. *ap.* Leutsch u. Schneidewin, *Paroem. Graec.* I. p. 165; cp. Diogenian. *ibid.* p. 311.

[2] ἐμπορικὸν πρᾶγμα, Strabo, x. 486; cp. Pliny, *N.H.* xxxiv. 4.

[3] See below, p. 260.

[4] Malalas *ap.* Migne, *Bibl. Patr. Gr.* vol. 97, p. 260. So Cedren. *Synops.* 243; *ibid.* vol. 121, p. 277.

[5] Plass, *Tyrannis*, p. 240.

land power to the east. The Peloponnesian expedition against Polycrates shows simply that the neutrals to the west did not yet realize who was their real enemy[1]. The danger from Persia only became apparent to European Greece when Darius invaded Scythia and Thrace[2].

There is every reason to believe that Polycrates supported Cambyses half-heartedly and under compulsion. He went over to the Persian side only when Cambyses was collecting a force against Egypt[3], or in other words when the Great King was advancing on the Mediterranean with an overwhelming force. He sent to his support only a disaffected contingent that was a source of trouble and weakness to him at home in Samos[3]. He met his death not so very long after, in an attempt to break away from Persia at what must have been the very first opportunity, just about the time when Cambyses fell ill[4].

On the whole therefore it seems best to accept as historical the account of the war between Cyrus and the Samians, since though only mentioned in late authors, it accords so well with all that is known of the period from early sources. It is ascribed to the period when Samos ruled the waves[5], which we have seen already to mean the reign of Polycrates, and this indication as to date agrees with the statement[5] that the war occurred at the end of Cyrus' reign. It brings Polycrates into a situation which alike in its patriotic and in its selfish side anticipates the attitude of Dionysius of Syracuse towards Carthage. But even this war may have been in part an attempt to maintain Samos in her commercial and industrial position. From the Samian point of view war with Persia meant first and foremost a struggle against Miletus. The island city and its neighbour on the mainland had long been rivals, and the supremacy of the one had meant the depression of the other. Miletus was now under the Persians and had made favourable terms with her conquerors. What Cyrus was aiming at in Anatolia is made sufficiently plain to us by the description in Herodotus of the way that he treated the conquered Lydians. They

---

[1] Hdt. III. 47, where observe the causes to which the war is attributed.

[2] Hence the relevance of the long account of the Thraco-Scythian expedition in the fourth book of Herodotus, immediately preceding the first attack upon Persia by European Greeks, that namely of Athens and Eretria during the Ionian revolt described in Book v.

[3] Hdt. III. 44. [4] Hdt. III. 120.

[5] Malalas, *loc. cit.*

were to bring up their children simply to play music and to become retail traders[1]. A similar account is given by Zenobius: "they say that Cyrus, having overcome the Lydians, charged them to become retail traders (καπηλεύειν) and not to acquire arms[2]." Zenobius says nothing about the music. There can be little doubt that the trading was the main thing. Both writers say that Cyrus' object was to prevent the Lydians breaking out into armed rebellion, and this may be true as far as it goes. But Cyrus did not treat all his rebellious provinces in this way. It looks as though he intended to make conquered Sardis, devoted entirely to trade and with the Persian army behind it, into the commercial capital of his kingdom, with Miletus as its chief seaport. This policy, if successful, would have been disastrous to the trade of Samos. May it not have been to prevent it that Polycrates organized the fleet and pursued the naval policy that won him such fame and unpopularity? We have an instance of rivalry between Polycrates and Sardis in the "laura" which he constructed at Samos, the significance of which is discussed below[3].

In any case Polycrates employed his fleet for commercial purposes as well as warlike. He traded with Egypt[4], which was the one Eastern country that was during most of his reign independent of Persia and open to Samian trade. The statement of Clytus the Aristotelian that "Polycrates the tyrant of the Samians from motives of luxury gathered the products of every country[5]" shows that Polycrates had a personal interest in the transport trade. There is unfortunately nothing to show that he employed his own vessels.

It is difficult again with the available evidence completely to identify the tyrant with Samian industry. He was the patron of Theodorus, who was famous not only as a jeweller, but also as a maker of metal vases[6]. The possible significance of this fact will be seen in a moment, when we proceed to examine the statements about

The tyranny of Polycrates and Samian industry.

[1] κιθαρίζειν τε καὶ ψάλλειν καὶ καπηλεύειν, Hdt. I. 155. So Justin, I. 7, iussi cauponias et ludicras artes et lenocinia exercere.
[2] Zenob. v. 1, Λυδὸς καπηλεύει, ap. Leutsch u. Schneidewin, *Paroem. Graec.* I. p. 115.
[3] pp. 76-7.
[4] Cp. Hdt. III. 39 with Diod. I. 95, 98.
[5] ὑπὸ τρυφῆς τὰ πανταχόθεν συνάγειν, Athen. XII. 540 c.
[6] Hdt. I. 51; Athen. XII. 514 f.

Polycrates' activities before he became tyrant. There is however no evidence that Polycrates was himself engaged in the Samian metal industries during his reign. For the woollen industries the evidence is stronger. Among the things which Athenaeus[1] declares that Polycrates, when tyrant, introduced into Samos are sheep from Miletus. Athenaeus is here quoting Clytus. Later in the same passage he quotes another writer, Alexis, as stating that the tyrant imported sheep from Miletus and Attica. The sheep were of course imported not for their mutton but for their wool: the wools of Miletus were particularly famous. During his reign Polycrates lent support to Arcesilaus III, king of Cyrene in "sheep-rearing Libya[2]" and himself probably a merchant prince[3], who when banished from his own dominions sought refuge with the Samian tyrant[4].

One reported act of Polycrates seems out of keeping with the view that he was a great merchant. "It is said that Polycrates struck a large quantity of local coins in lead and then gilded them and gave them to them in payment[5]." Herodotus, our authority for this statement, dismisses it as idle ($\mu\alpha\tau\alpha\iota\acute{o}\tau\epsilon\rho o\varsigma$). But it is supported by numismatic evidence[6], and the reason alleged for the issue in Herodotus is perfectly plausible. Polycrates was resorting to a desperate expedient for getting rid of an invader. Apart from the question of its truth, the report is valuable as indicating that Polycrates, like his contemporary Hippias, was credited with a tendency to make practical experiments with the coinage. This is borne out by another report, quoted by Suidas[7], according to which the Samaina reputed to have been invented by Polycrates was not a ship but a coin.

The tyranny of Polycrates and Samian coinage.

The two reports are not necessarily contradictory. The tyrant may have introduced both the ship and the coin, like Anaxilas, tyrant of Rhegium, who introduced the hare into his dominions

---

[1] Athen. XII. 540 c–d.

[2] Hdt. IV. 155; cp. *ibid.* 159.

[3] Arcesilaus II is represented on a famous kylix in the Louvre as presiding over the weighing and shipment of a cargo of silphium, and has in that connexion been called by Michaelis a silphium merchant, *Cent. Arch. Discov.* p. 235.

[4] Hdt. IV. 162–4.

[5] Hdt. III. 56. The recipients are Spartan invaders of Samos.

[6] Archaic Milesian hects of lead plated with electrum, Brandis, *Münz-wesen*, pp. 327–8; F. Lenormant, *La Monnaie dans l'Antiq.* I. p. 225.

[7] Suid. s.v. Σαμίων ὁ δῆμος.

and commemorated his action by putting a hare on his coins (fig. 9). The Samaina is found on extant Samian coins (fig. 9), some of which appear to have circulated in Samos itself about the middle of the fifth century, while others have been associated with the Samian refugees who migrated to the far West in 494 B.C. and occupied Messana in Sicily with the aid of Anaxilas of Rhegium, whose subjects they became. The type cannot be traced back to the days of Polycrates himself, but the numismatic evidence is not abundant enough to make that fact decisive. As far as it goes it even inclines slightly in favour of Suidas. If the coin type used by the refugees of 494 B.C. appears later on the coins of Samos itself, the fact is best explained by assuming that it was already in use in Samos before the earlier date. Moreover one of the coins generally associated with the refugees is inscribed with the letters A I, which have no obvious connexion with Messana or the Samians who went there, but which do on the other hand form the first syllable of the name Aiakes, the name of the Samian tyrant from whom the refugees fled to Messana. Aiakes was a nephew of Polycrates, so that if the A I coin is rightly ascribed to him the Samaina type is traced back to the family of Polycrates, if not to Polycrates himself. Aiakes had been restored to Samos by the Persians after their defeat of the Greek fleet at the battle of Lade. In that battle the Samian fleet, with the exception of the ships manned by the men who fled later to Sicily, had disgraced itself by deserting to the Persians. Aiakes profited by their proceedings but he can hardly have been proud of them. If he struck coins with the Samaina type it is more likely to have been because his uncle had done so before him than from any desire to commemorate either his own exploits, whether as a shipbuilder or a sailor, or those of his uncle, who so successfully defied the Persian power to which the nephew owed his throne[1].

Fig. 9. Samian coin with Samaina and Messanian coin with hare.

[1] On Aiakes see Hdt. VI. 13, 22, 25; on the Samaina coins see Head, *Hist. Num.*² pp. 153, 603-4; P. Gardner, *Samos*, p. 17, Pl. I. 17, 18; Babelon, *Rev. Num.* 1894, pp. 281-2, Pl. X.; v. Sallet, *Zeit. f. Num.* III. p. 135, v. p. 103.

In his domestic policy Polycrates won great fame as the promoter of great public works. "I have dwelt the longer on the Samians," says Herodotus[1], "because they have erected three works that surpass those of all the Greeks." The works in question are the harbour breakwater already mentioned, the huge temple of Hera, and the underground aqueduct constructed by Eupalinus of Megara[2]. Herodotus himself does not say who was responsible for these works being undertaken; but the context shows that the historian is thinking of the Samos of Polycrates. The first architect of the temple is given by him as Rhoecus, the partner of Theodorus, who worked for Polycrates. Great engineering activities in Samos about this time are indicated by the fact that the engineer who shortly afterwards bridged the Bosporus for Darius was a Samian[3]. The breakwater round the harbour is naturally ascribed to the time of the Samian thalassocracy under Polycrates. There is therefore little doubt that modern scholars and archaeologists have been right in identifying these great constructions with the "Polycratean works" referred to by Aristotle[4] as typical undertakings of a typical tyrant, the more so as there are numerous instances of early tyrants undertaking these particular kinds of work[5].

The public works of Polycrates during his tyranny, including an aqueduct and a harbour breakwater.

One work of a similar kind that Samos owed to Polycrates deserves at least a passing notice, namely the "laura" that he erected as a rival to what is called in Sardis the Ἀγκὼν γλυκύς[6]. Etymologically "laura" is probably to be connected with "labyrinth[7]."

---

[1] Hdt. III. 60.

[2] Fabricius, *Ath. Mitt.* IX. (1884), pp. 165 f.; *Jahrb.* IV. *Arch. Anz.* pp. 39–40; Wiegand, *Abhand. preuss. Akad. Phil. Hist. Class.* 1911; Dennis, *Academy*, 1882, Nov. 4, pp. 335–6; Guérin, *Patmos et Samos*, pp. 196–7. The great tunneled aqueduct that took the water through the mountain which separates the city from the source of the supply is still in existence.   [3] Hdt. IV. 87, 88.

[4] ἔργα Πολυκράτεια, Aristot. *Pol.* VIII. 1313 b; cp. Athen. XII. 540 d; Suet. *Calig.* 21 (regia).

[5] Water supplies: Cypselids at Corinth (Πειρήνη), Theagenes at Megara (the home of Eupalinus), Peisistratus at Athens (Καλλιρρόη). Temples: Corinth, Athens (the huge Olympiaeum completed by Hadrian 700 years later).

[6] Clearchus *ap.* Athen. 540 f.; cp. Ps.-Plut. I. 61, s.v. Σαμίων ἄνθη, καὶ Σαμιακὴ λαύρα *ap.* Leutsch u. Schneidewin, *Paroem. Graec.* I. p. 330.

[7] Burrows, *Discoveries in Crete*, pp. 117 f.; cp. Conway, *ibid.* pp. 227 f. The ancient derivations are interesting but not helpful: see *Et. Mag.* s.v. παρὰ τὸ λίαν ἔχειν αὔραν· ἢ δι' ἧς ὁ λαὸς ῥεῖ εἰς τὴν ὁδόν.

The word has various meanings¹. The laura at Samos appears to have been a place for buying and selling², possibly an early predecessor of the labyrinthine bazaars still in use in the great cities of the near East such as Smyrna, Cairo, and Constantinople³.

If Polycrates' laura was in fact a great bazaar, it is easy to imagine how it became a byword for luxury⁴ and worse things than that. The description of it by Clearchus as a place of ill-repute is plainly from a source unfriendly to the tyrant⁵.

The labour employed on these works appears to have been mainly free. Whatever the facts about the laura, the sums that Polycrates spent on his public works in general and the number of hands that he employed on them must have been very large. Of the life led by these employees we know little. Aristotle states that the object of the tyrant's works was "the employment and poverty of his subjects⁶." This implies that the work was ill-paid and unpopular. It is doubtful however whether Aristotle quite understood the social and economic conditions of sixth century Samos⁷. On the other hand no inferences as to the normal wages in the days of the tyrant are to be drawn from occasional instances of high payments made by him for exceptional work⁸. One fact however becomes plain from the statement in the *Politics*. The hands employed by Polycrates must have been mainly free men.

Like some tyrannical employers of labour in more recent times, Polycrates appears to have recognized the value of having his employees provided with amusements of not too elevated a type. Holidays and drunkenness appear to have been frequent under his

---

¹ Casaubon *ad* Athen. XII. cap. 10.

² Ps.-Plut. I. 61; cp. Athen. 541 a, Eustath. *ad Odyss.* XXII. 128.

³ See *Encyc. Brit.*¹¹ s.v. Bazaar: "Persian (bazar, market), a permanent market or street of shops or a group of short narrow streets of stalls under one roof." A similar picture is given by Radet, *Lydie*, pp. 298-9, of the Lydian γλυκὺς ἄγκων.

⁴ See Macarius VII. 55 *ap.* Leutsch u. Schneidewin, *Paroem. Graec.* II. p. 207, "Samian laura: of those indulging in luxury" (ἐπὶ τῶν εἰς τρυφὴν ἐκκεχυμένων); Ps.-Plut. I. 61 *ap.* eosd. I. p. 330, "of those indulging in extreme pleasures (ἐπὶ τῶν ὑστάταις ἡδοναῖς χρωμένων)."

⁵ It goes on to state that "Polycrates, the tyrant of luxurious Samos, perished through his intemperate mode of life."

⁶ ἀσχολίαν καὶ πενίαν τῶν ἀρχομένων, Aristot. *Pol.* 1313 b.

⁷ See above, pp. 26-32.

⁸ Athen. 540 d, μετεστέλλετο δέ, φησί, καὶ τεχνίτας ἐπὶ μισθοῖς μεγίστοις: Hdt. III. 131.

regime¹. The encouragement or permission of unprofitable amusements for the multitude is of course quite consistent with great severity in other directions², and more particularly with the suppression of the liberal forms of recreation popular among citizens of the better class³.

He maintained his power by means of mercenaries, native it should be noticed, as well as foreign⁴. These mercenaries were in all probability a development of the fifteen men at arms⁵ with which he had seized supreme power, and, like the original fifteen, they were presumably free men⁶.

The tyrant's mercenaries.

While on the subject of Polycrates' warlike achievements it is interesting to note that he did something to put military service on a sound financial basis by providing for the mothers of soldiers who fell in his service. The way he did so is described by Duris, a historian of Polycrates' own island, who was born about 340 B.C.⁷. "He gathered together the mothers of those who had fallen in war, and gave them to the wealthy among the citizens to support, saying to each, 'I give you this woman to be your mother.'" No provision was made for the widows; but from the Greek point of view this was hardly required. They would naturally be provided for by their second husbands⁸. The method of financing this popular measure recalls the Athenian

His pension scheme for the mothers of fallen soldiers.

---

¹ Athen. 541 a, ἔτι δὲ τῆς συμπάσης πόλεως ἐν ἑορταῖς τε καὶ μέθαις. The sentence is corrupt, but probably ἔτι=furthermore, and the subject is still Polycrates. It occurs in an extract from Clearchus that appears to deal exclusively with the Samian tyrant. If Polycrates is not the subject ἔτι is probably temporal, and the sentence described a state of affairs that had persisted from the time of the tyranny.

² Diod. I. 95, "behaving with violence both to the citizens and to strangers who sailed in to Samos."

³ Athen. 602 d, "there are some who regarded παλαῖστραι (wrestling schools) as counter-fortifications to their own citadels and set them on fire and demolished them, as was done by Polycrates the tyrant of Samos."

⁴ Hdt. III. 39 and 45.

⁵ Hdt. III. 120.

⁶ They consisted of "hired mercenaries" and "native bowmen," Hdt. III. 45.

⁷ *Ap.* Zenob. v. 64, s.v. Πολυκράτης μητέρα νέμει in Leutsch u. Schneidewin, *Paroem. Graec.* I. p. 146.

⁸ Cp. the story in Hdt. III. 119 of the woman who preferred to save her brother rather than her husband, because the latter was replaceable, but the former not.

liturgies. The measure itself points to the tyrant's troops having been free men.

One fact recorded of the times just after Polycrates' fall appears at first sight to offer a reason for assuming that Polycrates had relied on highly trained servile labour, which the city had found it a problem to deal with after his fall. A large number of slaves purchased the citizenship[1]. There is however a simpler explanation of this fact. Syloson, the brother of Polycrates, when restored by Persia, had almost annihilated the free population[2].

Polycrates the tyrant has therefore been shown to have taken some part in the commercial, the industrial and probably the financial activities of the city that he ruled.

Let us now see what is known about his career before he had made himself supreme in the state.

Before he became tyrant Polycrates already had a concern in the chief Samian industries.

Before he had become tyrant he used to get expensive coverlets and drinking vessels made, and lend them out to those who were holding weddings or entertainments on a particularly large scale.

These words are from Athenaeus[3]. It could scarcely be more definitely stated that Polycrates owed his throne to his wealth in coverlets and drinking vessels.

The coverlets (στρωμναί) are surely the manufactured article for which Polycrates subsequently introduced Milesian and Attic sheep. The word seems to denote a Samian speciality. A form of the corresponding verb (ἔστρωται) is used by Theocritus in the passage where he refers to the famous wools of Samos and Miletus[4].

It seems probable that Polycrates' brother and partner at first in the tyranny was also a merchant or manufacturer of woollen goods. At any rate after his banishment we find Darius wanting to buy a cloak (χλανίς) from him. According to Herodotus[5] it was the

---

[1] Suid. Σαμίων ὁ δῆμος.

[2] Strabo, xiv. 638; Heraclides, *F.H.G.* ii. p. 216; Zenobius, iii. 90 (*ap.* Leutsch u. Schneidewin, *Paroem. Graec.* i. p. 79), and Eustath. *ad Dion. Perieg.* 534, ἕκητι Συλοσῶντος εὐρυχωρίη; Suid. and Phot. s.v. Σαμίων ὁ δῆμος. Cp. Argos after the massacre of Cleomenes (about 494 B.C.): "Argos was so denuded of men that the slaves had the whole situation in their hands, ruling and administrating until the sons of the victims grew to manhood," Hdt. vi. 83.

[3] πρὸ δὲ τοῦ τυραννῆσαι κατασκευασάμενος στρωμνὰς πολυτελεῖς καὶ ποτήρια ἐπέτρεπε χρῆσθαι τοῖς ἢ γάμον ἢ μείζονας ὑποδοχὰς ποιουμένοις, Athen. 540 d.

[4] Cp. Tzetz. *Chil.* x. 347, τὸ παλαιὸν περὶ στρωμνὰς ἦν τῇ Μιλήτῳ φήμη.

[5] Hdt. iii. 139.

one that Syloson was at the moment wearing. The incident took place in Egypt. Syloson was one of the Greeks who followed Cambyses there after the Persian conquest. Some of these had come as traders (κατ' ἐμπορίην), some as soldiers, some as mere sightseers. Syloson, who was in the market place at Memphis at the moment of Darius' request, replied: "I am not selling this at any price; but I offer it you for nothing." What precisely Syloson was doing in the market place is unfortunately not certain. According to Grote[1] he was just walking there. The Greek is ἠγόραζε, which may mean "frequenting the market place," or "buying," or "selling in the market place." The incident suggests rather the last meaning, and that Syloson was in Memphis as a trader (κατ' ἐμπορίην) in cloaks (χλανίδες). The unromantic commercial aspect of the transaction between Syloson and Darius, which is already obscured in Herodotus' account, has quite disappeared in that of Strabo[2], who says simply that Syloson "made a present to Darius of a garment which he had seen him wearing and taken a fancy for..., and received the tyranny as a present in return."

The drinking vessels (ποτήρια) were almost certainly of metal. Ποτήρια of earthenware are only once[3] mentioned in the passages quoted in Liddell and Scott's *Lexicon*, whereas there are numerous passages in which ποτήρια are specifically stated to have been of metal[4]. In the case before us the fact that they were lent and for entertainments of special importance points strongly to metal[5]. We have just seen that Theodorus, who worked for Polycrates later in his career, was a maker of metal ποτήρια. It may well be the case therefore that Theodorus was something more to Polycrates than merely his crown jeweller and silversmith[6].

[1] Grote, III. p. 461. [2] Strabo, XIV. 638.
[3] Athen. XI. 464 a.
[4] Bronze, Hdt. II. 37; silver, gold, Hdt. III. 148; Boeckh, *C.I.G.* 138. 7, 19, 27.
[5] Cp. the borrowed metal vessels used for the entertainment of the Athenian envoys to Segesta just before the Athenian expedition to Sicily, Thuc. VI. 46.
[6] Some ancient authorities held that Theodorus flourished more than a century before Polycrates (Plin. *N.H.* XXXV. 43 (152); cp. Frazer, *Paus.* IV. p. 237). Theodorus is always associated with Rhoecus and the two names may have been borne in alternate generations by one family of artists. This would not require the Rhoeci to have flourished longer in Samos than the Wedgwoods have in Staffordshire. Whether or no this explanation holds, the divergence in dates points to the industry having flourished for a long time in the island. If one date for Theodorus is insisted on, that of Hdt. (I. 51), which makes him the elder contemporary of Polycrates, must be chosen.

The Samian silversmiths got their material from Tartessus[1]. Polycrates must therefore have had at least a second-hand interest in Samian shipping before his accession. In the outline of my views on the origin of the tyranny published in the *Journal of Hellenic Studies* for 1906 I observed that there was no evidence that Polycrates procured his silver in his own ships. That is still the case; but curiously enough only a few weeks after this observation was made, a find from Samos itself was published[2], which, with the learned and illuminating comments of the scholar who published it, has thrown fresh and interesting light on the close concern which the family of Polycrates already had in Samian shipping in the days when the future tyrant was still a child. The find consists of a headless seated statue[3] (fig. 10) that at once recalls the figures from Branchidae now in the British Museum[4]. The style both of the figure and of the lettering of the inscription attached to it point to a date about 550 B.C. The statue was dedicated by Aiakes the son of Bryson. Aiakes is not a common name. It was borne by the father of Polycrates. It is not improbable that, as L. Curtius maintains, the Aiakes who dedicated the statue was none other than the tyrant's father. The date suits exactly: so too does the inscription as ingeniously interpreted by Curtius. The actual words are:

Aiakes father of Polycrates is probably the Aiakes whom a Samian inscription appears to connect with sea-borne trade.

Ἀεάκης ἀνέθηκεν ὁ Βρύσωνος ὅς τῇ Ἥρῃ
τὴν σύλην ἔπρησεν κατὰ τὴν ἐπίστασιν.

The context makes it difficult to derive ἔπρησεν from πίμπρημι. Nor can ἐπίστασις well signify "dream" (visit by night), since the analogy of κατ' ὄναρ, κατ' ἐνύπνιον shows that in that case κατὰ would not be followed by the article. Curtius therefore takes ἔπρησεν as Ionic for ἔπρασσεν in the common sense of "exacted," "collected": for the single σ he compares Τειχιούσης for Τειχιούσσης, which actually occurs on one of the figures from Branchidae. The word σύλη he explains by reference to Herodotus IV. 152, which describes how the Samians, on their return from the voyage to Tarshish, "set apart the tithe of their gains, six talents, and let make

---

[1] Hdt. IV. 152.
[2] L. Curtius, *Ath. Mitt.* XXXI. (1906), pp. 151 f.
[3] Illustrated, *ibid.* pp. 151, 152, Pl. XIV.; *Amer. Journ. Arch.* XI. (1907), p. 84.
[4] *E.g.* Gardner, *Gk. Sculp.*, Fig. 8.

a copper cauldron after the manner of an Argive mixing bowl, and dedicated it in the Heraeum¹."

The gains from Tarshish, so Curtius suggests, may actually have been called σύλη, the idea of which word he thinks had grown to include all gains made by ventures on the sea. The name of Polycrates' brother Syloson is almost certainly to be derived from σῦλον (= σύλη, see above) and σῶν = σαῶν from σαώ = σῴζω (save)².

Fig. 10. Aiakes, father of Polycrates.

Curtius rightly observes that this name takes the connexion of Polycrates' family with σύλαι, sea-spoils, sea-gains, back to the time when Syloson received his name, that is, presumably, a generation or so before he and his two brothers, Pantagnotos and Polycrates, seized the tyranny of their native city.

[1] Hence perhaps the friendship of Polycrates with Arcesilaus of Cyrene; cp. Hdt. IV. 152, "It was from this action that the Cyreneans and Theraeans first struck up great friendships with the Samians."

[2] *Ath. Mitt.* xxxi. (1906), pp. 160, 161.

SAMOS

Polycrates is said by Herodotus to have owed his fall to an attempt to get money enough to rule all Greece.

The great wave of the Persian invasions of Europe, that began only a few years after Polycrates' death, and the rise of the Athenian empire after the Persians' final repulse, have somewhat eclipsed the glory of the Samian thalassocracy, which practically synchronized with the tyranny of Polycrates. During his reign he was unquestionably the most famous Greek in the whole Greek world, and his extraordinary series of unbroken successes was reported and discussed everywhere[1]. From the Greek point of view, according to which all excesses are to be avoided, whether of good things or of bad, he was too successful. The end could only be Nemesis or retribution. This feeling is expressed by Herodotus in the letter in which he makes the king of Egypt advise Polycrates to break the series by voluntarily giving up the thing that most he cared for[2].

The story goes on to tell how Polycrates was moved by the letter to cast away in the sea the most precious thing he possessed, a ring made by Theodorus, how the ring came back to him in the body of a fish served up at the royal table, and how Amasis "learnt that it is impossible for one human being to rescue another from the event that is to befall him[3]," and how accordingly he broke off his friendship with him, "that when some great and terrible accident overtook Polycrates, he might not himself be grieved at heart with the thought that it had befallen a friend[4]."

In all probability it was not Amasis who broke with Polycrates, but Polycrates who deserted Amasis when the Persian peril began to look irresistible[5]. But the dubious historicity of the incident only heightens its historical value: it shows that so far as the story of the end of Polycrates is false or inaccurate in point of fact, it has been altered to suit the requirements of Greek poetic justice and to make the way that Polycrates lost the throne a fitting requital for the way he had won and held it.

This is the story as given by Herodotus[6]. A new Persian satrap had been appointed at Sardis, who, learning that Polycrates aspired to rule "Ionia and all the islands," set a trap for him by pretending to need his help and promising in return much money. "As far as

---

[1] Hdt. III. 39, 125. [2] Hdt. III. 40. [3] Hdt. III. 43.
[4] Hdt. III. 43.
[5] So E. Meyer, *Ges. d. Alt.* II. p. 792; cp. above, p. 72.
[6] Hdt. III. 120 f.

money goes," the promise ran, "thou shalt be ruler of all Hellas." "When Polycrates heard this he was glad and willing. And since he greatly desired money, he first sent Maeandrius the son of Maeandrius to inspect...... But Oroetes, learning that the inspector was expected, did as follows. He filled eight chests with stones, except to a very slight depth just round the top, where on top of the stones he set gold." For the events that followed the precise words of Herodotus need not be quoted. Maeandrius was deceived. Polycrates crossed over to see Oroetes, was seized by him, and crucified.

It is important to remember how good are the sources for the history of the Samian tyranny. The famous Anacreon lived at Polycrates' court[1], and "all his poetry" was "full of references to him[2]." Practically all of it has perished, but it was accessible to the writers from whom we draw. Herodotus had conversed with Archias the Spartan, whose grandfather, also named Archias, had distinguished himself in the Spartan expedition against Polycrates, and whose exploits on that occasion had led to a permanent connexion between the Spartan family and the Samians[3].

Value of Herodotus on Polycrates.

As mentioned already in discussing the coins stamped with the Samaina, a son of Polycrates' brother Syloson was reinstated by the Persians as tyrant of Samos after the battle of Lade in 494 B.C. He is not heard of again, and in 480 B.C. a certain Theomestor "became tyrant of Samos, being set up by the Persians[4]." But even if the son of Syloson died immediately after his restoration, his reign still brings us down to times well within the memory of Herodotus' father. With sources like these it is highly likely that the main outlines of the facts have been preserved, and that where they have been improved on or added to, the changes or additions, whether conscious or unconscious, have been made to suit the general history of the period. Thus for example we should expect the facts about Polycrates' downfall to be in the main correctly reported: but the story of the letter from Amasis shows that we may expect touches to be added to emphasize the view that it was a visitation of Nemesis, an act of retribution on the part of the divine power.

[1] Hdt. III. 121.
[2] πᾶσα ἡ ποίησις πλήρης ἐστι τῆς περὶ αὐτοῦ μνήμης, Strabo, XIV. 638.
[3] Hdt. III. 55.
[4] Hdt. VIII. 85, IX. 90.

The account in Herodotus states that Polycrates fell because he hoped by means of boundless money to make himself tyrant of all Greece. The stress laid on money all through the narrative is remarkable[1]. According to all the laws of Greek psychology, the inference is surely this: that it was by means of his wealth that he had won and maintained his power.

[1] The wealth of Polycrates was still proverbial in the days of Plato, see *Meno*, 90a, and Stallbaum, *Platonis Meno, ad loc.*

Chapter IV. *Egypt*

Fig. 11. Psamtek I.

THE sixth century tyrants of Athens and Samos may be regarded with some probability as rulers who had come to their power by means of their wealth. Before proceeding to deal with the earlier Greek tyrants, as to whose antecedents the evidence is necessarily much more meagre and indecisive, it will be found convenient to turn our attention for a while to Egypt and Lydia. In both these states we shall find evidence, some of it very positive, that from the end of the eighth century onwards the kings were gaining and maintaining their power by means of their wealth. With both these states the Greeks of the seventh century were in close touch; from both they learned and borrowed much, since Egypt and the East had still much to teach them. The history therefore both of Egypt and Lydia is closely relevant at this period to that of the Greek world that they adjoined. It gives a context to the disconnected fragments of evidence that will have to be dealt with in some of the succeeding chapters, and makes it possible to fit them together into something resembling a significant whole.

Commercial and industrial developments in seventh century Egypt. Like Greece, Egypt had been through a dark period during the first three centuries of the first millennium B.C. After about two centuries of Libyan rulers (XXIInd and XXIIIrd dynasties) whose energies were often devoted to dealing with rival kings while subject princes spent the resources of the country in feuds among themselves, Egypt had fallen during the eighth century under an Ethiopian dynasty which she changed occasionally for Assyrian rule. But early in the seventh century, Egypt recovered its material prosperity. By the middle of the next century it is said to have been more prosperous than ever it was before[1], and this prosperity is reflected in the law of Amasis (570–526 B.C.) against unemployment[2] as also in the organization of industry into "more or less sharply defined classes or guilds[3]," in improved business methods and mechanical processes. The forms of legal and business documents became more precise[4]; the mechanical arts of casting in bronze on a core and of moulding figures and pottery were brought to the highest pitch of excellence[5]. Inscriptions of this epoch found in the gold-mining regions prove that the work of the ancient kings was taken up with renewed ardour[6]. The ports of Egypt were thrown open to the commerce of all the nations[7]. Strong fleets were maintained both in the Mediterranean and in the Red Sea[8]. An attempt was made by Pharaoh Necho (610–594 B.C.) to anticipate the Suez Canal by one connecting the Nile with the Red Sea[9]; and the exploits of Vasco da Gama were anticipated by a Phoenician ship that was sent out by this same Pharaoh Necho and circumnavigated Africa[10]. In these activities of Necho Sayce[11] sees an attempt to make Egypt the chief trading country of the world.

These great developments took place under a single dynasty, the XXVIth, which came from Sais on one of the western arms of the

---

[1] Hdt. II. 177; Plin. *N.H.* V. 11; Mela, I. 9 (60).

[2] Hdt. II. 177.

[3] Breasted, *Hist.*² p. 574, apparently an inference from Herodotus' inaccurate statement that a strict caste system prevailed among the Egyptians: only the priests became an exclusive caste, *ibid.* p. 575.

[4] Griffith, *Dem. Pap. Rylands*, III. p. 10.

[5] Griffith, *Encyc. Brit.*¹¹, Egypt, p. 87.

[6] Mallet, *Prem. Étab. des Grecs en Ég.* p. 292, quoting Erman u. Schweinfurth, *Abh. Ak. Berl.* 1885.

[7] Diod. Sic. I. 66.

[8] Hdt. II. 159; on technical progress in shipbuilding in seventh century Egypt see Mallet, *Prem. Étab.* pp. 99 f.

[9] Hdt. II. 158, IV. 42; cp. Aristot. *Meteor.* I. 14 (352 b); Strabo, XVII. 804; Diod. I. 33; Tzetz. *Chil.* VII. 446. A canal connecting the two seas appears (*pace* Wiedemann, *Hdt.* II. 158) to have been in use 700 years earlier under Seti I and Ramses II; see Petrie, *Hist.* III. p. 13; Maspero, *Hist. Anc.*⁶ p. 228. Necho's work was apparently completed by Darius (How and Wells, *ad Hdt.* II. 158).

[10] Hdt. IV. 42 and How and Wells, *ad loc.*; cp. Hdt. II. 159 on Necho's fleets of triremes on both the Mediterranean and the Red Sea.

[11] *Hdt.* I.–III. p. 338.

Delta[1]. The history of this dynasty can be traced back at Sais to the eighth century B.C., but the first of the family to rule all Egypt was Psammetichus (Psamtek), who reigned from about 664 to 610. Necho the father of this Psammetichus and grandfather of the Necho mentioned just above had been king or governor of Sais and Memphis under the Assyrian king Assurbanipal[2]. Psammetichus was driven into war and foreign politics to free his country from foreign invaders. The details of his warlike achievements do not here concern us. What does here concern us is to observe how he secured the power that enabled him to set about them.

Psammetichus I (664–610) rose to power

Early in his career, Psammetichus, so Herodotus informs us[3], had been one of twelve kings who had each received a twelfth of

---

[1] For convenience of reference I give here a list of the rulers with whom in this chapter we shall be concerned. The bracketed forms of the names are Egyptian. The dates are taken from Petrie's *History of Egypt*. In the case of acknowledged kings of all Egypt the number of their Dynasty is added after the date.

A. Saite rulers.

Tnefachthus (Tafnekht)	749–721
Bocchoris or (?) Anysis (Bakenranf)	721–715 (XXIV)
Stephinates or (?) Sethon (Tafnekht II)	715–678
Nechepsus (Nakauba)	678–672
Necho I (Nekau)	672–664
Psammetichus I (Psamtek)	664–610 (XXVI)
Necho II (Nekau)	610–594 (XXVI)
Psammouthis or Psammetichus II (Psamtek)	594–589 (XXVI)
Apries (Haa ab ra, Biblical Hophra)	589–570 (XXVI)
Amasis (Aahmes)	570–526 (XXVI)
Psammetichus III (Psamtek)	526–525 (XXVI)

B. Ethiopian rulers.

(Pianchi)	748–725 or later
Sabacon (Shabaka)	715–707 (XXV)
(Shabataka)	707–693 (XXV)
Taharqa (Biblical Tirhakah)	(701–)693–667 (XXV)
Ammeris (Amen Rud, Rud Amen, Nut Amen)	667–664 (XXV)

C. Dates of the dynasties.

XXIV (early Saite)	721–715
XXV (Ethiopian)	715–664
XXVI (Saite)	664–525

[2] G. Smith, *Assurbanipal*, pp. 20, 27, 28; cp. Petrie, *Hist.* III. p. 299, "Niku of Mempi and Sa'a."

[3] II. 151.

EGYPT

the country to reign over[1]. One day some bronze-clad Ionian and Carian freebooters were driven to Egypt by stress of weather. Psammetichus "made friends with the Ionians and Carians, and by great promises persuaded them to join him: and having persuaded them he thereupon, in conjunction with his supporters in Egypt and the mercenaries, put down the (other eleven) kings, and became master of all Egypt[2]."

according to Herodotus by means of Greek and Carian mercenaries,

The man who among twelve or more rivals[3] secured the monopoly of Greek and Carian mercenaries must have been a man of outstanding wealth. But this is not all our information about him. A fuller account is preserved in Diodorus[4]:

When the twelve had ruled Egypt for fifteen years it befel that the kingdom passed into the hands of one of them through the following causes. Psammetichus of Sais, who was one of the twelve kings, and ruler of the parts beside the sea, used to provide cargoes ($\phi o \rho \tau i a$) for the merchants, and particularly for Phoenicians and Greeks; by such means he disposed profitably of the products of his own land and secured a share of the products of the other nations, and enjoyed not only great wealth ($\epsilon \dot{v} \pi o \rho i a \nu$) but also friendship with nations and princes.

according to Diodorus by trading with Phoenicians and Greeks.

Could it be more plainly stated that Psammetichus owed his throne to his wealth and his wealth to trade?

The commercial origin of Psamtek's power can only be questioned by questioning the value of our authorities. The rest of this chapter will be devoted to showing that there is no reason for doing this, while there is much to confirm the passages just quoted.

Value of these statements of Herodotus and Diodorus.

Herodotus and Diodorus[5] had both visited Egypt and are among

---

[1] Herodotus (II. 147) says that these kings had been set up by the Egyptians themselves. It is generally recognized that his "dodecarchy" is an Egyptian description of the Assyrian administration, but the Assyrians may well have taken over a previously existing state of things, and the dodecarchy have developed out of the Libyan penetration of Egypt much as the heptarchy resulted from the Anglo-Saxon invasion of Britain.

[2] Hdt. II. 152.

[3] The Assyrian record gives twenty. Twelve may have been the number of kings in Lower Egypt (Mallet, *Prem. Étab.* p. 36, quoting Lenormant), or the total number at times (Wiedemann, *Hdt.* II. 147), or Herodotus may have got the number twelve from the twelve courts of the labyrinth that he erroneously ascribes to this period (Sayce, *Hdt. ad loc.*).

[4] Diod. I. 66.   [5] Diod. III. 11.

our best authorities. At first sight indeed they do not seem quite in agreement. But the story they tell is essentially the same. The difference is one of emphasis. Herodotus seizes on a single incident and makes much of the description of the Ionians and Carians as men of bronze. The point was worth emphasizing; for from the military point of view the first appearance of the heavy-armed hoplite in Egyptian history marked an epoch[1]. Diodorus contradicts Herodotus only in stating that it was not an accident that led Psammetichus to employ these foreign hoplites[2]. The rest of his narrative only supplements Herodotus, and the silence of Herodotus is no reason for thinking that the later historian was not drawing on good and early sources[3]. Even Herodotus could not incorporate in his history every scrap of knowledge that he possessed, and for Egypt in the seventh century there may well have been contemporary documents which were not consulted by Herodotus but were by Diodorus. Diodorus' account has in fact been accepted by a considerable number of modern scholars[4]. They point out that it agrees with the statement of Strabo about the Fort of the Milesians[5] that "in the days of Psammetichus the Milesians sailed with 30 ships and put in at the Bolbitine mouth, and disembarking built the foundation just mentioned."

Cp. Strabo on the Fort of the Milesians

There is one difficulty in this passage of Strabo. Psammetichus is described in it as the contemporary of Cyaxares king of the Medes, who reigned from 624 to 584 B.C., so that the Psammetichus referred to might be Psammetichus II (594–589). But Psam-

---

[1] Mallet, *Prem. Étab.* p. 39. Polyaen. VII. 3 (=Aristagoras and Theban tradition, Gutschmid, *Philol.* 1855, p. 692) makes Psammetichus employ Carians because an oracle had warned his rival to beware of cocks and "the Carians were the first to put crests on their helmets." Here too the armour is the main thing. The Egyptian warriors (μάχιμοι) were called Kalasiries and Hermotybies (Hdt. II. 164). According to Sayce, *ad loc.*, Kalasiries = armed with leather; but cp. How and Wells, *ad loc.*

[2] He says Psammetichus "sent for" mercenaries from Caria and Ionia.

[3] Diod. III. 11 quotes and praises two lost writers on Egypt, Agatharchides of Cnidus (second century B.C.) and Artemidorus of Ephesus (about 100 B.C.).

[4] *E.g.* Wiedemann, *Hdt.* II. 152; Meyer, *Ges. Alt.* II. p. 461 (but cp. I. p. 562); Mallet, *Prem. Étab.* pp. 37–8 (but cp. p. 41). Only Mallet, however, sees features typical of the rulers of the period and he quotes only Lydian and Phoenician parallels.

[5] Strabo XVII. 801; cp. Eustath. *Comment. ad Dion. Perieg.* 823 *ap. Geog. Gr. Min.* (Didot), II. p. 362; Strabo knew Egypt personally, cp. II. 118.

metichus in Strabo appears elsewhere always to mean the first and most important king of that name. Cyaxares too both from his date and his nationality is an odd person for a Greek writer to quote in order to indicate the date of an Egyptian king[1]. Hirschfeld is therefore probably right in rejecting this parenthesis as a learned but unintelligent gloss[2].

The Bolbitine mouth of the Nile is near the great lake and marshes of Bourlos[3]. Psammetichus I, before he overcame his rivals in Lower Egypt, is said by Herodotus[4] to have spent a period of exile in the marshes, and the marshes are shown by the context to have lain near the sea[5]. Thus quite apart from Diodorus, by simply comparing Herodotus and Strabo, a case may be made for thinking that the arrival of the bronze men from Ionia was not the accidental occurrence that Herodotus, after his way, makes it out to have been, but that it had some close connexion with the Milesians' Fort.

That Psammetichus made it his policy to cultivate "friendship with nations and princes[6]" in Asia Minor is sufficiently shown by the famous clay cylinder of Assurbanipal, king of Assyria (about 668–626 B.C.), which states[7] that

Assurbanipal on help sent to Psammetichus by Gyges of Lydia.

Gyges King of Lydia, a district which is across the sea[8], a remote place, of which the kings my fathers had not heard speak of its name...his forces to the aid of Psammetichus[9] of Egypt, who had thrown off the yoke of my dominion, he sent.

[1] Cp. however Pseudoscymn. 748–750 *ap. Geog. Gr. Min.* (Didot), i. p. 226, Ὀδησσός, ἣν Μιλήσιοι κτίζουσιν Ἀστυάγης ὅτ' ἦρχε Μηδίας. This method of dating might have its origin in some work that described the expansion of Greece and Media previous to the great clash of 490–479.

[2] *Rhein. Mus.* 1887, pp. 211 f.   [3] Mallet, *Prem. Étab.* p. 29.

[4] II. 151–2. Mallet, *Prem. Étab.* p. 38, cautiously quotes the Horus myth as a parallel for this flight. Nobody now would agree with Sayce (cp. Wiedemann, *Aeg. Ges.* p. 608) that "the story of Psammetichus' retreat in the marshes is clearly (*sic*) borrowed from the myth of Horus." It is far more likely that the story of Horus borrowed from the life of some early Egyptian ruler. Psamtek's flight to the marshes is as natural and well attested as that of Alfred or of Hereward, the latter of whom is suspiciously like Horus in name as well as in behaviour.

[5] In Diodorus' version of the same affair they are specifically stated to have done so.   [6] Diod. *loc. cit.*   [7] G. Smith, *Assurbanipal*, pp. 64, 66, 67.

[8] Radet, *Lydie*, p. 177, translates "où l'on franchit la mer."

[9] Assyrian Pisamiilki: see Mallet, *Prem. Étab.* p. 49, n. 1; but cp. Wiedemann, *Hdt.* II. 152.

The troops sent by Gyges may well have been none other than the Ionian mercenaries that made Psammetichus master of all Egypt[1]. The alliance of Psammetichus with Gyges adds to the probability that the Egyptian was responsible for the foundation and development of the Milesian settlement in his country, since we know that Gyges had allowed the Milesians to establish the Hellespontine Abydos in what was then Lydian territory[2].

If trade and riches raised Psammetichus to supreme power about the year 664 B.C. their influence was probably making itself felt in Egyptian politics at least some little while before that date. It will greatly strengthen the credibility of Diodorus on the early history of Psammetichus if this can be shown to have been in fact the case.

History of Psammetichus' predecessors:

In 701 B.C. Sennacherib made his famous expedition against Palestine and Egypt, which were saved only by the plague sent upon the Assyrian host by the Angel of the Lord[3]. According to the Egyptian version recorded in Herodotus the king of Egypt at this time was Sethon or Sethos, priest of Hephaestus. When the priest-king prepared to defend his country against the Assyrian "he was followed by none of the warrior class, but by hucksters and artizans and trades people[4]." No king of the name of Sethon is known either to the Egyptian monuments or to the Greek and Latin lists of the kings of Egypt: his individuality has been the subject of much controversy. Later in this chapter reasons will be given for thinking that he was a prince of the same city and probably of the same house as Psamtek. The point to be emphasized here is the appearance just at this period of a Pharaoh who rests his power on the support of the mercantile and industrial classes.

(i) Sethon in 701 B.C. based his power on "hucksters and artizans and trades people."

---

[1] Breasted, *Hist.* p. 566. This view is now commonly accepted. Against it, see Gutschmid, *Neue Beiträge Ges. Or.* pp. x.-xi.

[2] Strabo XIII. 590: see Mallet, *Prem. Étab.* p. 48, n. 1. Later in his reign Psamtek is said by Diodorus (1. 67) to have "made an alliance with the Athenians and some of the other Greeks"; but here we may follow Mallet (*ib.* p. 97; cp. pp. 212, 284) and suspect a reflexion backwards of events of the time of Psammetichus the Libyan (*circ.* 445 B.C.), who took part in the uprising against Persia in which Egypt received much help from Athens (Mallet, *ib.* p. 149, n. 3). On the very few examples from Naukratis of late Proto-Attic vases (Attic of about 600 B.C.) see Prinz, *Funde aus Naukratis*, pp. 75 f.

[3] Isaiah XXXVII. 36; II Kings XIX. 35; II Chron. XXXII. 21.

[4] Hdt. II. 141, ἕπεσθαι δέ οἱ τῶν μαχίμων μὲν οὐδένα ἀνδρῶν, καπήλους δὲ καὶ χειρώνακτας καὶ ἀγοραίους ἀνθρώπους.

Shortly before the days of Sethon another Egyptian king had won great fame by his recognition of the commercial tendencies of his age. This was Bocchoris the lawgiver, the solitary representative of the XXIVth dynasty, who appears for a time to have been recognized as king of Egypt until in 715 B.C. he was taken and burnt or flayed alive by his successor Sabacon, the first king of the Ethiopian (XXVth) dynasty[1]. Diodorus says that the laws concerning contracts were attributed to Bocchoris and that he brought more precision into the matter of contracts. These statements are illustrated in a remarkable way by actual business documents that have come down to us from that time[2].

(ii) King Bocchoris (d. 715 B.C.) and his commercial legislation.

A faience vase (fig. 12) with Egyptian scenes and the name of Bocchoris has been found in the Etruscan city of Tarquinii (Corneto)[3]. It is held by Maspero and v. Bissing to be of pure Egyptian workmanship[4]. Before its discovery the only evidence that Bocchoris had dealings with Europe was a reference in Plutarch[5] which makes Bocchoris the judge in a case involving a Greek hetaera named Thonis. The Plutarch passage is doubtful evidence, but the Corneto vase suggests that already in the reign of Bocchoris the Egyptians and perhaps the king himself already had dealings with the trading nations of the North. This would fit well with the fact that Bocchoris was probably the predecessor of a king whose following consisted

---

[1] Africanus and Euseb. *F.H.G.* II. p. 593; John of Antioch, *F.H.G.* IV. p. 540.

[2] Their significance is well put by Griffith, *Dem. Pap. Rylands*, III. pp. 9–10; cp. Moret, *de Bocchori*, pp. 76 f. quoting Revillout, *Précis droit égy.* pp. 190 f. The Diodorus passages are from I. 94 and I. 79; cp. also Plut. *Demetr.* 27 and Clem. Alex. *Strom.* IV. 18, Bocchoris as clever judge in a claim for payment; Iambl. (Didot, *Erot. Scrip.* p. 517) on Bocchoris' skill in assessment of values (cup, nosegay, kiss). Moret is scarcely right in saying (*de Bocch.* p. 55) that every kind of story is told to illustrate the wisdom of Bocchoris: cp. Revillout *ap.* Moret, p. 78, "Bocchoris avait voulu surtout faire un code commercial." Diod. I. 94 places Bocchoris fourth among the reputed lawgivers of Egypt. No similar measures are attributed to any of the earlier three.

[3] Schiaparelli, *Mon. Ant.* VIII. pp. 90–100 and Tav. II. The context in which the vase was found (Poulsen, *Orient u. frühgriech. Kunst*, pp. 125–6) recalls the Regulini-Galassi and Bernardini graves.

[4] See Poulsen, *Orient u. frühgr. Kunst*, p. 64; cp. Kinch, *Vroulia*, p. 249. Schiaparelli, Revillout (*Quirites et Ég.* p. 4), and Moret (*de Bocch.* pp. 27–8) think it of Phoenician make and provenance.

[5] Plut. *Demetr.* 27.

Fig. 12. Vase with cartouche of Bocchoris found at Tarquinii.

of hucksters and artizans and trades people. Bocchoris himself is said by Diodorus to have been reputed the most money-loving of men[1].

Bocchoris' father Tafnekht[2], the first of the Saite princes (749–721 B.C.), is not known to have had any commercial interests or connexions. He is best remembered for his struggle against Pianchi, the first Ethiopian ruler to claim the throne of the Pharaohs. Of this struggle we have Pianchi's own version, preserved in the famous Pianchi stele. While Tafnekht's partizans were holding Memphis against the Ethiopians we hear of the employment of artizans and master masons as soldiers[3]. The force however is stated to have been small, and it is not quite certain which side it was fighting on. Tafnekht, when the struggle went against him, retired to "the islands of the sea," from whence he was able to negotiate with Pianchi in complete safety. Tafnekht himself described the situation not without tact in a letter to Pianchi: "To whatsoever city thou hast turned thy face, thou hast not found thy servant there, until I reached the islands of the sea, trembling before thy might, and saying 'his flame is hostile to me.'" Eventually he submitted to the Ethiopians, but the submission seems to have been little more than nominal. Pianchi after receiving it is no more heard of in the Delta, and Tafnekht, to judge from the position held after him by his son Bocchoris, must have regained considerable power.

(iii) Tafnekht, father of Bocchoris, resisted the Ethiopians thanks apparently to his command of the sea.

This may have had its base in naval supremacy. In the ancient list of thalassocrats, or states that successively ruled the waves, preserved to us by Syncellus, Eusebius and Jerome, the thalassocracy of Egypt falls at about this period. The only list that gives a precise date is that of Jerome, who puts it between 783 and 748 B.C. But the lists give the duration of each thalassocracy as well as absolute

---

[1] πάντων φιλοχρηματώτατον (Diod. I. 94), a trait quite reconcilable with the statement of Zenobius (II. 60), that he was remembered for his justice (cp. Suid. s.v. Βάκχυρις) and ingenuity (ἐπίνοια) as a judge. The statement of Aelian that Bocchoris was hated by his countrymen (*H.A.* XI. 11; cp. Plut. *Vit. Pud.* 3, φύσει χαλεπός) proves only that he, like Solon and Cypselus, excited different feelings in different quarters: nobody would now follow Wiedemann (*Aeg. Ges.* p. 579) and quote it against reports favourable to him, as a proof that neither are of any use for serious history.

[2] Manetho, *F.H.G.* II. pp. 592–3; see further below, p. 100, n. 4.

[3] Breasted, *Records*, IV. 858; J. de Rougé, *Chrestom. Egypt*, IV.

dates, and, as pointed out by J. L. Myres, if, instead of following the dates in years from Abraham, we calculate from the duration of the various thalassocracies, working backward from the period of the Persian wars, then the end of the Egyptian supremacy falls not in 748 but in 725[1]. This dating makes Tafnekht a thalassocrat[2], and explains how he was able to stand up against Ethiopia and the comparatively little damage that he sustained in spite of his military failures. In 715 we find another Ethiopian invading the Delta. The new prince of Sais, Bocchoris, presumably had no impregnable naval base. He was caught by the Ethiopian Sabacon and burnt or flayed alive[3]. It is only when Psamtek formed alliances with the naval power that had replaced Egypt that the Saite princes fully regained the throne of the Pharaohs. This time their power had a sounder financial basis. It lasted for nearly a century and a half, and was then suddenly destroyed at its zenith by irresistible forces from without. On the reckoning which ends Egyptian naval supremacy in 725 B.C. the command of the sea when Psamtek was building up his power was in the hands of the Carians. It is precisely the Carians, along with the Milesians (who on the same reckoning were thalassocrats from 725 to 707 B.C.), who are said by all our ancient authorities to have been the basis of Psamtek's power[4].

If the king who ruled Egypt in 700 B.C. based his power on the trading and industrial classes, and a king who reigned twenty years

---

[1] *J.H.S.* xxvi. p. 103; cp. pp. 91–2, 94 f. The main divergence is in the Lesbian thalassocracy, where the Armenian version of the canon of Eusebius gives the dates ann. Abr. 1345–1441 (=96 years), whereas Jerome gives the duration as 68 years.

[2] Note that he probably began his career at a small town near Canopus, E. de Rougé (quoting Brugsch), *Inscr. Hist. Pianchi ap.* Maspero, *Bibl. Égypt.* xxiv. p. 290. De Rougé notes that Tafnekht's name has no cartouche and no qualification announcing royal birth and from these facts argues that he was of comparatively humble origin.

[3] Note that the unrevised dating of the Egyptian thalassocracy makes it fall into the reign of Bocchoris as dated by Eusebius, Fotheringham, *J.H.S.* xxvii. p. 87.

[4] Cp. perhaps Steph. Byz. Ἑλληνικὸν καὶ Καρικόν, τόποι ἐν Μέμφιδι ἀφ' ὧν Ἑλληνομεμφῖται, ὡς Ἀρισταγόρας. *ibid.* Καρικόν· τόπος ἰδιάζων ἐν Μέμφιδι, ἔνθα Κᾶρες οἰκήσαντες ἐπιγαμίας πρὸς Μεμφίτας ποιησάμενοι Καρομεμφῖται ἐκλήθησαν. Cp. Polyaen. vii. 3, ἀπὸ τῶν Καρῶν ἐκείνων μέρος τι τῆς Μέμφεως κέκληται Καρομεμφῖται. These Caromemphites and Hellenomemphites are generally recognized as descendants of Psamtek's mercenaries who were transplanted by Amasis to Memphis (Hdt. ii. 154).

CH. IV EGYPT 97

earlier drew up the first commercial code in Egypt, while under the predecessor of this latter king Egypt had been supreme at sea, then by 670 B.C. conditions may well have been favourable for the commercial activities of Prince Psammetichus as described by Diodorus. But still more will this have been so if, as seems likely, both Sethon and Bocchoris were Saite princes of the same house as Psammetichus himself. The evidence is weak and inconclusive and for that reason difficult to summarize shortly. But the conclusions that it seems to point to are sufficiently important to make the attempt worth while.

Tafnekht and probably Bocchoris and Sethon were (not kings of all Egypt but) princes of Sais, the city of Psammetichus, and belonged possibly to the same family as Psammetichus.

One point seems fairly certain. Sethon was not the name of the conqueror of the Assyrians. Far more probably it was his title, a graecized form of the priestly title stm, stne, setmi, or satni[1]. If his actual name is still doubtful, it is not for lack of suggestions. Sethon has been identified with (a) Khamois son of Ramses II[2], (b) Shabaka, first king of the Ethiopian dynasty[3], (c) Shabataka, successor of Shabaka[4], (d) Taharqa, the Biblical Tirhaka[5].

These identifications are all untenable, the first two on account of their dates, the rest because they make Sethon an Ethiopian. The warrior class that refused to support Sethon was Ethiopian in sympathy and not likely to desert an Ethiopian[6]. The Sethon story glorifies the god Ptah (Hephaestus) of Memphis whereas the Ethiopian dynasty was devoted to Amon of Thebes[7]. Griffith indeed suggests that Taharqa, who became king of Ethiopia and Egypt after 700 B.C., may at the time of Sennacherib's defeat have represented the reigning king Shabataka in Lower Egypt, possibly with the title of priest of Ptah at Memphis[8]. But there is no evidence for this having been so, and the picture of Taharqa as a king with no real soldiers at his back is not easily explained. On the contrary,

[1] Griffith, *High Priests of Memphis*, p. 8, who compares the Herodotean king Pheron of Egypt (Hdt. II. 111) who plainly is simply a nameless Pharaoh.

[2] See below, p. 101.

[3] So apparently Breasted, *Hist. Eg.*[2] pp. 552-3.

[4] Wiedemann, *Aeg. Ges.* p. 587; Lauth, *Aeg. Vorzeit*, p. 439 f.; Oppert, *Rapp. Eg. et Assyr.* pp. 14 n. 1, 29 n. 1, quoting Brugsch.

[5] Joseph., *Antiq. Iud.* x. 1. 4 (17); cp. Petrie, *Hist. Eg.* III. p. 296.

[6] Cp. Hdt. II. 30.

[7] Griffith, *High Priests of Memphis*, p. 10.

[8] *Ibid.*

U. T. 7

as pointed out long ago by Lepsius[1], the Biblical account[2] appears to differentiate Pharaoh king of Egypt, whom it calls a broken reed, and Tirhaka king of Ethiopia. Similarly the Assyrian cylinders distinguish the kings of Egypt from the king of Miluhhi = Meroe = Ethiopia[3]. The kings of Egypt who are thus referred to in the plural[4] are plainly the rulers who at the period divided among themselves the lands of the Delta. The evidence all points to the conclusion that Sethon was one of these Delta chiefs, and presumably one of the most important of them, who acknowledged when forced to the suzerainty of Ethiopia or Assyria as the case might be, but did his best to keep clear of both great powers.

It is not improbable that Sethon belonged to the same family as Psammetichus, or at any rate that he was one of his predecessors on the throne of Sais. As starting-point for identifying him we have two facts. He was high priest of Ptah and he was alive in 701 B.C. A generation earlier the title Sem of Ptah was borne by Tafnekht, the chief of Sais from about 749 to 721 B.C.[5] who led the Delta in its struggle against the Ethiopian Pianchi[6]. A generation after Sethon the Assyrian cylinders[7] describe Necho I (672–664 B.C.) the father of Psammetichus I as king not only of Sais but also of Memphis, the home of the Sethon tradition. A whole line of Saite rulers may be traced from Tafnekht onwards to Psammetichus I[8]. All of these kings seem to have been something more than mere local rulers. The Pianchi stele makes it plain that Tafnekht aimed at becoming king at least of the whole of Lower Egypt. Bocchoris, the solitary king of the XXIVth dynasty, has been discussed already. Stephinates, Nechepsus, and Necho I appear in Africanus[9] as the first three kings of dynasty XXVI, Psam-

[1] *Königsbuch*, p. 47.
[2] II Kings xviii. 21; xix. 9; Isaiah xxxvi. 6; xxxvii. 9.
[3] Schrader, *Cun. Inscr. and O.T.*, (marginal) pp. 292, 303; cp. 357. This fact by itself is fatal to Sourdille (*Hdt. et la relig. de l'Ég.* p. 141) when he places Sethon on his index mythologique on the ground that Shabataka was king of Egypt at this time.
[4] Hence the equation with Shabataka, while Tirhaka is equated (Oppert, *Rapp. Égy. et Assyr.* p. 29) with the king of Meroe, is impossible, quite apart from its making nonsense of the reference to the bruised reed.
[5] Petrie, *Hist. Eg.* III. p. 312; Griffith, *Dem. Pap. Rylands*, III. p. 6.
[6] Griffith, *High Priests of Memphis*, p. 10; Breasted, *Records*, IV. 830 (Pianchi stele).
[7] G. Smith, *Assurbanipal*, p. 20.
[8] See above, p. 88, n. 1.
[9] *F.H.G.* II. p. 593.

metichus I coming fourth on the list. This statement is not discredited by the fact that other writers[1] begin the dynasty with Psammetichus, while Eusebius[2] puts Stephinates second, after Ammeris the Ethiopian. The three versions need not be mutually exclusive. Psammetichus was unquestionably the first of the Saites to win for his house the undisputed kingship of all Egypt. Hence the position generally assigned to him. In another way too he represented a new departure dynastically. He appears to have had family connexions with Ethiopia, and to have consistently aimed at an entente with the Ethiopian royal house[3], who may have originally left him a free hand in the Delta from the desire to put a buffer state between Ethiopia and Assyria. Ammeris appears to be a Greek form of (Ta) Nut-Amen, Rud-Amen, or Amen-Rud, as the last of the Ethiopian kings is variously called[4]. His appearance at the head of the XXVIth dynasty is a record of its Ethiopian connexions at this time[5]. Africanus on the other hand, following Manetho, who was himself an Egyptian, records Psamtek's ancestry in the direct line, and regards them, rather than any Ethiopian or Assyrian conquerors, as the lawful kings of the whole country[6].

We are now in a better position for trying to identify the Sethon of Herodotus. This Saite dynasty was probably represented at the

[1] Hdt. II. 151; Diod. I. 66; the Apis stelai.
[2] *F.H.G.* II. p. 594.
[3] Psamtek's daughter Nitokris was adopted by Shepnepet, daughter of Taharqa (or, according to J. de Rougé, *Ét. sur les textes géogr. du temple d'Edfou*, p. 62, of Pianchi), sacerdotal princess of Thebes, Breasted, *Records*, IV. 935 f.; cp. E. de Rougé, *Notice de quelques textes hiérogl. publ. par M. Greene, ap.* Maspero, *Bibl. Égypt.* XXIII. pp. 70 f.; J. de Rougé, *Ét. sur les textes géogr. du temple d'Edfou*, pp. 59–63; neither of whom understood that N. was daughter of S. only by adoption. From the omission of the revolt of Gyges and Psamtek from the earlier Assurbanipal cylinders and the statement that Miluhha (Ethiopia) revolted with Saulmugina (brother of Assurbanipal), G. Smith, *Assurbanipal*, p. 78, cp. pp. 154–5, infers that the revolt of Gyges and Psammetichus took place at the time of the general rising against Assyria, which means that Psammetichus was allied with Ethiopia at that time. His early flight into Syria, Hdt. II. 152, is to be connected with his father's policy rather than with his own.
[4] Against this identification see Maspero, *Hist. Anc.*[5] p. 459, n. 3; E. de Rougé, *Textes pub. par M. Greene, ap.* Maspero, *Bibl. Égypt.* XXIII. pp. 74–75.
[5] Psamtek himself acknowledged the Ethiopian Taharqa as his predecessor: Wiedemann, *Aeg. Ges.* p. 600.
[6] There can be no doubt that the reigns of rival rulers of the period largely overlap. Otherwise, as pointed out long ago by Gutschmid (*Philol.* 1855, p. 659), we have Psamtek I surviving his father for over 100 years.

time of Sennacherib's invasion by Stephinates. In Africanus his reign as first king of the XXVIth dynasty begins later, about 685 B.C. But this leaves a gap of 30 years with no recorded rulers of Sais and Memphis. Petrie's explanation of this hiatus may be right. He thinks that Stephinates was probably son and successor of Bocchoris, but that after Bocchoris had been crushed and burnt by the Ethiopians in 715 B.C. the Saite power remained for some time a very broken reed. It is therefore not unlikely that the Stephinates of Manetho is the Sethon of Herodotus. No prince of the name appears on Egyptian monuments, but it has been plausibly suggested by Petrie[1] that Stephinates is another Tafnekht with perhaps a sigma carried over by a Greek copyist from some word before his name. May we not guess what this word was? The first Tafnekht styled himself Sem of Ptah. The story of Satni Khamois[2] shows that the title might be prefixed to the personal name. May not the strange form Stephinates be simply a Greek corruption of Satni Tafnekht or, as the name is sometimes transcribed, Tefnakhte[3]?

A family connexion between Bocchoris and the later Saites is harder to establish. In support of it there are these facts: a Samtavi Tafnekht appears among the officials of Psamtek I; and, as the name Tafnekht was borne by the father and predecessor of Bocchoris[4], this Samtavi Tafnekht has been recognized by Petrie[5] as "doubtless a brother or cousin of the king." The name Bakenranf itself is borne by another of Psamtek's officials[6], who may well be the Bocchoris son of Neochabis (Nekauba) mentioned by Athenaeus[7], in which case he would have been an uncle of the reigning king[8].

[1] *Hist. Eg.* III. p. 318. [2] Below, p. 101.
[3] *E.g.* by Breasted.
[4] Diod. I. 45; Plut. *de Is. et Os.* 8 (*Moral.* 354); cp. Moret, *de Bocch.* pp. 6–8, quoting Mariette and Maspero; Breasted, *Records*, IV. 811, 884, *Hist.*[2] p. 546; Griffith, *Dem. Pap. Rylands*, p. 6. The Pianchi stele mentions one son of Tafnekht as killed in Pianchi's campaign against Tafnekht, and another as spared by him (Breasted, *Records*, IV. 838, 854; cp. Moret, *de Bocch.* p. 6, n. 2).
[5] *Hist. Eg.* III. p. 334.
[6] *Hist. Eg.* III. p. 327. [7] Athen. x. 418 *e*.
[8] In Diod. (I. 45) and Plut. (*de Is. et Os.* 8) Tnefachthos, the father of Bocchoris, is said to have accidentally discovered while campaigning against the Arabians the joys of the simple life. In Athen. (418*e*) Neochabis and his son Bocchoris are said both to have been moderate in their diet ($\mu\epsilon\tau\rho i\alpha$ $\tau\rho o\phi\hat{\eta}$ $\kappa\epsilon\chi\rho\hat{\eta}\sigma\theta\alpha\iota$). But even if we have here variants of a single story, it would be no proof that we are up against the same individuals.

A direct connexion between the XXIVth and XXVIth dynasties has indeed been often suspected[1]. They may stand to one another much as the English Lancastrians to the Tudors, separated by a period of eclipse and by the alliance with their rivals that was made in each case at the period of the restoration[2].

It was probably during this period of eclipse that two popular stories of an earlier date were revised and received the shape in which they have come down to us[3], and in which also they very possibly have a bearing on the history of the Herodotean Sethon. Their hero is Satni Khamois, son of Ramses II, who protects the king his father not by force of arms but by learning and magic.

Popular stories of Satni Khamois, which probably reflect the atmosphere of Sais under Sethon,

Satni and Sethon both save their country where the military had failed. "The military chieftains of the chief ones of Egypt were standing before him (Pharaoh Usimares) each one according to his rank at court" when the Ethiopian came and threatened to "report the inferiority of Egypt in his country, the land of the Negroes." And just as the captains and the courtiers proved helpless against the Assyrians in the days of Sethon, so did they against the Ethiopians in the days of Satni. This is the connecting link. The value of the Satni story for the history of Sethon is that it probably gives the atmosphere of the Sethon period, and that being so it helps to show that Sethon was already pursuing in many ways the Saite policy. Griffith for instance has observed that Satni is not presented in a very heroic light. But neither did any of the later Saites adopt the heroic pose. Nothing could be less like the grand monarque than Psamtek as pictured on a relief in the British Museum (above fig. 11)[4] or Amasis as pictured in the pages of Herodotus[5]. The same picture of Amasis is presented to us by the popular Egyptian stories. "Is it possible," his courtiers ask, "that if it happens to the king to be

recall in tone those told of Amasis, the last great Saite pharaoh.

---

[1] It is implied by Breasted, *Hist.*² p. 556, when he calls Necho I "doubtless a descendant of Tefnakhte."

[2] Necho I enjoyed the favours of the Assyrian conqueror (G. Smith, *Assurbanipal*, pp. 20, 23, 27–28), but his revolt shows that he was making a virtue of necessity.

[3] Translated Griffith, *High Priests of Memphis*, chaps. II., III.: Maspero, *Pop. Stories*, pp. 115 f.

[4] Petrie, *Hist.* III. fig. 139.

[5] Hdt. II. 173; cp. Athen. VI. 261 c, X. 438 b.

drunk more than any man in the world, no man in the world can approach the king for business[1]?"

Amasis, who was virtually the last of the Saites, is said to have been a man of the people[2]. In the days of Sethon (Satni Tafnekhte), who perhaps heads the dynasty, a story of the Satni Khamois cycle told how that royal prince had personally visited the kingdom of the dead to learn the lesson of Dives and Lazarus[3].

This concludes our examination of the history of the early Saites. It points to a consistent policy carried out with a remarkable combination of perseverance and versatility by a succession of rulers who may have been all of a single family and who certainly inherited in unbroken succession the same aims and the same essential method of attaining them, which was marked out for them by the place and the age they lived in. The Saite power grew to be supreme in Egypt while Ethiopians and Assyrians were contending for the land. From force of circumstances Sais had to be a military power. But the city owed its victory over its rivals between 721 and 670 B.C. first and foremost to the fact that it lay off the main track of war. As always when Egypt is involved in a great war it is the Eastern frontier that faces the main enemy. Sais was not always able to remain neutral, but lying right away in the West it was able at least to preserve and even to develop its commerce. It seized its

Conclusions as to the early history of the Saite dynasty.

---

[1] Maspero, *Pop. Stories*, pp. 281–2; the story, however, is Ptolemaic and may be influenced by Hdt.; cp. Wiedemann, *Hdt.* II. 173. E. Meyer, *Ges. Aeg.* p. 366, n. 1, uses the demotic stories about Amasis' drunkenness as proof that the Saite Pharaohs were not popular with their Egyptian subjects. It might as well be argued that Edward VII must have been unpopular in England because the masses like to associate him with horse-racing and cigars. When the Egyptians represented Amasis as drunken they paid him the compliment of making him like themselves. The catastrophe of 525 B.C. was helped on by the drunkenness of the servants sent by Amasis to capture Phanes the captain of the Greek mercenaries when he was on his way to desert to Persia (Hdt. III. 4). The Egyptian who "complained before his majesty King Cambyses on the subject of all the strangers who dwelt in the sanctuary of Neith (at Sais) to the end that they might be expelled" (so-called demotic chronicle, *ap. Rev. Égy.* 1880, p. 75) is a better witness as to the policy of Cambyses than as to the unpopularity of Amasis; cp. the sequel: "His Majesty ordained: expel all the strangers who dwell in the sanctuary of Neith: destroy their houses."

[2] Hdt. II. 172; Hellanicus, *F.H.G.* I. p. 66; but cp. Revillout, *Rev. Égypt.* 1881, pp. 96–98.

[3] *Pop. Stories*, pp. 151 f.

opportunity and did so. The commercial code of Bocchoris, the hucksters and artizans and tradespeople of Sethon, and the cargoes of Psammetichus mark three great stages in the development, at the end of which, to quote the words of Maspero, "the valley of the Nile becomes a vast workshop, where work was carried on with unparalleled activity[1]."

All these considerations lend a general probability to the narrative of Diodorus. They do not however specially confirm his statements about Psamtek's trading with the Greeks. Greek commerce in Egypt in the days of the Saites is bound up with the name of Naukratis. "In the days of old," says Herodotus[2], "Naukratis was the only emporium in Egypt. There was none other." This is an overstatement the origin of which will be seen when we come to deal with Amasis, the last but one of the Saite Pharaohs. But it implies that Naukratis eclipsed in importance all the other Greek trading stations in the country. It concerns us therefore to enquire what was the position of Naukratis in the days of Psammetichus. The question has been much disputed, especially since the eighties of the last century, when the site was excavated by Petrie and Ernest Gardner, and an account of the city was published by Petrie[3] based on the literary sources and the results of the dig. As however some of the excavators' archaeological conclusions have been challenged in many quarters, and as too some important archaeological evidence has only recently come to light, it may be worth while to summarise briefly the whole body of available material.

Sais and Greece: foundation of Naukratis:

S. Jerome under the date Olymp. VII 4 (= 749 B.C.) says "the Milesians held the sea for eighteen years and built in Egypt the city of Naukratis[4]." This statement agrees with Stephanus Byzantinus[5] who calls Naukratis "a city of Egypt from the Milesians who were at that time supreme at sea." Jerome and Stephanus are in harmony with Polycharmus[6] who mentions a certain Herostratos as living at Naukratis and trading there and making long voyages in the XXIIIrd Olymp. (688 B.C.). But there are other writers who put the foundation later. Strabo, in the passage

(a) literary evidence;

---

[1] *Hist. Anc.*[5] p. 531. Maspero refers to the evidence of excavations; Malle *Prem. Étab.* pp. 52–53.

[2] Hdt. II. 179.
[3] *Naukratis*, I. pp. 1 f.
[4] Hieron. VIII. (Migne), pp. 365–6.
[5] s.v. Naukratis.
[6] *Ap.* Athen. XV. 675

already referred to[1], after describing the foundation of the Milesians' Fort in the days of Psammetichus, continues: "and eventually they sailed up to the Saite nome and after defeating Inaros in a naval engagement they founded the city of Naukratis." Lastly we have Herodotus[2] stating that King Amasis (570–526 B.C.) "gave the city of Naukratis for Greeks who came to Egypt to dwell in," an assertion that taken by itself might mean that Naukratis was founded in or after 570 B.C.[3]

One further witness remains to be cited. Sappho wrote a poem reproaching her brother Charaxos for his devotion to a Naukratite hetaera named Doriche, with whom he had fallen in love when bringing Lesbian wine to Naukratis by way of trade[4]. Among the papyri discovered by Grenfell and Hunt at Oxyrhynchus is a fragment containing sixteen mutilated Sapphic lines that almost certainly form part of this very poem[5]. This means that Naukratis had already grown to be a pleasure city in the days of Sappho. Unfortunately her dates are not absolutely certain. A recent heresy brought her down to the reign of Amasis, but her floruit is generally given as the end of the seventh century, and there seem to be no sufficient reasons for not accepting that date.

Such is the literary evidence. No single item of it is decisive for an early occupation. Those which are definite can be questioned on point of fact. Sappho, whose evidence alone cannot be so questioned, may conceivably have written after 570. Combined however they make it probable that Naukratis rose to importance before the days of Amasis, and that Herodotus either confused the foundation of the city with that of the Hellenium[6] or else did not intend his words "gave the city for Greeks who came to Egypt to dwell in" to imply that the Milesians were not there in force before the granting of this concession[7]. Nevertheless, if we were limited

---

[1] Strabo, XVII. 801.   [2] Hdt. II. 178.

[3] Plutarch, *Sept. Sap. Conviv.* 2 (*Moral.* 146), speaks of a certain Niloxenos the Naukratite as entertained by Periander. If the setting of the dialogue was strictly historical, this would be evidence for the existence of Naukratis before 590 B.C. But Amasis is introduced as reigning in Egypt and Croesus apparently as already King of Lydia, so that chronological inferences from this fictitious dialogue would be rash.

[4] Strabo, XVII. 808; cp. Hdt. II. 135; Athen. XIII. 596b; Suid. s.v. Ῥοδώπιδος ἀνάθημα.

[5] *Oxyr. Pap.* I. pp. 10–13.   [6] So Gutschmid, *ap.* Wiedemann, *Hdt.* II. 178.

[7] It is forcing the sense of Herodotus' words to regard them, as does Petrie,

to these literary sources, we could not be certain that where Diodorus seems to supplement his predecessors he was not merely adding details that they appear to imply. That is in fact the view of his narrative that some modern scholars apparently hold[1]. Even if this were so, his additions would still have a certain value. If Diodorus, writing in the first century B.C., read between the lines of Herodotus the same unstated implications that have been read there in recent times, the coincidence points to the probability that this reading is not altogether wrong[2].

That is as far as the texts take us. For further light we must look to archaeology. The new light began by increasing the perplexity. Petrie and Gardner both claimed that their excavations at Naukratis proved that it had been an important Greek city from the middle of the seventh century. But their main arguments were before long shown to be mistaken, and somewhat naturally it began to be assumed that they must be wrong in their conclusions.

(b) archaeological evidence:

Petrie[3] based his arguments on the following observations. In the South part of the town he came across what he described as a scarab factory. There were numerous scarabs of Psamtek I, some of Psamtek II, and some that are probably of Apries; but none of Amasis. This seems to date the factory from well before 610 till after 589. Two feet beneath the factory was a burnt stratum of plain potsherds which must take us back a good way further, to at least 650 B.C. and probably earlier. The scarabs are imitation Egyptian and are taken by Petrie to be Greek. Further South, but also within the area of the burnt stratum, there is a large enclosure which he describes as surrounded by a strong brick wall. This he identified with the Hellenium, where Herodotus states that nine Greek cities had quarters assigned to them by Amasis. The dimensions of the bricks point to the early Saite period.

(i) excavations of Petrie, who dated Naukratis from the time of Psammetichus I;

Nauk. i. p. 4, as proof positive of a pre-Amasis occupation. Still less is Kirchhoff justified (*Stud. Gr. Alph.*[4] p. 47) in regarding them as proving that there were no Greeks in Naukratis before the reign of Amasis.

[1] *E.g.* Mallet and E. Meyer.

[2] I was first led to apply to Egypt my views about the Greek tyranny, before I had read Diodorus on Psammetichus, from Herodotus' account of Sethon and his following of tradesmen and artizans; above, p. 92.

[3] *Nauk.* i. pp. 5, 6, 21.

But in 1899 and 1903 further work was done at Naukratis by Hogarth which led him to the following conclusions. Petrie's Hellenium is wrongly identified: it is not a walled enclosure: what Petrie took for walls is simply débris of houses[1]. The real Hellenium is to be found in what Petrie called the North Temenos[2]. All Petrie's evidence for a seventh century Naukratis comes from his scarab factory and his "Great Temenos," both in the South part of the town, which is marked off by the occurrence there of the burnt stratum already referred to, and is shown by the finds to have been the Egyptian quarter of the town[3]. The Greeks would naturally have separate quarters and occupy the Northern seaward end of the town[4]. The scarabs, it is maintained, may well be of Phoenician make[5].

(ii) further excavations by Hogarth invalidated Petrie's arguments;

The early arrival of the Greeks in Naukratis has been thought by Ernest Gardner to be confirmed by the numerous inscriptions, some painted but most (about 700) incised, on the pottery from the site[6]. His arguments were criticized by Hirschfeld and Kirchhoff[7] and have received little support[8]. In some of them the lettering appears very crude and primitive; but this may be due simply to the fact that they are scratched by hasty and unskilled hands. They are not more archaic in appearance than some of the graffiti on vases from Rhitsona (Mykalessos) in Boeotia, of which the earliest must be dated in the middle of the sixth century, while others are contemporary with the finely written signatures of Teisias, who flourished

(iii) arguments from the vase inscriptions shown to be indecisive.

---

[1] *J.H.S.* xxv. pp. 110 f.

[2] *B.S.A.* v. p. 39 f.; *J.H.S.* xxv. p. 109; cp. especially the finds there of vases dedicated "to the gods of the Greeks" and also to various different individual Greek deities. The size of the bricks dates this enclosure as earlier half of sixth century, *B.S.A.* v. p. 35.

[3] *B.S.A.* v. pp. 41 n. 2, 48; *J.H.S.* xxv. p. 107. In 1899 there was found in Petrie's "Great Temenos" a fourth century Egyptian inscription that speaks of "Pi-emro which is called Naukratis." This is, however, *pace* Hogarth, *J.H.S.* xxv. p. 106, evidence not for but against thinking of Piemro Naukratis as a double town like Buda-Pesth rather than as a bilingual like Swansea Abertawe.

[4] *J.H.S.* xxv. p. 107; *B.S.A.* v. p. 43.

[5] *B.S.A.* v. p. 49.   [6] *Nauk.* I. pp. 54 f.

[7] Hirschfeld, *Rhein. Mus.* 1887, pp. 215–219; Kirchhoff, *Stud.*[4] p. 44 f.; cp. Edgar, *B.S.A.* v. pp. 50 f. For Gardner's reply see *Nauk.* II. pp. 70 f. For a *résumé* of the epigraphical evidence see E. S. Roberts, *Gk. Epig.* I. pp. 159 f., 323 f.

[8] Wiedemann accepts them, *Hdt.* II. 178.

at the end of the sixth century[1]. Gardner is certainly wrong in thinking that the lettering of any of his inscriptions proves a seventh century date. But on the other hand, as well remarked by Edgar[2], all that his critics have proved is that none of the inscriptions are *necessarily* so early. It by no means follows that they are necessarily not. But even supposing that the Naukratite graffiti are all sixth century, it does not follow that Greek Naukratis was of no importance till then. Both Gardner and his critics and likewise Mallet[3] discuss the inscriptions with too little reference to the particular sherds on which they are inscribed. Thirty years ago, when the study of archaic Greek pottery was still in its infancy, this was perhaps inevitable. But in the present state of our knowledge the style of the potsherds would be a natural starting-point for dating the graffiti. Unfortunately the information on this point given by Gardner is inadequate, and the Naukratite finds have been so dispersed, that the task of collating sherds and graffiti must now wait for someone who can devote to it his undivided time and attention[4].

Under these circumstances the best that can be done is to turn to some more recently excavated site. At Rhitsona the graffiti are nothing like so numerous as at Naukratis. Still they

---

[1] *B.S.A.* xiv. p. 263.   [2] *B.S.A.* v. p. 52.   [3] *Prem. Étab.* pp. 167 f.
[4] Hogarth's publication of the additional inscriptions found in 1903 is still more deficient. Edgar's account of those found in 1899 is better, though by no means adequate. Of 108 probable dedications (some are too fragmentary to be certain), 48 are on vases (black glaze, black figure, red figure) that cannot have been made before the reign of Amasis, 33 are on cups of types that certainly lasted into his reign, 6 on Naukratite fragments (phase not stated), 2 on (late) Milesian. The rest are on fabrics difficult to date from the meagre descriptions. Unfortunately this collection is not typical. It is to be regretted that Edgar thought it "unnecessary to state the provenance of each separate inscription" (*B.S.A.* v. p. 53). Sixteen have dedications to the gods of the Greeks, and only two to Apollo. We may conclude that a large percentage come from the Hellenium and are therefore after 570. But this does not prove a late date for graffiti generally. Of the sixteen dedications to the gods of the Greeks fifteen are on black figure or black glaze vases: the other is on one of the 33 cups mentioned above. This fact suggests that the dedications generally could have been dated from the vases they are inscribed on if the data had been made available, and that Gardner was fairly right in his main conclusion although wrong in his method of reaching it. Of the Milesian fragments one has a dedication to Apollo, of the Naukratite two (both from the old Southern "Temenos") are to Aphrodite. It is significant that among the finds of the reign of Amasis "the early local pottery was disappointingly scarce" (*B.S.A.* v. p. 57). It is surprising that the excavators did not draw the obvious conclusion.

are numerous enough to justify certain observations. Some 50 examples have been found[1]. All of them are on vases of the sixth century. Not one occurs on the numerous vases of the seventh century also found on the site[2]. Plainly in Boeotia the fashion of scratching inscriptions on pottery only became prevalent[3] in the sixth century. By itself therefore the absence of seventh century Greek graffiti from Naukratis would no more prove the absence of seventh century Greek worshippers[4] than the corresponding absence from Rhitsona proves the absence of seventh century graves. At the other end of the period Edgar has already noticed that "the practice of dedicating vases in the temples appears to have almost died out at Naukratis before the middle of the fifth century[5]." Edgar makes this remark at the end of his discussion of the inscriptions found in 1899. He is apparently thinking of inscribed dedications. Elsewhere, discussing the pottery discovered during the same dig, he mentions late red figure (*i.e.* about 450 B.C. onwards) as plentiful and black glazed pottery with stamped ornaments inside as particularly common. This latter ware dates from about the middle of the fifth century, but its main vogue is later still[6]. Unfortunately not a sherd of this latter ware from Naukratis has been published, and not a word is said as to its distribution over the site. It was customarily offered to the dead at Rhitsona. It may well have been offered to the gods at Naukratis[7]. There is of course no need to assume that the fashion of inscribing vases came in and went out simultaneously in Naukratis and Mykalessos. Boeotia was often behind the times, the Ionians of the seventh and sixth centuries generally ahead of them. But the Boeotian evidence shows how cautiously the Naukratite graffiti must be used for determining the date of the first Greek settlement.

[1] *B.S.A.* XIV. p. 263; *J.H.S.* XXIX. p. 320; Ure, *Black Glaze Pottery*, pp. 59–61. Others still unpublished from Burrows' excavations of 1909.

[2] For later Boeotian examples see *Ath. Mitt.* XV. pp. 412–413 (Theban Kabeirion) and probably those from Mt Ptoon alluded to in *B.C.H.* IX. 479, 523.

[3] Occasional earlier inscriptions are no evidence against this later dating for the beginning of the real vogue.

[4] The inscriptions are largely dedications to deities.   [5] *B.S.A.* V. p. 57.

[6] Ure, *Black Glaze Pottery*, pp. 32 f.

[7] Three of the stamped black sherds from Naukratis (*B.S.A.* V. p. 56, nos. 113–15) are inscribed, one with a very secular inscription, one with a Cypriote abbreviation, and one with what may be the beginning of a dedication. The secular inscription on one example of a very common fabric is no argument against the use of other examples for religious purposes.

Nor is there anything against a seventh century date in the absence of proto-Corinthian pottery[1], which is so prevalent on the mainland in seventh century Greece. Edgar indeed[2] infers from this absence that the fabric must have been obsolete by the time the Greeks came to Naukratis. This argument cannot be maintained. Kinch notices that there is none of this ware in a chapel that he excavated at Vroulia in Rhodes and in which he found a good deal of seventh century Greek pottery[3]. Within the proto-Corinthian sphere of influence the style lasted on side by side with its successors all through the sixth century[4]. This late proto-Corinthian ware is equally conspicuous by its absence from Naukratis. To push Edgar's argument to its logical conclusion we should have to doubt the existence of Naukratis in the days of Amasis himself[5]. Of the twelve Greek cities that had quarters in Naukratis in the days of Amasis only one, Aegina, belonged to European Greece. For the little known history of this Aeginetan settlement the absence of proto-Corinthian may be of significance. Beyond that it is not.

(iv) The absence of proto-Corinthian pottery proves little.

So far then all that has been proved is that both Petrie and Gardner fixed partly on the wrong material for deciding whether Naukratis was a Greek city of importance in the days of Psammetichus I. And even here on one important point the criticism of them has been shown to be ill founded. Edgar doubted the Greek character of the scarab factory: but not only are the types on some of the scarabs of Greek origin, but a faience fragment from the site shows fragments of a Greek inscription placed on it before the glazing of the vase[6], a fact that can hardly be explained except by assuming a Greek maker.

A great advance was made by Prinz, whose monograph *Funde aus Naukratis* marked the first adequate treatment of the pottery. The earlier controversies about the date of Naukratis had made little appeal to the potsherds that from their mere numbers

---

[1] The vases so classed by Prinz, *Funde aus Naukratis*, p. 69, do not belong to the style (cp. Kinch, *Vroulia*, pp. 134 f.). His conclusions *ib.* p. 72 therefore do not hold.

[2] *B.S.A.* v. p. 57.   [3] Kinch, *Vroulia*, p. 26.

[4] Cp. Rhitsona, *passim*.

[5] Cp. also Daphnae, which flourished contemporaneously with Corinthian and some phases of proto-Corinthian pottery, but yielded no remains of Corinthian nor, apparently, of proto-Corinthian: Petrie, *Tanis*, II. p. 62.

[6] Brit. Mus. 1886, 6–1. 40; Prinz, *Funde aus Nauk.* p. 102.

offer the most valuable evidence that has been yielded by the site.

(v) Positive evidence for an early foundation comes from the pottery actually found, viz.:

Edgar indeed observed in 1905[1] that it seems very doubtful whether all the fragments from the Naukratite temples can be as late as 570. There is at least a probability that some of the temples, especially that of the Milesian Apollo, date from the earlier [*i.e.* Hogarth's Egyptian] days of the town.

But apparently the question was still regarded as "primarily a question of historical criticism[2]." Since Prinz's monograph appeared the pottery has taken the first place in the discussion, and it has now finally confirmed the earlier dating.

Milesian (?) (fig. 13),

Much of the pottery belongs to the well-marked style known generally as Rhodian or Milesian[3] (fig. 13) which had its chief vogue in the seventh century and the first part of the sixth[4]. The crucial point however for our immediate enquiry is to know how long the style may have survived. When Prinz states[5] that it is hard to imagine the style surviving as a competitor of the developed black figure (*i.e.* sixth century) style he is treading on dangerous ground. The earlier ware has a charm of its own. The excavations at Rhitsona show that, in Greece Proper at any rate, old styles of pottery often lasted long after a new style had been introduced, and that a white ground ware with no human figures[6] maintained itself all through the sixth century. Against any such survival of the fabrics under discussion there is however the fact that at Berezan in South Russia it does not occur with Attic black figure of the style that spread all over the Greek world by the middle of the sixth century[7]. At Naukratis itself it is said not to have been found in the Hellenium erected very soon after 570 B.C., a fact which points to its vogue having ended by about that date[8]. On the other hand fragments, mainly of a later phase, have been found in Samos in a cemetery that can hardly go back beyond the middle of the sixth century[9]. The Samian

---

[1] *J.H.S.* xxv. p. 136.   [2] Edgar, *B.S.A.* v. p. 52.

[3] See *e.g. Nauk.* I. Pl. IV. 3.

[4] Wiegand, *Sitz. Preuss. Akad.* 1905, pp. 545–6; *Arch. Anz.* 1914, p. 222, p. 219, figs. 29–31; Kinch, *Vroulia*, pp. 194–231.

[5] *Funde aus Nauk.* p. 37.

[6] The Boeotian Kylix style of *B.S.A.* xiv. pp. 308 f., Pls. VIII. and XV.

[7] *Arch. Anz.* 1904, p. 105; 1905, p. 62; 1910, p. 224.

[8] A. J. Reinach, *Journ. d. Sav.* 1909, p. 357.

[9] Boehlau, *Nekrop.* Taf. XII. 2, 4, 5, 6, 8, 9, 11; cp. pp. 30, 31.

material is however scanty[1] and hardly demands any modification of the conclusions suggested by the rest of the evidence.

Fig. 13. Rhodian or (?) Milesian vase found at Naukratis.

Though generally known as Rhodian this ware was probably made at Miletus[2]. It is the dominant ware in archaic Miletus[3] and has been found all over the Milesian sphere of influence, including

[1] An important fact, not sufficiently taken into account by Boehlau and his followers.
[2] Boehlau, *Nekrop.* p. 75; Prinz, *Funde aus Nauk.* p. 33.
[3] *Sitz. Preuss. Akad.* 1905, p. 545.

the East coast of the Aegean, Rhodes, Rheneia, the Black Sea, and to some extent Sicily and Italy (*via* Sybaris?). It has seldom been found outside it, scarcely any being recorded from Greece Proper. The occurrence at Naukratis in large quantities of what is probably seventh century Milesian pottery is distinctly in favour of a Milesian occupation in the reign of Psammetichus[1].

Fikellura (Samian?) (fig. 14),

Another fabric of the end of the seventh century and beginning of the sixth that is well represented at Naukratis is the so-called Fikellura[2]. This ware is similar to the later phases of the "Milesian" that show full silhouettes, incisions, and a comparative absence of fill ornament. Its distinguishing mark is the zone of crescent-shaped ornament that never appears in the "Milesian" style. Its date is sufficiently established by its occurrence at Daphnae[3], which had its Greek garrison removed by Amasis almost certainly in connexion with his concentration of Greeks in Naukratis[4]. This ware is assigned by Boehlau to Samos[5], but Perrot[6] well observes how rash it is to draw wide general conclusions from the meagre finds published in Boehlau's *Aus ionischen und italischen Nekropolen*.

Corinthian (figs. 22, 34),

Corinthian sherds are also fairly frequent at Naukratis[7]. This ware prevailed in the seventh century and early sixth and survived till the end of the sixth century in certain stereotyped forms. Some of the examples from Naukratis appear to be fairly early; *e.g.* the aryballi with four warriors[8] belong to

---

[1] The ware has often been called Rhodian and more recently (Kinch, *Vroulia, passim*) Camirian. Rhodes has produced far the most specimens, but probably only because tomb-robbing has been particularly prevalent in the island. Rhodian provenance is maintained by Poulsen (*Orient u. frühgr. Kunst*, p. 91), but on dangerous stylistic grounds. His treatment of the Russian finds is particularly unconvincing. All the same Perrot does well (*Hist. de l'Art*, IX. pp. 390, n. 2, 403 f.) to remind us that the Milesian attribution is not a certainty.

[2] Prinz, *Funde aus Nauk.* pp. 39 f.

[3] Petrie, *Tanis*, II. Pls. XXVII., XXVIII.

[4] Petrie, *Tanis*, II. pp. 51, 52 (quoting Hdt. II. 30, 154). Duemmler's doubts as to the identity of Daphnae and the Greek "Camps" (*Jahrb.* x. p. 36) seem somewhat superfluous.

[5] Boehlau, *Ion. Nekrop.* pp. 52 f.; cp. Edgar, *Cat. Vases, Cairo*, pp. 10, 13, 14.

[6] *Hist. de l'Art*, IX. p. 404.

[7] Prinz, *Funde aus Nauk.* pp. 73–74.

[8] *C.R.* II. 233 *e*, Oxford Ashmolean Museum, G. 127. 2, 3 (the latter two excavated 1903). For an illustration of this type see *J.H.S.* XXX. p. 354, fig. 18.

CH. IV   EGYPT   113

a type that was very prevalent about 600 B.C. but had died out before Black Figure came in[1].

Attic
(fig. 41)

The earliest examples of Attic pottery from Naukratis[2] likewise go back to the very beginning of the sixth century. They belong to a series of amphorae called Netos amphorae from the name of a centaur painted on one of them

Fig. 14. Fikellura or (?) Samian vase found at Daphnae (Defenneh).

in Attic lettering. Their general archaic appearance and the survival of the fill ornament show that they must be considerably earlier than the François vase or the earliest Panathenaic amphorae, which date from about 565 B.C. Prinz puts them back to about 600.

[1] See the evidence of the Rhitsona grave catalogues, *B.S.A.* XIV.; *J.H.S.* XXIX., XXX.
[2] *Nauk.* I. Pl. VI. 1, 2; II. Pl. IX. 5; cp. Prinz, pp. 75 f.

and Naukra-
tite (fig. 15),

For dating the Greek settlement at Naukratis this probably imported ware is of less importance than a very distinctive style of painted pottery[1] that was found there in far larger quantities than any of the fabrics just mentioned, and was almost certainly made by Greeks in Naukratis itself[2].

For the dating of this pottery Naukratis offered no certain data. The decisive evidence is derived from Naukratite vases recently found in three other sites, Vroulia in Rhodes, Rhitsona (Mykalessos) in Boeotia, and Berezan in South Russia. Vroulia was excavated by Kinch in 1907 and 1908. The finds were fully and sumptuously published in 1914. They led him to believe that the site was occupied only from the first third of the seventh century B.C. to about 570–560[3]. Among them were fragments of nine Naukratite cups, none of them particularly early examples of the style, and of one vase in what seems to be a late development from it. The decoration of the Vroulia Naukratite seems moreover to correspond to one of the earlier phases of the Milesian (?) pottery from the same site.

The Vroulia evidence is confirmed by that of the Naukratite chalice (fig. 15) unearthed at Rhitsona just at the time when Vroulia was being excavated by Kinch. The vase, which is almost complete, belongs to a late phase of the style[4]. Fill ornaments have almost disappeared. Red and incisions are abundantly used for details. The vase was found with some hundreds of others in a single interment grave that cannot be dated much after 550 and may be a little before that date[5]. A Naukratite vase cannot have been made to order for a Boeotian funeral. The Rhitsona chalice by itself renders it practically certain that the making of Naukratite ware at Naukratis began long before the accession of Amasis.

Finally at Berezan on the Black Sea the Russian excavators report that in 1909 Naukratite pottery was found along with Rhodian (= Milesian), Fikellura and Clazomenae wares in the lowest stratum of the excavations, which they date seventh to sixth century, whereas Attic pottery of the middle of the sixth century

[1] *E.g.* Petrie and Gardner, *Nauk.* I. Pl. V. and (coloured) *J.H.S.* VIII. pl. 79.
[2] *Nauk.* I. p. 51; II. p. 39: cp. Prinz, pp. 87 f.
[3] *Vroulia*, pp. 7, 34, 89.
[4] *J.H.S.* XXIX. pl. 25 and pp. 332 f.
[5] Cp. Buschor, *Gr. Vasenmal.*[1] p. 81; Frickenhaus, *Tiryns*, I. p. 53.

(especially Kleinmeister kylikes) first appears in a higher stratum (sixth to fifth century B.C.)[1].

all pointing to a foundation in the seventh century. In the face of all this evidence it becomes highly probable that Naukratite pottery began to be made before the end of the seventh century[2]. It is against all likelihood to suppose that the first thing the Greek settlement at Naukratis did was to start a large pottery, which proceeded at once to turn out a highly original kind of

Fig. 15. Naukratite vase found at Rhitsona in Boeotia.

ware. And in point of fact we have seen that the finds include a good quantity of an earlier style of pottery, that takes us back well

[1] *Arch. Anz.* 1910, pp. 224-5; 1914, p. 227.

[2] Its absence from Daphnae, the military station from which the Greeks were removed by Amasis soon after 570 B.C., was formerly thought to indicate that at that date it had not yet been invented or at least not yet become popular. But the chief wares found at Daphnae, including the typical (Clazomenian?) Daphnae ware, and excepting only a peculiar local type of situla, are not uncommon at Naukratis (*B.S.A.* v. pp. 60-61). This could hardly be the case, at least not to the same extent, if Naukratis started only when Daphnae ceased. We must seek some other explanation of the lack of Naukratite at Daphnae. May it not have been simply that such delicate ware was ill-suited for a camp? The Naukratite cups show a fabric as fragile as the modern teacup.

into the reign of Psamtek. We have seen too that this pottery, which is one of the starting-points of the Naukratite style, is probably Milesian.

A further proof of early Milesian influence at Naukratis remains to be mentioned. At one spot in the excavations literally hundreds of vases were found with incised dedications to Apollo[1]. Some ten of these speak of the Milesian Apollo, the god to whom Necho the son of Psammetichus made an offering after the victory over Josiah at Megiddo[2]. The Milesian sherds that it is natural to put into the seventh century come largely from this spot. Herodotus tells us that the Milesians did not have quarters in the Hellenium but occupied a separate temenos. The spot where these sherds and inscriptions were found is unquestionably the site of this temenos. As to why the Milesians thus kept apart there can be little doubt that Petrie gives the right explanation. It means that they were there before the cities that shared the Hellenium[3]. The finds show that their occupation was already on a considerable scale before the end of the seventh century.

Evidence as to Naukratis based on differences observed in different parts of the site, viz. (a) the temenos of the Milesians,

Two other cities had separate temene, namely Samos and Aegina[4]. The Samian has been identified by a find of sherds dedicated to the Samian goddess Hera. But there is from this temenos no mass of pottery that takes us back into the first half of the sixth century or the second of the seventh, as there is from the Milesian. "Fikellura" ware that is very possibly Samian[5] and that may date from about 600 B.C. was indeed found, but not in quantities like the Milesian[6]. The scanty finds may be due to Arab farmers who had removed much earth from the Samian temenos before the excavations began[7]. But the finds as we have them, with inadequate accounts of the exact spots

(β) the temenos of the Samians,

---

[1] Over 350; *Nauk.* I. pp. 60 f.   [2] *Nauk.* I. p. 11.

[3] Its central and crowded position is (*pace* Edgar, *B.S.A.* v. p. 53) no argument against this view, but rather the reverse, especially if it is remembered that Miletus and presumably as a consequence the Milesian part of Naukratis was in a bad way in the days of Amasis.

[4] On the evidence of excavation as to these temene see Prinz, *Funde aus Nauk.* pp. 12–13.

[5] Note, however, Perrot's comments, *Hist. de l'Art*, IX. p. 415.

[6] Prinz, pp. 39–42; *B.S.A.* v. pp. 41, 60.

[7] *Nauk.* II. p. 60.

they come from, hardly make it likely that the Samian temenos was an early establishment[1]. True Herodotus[2] tells the tale of a Samian ship that set sail for Egypt between 643 and 640 B.C. But it got to Spain by mistake, a fact which suggests an imperfect knowledge of the route it wished to take. A Samian nymph appears in a fragment of the "Foundation of Naukratis" of Apollonius Rhodius[3]. But we only know that she once went to a festival at Miletus and was there carried off by Apollo.

(γ) the temenos of the Aeginetans,

Of the Aeginetan temenos no trace has been found. It might be suggested that the Aeginetans had not the habit of inscribing their dedications. But the absence of proto-Corinthian finds favours the view that this temenos was not unearthed. It is idle therefore to speculate on its date and importance[4].

In any case we have good reason for interpreting the written texts in the sense that the Milesians' Fort made way for the Greek Naukratis during the reign of Psammetichus. This is historically important. The Milesians' Fort may have been a fortified trading station[5]: but it never had the commercial importance of Naukratis. If, as we have just seen good evidence for believing, Greek Naukratis was already a considerable place before Psamtek's death and owed the fact to Psamtek himself, then there is an increased probability that Diodorus is right when he says that Psamtek owed his throne to commercial dealings with traders from across the sea.

(δ) the Egyptian quarter, with its early temple of Aphrodite

There are two further points in which the Naukratis excavations bear out the texts that support this view. Hogarth has shown that South Naukratis was the Egyptian quarter, and that it goes back probably to before King Psamtek's reign. We have seen too that as early

---

[1] There is little evidence for the attractive suggestion (A. G. Dunham, *Hist. Miletus*, p. 68) that the establishment should be connected with the victory of the Samian side and the defeat of the Milesian in the (seventh century) Lelantine war. [2] IV. 152.

[3] Athen. VII. 283 e. Hirschfeld may be right in inferring that Apollonius took the foundation of Naukratis back to mythical times (*Rhein. Mus.* 1887, p. 220).

[4] Prinz, *Funde aus Nauk.* p. 75, connects with it the Corinthian sherds, some of which are much earlier than Amasis. Better evidence for early Aeginetan dealings with Naukratis are the Naukratite sherds, some of them of the earliest phase, found in Aegina, Prinz, p. 88.

[5] Hirschfeld, *Rhein. Mus.* 1887, p. 212; E. Meyer, *Ges. Aeg.* p. 368; Prinz, *Funde aus Nauk.* p. 1.

as 688 B.C. the Greek merchant Herostratos is said to have made offerings at Naukratis in the temple of Aphrodite. There is only one spot at Naukratis that compares with the Milesian temenos for early Greek finds, and that spot is marked by a long series of dedications to Aphrodite[1] incised or sometimes painted on the pottery, which includes Milesian, Naukratite, Ionian buff and black, and other seventh and sixth century wares. The site of this temenos has a significance that seems to have been overlooked. It lies just on the borders[2] of the black stratum area that appears to mark the limits of the original Egyptian town. When excavations were resumed in 1899 there was discovered in the North part of the town a second Aphrodite shrine forming a sort of side chapel to the real Hellenium[3]. The earliest finds from this Northern Aphrodite shrine date from the earlier part of the fifth century[4]. May not the position of the earlier and more southerly shrine be due to the fact that it was founded before the occupants of the Milesians' Fort had moved to Naukratis and established a Greek quarter there? In other words, may we not see in it a confirmation of Polycharmus[5] when he speaks of a Greek as offering an image of Aphrodite in a temple of that goddess at Naukratis in 688 B.C.? The fact that the Aphrodite site was not burnt is no proof that it did not form part of the earliest settlement. The men from the Milesians' Fort who defeated Inaros may well have spared the Greek sanctuary when they burnt the rest.

The voyage of Herostratos was held in remembrance at Naukratis because of a statuette of Aphrodite that he dedicated in her temple as a thank-offering for having saved him during a storm. The statuette was a span long and of archaic workmanship, and had been bought by him at Paphos during the voyage. When the storm arose the people on board had betaken themselves to this eikon and prayed it to save them. The goddess heard their prayers and gave them a

and the statuettes of the goddess found on the temple site.

---

[1] Over 100 are recorded, *Nauk.* II. p. 62 f.; others, *B.S.A.* v. p. 41.

[2] Not apparently on it: cp. *Nauk.* II. pl. 3 (section of the site down to the basal mud with no black stratum marked); *B.S.A.* v. p. 44 (spoken of as at South end of Greek quarter); *J.H.S.* xxv. p. 107. Considering that the temple lies so very near the scarab factory and due West of it and that the line of cleavage between Greek and Egyptian runs East and West it is strange that no explicit statement is made on this point.

[3] *B.S.A.* v. pp. 38, 44. [4] *J.H.S.* xxv. p. 114.

[5] Athen. xv. 675 f.

sign by suddenly filling the ship with a most fragrant perfume. The story is discussed by Gardner[1] in his chapter on the statuettes from the temenos of Aphrodite, which include a number that may represent the Paphian goddess. But he makes no reference to the statuette that probably has the closest bearing on the tale. The upper half is of the normal draped female type, but the lower shows simply the form of an alabastron. The whole is a perfume vase[2]. This particular example (fig. 16) cannot be earlier than the end of the sixth century. The type however is shown both by the style and the context of other examples to go back to the seventh century, and probably to the earlier part of it. The home of the type is thought by Poulsen[3] to be Cyprus. An object that combined the functions of an eikon and a smelling-bottle might indeed work miracles in a storm. It is tempting to believe that such was in fact the image that saved Herostratos. The miracle takes place just at the period when this type of figurine was started. If we are right in associating the two, then we are further justified in thinking that Polycharmus may have had some solid grounds for his dating as well as for the rest of his account.

Fig. 16. Perfume vase found at Naukratis.

Evidence of large jars used for merchandise.

The other point concerns the large plain jars that were found on the site[4]. Many of these are of Egyptian forms. But others, of which one is shown in fig. 17, are unmistakably Greek. This jar was found in the burnt deposit in the South end of the city, which represents the earlier Egyptian settlement on the site[5]. These large jars were

[1] *Nauk.* II.   [2] *Nauk.* II. Pl. XIV. 11.

[3] *Orient u. frühgr. Kunst*, pp. 93–99 (Cyprus for examples with an Oriental character, Rhodes for those that are purely Greek). An example found at Polledrara (Vulci) comes from a grave ("tomb of Isis," Montelius, *Civ. Prim. en Ital.* Sér. B, pl. 266. 3) that contained also a scarab of Psammetichus I and is probably to be dated in the second half of the seventh century.

[4] *Nauk.* I. Pls. XVI., XVII. For Pl. XVI. 4 see below, fig. 17.

[5] *Nauk.* I. p. 21; cp. p. 42; but cp. Petrie, *B.S.A.* v. p. 41, "I found nothing but Egyptian South of Aphrodite."

used by the Greeks for the transport of wine, oil and the like[1]. In jars such as these Sappho's brother must have brought to Naukratis the wines of Lesbos, and they must have figured largely in the cargoes brought by Greeks and Phoenicians[2] to Psamtek in exchange for the cargoes that they received from Psamtek in the days when he was building up his power[3].

Conclusions about early Naukratis. To sum up our conclusions about Naukratis: texts and excavations confirm and supplement one another to the effect that there was an Egyptian settlement from the beginning of the seventh century, that Greek traders found their way there almost from the first, and that about the middle of the seventh century the Greek trading settlement became of considerable importance[4] through the removal to it of the occupants of the Milesians' Fort[5]. Finally about 569 B.C. we have the concentration in the city of all the Greek traders in Egypt.

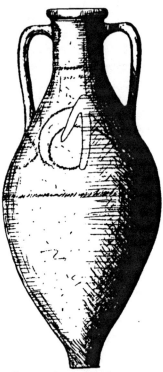

Fig. 17. Greek wine jar found at Naukratis.

[1] Prinz, *Funde aus Nauk.* p. 84. Prinz, *ibid.* pp. 86–87, regards some of the early jars from Naukratis as Ionian, comparing the shapes of painted Ionian jars. Whether, as Prinz thinks (*ibid.* p. 13), they prove an early Greek settlement in the South quarter is another question.

[2] For Phoenician remains at Naukratis see *B.S.A.* v. p. 49, where they are probably overestimated; cp. Prinz, *Funde aus Nauk.* p. 102.

[3] For connecting jars of this sort with Greco-Saite trade cp. perhaps Epiphan. *de Mens. et Pond.* 182 d ὁ ἀληθινὸς Σαΐτης ξεστῶν ἐστι κβ (=44 kotylai).

[4] For a more modest estimate of early Naukratis see Mallet, *Prem. Étab.* p. 178. The view of Kahrstedt (Pauly Wissowa, s.v. Herostratos) and Hirschfeld (*Rhein. Mus.* 1887, p. 219) (cp. Endt, *Ion. Vasenmal.* p. 68), that Greek Naukratis dates only from 570, is untenable.

[5] One great gap in the evidence would be filled if ever the site of the Milesians' Fort was found and excavated.

The Greek traders were concentrated by Amasis in Naukratis as a concession to the Egyptians with whom they had grown more and more unpopular owing to their influence and success. Amasis had risen to power as the leader of an anti-Greek agitation[1], and, as Petrie pointed out[2], the concentration was an anti-Greek move[3]. But Amasis cleverly contrived that it should be not unpopular, but even the reverse, with the Greeks. Naukratis as a monopoly city enjoyed an immense reputation during Amasis' long and prosperous reign. But the Amasis tradition cannot conceal the fact that the time when Greek traders got the freest welcome in Egypt was that of Psammetichus, when Greek hoplites were being employed to establish the Saite dynasty as rulers of all Egypt.

The position of Naukratis under Amasis contrasted with its position under Psammetichus.

In the early days of Psammetichus, when he was overthrowing the dodecarchy, his Greek merchants and his Greek soldiers probably had their headquarters together, in the Milesians' Fort. At Naukratis the military element does not appear. From about 650 B.C. till shortly after the accession of Amasis in 570 the Greek mercenaries are found quartered in a place called The Camps at Daphnae on the most Easterly (Pelusian) arm of the Nile[4]. The history of the transition from the Milesians' Fort to Daphnae is obscure[5]; but in a broad sense there can be little doubt that the Fort was as much the parent

Daphnae and the Greek mercenaries

---

[1] See below, pp. 122–3.

[2] Petrie, *Hist. Eg.* III. pp. 351–2; *Tanis*, II. pp. 51 f.; cp. Mallet, *Prem. Étab.* pp. 129–130.

[3] Sharpe, *Hist. Eg.*⁶ I. p. 167, thought it directed against Tanis, Mendes and Bubastis; but there is nothing to show that Amasis had anything to fear from these seats of earlier dynasties in the Eastern part of the Delta.

[4] Hdt. II. 154; cp. II. 30; Diodorus (I. 67) dates the foundation of The Camps after Psamtek's victory. The site confirms the date. Daphnae could become the military base of the Saite prince only after he had disposed of the dodecarchy and was mainly concerned with the Assyrian peril; see Petrie, *Tanis*, II. p. 48.

[5] Whether troops were actually transferred from the "Fort" to the "Camp" is doubtful. There is little trace of Miletus at Daphnae, where the Greek pottery appears to have been mainly from Samos (Fikellura ware, Petrie, *Tanis*, II. pls. 27, 28) and Clazomenae (Daphnae ware, *ibid.* pls. 29–31). The marked differences between the pottery finds at Naukratis and Daphnae are now generally recognized as being local, not temporal, except in so far as the Daphnae series ends earlier. But the fact of these local differences still awaits a satisfactory explanation. Cp. above, p. 115, n. 2.

of the camp at Daphnae as of the emporium at Naukratis. Naukratis and Daphnae, the Greek emporium and the Greek camp, were alike essential to the Saite Pharaohs, and both had plainly gone far in their development and organization early in Psamtek's reign.

and the Egyptian warrior caste. How closely the two were associated may be realized from the consistent attitude of the Saite Pharaohs towards another element of the population. The Ionian and Carian bronze men were not the first mercenaries to form the basis of a Pharaoh's power. The XXIInd and XXIIIrd dynasties (c. 943–735 B.C.) had rested their power on their mercenaries from Libya. These Libyan mercenaries had developed into a caste of professional soldiers and were still in the land[1]. It is noteworthy that no Saite, with one possible exception nearly 100 years after Psamtek's accession, ever attempted to use them either for securing or for maintaining his power. Mallet notes that for the time before Psammetichus the monuments often show commanders of Libyan mercenaries bearing high titles, but that from his reign onwards there is no similar instance[2].

Meyer[3] is probably right in suspecting that this warrior class (μάχιμοι) formed Psamtek's bitterest opponents. Eventually a large body of them deserted and took service with the king of Ethiopia, and Psamtek seems to have made no determined effort to prevent them[4]. The one exceptional case in which the Libyan warrior class may possibly have placed a Saite on the throne is that of Amasis (570–526 B.C.)[5], who overthrew his predecessor Apries (589–570)

---

[1] Meyer, *Ges. d. Alt.*[1] I. 384; cp. Mallet, *Prem. Étab.* pp. 43, 80. Mallet, *ibid.* pp. 79–80, makes Herodotus' μάχιμοι a sort of militia, but this hardly suits their description as a caste. Egyptian documents do indeed show that, in spite of Herodotus II. 164, VI. 60; Plato, *Tim.* 23–24; Isocr. *Bus.* 15–17 (224); Diod. I. 28, 73–74; Strabo XVII. 787; there was no hard caste system in ancient Egypt; cp. Wiedemann, *Hdt.* II. 164; Mallet, *Prem. Étab.* p. 411. But the μάχιμοι, though not a caste, were plainly a sharply defined class.

[2] *Prem. Étab.* p. 80.

[3] *Ges. d. Alt.*[1] I. 561.

[4] Hdt. II. 30; Diod. I. 67; Strabo XVI. 770 and XVII. 786 (where they are said to have been still in Ethiopia in the days of the historian); Pliny, *N.H.* VI. 35 (30); Ptol. *Geog.* IV. 7 (Didot, I. p. 783); Hesych. s.v. Μαχλαίονας. On the authenticity of this story see Wiedemann, *Hdt.* II. 30, pp. 128 f., *Ges. Aeg.* pp. 137–8 (sceptical); Mallet, *Prem. Étab.* pp. 77 f. Herodotus says there were 240,000, Diodorus over 200,000. These numbers will not now be regarded as sceptically as they were in the last century.

[5] Wiedemann, *Hdt.* II. 161; Breasted, *Records*, IV. 1000, 1001.

by leading the native population against the Greek mercenaries[1]. But, as Herodotus tells us, he was soon driven to "become a philhellene[2]." Petrie thinks that Amasis was converted under pressure of the Persian peril, and in support of this view quotes the alliance of Amasis with Croesus[3], Polycrates[4], and the Greek Battus of Cyrene[5], as also his friendship with Delphi[6].

This point of foreign policy no doubt had its weight in the years that saw the rise of Cyrus and his overthrow of Media in 549 B.C., Lydia in 546, Babylon in 538 (?). But it was not the cause of his conversion. Amasis became Pharaoh in 570. In the sixth year of his reign he made an edict that contained the following words: "Let the Ouinin (= Ionians) be given place of habitation in the lands of the nome of Sais. Let them take to their use ships and firewood. Let them bring their gods[7]." Long therefore before the rise of Persia Amasis had realized how impossible it was to maintain his position otherwise than by coming to an understanding both with the Greek merchants and the Greek mercenaries. Philhellenism was in fact an essential part of Saite policy. Necho (610-594 B.C.), the son and successor of Psammetichus I, sent offerings to Apollo at Branchidae (Miletus) after his victory over Josiah of Judah and the Syrian fleet[8]. Psammetichus II (594-589) died probably as a child: to his reign are probably to be assigned the Abu Symbel inscriptions[9] scratched by Greek soldiers on monuments far up the river by Elephántine. The people of Elis are said to have appealed to him or his government on a point respecting the Olympian games[10]. Apries (589-570), who fell foul of his Greek troops, had 30,000 Ionians and Carians under arms[11]. A small Greek vase found at Corinth[12] has the cartouche of Apries. It is in the form of a

[1] Hdt. II. 169; Diod. I. 68; Petrie, *Hist. Eg.* III. 351-2; Breasted, *Records*, IV. 1003.   [2] Hdt. II. 178.
[3] Hdt. I. 77; cp. Xen. *Cyrop.* VI. 2. 10.   [4] Hdt. III. 39.
[5] Maspero, *Passing of the Empires*, p. 645; cp. Plut. *Mor.* 261 (*Mul. Virt.* 25).
[6] Hdt. II. 180.
[7] From a demotic chronicle published by E. Revillout, *Proc. Soc. Bib. Arch.* XIV. (Mar. 1892), pp. 251-4; cp. *Rev. Égyptol.* 1880, p. 60.
[8] Hdt. II. 159; Hirschfeld, *Rhein. Mus.* 1887, p. 219, suggests that the fleet with which Necho defeated the Syrians may have owed much to the Milesians' Fort.
[9] Cp. Hdt. II. 161; Lepsius, *Denkm.* III. 274 *d,e*; Roberts, *Gk. Epig.* I. 151 f.
[10] Hdt. II. 160; according to Diod. I. 95, the appeal was made to Amasis.
[11] Hdt. II. 163; Diod. I. 68.
[12] Heuzey, *Fig. Ant.* pl. 7. 2; Mallet, *Prem. Étab.* fig. 27; Prinz, *Funde aus Nauk.* p. 107.

helmeted head (fig. 18). The vase is of faience (so-called). It was probably made at Naukratis, perhaps in Petrie's scarab factory, and gives us a contemporary picture of one of Apries' Greek mercenaries, or at least of the top part of his equipment.

Amasis accordingly became a friend of the Greeks and remained so till he died. The Greeks reciprocated his friendship. The feelings of the Naukratite traders towards him are reflected plainly enough in the pages of Herodotus[1]. The Greek mercenaries supported him loyally to the end of his long reign, and in spite of the treachery of their commander Phanes they fought gallantly at Pelusium in 525 B.C. when Psammetichus III, the last of the Saites, was overthrown by the Persians. Under the military rule of Persia the Libyan warrior class recovered its old position[2].

Fig. 18. Corinthian vase with cartouche of Apries.

Thus we have seen the Saite dynasty rising to power by means of Greek merchandise and Greek mercenaries and maintaining its power by the same means. Its general policy follows the same lines as that of the tyrannies that sprang up at this time all over the Greek world. Herodotus with his usual insight recognized this fact when he put into his history the story of the friendship between Amasis and the Samian tyrant Polycrates. Amasis was probably not the first of the Saites to have a Greek tyrant for his friend. Cordial relations with Thrasybulus, the tyrant of Miletus, are suggested by Necho's offerings to the Milesian Apollo, and the friend of Thrasybulus must have been also the friend of the Corinthian tyrant Periander. It has often been assumed, and not without reason, that Periander's successor was called Psammetichus from some personal connexion with the lord of Sais.

Personal relations between Saite sovereigns and Greek tyrants.

---

[1] For Amasis and trade cp. Plut. *Sept. Sap. Conv.* 6 (*Moral.* 151), ἐκείνῳ γὰρ (sc. 'Αμάσιδι) ἂν γένοιτο πλέονος ἀξία τῆς ἐμπορίας ἡ παρενθήκη.

[2] Mallet, *Prem. Étab.* p. 414.

Psammetichus I is the first individual known to have borne that name. It is possible therefore that it may have had some special appropriateness to his own or his father's career[1]. One of the most probable interpretations of the name is "man (vendor) of mixing bowls." The choice seems to lie between this interpretation and "man (vendor) of mixed wine" (*i.e.* wine mixed with spices, etc.). Which of these is to be preferred depends on the interpretation of the root mtk[2]. In hieratic writing the phonetic symbols are sometimes followed by a "determinative" symbol or pictograph, placed at the end to prevent misunderstanding. The determinative for mtk is the picture of a vase, as seen for instance in *Rylands Library Demotic Papyri*, p. 201. The vase has a barrel or pear-shaped body, narrow neck, and broad flat mouth, ᛘ. The particular shape must not be pressed, and the picture may be meant to denote not the vase but its contents. But it must mean one or the other[3]. Griffith thinks it denotes the contents, his reasons

The name Psammetichus.

[1] Cp. Griffith, *Dem. Pap. Rylands*, III. p. 44, n. 5.
[2] *Ibid.* p. 201. The word analyses p (article)—san (man, vendor)—mtk.
[3] Earlier Egyptologists derived the word quite differently, explaining it as Libyan (*e.g.* v. Stern, *Z. f. Aeg. Spr.* 1883, pp. 24 f. and references, *ad loc.*) or Ethiopian (=son of the Sun), (Brugsch, *Ges. Aeg.* pp. 731 f., but cp. Wiedemann, *Aeg. Ges.* p. 623). Meyer, *Ges. Aeg.* p. 363, describes it simply as "not Egyptian," presumably as not occurring before the Saite period. But this is no argument if the name was till then extremely plebeian. Petrie rejects "man (vendor of) mixing bowls," as manifestly absurd and analyses P-sam-te-k=the (Egyptian) lion's (Upper Egyptian) son (Ethiopian) the (Ethiopian suffix) (*Hist. Eg.* III. p. 320, accepted as probable by How and Wells, *ad Hdt.* II. 151). He compares Shaba-ta-ka (Ethiopian dynasty, 707–693)=wild cat's son the; but this is no parallel for the real difficulty, which is the extraordinary hybrid composition. Linguistic hybrids are legion. Our own forefathers enriched Latin with the word quicksethedgavit. But so complicated a hybrid as Petrie implies cannot be considered seriously without some very solid evidence for really parallel monstrosities. Spiegelberg (*Orient. Litt. Zeit.* 1905, p. 560), after arguing convincingly against Petrie, accepts "bowl vendor" as a popular etymology, but rejects it as the real meaning, "denn kein König wird Mischkrughändler heissen wollen." He explains the word as really meaning "man of the god Mtk"; only no such god is known. Even if there were, Spiegelberg's explanation cuts both ways. If, as the evidence has shown, there is a probability that Psammetichus I had really been a vendor of something like mixing-bowls, and got his name from his occupation, some such aristocratic explaining away of the plebeian name may perhaps have induced him and his successors to keep it, just as Mrs Snooks in one of Wells' stories became more than reconciled to her name after it had been explained as an abbreviation of Sevenoaks and spelt accordingly.

being these[1]: mtk is a Coptic root meaning "mix" and has a Hebrew equivalent meaning "mixture" (wine mixed). This meaning "seems to fit all requirements[2]," *i.e.* it suits the story of the libation which led Psammetichus to become king[3], and also the tales of the low and bibulous ($\phi\iota\lambda o\pi \acute{o}\tau\eta\varsigma$) origin of Amasis[4]. Griffith's interpretation rests ultimately on the philological point, and on the assumption that the root in Egyptian must have precisely the same meaning as in Coptic and Hebrew. I am indebted to the writer himself for the information that this is not always the case. Apart from philology "mixed wine" may suit all requirements[5]: but does it do so quite as well as "mixing bowl"? The whole point of the story of Psammetichus' libation depends not on the wine but its receptacle. On either interpretation however it is sufficiently remarkable that the ruler who is said to have risen to power by trade should have had so mercantile a name. Griffith does not forget the possibility that the name may have been the source of the stories[6]. The two possibilities are not mutually exclusive. A merchant prince may be proud of his origin: but that fact will not always prevent other people from telling good unofficial stories about his early days.

[1] *Dem. Pap. Rylands*, III. pp. 44, n. 5; 201, n. 3.
[2] *Ibid.* p. 201, n. 3.   [3] Hdt. II. 151.
[4] Griffith, *ibid.* p. 44, n. 5, quoting Hdt. II. 174; cp. Ael. *V.H.* II. 41; Athen. VI. 261, X. 438.
[5] There is little evidence for a trade in mixed wine. The ancient Greeks habitually drank mixed wine, but the mixing was done at home. In England there is no wholesale trade in claret cup. But note Mod.Gk. $\kappa\rho a\sigma \acute{\iota}$, =mixture, the normal word for wine.
[6] *Ibid.* p. 44, n. 5.

Chapter V. *Lydia*

"Yes, ready money is Aladdin's lamp."—BYRON.

Tyranny and coinage both said to be of Lydian origin.
IN an enquiry into the connexions between the new form of government and the new form of wealth that both arose at the opening of the classical epoch Lydia has a special interest and importance for the reason that both coinage and tyranny are said on good authority to have been of Lydian origin. Considering how much Lydia was then in the background of the Greek world this fact by itself is suggestive. It becomes important to determine the dates, and connexions if any, of the first Lydian tyrant and the first Lydian coins. It should be said at once that no Lydian ruler has been credited with the invention of coinage, and that no very definite conclusions can be drawn from the available material. The evidence is however sufficiently suggestive to repay a careful examination.

a   *b*

Fig. 19. Coins of (*a*) Gyges (?), (*b*) Croesus.

Date of the earliest coins.
Both the date and the place of the final evolution of a metal coinage are the subject of much dispute. Among writers of a generation or more ago the question of date was mainly a matter of speculation as to how long an interval was required between the earliest silver coins with a type in relief on both sides, which on grounds of style, epigraphy, and circumstances of find can be dated with fair accuracy to about the middle of the sixth century, and the primitive electrum pieces punched on one side and striated on the other (fig. 19. *a*) that probably belong to the earliest issues of Lydia. Most of the leading numismatists allowed some three or four generations and assigned the earliest

coins to the earlier part of the seventh century[1]. But more recently facts have come to light which point to the possibility of an earlier and perhaps a considerably earlier date. A round dump of silver weighing 3·654 grammes was found by Sir Arthur Evans at Knossos in a stratum that cannot, he says, be dated later than the twelfth century B.C., and two similar dumps of gold weighing 4·723 and 4·678 grammes along with a third of elongated shape weighing 8·601 were found during the British Museum excavations at Enkomi in Cyprus, a site which according to Evans must be dated equally early[2]. These few Cretan and Cyprian dumps are no argument against the mass of material which points to a great numismatic development at a date not so very far removed from 700 B.C. But they do shift the balance of probability backward and make a date in the eighth century as likely as one in the seventh. The same conclusion is suggested by the recent British excavations of the famous temple of Artemis at Ephesus[3]. There, below the temple erected in the days of Croesus and to which he contributed the sculptured column now in the British Museum, the excavators found remains of three earlier structures. While clearing out these early buildings they found 87 electrum coins. Twenty of these were extracted from between the slabs of the earliest of the three buildings, five (including four of the lion type) were extracted from underneath the foundations of the second building, and all low down within the area of these three early structures. The total evidence points to all the 87 coins being not later than the time of the first of the three buildings, *i.e.* well before the time of Croesus. The series begins with the striated type (above fig. 19. *a*) that is generally regarded as the most primitive of all, while far the commonest type (42 coins) is the lion's head of the style usually attributed to Alyattes[4].

From the latest building to the earliest coin means a considerable period, and may well take us back into the eighth century. General historical considerations are however against going back too far

[1] Babelon, *Rev. Num.* 1894, pp. 267 f.; Th. Reinach, *L'Hist. par les Monnaies*, pp. 32-3; Head, *Hist. Num.*² p. 643; Macdonald, *Coin Types*, pp. 6-8; Radet, *Rev. des Univ. du Midi*, 1895, p. 120; Busolt, *Gr. G.*² I. p. 493.

[2] Evans in *Corolla Numismatica B. V. Head*, pp. 363-7; Ridgeway, *Compan. Gk. Stud.*² p. 537.

[3] *Brit. Mus. Excavations at Ephesus* (1908), chaps. IV., V.

[4] Three have the | ꟼꟻΛAꟻ inscription that Six explained as an abbreviation of Alyattes' name, *Num. Chron.* 1890, pp. 203 f.

CH. V   LYDIA   129

into the eighth century. It was only in the course of that century that brigandage and piracy gave place to trade and commerce and the first traces can be discovered of the great renaissance that led to Classical Greece. If the earliest coins were struck by Lydia they are more likely to have been issued in the second half of the century than the first, since the establishment of the second Assyrian empire in 745 B.C. probably gave a great impetus to Lydian trade. This, however, is assuming the claims of Lydia to the "invention." They have been frequently challenged and before proceeding it is necessary briefly to examine them.

The Lydians are only one of several peoples and cities that were credited by the ancients with the invention of coinage. This uncertainty was inevitable. Coinage was not invented but evolved[1]. But it is probable that in the final stage of the evolution some one state was a little ahead of the rest, and put in this form the Lydians have a good claim to the invention. They have in their favour our two best and oldest witnesses, Xenophanes and Herodotus[2], the latter of whom recognized their outstanding position as traders and plainly sees in it the explanation of their leading position in the evolution of coined money[3]. The facts as far as we know them bear these authorities out. Lydia contains Mt Tmolus and Mt Sipylus and the river Pactolus, the main sources of the supply of the metal in which the most primitive coins were struck. It was probably just about this period that the Lydian electrum mines began to be worked[4] and the electrum of Sardis gained the fame it still enjoyed in the days of Sophocles[5]. The kings of Lydia from the beginning of the seventh century onward were famous for their wealth[6]. The touchstone used by the ancients for testing the precious metals came likewise from Mt Tmolus, and was called "Lydian stone[7]." Further-

The evidence for attributing them to Lydia.

[1] Babelon, *Origines*, pp. 181 f.
[2] Xen. *ap*. Poll. IX. 83; Hdt. I. 94.
[3] Cp. Th. Reinach, *Hist. par les Monn.* p. 32. Cp. also the account of the invention of money in *Rep.* II. 371, where Plato connects it with the rise of middlemen.
[4] See below, p. 148.   [5] Soph. *Antig.* 1037.
[6] Strabo XIII. 626 (cp. XIV. 680); Archilochus, quoted below, p. 134; cp. Justin I. 7.
[7] Bacchyl. ed. Jebb, fr. 10 (Λυδία λίθος μανύει χρυσόν); Theophr. *de Lap.* 4; Pliny, *N.H.* XXXIII. 43; Pollux VII. 102; Hesych. s.v. βασανίτης and χρυσῖτις λίθος; cp. Ridgeway, *Num. Chron.* 1895, pp. 104 f.

U. T.   9

more, the Lydians occupied a unique position for purposes of trade. Sardis, their capital, was the place where the great trade-route from the further East, the "royal road," as Herodotus calls it[1], branched out to reach the various Greek cities on the coast[2].

In the face of this evidence it is hardly necessary to examine in detail the arguments of the modern sceptics who have disputed Lydia's claim. In many cases they start from the baseless assumption that so remarkable an invention cannot but be due to the quick-witted Greeks[3]. True, the earliest electrum coins are said to have been found mostly along the Eastern shore of the Aegean, but it does not follow that that is where they were all struck. Gold pieces were common enough in Greece in the first half of the fourth century B.C., but they had nearly all been struck in Persia. 30,000 Darics (fig. 8) were distributed among the Greeks by the Great King's agents in one single year[4]. The two staters of gold that each of the Delphians received from King Croesus[5] were undoubtedly Crœseids[6].

Again, the modern market for ancient coins has been largely restricted to the coast. Because a coin was bought in Smyrna it does not follow that it was found there. Of Sardis itself we still know too little to speak with any assurance[7]. But the absence of

---

[1] Hdt. v. 52 f.; cp. Radet, *Lydie*, pp. 23 f. and references p. 23, n. 1.

[2] Radet, pp. 31 f. On the political importance of the great highways of trade in Lydia see Radet, *Lydie*, pp. 108 (tolls along caravan routes in eighth century B.C., Nic. Dam. *F.H.G.* III. p. 381, fr. 49), 227–8 (ferry tolls levied by the state under the dynasty founded by Gyges, and state compensation for damage done by the flooding of the waterways, Xanthus, *F.H.G.* I. p. 37, fr. 4).

For Sardis as geographically more likely than any coast city to have evolved a metal coinage see Radet, *Lydie*, p. 156; Th. Reinach, *Hist. par les Monn.* p. 22. For the contrary view see Babelon, *Rev. Num.* 1895, pp. 352 f., *Origines*, p. 218.

[3] E.g. P. Gardner, *Gold Coinage of Asia*, p. 4, *Hist. Anc. Coin.* p. 69; Brandis, *Münzwesen*, p. 201; cp. also Radet, *Lydie*, p. 293.

[4] Plut. *Apophth. Lac.*, *Agesil.* 40 (*Mor.* 211 b).

[5] Hdt. I. 54.

[6] The fact that 73 out of 87 early electrum coins found recently in the Artemision at Ephesus are of types usually assigned to Lydia is thus no argument against the usual attribution. Of the rest two are Phocaean, two possibly Phocaean, four possibly belong to Cyme, one perhaps to Ephesus, while five are quite uncertain. Head, *Brit. Mus. Excav. Ephesus*, pp. 79 f.

[7] F. Lenormant, *Monn. royal. de la Lydie*, p. 28, quotes two early electrum coins, one *obv.* striated, *rev.* three incuses, as found in the Plain of Sardis, the other, *obv.* four petals, *rev.* one incuse, as found at Nymphi, about 12 miles inland from

finds, even at Sardis, would not be decisive, since on Radet's theory the Lydian coinage was intended mainly for export, just as appears later to have been the case with the silver tetradrachms of Smyrna, Myrina, Cyme, Lebedos, Magnesia ad Maeandrum and Heraclea Ioniae, which are rarely found near their place of origin, but with few exceptions are brought from different parts of Syria[1].

More serious are the criticisms which do not altogether reject Xenophanes, but explain him away by means of an interpretation of Herodotus I. 94 first put forward by J. P. Six and later developed by Babelon[2]. Six maintained that when Herodotus there states that the Lydians were the first to strike and use coins of gold and silver, the reference is to the concurrent issue of coins in the two separate metals, or, in other words, to the coinage of Croesus (fig. 19. *b*), who is generally admitted to have been the first to give up electrum in favour of separate issues of gold and silver. But though it is true that "coins of gold and silver" cannot mean "coins of electrum," it by no means follows that Herodotus is referring to the beginnings not of coinage but of bimetallism. Babelon is right in insisting on the exact words used by Herodotus, but in his interpretation of them he takes perhaps too little account of the type of fact usually recorded by the historian. Which is Herodotus more likely to give us? An inaccurate version of a fundamental fact like the invention of coined money? Or a pedantically accurate statement about an experiment in bimetallism that was after all of quite secondary importance? Other things being equal we should surely always prefer the interpretation which gives us the former, and there is nothing to prevent us from doing so in the present case. Assume that Xenophanes means what he says and that his statement represents the prevalent tradition, and it is easy to see how Herodotus came to use the precise words that he did.

"The Lydians," he begins, "were the first to strike and use coins." We must remember who it was that he was writing for. His readers would be found mainly in the free cities of European Greece. Down to the days when he ended his history these European

Smyrna. An electrum third (67. 6 grains) *obv.* lion's head, *rev.* one incuse, *Brit. Mus. Coins, Lydia,* p. 2, no. 4, is said to have been found at Ala Shehr (Philadelphia), 30 miles S.E. of Sardis.

[1] Borrell, *Num. Chron.* VI. (1843), p. 156; cp. *Brit. Mus. Coins, Troas,* etc. p. lvii.

[2] *Num. Chron.* 1890, p. 210, n. 69; cp. Babelon, *Rev. Num.* 1895, pp. 354 f., *Origines,* pp. 215 f.

Greeks had coined almost exclusively in silver. On the other hand the coinage of Lydia and the other Persian satrapies of Asia Minor consisted of Darics of gold and shekels of silver, and people in those parts doubtless remembered that this coinage in the two metals went back to the days of the Lydian kings. It is a fundamental principle with our historian never to omit any fact that he can possibly insert. In this case an extra fact can be inserted in three words, χρυσοῦ καὶ ἀργύρου, and almost inevitably the words go in. Possibly he had forgotten for the moment the primitive pieces of electrum: it is equally possible that accuracy was sacrificed to fulness of information. Another way of meeting Babelon's difficulty is suggested by Babelon's own article. It is generally assumed that the first coins struck in Asia Minor were all of electrum, and that electrum later gave way to gold and silver. But Babelon[1] quotes an example of what is generally regarded as the earliest Lydian electrum type (*ob.* striated, *rev.* three small stamps as on silver spoons) that appears from its specific gravity to contain 98 per cent. silver and weighs 10·81 grammes. This latter is the unit of the so-called Babylonian standard, which is employed almost exclusively for silver, the only exception being a gold issue of Croesus. It is true that the coin has a yellow tint, and that it may contain more than 2 per cent. gold, if the light specific gravity is due partly to the presence of copper[2]. There are cases too of what seem to be unquestionable electrum coins with a very low percentage of gold, *e.g. Brit. Mus. Cat. Coins of Ionia*, p. 47, nos. 2, 3, Ephesian thirds of the normal Phoenician standard, one with only 14 per cent. gold to judge by the specific gravity, the other actually with only 5 per cent. But the combined evidence of weight and specific gravity gives strong support to Babelon's view that the coin must have been intended to pass as silver[3]. Babelon assigns this piece to Miletus, but on no sufficient grounds. As he himself points out[4], the weight is exactly that of

---

[1] *Rev. Num.* 1895, p. 303; *ib.* Pl. VI. 3.

[2] Head, *Brit. Mus. Coins, Ionia*, p. xviii.

[3] Head, *Hist. Num.*² p. 643, Ridgeway, *Metal. Curr.* p. 293, and others have stated that the 168 gr. standard was in regular use for early electrum, but their only evidence appears to be this one coin; cp. Head, *ib.* p. xl., who notes that no divisions of this standard are known in electrum. They are fully represented in Lydian gold and silver. Others, *e.g.* Radet, *Lydie*, p. 233, explain it as a three-quarter stater of the Phoenician standard normally employed for Lydian electrum, but a three-quarter stater is most unlikely. Nobody has suggested that the coin was meant to pass as gold. [4] *Rev. Num.* 1895, p. 303.

the silver coins of Croesus, a weight which in Ionia prevailed only at Colophon and Erythrae in the fifth century and at Miletus in the third[1], and in these three cases was borrowed from the Persian siglos (shekel), which latter was the direct successor of the silver coins of Croesus. The earliest silver coins assigned by Head to Miletus are struck on the Aeginetan standard (185 grains)[2]. In short, if it seems probable that this piece is silver, *a fortiori* is it probable that it is Lydian, and if, as the evidence all tends to show, this is the case, the importance of the piece at once becomes obvious. It means that from the earliest period of their coinage the Lydians struck not only in electrum but also in silver. Now for Herodotus electrum was only a variety of gold. His name for it is "white gold" (λευκὸς χρυσός), and he appears to regard it as gold of a particular quality, just as Bonacossi does the gold of China when he describes it as "pâle, mou et ductile[3]."

When therefore Herodotus speaks of the Lydians as the first to coin in gold and silver he may well mean white gold and silver and be referring, like Xenophanes, to the original "invention" of coined money. But even if Babelon is right, there is still no decisive reason why we should not ascribe to the Lydians the original "invention" as well as the first bimetallic development. Thus Xenophanes and Herodotus may be regarded as pointing to Lydia as the first country to strike coins, and after all they were in a fairly good position for ascertaining the facts[4]. Certainty is perhaps hardly attainable. But that does not justify a completely sceptical attitude. It is the reverse of scientific to treat an epoch illuminated by many half lights as though it was one of total darkness. The safest course in such a case is to operate with probabilities.

The claim of Lydia to have been the original home of tyranny is based on similar evidence that needs to be similarly used. The earliest authority for it is Euphorion (third century B.C.), who says that the first ruler to be called

The origin of the title tyrant.

---

[1] Head, *Brit. Mus. Coins of Ionia*, p. xxxviii.

[2] *Ibid.* p. 184, nos. 6–11. Babelon himself ascribes three small early silver pieces to Miletus (his nos. 18, 23, 39 = Pl. VI. 7, 10, 17). They weigh 1·26 grammes, 1·75 grammes, 1·10 grammes and are hardly helpful from the metrological point of view.

[3] *La Chine et les Chinois* (1847), p. 173; this, though he refers *ibid.* to ingots of silver mingled with gold dust, called "syce," of which the literal translation is "fine silk."

[4] See further, Radet, *Lydie*, pp. 155 f.; Macdonald, *Coin Types*, pp. 6–8.

tyrant was Gyges, who began to reign in the XVIIIth Olympiad (708–704 B.C.)[1]. The statement has been doubted as being perhaps only an inference from Homer and Archilochus drawn by later writers[2]. Homer does not use the word τύραννος. It first appears in Archilochus, and apparently the tyrant that Archilochus had in mind was his contemporary[3] Gyges:

> I care not for golden Gyges...
> I long not for a great tyranny[4].

But even if only an inference from this source the statement may still be of some value. The word tyrant is not Greek and may be Lydian[5]. A new title does not necessarily imply a new form of government; but if there is independent evidence for thinking that a new form of government arose just at this time, then that evidence will be corroborated by the appearance of a new title; and if that title has a particular local origin, it becomes of particular interest to examine the history of the rulers of the region where the change arose.

As our evidence leaves it uncertain whether Gyges was the first

[1] *F.H.G.* III. p. 72, fr. 1; so *Et. Mag.* and *Et. Gud.* s.v. τύραννος.
[2] Cp. Hippias of Elis, *F.H.G.* II. p. 62; Schol. Aesch. *P.V.* 224; Plut. *Vit. Hom.*, Didot v. p. 153.
[3] Hdt. I. 12.
[4] *Ap.* Aristot. *Rhet.* III. 17 and Plut. *De Tranqu. An.* 10 (*Mor.* 470c). The two lines quoted above were not consecutive. Plutarch quotes them thus:

οὔ μοι τὰ Γύγεω τοῦ πολυχρύσου μέλει
καὶ   οὐδ' εἱλέ πω με ζῆλος, οὐδ' ἀγαίομαι
θεῶν ἔργα, μεγάλης δ' οὐκ ἐρέω τυραννίδος.

But the καὶ appears to connect two extracts from a single passage. Aristotle, who quotes only οὔ μοι τὰ Γύγεω, states that the passage was put by Archilochus into the mouth of Charon the carpenter (τέκτων).
[5] Cp. *Et. Gud.* quoted above, defended by Radet, pp. 146–8. -αννος, so R. S. Conway writes to me, is neither Greek nor Latin, but occurs often in Etruscan (=Lydian?) and several times in Lycian: "tyrant" is derived from "Tyrrhenian" (=Etruscan) by Philochorus (*ap.* Schol. Lucian, *Catapl.* 1: τύραννος εἴρηται ἀπὸ τῶν Τυρρηνῶν...ὥς φησι Φιλόχορος. οἱ οὖν Ἀθήνησι ῥήτορες ἔθος ἔχουσι τοὺς βασιλέας τυράννους καλεῖν ἀντὶ τῆς παρ' αὐτοῖς βίας τῶν Τυρρηνῶν: the reference is to the Tyrrhenians of Lemnos and Imbros), Tzetzes, *Chil.* VIII. 890–1 (ἐκ τούτων καὶ τὸ τύραννος ὁμοίως ἐπεκλήθη· βίαιοι γὰρ οἱ Τυρρηνοὶ καὶ θηριώδεις ἄγαν), Verrius Flaccus (*ap.* Festum s.v. turannos, ed. Teubner, p. 484, a cuius gentis (sc. Tyrrhenicae) praecipua crudelitate etiam tyrannos dictos ait Verrius), and the *Et. Mag.* (ἤτοι ἀπὸ τῶν Τυρσηνῶν· ὠμοὶ γὰρ οὗτοι). On Vedic affinities of the word τύραννος see Peile, *ap.* Jebb, *Soph. O.T.* p. 5.

ruler of his kind to arise in Lydia or merely the first to find a prominent place in Greek literature and as further we find unusual steps for securing the throne attributed to Lydian rulers of about the middle of the eighth century it will be well to begin at this earlier date.

According to the story told by Nicolaus Damascenus[1], Damonno, the wife of Cadys, whose reign is ascribed to the middle of the eighth century[2], after her royal husband's death won over by her wealth a large number of Lydians, expelled her brother-in-law Ardys, and then married her lover Spermos and proclaimed him king. When banished by Spermos and Damonno, Ardys goes into business at Cyme as a waggon-builder (ἁμαξοπηγῶν) and is keeping a hotel (πανδοκεύων) there when called back to the throne of Sardis. He is brought back by a tavern-keeper or retail trader (κάπηλος) named Thyessos[3], who as his reward asked and received that this inn or shop (καπηλεῖον) should be exempt from paying dues (ἀτελές) and after a time became rich from his shop-keeping (καπηλεύειν) and as a result established near it a market and a shrine of Hermes[4]. The part played in this story by innkeepers may, at first sight, seem odd. But as pointed out by Radet[5] in discussing the word κάπηλος, innkeeper was probably synonymous with merchant in the days of Ardys (766-730 B.C.)[6], when Lydia was already becoming a great highway of commerce between Further Asia and the Aegean[7]. The Lydian merchants of the period must have seen the advantage of providing food and shelter for the members of the caravans with whom they traded. Waggon-building, which was one of the occupations of the banished Ardys[8],

<hr />

[1] *F.H.G.* III. p. 380.   [2] Radet, *Lydie*, p. 79.

[3] *F.H.G.* III. pp. 380-1; cp. Steph. Byz. s.v. Θυεσσός, "πόλις Λυδίας...ἀπὸ Θυεσσοῦ καπήλου."

[4] *F.H.G.* III. pp. 381-2. The scene of the story is doubtless Hermocapelia, put by Pliny, *N.H.* v. 33, in Pergamene territory, by Hierocles 670, Teub. p. 21, in the eparchy of Lydia. Schubert, *Könige v. Lydien*, p. 20, identifies Thyessos with Hermes himself.

[5] *Lydie*, p. 98.

[6] Radet, *Lydie*, p. 79; *Rev. des Univ. du Midi*, 1895, p. 117.

[7] Radet, pp. 95 f. and *Rev. des Univ. du Midi*, 1895, pp. 118-9 (foundation of Sinope by Milesians, 756 B.C., implies knowledge on part of Miletus of great eastern caravan routes).

[8] Heraclides, *F.H.G.* II. p. 216, fr. 11.

is part of the same activity, connected with the famous road that did as much to make the fortunes of ancient Lydia as railways will some day do to revive them in the future.

If the narrative of Nicolaus is to be believed, then, as recognized some time ago by Gelzer[1], the Lydian leaders of the period appear as great merchants and men of business, and more than that, it is as such that the rulers secure the throne, and a not unnatural inference is that it was the spread of this new type of merchant prince from Lydia Westward over the Greek world that caused the spread at the same time of the Lydian title. There is nothing improbable in the assumption that Lydian history of this period was preserved in a fairly authentic form. True our extant authorities are late and their sources uncertain, and the story of Spermos has perhaps an excessive resemblance to that of Gyges and the wife of his predecessor Candaules[2]. In both cases the usurper marries the wife of his predecessor and owes to her his throne. The close relations between Ardys and the Greek Cyme recall those between the house of Gyges and the tyrant house of Melas at Ephesus, which latter is very plausibly explained by Radet[3] as based on their common business interests. But these resemblances do not prove that the two narratives are not both true. The two queens may have responded in the same way to similar semi-matriarchal surroundings, and the two princes have found similar solutions for the same commercial problem. If the Damonno Ardys story is not history we have no Lydian history of that age. But even so it is of value as reflecting conditions that prevailed at the beginning of the seventh century and possibly went back to the period to which the story is ascribed.

Chronologically we ought next to deal with Gyges himself. Unfortunately his history, and more particularly the part that tells how he won the throne, has been much obscured by legend. We shall examine it with a better prospect of disinterring the facts if first we review certain later incidents of Lydian history.

[1] *Rhein. Mus.* xxxv. (1880), p. 520.

[2] Hdt. I. 7 f.; Plut. *Mor.* 622 f; Justin I. 7. In Nic. Dam. *F.H.G.* III. pp. 384–5 she does not aid Gyges.

[3] *Lydie*, p. 134; cp. Nic. Dam. *F.H.G.* III. pp. 396, 397, fr. 63, 65; Ael. *V.H.* III. 26. The Ephesian connexion is (*pace* Radet) only attested for the later rulers of Gyges' house. Cp. Gelzer, *Rhein. Mus.* xxxv. p. 521. Cp. too with the attempt to poison Cadys the attempt to poison Croesus, Plut. *de Pyth. Orac.* 16 (*Mor.* 401).

The century that followed Gyges is for this purpose not very
illuminating. A great part of it is taken up with the
national struggle against the Cimmerian invaders.
The kings of the house of Gyges appear to have led this struggle
well, and as a natural result their power was seldom called into
question. It is only before the accession of Croesus, the last king
of the line, that active steps appear to have been necessary to secure
the throne. The reason was not any anti-monarchic movement, but
rivalry between two sons or possibly grandsons of the old and perhaps
senile King Alyattes. None the less, the steps taken by the rivals
are not without significance. The story is told[1] that shortly before
Alyattes' death Croesus, the subsequently successful
rival, had borrowed largely from a very rich man[2]
in Ephesus in order to appear before the old king
with a levy. Before resorting to the rich Ephesian,
Croesus had appealed to a certain "Sadyattes the merchant, the
richest man in Lydia," who had refused to lend to him for the
reason, as it subsequently turned out, that he was backing the other
candidate for the throne, Croesus' half-brother, the half-Greek
Pantaleon[3]. Croesus' poverty, we are informed, was due to spend-
thrift habits. But it is doubtful whether his lavishness at this period
was simply youthful dissipation, and not rather part of a systematic
policy.

Later rulers of Lydia.

Financial dealings of Croesus before he became king.

Only a few years later Peisistratus of Athens "rooted his tyranny"
on revenues from mines. Reasons have been given above[4] for
thinking that he was already endeavouring to do so. May not
Croesus have been pursuing a similar course? Later in his career,
when he wanted to win the special favour of Delphi, "he sent to
Pythîo, ascertained the number of Delphians, and presented each
one of them with two staters of gold[5]." The staters of Croesus

---

[1] Nic. Dam. *F.H.G.* III. p. 397, fr. 65; cp. Ael. *V.H.* IV. 27; Hdt. I. 92. For a different version or phase of the struggle see Plut. *de Pyth. Orac.* 16 (*Mor.* 401).

[2] Babelon, *Origines*, p. 105, calls him a banker, on what authority I cannot discover: Nic. Dam. calls him simply εὖ μάλα εὐπόρου.

[3] Note that Sadyattes (*ap.* Suid. (s.v. Κροῖσος), Alyattes) bears a royal name, and that he is almost certainly the rival (ἀντιστασιώτης) of Croesus of Hdt. I. 92. A *var. lect.* in Nic. Dam. has ἔπαρχος (governor) instead of ἔμπορος (merchant). Sadyattes may therefore well have been a great noble: but that is no reason, *pace* Gelzer, *Rhein. Mus.* XXXV. 520, for not assigning the chief rôle to his wealth.

[4] Pp. 37 f.   [5] Hdt. I. 54.

(above fig. 19. *b*) were among the most famous coins of antiquity[1]. Reference is made in the *Mirabiles Auscultationes* to gold mines that he worked[2]. His wealth was proverbial[3]. Most of it he inherited from his predecessor[4]: but the wise old Alyattes knew that it was the root of his power and clung to it till his death. For the rivals it is a question who can secure it first and in the meanwhile carry on best without it. Both try to borrow on a princely scale, and to judge by the issue Croesus was the more successful. "As a result of that proceeding he got the upper hand of his calumniators[5]." He became king, and his government is described by Radet[6] as "une puissante monarchie régnant par la force de l'or."

This is all conjecture, but it is borne out alike by Croesus' own behaviour and by the advice to Cyrus that is put into his mouth after he has become the captive and the counsellor of the Persian king.

The first thing that Croesus did after securing the throne was to put Sadyattes to death and to confiscate his possessions[7]. By itself this might be taken simply as part of something corresponding to a normal process of attainder. But the Sadyattes incident must be read in the light of the advice that Croesus is represented as having subsequently given to Cyrus, the gist of which is that Cyrus is to beware above all things of the richest of his subjects[8]. The speech is of course pure fiction: so too is very possibly the whole story of the intimacy between Croesus and his conqueror[9]. But all the same Croesus is Herodotus' embodiment of the wise and experienced ruler of the sixth century, the century during which the historian's father was born only a little way from the borders of Croesus' kingdom. If in the pages of Herodotus he is made to regard wealth

Croesus bids Cyrus to suspect a rival in the richest of his subjects.

---

[1] Poll. III. 87, *Brit. Mus. Coins, Lydia*, p. xx.
[2] Aristot. (?) *Mirab. Ausc.* 52 (834 *a*).
[3] Strabo XIII. 626; Justin I. 7.
[4] Strabo, *ibid.*; Hdt. I. 92.   [5] Nic. Dam. *F.H.G.* III. fr. 65 end.
[6] *Lydie*, p. 242.
[7] The ἀνὴρ ἐχθρός of Hdt. I. 92 is almost certainly the Sadyattes of Nic. Dam. See Gelzer, *Rhein. Mus.* XXXV. 520; Schubert, *Könige v. Lydien*, p. 61.
[8] Hdt. I. 88–89; the story is repeated but with the point omitted, Diod. IX. 33.
[9] Cp. Bacchyl. III., the earliest reference to the fall of Lydia, written for Hiero of Syracuse in 468 B.C., where Croesus is made during the sack of Sardis to immolate himself and his family and to be saved by Zeus and carried off by Apollo to the land of the Hyperboreans.

CH. V   LYDIA   139

as the basis of political power, it must be because the historian believed such to have been in fact the case. Of the evidence that may have led him, and with good reason, to this belief, one item may have been derived from the colossal tomb of Croesus' predecessor Alyattes, which according to the account given by Herodotus

The tomb of Croesus' father had been erected by tradesmen, artizans, and "working girls."

was constructed by the tradesmen and artizans and prostitutes (οἱ ἀγοραῖοι ἄνθρωποι καὶ οἱ χειρώνακτες καὶ αἱ ἐνεργαζόμεναι παιδίσκαι)[1]. Presumably these were the classes who had most benefited or at least been most affected by Alyattes' rule, and on whose support he had mainly depended[2]. The largest part of the tomb is said by Herodotus to have been built by the "working girls" (= prostitutes) but too much attention need not be paid to this typical instance of Herodotean "malignity." Strabo's report that the tomb was said by some to be that of a harlot (πόρνης) is equally suspicious. It may possibly have arisen from the obscene symbols that appeared on various parts of the monument, including its summit. Possibly the builders of the tomb got mistaken for its occupant. The reverse process is less likely, as it leaves the tradesmen and artizans unaccounted for[3].

In conformity with the policy that Herodotus puts into the

Revolt from Cyrus of Pactyes who had all the gold from Sardis.

mouth of Croesus, Cyrus was careful before he returned from Lydia to Persia to separate the political and financial power in his new conquest:

Sardis he entrusted to Tabalos, a Persian gentleman, but the gold both of Croesus and the other Lydians he gave to Pactyes, a man of Lydia, to look after (κομίζειν)....But when Cyrus had marched away from Sardis, Pactyes caused the Lydians to revolt from Tabalos and Cyrus, and going down to the sea, as was but natural since he had all the gold

---

[1] Hdt. I. 93; cp. Hipponax, fr. 5 παρὰ τὸν Ἀττάλεω τύμβον κ.τ.λ. (an almost contemporary reference); Strabo XIII. 627. For excavations of this monument see *Abb. Preuss. Akad.* 1858, pp. 539 f. and Pls. IV. (tomb) and V. (pottery from the tomb). The pottery suits very well the period of the Mermnad dynasty.

[2] Radet, *Lydie*, p. 226, infers for the time of Croesus corporations of artizans (potters, boot-makers, dyers, etc.) such as existed in Lydia in the time of the Roman empire, but his suggestion is too speculative to build on.

[3] Strabo XIII. 627; cp. Athen. XIII. 573 a, "Clearchus in Book I. of his *Erotica* says Gyges, king of Lydia,...when (his mistress) died, gathered all the Lydians of the land and raised what is called the tomb of the hetaera." This looks like the version preserved by Strabo with details borrowed from Herodotus: note that the work is here ascribed to Gyges.

from Sardis, he proceeded to hire mercenaries and persuaded the population by the sea to join his expedition[1].

Xerxes and the rich Lydian Pythes. In the days of Xerxes the richest of all the Lydians was Pythes the son of Atys. After Xerxes himself, Pythes was the richest man known to the Persians of that day. His wealth amounted to 2000 talents of silver and 3,993,000 golden Darics[2]. He held some sort of rule under the Great King at Kelainai in Phrygia and owed his enormous wealth to his mines, in which the citizens of his dominions were forced to labour. When Xerxes reached Kelainai on his way to invade Greece, Pythes offered to present the whole of this immense sum to the king[3]. So stupendous a present requires a special explanation. It is not like "the gold plane tree and the vine" that Pythes had given earlier to King Darius. It looks as if he had suddenly discovered with intense alarm that Xerxes, like Cyrus before him, feared nothing so much as a man of extraordinary wealth, and as if this present was a desperate attempt to disarm the Great King's suspicions. The father of Pythes bore the same name as one of the sons of Croesus, and Pythes himself has been thought by some modern scholars to have been the grandson of Croesus[4]. The name Pytheus (Pythes) might be due to Croesus' relations with Delphi[5].

Radet suggests that the first coins were struck by the first tyrants, The evidence so far adduced has pointed to the following conclusions: metal coinage reached its final evolution in Lydia, probably in the second half of the eighth century B.C.; the title tyrant reached Greece from Lydia probably early in the seventh century; from the middle of the eighth century down to the end of the age of the tyrants all the rulers or would-be rulers of Lydia of whom we have any relevant information regarded money as the basis of political power. In the face of these facts it is not surprising that Radet, the scholar who has devoted most attention in recent years to this period of Lydian history, should have expressed the opinion that the earliest tyrants were also the first coiners[6].

---

[1] Hdt. I. 153–4.
[2] Hdt. VII. 27, 28.
[3] Hdt. VII. 27, 28; Plut. *de Mul. Virt.* 27 (*Mor.* 262); Polyaen. VIII. 42.
[4] Gelzer, *Rhein. Mus.* XXXV. p. 521.
[5] How and Wells, *Hdt.* VII. 27.
[6] *Lydie*, pp. 155 f., and particularly pp. 162–3.

The rest of this chapter will be devoted to examining and very tentatively developing this suggestion.

Radet attributed the earliest coins to Gyges and imagined them as having been struck when Gyges was already on the throne[1]. He wrote however before Enkomi, Knossos, and Ephesus had suggested the possibility of an earlier date for the earliest coins, and he does not consider the possibility that it may have been quite as much a case of the coins making the tyrant as the tyrant making the coins. No certainty is to be looked for on this point, but for arriving at the greatest available probability it will be well for a moment to turn to the brilliant and convincing account of the last stages in the evolution of metal coinage published by Lenormant and developed by Babelon. Lenormant's account of the circumstances in which stamped pieces of precious metal of definite weight first came into circulation cannot be given better than in his own words:

<small>Lenormant that they were private issues.</small> Pour la commodité du commerce, auquel ils servent d'instrument habituel d'échange, on donne à ces lingots des poids exacts...de $\frac{1}{2}$ à 10 taels en or, de $\frac{1}{2}$ à 100 taels en argent. Mais leur circulation et leur acceptation n'ont aucun caractère légal et obligatoire. L'autorité publique n'a point à y intervenir et ne leur donne aucune garantie. Ces lingots ne portent aucune empreinte si ce n'est en certains cas un poinçonnement individuel, simple marque d'origine et de fabrique, qui quelquefois inspire assez de confiance pour dispenser de la vérification du titre du métal, lorsque c'est celle d'un négociant assez honorablement connu. La facilité avec laquelle on accepte le lingot à tel ou tel poinçon tient donc entièrement au crédit personnel de celui qui l'a marqué[2].

The passage just quoted describes not a theory of Lenormant's but the actual practice of the Chinese empire[3]. A similar currency of ingots stamped by merchants or bankers has been used in many

---

[1] Early in his reign before the Cimmerian invasions (on which see Gelzer, *Rhein. Mus.* xxx. pp. 256 f.), *Lydie*, p. 166. So Cruchon, *Banques dans l'Antiq.* pp. 15-16.

[2] *Monn. dans l'Antiq.* I. p. 110; cp. Babelon, *Origines*, pp. 39-40.

[3] Cp. Babelon, *Origines*, p. 94, quoting Terrien de la Couperie, *Brit. Mus. Cat. Chinese Coins*, p. 4, on period before fourth century A.D. So also *ibid.* (*Cat. Chinese Coins*), p. xlviii. 5. Bonacossi, *La Chine et les Chinois* (1847), pp. 172-3, says there is no government mint: the precious metals are formed into ingots by private bankers: these ingots bear the name of districts, bankers, etc. To the present day Chinese bankers stamp foreign coins with their own countermarks, Babelon, *Origines*, pp. 121-2.

other parts of the world, *e.g.* Japan[1], Java[2], India[3] and Russia[4]. Reversions to the practice of private coinage have been frequent in America[5]; "for a long time the copper currency of England consisted mainly of tradesmen's tokens," used largely by manufacturers to pay the wages of their workpeople[6]. The earliest coins of Asia Minor are regarded by the French savants as private issues of a similar kind to those just quoted. The small stamps of which several often appear on an early electrum coin (*e.g.* above fig. 19. *a* right) are regarded by them as marks or countermarks of bankers or merchants. Babelon[7] points out that these stamps cannot be identified as the types of towns or kings; that in one case no less than six of them are found on a single coin[8]; and that they continue to be put on to the state coinage of Darius. The case for Lydia therefore rests largely on analogies, and analogies can never be quite conclusive. Some even of these must be used with caution, *e.g.* those from Russia and Merovingian France, where it is difficult to be sure that they do not represent a stage of decadence rather than development. But decadence is often another name for reversion to type, and some of the instances already quoted, *e.g.* those from China and India, are sufficiently remote to be safely trusted. The total effect of the evidence marshalled by Lenormant and Babelon is impressive, and certainly no other view offers so satisfactory an explanation of the distinguishing features of the earliest

---

[1] Babelon, *Origines*, pp. 41, 42.

[2] Babelon, *Origines*, p. 98.

[3] E. Thomas, *Chron. Pathan Kings Delhi*, p. 344 (cp. E. Thomas, *Anc. Indian Weights*, p. 57, n. 4), goldsmiths and merchants struck coins in fourteenth century A.D.; J. Malcolm, *Mem. Central India*, II. 80, similar issues still in 1832 but with permit from central government; cp. Babelon, *Origines*, p. 95.

[4] Babelon, *Origines*, p. 83, at Kieff and Novgorod in the Middle Ages ingots weighing rouble or multiple stamped, sometimes with name, by merchants, bankers or goldsmiths. This practice arose before the Russian government first struck coins. On Greek and Roman stamped ingots see Saglio, *Dict. d. Antiq.* s.v. Metalla, p. 1865; all appear to be centuries later than the invention of money, on which accordingly they throw no light.

[5] Babelon, *Origines*, p. 100; *e.g.* Chalmers' shillings struck by a goldsmith named Chalmers in 1783, numerous private issues in California, 1831–1851, with the legend "native gold" or "pure gold" and the name and sometimes address of the striker.

[6] Jevons, *Money*^{23}, p. 65.

[7] *Origines*, pp. 110 f.

[8] *Ibid.* p. 123.

Greek coins. Their view has already won partial acceptance[1]. There are of course gaps in the evidence, notably as to the circumstances of the nationalization of the coinage. But this is not very surprising if, as the stories of Damonno and Ardys suggest, it was in a succession of financial struggles for the throne that the control of the mint came gradually to be synonymous with the kingship. When the two were finally equated is a matter of conjecture. The chief part in the process may perhaps have been played by the tradesman king Ardys, but on the whole it seems likely that it was Gyges who completed the evolution of metal coinage by making it the prerogative of the state after he had first used it to obtain the supreme power. His career falls early enough to make this possible[2], and the gold of Gyges attained proverbial fame[3].

Gyges.

Herodotus indeed seems to discountenance the view that Gyges was ever a merchant or banker, since he describes him as serving as a guardsman (αἰχμοφόρος, δορυφόρος) under his predecessor

[1] Head, *Hist. Num.*² pp. lvii. and 644–5, dates private issues 687–610; P. Gardner, *Gold Coinage of Asia*, p. 9, attributes the first state coinage anywhere to Croesus, against which view see the whole of the present chapter. Gardner's own objection to his own theory, based on the ΦαλΦει coins, is not cogent. Alyattes might, of course, have struck coins as a private venture. The late King George of Greece traded largely in wine grown on the royal estates, but the wine was in no sense a state beverage; cp. also Cruchon, *Banques dans l'Antiq.* pp. 11 f. For Babelon himself see further *Rev. Num.* 1895, pp. 332–3, on the early electrum coin, obv. stag, φανος ἐμι σεμα; rev. one oblong incuse between two square, which Babelon ascribes to Ephesus and suggests was issued by "one of those rich bankers who lent to kings and whose safes were filled with precious metals"; see Hdt. VII. 27–29; but cp. Macdonald, *Coin Types*, p. 51. Against Babelon's view has been urged the fact that his supposed collections of private marks on such coins as our fig. 19. *a* (p. 127) form in each case a single group all stamped together. But such a stereotyped grouping on the earliest extant specimens is no argument against his explanation of the origin of these curious marks, which on other very early coins occur in positions which show them to be counter-stamps: see e.g. that on the back of the tortoise of our fig. 20. *b*.

[2] His accession is variously dated 716 B.C. (Hdt.), 708 (Euphorion), 698 (African.), 687 (Euseb. Arm. vers.); he was still alive after 660 B.C. and perhaps after 650 (Geo. Smith, *Assurbanipal*, pp. 64–68; cp. *ibid.* pp. 341–2, Winckler, *Altorient. Forsch.* VI. pp. 474 f., 494 f.).

[3] The Γυγάδας χρυσός of Poll. III. 87 and VII. 98 was not, *pace* Radet, *Lydie*, p. 162; *Rev. d. Univ. du Midi*, 1895, p. 119, necessarily or even probably coined, but the history of Croesus shows that a king who unquestionably coined might yet be famous for his uncoined gold. Archilochus calls Gyges "the golden."

Candaules[1]. But Schubert[2] is probably right in putting only a limited confidence in this part of our account of his career, which he shows to have been derived from Delphi. He even suggests[3] that Gyges had bought up Delphi before, with a view to his accession, just as Croesus endeavoured to purchase the favour of Apollo before his attempted conquest of Persia[4]. If there is any truth in this plausible suggestion, then the guardsman part of the story may well have been a half-truth emphasized to hide Gyges' commercial antecedents, and Gyges may have secured the throne mainly through his wealth.

It is true that Gyges as tyrant fought against the Cimmerians who at this time were sweeping over Asia Minor, and that later in his reign he rebelled against Assyria[5]. From time to time he invaded the Greek cities on the coast. He may even have taken military measures to secure the throne, if, as Radet argues[6], his accession meant the overthrow of a Maeonian domination and the substitution for it of a Lydian. All this however is no proof of particular militarism. The wars against the Cimmerians were defensive. The revolt from Assyria was an indirect result of the Cimmerian wars.

---

[1] Hdt. I. 8, 91; cp. Xanthus, *ap.* Nic. Dam. *F.H.G.* III. fr. 49, p. 383 ἐκέλευσε (τὸν Γύγην) μετὰ τῶν δορυφόρων εἶναι.

[2] *Könige von Lydien*, p. 30.

[3] *Ibid.* p. 34; cp. Athen. VI. 231 *e*, "The Delphian dedications of silver and gold were started by Gyges the king of the Lydians (ὑπὸ πρώτου Γύγου...ἀνετέθη): before his reign the Pythia had neither silver nor gold, as is stated by Phanias the Ephesian and Theopompus," and Hdt. I. 13, 14, "he won the throne and was confirmed on it by the Delphic oracle"..."In this way the Mermnadae won the tyranny...and Gyges, having become tyrant, sent offerings to Delphi not a few, but most of the silver offerings at Delphi are his, and besides the silver he offered vast sums of gold."

[4] "He is dedicating golden bricks to the Pythian as payment for his oracles," Lucian, *Charon*, 11; Hdt. I. 50 f.; "we may suppose that the liberality of Croesus was intended to secure the Lacedaemonian alliance through Delphic influence," How and Wells, *Hdt.* I. 53 (doubtless in view of Xen. *Cyr.* VI. 2. 11 (news is brought to Cyrus) "that Croesus had sent to Sparta about an alliance"); μέγιστα θνατῶν ἐς ἀγαθέαν ἀνέπεμψε Πυθώ (Κροῖσος), Bacchyl. III. 61–62.

[5] Smith, *Assurbanipal*, pp. 64–68.

[6] *Lydie*, pp. 57 f.; cp. Plut. *Qu. Gr.* 45 (*Moral.* 302), "when Gyges revolted and made war on him (Candaules)": cp. also Hdt. I. 13, "when the Lydians much resented the way Candaules was treated and took up arms." But Herodotus goes on to say that the two factions came to an understanding to refer the dispute to Delphi.

If Gyges took the aggressive against the Greeks[1], his motive was probably commercial. He wanted "to secure for the Lydian caravans a free and sure outlet for their goods[2]." These Greek wars were seldom carried to extremes[3]. As regards the fighting by which he is said to have seized the throne note that his troops, in part at least, were Carian mercenaries[4].

Immediately after establishing himself by these violent means Gyges "sent for his various friends and enemies. Those whom he thought would oppose him he did away with; but to the rest he gave presents and made them mercenaries[5]."

A confirmation of this same view as to the origin of Gyges' power is possibly to be found in the story of Gyges and his ring. In this famous story, as told by Plato[6], Gyges was a shepherd who discovered in the earth a magic gold ring, which gave him the power of invisibility and enabled him to enter the palace, slay the king, and procure his own accession. As happens so often when a story of the order of the *Arabian Nights* is applied to a historical personage, the immediate problem is to discover not the origin of the story, but the points about the historical character that caused the story in question to get attached to him.

The ring of Gyges

---

[1] Hdt. I. 14; *F.H.G.* III. Nic. Dam. fr. 62; IV. p. 401, fr. 6; Paus. IV. 21, 5; IX. 29, 4; Suid. s.v. Γύγης and Μάγνης.

[2] Radet, *Lydie*, p. 214; cp. *ib.* 243 on the commercial necessities that drove Croesus to make war on Cyrus when the Persians, "who are accustomed to make no use of markets and have no market at all" (Hdt. I. 153), threatened the great trade routes of the East.

[3] Radet, *Lydie*, p. 171; cp. Hdt. I. 17, on the way Sadyattes and Alyattes warred against Miletus, and also Ael. *V.H.* III. 26; Polyaen. VI. 50 on Croesus' war with Ephesus.

[4] Plut. *Qu. Gr.* 45 (*Moral.* 302a): ἦλθεν Ἀρσηλις ἐκ Μυλέων ἐπίκουρος τῷ Γύγῃ μετὰ δυνάμεως, καὶ τὸν Κανδαύλην...διαφθείρει. This notice is "historisch wertlos," Meyer, *G. d. A.* I. p. 547, following Duncker, *G. d. A.*[5] I. p. 488, but cp. Gelzer, *Rhein. Mus.* XXXV. p. 528; Schubert, *Könige v. Lydien*, p. 33; Radet, *Lydie*, pp. 124 f., 133 f., 136, n. 2. It is more than a coincidence that Carian mercenaries become famous just at this time: cp. Archilochus. In Lydia, as in Egypt (pp. 89, 123), mercenaries, in great part Greek, play an important part throughout the period of the tyrant dynasty. Croesus raised a force of mercenaries before he became king, Nic. Dam. fr. 65, *F.H.G.* III. p. 397; mercenaries fought for Croesus against Cyrus, Hdt. I. 77; cp. Radet, *Lydie*, p. 261.

[5] Nic. Dam. fr. 49; *F.H.G.* III. p. 385.

[6] *Rep.* II. 359d; cp. Cic. *de Off.* III. 9 (38); Suid. s.v. Γύγου δακτύλιος.

We may begin by dismissing the shepherding, since Gyges belonged to an ancient and princely family[1].

The fact or facts that caused Gyges to be associated with the story probably had some connexion with the magic ring and its discovery in the earth. It has for instance been suggested that the real magic of the ring of Gyges lay in the signet that serves as a passport and reveals or conceals a man's identity according to the way he wears it. Radet[2] pictures Gyges as a sort of major domo to Candaules, and the ring as the emblem of his power. Explanations of this kind are not without plausibility; they are right in taking notice of the signet[3]; but they ignore one essential detail of the story namely the marvellous discovery of the ring, nor do they go to the root of the matter, if, as the story plainly implies, the ring of Gyges is to be equated with the real source of his power. From this last point of view it becomes probable that Radet has come very much nearer the truth in another passage, where he says: "Gygès et ses successeurs ont possédé un merveilleux talisman: la science économique[4]." There is a point about the ring story that tells strongly in favour of some explanation on the lines of this second suggestion of Radet's. The hero of the story is not always Gyges: in Pliny[5] it is Midas the king of Phrygia who was overthrown by the Cimmerians a generation before they overthrew Gyges[6]. It is of course possible that Pliny is merely making a mistake about the name. But it is equally possible that a genuine tradition attributed the ring to Midas. Midas has much else in common with Gyges and the points of resemblance deserve to be noticed. His kingdom, like that of Gyges, was famous for its precious metals[7]. Like Lydia it occupied an

explained by Radet as "la science économique."

---

[1] Nic. Dam. *F.H.G.* III. p. 382; cp. Gelzer, *Rhein. Mus.* XXXV. pp. 515 f.; Radet, pp. 80 f.; cp. also Hdt. I. 8.

[2] *Lydie*, pp. 89, 120.   [3] Cp. below, pp. 149 f.

[4] *Lydie*, p. 224. For Gyges' invisibility Radet, p. 153, compared that of Deiokes the Mede who, when he became king, withdrew himself from the sight of his subjects, ὁρᾶσθαι βασιλέα ὑπὸ μηδενός, Hdt. I. 99.

[5] *N.H.* XXXIII. 4.

[6] Gelzer, *Rhein. Mus.* XXX. pp. 256 f. According to Eusebius Midas became ς in B.C. 738.

and Hammer, *Zeits. f. Num.* XXVI. 4; Midas himself worked the mines of much ... rmion, Strabo XIV. 680. The fame of the Phrygians as metal workers ... goes ... k to mythical times, see Schol. Ap. Rhod. I. 1129, with which cp. Diod. dispute to ... n. Alex. *Strom.* I. p. 360 (132 edit Sylburg.).

important part of the great caravan route¹. Midas was the golden king still more than Gyges. His touch turned all things into gold until he was freed from this disastrous power by bathing in the Pactolus, the river from which the Lydians got so much of their electrum². According to one account coins were first struck by "Demodike of Cyme, daughter of Agamemnon king of the Cymaeans, after her marriage with Midas the Phrygian³." Midas, like Gyges, sent rich presents (bribes?) to Delphi⁴. In short the great point of resemblance which Midas bears to Gyges lies in his enormous wealth and the ways in which he appears to have acquired and used it⁵. It may be that this implied the possession of the magic ring⁶.

With the story of the finding of the ring cp. stories of finds in mining districts.

The circumstances of the find recall two anecdotes in the *Mirabiles Auscultationes*⁷, located the one in Paionia the other in Pieria, in which, as in the Gyges story, we have the rains, the chasms, the find of gold and the taking of it to the palace. In at least one of the two cases the find is treasure trove, like the ring of Gyges. But the point to be noticed is that both Paionia and Pieria are in the famous mining district that played so great a part in the history of Athens and Macedonia. Considering the fame of the

---

¹ Note that Kelainai (the home of the rich Pythes, above, p. 140), which lies in East Phrygia near the source of the Maeander, occupied "a central point from which trade routes radiated in every direction. It became a commercial junction where goods arriving by caravan routes from the East were packed in chests to be forwarded to various sea ports." These words (Head, *Hist. Num.*² p. 666) refer to Apamea, which, from its occupation, was nicknamed Kibotos (Box), but Apamea was only a revised version of Kelainai, which lay on the heights above it and was supplanted by the lower city in the time of Antiochus I.

² Ovid, *Met.* XI. 100 f.; Hyginus, fab. 191.

³ Poll. IX. 83; so Heraclides, *F.H.G.* II. p. 216; Radet, p. 160, acutely argues from the association here of Cyme and Phrygia that this account associates the invention of money with the great caravan route, of which Cyme was the main terminus before the rise of the Lydian Mermnadae, about which time it was replaced by Ephesus, the Greek city with which the Lydians maintained the most friendly terms; cp. Ramsay, *J.H.S.* IX. (1888), pp. 350 f., followed by S. Reinach, *Chroniques d'Orient*, I. p. 574, Radet, *Lydie*, p. 172.

⁴ Hdt. I. 14.

⁵ Polyaen. VII. 5 makes Midas secure his throne (Μίδαν τύραννον ἀνηγόρευσαν) "by pretending to celebrate by night rites in honour of the great gods."

⁶ On Midas and the ring see also K. F. Smith, *Amer. Journ. Phil.* XXIII. p. 273.

⁷ Aristot. (?) *Mirab. Ausc.* 45, 47 (833 b).

mines of Lydia it is natural to ask whether they did not play their part in the evolution of the story of the ring. Stories of men buried in the mines of Lydia did actually exist. One of them, told in the *Mirabiles Auscultationes*, shows that in Lydia, as in the region of Mt Pangaion and the river Strymon, chasms containing skeletons and gold were not unlikely to be mine shafts, and the power secured by their discoverer to be simply the power of suddenly and perhaps secretly acquired wealth.

As to the date at which Tmolus was first mined nothing is known except that the workings were disused in the days of Strabo[1]. It may well have been worked from the earliest days of Gyges if, as is probable, he mined at Pergamus and further afield[2]. Lydians mining in those regions would hardly be neglecting mines so near their own capital, the more so as they would be directed to them by following the golden stream of the Pactolus[3].

In the face of these facts it is tempting to go one step further than Radet when he explains Gyges' talisman as economic science. We are reminded of Byron's description of the most potent of talismans:

> Yes, ready money is Aladdin's lamp[4].

Gyges, it is true, discovered a ring, not a lamp, but the particular form of his talisman only adds point to the Byronic interpretation.

Rings as money. Till somewhere about the time of the story rings were probably ready money in the literal sense of the phrase[5]. In many parts of the world before the introduction of a regular stamped coinage trade had been conducted largely by means of rings of specific weight[6].

---

[1] Strabo XIII. 591, XIV. 680. See also Radet, *Lydie*, p. 44, on Eurip. *Bacch.* 13.

[2] Strabo XIII. 590–1, XIV. 680; cp. Xen. *Hell.* IV. viii. 37.

[3] It is not known when the river was first exploited, but an early date may be safely assumed. The gold washings of the Phasis are said to have been the objective of the Argonauts (Strabo XI. 499; cp. Hammer, *Zeits. f. Num.* XXVI. p. 4). In Egypt "gold of the water," *i.e.* river gold, is recorded about 1200 B.C. (Lepsius, *Abb. Berl. Akad.* 1871, p. 35). The Pactolus washings went back at least some generations beyond Croesus (Strabo XIII. 626; cp. Dio Chrys. *Orat.* 78, Teubner, p. 280).

[4] *Don Juan*, XII. xii. For Gyges and Aladdin see K. F. Smith, *Amer. Journ. Phil.* XXIII. p. 271.

[5] E. Meyer, *Ges. d. Alt.* I. p. 580; cp. Regling *ap.* Pauly Wissowa s.v. Geld, p. 972.

[6] Ridgeway, *Orig. Metallic Currency*, pp. 35 f., 44, 82, 128, 242, 399 f.; Babelon, *Origines*, chap. II. The rings appear not to have always a fixed weight,

Much of the evidence for this use takes us back well into the second millennium. Some of the localities where it is known to have prevailed earliest were connected with Lydia at this time. Egypt was the ally of Gyges, the Hittites were the predecessors of the Lydians in the land of Lydia. Troy probably formed part of Gyges' dominions[1]. The book of Genesis specifically associates ring money with caravans[2]. It is therefore probable that rings circulated in Lydia itself until they were supplanted by the new stamped coins, which may have owed their shape to its convenience for stamping.

With Gyges' ring cp. perhaps Pheidon's spits, the Attic obol and drachma, and the Roman as.

In Argos, according to a tradition which is defended in the next chapter, the stamped coinage was preceded by a currency of metal spits (below, fig. 21): if the tradition is to be trusted, these spits remained permanently associated with the name of the tyrant who displaced them by coined money. Have we a parallel in the case of the Gyges story? Is its hero the inventor of the new stamped coinage and has his name become associated with the rings that he displaced? It is perfectly possible that the new coins were at first regarded as so many rings' worth of precious metal. The name νόμισμα implies that the stamped coin had won general acceptance; it would of course be quite appropriate to a currency in rings or kettles or cows; but there is no evidence of its use previous to the introduction of a stamped metal coinage, and it was probably the general acceptance of this latter that gave rise to the word. To call the earliest Lydian coins rings (δακτύλιοι) would be precisely like calling the earliest coins of Athens spits (ὀβελοί) or bundles of spits (δραχμαί) or the earliest coins of Rome bars (asses). If obol and drachma and as survived while δακτύλιος did not, the fact is sufficiently accounted for by the histories of Athens, Rome, and Lydia.

The explanation just offered of the ring of Gyges omits one detail that is essential to the story as told by Plato. *But if so, why is the ring a seal ring?* Plato's ring is a signet ring, and it is the seal (σφραγίς) that does the magic. Babelon holds that the seal makers (δακτυλιογλύφοι) of the period were probably also the coin strikers. But if we are to follow one of our own leading numis-

but the ring, especially if not closed, is a very convenient form for weighing, v. Bergmann, *Num. Zeits.* 1872, pp. 172–4.

[1] Strabo XIII. 590, see above, p. 148.
[2] Genesis XXIV. 22; cp. Job XLII. 11.

matists, G. Macdonald, the connexion between seal and coin was closer than this. Originally, according to him[1], coins were simply pieces of sealed metal.

"Coins are pieces of sealed metal." The minting of money in its most primitive form was simply the placing of a seal on lumps of electrum that had previously been weighed and adjusted to a fixed standard: the excessive rarity of coins that have only a striated surface on the obverse proves that this primitive stage was of short duration[2].

Greek seals were normally attached to rings[3]. The definition of a coin as a piece of sealed metal was started by Burgon, who used it as an argument for the religious character of coin types and described the seal as "the impress of the symbol of the tutelar divinity of the city[4]." Macdonald very rightly rejects the theory, so widely current before the appearance of Ridgeway's *Metallic Currency*, that all coin types had a religious origin. But he himself proceeds to hang on to the seal theory views of his own that are equally untenable, at least in the sweeping form in which he states them. He assumes that the seal must be always that of a state or king or magistrate, and that the device is usually heraldic. The latter point does not concern us here[5]: the former does, since it is incompatible with the views of Babelon and Lenormant that the earliest coins were not state issues. But the seal theory does not depend on the nature either of the seals or of the sealers. There is no reason why we should not accept Babelon and Lenormant on the private character of the earliest coins simultaneously with Burgon and Macdonald on the character of the first coin types as being simply seals. Indeed some of the evidence collected by Macdonald positively suggests that we should. In the fifth and fourth centuries B.C. at Athens public property was stamped with the public seal, τῷ δημοσίῳ σημάντρῳ[6]. The same practice was followed in the fifth century

---

[1] Macdonald, *Coin Types*, p. 52; cp. Brandis, *Zeits. f. Num.* I. p. 55.

[2] Macdonald, *Coin Types*, p. 46.

[3] Cp. Diog. Laert. I. 2. 9 (from a law of Solon's), δακτυλιογλύφῳ μὴ ἐξεῖναι σφραγῖδα φυλάττειν τοῦ πραθέντος δακτυλίου.

[4] See Macdonald, *Coin Types*, p. 45.

[5] I incline to the view that the types are in part heraldic (*e.g.* the lion), but I see nothing in Macdonald's arguments to invalidate Ridgeway's illuminating explanation of many early coin types as indicating the previous unit of exchange (*e.g.* tunny fish or tortoise shell; cp. Ridgeway, *Cambridge Companion to Greek Studies*, § 503).

[6] Xen. *de Vect.* IV. 21, referring to public slaves; Ael. *V.H.* II. 9 (Samian prisoners branded with an owl).

at Samos[1], and perhaps at Syracuse[2]. This use of public seals to stamp public property suggests corresponding private seals similarly used. At this point the literary evidence fails us, but archaeological documents come to our aid.

Metal was not the only material that the ancients stamped in this way. Wine jars, bricks, and tiles were similarly stamped. Thousands of these stamps have come down to us, and many of them bear city symbols and a magistrate's name. But they often bear also the name of the maker, and the Danish scholar Nilsson[3], who has made a thorough study of them, is inclined to regard them as essentially the seals of private manufacturers. The magistrate's name may merely indicate the date: the state symbol may mean that the state was the consignee, or that the manufacturer enjoyed some sort of state protection, or was subjected to state taxation and control.

If then such was the history of the stamp as applied to bricks and wine jars, we have a further reason for thinking that stamps as applied to the precious metals may have originally been put on them by private owners. May we not here have the true explanation of the marvellous seal of Gyges' ring? May not the owner of this ring have been the first person to use his signet for stamping coins of metal, and may not this fact be the origin of the stories about its marvellous powers?

Whether this person was Gyges is another question. His claim to the ring is not beyond dispute. We have seen already that it is sometimes attributed to Midas. Even in the story as told by Plato the MSS. make the hero "the ancestor of Gyges," not Gyges himself, and the fact that in other writers and elsewhere in the *Republic*[4] the ring is called the ring of Gyges is not in itself decisive. Both the ring and its magic powers may have passed from hand to hand. But if the evidence and opinions that have been adduced in this chapter have any value, our interpretation of the ring story does not depend on establishing Gyges as the original owner.

Let us now revert for a moment to the illuminating theory of

[1] Photius, *F.H.G.* II. p. 483.

[2] Plut. *Nikias*, 29, the captive Athenians in 413 were branded on the forehead with a horse, but after being branded they were sold as domestic slaves (οἰκέται), which makes it possible that the branding was an act of simple revenge.

[3] *Timbres Amphoriques de Lindos*, Copenhagen, 1909.

[4] Cic. *de Off.* III. 38; Lucian, *Nav.* 42, *Bis Acc.* 21; Philostratus, *Vit. Apoll.* III. 8; Plato, *Rep.* 612 b. The version which makes the hero an ancestor of Gyges is found in Proclus, *Comm. in Remp.* 614 b (Teubner, II. p. 111).

Babelon that the striking of coins was at first a private undertaking of merchants or miners or bankers, and that the final step in the evolution of a gold and silver coinage was reached only when this business of stamping and issuing the pieces was taken over by the state. We are entirely without record of the actual transference that the theory implies. Babelon assumes that the government created the monopoly. This chapter suggests a modification of Babelon's view in one important point, namely that it was not the government that made the monopoly, but the monopoly that made the government. As in the case of Babelon's own main thesis, we are forced to trust largely to analogies. But the analogies are striking, and they strike in two directions. We have first the commercial or financial antecedents of the rulers of this period both in Lydia and in various Greek states: and secondly we have the history of later Lydian rulers and aspirants to the throne, notably Croesus and Sadyattes, Cyrus and Pactyes, Xerxes and Pythes. The moral of their stories is that no ruler could feel safe at Sardis until he had secured some sort of financial supremacy. When we further consider that Gyges was famous for his gold[1], and that his gold and his tyranny are spoken of by Archilochus, probably in the same breath, then apart from speculative interpretations of the story of the ring, there is at least a clear possibility that the monopolist policy of Croesus and his successors goes back at least to Gyges and perhaps even a generation or so earlier, to some such ruler as Ardys or Spermos, and that it was the monopoly in stamped pieces of electrum that brought the first tyrant to the king's palace and placed him on the throne[2].

[1] Pollux III. 87, VII. 98.

[2] Babelon, in his account of the origin of money, rightly points out (*Origines*, p. 167) that "in general the prince has at his disposal a greater quantity of precious metal than any banker or merchant." This fact does not however affect our argument. As Babelon himself goes on to observe, the princes of this period, like modern monarchs in the East, "had in reserve in their treasuries enormous quantities of gold and silver ingots." He cites Midas, Alyattes, Croesus and Darius as coining according to their various requirements from this reserve. But there is a point that Babelon does not touch. What started these monarchs coining? If, as Babelon assumes, it was simply the fact that the previous private coiners supplied bad coins, the position of coins is on a par with that of any other commodity. We might expect to hear of kings who became butchers and bakers to ensure their subjects good bread and good meat. It is therefore more than doubtful whether the initiative is likely to have come generally from the ruling sovereign. To imagine again a popular clamour for state control, as is done by Babelon, *ibid.* pp. 168–9, is probably

an anachronism. The platform would be too constructive and original for a popular agitation. As a general rule constructive movements begin or at least take shape with outstanding individuals. Parallels from later periods, such as quoted by Babelon, p. 171, are dangerous. A populace can of course clamour for the restoration of lost rights and advantages, that of a state coinage among the rest. In the days that we are considering no precedents could be quoted for a state currency. On the other hand, the situation as conceived either by Babelon or myself implies outstanding individuals in the mercantile class. It is surely among these that it is most natural to look for the beginnings alike of a state coinage and of the new statesmanship that sprang up with it. This need not, of course, imply that occasionally a monarch of the old regime did not grasp the situation and himself institute a state coinage. Pheidon of Argos is a case in point.

Chapter VI. *Argos*

τὰν ἀρετὰν καὶ τὰν σοφίαν νικῶντι χελῶναι.

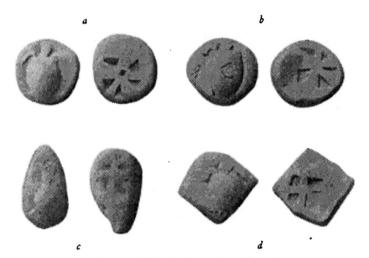

Fig. 20. Early Aeginetan "tortoises."

"Tyranny" of Pheidon the legitimate sovereign "who created for the Peloponnesians their measures" (Herodotus),

Our earliest account of the one tyrant of Argos is found in Herodotus and runs as follows: "and from the Peloponnesus came Leokedes the son of Pheidon the tyrant of the Argives, that Pheidon who created for the Peloponnesians their measures and behaved quite the most outrageously of all the Greeks, who having removed the Eleian directors of the games himself directed the games at Olympia[1]." Pheidon belonged to the royal house of Temenos[2], and appears to have succeeded to a hereditary throne in the ordinary way. Nevertheless he is deliberately classed by Aristotle as a typical tyrant[3].

Some years ago I suggested that it was Pheidon's "invention" of measures rather than his outrageous behaviour or his warlike achieve-

---

[1] Hdt. VI. 127. [2] See below, pp. 156–158.
[3] Aristot. *Pol.* VII. (V.), 1310b.

CH. VI ARGOS 155

ments that caused him to be regarded as a different kind of ruler from his forefathers—as a tyrant instead of a king[1].

Herodotus speaks of him simply as the man who made their measures for the Peloponnesians. But Ephorus and later writers declare that Pheidon invented a system of weights as well as measures, and, most important of all, that silver was first coined by him in Aegina[2]. The reign of Pheidon probably covered the first third of the seventh century. Thus in Greece Proper as in Asia Minor there is evidence for ascribing the earliest coins to the earliest tyrant. If there is any weight in the Argive evidence, then the accounts mutually confirm one another, and it becomes distinctly improbable that the association of coinage and tyranny was a mere accident.

and also, according to Ephorus, struck in Aegina the first silver coins.

Pheidon the European counterpart of Gyges.

Unfortunately the evidence as regards Pheidon is all very much disputed. The greater part of this chapter will therefore be devoted to examining its credibility and endeavouring to show that the doubts that have been cast upon it are not well founded, that on the most probable showing the reign of Pheidon opened the epoch known as the age of the tyrants, that Pheidon lived just about the time when the first coins were struck in Aegina,

The evidence for Pheidon is disputed. This chapter is devoted to maintaining its credibility.

---

[1] *J.H.S.* xxvi. p. 140. Note that in later times Pheidon was regarded as a typical miser, οἱ λοιποὶ τῶν ᾿Αθήνησι νεοπλούτων Φείδωνός τε εἰσι καὶ Γνίφωνος μικροπρεπέστεροι, Alciphron, III. 34, where, however, the statement may be an inference from the name.

[2] Strabo VIII. 376, "Ephorus says that in Aegina money was first coined by Pheidon"; *Marm. Par.* (Jacoby) under 895 B.C. "Pheidon the Argive...made a silver coinage in Aegina (ἀφ' οὗ Φείδων ὁ ᾿Αργεῖος ἐδήμευσε τὰ μέτρα καὶ σταθμὰ κατεσκεύασε καὶ νόμισμα ἀργυροῦν ἐν Αἰγίνῃ ἐποίησεν)": *Et. Mag.* s.v. ὀβελίσκος, "the first of all men to strike a coinage was Pheidon the Argive in Aegina"; Eustath. *Comm. Iliad.* II. 562, "silver was first coined by Pheidias (sic) there (sc. in Aegina)." So, but with no mention of Aegina, and an implication of other metals besides silver, Strabo VIII. 358, "and he (sc. Pheidon) invented the measures called Pheidonian, and weights, and a stamped coinage, particularly that in silver," and Pollux IX. 83, "whether Pheidon the Argive was first to strike money or Demodike of Cyme when married to Midas of Phrygia or Erichthonios and Lykos or the Lydians or the Naxians." Aelian, *V.H.* XII. 10, in a list of Aeginetan achievements mentions their invention of money: he has no occasion to mention Pheidon but rather the reverse, so that no conclusion can be drawn from the omission of the name.

and that the institution of the Aeginetan weight system was the direct result of an Argive occupation of the island.

One or two points may be assumed to start with as generally admitted. The Aeginetan "tortoises" (fig. 20) were the first coins struck in European Greece[1], and they were first struck fairly early in the seventh century[2]. The points that have been most disputed are the date of Pheidon and his connexion with Aegina and the Aeginetan coinage. It is the date that is the real centre of the controversy, and it will be best to deal with it first and to begin by briefly recalling the evidence and arguments.

Date of earliest Aeginetan coins.

Evidence for the date of Pheidon:

(i) The later genealogies[3] which make Pheidon seventh from Temenos and eleventh from Heracles and thus put him early in the ninth century have been shown by Busolt[4] to be due to fourth century tamperings with the pedigree of the royal house of Macedon. In ascribing the foundation of the Macedonian dynasty to a certain Karanos, who according to Theopompus was a son of Pheidon, according to Satyrus a son of Pheidon's father[5], they were influenced by the incurable Greek belief in

(1) from genealogies:

---

[1] For Aegina as the first place in Greece to coin see Pindar, *Isthm.* IV. (V.), 1–3:

Μᾶτερ Ἀελίου πολυώνυμε Θεία
σέο γ' ἕκατι καὶ μεγασθενῆ νόμισαν
χρυσὸν ἄνθρωποι περιώσιον ἄλλων.

The statement of the *Et. Mag.* s.v. Εὐβοικὸν νόμισμα that "Pheidon king of Argos struck a gold coinage in Euboea, a place in Argos," is manifestly a hopeless confusion. For the Aeginetan tortoise as the coin of the Peloponnesus see Pollux IX. 74.

[2] *Pace* Macan, *Hdt.* IV.–VI., vol. I. p. 382. See *e.g.* Hill, *Hist. Greek Coins*, p. 4; Regling *ap.* Pauly Wissowa s.v. Geld, p. 975; about the middle of the seventh century, Head, *Hist. Num.*[2] p. 394; rather after than before 650, Willers, *Roem. Kupferpräg.* pp. 8–9, Svoronos, *J. I. d'A. N.* v. p. 44; about 620 Earle Fox, *Corolla Num. B.V. Head*, pp. 40, 46; there is no specific evidence either way, but the earlier date seems much more probable, particularly since the discovery of the Cretan and Cyprian dumps and the coins from Ephesus discussed in the preceding chapter.

[3] Satyrus, fr. 21, *F.H.G.* III. p. 165; Marm. Par. *F.H.G.* I. pp. 546–7. Theopompus (*ap.* Diod. VII. fr. 17 and Syncellus, *F.H.G.* I. p. 283) makes Pheidon sixth from Temenos, but this may be due to the accidental omission of a name. For fifth century pedigrees of the royal house of Macedon see Hdt. VIII. 137–9.

[4] Busolt, *Gr. G.*[2] I. p. 616.

[5] On Karanos see also Justin VII. 1. How and Wells, *ad* Hdt. VI. 127, refer wrongly to Theopompus as making Karanos a brother of Pheidon.

symmetry which required the Macedonian royal family to be as old as that of its great rivals the Medes which latter, following Ktesias, they dated from 884 B.C.[1]

(ii) The genealogy that makes Pheidon tenth from Temenos and thus puts him about the middle of the eighth century can be traced back only to Ephorus[2]. In other words, as already pointed out by Bury[3], its credibility depends in great measure on that of the writer who is also our earliest authority for the statement that Pheidon coined in Aegina[4].

(iii) Yet a third statement as to Pheidon's family is that of Herodotus[5]. According to Herodotus Leokedes son of Pheidon was one of the suitors of Agariste at Sicyon early in the sixth century. The statement occurs in a plainly romantic setting, and must not be pressed too far. It may however be fairly claimed as an argument against a date as early as 750. Even admitting the possibility that παῖς (son) in the singular may be loosely used for ἀπόγονος (descendant)[6], yet it remains highly unlikely that Herodotus would have mentioned Pheidon at all in connexion with Leokedes if he regarded them as separated by over 150 years[7].

Lehmann-Haupt[8], who, in spite of all the difficulties just summarized, dates Pheidon eighth Olympiad (748 B.C.)[9], imagines an obscure Pheidon, father of Leokedes, and formulates as a characteristic of Herodotus the practice of assigning the deeds of famous

---

[1] Hence the date 894 B.C. assigned to Pheidon by the Parian Marble.

[2] Strabo VIII. 358; cp. Paus. II. 19. 2.

[3] *Pindar, Nem.* p. 255.

[4] See further Busolt, *Gr. G.* I.[2] p. 619, n. 2, and text. Long pedigrees are not in any case infallible material for arriving at a precise date. There is always *e.g.* the possibility that here and there a son who died before his father may have been left out of the list. A pedigree of the house of Hanover might easily omit Frederic the father of George III, as is in fact done by Thackeray, who, in chapter XXX. of the *Virginians*, speaks of Queen Victoria's great grandfather, meaning George II.

[5] Hdt. VI. 127.

[6] Cp. Schol. Pindar, *Ol.* XIII. 17, παῖδας εἶπεν...ὡς ἀπογόνους. The usage is poetical, and if accepted here might point to a poetical source for the Agariste story.

[7] Bury, *Pindar, Nem.* pp. 255–6. Bury's arguments are scarcely affected by the question (Macan, *Hdt.* IV.-VI., vol. I. *ad* VI. 127. 11; cp. *ibid. ad* VI. 127. 2) whether an Argive and Dorian suitor for Agariste is conceivable.

[8] *Ap.* Gercke u. Norden, *Einleit. i. d. Altertumsw.* III. pp. 80–105.

[9] See below, p. 159.

men to obscure namesakes. Besides Pheidon he quotes only Philokypros, tyrant of Soli and friend of Solon, whom he proceeds, in direct contradiction of Herodotus[1], to differentiate from the father of the Aristokypros who fell during the Ionic revolt. His view is discredited by the one illustration that he quotes in its support. Solon's young friend need not have been born before 608 B.C., and the son of a man born in that year might well be alive in 498 B.C. Even if Herodotus is mistaken on this point, his mistake would only illustrate the comparatively narrow margin of error to which his anachronisms on matters of this kind are limited.

There is yet another group of statements bearing on Pheidon's pedigree. Pausanias says that the last king of Argos was Meltas son of Lakedes[2]. The latter is equated by Beloch[3] with the Leokedes of Herodotus[4]. Meltas is said by Pausanias to have been tenth in descent from Medon, grandson of Temenos. Pheidon, as has been noted already, is described by Strabo as tenth in descent from Temenos himself. Thus Strabo, Pausanias, and Herodotus might be taken as mutually confirming one another, if we accept Herodotus literally, and make Pheidon father of Leokedes and consequently grandfather of Meltas. As there was still a king of Argos in 484 B.C.[5], and there is nothing to show that the office did not continue well after that date, Beloch's argument brings Pheidon well down into the sixth century. But as it allows only twelve generations from the Dorian invasion under Temenos to the indeterminate date after 480 B.C. when kingship was completely abolished, it only helps to emphasize the fact that Argive royal pedigrees are not a safe guide for determining Pheidon's date[6].

[1] Hdt. v. 113. [2] Paus. II. 19. 2.
[3] Beloch, *Gr. G.*² I. ii. pp. 193 f., following Wyttenbach: see Hitzig and Bluemner, *Paus.* II. 19. 2.
[4] He is perhaps to be equated also with the luxurious Lakydes, king of Argos, of Plut. *Mor.* 89e.
[5] Hdt. VII. 149.
[6] Cp. Paus. IV. 35. 2, Damocratidas, king during the second Messenian war who does not appear in Theopompus' list. Plut., *de Fort. Alex.* 8 (*Mor.* 340c), actually declares that the Heraclid royal family became extinct, and that a certain Aegon was indicated by the oracle to succeed them. Of this dynastic change there is no hint in Theopompus. Modern sceptics again, distrusting every statement about Pheidon not contained in Hdt. VI. 127, have doubted Pheidon's royal descent, regarding it as an invention of Theopompus, beyond whom it cannot be traced. But if we assume that Theopompus glorified Pheidon to please the Macedonian royal family, we must suppose that the latter were anxious from

(2) from his interference at the Olympian games.

The assertion of Pausanias[1], that Pheidon interfered with the eighth celebration of the Olympian games, is not to be reconciled with a seventh century date. But serious doubts have been thrown on Pausanias' dating, which may very possibly have been influenced by the Macedonian genealogies, in which case it is no confirmation of the date arrived at by reckoning Pheidon tenth from Temenos. The arguments for emending eighth to twenty-eighth are weighty[2]. Pausanias' exact statement is that "at the eighth Olympian festival the Pisatans called in Pheidon...and celebrated the games along with Pheidon[3]." But Strabo declares it to be "more probable (ἐγγυτέρω τῆς πίστεως) that from the first Olympiad till the twenty-sixth the presidency both of the temple and the games was held by the Eleians[4]." Julius Africanus likewise knows nothing of any disturbance at the eighth Olympiad, but records one at the twenty-eighth.

The difficulties in accepting the twenty-eighth Olympiad, as set forth by Unger[5], are not very impressive. He argues that at the twenty-eighth Olympiad the Eleians had arms[6], whereas Pheidon made his attack "when the Eleians were without arms[7]," and that, as the Pisatans celebrated the twenty-seventh Olympiad, Pheidon in the twenty-eighth would have displaced not the Eleians, but the Pisatans. But when Strabo says that the Eleians were without arms, he or his source may mean that their Dymaean war left them unequipped for home defence. Assume that this was so and that they were preoccupied with their Dymaean war both in 672 B.C.

the beginning to have their connexion with Pheidon brought into prominence, which would hardly have been the case if Pheidon had been regarded as an upstart; cp. Hdt. VIII. 137.

[1] Paus. VI. 22. 2.

[2] First suggested by Falconer, *ad* Strab. VIII. 355, and first fully discussed by Weissenborn, *Hellen*, pp. 18 f.; accepted by Busolt, Bury, and Macan, and by many earlier scholars, see E. Curtius, *Gr. G.* 1.[6] p. 660, n. 72.

[3] Paus. VI. 22. 2. [4] Strabo VIII. 355.

[5] Unger, *Philol.* XXVIII. (1869), pp. 399 f., followed by Duncker, *Ges. d. Alt.* v.[5] p. 546; Holm, *Hist. Greece* (Eng. trans.), I. p. 213; Reinach, *L'Hist. par les Monnaies*, p. 35; Radet, *Rev. Univ. du Midi*, 1895, pp. 120–1; P. Gardner, *Earliest Coins of Greece Proper*, p. 7; and very tentatively by Head, *Hist. Num.*[2] p. xliv.

[6] *Philol.* XXVIII. pp. 401 f.; Euseb. *Chron.* I. 33, Olymp. 28, "the Eleians being occupied through their war against the Dymaeans."

[7] Strabo VIII. 358.

and in 668 B.C., and the whole situation is explained easily. At the twenty-seventh celebration the Pisatans unaided might secure the presidency by a surprise attack. It would be at the next festival, when the Eleians were forewarned, that the Pisatans would need Pheidon's help to displace them at Olympia. Weaker still is Unger's argument that a notice about Pheidon may have fallen out in Eusebius under Olymp. VIII, as one has in the same chronicle about the emperor Caligula.

We may indeed with Mahaffy[1] and Busolt[2] doubt whether these early parts of the Olympian victor lists are contemporary records. But it is easy to be unduly sceptical. Mahaffy, for instance, is inclined to argue that the Olympian lists cannot have existed in the fifth century because they are not then used for purposes of dating. He assumes that Hippias who made his edition of the list in 370 B.C. can have had little more evidence at his disposal than Pausanias, who lived over five hundred years later. Plutarch[3], whom he quotes as discrediting the list, merely expresses an opinion which is no more final than that of Mahaffy himself. If our chronological data are untrustworthy, we are thrown back on Pheidon's achievements for determining his date, a position long ago maintained by C. Mueller[4]. Regarded as a fact of indeterminate date Pheidon's interference at Olympia is more likely to have been remembered if it was not made so early as the close of the eighth century, when the festival had not yet attained its subsequent reputation[5].

Pheidon probably contemporary with the earliest Aeginetan coins.

The evidence as to Pheidon's date is therefore quite compatible with the statement that makes him the first to strike coins in Aegina. For if it be allowed that he may have lived in the first half of the seventh century, there would be nothing unique in his having his mint away from his capital in an outlying but commercially important part of his dominion. Ridgeway and Svoronos have already compared the Romans, who struck their first coins in Campania[6], and the Ptolemies who coined very largely in Cyprus[7].

[1] *J.H.S.* II. pp. 164-178. [2] Busolt, *Gr. G.*² I. p. 586. [3] Plut. *Numa*, 1.
[4] C. Mueller, *Aeginetica*, p. 58, ignored by Jacoby, *Marm. Par.* (1904), pp. 158-162.
[5] See further, Bury, *Pindar, Nemeans*, pp. 253-4, and *ibid.* Bury's discussion of the tyrants' connexions with the great games.
[6] Ridgeway, *Orig. Met. Curr.* p. 216.
[7] Svoronos, *J. I. d'A. N.* v. (1902), p. 44: their other main mint was at Alexandria.

But had Pheidon anything to do with Aegina and its coinage? Against the statements of Ephorus and later writers must be set the silence of Herodotus, who makes no reference either to coins or to Aegina in his account of Pheidon. This omission, combined with the diversity of views as to Pheidon's date, has led to a general distrust of Ephorus, so much so that the majority of the most competent authorities are either agnostics[1] or utter unbelievers[2].

Did he strike them?

Herodotus' silence is not by itself a serious argument for rejecting the additions of the later historians. It should be remembered that his whole account of Pheidon in VI. 127 extends to barely four lines. He can hardly be expected to state at all completely even the main facts about so important a personality in so short a space. To assert, as has been done recently[3], that Herodotus *knew* nothing about a coinage issued by Pheidon is to beg the question.

To the fifth century Greek, for whom Herodotus wrote, the origin of the system of weights on which the Aeginetan coins were struck may have been of greater interest than the remoter question of an invention which they doubtless all took for granted. Peloponnesian weights and measures stood for the lack of standardization in all matters metrical from which Herodotus and his hearers must have suffered daily.

There is no need to pursue these criticisms in further detail. They start with various assumptions as to Pheidon's date. Some of them would be found to be mutually destructive. Nearly all of them overestimate the difficulties raised by the apparent lack of confirmation of Ephorus in earlier writers. It is by no means certain that his statements about Pheidon's connexion with the Aeginetan coinage must be a fanciful expansion of Herodotus VI. 127. There are in fact two lines of evidence that point in quite the opposite direction. One of them rests on notices about the Argive Heraeum supplemented by recent finds on the site; the other is based on a new interpretation of a passage in the fifth book

---

[1] *E.g.* Head, *Hist. Num.*² pp. xliv, 394–5; G. F. Hill, *Hist. Greek Coins*, p. 4; cp. Babelon, *Origines*, pp. 211–3; Earle Fox, *Corolla Numis. B. V. Head*, p. 34.

[2] *E.g.* Th. Reinach, *Rev. Num.* 1894, pp. 2–3; P. Gardner, *Earliest Coins Greece Proper*, p. 8; F. Cauer *ap.* Pauly Wissowa s.v. Argolis, p. 733; Macan, *Hdt.* IV.–VI. vol. I. p. 382; How and Wells, *Hdt.* vol. II. pp. 117–8.

[3] Lehmann-Haupt, *Hermes*, XXVII. (1892), p. 557; Beloch, *Gr. G.*² I. ii. p. 196.

of Herodotus. It will be necessary to examine in some detail the evidence from these two sources.

<small>A. Evidence from the Argive Heraeum.</small> In the famous temple of Hera, the Argive Heraeum, that lies between Argos and Mycenae, there was preserved a dedication that was said to have been made by Pheidon in commemoration of his coinage. The notice is preserved only in the mediaeval *Etymologicum Magnum*. It runs: "Pheidon the Argive was the first of all men to strike a coinage in Aegina, and on account of this coinage he called in the spits (ὀβελίσκοι) and dedicated them to the Hera of Argos." There is nothing suspicious in this notice. The word drachma means a handful, and according to Plutarch a drachma is a handful of obols (spits or nails), which in early times were used as money[1]. In modern times nails are said to have served as a coinage in both Scotland and France[2]. Plenty of evidence is to be found in antiquity for offerings of disused objects to the gods[3]. The ultimate source for the statement of the *Etymologicum Magnum* may well be the official guide at the Heraeum itself. Temple traditions are not always above suspicion. All the same the indications of a Pheidon tradition

---

[1] Plut. *Lys.* 17; Pollux VII. 105; IX. 77–8; cp. Plut. *Fab. Max.* 27; Hdt. II. 135; and perhaps Caes. *B.G.* v. 12 (reading "taleis" as against "anulis").

[2] Jevons, *Money*[3], p. 28.

[3] See Homolle *ap.* Saglio, *Dict. Ant.* s.v. donarium, pp. 374, n. 155 and 378. It is hardly surprising (*pace* Th. Reinach, *Rev. Num.* 1894, p. 5) that no instance there quoted is contemporary with the first recorded event in Greek history. Nor is Reinach's psychology sound when he maintains (*ibid.*) that giving away what one no longer needs is an action that by its sentimental or archaeological character betrays a rather recent epoch. Reinach, *Rev. Num.* 1894, pp. 1–8, notes that the ancients often kept in their temples samples of weights and measures and quotes examples from Athens, Delos, Lebadea, Rome (see also Homolle *ap.* Saglio, *Dict. Ant.* s.v. donarium, n. 176), whereas there is no other certain instance of the dedication of a disused currency (Paus. x. 14. 1, dedication at Delphi of double axes by Periklytos of Tenedos, is so interpreted by Babelon, *Origines*, pp. 75 f., 208, but see Regling *ap.* Pauly Wissowa s.v. Geld, p. 974 and references *ibid*. Coins have been found in temples superscribed ἀνάθεμα (dedication) and ἱαρόν (sacred), Babelon, *Origines*, p. 208, but these may be nearer in intention to the modern offertory than to Pheidon's reputed dedication). He therefore maintains that the ὀβελίσκοι were not called in by Pheidon, but first issued by him: Pheidon's invention thus becomes something that happened in Argos not in Aegina, and must be put back at least into the eighth century. Reinach accordingly dates the tyrant eighth Olympiad (748 B.C.). His conjecture only carries weight if that is regarded as the most probable date for Pheidon, against which see above, pp. 159–160.

preserved in the Argive Heraeum are valuable, because they show a source from which Ephorus might very well have supplemented Herodotus far older and more valuable than his own imagination.

This however does not end the evidence of the Argive Heraeum. Some thirty years ago the site was excavated by the American School of Archaeology at Athens. Among the finds was a bundle of iron spits or rods about four feet long (fig. 21) which Svoronos[1] has plausibly associated with the ὀβελίσκοι of the *Etymologicum Magnum*.

The Americans ascribed the foundation of the Heraeum to the Mycenaean period, so that the dedication of the spits could be put anywhere in the three centuries that form the limit of controversy as to Pheidon's date. But more recently this dating has been shown to be mistaken by the Germans who excavated Tiryns. Whole series of miniature vessels which the Argive Heraeum excavators had regarded as Mycenaean were shown by the Tiryns excavators to be seventh century or later, and when one of them, Frickenhaus, visited the Argive Heraeum, he found fragments of Geometric and proto-Corinthian pottery in positions which proved the sherds to be older than the temple foundations. From this fact he argues conclusively that the abundant series of dedications at the Heraeum

Fig. 21. Bundle of spits found in the Argive Heraeum.

---

[1] Svoronos, *J. I. d'A. N.* IX. (1906), pls. X.–XII. For connecting iron spits with the coinage at Argos cp. perhaps the Argive iron coins of usual shape and type, Koehler, *Ath. Mitt.* VII. pp. 1–7, dating, however, only from the fourth century B.C.

begin in the seventh century. Pheidon's ὀβελίσκοι cannot therefore go further back than that[1]. The Mycenaean objects from the Argive Heraeum site must all come from a small secular settlement that preceded the temple. The latter becomes possibly contemporary with Pheidon himself.

This is a fact of possible significance. It suggests that the Heraeum may have been the religious centre of Pheidon's imperial policy, a sort of religious federal capital carefully placed away from the chief cities of the Argolid much as the federal capital of Australia has been placed away from the capitals of the various Australian states. It looks indeed as though the analogy may have been closer still, and that Pheidon was the builder of his federal capital. If so his date was some time, probably early, in the seventh century.

This ends the evidence of the Heraeum and brings me to the most important section of my argument. We have just seen how little need there is to mistrust Ephorus simply because he does not exactly reproduce Herodotus. All the same the earlier writer is of course by far the more reliable. The account of Pheidon's coinage in Aegina would gain enormously in credibility if any evidence for it could be found in the pages of Herodotus. Modern writers without exception have taken it for granted that no such evidence is to be found. In this I believe them to have been mistaken. There is a passage in the fifth book which, though it does not mention Pheidon's name, I believe to describe the conquest by him of Aegina and the institution as a result of that conquest of the weight standard on which the earliest Aeginetan coins were struck. If my explanation has not been anticipated, there is no reason for surprise. The passage contains references to pottery, ships, dress, and jewellery, and my interpretation of it is based on archaeological evidence much of which has only quite recently become available.

B. Fresh evidence from Herodotus.

---

[1] *Tiryns*, I. p. 114. It does not follow simply from this that they were demonetized offerings, and not standard samples. Spits on the new standard may have circulated concurrently with the new silver coinage. In Thebes and Sparta very heavy iron spits were used as currency as late as the fourth century, Plut. *Fab. Max.* 27; *Lysand.* 17. On the other hand the spits published by de Cou in the *Argive Heraeum* (vol. II. pp. 300-323, pls. CXXVII.-CXXXII.; cp. vol. I. p. 63), appear to be mainly of the Geometric period, and discountenance the view that a spit currency was instituted by Pheidon and went on after him.

In the passage of the fifth book which we are now to examine
Herodotus[1] is explaining the origin of the hatred that
existed between Athens and Aegina in 500 B.C.
Aegina had once been subject to Epidaurus[2]. Then
the Aeginetans, having built triremes and made themselves masters of the sea[3], revolted. Through their revolt they got embroiled with the Athenians, who had at that time very close relations with Epidaurus. At the suggestion of the Epidaurians, the Athenians sailed against Aegina. The Aeginetans appealed to Argos, and with the help of an Argive force that crossed undetected from Epidaurus, utterly defeated the Athenians in a land battle on the island. The various measures[4] taken in common by the Aeginetans and the Argives immediately after the war suggest that Aegina, when she had revolted from Epidaurus, became in some sort a confederate, or possibly a subject, of Argos[5]. We may assume too that Argos secured some sort of control over Epidaurus in the course of the war. Otherwise it is inconceivable that an Argive force should have set out from Epidaurus with the double purpose of aiding Epidaurus' revolted subjects and attacking those very Athenians, whose expedition against the island had been suggested by the Epidaurians themselves[6]. The crushing defeat that the Athenians sustained may have been due to the collapse of her Epidaurian allies.

Herodotus, v. 82 f. describes an Argive intervention in Aegina,

One further point about Herodotus' narrative should be noticed. There is nothing in it to suggest that at the time when the Aeginetans revolted from the Epidaurians, either of them was dependent on Argos. The narrative points rather to a previous confederation or dominion in which the chief cities were Epidaurus, Aegina, and not Argos but Athens. Are there any indications as to when all this occurred?

The reference is to a time considerably[7] previous to 500 B.C. Macan thinks that the most probable date for the expedition to

---

[1] v. 82–89.

[2] Hdt. v. 83; cp. VIII. 46 and Paus. II. 29. 5.

[3] Hdt. v. 83. "The thalassocracy might be local and relative to Epidaurus," Macan, *ad loc.*

[4] Hdt. v. 88.

[5] Hence too, *pace* How and Wells, it is improbable that the Argives who helped Aegina were merely mercenaries.

[6] Hdt. v. 84.

[7] Cp. ἐκ τόσου, Hdt. v. 88 (89), and Macan, *ad loc.*

Aegina is somewhere in the lifetime of Solon or Peisistratus[1]. He

generally ascribed to the first half of the sixth century, points to various circumstances that certainly might well have led to a collision between Athens and Aegina during that period[2]. All the same it is difficult to accept a date within those limits. The Aeginetans are not likely[3] to have been dependent on Epidaurus after it was conquered by Periander, about 600 B.C.[4] If therefore the revolt from Epidaurus and the Athenian invasion are incidents in one and the same struggle, both must go into the seventh century. Macan prefers to assume a long interval between these two events. But Herodotus gives no hint of one. On the contrary, his narrative hangs excellently together as a description of successive and correlated incidents in a single struggle. Not only so, but even if the invasion be separated from the revolt, it is difficult to believe that it occurred after 590. So crushing a defeat for the Athenians, who themselves admitted that only one of their number got back to Attica[5], could hardly have taken place in the time of Solon or Peisistratus without being associated with their names. After all, a fair amount is known about sixth century Athens. There are no traces of any such overwhelming disaster, or of the inevitable set back that would have followed it. The relations of Athens to Argos during the period seem to have been friendly rather than the reverse. Peisistratus had Argive mercenaries, not to speak of an Argive wife[6]. Argive support of Peisistratus is of course quite consistent with hostility to the government that Peisistratus overthrew. It has indeed been suggested[7] that the Aeginetan expedition took place while Peisistratus was in exile. But, apart from the entire absence of evidence, and all the other difficulties involved by a sixth century

---

[1] Macan, *Hdt. IV–VI*. vol. II. p. 106; cp. How and Wells, *Hdt.* v. 86. 4; so C. Mueller, *Aeginetica*, p. 73 ("coniectura satis uaga"), *F.H.G.* II. p. 481; Duncker, *Ges. d. Alt.* IV.¹ p. 312, n. 1; Helbig, *Homer. Epos.*² p. 162; Hirschfeld *ap.* Pauly Wissowa s.v. Aigina, p. 966; Amelung, *ibid.* s.v. χιτών, p. 2327; Studniczka, *Altgr. Tracht*, p. 4; Abrahams, *Gk. Dress*, p. 39.

[2] Macan, *Hdt. IV–VI*. vol. II. p. 106, successful war with Megara, conquest of Salamis, new coinage, development of trade and commerce, patronage of Delos.

[3] *Pace* Duncker, *Ges. d. Alt.* VI.⁵ p. 52.

[4] How and Wells, *Hdt.* v. 84. 1.

[5] Hdt. v. 87.

[6] Hdt. I. 61; Aristot. *Ath. Pol.* 17; cp. Hdt. v. 94; Plut. *Cato Mai.* 24.

[7] Studniczka, *Altgr. Tracht*, p. 4.

date, this suggestion means that Peisistratus sought a bodyguard and wife in the most unpopular quarter imaginable, hardly a probable proceeding on the part of a ruler so tactful and popular as Peisistratus must have been.

A date late in the seventh century is rendered unlikely by what is known of Procles of Epidaurus[1], the father-in-law of Periander, who ruled Epidaurus during the last part of the seventh century[2], apparently as a dependent of the Corinthian tyrant, by whom he was eventually deposed. C. Mueller indeed[3] claims Aegina for Procles, but only on the more than dubious evidence of a more than dubious story of Plutarch's, which tells how Procles once used an "Aeginetan stranger" to get rid of the corpse of a man whom he had murdered for his money[4].

On the whole the narrative seems to fall best into the first half of the seventh century. That is the time that best suits the naval situation during the war, and the effect that it is said to have had upon costume, ornament, and pottery. As the archaeological evidence for all these points is based largely on the evidence of the pottery, it will be best to take the pottery first.

but more probably to be dated early in the seventh, as shown by archaeological evidence on allusions in the narrative to:

In the temple of Damia and Auxesia on Aegina it became the practice (νόμος) after the war "to introduce into the temple neither anything else Attic nor pottery, but to drink there henceforth only out of native jars[5]." Herodotus mentions this embargo on Attic pottery only as applied to the one temple on Aegina[6]. But he states that it was observed by Argives as well as by Aeginetans, which points to the

(i) pottery,

---

[1] Hdt. III. 50–52; Her. Pont. *ap.* Diog. Laert. I. 7. 1; Paus. II. 28. 8; Athen. XIII. 589 f.

[2] His father-in-law is said to have perished in the second Messenian war; cp. Diog. Laert. I. 7. 1 with Strabo VIII. 362; Paus. IV. 17. 2, 22. 7.

[3] *Aeginetica*, pp. 63–73.

[4] Plut. *de Pyth. Or.* 19 (*Moral.* 403). Neither Plutarch's story nor Mueller's inference is confirmed by the fact that the story of the wooing of Procles' daughter is quoted by Athenaeus XIII. 589 f. from "Pythaenetus in his third book about Aegina."

[5] Hdt. V. 88; cp. Athen. XI. 502 c.

[6] This fact is obscured by Hoppin's translation of the passage, *Argive Heraeum* II. p. 175, who renders τῶν θεῶν τούτων "their gods," ἱρόν "temples," and omits αὐτόθι.

possibility that the practice prevailed in Argos as well as Aegina. Macan goes as far as to suggest that it is an "understatement and pseudo-explanation of a measure or custom for the protection of native ware from Attic competition[1]." The other measures recorded in this connexion, the changes in Attic dress and in Peloponnesian brooches, support Macan's suggestion. But in the matter of dating he follows earlier writers who, using very inadequate material, came to conclusions which can now be shown to be improbable. They date this embargo in the middle of the sixth century. But in Aegina at any rate Attic pottery continued to be imported throughout the second half of the sixth century, while in Argos, where the evidence is less decisive and abundant, there is no sign of a cessation of Attic imports about 550 B.C. On the other hand both in Argos and Aegina there does appear to be an abrupt cessation of Attic imports early in the seventh century. As, further, the general history of Greek pottery shows that an Argive-Aeginetan embargo on Attic pottery would have had a strong commercial motive early in the seventh century and none in the middle of the sixth, there is a strong presumption that the date of the embargo was not the middle of the sixth century but somewhere about the beginning of the seventh. To examine the archaeological evidence here in detail would take us too far from our main enquiry. It will be found presented in full in an appendix[2].

(ii) sea-power and ships, The war was a great disaster for Athenian naval power. Now the period of greatest eclipse for Athens from this point of view was the seventh century. Throughout it there is no indication whatever of naval activity at Athens, except a possible war against Mitylene. Even that must be put at the earliest close on the year 600 B.C., and is to be regarded as announcing the beginning of the new epoch of activity in the sixth century[3]; and against it must be set the failure in the struggle with Megara for Salamis[4]. This had not been the naval position of Athens earlier. During the dark ages she appears to have been a considerable naval power. A tradition preserved by Plutarch makes Athens succeed

---

[1] Macan, *Hdt. IV.–VI. ad loc.*; cp. How and Wells, *ad loc.*

[2] Below, Appendix B.

[3] Cp. its continuation, if continuation it was, under the tyrants. For Athens with no fleet about 650 B.C. see B. Keil, *Solon. Verfass.* p. 94. For Athens and Mitylene, E. Meyer, *Ges. d. Alt.* II. sect. 402, n.

[4] E. Meyer, *ibid.* sect. 403 n.

Crete in the command of the sea[1]: naval power is implied in Theseus' expedition to Crete; a poem of Bacchylides[2], which is illustrated by a vase painting of Euphronios[3], tells how Theseus went to the depths of the sea to fetch up the ring of Minos, and the story has been brought by S. Reinach into connexion with rings such as those of Polycrates and the doges of Venice, and explained as symbolizing the winning by Theseus of the sea which had been previously the bride of Minos[4].

The date of these events must not be pressed. The period of this sea-power is plainly the dark age that followed the breaking up of the Cretan and Mycenaean civilization. It is the period of the pottery known as Geometric, and the Athenian Geometric, the Dipylon ware, again and again shows pictures of ships. Thirty-nine examples are quoted by Torr[5], enough, as pointed out by Helbig[6], to prove the important rôle played by the Athenian navy in the life of Athens of that age. The Dipylon ships, as remarked twenty years ago by Helbig[7], show that already in the eighth century Athens was preparing to found her power on her navy. It requires some such catastrophic explanation as has just been offered to account for her complete set back in the seventh.

(iii) dress.

One result in Athens of the reverse in Aegina, so Herodotus declares, was a revolution in the dress of the Athenian women, who gave up the Doric costume, which was made of wool and fastened with pins, and adopted in its place the Ionic, which consisted of sewn garments made of linen. The passage is a *locus classicus* among writers on Greek dress, and it must be at once admitted that nearly all of them accept a date late in the

---

[1] Plut. *de Exil.* 10 (*Moral.* 603) (Cyclades settled first by the sons of Minos, later by those of Kodros and Neilos); Plut. *Solon*, 26 (Aipeia in Cyprus founded by a son of Theseus).

[2] Bacchyl. XVI.; cp. Paus. I. 17. 3. Theseus fetches the ring to prove himself a true son of Poseidon, and brings with it a crown.

[3] Perrot et Chipiez, x. pl. ix.; Buschor, *Gr. Vasenmal.*[1] fig. 113.

[4] S. Reinach, *Cultes Mythes et Relig.* II. p. 218. Theseus' connexion with Troezen, Paus. I. 27. 7, points to the Athens of the period as powerful in the Saronic Gulf.

[5] *Rev. Arch.*[3] xxv. (1894), pp. 14-15. Add *Arch. Eph.* 1898, pl. v. 1 (Eleusis).

[6] *Mém. Acad. Inscr. et B.-L.* XXXVI. (1898), p. 390.

[7] *Ibid.* p. 421, based on Brueckner and Pernice, *Ath. Mitt.* XVIII. (1893), p. 153. For further discussion of this naval question see below, Appendix C.

first half of the sixth century¹. So late a date seems to me to be untenable. It can be reconciled neither with the statements of Thucydides on the subject of Athenian dress², nor with the evidence of extant monuments³. The sumptuary laws on women's dress passed by Solon in 594 B.C.⁴ were plainly directed against the Ionian costume. They show that it must have reached Athens by about 600 B.C. and offer no evidence that it had not done so considerably earlier. Bury dates the introduction of Ionian dress into Athens "c. 650(?)⁵."

After the war the Argives and Aeginetans make their brooches "half as big again." Among the Aeginetans and Argives as a result of their victory over Athens a change was introduced in what Herodotus calls the "measure" (μέτρον) of Aeginetan and Argive brooches (περόναι). Herodotus states that this change affected both the dedications at the temple of Damia and Auxesia⁶, and also the general manufacture and use. The way he tells the story explains why he goes beyond the temple when speaking of the pins, but does not do so in the case of the pottery. The exclusion of Attic pottery from the Aeginetan temple, or rather the exclusive use for temple purposes of local ware, was in Herodotus' days a ritualistic survival. The large brooches on the other hand had continued in general use. "Now the women of Argos and Aegina even to my own days wore brooches of increased size." Very possibly Herodotus had himself noticed them. It is the account of this change in the "measure" of the Aeginetan and Argive brooches that confirms the connexion of Pheidon with the origin of the Aeginetan coinage.

The new practice was in Herodotus' own words: "to make the brooches half as big again as the then established measure." It is probably significant that, both before and after the change, the brooches have a standard "measure." The tendency of articles of jewellery in early periods to be of a fixed weight is a familiar one. Numerous instances are quoted in Ridgeway's *Origin of Metallic*

---

¹ *E.g.* Lady Evans, *Greek Dress*, pp. 24 and 29; cp. p. 28: Studniczka, *Ges. Altgr. Tracht*, pp. 13, 29; Helbig, *Epos.*² pp. 162–163.

² See below, Appendix D.

³ A paper on this subject is being prepared by my wife.

⁴ Plut. *Sol.* 21.

⁵ Bury, *Hist. Greece*², p. 174.

⁶ Cp. the 346 iron brooches (peronai) in the extant (fifth century) inventory of this temple, Furtwaengler, *Berl. Phil. Woch.* 1901, pp. 1004-5, 1597-9.

Currency¹. Not only so, but these fixed weights are repeatedly found corresponding with or anticipating the coin standards of the places they belong to.

It may be objected that the word μέτρον does not mean weight. This is so when it is contrasted with σταθμός²; but it appears to have been used also in a more comprehensive sense³. The Athenian μετρονόμοι⁴ must have inspected weights as well as measures. μέτρον is presumably applied to both, and to a fifth century Greek there would be no question of its referring to anything but weight when applied to jewellery⁵.

The change introduced by the Argives and Aeginetans after driving the Athenians from Aegina was to make the "measure" of their brooches half as big again as what it had previously been. Now this is approximately the relationship in weight of the earliest Aeginetan drachmae to the earliest drachmae struck on the Euboeic standard. Later, in Herodotus' own times, the relative weights were four to three. But the earliest Aeginetan drachmae weighed a little more than those of later issues⁶. On the other hand, as stated by Percy Gardner⁷ in discussing Solon's "augmentation" of the Athenian coins, the earliest Attic or rather Euboeic drachma⁸ weighed less

The Aeginetan drachma was half as big again as the Attic.

---

¹ Rings, pp. 35, 394; ear-rings, p. 35; fibulae (but not with pins), p. 42. Add Brit. Mus. Cat. Jewellery, early Greek fibula no. 1089 (Rhodes); Furtwaengler, Winckelmannspr. 1883, pp. 5-10, archaic Greek gold ornaments found at Vetterfeld, all apparently weighing some multiple of the Attic drachma. On the whole question of ring money, see above, chapter v, p. 148. Ridgeway is criticized by Svoronos, J. I. d'A. N. IX. p. 184, who, however, admits the main fact that "goldsmiths habitually make their ornaments from a specific weight of metal in agreement with the prevalent standard of weight." We must of course beware of arguing from the practice of places like modern Nigeria, where the native jewellers are in the habit of making up rings and other objects out of coins supplied for the purpose by their customers, see e.g. J. W. Scott Macfie, Rev. d'Ethn. et de Sociol. 1912, p. 282.

² As in Aristot. Ath. Pol. 10, "the increase of the μέτρα and of the σταθμοί."

³ Pheidon's invention is described by Pliny, N.H. VII. 57 as concerning "mensuras et pondera."

⁴ Suid. s.v.; Harpocrat. s.v.   ⁵ Cp. the Delos inventory.

⁶ E.g. (didrachms), J. I. d'A. N. 1912, pp. 17, 18, nos. 1727, 1728, 1732 (12·06, 12·14, 12·26); Hermes, XXVII. p. 558 (13·44); cp. Head, Hist. Num.² p. xlv. Note, however, Willers, Roem. Kupf. p. 9, in Brit. Mus. 38, very archaic weigh 11·713; 20 more advanced weigh 12·266.

⁷ P. Gardner, Hist. of Anc. Coinage, p. 152.

⁸ E.g. J. I. d'A. N. 1912, pp. 1, 3, drachmae nos. 1038, 1044, 1083, 1093 (3·60, 4·12, 4·10, 3·95), didrachms nos. 1042, 1043 (8·48, 8·20).

than those of post-Solonian times. The weight of the Aeginetan drachma as determined from the early didrachms quoted above (p. 171, n. 6) is just over six grammes, as compared with the 5·85 grammes of later issues, while that of the earliest Attic Euboeic drachma as determined from the coins of p. 171, n. 8 is just over four grammes, as compared with the 4·26 grammes of later issues[1].

Thus the original Aeginetan drachma seems to have been just half as heavy again as the earliest Attic[2]. This ratio is accepted by Ridgeway[3], who regards it as invented to make ten silver pieces worth one gold when gold was fifteen times as precious as silver, while later, when silver rose to be worth 3/40 of its weight in gold, the silver pieces were slightly diminished in weight, in order that ten of them might still be the equivalent of one of gold[4].

Let us now return to the one passage of Herodotus, in which he refers by name to the Argive tyrant.

Summary of the evidence of Herodotus.

In that passage he speaks of Pheidon as "the man who made their measures for the Peloponnesians[5]." The force of the definite article that precedes the Greek μέτρα has not always been sufficiently stressed. More than one recent writer begins his discussion of the passage by translating τὰ μέτρα "*a* system of measures." The subsequent argument has naturally suffered. τὰ μέτρα can be no other measures than those associated with the Peloponnesus in Herodotus' own days, namely those of the famous Aeginetan standard, employed in particular for the coinage of the island[6]. Other scholars have regarded the statement

---

[1] Of the weights found at Naukratis, Petrie, *Naukratis*, I. pp. 83–4, 87, notes that the earliest Aeginetan are the heaviest, the earliest Attic the lightest.

[2] According to Pollux IX. 76, the Aeginetan drachma contained ten Attic obols, and was thus a little *more* than half as heavy again as the Attic drachma, which contained six Attic obols. This statement is not easily explained. It is doubtful what period it refers to.

[3] Ridgeway, *Metallic Currency*, pp. 219–228; cp. *ibid.* 307, 311, and *J.H.S.* VIII. (1887), pp. 140 f.; cp. also, Head, *Hist. Num.*² p. 395.

[4] For the gradual rise in value of silver, see Reinach, *Hist. par les Monnaies*, pp. 72–3; in 438 B.C. gold was to silver as 14 : 1, in 408 as 12 : 1, in 356 as 10 : 1. For the fall in weight of the Attic silver pieces struck on the gold standard, cp. the fall from the Homeric gold talent of 135 grains to the Persian gold Daric of 130 grains, Ridgeway, *Met. Curr.* p. 126.

[5] Hdt. VI. 127; cp. Pliny, *N.H.* VII. 57. 7; Euseb. *Chron.* anno Abrahami 1201; Jerome, anno Abrahami 1198.

[6] Pollux IX. 74.

that Pheidon struck the first coins in Aegina as merely an amplification by later writers of these very words. They argue that "the measures" plainly meant the Aeginetan standard, and so suggested the famous Aeginetan coinage. This latter view assumes of course that the amplifications of Ephorus are not to be found in Herodotus himself. But what are the facts? The establishment of Aeginetan measures in the Peloponnesus are alluded to by Herodotus not only in the passage about the Argive tyrant in Book VI but also very possibly in the passage in Book V that describes the early Argive expedition to Aegina. In this latter passage the measures are said to have been the result of the expedition. Both expedition and tyrant are probably to be dated early in the seventh century. That is also the date to which numismatists generally assign the first drachmae struck in Aegina, struck too on a standard that, like that of our brooches, was half again as great as that previously in use.

Sceptical views on these chapters of Herodotus stated and answered.
It is hard to avoid the inference that when the fourth century writers say that Pheidon coined in Aegina, they are faithfully reporting a genuine tradition.

It has indeed been maintained that the whole Herodotean account of the early relations of Argos, Aegina, and Athens is unhistorical[1]. The arguments brought forward to support this destructive view are: (i) that the episode is timeless and its timelessness must be due to its unhistorical character, (ii) that it must be unhistorical because it cannot, as alleged by Herodotus, have been the cause of the war of 487 B.C., which must have been due to the natural rivalry of the two neighbouring states. As regards the first of these two arguments, the preceding pages have, it is hoped, shown that the episode is not timeless: as regards the second, it is enough to point out that it assumes that war cannot breed war, that no war can be due to two causes, and that an incident cannot be historical if it is alleged as leading to results that it cannot have in fact produced. The fact that arguments such as these were accepted for publication in a periodical of high repute less than a generation back shows how much the whole world of scholarship was infected by the spirit of uncritical scepticism that has left its mark in some quarters on that of the present age.

Others again like Wilamowitz[2] regard the narrative of Herodotus

[1] Koehler, *Rhein. Mus.* XLVI. (1891), p. 3.
[2] Wilamowitz, *Aristot. u. Athen.* II. pp. 280–288; so E. Meyer, *Ges. d. Alt.* II. sect. 341 n. (p. 538).

v. 82–88 as simply a reflexion backwards of the state of affairs existing in 487 B.C.[1], when Athens attacked Aegina, and the Aeginetans "called to their aid the same people as before, the Argives[2]." They argue that (i) the story is our only evidence for hatred between Athens and Aegina much before 506 B.C., (ii) the Argive-Aeginetan brooches as compared with the broochless Athenian costume[3], the embargo on Attic pottery at the Aeginetan temple, and the posture of the kneeling statues (pleading before the Athenian invaders) may all have been referred in Herodotus' days to the existing hatred and recent wars between Athens and Aegina, (iii) Herodotus puts back the Athenian disaster into the timeless period because the miracle and the change of costume required an early date, and the story does not fit the war of 487 B.C., since the famous Sophanes[4], who fought in it, lived till 464. Herodotus, they say, gives no account of a disaster to the Athenian fleet in 487 because he had used it up for this early reflexion.

Of these points (i) is answered by the whole of this chapter, (ii) and (iii) fall with (i), besides which (ii) contains many improbabilities, *e.g.* that the pottery in an Aeginetan temple should without historic reason have suggested to any fifth century Greek an early war with Athens, while (iii) assumes an Athenian disaster in 487 B.C., whereas Thucydides declares that Athens was successful in that war[5].

There is nothing suspicious in the Aeginetans having twice in two hundred years attained some sort of thalassocracy, and having on both occasions come as a result into collision with Athens. It is perfectly natural for the Aeginetans on a second occasion to appeal to allies who had previously helped them so effectively and with such profit to themselves. Macan[6] observes that the Herodotean account of the feud between Athens and Aegina is remarkably uninfluenced by contemporary politics and interests. He suggests[7] dating the subjection of Aegina to Epidaurus to the reign of Pheidon, and the revolt of the island from Epidaurus to the time of Pheidon's fall. But why in that case does the account speak of a revolt from

---

[1] Hdt. vi. 87–93.   [2] *Ibid.* vi. 92.
[3] Cp. Soph. *O.T.* 1269; Eurip. *Hec.* 1170.
[4] Hdt. vi. 92, ix. 73–5.
[5] Thuc. i. 41; cp. the inscription *ap.* Koehler, *Rhein. Mus.* XLVI. (1891), p. 5, n. 1.
[6] Macan, *Hdt. IV–VI.* vol. ii. p. 103.   [7] *Ibid.* p. 106.

Epidaurus, if it was really a revolt from the famous Argive tyranny? The whole narrative finds a more appropriate setting if regarded as one chapter in the history of Pheidon himself.

Only, why in this case is the name of Pheidon nowhere mentioned? It is one thing to omit details in a biography four lines in length. It is quite another to omit so prominent a name in a narrative that runs to seven whole chapters. But the omission, though at first sight surprising, is capable of explanation. The Herodotean story appears to have been derived from the temple of Damia and Auxesia[1]. It was told Herodotus not in connexion with any royal monument, but to explain certain offerings of pottery and jewellery that he saw in the temple. Not a single personal name occurs in the whole narrative, and there is no particular reason why there should. There may actually have been motives for not introducing them. The account of the events given to Herodotus in the Aeginetan temple of Damia and Auxesia would naturally not emphasize the part played by the Argive tyrant. The Athenian version, to which also Herodotus alludes, would have still better reason for trying to forget the name of Pheidon. If my whole interpretation of these events is not entirely wrong, Pheidon dealt the Athenians what was probably the most crushing blow they had ever received down to the days when Herodotus wrote his history. The personal name may be omitted from the same motive that made the Athenians speak of the Aeginetan drachma as the "fat" drachma, which they are said to have done, "refusing to call it Aeginetan out of hatred of the Aeginetans[2]." Sparta again had taken sides against Pheidon at Olympia[3], and would have had no interest in perpetuating the name of the man who had almost barred their way to the hegemony of the Peloponnese.

Ephorus' account of Pheidon's conquests and inventions is derived neither from Attic nor from Aeginetan sources. As seen already[4] the source of his statement about Pheidon coining in Aegina was most probably the Argive Heraeum. Herodotus claims to use Argive sources, but for him the war is primarily a matter between the Athenians and the Aeginetans, whose subsequent hatred of one another it is intended to explain. Thus we appear to have three

Why Pheidon is not mentioned in them.

---

[1] Cp. Macan, *Hdt. IV–VI.* vol. II. p. 107.
[2] Pollux IX. 76. [3] Strabo VIII. 358.
[4] Above, pp. 162–4.

rival or even hostile traditions confirming one another, so that the variety of sources adds in a real way to the credibility of the resultant narrative.

Pheidon and Aegina, further evidence from Ephorus: Pheidon recovered the lot of Temenos, which included Aegina.

The notices about the coinage are not the only evidence for associating Pheidon with Aegina. According to Ephorus "he completely recovered the lot of Temenos, which had previously been split into several parts[1]." Temenos appears in the genealogies as great great grandson of Heracles, and founder of the Dorian dynasty at Argos[2]. He and his sons and his son-in-law between them are represented as securing the greater part of the North-east Peloponnese. Aegina fell to his son-in-law Deiophontes, who went to the island from Epidaurus[3].

The operations described in Herodotus v. 82–88, by which the Argives crossed from Epidaurus and drove the Athenians out of Aegina and put an end to the Epidaurians being tributary to Athens[4], are almost beyond doubt to be identified with the recovery by Argos of the portion of the lot of Temenos that had been secured by Deiophontes.

Traces of this recovery in other passages of Herodotus.

It is true that this account of the recovery of the lot of Temenos is first certainly met with in Strabo, whose authority is only the fourth century Ephorus. But there are hints that Ephorus is here to be trusted. There is the evidence of Herodotus that from an unspecified earlier date down to about 550 B.C. the Argives had possessed the whole east coast of the Peloponnesus and "the island of Cythera and the rest of the islands[5]." The most likely period for Argos to have acquired this territory is the reign of Pheidon. Pheidon according to Strabo[6] "had deprived the Spartans of the hegemony of the Peloponnese," and it is the Spartans who shortly before Croesus

---

[1] *Ap.* Strabo VIII. 358. [2] Plato, *Laws*, III. 683 c–d; Diod. VII. 13.

[3] Strabo VIII. 389; Paus. II. 29. 5, VII. 4. 2; cp. Hdt. VIII. 46, but contrast Schol. Pind. *Ol.* VIII. 39, "a certain Triakon of Argos settled Aegina." Mueller, *Aeginetica*, p. 67 reconciles the two versions by stating that Deiophontes, "per Triaconem Aeginam occupaverat." Triakon appears in Tzetzes, *Chil.* VII. 133 (ll. 317, 319) as developing Aeginetan shipping after Aeacus:

ὁ Αἰακὸς κατάρξας δὲ ποιεῖν αὐτοῖς ὁλκάδας
ὥσπερ καὶ μετὰ θάνατον τοῦ Αἰακοῦ Τριάκων.

[4] The troubles that led up to the war had begun with a refusal of the Epidaurians to make their annual payment to Athens, Hdt. v. 82, 84.

[5] Hdt. I. 82. [6] Strabo VIII. 358.

asked for their help, had wrested from the Argives "Cythera and the rest of the islands." About 668 B.C., *i.e.* probably in Pheidon's reign, the Argives had beaten the Spartans in the battle of Hysiae, which decided the possession of the strip of coast land south of the Argolid[1].

Aegina is not mentioned in these proceedings, but C. Mueller may be right in including it among "the rest of the islands[2]." The Hysiae campaign is roughly contemporary with the second Messenian war, in which Argos took part against the Spartans[3], and of which indeed it may have been an incident. Now in that war the Samians took part by sea against the Argives[4], and it is natural to connect this action of theirs with their repeated attacks on Aegina in the days of the Samian King Amphikrates, at some period indefinitely before the reign of Polycrates. The Samians were certainly a naval power in the first half of the seventh century. The four triremes built for them in 704 B.C. marked for Thucydides an epoch in naval history[5]. About 668 B.C. Kolaios the Samian made his famous voyage beyond the Straits of Gibraltar to the Spanish seaport of Tartessus, a voyage that implies much previous naval enterprise on the Samians' part. The rivalry with Aegina was probably commercial. Kolaios and his crew returned from the "silver rooted streams" of the Tartessus river[6], having "made the greatest profits from cargoes of all Greeks of whom we have accurate information, excepting Sostratos the Aeginetan: for it is impossible for anyone else to rival him[7]." Samian attacks on Aegina are thus particularly likely to have happened about the time of the second Messenian war.

A century ago C. Mueller[8] argued that some event or other connecting Samos with Aegina must have been closely connected

---

[1] Paus. II. 24. 7.

[2] C. Mueller, *Aeginetica*, p. 53.

[3] Strabo VIII. 362; Paus. IV. 14. 8, 15. 1, 7, 17. 7. Beloch and his followers, *e.g.* Costanzi, *Riv. Stor. Ant.* v. p. 522, follow their general practice and post-date the war.

[4] Hdt. III. 47.

[5] Thuc. I. 13.

[6] παγὰς ἀργυροριζους, Stesich. fr. 4 (5). The river is the Baetis (Guadalquivir).

[7] Hdt. IV. 152. For Aeginetan aspirations towards the Spanish Eldorado, see perhaps Pindar, *Nem.* III. 21, IV. 69.

[8] C. Mueller, *Aeginetica*, p. 73.

with the revolt of Aegina from Epidaurus, since the revolt was described in the *History of Samos* of the Samian historian Duris (born about 340 B.C.)[1]. From this he proceeds to advocate a date for the revolt not very long before the war between Samos and Aegina of 520 B.C. Arguments based on the laws of digression observed by a writer whose works are known to us only in a few fragments need to be used with caution. If Duris is any indication whatever for the date of the revolt, he leaves an open choice between the time of the war of 520 B.C. and that of the days of King Amphikrates; and as between these two the evidence shows that the earlier is probable while the latter is almost impossible.

As independent evidence these hints would be of scarcely any value. As confirmation of a definite but disputable statement their value is considerable.

Summary of Pheidon's activities according to Strabo (=Ephorus). The recovery of ancestral domains is a favourite euphemism among military conquerors for their policy of annexation. The chronology, both relative and absolute, of Strabo's summary of Pheidon's career has every appearance of authenticity. Pheidon first recovers the lot of Temenos, then "invents" his measures and coinage, and after that attempts to expand eastwards and southwards to secure the whole inheritance of Heracles, or in other words aims at the suzerainty of the whole Peloponnese, and to that end celebrates the Olympian games. This last event is probably to be dated 668 B.C. The coinage must be put indefinitely earlier in his reign, a perfectly reasonable date on numismatic and historical grounds, and the recovery of the lot of Temenos a few years earlier still.

The date thus reached is confirmed by the histories of the two other leading cities of this part of the Peloponnese, Sicyon and Corinth.

---

[1] *F.H.G.* II. p. 481. Duris makes the Spartans take the place of the Argives, and the hapless Athenian is blinded before being put to death. Duris, however, is plainly based on Herodotus: Spartans are substituted for Argives as the enemies of Athens under fifth century influence, and a little archaeology is thrown in, borrowed perhaps from Thucydides, I. 6. The position of the story in the narrative of Duris might indicate his view (not necessarily correct) as to its date, but we know only that it occurred in the second book of his Horae (Schol. Eurip. *Hec.* 915, where the fragment is preserved, "ἐν τῷ ιδ τῶν Ὡρῶν"; "recte procul dubio Hullemanus ἐν τῷ β," *F.H.G. ad loc.*), which mentioned events of the sixth century, and may have dealt with the seventh also.

Sicyon formed part of the lot of Temenos, and was held by his son Phalkes[1]. About 670 B.C. the city fell under the tyranny of the able and powerful family of Orthagoras, whose policy was marked by extreme hostility to Argos[2]. Pheidon plainly can have had no footing in Sicyon during the rule of the Orthagorids. But the unusual stability and popularity of the tyranny at Sicyon have often been explained, not without reason, as due to its popular anti-Dorian policy. During the second Messenian war, which Pausanias dates 686–668 B.C.[3], so that the rise of Orthagoras coincides with its conclusion, the Sicyonians appear to have acted in close co-operation with the Argives[4]. The position and policy of the Sicyonian tyrants becomes particularly comprehensible if they had risen to power as leaders of a racial uprising that put an end in the city to a Dorian ascendancy that dated originally from the days of Temenos[5] and had been revived by Pheidon[6].

Pheidon and other parts of the lot of Temenos: (i) Sicyon.

Whether Corinth formed part of the lot of Temenos is uncertain. Probably it did. Strabo and Ptolemy exclude the city from the Argolid[7]. But on the other hand Homer speaks of it as being "in a corner of horse rearing Argos[8]," and Pausanias states that "the district of Corinth is part of Argolis[9]," and that he believes it to have been so in Homeric times[10]. The

(ii) Corinth.

[1] Paus. II. 6. 7, 7. 1, 13. 1; cp. Strabo VIII. 389.

[2] Hdt. v. 67, war of Cleisthenes, the third tyrant of the family, with Argos, and his device for inducing the Argive hero Adrastus, who was buried in Sicyon, to quit the city.

[3] Paus. IV. 15. 1, 23. 4. This is firmer evidence, *pace* Hicks, *Cambridge Comp. Greek Stud.*[1] p. 58, n. 3, than Plut. *Moral.* 194 (*Reg. et Imp. Apoph.*), where Epaminondas, speaking in 369 B.C., declares "that he had refounded Messene after an interval of 230 years." Plutarch may equally well be used as evidence that the extinction of archaic Messene did not synchronize with the end of the second Messenian war.

[4] Paus. IV. 15. 7, 17. 7.

[5] Cp. Paus. II. 6. 7, 7. 1: "Phalkes, son of Temenos with his Dorians seized Sicyon,"..."from that time the Sicyonians became Dorians and formed part of Argolis."

[6] For its lapse in the interval see references below, p. 183, n. 3. On the tyranny at Sicyon, see below, chapter IX.

[7] Strabo VIII. 389, cp. 369, 335; Ptol. III. 14. 33, 34.

[8] *Il.* VI. 152, ἔστι πόλις Ἐφύρη μυχῷ Ἄργεος ἱπποβότοιο.

[9] Paus. II. 1. 1.

[10] Paus. II. 4. 2 (trans. Frazer). "Like every attentive reader of Homer, I am persuaded that Bellerophon was not an independent monarch, but a vassal of

conflicting statements of these excellent authorities are best reconciled by supposing them to be referring to different periods. If this is so, and if, as well might be, all the domains of Homeric Argos passed to its first Dorian lord, then Corinth formed part of the lot of Temenos. A Temenid Corinth is perhaps implied in Apollodorus[1], where Temenos, the two sons of Aristodemus, and Kresphontes "when they had conquered the Peloponnese, set up three altars of Zeus Patroos and sacrificed on them and drew lots for the cities. The first lot was Argos, the second Sparta, the third Messene."

For connexions between Pheidon and Corinth we have only a story told by Plutarch and a Scholiast on Apollonius Rhodius[2] of which the salient points are that (*a*) Pheidon tries to annex Corinth; (*b*) the Bacchiads and Archias are the pro-Argive party; (*c*) the fall of the Bacchiads (which led to the rise of the tyrant Cypselus) meant the overthrow of Argive influence.

So far the story is all of a piece, and supports the view that the simultaneous establishment of Cypselus in Corinth and Orthagoras in Sicyon may have been part cause and part result of the fall of Pheidon and the breaking up again of the lot of Temenos. Such a suggestion harmonizes well with the friendship that existed between the Corinthian and Sicyon tyrants[3].

There are however chronological difficulties in this interpretation of the Pheidon Archias story. In the story (i) the fall of the Bacchiads is made contemporary with the foundation of Syracuse, *i.e.* it must presumably be dated about 734 B.C.[4]; (ii) Pheidon is put

Proetus, king of Argos. Even after Bellerophon had migrated to Lycia, the Corinthians are known to have been still subject to the lords of Argos or Mycenae. Again, in the army which attacked Troy, the Corinthian contingent was not commanded by a general of its own, but was brigaded with the Mycenaean and other troops commanded by Agamemnon."   [1] Apollodorus II. 8. 4.

[2] Plut. *Amat. Narr.* B (*Moral.* 772); Schol. *ap.* Rhod. *Arg.* IV. 1212; see also Diod. VIII. 10; Alex. Aetol. *Anth. Lyr.* I. 208; Max. Tyr. (ed. Teubner), XVIII.: cp. Wilisch, *Jahrb. Class. Phil.* 1876, pp. 586 f.

[3] Cleisthenes, the tyrant of Sicyon, regarded with particular favour one of his daughter's suitors, "because he was related by descent to the Cypselids of Corinth," Hdt. VI. 128 (quoted by Grote in this connexion). For friendship between Corinth and Sicyon at this time, see perhaps also Nic. Dam. *F.H.G.* III. p. 395; cp. Wilisch, *Goett. Gel. Anz.* 1880, II. p. 1195.

[4] Thuc. VI. 3, 4; Thucydides must be preferred to Strabo VI. 269, 267, who says the first Greek cities in Sicily included Syracuse, and were founded in the tenth generation after the Trojan wars (*i.e.* about 800 B.C., E. Meyer, *Ges. d. Alt.* II. sect. 302 n.).

some time before this event, his contemporary Habron being grandfather of Archias' favourite Actaeon: the Marmor Parium enters Pheidon before Archias.

In a highly romantic narrative like that of Archias and Actaeon the last thing to be looked for is a reliable and exact chronology. Impossible dates may mean impossible statements; but on the other hand they may mean merely a confusion of facts of different dates, or again, the facts may be coherent, and the dates just simply wrong.

In the present case, except for the relative dating of Archias and Pheidon, the historic background is perfectly coherent, if the events are put early in the seventh century. To accept the 750 date for Pheidon sets him right in relation to Archias, but leaves the rest of the story in the air. There is indeed always the refuge of assuming a double banishment of the Bacchiads. But the idea of a double banishment, traces of which might easily be discovered by the reduplicating school of historians, is deservedly suspect, and may have arisen from a double dating due to double dating of Pheidon. If there really were two banishments, the story better suits the second.

Neither Plutarch nor the Scholiast on Apollonius gives any absolute dates; and those of the Parian Marble, which does, are impossible. The Marble dates Pheidon 895 B.C. and Archias 758. Pheidon is also indeed made contemporary with an Athenian who according to Castor held the office of king from 864 to 846 B.C.[1] From 846 to 758 is a possible, though improbably long interval between Pheidon and Archias, if as the story tells us, the latter had as favourite the grandson of one of Pheidon's contemporaries; but even so the dating is so unsatisfactory, that the latest editor of the Parian Marble[2] has suggested transposing Archias and Pheidon. But, apart from other difficulties, the resultant early date for Archias is altogether against the evidence. There is no need to put him back into the ninth century merely because it is not unlikely that Greeks at that period were already making their way to Sicily. The antedating of Pheidon has already been accounted for, and he appears to have taken back Archias with him part of the way.

The date of Archias is a problem any way. But it is not difficult to suggest a possible chronology. Pheidon's fall[3] was probably rapid (a proof of his hubris). His rise was probably slow. Being a

[1] Jacoby, *Marm. Par.* p. 158.   [2] *Ibid. ad loc.*
[3] See perhaps Plato, *Laws*, 690 d–e.

hereditary monarch, he may well have ruled for fifty years, from about 715 to 665 B.C. It was early in his career that he began to carry out his designs on Corinth. Archias, who had founded Syracuse in 734, gave him support. We are told no details, but the alliances of the period of the second Messenian war and the naval struggle in the Saronic Gulf must have supplied abundant motives and inducements. Bacchiad government under Argive protection continued till Pheidon fell, which meant also the fall of the Bacchiads themselves. They withdrew to the far west. Demaratus penetrated as far as Tarquinii. Large numbers doubtless settled at Syracuse. The order of events just outlined coincides entirely with the extant narratives, except in the one matter of Syracuse, and there the divergence is very comprehensible. The founder of Syracuse had supported Pheidon. Pheidon's fall had led to a great influx of pro-Argive Corinthians into Syracuse, and threw Archias back entirely onto his Sicilian colony. If this is what really happened, it would not be surprising if the fall of Pheidon came to be regarded as having led to the original foundation of Syracuse.

Pheidon of Corinth: is he identical with the Argive? The chief doubt however as to the historical truth of the Argive tyrant's interference in Corinth is caused by certain references to a Corinthian Pheidon, described by Aristotle as "one of the earliest lawgivers[1]." When an Argive Pheidon is reported as making his appearance in Corinthian history, is it a mistake due to the confusing of two separate personalities? If two existed, they were unquestionably confused. A Pindar Scholiast says that "a certain Pheidon, a man of Corinth, invented measures and weights[2]."

But there is an alternative possibility. The Corinthian Pheidon may be only one aspect of the Argive: this is suggested by the Pindar Scholiast later in the same ode, where he says that "the Pheidon who first struck their measures ($\kappa \acute{o} \psi \alpha \varsigma \; \tau \grave{o} \; \mu \acute{\epsilon} \tau \rho o \nu$) for the Corinthians was an Argive[3]." Too much stress must not be laid on such very confused statements[4]. At best they can only corroborate other and

[1] Aristot. *Pol.* II. 1265 *b*. [2] Schol. Pind. *Ol.* XIII. 20. [3] *Ad Ol.* XIII. 27.
[4] A quotation at length is needed to illustrate our authority's mentality. He explains τίς γὰρ ἱππείοις ἐν ἔντεσσιν μέτρα ἐπίθηκε, *Ol.* XIII. 27, thus: "by gear he is meaning quarts and bushels owing to their hollowness...now of this gear for measures he says that the Corinthians were the inventors. But why did he call them equestrian? Because Pheidon, who first struck their measures for the Corinthians, was an Argive, and the poets call Argos equestrian: Eurip. (*I.T.* 700), 'when to Hellas and to equestrian Argos thou dost come'."

better evidence. This however is not altogether lacking. When Karanos, the kinsman of Pheidon, went to Macedonia and occupied Edessa and the lands of the Argeadae[1], Bacchiads from Corinth settled near by among the Lynkestai[2].

A lawgiver who was "one of the earliest" can have arisen in Corinth only before the establishment of the tyranny in 657 B.C. On the other hand lawgivers seem to have been mainly a seventh century phenomenon in Greece, and the most natural time for one to have been appointed in Corinth is when the Bacchiad nobility was losing its ascendancy, a process which may be imagined as beginning early in the seventh century or at the end of the eighth. Plutarch describes Pheidon's designs on Corinth as formed at the beginning of his career. Everything points to the Argive tyrant having had a long reign. There is nothing improbable in the supposition that the rival factions in Corinth invited to act as their lawgiver a young sovereign of unusual ability who ruled a city of great traditions but not at the time particularly powerful[3]. I have already suggested the course taken by events in Corinth after Pheidon had once secured a position in the city. One passage remains to be quoted that makes it still more probable both that the Corinthian lawgiver was the Argive tyrant, and that events in Corinth took something like the course that I have suggested. According to Nicholas of Damascus[4] Pheidon out of friendship went to the help of the Corinthians during a civil war: an attack was made by his supporters, and he was killed[5]. An intimate connexion from the beginning of his career with the great trading and manufacturing city of the Isthmus would go far to explain the commercial and financial inventiveness that was the distinguishing feature of this royal tyrant[6].

[1] Justin VII. 1; cp. above, p. 156.   [2] Strabo VII. 326.

[3] For the lot of Temenos having been really dissipated, see Paus. II. 26. 2, 28. 3; VIII. 27. 1; II. 36. 5; III. 7. 4; IV. 8. 3, 14. 3, 34. 9.

[4] F.H.G. III. p. 378, fr. 41.

[5] The Argive tyrant's overlordship in Corinth is accepted, but put into the eighth century by Unger, Philol. XXVIII. pp. 399 f., XXIX. pp. 245 f., and Wilisch, Neue Jahrb. 1876, pp. 585 f.

[6] Svoronos, J. I. d'A. N. v. p. 42 states that some of the earliest "tortoises" are bad money ($\kappa i\beta\delta\eta\lambda a$), and suggests that Pheidon debased the coinage when his prosperity began to diminish towards the end of his reign. This suggestion has no direct confirmation, but it harmonizes with what is known of the fall of the tyranny in other places, notably Athens, where it coincides with the loss of the Paionian mines, and Rome, where Tarquin fell, "exhaustus munificentia publicorum operum."

Chapter VII. *Corinth*

ἡ μὲν δὴ πόλις ἡ τῶν Κορινθίων μεγάλη τε καὶ πλουσία διὰ παντὸς ὑπῆρξεν, ἀνδρῶν τε ηὐπόρησεν ἀγαθῶν εἴς τε τὰ πολιτικὰ καὶ εἰς τὰς τέχνας τὰς δημιουργικάς. STRABO VIII. 382.

Mercantile and marine developments at Corinth quoted by Thucydides to illustrate the conditions that led to the rise of tyrannies.
IN the passage of Thucydides[1] in which he associates the origin of tyranny with the acquisition of wealth, one other development is mentioned as characteristic of the age. "Greece began to fit out fleets and took more to the sea."

If the views expressed in the last chapter are not entirely mistaken, then in Greece Proper the earliest phases of all these developments, in politics, in industry, and in commerce by land and sea, are all to be associated with Pheidon of Argos. But on the same showing Pheidon was a man born rather before his time and not quite in the right place.

The town marked out by its situation[2] to develop the new tendencies to the fullest was Corinth, and it is in fact from Corinth that Thucydides draws his illustration, mentioning in this connexion the shipbuilding of the Corinthian Ameinokles about 704 B.C. and the naval battle between Corinth and Corcyra of about 664 B.C.[3] He says nothing about Corinthian tyrants, but the description of the situation at Corinth is simply a paraphrase of that of the general situation that led to tyrannies[4]. Corinth is chosen to exemplify the normal course of things in a seventh century Greek town, and it may be taken as certain that Thucydides regards the tyranny at Corinth as the outcome of the mercantile and maritime developments described in the passage just quoted.

Only, what was the personal relationship of the tyrants to the new developments?

[1] I. 13.
[2] Cp. Livy XXXIII. 32; Val. Max. IV. 8. 5; Aristid. *Isthmic.* p. 102.
[3] Thuc. I. 13; cp. Strabo VIII. 378.
[4] cp. δυνατωτέρας γενομένης τῆς Ἑλλάδος καὶ τῶν χρημάτων τὴν κτῆσιν ἔτι μᾶλλον ποιουμένης τυραννίδες ἐν ταῖς πόλεσι καθίσταντο, τῶν προσόδων μειζόνων γιγνομένων with οἱ Κορίνθιοι...χρήμασί τε δυνατοὶ ἦσαν...καὶ ἐμπόριον...:-ἀρέχοντες δυνατὴν ἔσχον χρημάτων προσόδῳ τὴν πόλιν.

Before attempting to answer this question, one important addition may be made to Thucydides' picture of the state of things in the city when the tyranny arose. Corinth was not engaged only in commerce and shipping. She was also a great industrial centre. In the chapter on Argos reasons have been given for thinking that the tyrant Pheidon flourished just at the time when pottery of the style called for want of a better name proto-Corinthian

Seventh century Corinth was also a great industrial centre, especially for pottery.

Fig. 22. Corinthian vase found at Corinth.

was enjoying a great vogue in a great part of the Greek world, that much at least of this ware was made in Pheidon's dominions, and that Pheidon took political measures to crush or cripple rival centres. Towards the middle of the seventh century proto-Corinthian ware was eclipsed by a new style, which with good reason has been named Corinthian[1]. This new style became so popular that the invention of the potter's wheel was ascribed to a Corinthian[2].

Fig. 23. Corinthian terra cotta tablet depicting a potter at his wheel

Fig. 24. Corinthian terra cotta tablet depicting the interior of a kiln.

Corinthian vases of this period show one of the most decorative and distinctive styles of pottery that has ever been invented. The style of decoration somewhat recalls oriental carpets, and it was long ago plausibly suggested that oriental carpets or tapestries furnished

[1] Cp. perhaps the tradition which makes the artist Butades migrate from (proto-Corinthian?) Sicyon to Corinth. Pliny, *N.H.* xxxv. 43 (12).

[2] Pliny, *N.H.* vii. 57 (56), figlinas (inuenit) Coroebus Atheniensis, in iis orbem Anarcharsis Scythes, ut alii Hyperbius Corinthius. Schol. Pind. *Ol.* xiii. 27 (on achievements of Corinthians), Δίδυμος δέ φησι δηλοῦσθαι τὸν κεραμεικὸν τρόχον ἐκ μεταφορᾶς.

the models for the Corinthian vase painters[1]. Two jugs in this style, one from Corinth itself[2], the other from Corneto (Tarquinii), are shown in figs. 22 and 34. Votive tablets of the sixth century B.C. have been found at Corinth that depict various stages of the manufacture. Two are here reproduced (figs. 23, 24). This very distinctive pottery made its way over a great part of the Greek world[3]. It has been found in large quantities all over Sicily, South Italy and Etruria, in many parts of Greece Proper, and in many places further east[4].

Cypselus established himself as tyrant in 657 B.C. at the height of these great developments of Corinthian industry, trade, and shipping. It has been noticed by Busolt[5] that 657 is also the year of the conquest of Sardis by the Cimmerians. The disturbances in Asia Minor may have enhanced the importance of the western trade, in which Corinth was particularly concerned[6]. They may incidentally have removed, at least for the time being, a very powerful commercial rival, since Corinth and Lydia appear to have been engaged in much the same industries, namely weaving, dyeing, metallurgy, horse rearing and the making of ointments, in addition to pottery, a fact that can hardly have been accidental[7], and points to Corinth having been influenced by Lydia. Both before and after the Cimmerian invasion Lydia and Corinth appear to have been on excellent terms[8]: but this would not prevent Corinthian merchants from growing more prosperous through Lydia's troubles[9].

Cypselus becomes tyrant at the height of these developments.

---

[1] Birch, *Hist. Pott.* p. 185. For Corinthian textiles see Barth, *Corinth. Comm.* pp. 22 f. quoting Athen. I. 27 *d*, XII. 525 *d*., XIII. 582 *d*, Aristoph. *Ranae* 440. For general industrial activities see Strabo 382, γραφική τε καὶ πλαστικὴ καὶ πᾶσα ἡ τοιαύτη δημιουργία; Oros. v. 3, officina omnium artificum atque artificiorum.

[2] From recent excavations of the American School. I am indebted for the photograph to Miss A. Walker.

[3] Cp. below, p. 242.

[4] *E.g.* 79 vases in one grave in Rhodes, *Jahrb.* I. 144.

[5] *Gr. G.*² I. 459, n. 6.

[6] See for instance the story of Demaratus and Tarquinii, discussed in the chapter on Rome.

[7] Bluemner, *Gewerb. Tätig.* 35–37; Wilisch, *Jahrb. Gym. Zittau*, 1901, p. 7.

[8] Gyges used the Corinthian treasury at Delphi (Hdt. I. 14). Periander sent slaves to Alyattes (Hdt. III. 49).

[9] The revolts from Corinth of Corcyra and Megara are also associated by Busolt (*Lakedaim.* I. 200) with the rise of Cypselus. If they helped it, it was probably by discrediting the ruling Bacchiads.

Whether the rise of Cypselus had any connexion with the beginnings of Corinthian coinage is a matter of dispute. Busolt[1] dates the earliest issues some half century later than the establishment of the tyranny.

Cypselus and the beginnings of Corinthian coinage.

Head[2] on the other hand makes the coinage and the tyranny begin approximately together and he is supported by Percy Gardner[3], who dates the earliest coins of Corinth in the early part of the seventh century but after 665 B.C.

Fig. 25. Coins of Corinth.

If, then, as seems probable, the English numismatists are nearer the truth than the German; the first issues of "colts," as the coins were colloquially called from the winged horse that they bore, may have played their part in helping Cypselus to the tyranny. The traces of Lydian influence support this view. But on the other hand Corinth, whose trade was so preponderatingly with the west, may, like its colony Corcyra, have felt the need of a coinage only comparatively late. Where the main facts are so obscure and particulars are completely wanting it is idle to carry speculation further.

For evidence as to Cypselus' personal relationship to the commercial developments of his age we must look elsewhere. Some modern writers have indeed despaired of recovering any picture of the personal history of a ruler who is variously described by our

---

[1] *Gr. G.*² I. 627 (where "seventh" century is a misprint for "sixth"; cp. p. 651); cp. p. 499 and Wilisch, *Jahrb. Gym. Zittau*, 1901, p. 25.

[2] *Brit. Mus. Cat. Coins Corinth*, p. xviii; *Hist. Num.*² ad loc.

[3] *Earliest Coins Greece Proper*, pp. 22 f.

best authorities as having ruled mildly[1] and with bloodthirsty severity[2]. This attitude is quite unnecessary. Both statements are in themselves quite credible as contemporary accounts of the same regime from different points of view. Still, by themselves they do not take us very far. Fortunately we are better informed in other directions.

His personal relationship when tyrant to the commercial developments of his age.

Of the Corinthian colonies in Western Greece, that lined the trade route to Sicily and Italy and the Furthest West, Leukas, Ambracia and Anaktorion were founded by Cypselus[3]. Leukas was converted by him from a peninsula into an island for the greater convenience of navigation[4].

Cypselus is said to have taxed his subjects heavily. This statement is taken from the pseudo-Aristotelian *Oeconomica*[5], a work of no great authority for our early period. The tax is associated by Suidas[6] with the dedication of a colossus of beaten gold which "Didymus says was made by Periander" (not Cypselus) "with the object of checking the Corinthians in their luxury and arrogance." Theophrastus, so Suidas also states, called the statue the colossus not of Cypselus but of the sons of Cypselus (Κυψελιδῶν). The statement of the *Oeconomica* must therefore be taken with reserve. But the story of Cypselus' heavy taxation states also that the tyrant made his subjects work and prosper and able to pay the taxes[7].

Whatever the truth about the colossus the fact remains that the fame of Cypselus was largely eclipsed by that of his son and successor Periander, who was actually claimed by some writers as one of the seven sages of early Greece[8]. This is unfortunate when we are searching

Personal relationships of his son Periander to these same developments.

---

[1] Aristot. *Pol.* VII. (V.), 1315b; Nic. Dam. *F.H.G.* III. p. 392.

[2] Hdt. v. 92. 21.

[3] For full references see Busolt, *Gr. G.*² I. pp. 642–3.

[4] Strabo x. 452; cp. Busolt, *Gr. G.*² I. 642, who quotes also Strabo I. 59, Polyb. v. 5. 12.

[5] Aristot. *Oecon.* II. 1346a–b.   [6] Suid. s.v. Κυψελιδῶν ἀναθήματα.

[7] Cp. Knapp, *Korrespondenz-Bl. Gelebrt-Schulen Wuerttembergs*, 1888, p. 120, n. 1, who compares fourteenth century Italian tyrants.

[8] Plut. *de Ei ap. Delph.* 3 (*Moral.* 385); Dio Chrys. XXXVII. 456M (103 R); Plato, *Ep.* 2. The unfriendly Nic. Dam. *F.H.G.* III. p. 393, quotes this view, but adds τὸ δὲ οὐκ ἦν; cp. Plato, *Rep.* I. 336; *Protag.* 343a. Appian (*bell. Mithr.* 28) does not mention Periander, but accepts his claim: "of the seven sages so called all who engaged in active life ruled and tyrannized more savagely than the normal tyrant (ὠμότερον τῶν ἰδιωτικῶν τυράννων)."

for origins, since Periander is said to have changed the character of the sovereignty[1]. Even if the authorities who made this statement are not particularly good, still it must be taken as in some part true. The son born in the purple can never succeed exactly to the position of the father who founded the house. Luckily however we are told the nature of Periander's change. He regarded himself as a soldier and sought to make Corinth a great military power, whereas Cypselus had been a man of peace with a peaceful policy[2]. So far therefore as Periander's policy was not directly or indirectly military, there is no need to assume a break with that of his father.

He maintained and enlarged the colonial empire of the city[3]. As regards Corinthian trade under Periander we are told that his public revenues were all derived from its taxation[4]: but everything shows that he did not follow the Bacchiads and tax it ruthlessly. Rather he seems to have aimed at increasing his revenues by fostering commerce. Corinthian shipping, with which the trade of the city

[1] "Periander first changed the government (πρῶτος μετέστησε τὴν ἀρχήν)," Heraclides, *F.H.G.* II. p. 213; "Periander, the son of Cypselus king of Corinth, received the kingdom by inheritance from his father and out of savagery and violence turned it into a tyranny," Nic. Dam. *F.H.G.* III. p. 393; "they say that Periander the Corinthian was originally popular (δημοτικόν), but afterwards changed his policy and became tyrannical," Greg. Cypr. III. 30 = Leutsch, *Paroem. Gr.* II. p. 89; cp. (almost the same words) Schol. *Hipp. Maj.* 304 E; cp. also Diog. Laert. I. 7. 5. Hdt. v. 92. 23 regards Periander's early mildness as a change from Cypselus, but his account is frankly anti-Cypselid.

[2] "Cypselus was a demagogue and throughout his reign remained without a bodyguard: but Periander proved tyrannical but warlike," Aristot. *Pol.* VII. (v.), 1315b, where Cypselus' alleged demagogism is probably only a late inference from a genuine tradition that he was not a soldier: see chap. I. p. 31. The passages quoted in the last note from Heraclides and Nicolaus go on at once to mention that Periander instituted an armed bodyguard, and Nicolaus adds that "he made repeated campaigns and was warlike." This statement may be accepted though the context of the last passage shows that the picture of the tyrannical Periander is influenced by the conception of the tyrant as a military despot prevalent since Aristotle (see chap. I. pp. 28 f.). The maxim καλὸν ἡσυχία (peace is a good thing) is attributed to Periander by Diog. Laert. I. 7. 4, but such utterances are notoriously quite consistent with the most aggressive military policy.

[3] Nic. Dam. *F.H.G.* III. p. 393 (a son of Periander founded Potidaea); cp. How and Wells, *Hdt.* vol. II. p. 341 on Potidaea and Epidamnus (founded 626 B.C. Euseb.; cp. Thuc. I. 24) as controlling the great road from Durazzo to Salonika. The road traversed the land of the Lynkestai, whose kings claimed Corinthian descent, Strabo VII. 326.

[4] Heraclides, *F.H.G.* II. p. 213.

was inseparably bound up, certainly owed much to him. "He built triremes and plied both seas[1]." This last statement seems intended to contrast Periander with his father, whose activities had been mainly in the west. Periander on the other hand is found acting in close concert with Thrasybulus the tyrant of Miletus[2]. He has been suspected of slave-dealing with Lydia[3], and acted as arbitrator between that state and Miletus[4]. He had a nephew who bore the name of a king of Egypt[5]. In order the better to "ply both seas" he is said to have wanted to cut a canal through the Corinthian Isthmus[6]. Here too he was following in the footsteps of his father who had "velificated" Leukas.

It is interesting therefore to notice the emphasis laid on Periander's wealth[7], and to recall the social legislation attributed to him by

[1] Nic. Dam. *ibid.*

[2] Hdt. v. 92; Aristot. *Pol.* III. 1284a, VII. (v.), 1311a; Dion. Hal. IV. 56. Myres, *J.H.S.* XXVI. pp. 110 f. makes Periander an active partner in the Milesian thalassocracy, which he dates at this period. Reasons for not accepting Myres on the Milesian thalassocracy are suggested in the chapter on Egypt, but his account of Periander's naval support of Thrasybulus is valuable and convincing. Myres quotes the story of Arion and his wonderful adventure with the pirates and the dolphins on the Corinthian merchant ship that was bearing him to Periander's court, Hdt. I. 23-4; Plut. *Sept. Sap. Conv.* 18 f. (*Moral.* 161).

[3] Hdt. III. 48, 49; Nic. Dam. *F.H.G.* III. pp. 393-4; Plut. *de Mal. Hdt.* 22, 23 (*Moral.* 859-861); Diog. Laert. I. 7. 2. Hence Movers, *Phoen.* II. iii. 109, calls Periander a slave dealer; so also Wilisch, *Gœtt. Gel. Anz.* 1880, p. 1202, *Jahrb. Gym. Zittau*, 1901, p. 22, n. 9, who refers also to Hdt. VIII. 105 (on Panionios the Chian who in the early part of the fifth century "made his living" by mutilating boys whom "he took and sold at Sardis and Ephesus for great sums"). Wilisch infers also, *ibid.* p. 22, from the ἱερόδουλοι or consecrated prostitutes of the Corinthian temple of Aphrodite, an import from Asia to Corinth of female slaves: see Athen. XIII. 573; Strabo VIII. 378 and perhaps 347. This view is not necessarily contradicted by Heraclides, who declares (*F.H.G.* II. p. 213) that Periander drowned all the procuresses in the city (Steinmetz however reads ἀπέδυσε, stripped). Heraclides is not indeed discredited by the fact that Athenaeus x. 443 a, makes not only Periander but also Cleomenes or Cleomis tyrant of Methymna dispose of loose women in this Napoleonic way. The double assignation decides neither whether the story is true or false nor which way went the borrowing. But Wilisch and Heraclides may both be right. A tyrant who traded in prostitutes might yet be most severe on unlicensed prostitution.

[4] Busolt, *Gr. G.*[2] II. 466.   [5] See below, pp. 212-4.

[6] Diog. Laert. I. 7. 6; cp. E. Curtius, *Pelop.* I. 13; Gerster, *Isthme de Corinth*, *B.C.H.* VIII. (1884), pp. 225 f.

[7] Cp. the epitaph, Diog. Laert. I. 7. 3,

πλούτου καὶ σοφίης πρύτανιν πατρὶς ἥδε Κόρινθος
κόλποις ἀγχίαλος γῆ Περίανδρον ἔχει.

Nicolaus Damascenus, according to whom the tyrant "forbad the citizens to acquire slaves and live in idleness, and continually found them some employment[1]." Heraclides[2] and Diogenes Laertius (quoting Ephorus and Aristotle)[3] state that he did not allow anybody and everybody to live in the city. Their statement is capable of many interpretations. It may mean that Periander sought to control labour in the city or to prevent the rural population from quitting the land for the superior attractions of life in the great industrial centre.

In short from first to last the tyranny at Corinth is seen taking an active part in guiding the industrial, commercial and maritime activities of the city[4]. This however is what might be expected from any able government at the period, and nobody has ever questioned the Cypselids' ability. The previous government, that of the aristocracy of the Bacchiads, had "exploited the market with impunity[5],"

---

[1] *F.H.G.* III. p. 393; cp. Heraclides, *F.H.G.* II. p. 213, "putting a complete stop to the acquisition of slaves and to luxury." These statements are treated sceptically by Busolt, *Gr. G.*² I. p. 646 (mainly on the dangerous ground that Periander's behaviour is too typical to be true), and by Poehlmann, *Grundr. Gr. G.*¹ 62, ⁴79, but accepted or defended by Knapp, *op. cit.* p. 119; Duncker, *G. d. A.* VI.⁵ 63; Wilisch, *Jabrb. Gym. Zittau*, 1901, p. 17; cp. p. 12; Meyer, *G. d. A.* II. 621; Beloch, *Gr. G.*² I. i. p. 270. These writers mainly explain the measures as intended to protect small home industries against large slave factories (so Busolt, *Lakedaim.* p. 201). Porzio, *Cipselidi*, p. 235, n., rightly points out that the authors who preserve this notice did not so understand it, but wrongly maintains that this fact is fatal to the explanation. Porzio's own explanation (that the Cypselids' taxation led to discontent which endangered the tyrants whose "main care was therefore to empty the city by forcing their subjects to live solitary and scattered in the country," *ibid.* p. 236) runs counter to the facts, which show that cities increased under the tyranny.

[2] *F.H.G.* II. 213.   [3] Diog. Laert. I. 7. 5.

[4] Cp. Wilisch, *Jabrb. Gym. Zittau*, 1901, p. 13, "promotion of home industries, attitude towards slave labour, introduction of the coinage, these were the main questions for the government of the Cypselids, especially Periander"; so Busolt, *Lakedaim.* I. 202, 211.

[5] Strabo VIII. 378; cp. Barth, *Corinth. Comm.* p. 14. Strabo calls the Bacchiads tyrants, probably in the later sense of bad despotic rulers. Note, however, that he associates their "tyranny" with great wealth and commercial connexions. "The Bacchiads too became tyrants, and being wealthy and many and of distinguished family for some two hundred years they held rule and exploited the market with impunity. These Cypselus put down and himself became tyrant.... Of the wealth associated with this house there is evidence in the dedication of Cypselus at Olympia, a hammered gold statue of large size." Busolt, *Lakedaim.* I. 201-3, thinks that the Bacchiads had the industry of Corinth in their own

CORINTH

and very possibly this short-sighted policy had hastened and helped their fall[1].

But how precisely were they overthrown? What was the career of Cypselus previous to his obtaining the tyranny?

Before he became tyrant Cypselus was probably polemarch,

According to Nicolaus Damascenus, who based himself largely on the fourth century Ephorus[2], Labda, the mother of Cypselus, belonged to the Bacchiad aristocracy, but owing to a personal deformity[3] she had married beneath her. Her husband, Eetion, is variously said to have been descended from the pre-Hellenic Lapithae of Thessaly[4] and from a non-Dorian stock of Gonussa above Sicyon[5]. In any case, as observed by How and Wells[6], Eetion belonged to the pre-Dorian "Aeolic" population of Corinth[7]. The Bacchiad aristocracy was extremely exclusive. Its members married only among themselves. Consequently the official oracles prophesied evil from this union, and when a son was born of it, the government sent agents to destroy the child. But

---

hands, and that they employed in it numerous slaves who proved irresistible competitors to the crowd of *petit bourgeois*, and that Cypselus made himself tyrant by putting himself at the head of the latter. Servile competition was put out of the way when Cypselus had made himself tyrant, and the working classes of the citizen population were occupied in numerous public works. Busolt rightly recognizes the commercial element in Cypselus' power, but the evidence is all against a highly organized servile industry at this early date; in Corinth itself the legislation against servile labour is attributed to Periander, and the date of the legislation is a good indication of the date at which servile labour first seriously threatened free; the exploiting of the market by the Bacchiads is not evidence for commercial undertakings on the part of the Bacchiads, but rather of their having held aloof from commerce.

[1] This suggestion is quite consistent with the vague statement of Aelian, *V.H.* I. 19, that they fell "through immoderate luxury" (διὰ τρυφὴν τὴν ἔξω τοῦ μέτρου).

[2] Busolt, *Gr. G.*² I. p. 637; E. Meyer, *Rhein. Mus.* 1887, p. 91.

[3] *Et. Mag.* βλαισός· ὁ τοὺς πόδας ἐπὶ τὰ ἔξω διεστραμμένος καὶ τῷ Λ στοιχείῳ ἐοικώς· διὰ τοῦτο καὶ Λάμβδα ἐκαλεῖτο ἡ γυνὴ μὲν Ἠετίωνος μήτηρ δὲ Κυψέλου τοῦ Κορίνθου τυράννου. Knapp, *op. cit.* p. 33, notes that Bacchis, ancestor of the Bacchiads, was also lame, Heraclid. *F.H.G.* II. p. 212.

[4] Hdt. v. 92. 7.   [5] Paus. II. 4. 4; cp. v. 18. 7.

[6] *Hdt. ad loc.*

[7] Thuc. IV. 42. His family lived at Petra, Hdt. v. 92. 7, which has led Knapp, *op. cit.* pp. 33–34, n. 5, to compare Cypselus with the Paladin Roland who was son of Charlemagne's sister Bertha and a poor knight named Milo. Roland was born among the rocks and was called Roland because he rolled across the cave in which he was born.

U. T.

the infant melted the hearts of its would-be murderers, and instead of killing it they went back and reported that they had done so. The infant was sent away by its parents to Olympia, and was brought up first there and then at Cleonae. Encouraged by a Delphic oracle Cypselus returned to Corinth, became very popular, was elected polemarch, and made himself still more popular by refusing to imprison citizens and remitting in all cases his part of their fines. Finally he headed a rising against the unpopular Bacchiads, killed Patrokleides, who was king at the time, and was made king in his stead. He ruled mildly, neither maintaining a bodyguard nor losing the people's favour[1].

Such is the account given by Nicholas of Damascus. For the greater part of it we have no earlier authority. But once more we must be on our guard against too hasty scepticism. Ephorus, who is generally admitted to have been the source of this account, was not further removed from Cypselus than this age is from Cromwell. Cypselus was the foremost man of his age in all Greece. We need to be very sceptical of such scepticism as that of Busolt[2], who argues that Cypselus cannot have been polemarch before he became tyrant because if his parentage was not known he would not have been eligible, while if it was he would not have been elected[3]. As pointed out many years ago by Wilisch[4], such arguments are dangerous when applied to times of which so little is known. The aristocracy which fell in 657 B.C. may have begun to totter some time earlier. Given the requisite gaps in our knowledge, Busolt's line of argument might be equally well used to discredit the received tradition about the Victorian age in England on the ground that it contains the highly improbable statement that the leader of the aristocratic party was an Italian Jew.

Ephorus seems to have been used by Aristotle[5]. It would be rash indeed to follow Busolt[6] and agree that such a source may yet be valueless. Aristotle is not to be treated in this way. The whole

---

[1] *F.H.G.* III. pp. 391–2.   [2] *Gr. G.*² I. p. 636, n. 2.
[3] Cp. Schubring, *de Cypselo* (Goettingen, 1862), pp. 62 f.; Wilisch, *Goett. Gel. Anz.* 1880, p. 1198.
[4] *Goett. Gel. Anz.* 1880, pp. 1196–1197.
[5] Wilisch, *Goett. Gel. Anz.* 1880, p. 1197; Knapp, *op. cit.* p. 115; Busolt, *Gr. G.*² I. p. 637, quoting Ar. *Pol.* VII. (v.), 1310 b, Κύψελος ἐκ δημαγωγίας.
[6] *Gr. G.*² I. p. 637. So more recently Porzio, *Cipselidi*, p. 180, who thinks the Ephorean version a mere amplification of Herodotus. In uncritical incredulity Porzio rivals Pais (see *e.g. op. cit.* pp. 164–5 and cp. below, pp. 236 f.).

character of his work forces us to start with the assumption that he had some idea of the difference between myth and historical tradition. We always know the reasons why modern scholars are sometimes inclined to discredit him. We do not always know the reasons that led Aristotle to accept as facts what he so accepts. What we do know is that the material on which he based his statements was far more ample than that which is now at our disposal. Even for a period so comparatively remote from him as the seventh century B.C. Aristotle must have been able to collect much evidence of one sort or another to confirm him alike in his doubts and his beliefs[1].

For eighth century Corinth Aristotle and his contemporaries probably[2] had the poems of the Corinthian Eumelos, a ποιητὴς ἱστορικός[3] who flourished about 750 B.C. and wrote among other works an epic called Κορινθιακά. A prose history of Corinth (Κορινθία συγγραφή) was also ascribed to him. The ascription is doubted by Pausanias[4], not without reason, but it may still have been a document of some value and antiquity. The same is true of the "didactic poem in two thousand lines" ascribed by Diogenes Laertius to Periander himself[5]. We are learning to take our ancient records more on their face value than was done by our grandfathers in the nineteenth century. The classical historians, using the word in its widest sense, are still suffering from the reaction against the doctrine of verbal inspiration.

The story of the infant Cypselus is put by Plutarch[6] into the mouth of a certain "Chersias the poet," who is represented as having during a banquet given by Periander "mentioned others whose lives

---

[1] Cp. Wilisch, *Goett. Gel. Anz.* 1880, pp. 1198–9, quoting Plut. *de Mal. Hdt.* 22 (*Moral.* 860), Strabo XIII. 600.

[2] Wilisch, *Eumelus* (Zittau, 1875). The Κορινθιακά were known to Theopompus (*b.* 380 B.C., quoted eight lines, Tzetz. *ad Lyc.* 174) and Apollonius Rhodius (*b.* 265 B.C., used them for his *Argonautica*). To judge from slight extant fragments they dealt with the mythical period. But even so they may well, when complete, have contained material for eighth century Corinthian history. They were not known to Pausanias in the original; Paus. II. 1. 1.

[3] Tzetzes, *ad Lyc.* 174; Schol. Pind. *Ol.* XIII. 74.

[4] Paus. II. 1. 1. Groddech and Wilisch think the συγγραφή a prose précis of the ἔπη.

[5] ὑποθήκας εἰς ἔπη δισχίλια, Diog. Laert. I. 7. 4; cp. Suid. s.v. Περίανδρος· ὑποθήκας εἰς τὸν ἀνθρώπειον βίον, ἔπη δισχίλια. The maxims quoted by Diogenes as from this work are utterly commonplace, but they might none the less be derived from a poem or collection as valuable as that of Theognis.

[6] Plut. *Sept. Sap. Conviv.* 21 (*Moral.* 163).

had been saved when despaired of and in particular Cypselus the father of Periander." One of the sceptics[1] has recently accepted this Chersias as historical and imagined Plutarch as here making use of a poem of his which he proceeds to explain as a fiction invented to give an appearance of legitimacy to the Cypselids. The explanation is quite gratuitous. It is true that Diogenes Laertius[2] speaks of Periander as "of the race of the Heraclids." But Chersias in Plutarch does not mention even the parents of Cypselus, much less his remote ancestors, and there is no evidence that he had them in mind[3]. The poem itself is a doubtful item. The only inference to be drawn from Plutarch is that to his readers the poem (assuming its existence) probably seemed in keeping with the scene. It is however well to be reminded that even Plutarch had much more literary material to draw from for this early period than have the moderns.

On the whole therefore the safest attitude towards the narrative of Nicolaus will be one of benevolent agnosticism. No doubt he had a tendency to rationalize half or wholly mythical stories. It is not improbable that he did this to some extent in his account of the infant Cypselus with which we can compare the version of Herodotus. But when he makes a simple statement of commonplace fact, as, for instance, that Cypselus was polemarch before he became tyrant, the most prudent and the most critical course is to accept it as probably true[4]. The reason why the record of this fact was preserved is not far to seek. The fourth century historians seized on the name as evidence that Cypselus was in fact as well as in name a ruler of the same order as Dionysius, who started his career as a military demagogue. But the context

but that is no evidence of military power. Cypselus cannot have been a military despot.

shows that the polemarch was not in this case a military officer[5], and we know by implication that Cypselus was not a warlike person, for the record of how Periander changed the character of the government goes on to say that he *became*[6] warlike. And,

---

[1] Porzio, *Cipselidi*, p. 195. [2] Diog. Laert. I. 7. 1.

[3] On the family of Cypselus see above, p. 193. The accounts make it on the father's side older than that of the ruling Bacchiads.

[4] Cp. Wilisch, *Goett. Gel. Anz.* 1880, p. 1198, Knapp, *op. cit.* p. 41 (who realizes that ancient lists of Corinthian magistrates may have survived till the days of Ephorus and been used by him).

[5] Polemarch was a common title (Knapp, *op. cit.* p. 39). The duties of the office varied and were by no means always military: see Schubring, *de Cyps.* pp. 62–63, quoting Sparta, Athens, Boeotia, Aetolia (Polyb. IV. 18. 2).

[6] Aristot. *Pol.* VII. (v.), 1315 b.

as remarked long ago by Schubring[1], if the tenure of the polemarchy is historical, still it was not the means by which Cypselus reached the tyranny, but rather like the murder of the Bacchiad Patrokleides, a sign and token that he was already in a position to seize it.

What then was the basis of his power? The only possible evidence is to be found in the story Nicolaus therefore brings us little nearer to understanding the basis of the future tyrant's power. Our only hope of doing this lies in Herodotus, who tells the story of the infant Cypselus with certain details omitted by Nicolaus but which probably contain the essence of the story. According to Herodotus[2] Cypselus was the child from the cypsele in which as an infant his mother had concealed him from his would-be murderers. If we

which makes Cypselus the child from the cypsele. are to believe Plutarch, the story of the cypsele could still in his days be traced back to the days of Periander[3]. It is easy to point out[4] that we are here up against a widespread story of which different versions have been attached to such different names as Sargon of Akkad (c. 3800 B.C.[5]), Moses, Romulus and Cyrus[6]. But even if we accept a common origin for all these stories, we are not very much further on. We should still have to determine why and how Cypselus found a place in the series. But it must not be too hastily assumed that the

What is a cypsele? Not, in spite of some ancient and modern authorities, either an ark or a wooden chest. cypsele of Cypselus has anything at all to do with the ark that Pharaoh's daughter found on the banks of the Nile[7] or the "alueus" discovered by the shepherd Faustulus on the banks of the Tiber. In both these cases[8] the vessel could float and was discovered by a river side. Cypselus was not discovered.

---

[1] *de Cypselo*, p. 64.   [2] Hdt. v. 92.

[3] *Sept. Sap. Conv.* 21 (*Moral.* 163–4). Periander's court poet Chersias (above, p. 195) tells of Cypselus "whom those who were sent to destroy him when a new born child refrained from slaying because he smiled on them. And afterwards they repented and sought for him, but did not find him, since he had been put away by his mother in a cypsele."

[4] As is done by Porzio, *Cipselidi*, p. 198.

[5] Sayce, *Encyc. Brit.*[11] s.v. Babylonia and Assyria, p. 103; Maspero, *Hist. Anc.*[5] pp. 157–8.

[6] For other parallels cp. Bauer, *Sitz. Ak. Wiss. Wien*, vol. 100 (1882), pp. 553 (German), 557 (Indian).

[7] The fact that Cypselus smiled before being put in his cypsele while Moses cried when left in his ark hardly proves the identity of the legends, *pace* Knapp, *op. cit.* 1888, p. 32, n. 1.

[8] As also in those quoted by Bauer, *Sitz. Ak. Wiss. Wien*, vol. 100, pp. 553, 557.

That is the whole point of the story. He was not exposed in a river or sea like Romulus or Perseus. And it is more than doubtful whether a cypsele has any connexion whatever with an alueus or ark. It is true that they are more or less identified by our ancient authorities. Pausanias[1], who wrote his guide to Greece in the second century A.D., professed to have seen at Olympia the very cypsele in which Cypselus had been hidden and from which he was said to have got his name. It was a coffer (λάρναξ) of wood and ivory elaborately carved. The description leaves no doubt that it was of archaic Corinthian workmanship of the time of the tyrants or not much later[2]. But it is extremely doubtful whether this carved box was a cypsele or had any original connexion with the cypsele story. Plato[3], Aristotle[4], and Plutarch[5] all refer to the dedications of the house of Cypselus without alluding to this object. Herodotus says nothing about the cypsele having been dedicated. For Strabo[6] the chief dedication of Cypselus was a "golden hammered Zeus." Dio Chrysostom[7] (about 100 A.D.) refers to what Pausanias calls the cypsele of Cypselus, but describes it simply as the "wooden box (ξυλίνη κιβωτός) dedicated by Cypselus." From Pausanias himself it is plain that the object was not by any means what the Greeks of his time understood by a cypsele. His statement[8] that the ancient Corinthians called a coffer a cypsele raises a suspicion that nobody else ever did. It is probably only an inference drawn by the traveller from the fact of this particular coffer being so called by the guides at Olympia[9].

---

[1] Paus. v. 17. 5.

[2] Note *e.g.* the human-legged centaurs, the winged Artemis, and the misreadings by Pausanias of inscriptions plainly in the archaic Corinthian alphabet (with its σὰν κίβδηλον ἀνθρώποις), Paus. v. 19. 7, 19. 5; Stuart Jones, *J.H.S.* XIV. p. 40.

[3] *Phaedrus*, 236 b and schol. *ad loc.*

[4] *Pol.* VII. (v.) 1313 b.

[5] *Sept. Sap. Conv.* 21 (*Moral.* 164), "and found him not, since he had been put into a cypsele by his mother. Wherefore Cypselus built his house at Delphi." The omission here is particularly striking. Plutarch, living in Boeotia, has a reason for referring to offerings at Delphi rather than at Olympia: but the counter-motive for quoting Olympia would surely have been stronger still if Plutarch had believed that the actual cypsele was there.

[6] VIII. 353, 378. No other dedications by Cypselus are mentioned.

[7] *Or.* XI. 163 M. (325 R.). [8] v. 17. 5.

[9] So Hitzig, *Pausan. loc. cit.* (vol. II. p. 396); Schubring, *de Cyps.* p. 26 f.; Overbeck, *Abh. Saechs. Ges. Wiss.* 1865, p. 611. The equation of cypsele with coffer was

CH. VII   CORINTH   199

The Olympian larnax does not at all correspond to the picture of a cypsele suggested by the ancient notices on the subject, which, quite apart from the light they may possibly throw on Cypselus, deserve a more detailed examination than they have hitherto received[1].

Meanings of the word "cypsele" given by the ancients.

The meanings of the word given by the ancients are as follows:

(1) A wine vessel[2],

(2) A vessel to receive wheat or barley[3],

(3) Part of a furnace[4],

(4) A beehive[5],

(5) Vessels for sweet condiments[6], or receptacles for such vessels[7],

(6) The hole of the ear[8],

(7) Wax in the ears[9].

This literary evidence may be supplemented from a numismatic source. Some fourth century B.C. coins of the Thracian Cypsela[10] show a more or less cylindrical vessel with two small vertical handles[11]. A similar vessel, resting on what is probably a grain of corn, is shown on

Cp. coins of Cypsela.

accepted without question by many scholars of the last century, *e.g.* Preller, *Arch. Zeit.* 1854, p. 297; Klein, *Sitz. Ak. Wiss. Wien,* CVIII. pp. 56, 69 f.; Plass, *Tyrannis,* p. 151; Duncker, *G. d. A.* VI.[5] pp. 39, 40; Curtius, *Gr. G.*[6] I. pp. 262–3; Holm, *Gk. Hist.* I. 307 (cp. *ibid.* Pref. p. v. where Holm claims to have endeavoured to bring into clear relief what may be regarded as proved and what as hypothesis).

[1] See *e.g.* Bluemner's despairing agnosticism, *Woch. Kl. Phil.* 1885, p. 609.

[2] Suid. s.v.

[3] Suid. s.v.; Schol. Aristoph. *Pax,* 631; Hesych. s.v.; Schol. Lucian, *Lexiphanes,* 1.

[4] Hesych. s.v.

[5] Aristot. *H.A.* IX. 627 b (in form κυψέλιον); Plut. *de Exil.* 6 (*Moral.* 601); Suid. s.v.; Hesych. s.v.

[6] Pollux x. 92.

[7] Pollux VI. 13.

[8] Suid. s.v.; Hesych. s.v.; Pollux II. 85.

[9] Pollux II. 82, so *ibid.* II. 82, 85, κυψελίς; Hesych. s.v. κυψέλαι, κυψελίς; Schol. Aristoph. *Pax,* 631; Lucian, *Lexiphanes,* 1, and Schol. *ibid.*; cp. Alex. Aphrod. *Prob.* II. 63; Cassius Iatrosoph. *Prob.* 32.

[10] Steph. Byz. s.v. For other references see Pape, *Gr. Eigennamen,* s.v. Schubring, *de Cypselo,* p. 14, thinks the Thracian Cypsela founded by Miltiades of the Chersonese and named after his father Cypselus, a relation of the Corinthian.

[11] *Abh. Bay. Ak., Phil. Class.,* 1890, pl. I. 7, 8.

other coins of the same century and from the same district[1]. The vessel has very plausibly been identified as a cypsele.

Inferences as to size, shape, and material.
At first sight the various uses of the word appear rather miscellaneous, especially if we include (6) and (7). But (6) and (7) need not be brought in. They are late uses derived from (4)[2]. Meaning (5) is probably to be eliminated on the same grounds. This leaves us with (1) to (4), all of them vessels of large size, a feature implicit in the Cypselus legend and confirmed by the ancient lexicographers[3].

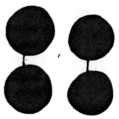

Fig. 26. Coins of Cypsela.

For the material of cypselae under meanings (1) to (5) the only written evidence is found in (i) schol. Aristoph. *Pax* 631, which says that "cypselae were not only woven (πλεκταί) but also of pottery (κεραμεαῖ)," (ii) a scholiast to Lucian, *Lexiphanes*, 1, which explains the cypsele as (a) "the narrow-mouthed unpitched vessel of pottery," (b) an earthenware vessel, (c) [addit. C] "the name is also given to a sort of woven vessel," (iii) Hesychius, who explains a cypsele as a wickerwork beehive.

These statements quite suit the list of uses. As between the two materials mentioned the Aristophanes scholiast gives the impression that the commoner was wicker or basket work. But in the Lucian scholiast wickerwork is only an afterthought added by a later hand. The Lucian scholiast is probably more correct. Pottery is a natural material for every kind of cypsele. Cypselae (1) and (3) can never have been of basketwork, and for (5) it looks a most unlikely material, though we know too little about ancient spice vessels to speak with certainty. For (2) it is suitable enough, but the cypselae of the Thracian coins, which the emblem of the grain of corn shows to have been probably corn jars, point in the other direction. Their shape suits either terra cotta or metal but not wickerwork. The

---

[1] *Abh. Bay. Ak., Phil. Class.*, 1890, pl. I. 6; Imhoof, *Monn. Gr.* pls. C 5, C 6, C 7 and pp. 51, 52. These coins have been found mainly in the Hebrus valley, some of them during the construction of the railway from Adrianople to Aenus.

[2] Pollux II. 86 says that "physicians invented these names. Aristotle thought the parts of the ear to be nameless except the lobe."

[3] Suid. s.v. and Schol. Aristoph. *Pax*, 631 speak of a "six bushel kypsele" (ἑξμέδιμνος κυψέλη).

probable use practically excludes metal[1]. (4) is according to Hesychius a "plaited beehive," *i.e.* a hive of basketwork, and this statement is accepted by M. Pottier[2]. No doubt it was true at the time when it was made. But is it so certain that the earliest cypsele beehives were of basketwork? The first reference to beehives is in the *Odyssey*, which describes hives of stone in the shape of vases (κρητῆρες and ἀμφιφορῆες)[3]. These Homeric beehives must have been either prototypes or glorifications of hives of earthenware[4], and it is tempting to classify these latter with the cypsele form of hive, especially in the light of the cypsele on the Thracian coins, which has much the shape of a mixing bowl except that the handles are of a type more frequent on the amphora. These coins are of the first half of the fourth century. Our literary authorities are all much later. Most of them mention earthenware beehives only to condemn them[5]. Presumably they were out of fashion. Basketwork hives[6] on the other hand are spoken of without condemnation. When therefore they define the cypsele beehive as a basketwork beehive, they practically mean a round or vase-shaped hive like the "little pail where the bee distils his sweet flow" of Antiphilus[7], as distinguished from the rectangular form that was also much in use[8].

[1] For terra cotta corn jars cp. probably Hor. *Ep.* I. vii. 29 f. Earthenware offers the best protection against damp as well as rodents.

[2] Saglio, *Dict. d. Ant.* s.v. citing also Suid., *Et. Mag.*, Plut. *Mor.* 601 c.

[3] *Od.* XIII. 105; cp. Porphyr. *de Antro Nymph.* 17.

[4] Bluemner's view that the poet meant simply natural holes in the rock may be right, but his inference that the passage is no evidence for artificial hives is absurd, especially in the light of the stone looms (ἰστοὶ λίθεοι) described in the same passage and actually quoted by Bluemner (*ap.* Hermann, *Lehrb. Gr. Antiq.*³ IV. p. 120, n. 1).

[5] Varro, *de Re Rust.* III. 16. 15, (alui) deterrimae fictiles; Columella IX. 6, deterrima conditio fictilium; Pallad. I. 38, (aluearia) fictilia deterrima sunt.

[6] Varro, *de Re Rust.* III. 16. 15, ex uiminibus rotundos; Pallad. I. 38, salignis uiminibus.

[7] γαυλοῦ δὲ σμικροῖο, τόθι γλυκὺ νᾶμα μέλισσα | πηγάζει, *Anth. Pal.* IX. 404.

[8] "Ex ferulis quadratas," Varro, *de Re Rust.* III. 16. 15; "the best are those made of boards," Florentinus, *Geopon.* XV. 2. 7; cp. *ibid.* 2. 21, "Juba king of the Libyans says bees should be kept in a wooden box (ἐν λάρνακι ξυλίνῃ)"; "figura cerarum talis est qualis et habitus domicilii; namque et quadrata et rotunda spatia nec minus longa suam speciem uelut formae quaedam fauis praebent," Columella IX. 15. 8. For possible earlier evidence for square hives see Aristoph. *Vesp.* 241 with Schol. *ad loc.* In Theocr. VII. 78 f. bees occupy

This is assuming that cypselae were never rectangular, but the assumption seems fairly safe. Neither plaiting nor pottery adapts itself to rectangular shapes. Wine vessels are not usually square. The cypsele of the coins is not rectangular.

Fig. 27. Attic vase painting, perhaps depicting a cypsele.

Fig. 28. Attic vase painting, perhaps depicting a cypsele.

There remains the "certain part of a furnace" referred to by Hesychius. Whatever this may have been, it is most unlikely that

a large rectangular box (λάρναξ) of sweet cedar wood, but they are taking part in a miracle and it would be rash to generalize from their behaviour. See further Pauly Wissowa s.v. Bienenzucht.

CH. VII   CORINTH   203

it was rectangular for the simple reason that ancient Greek furnaces appear from extant pictures to have no rectangular parts that could possibly be so identified. Pictures of ancient Greek furnaces are numerous, and it is surprising that no attempt seems to have been made to discover a cypsele in any of them, for it is not unlikely that some of these pictures do in fact depict it, and in that case they show us the earliest form of the object of which we have any precise record.

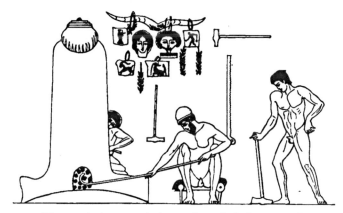

Fig. 29. Attic vase painting, perhaps depicting a cypsele.

Probable pictures of a cypsele on sixth-century Attic vases, depicting it as a large terra cotta vase.

In Saglio's *Dictionnaire des Antiquités*, s.v. Fer, figs. 2964, 2965, (here figs. 27, 28), pictures are reproduced from two black figure vases that depict furnaces being used, in all probability for treating iron[1]. On the top of either furnace is depicted what de Launay describes as a "sorte de vase, sans doute de terre cuite[2]." A similar vase is shown *ibid.* s.v. Caelatura, fig. 937[3] (here fig. 29) on top of what the context shows to be the furnace of a bronze foundry[4]. This latter picture is on an

---

[1] Iron rather than copper is suggested by the heavy hammers in the picture, but cp. below, n. 4.

[2] Saglio s.v. Fer, p. 1090. Bluemner, *Gewerbe u. Künste*, IV. p. 363, with unnecessary vagueness calls it an Aufsatz. But *ibid.* p. 331 he calls the vase on Saglio, fig. 937 a "gefäss- oder kesselartiger Aufsatz."

[3] =*Berl. Cat. Vases*, 2294; the whole vase in colours Gerhard, *Trinkschalen*, Pls. XII., XIII.

[4] Mau, *ap.* Pauly Wissowa s.v. fornax, calls all three furnaces (*i.e.* Saglio, figs. 937, 2964–5) Schmiedeöfen and says they served a double purpose, partly

early red figure vase[1]. In all three cases the "sort of vase" is very large, as is shown by comparing it in size with the human figures in the picture. In short both in size, shape, use and probably material it answers to the written descriptions of one variety of cypsele. What it does not so well answer to is the vase represented on the coins of Cypsela, which is tall and cylindrical and shows two vertical handles. Fortunately there is a connecting link between the two forms. In the Berlin Museum there is an actual stove of terra cotta, said to have been found in the sea off Iasos (coast of

---

to raise iron to a glowing heat for the smithy, partly to smelt metals more easily molten (*e.g.* copper, bronze). On these vases as melting pots cp. Gerhard, *Trinkschalen*, p. 22 (Schmelzkessel); Furtwaengler, *Berl. Cat.* 2294 ["above, a round cauldron with lid (inside it metal?)"]. So Saglio and de Launay *ap.* Saglio *Dict. d. Ant.* s.v. Caelatura, p. 790, ferrum, p. 1090, n. 6. For the way metals may have been smelted in these vases cp. Diod. III. 14 (from Agatharcides, describing the mining and working of gold in "Furthest Egypt" (περὶ τὰς ἐσχατιὰς τῆς Αἰγύπτου) under the Ptolemies). When the metal has been pounded and washed and the gold dust (ψῆγμα) is left behind "finally other skilled workmen (τεχνῖται) take what has been collected and cast it into earthenware pots (εἰς κεραμεοὺς χύτρους); and mixing in the right proportions lumps of lead and grains of salt and further a little tin and some barley bran, they put that in too, and having made a well fitting lid and carefully sealed it (περιχρίσαντες) with clay, they heat it on a furnace for five days and nights without a break. Then letting it cool they find nothing left in the vases (ἀγγείοις) but the gold." If the process thus described is open to criticism it should be remembered (Bluemner, *Gewerbe u. Künste*, IV. 132) that Diodorus was not a metallurgist, and that ancient methods were probably far from perfect, even of their kind. Bluemner, *ibid.* IV. p. 363, regards Saglio 2964 (above, fig. 27) as a smithy. For κάμινος = smithy cp. *e.g.* Lucian, *Prometh.* 5. But the furnace here is too big and elaborate for a smithy. None of our three vase pictures shows an anvil. What Bluemner *ibid.* calls a small anvil is too small to be an anvil at all; cp. the lump of iron in the same picture and also Bluemner's own fig. 53, which shows an anvil of a natural size; cp. too the similar projections to Bluemner's supposed anvil in the corresponding position on the furnaces of our other two vase pictures, both of which projections are obviously not anvils. The picture of an unquestionable smithy, Bluemner, fig. 53, shows a quite different type of furnace, not half a man's height, called in Bluemner "ein niedriger konisch geformter Schmelzherd." The heavy hammers in Saglio, *Dict. d. Ant.* fig. 2964, do not prove a smithy; they may have been used for various other purposes, *e.g.* breaking up the ore; cp. Diod. V. 13 (Aithalia in Etruria), τοὺς λίθους καίουσιν ἔν τισι φιλοτέχνοις καμίνοις...(καὶ)...καταμερίζουσιν εἰς μεγέθη σύμμετρα......ταῦτα ἔμποροι κομίζουσιν εἰς τὰ ἐμπόρια. Or smelting and forging may have gone on simultaneously in the same works.

[1] Style of Brygos, Furtwaengler, *Berl. Cat. Vases*, p. 596.

Asia Minor)[1]. It is about ·50 m. high and of a common enough type[2], though it is rare to find one so well preserved[3]. What however gives the Iasos example its importance is a vase ·13 m. high and ·192 diameter, of the same dark brown micaceous clay as the stove itself, that was found along with it and fits so well on top of it that it must unquestionably have formed part of the complete article[4]. Here we have a vase of considerable size that in shape has resemblances to the vases on the coins of Cypsela, but in its bulging sides deviates from them in the direction of our conjectured cypselae of the vase paintings. In position, and in use as the receptacle for material to be heated, it corresponds with these latter. Though comparatively large, it must remain doubtful whether it is large enough to be a cypsele. But in any case it helps to connect the vases of the Cypsela coins with the "part of a furnace" of the vase paintings, and to make it probable that the latter was made of pottery and that both are rightly identified as cypselae. The objects on the vase paintings differ from all our other hypothetical cypselae in having no handles; even the beehive cypsele has been connected with craters and amphorae, both of which normally have two handles. But it is use as often as shape that determines the name of a vase,

Fig. 30. Vase on stove found at Iasos.

[1] Winter, *Jahrb.* XII. pp. 160 f. and fig. 1.
[2] Conze, *Jahrb.* v. pp. 118 f.
[3] For well preserved examples see those figured by Conze, *Jahrb.* v. pp. 134, 137.
[4] Dumont had already inferred that these stoves were regularly intended "à soutenir les plats ou les autres ustensiles qu'on plaçait sur ces sortes de réchauds." See *Jahrb.* v. p. 135, and Conze, *ibid.* Neither writer suggests cypselae.

and from the point of view of use the Iasos vase is probably to be classed with a vase figured on a Greek funeral relief (fig. 31)[1]. Here we have an object very similar in shape to our conjectured cypselae of the vase paintings, resting on what Dumont[2] called a réchaud. Its size may be judged by comparing it with a human head from the same relief. There is no *a priori* reason why the ancient cypsele, like the modern glass or bottle or cup or mug, should not show much diversity in the matter of handles and of shape generally.

Fig. 31. Relief, perhaps depicting a small cypsele.

The evidence just collected suggests that such was in fact the case, and it becomes the more likely when we remember that we are dealing with a period of some centuries. The Cypsela coins date only from the fourth century. The portable stoves of the Iasos type are later still[3]. The funeral relief with the vase and réchaud is dated by Dumont in the first century A.D.[4]

[1] *Rev. Arch.* 1869, II. Pl. XVII.
[2] *Ibid.* II. p. 423.
[3] Third to second century B.C., Conze, *Jahrb.* v. pp. 138-9.
[4] *Rev. Arch.* 1869, II. p. 432.

CH. VII   CORINTH   207

On the other hand the vases depicting the cypsele that forms part of a furnace¹ belong to the fifth or sixth century B.C., and thus bring us to within measurable distance of Cypselus himself². A cypsele of this description would be an admirable hiding-place for a baby, provided it was technically speaking a good baby, not given to crying³. Eventually, as has been seen, the box version of the story won the day: but from the Greek point of view there would be nothing impossible in a version which hid the child in an earthen jar. Eurystheus⁴ sought safety from Heracles in a πίθος or jar. In the seventh and sixth centuries infants were usually buried in large terra cotta vases not unlike those we are here considering. In the fifth century Aristophanes represents a supposititious child as introduced into the house in an earthenware pot⁵.

In short everything points to the cypsele of Cypselus having been a large vessel of pottery. May not Herodotus after all be right when he says that the tyrant got his name from the cypsele? The story of the attempted murder and the ten bad men may be older than Cypselus. But if so we have to explain how it came to be attached to the Corinthian tyrant. Is it not possible that it was given to him as being ἐκ τῶν κυψελῶν (just as later the demagogue Hyperbolus, who had spent his early days in a lamp factory, was spoken of as the man from the lamps, οὐκ τῶν λύχνων⁶) or in other words to denote his connexion with the Corinthian potteries which at this period were supplying a great part of the civilized world?

Was Cypselus (the child from the cypsele) a potter who got his name from his occupation?

Evidence for the plausibility of this suggestion. (i) Such names do occur, notably among potters.

Hyperbolus does not offer the only analogy for this suggestion or even the closest. In the chapter on Rome⁷, when tracing the source of the power of the Tarquins, we shall have occasion to examine the story of the Corinthian potters Eucheir and

---

¹ Above, figs. 27, 28, 29.

² Similar cypselae are perhaps depicted on the Corinthian terra cotta tablets from Penteskuphia, *Berl. Cat. Vas.* nos. 616, 631, 802; but see Furtwaengler, *ad loc.*

³ Cp. Plut. *Sept. Sap. Conv.* 21 (*Moral.* 164). Cypselus erected the house in Delphi believing that it was a god who on that occasion prevented his crying.

⁴ Pauly Wissowa s.v.

⁵ *Thesm.* 505 f. The Scholiast explains that the pot was used "because they used to expose children in pots."

⁶ Aristoph. *Clouds*, 1065.   ⁷ See below, pp. 217, 244–5.

Eugrammus, who lived just at this period and whose names meaning "skilful with the hand" and "skilful at painting" are palpably derived from their occupation[1].

Cypselus may possibly have adopted, or inherited from the founder of the firm, a cypsele as his badge or emblem, and this may have been the immediate origin of his name. These personal or family badges or arms were widely used in ancient Greece. Among the many found on the Heraclean tables[2] a κιβώτιον (box) occurs three times. A κιβώτιον is not a cypsele; but it is a similar object and shows that a cypsele might have been similarly used. The emblems as a rule seem to be entirely arbitrary and unconnected with the bearer's name or occupation. But the word κιβωτός (in the original non-diminutive form) became the nickname of Apamea in Phrygia from the fact that so much packing was done in that great centre of trade[3].

If Cypselus was originally a potter he may be compared with Agathocles, tyrant at the end of the fourth century of Syracuse, the great daughter city of Corinth. Agathocles is said to have been the son of a potter[4].

(ii) Agathocles, tyrant of Syracuse, is said to have been a potter,

According to Diodorus Siculus, the Delphic oracle prophesied over the infant Agathocles (as it had over Cypselus) that "he would be the cause of great misfortunes" to his country: and as a result of the prophecy it was resolved to do away with the

[1] Cypselus may have been chosen rather than a more general name or a name derived from some other shape, owing to the huge size of the cypsele. Modern potters have a great respect for a man who can throw a particularly large vase. So, too, had the ancients, as is shown by the proverb ἐν τῷ πίθῳ τὴν κεραμείαν ἐπιχειρεῖν μανθάνειν, Plato, *Gorg.* 514 e. What is probably the earliest allusion to actual Corinthian vases in all Greek literature speaks of a parasite hurrying to dinner and not stopping to admire his host's κάδοι. "οὐδὲ δοκιμάζω τοὺς Κορινθίους κάδους," Diphilus *ap.* Athen. VI. 236 b. The κάδος was a vessel of large size and might be of pottery; cp. Athen. XI. 472 e, 473 b and especially Κλείταρχος ἐν ταῖς Γλώσσαις τὸ κεράμιόν φησιν Ἴωνας κάδον καλεῖν. For the archaic period the large number of furnaces depicted on the Penteskuphia tablets suggests that the furnace cypsele may have been an article of much importance, assuming that all the furnaces were provided with cypselae for use as occasion required. Their comparatively rare appearance in the pictures is sufficiently explained on artistic grounds if the flames blazed up better when they were removed.

[2] *C. I. G.* III. pp. 709–10, where the word, *e.g.* τρίπους, precedes the name.

[3] Head, *Hist. Num.*[2] p. 666.

[4] Diod. XIX. 2; Justin XXII. 1; Plut. *Reg. et Imp. Apophth.* s.v. (*Moral.* 176); Athen. XI. 466 a; Amm. Marc. XIV. fin.

CH. VII   CORINTH   209

child, who however was saved by its mother. Eventually the father was told that the child had been saved, and took it back, and "being poor he taught Agathocles the potter's trade (τὴν κεραμευτικὴν τέχνην) while he was still a boy." This story is probably to be traced back to Timaeus, who is quoted by Polybius[1] for the statement that Agathocles was a potter, and is the only source of Diodorus actively hostile to the tyrant, by whom he had been banished from Sicily[2].

Plainly in great part at least the story of the young Agathocles is a piece of malicious fiction. What is its prototype? I cannot help suspecting that it is Cypselus himself. It is true that there is no cypsele or larnax in the story, and Bauer[3] connects it with the legends of the youthful Cyrus and infant Romulus. But neither is there an animal to suckle the infant, which the experts state to be the essential feature of the Cyrus Romulus cycle[4]. The oracle and the rescue by the mother are both salient incidents of the Cypselus story. In the Cyrus story we have dreams and their interpretation by Magians, not nearly so close an analogy. The dreams too indicate only the greatness of the child that is to be born. The Cypselus story indicates, like that of Agathocles, the harm the child will do[5]. Agathocles grew up in the days when the great name in Sicily was that of the Corinthian Timoleon. The thoughts of Sicily were all turned towards Corinth, and we find this rapprochement reflected in the Syracusan coins of the period, which show the Corinthian types of the helmeted goddess head and Pegasus[6]. What more natural therefore, especially for the banished Timaeus,

in what is probably a fiction intended to suggest a comparison with Cypselus.

[1] XII. 15, XV. 35.
[2] Bauer, *Sitz. Ak. Wiss. Wien*, vol. 100, pp. 564–5; cp. Tillyard, *Agathocles*, p. 13, n. 2.
[3] *Ibid.*, so Schubert, *Agathokles*, p. 29 (quoting Ferrari, *Agathokles*, p. 10 (1872)), Tillyard, *Agathocles*, p. 26.
[4] The bees that are said to have settled on the hips of a stone statue of him set up by his mother when he was well over seven years old are, *pace* Schubert, *Agathokles*, p. 30, hardly a substitute.
[5] Cp. *e.g.* Hdt. v. 92. 10, πολλῶν δ' ὑπὸ γούνατα λύσει (oracle about Cypselus) and *ibid.* 92. 16, ἔδει ἐκ τοῦ Ἠετίωνος γόνου Κορίνθῳ κακὰ ἀναβλαστεῖν with Diod. XIX. 2, ἐξέπεσε χρησμὸς ὅτι μεγάλων ἀτυχημάτων ὁ γεννηθεὶς αἴτιος ἔσται Καρχηδονίοις καὶ πάσῃ Σικελίᾳ. In this point the Romulus story is still more remote from the Agathocles than is that of Cyrus.
[6] Head, *Hist. Num.*[2] p. 179.

than to compare Agathocles with Cypselus[1]? It is not impossible that from this seditious analogy there grew up the story that Agathocles was the son of a potter[2]. The alternative is to accept Agathocles' early connexion with "the wheel, the clay, and the smoke[3]" of the pottery as a historical fact: but this is less likely. Polybius himself warns us against accepting Timaeus on Agathocles as truthful history, and seems himself to suspect his own quotation about the tyrant having been a potter in his early days. The elder brother of Agathocles was a prominent statesman and soldier in Syracuse early in his career, before the younger brother had risen to the tyranny: Agathocles himself appears early in his career to have reached high rank in the army and to have lived in intimate relations with some of the Syracusan nobility[4]. The tyrant's father was banished from Rhegium in the days when that city was under Dionysius of Syracuse, from which fact Beloch[5] reasonably infers that he was a distinguished personality. Beloch supposes that Agathocles inherited a big pottery business. If this view is right, then the pottery does not seem to have greatly helped the future tyrant in his public career, which from first to last was essentially military. Still, though the capitalist tyrant was already a thing of the past in Greece Proper, Sicily was in some ways younger than the mother country, and it is not impossible that Agathocles possessed a pottery, and that it played a part, though not the leading one, in helping him on to the throne. Agathocles was the contemporary of the Roman Appius whose suspected attempt at a financial

---

[1] Cp. Hdt. v. 92. 21: "when Cypselus became tyrant this is the sort of man he proved: many of the Corinthians he banished, etc." Agathocles and Cypselus both reigned about the same length of time, a fact that would attract Timaeus, who was excessively interested in such coincidences or parallels of time (Tillyard, p. 14). [Cypselus reigned 657-627; Agathocles' reign is usually dated 317-289; but cp. *Ath. Mitt.* xxii. p. 188 (new fragment of Marmor Parium), 319/8, Ἀγαθοκλῆν Συρακόσιοι εἵλοντο αὐτοκράτορα στρατηγόν, which may indicate what Agathocles himself regarded as the date of his accession.]

[2] But cp. Schubert, *Agath.* p. 31, "wie man darauf kam, den Karkinos (father of Agathocles) gerade zum Töpfer zu machen, lässt sich natürlich nicht mehr erkennen." Schubert, *ibid.* pp. 26 f., discovers two sources for the story of the tyrant's early days, and ascribes the pottery making to one (Timaeus), and to the other the rescue of the infant from attempted murder. His division appears to be very arbitrary.

[3] Polyb. xv. 35.

[4] Diod. xix. 3; cp. Tillyard, *Agath.* p. 28; Schubert, *Agath.* p. 31.

[5] *Gr. G.* iii. i. 186, n. 3.

despotism is discussed in the chapter on Rome. Before his accession he is described as having become very rich: but his riches are attributed to his marriage[1]. The evidence about Agathocles' early career is not decisive. But on any interpretation it lends plausibility to the view that Cypselus started life as a potter.

In the whole of this long discussion as to how Cypselus acquired **Cypselus as a** his name it has been assumed that Herodotus was **common noun.** right in declaring that he derived it direct from cypsele. The fact that there is a common noun cypselus hardly affects this assumption. It is true that the cypselus is a bird, but the bird in question is shown by Aristotle's account of it[2] to be either the house-martin[3] or some similar species[4] that derives its name from its clay-built nest. The cypselus is in fact the potter-bird.

But are we right in our main assumption? There is of course **King Cypselus** an alternative possibility. The story of the infant **of Arcadia.** Cypselus may have been attached to him solely to explain his unusual name. Schubring's instances of stories that he thinks to have arisen in this way are neither convincing in themselves nor altogether analogous[5]. But there is one fact that offers more solid grounds for not accepting Cypselus as a name that the tyrant derived from his occupation. An early king Cypselus of Arcadia is mentioned by Pausanias[6].

This is a genuine difficulty. But there are several ways of meeting it. It is for instance quite conceivable that two different individuals should have independently earned the same nickname. The name need not have been used in the same sense on both occasions. The cypselus is not only the potter-bird. It is also one of the most conspicuous of migrants[7]. It may have been from this latter point of view that the name was thought appropriate for a king of the period of the great migrations.

---

[1] Diod. XIX. 3; Justin XXII. 1.   [2] *Hist. Animal.* IX. 618 a.

[3] So Aubert and Wimmer ad *Hist. Animal.* IX. 108.

[4] Mr W. Warde Fowler has suggested to me that the cypselus is the Rufous or Eastern Swallow, which builds a more elaborate nest than the House Martin and has not the white rump that so distinguishes the House Martin but is absent from Aristotle's description of the cypselus.

[5] Πάγασαι, Κορυθείς, *de Cypselo*, pp. 29 f.

[6] Paus. IV. 3. 6; VIII. 5. 6, 29. 5; cp. Polyaen. I. 7 (Cypselus' stratagem against the Heraclids); Nic. Dam. *ap. F.H.G.* III. p. 377; Athen. XIII. 609 e.

[7] As a traveller according to Pliny, *N.H.* X. 55 (39), it excelled even the other birds of the swallow tribe.

If this be thought unlikely we might borrow a page from the sceptics and throw doubts upon the Arcadian's historical existence. We might explain him away as the eponymous hero of the Arcadian Cypsela[1]. Or again, it might be pointed out that he is said to have been an ancestor of his Corinthian namesake's daughter-in-law, Melissa the wife of Periander[2]. The Arcadian Cypselus might then be disposed of as a creation of the pedigree-mongers of the period when the marriage between Melissa and Periander took place[3].

There is another name in the pedigree of the Corinthian tyrants from which historical conclusions have frequently been drawn. According to Aristotle the third and last of the tyrants (587–584 B.C.) was called Psammetichus, a name which, as we have seen already, was borne by the first Pharaoh of the Saite (twenty-sixth) dynasty, which appears to have based its power largely on foreign mercenaries and foreign trade, both mainly Greek[4]. The Egyptian name of the Corinthian tyrant has rightly been held to establish some sort of connexion between the two states during the age of the tyrants. It has often been assumed[5] that Psammetichus of Corinth got his name directly from the Egyptian royal family. No certainty is to be had on this point. The name, though unknown before the time of Psammetichus I, appears to have become common during the twenty-sixth dynasty[6]. A Greek mercenary named Psammetichus son of Theocles commanded the expedition which has left us the graffiti of Abu Symbel[7]. The name and position of the son of Theocles show that the Corinthian tyrant might have got his Egyptian name through a Greek intermediary. But on the other hand there is a fair probability that the governments of Corinth and Egypt at this period were in touch with one another either directly or through their common friend Miletus[8].

The third tyrant of Corinth, whom Aristotle calls Psammetichus,

---

[1] Steph. Byz. s.v., an outpost fortified by the Mantineans, Thuc. v. 33.

[2] Paus. VIII. 5. 4 f.; Diog. Laert. I. 7. 1.

[3] Niese, *Hermes*, XXVI. p. 30, thinks the Arcadian pedigree of Melissa a late invention, but his argument from the silence of Herodotus is of very little weight.

[4] See above, Chapter IV.   [5] *E.g.* by Bury, *Hist. Greece*², p. 152.

[6] *E.g.* the priest Psammetichus, Breasted, *Records*, IV. 1026–9 (*circ.* 610–544 B.C.). For a list of its bearers see Wiedemann, *Aeg. Ges.* p. 623.

[7] See above, p. 123: written probably between 594 and 589 B.C.

[8] In Naukratis, which became under Psammetichus of Egypt the chief Greek trading-centre in the country, Corinthian potsherds take the second place among

But the really curious point about a Cypselid being called Psammetichus lies in the meaning of the name, which, as seen above[1], is most probably to be interpreted "man (vendor) of mixing bowls." If this interpretation is correct Psammetichus and Cypselus are synonyms. Now the modern historians generally follow Aristotle[2], and give the name of the last tyrant of Corinth as Psammetichus. But our other ancient authority, Nicolaus of Damascus[3], states that Periander was succeeded by a second Cypselus, "who came from Corcyra and became tyrant of Corinth until certain of the Corinthians combined and slew him....and freed the city." Psammetichus is called by Aristotle the son of Gorgos, Cypselus II is described by Nicolaus as son of Periander's brother Gorgos[4]. A Psammetichus son of Gorgos is mentioned by Nicolaus as having been sent to Corcyra by Periander. The same author makes Cypselus II come from

an Egyptian name meaning probably "vendor of bowls,"

is given by Nicolaus the name of Cypselus,

the vase finds of the earlier period of the Greek settlement, Milesian coming first (Prinz, *Funde aus Nauk.* p. 75), though note that Corinth was not among the Greek cities that had an establishment at Naukratis, the Aeginetans being the only European Greeks to possess one. On Egypt and Miletus see above, Chapter IV. To the evidence usually quoted for Egyptian influence on Periander we should perhaps add a story told by Diog. Laert. I. 7. 3. When Periander was an old man he is said to have provided for his own death and burial in the following way. He directed two men to kill and bury a man they would meet on a certain night at a certain lonely spot. He arranged with four others that they should kill these two on their way back. The four in their turn were to be disposed of in like manner by a larger band. At the appointed hour Periander himself went to the spot to which the two had been directed and was there killed and buried by them. The essence of this story is that Periander took extraordinary precautions to prevent anyone knowing the place of his burial. Such precautions at once recall Egypt. Can the story have originated as a skit on Periander's Egyptianizing tendencies?

[1] Above, p. 125.   [2] *Pol.* VII. (v.), 1315 b.   [3] *F.H.G.* III. p. 394.
[4] In Aristotle Gorgos is Susemihl's emendation for Gordios. In Plutarch's *Sept. Sap. Conv.* 17 (*Moral.* 160) Gorgos (Didot, Gorgias) brother of Periander takes part, and the name occurs too often to be a mistake for some quite different name. Nic. Dam. *F.H.G.* III. p. 393 mentions a Gorgos son of Periander who broke his neck when chariot racing. There can be little doubt that in all these passages the same name should be read, and that that name should be Gorgos, which appears on Ambracian coins as that of a local hero. See *Mon. Ined. Inst.* I. pl. XIV. nos. 1, 2. The name Gordios was much used in the Phrygian royal family. But as in Aristot. *Pol.* 1315 b it is probably only an intrusion for the less familiar Gorgos it is no evidence for connexion between the Cypselids and the house of Midas.

Corcyra to succeed Periander on the throne of Corinth. It is hard to avoid the conclusion reached by Busolt[1] that Cypselus II and Psammetichus are one and the same person. But need we follow Busolt further[2] and assume that Psammetichus changed his name to Cypselus on his accession? Psammetichus I of Egypt in his early days when he was a vassal of Assyria, appears to have received from his overlord the Assyrian name of Neboshazban[3]. Possibly therefore the Egyptian king might take it as a compliment if a Greek adopted an Egyptian name. But even this is doubtful. The Saites would not be extremely anxious to follow the practices of Assyria and Babylon: the Greeks did not readily change their names. On the other hand the Greeks loved to find equivalents between Greek names and Egyptian, as we see most markedly in their treatment of Greek and Egyptian gods[4], and heroes[5], and likewise of Egyptian place-names[6]. Is it not therefore rather more probable that from beginning to end the last of the Corinthian tyrants bore the name of his grandfather, according to the familiar Greek custom, and that Cypselus and Psammetichus were employed consciously as the Greek and Egyptian forms of one and the same name[7], both alike meaning "man of pots."

which suggests that the two names were regarded by their bearer as synonyms meaning vendor of pots.

It may of course have been an accident that of the three names borne by the three tyrants of the Greek potteries two should be derived from words denoting some species of pot: but if so it is a very curious one.

---

[1] *Gr. G.*² I. p. 657, n. 4.   [2] *Ibid.* So Knapp, *op. cit.* pp. 123–4.

[3] Geo. Smith, *Assurbanipal*, p. 28. The identification is not certain, but we find Neboshazban where we should look for Psammetichus: the Assyrian practice is illustrated, in a repetition of this very sentence in question, by the double name of Neboshazban's fief: "and Neboshazban his (*i.e.* Necho's) son in Athribis, which Limir-patesi-Assur is its name, to the kingdom I appointed" (*ibid.* pp. 46–47).   [4] *E.g.* Plato, *Tim.* 21 *e*, Neith = Athena.

[5] *E.g.* Chem Peh'-resu (?) = Perseus, Wiedemann, *Hdt.* II. pp. 368–9.

[6] Phacussa atque Mylonpolis sunt Graeca nomina ex Aegyptiacis translata, Gutschmid, *Philol.* x. p. 528.

[7] There is of course the alternative possibility (assumed by Duncker, *G. d. A.* VI.⁵ p. 72, n. 1), that one of the names is merely a mistake. The Lycophron son of Periander of Herodotus is plainly the Nikolaos of Nic. Dam. *F.H.G.* III. p. 393.

Chapter VIII. *Rome*

"All the historical labours bestowed on the early centuries of Rome will, in general, be wasted."—Sir George Cornewall Lewis, *On the Credibility of Early Roman History* (1855), vol. II. p. 556.

1. The narrative as to how the Tarquins are said to have gained, held, and lost the throne.

AT the time of the birth of Herodotus, which took place about the year 484 B.C., Polycrates, Peisistratus, and Croesus had been dead less than fifty years: in Corinth and Sicyon it was not more than a century since the tyranny had been suppressed. The historian had probably met people who remembered the tyrants of Samos and Athens: he may possibly have talked with old men from the cities of the Isthmus whose fathers had told them of personal experiences under Cleisthenes, or Periander.

The case with the Tarquins, the tyrant kings of Rome, is very different. There is nothing even approximating to contemporary literary evidence for their history, or even for their existence. In recent times their whole claim to be regarded as historical has been disputed. It may therefore seem something like begging the question to proceed at once to collect evidence for the narrative before clearing the ground by discussing its authenticity. There are however two reasons for following that course. The first is that the question of authenticity can be more easily discussed after the narrative has been called to mind. The other is that the value of the story for this enquiry does not altogether depend on the Tarquins' historicity[1].

According to the extant narratives[2] king Tarquinius Priscus was the son of a Corinthian named Demaratus who had settled in the Etruscan city of Tarquinii, the modern Corneto, some fifty miles

---

[1] See below, p. 256.
[2] Polyb. VI. fr. ii.; Strabo V. 219–20, VIII. 378; Dion. Hal. III. 46; Diod. VIII. 31; Cic. *de Rep.* II. 19–20 (34–36); Schol. Bob. ad Cic. *pro Sulla*, 22; Livy I. 34, IV. 3; Florus, *Epitome Liui*, I. 5. 1; Pliny, *N.H.* XXXV. 5, 43; cp. XXXIII. 4; Aurel. Vict. *de Vir. Ill.* 6; cp. *C.I.L.* I. i. p. 43 and *Roem. Mitt.* XIX. p. 117 (acta triumphorum Capitolina), L. TARQUINIUS. DEMARATI. F. PRISCUS; *C.I.L.* XIII. 1668 (Claudius at Lyons); Zonaras VII. 8.

north of Rome. The fullest of these narratives, that of Dionysius, makes Demaratus sail to Italy "intending to trade, in a private merchant vessel, and with a cargo of his own: having disposed of his cargo in the cities of the Etruscans...and acquired great gains,...he continued to ply the same sea, conveying Greek cargoes to the Etruscans and bringing Etruscan goods to Greece, and became the possessor of very great wealth ...and when the tyranny of Cypselus was being established...he quitted Corinth and set up a house in Tarquinii, which was then a great and prosperous city." All this property was left by Demaratus to his son Lucumo, the future Lucius Tarquinius, "who, receiving his father's great wealth, resolved to engage in politics and take a part in public life and to be one of the foremost men of his city[1]." He is described as migrating to Rome for the specific reason that there seemed more prospect there of his wealth leading to high political power, and as finding there the opportunity he was looking for. "At Rome," says Livy[2], "his wealth brought him into prominence." So Dionysius[3]: "He very soon became friends with the king (Ancus Martius), making him presents and supplying him with funds for his military requirements...he also secured many of the patricians by his benevolences, and won the favour of the common people by his courteous greetings and the charm of his discourse and by contributions of money." Similarly Aurelius Victor[4]: "by his money and his industry he secured high position." So too Diodorus[5], speaking of Tarquin's rise to prominence in Rome: "being very wealthy he helped many of the poor by giving them money." Still more specifically our oldest authority, Polybius[6], says "Lucius, the son of Demaratus the Corinthian, set out for Rome trusting in himself and his money."

Tarquinius Priscus, son of a rich Corinthian trader named Demaratus, settles at Rome and by means of his wealth secures the throne.

These passages are enough to show that according to all our best extant authorities, and therefore presumably according to some earlier common source, Tarquinius Priscus owed his throne to

---

[1] Dion. Hal. III. 47; cp. Livy I. 34, Lucumoni contra...cum divitiae iam animos facerent.
[2] Livy I. 34.
[3] Dion. Hal. III. 48.
[4] de Vir. Ill. 6.
[5] Diod. VIII. fr. 31.
[6] Polyb. VI. fr. ii. 10. Polybius insists on this point: πιστεύων αὑτῷ τε καὶ τοῖς χρήμασι...διὰ τὴν χορηγίαν...μεγάλης ἀποδοχῆς ἔτυχε...τῇ τοῦ βίου χορηγίᾳ μεγαλοψύχως εἰς τὸ δέον ἑκάστοτε καὶ σὺν καιρῷ χρώμενος.

his previous wealth. The writers just quoted apparently pictured Tarquin as a royal favourite who used his great wealth and ability to pave the way in the palace for his own succession[1], or possibly as merely a wealthy demagogue[2], but there are indications in the accounts that have come down to us that Tarquin's power may have had a somewhat different basis.

When Demaratus was making[3] his fortune in Etruria, he was probably, if the story has any historical foundation, a great employer of labour. Strabo speaks of the "large number of skilled workmen" who accompanied him from Corinth[4]. Pliny speaks of the Corinthian as accompanied by the potters (fictores) Eucheir and Eugrammus[5]. As Tarquin is made by both Livy[6] and Dionysius[7] to succeed to all his father's possessions, the received accounts may be taken as implying that he too was master of "a large number of skilled workmen." That this is the intention of our narrative is borne out by Dionysius' account of the migration of Lucumo, as the subsequent Tarquinius was then called, from Tarquinii to Rome. "He resolved to migrate thither collecting up all his money ...and taking all who were willing of his friends and relations: and there were many eager to go with him[8]." On his arrival at Rome the king "assigned him and the Etruscans who had come with him to a tribe and curia ($\phi\upsilon\lambda\dot{\eta}\nu$ $\tau\epsilon$ $\kappa\alpha\grave{\iota}$ $\phi\rho\alpha\tau\rho\acute{\iota}\alpha\nu$)."

Demaratus and Priscus were great employers.

[1] Cp. Diod. VIII. fr. 31, "he was introduced to the king, Ancus Martius, and became his greatest friend, and helped him much in the administration of the kingdom"; Dion. Hal. III. 48, "he very soon became friends with the king"... "being held in high honour by the king"; also the passage from the same chapter quoted above; Livy I. 34, Tarquinius gets himself made guardian of Ancus' young sons; Aur. Vict. *de Vir. Ill.* 6, "he even secured the friendship of King Ancus."

[2] Cp. Diod. VIII. fr. 31,"making himself agreeable to everyone ($\pi\hat{a}\sigma\iota$ $\pi\rho o\sigma\phi\iota\lambda\hat{\omega}s$ $\dot{o}\mu\iota\lambda\hat{\omega}\nu$)"; Dion. Hal. III. 48,"by courteous greetings and ingratiating discourses" (cp. VI. 60, "every tyrant develops out of a mob flatterer"); Livy I. 34, "benigno alloquio, comitate inuitandi," I. 35, "he is said to have been the first to canvass for the throne and to have made a speech designed to win over the plebeians."

[3] Or perhaps rather increasing; cp. Strabo VIII. 378, "Demaratus...brought such great wealth from home to Etruria that he became ruler of the city that received him, and his son was actually made king of Rome."

[4] Strabo V. 220.

[5] Pliny, *N.H.* xxxv. 43 (12); so (multo uero elegantius) Val. Max. III. 4. 2.

[6] Livy I. 34. 2, "bonorum omnium heres," so also 34. 4.

[7] Dion. Hal. III. 47, $\kappa\lambda\eta\rho o\nu\acute{o}\mu o\nu$ $\dot{a}\pi\acute{a}\sigma\eta s$ $\tau\hat{\eta}s$ $o\dot{v}\sigma\acute{\iota}as$.

[8] Dion. Hal. III. 47.

This whole description implies that Lucumo's fellow-emigrants were free men: nothing is said as to their occupations. On the other hand the narratives of his father's migration to Tarquinii make no statement as to whether the "skilled workmen" who accompanied him were free men or slaves. But the temptation to equate the two bodies is considerable. Later on, when on the throne, the Tarquins are represented as employing free skilled labour on a large scale. The object alleged by Livy for the first Tarquin's numerous public works was "that the people might be as much employed at home as they had been in the army[1]." The Roman army did not include slaves.

Their employees were probably free men.

About the Tarquins as large employers of free labour we shall find more precise and significant statements when the story of Superbus comes to be discussed. But in the accounts of Priscus there is one further statement that associates him closely with the trade of Rome. "The same king," says Livy[2], speaking of Priscus, "apportioned sites round the forum for private individuals to build on, and erected arcades and shops." So Dionysius[3]: "he adorned the forum by surrounding it with workshops and arcades (ἐργαστηρίοις καὶ παστάσι)." It is surely somewhat remarkable that King Tarquin should be thus associated with the building of shops.

Between the first and the last of the Tarquins our accounts are unanimous in inserting Servius Tullius. Livy and Dionysius[4] make him the son-in-law of Priscus. Servius, who is thus assigned to both the period and the family of the Tarquins, is stated by several authors to have been the first to issue coins at Rome. Varro[5] for instance informs us that "they say that silver coinage was first struck (flatum) by Servius Tullius." So Pliny[6]: "King Servius was the first to stamp (signauit) bronze"; and again Cassiodorus[7]: "King Servius is said to have been the first to strike a coinage (impressisse monetam) in bronze."

Priscus is succeeded by Servius Tullius, who is said to have been the first at Rome to strike coins.

[1] Livy I. 38, "ut non quietior populus domi esset quam militiae fuisset."
[2] Livy I. 35.
[3] Dion. Hal. III. 67. On the forum shops see also Livy XXVI. 27; Varro, *L.L.* VI. 59.
[4] Livy I. 39; Dion. Hal. IV. 1 (but cp. IV. 2; Pliny, *N.H.* XXXVI. 70 (204)).
[5] *Ap.* Charisii, *Art. Gramm.* I. p. 105, ed. Keil.
[6] *N.H.* XVIII. 3, XXXIII. 13.   [7] *Variae*, VII. 32.

Possible historical basis for this statement.
These statements cannot be accepted just as they stand. Silver coins were first struck in Rome in 268 B.C., and the first round copper coins, the large *aes graue* with a Janus head on one side and a ship's prow on the other, are now unanimously assigned to the middle of the fourth century[1]. There is however nothing to preclude the possibility of important monetary innovations or reforms by a sixth century king of Rome. Copper has been found in Central Italy in various forms that point to a copper currency prior to the introduction of the round *aes graue*. There are the rough pieces known as *aes rude*, the objects of various simple shapes but entirely devoid of decoration known as *aes formatum*, and the pieces rectangular in shape and marked with a type known as *aes signatum*[2]. Though the extant examples of *aes signatum* are plainly on stylistic grounds to be assigned to long after the regal period, and though the objects discovered along with finds of *aes rude* do not point to a very early date[3], it would be rash to say that either *aes rude* or *aes signatum* or for that matter *aes formatum* was not as early in origin as the sixth century[4]. Willers[5] dates the use of *aes rude* from 1000 B.C. to the fourth century, and supposes some developments during the period, one of which, *e.g.* the kuchenförmig (bun-shaped) variety of *aes formatum* or the "bars with various patterns," may possibly be due to Servius. If Servius is to be associated with *aes formatum* the "bun-shaped" pieces have perhaps not quite so good a claim as those to which Haeberlin[6] gives the name tortenförmig (something like the flat round weights with a flange that are made to fit into one another), since these latter appear from the full data that Haeberlin has collected to be characteristic of S. Etruria: they have been found mainly at Caere, Tarquinii, and Castelnuovo di Porto (between Rome and Falerii), *i.e.* in great part at places with which Rome had particularly close connexions.

But neither the "kuchenförmig" nor the "tortenförmig" *aes formatum* suits the literary evidence so well as Willers' "bars with

[1] See Samwer, *ält. roem. Münzwesen*, p. 43; T. Frank, *Class. Phil.* XIV. (1919), pp. 314 f.

[2] For copious illustrations see Haeberlin's sumptuous *Aes Grave*.

[3] See *e.g.* Pasqui, *Notiz.* 1897, pp. 265 *p*, 267 *a* (Praeneste).

[4] *Aes rude* is recorded among the finds of the earlier stips at Conca (Satricum in South Latium) which appears to belong exclusively to the seventh and sixth centuries B.C., *Notiz.* 1896, pp. 29–31, 101.

[5] *Roem. Kupferpräg.* pp. 21–22.   [6] *Aes Grave*, p. 5.

various patterns." These appear to constitute the most primitive form of *aes signatum*. Pliny's precise account[1] of Servius' innovation is that he introduced *aes signatum* in place of the earlier *aes rude*. Pliny indeed goes on to say that Servius' money "signatum est nota pecudum[2]." Among extant pieces this description is applicable only to certain fully developed examples of the quadrilateral *aes signatum*[3], that, as remarked already, have to be assigned to a later date: but whereas Pliny's statement about Servius and *aes signatum* is based on Timaeus (Sicily, third century B.C.), it is quite uncertain whether

Fig. 32. *Aes signatum*.

the remark about "nota pecudum" is to be referred to the same respectable authority. Pliny's own words are: "Seruius rex primus signauit aes. antea rudi usos Romae Timaeus tradit. signatum est nota pecudum."

Assume a historical basis for the accounts of Servius' connexion with the Roman currency[4], and the motive for his activity in this direction is not far to seek. Just about the period to which his reign is dated Greek coins began to penetrate Etruria. They belong

[1] *N.H.* xxxiii. 13.
[2] xxxiii. 13, so xviii. 3, ouium boumque effigie.
[3] E.g. *Brit. Mus. Rep. Coins*, I. p. 3.
[4] As is done by Babelon, *Origines*, pp. 186 f., who quotes as a possible example of regal "aes signatum," Garrucci, pl. XVII. figs. 1 *a*, 1 *b*; but cp. *ibid.* p. 195, where he much antedates the earliest silver coins of Rome.

mainly to Phocaea and the Phocaean colonies[1]. Now "in the days of King Tarquinius," so Justin[2] tells us, "Phocaeans from Asia put in at the mouth of the Tiber and formed a friendship with the Romans." The Phocaean coinage may well have led to some reform or regulation of the home currency, though the statement of Aurelius Victor[3] that "he (*i.e.* Servius) established weights and measures" may perhaps come nearer to the truth than the more detailed assertions about striking a coinage that have been already quoted. Even if this was all that Servius did it is enough to make him stand out as a commercially minded statesman since he is represented as the first ruler in Rome to regulate units of exchange[4].

The chief positive objection to a sixth century date for even the most primitive form of metallic currency is the fact that down to the time of the XII tables (450 B.C.) all fines were paid in cows and sheep[5]. But evidence of this sort may be given too much weight. As pointed out by Ridgeway[6], "even in a great commercial Greek city like Syracuse, the cow formed the basis of assessment in the reign of Dionysius (405–367 B.C.)." Syracuse had minted masterpieces of silver coinage some time before Dionysius was born.

Enough has been said to indicate the possible significance of the accounts of king Servius and his copper coins. Too little is known about either the king himself or the sixth century currency to build much upon their reputed connexion. The matter is not one of first importance for our enquiry. There can be no question of a revolution in the currency, such as there are reasons for attributing to Gyges, Pheidon, Peisistratus, and probably others of the early Greek tyrants[7].

---

[1] Mueller-Deecke, *Etrusker*, I. p. 382.

[2] Justin XLIII. 3. The traditional date is 600 B.C. Cp. the statements as to Servius' intercourse with Ephesus, Livy I. 45; Dion. Hal. IV. 25–26 (quoting an ancient inscription); Aur. Vict. *de Vir. Ill.* 7. The Phocaeans expelled from Corsica about 537 B.C. ultimately settled at Velia near Paestum, a fact that has led Pinza, *Bull. Comm.* 1898, p. 269, to see a Phocaean quarter in the Velia at Rome: he compares the Vicus Tuscus, but even so the evidence hardly justifies the inference.

[3] *de Vir. Ill.* 7.

[4] Cruchon, *Banques dans l'Antiq.* pp. 13, 14, 16, so regards him, and compares the laws of Manu (fourteenth century B.C.).

[5] Cic. *de Rep.* II. 60 (35); Gellius XI. 1, 2; Festus s.v. peculatus.

[6] *Compan. Lat. Stud.* sect. 685.

[7] On the whole question of the origin of Roman coinage see most recently Haeberlin's *Aes Grave*, especially pp. 1–6, and Grueber, *Brit. Mus. Coins*

The census of Servius.

Reforms or innovations in the currency are quite in keeping with the other activities ascribed to Servius. The step most commonly associated with his name is the institution of a census, "ex quo belli pacisque munia non uiritim, ut antea, sed pro habitu pecuniarum fierent[1]."

Servius and the collegia opificum.

Another institution that has been attributed to Servius is that of the collegia opificum or unions of workmen[2]. The early history of these collegia is obscure: Plutarch attributes the eight earliest of them (carpenters, potters, tanners, leather-workers, dyers, coppersmiths, goldsmiths, flute-players) to Numa[3]. The two versions may both have a historic basis if we suppose that the collegia as private corporations go back into the early regal period and that later they passed under state control[4]. This view is of course incapable of proof. The evidence limits us to conjecture[5]. But one point seems fairly certain. The collegia must have lost importance when slave labour came to be much used[6].

Servius is constantly accused of having secured the support of the poor by gifts and benevolences[7], and special mention is

Rom. Rep. vol. I., especially p. 1, n. 1, p. 3, n. 1. The introduction of money of bronze and iron was attributed by Suetonius to Numa, Suid. s.v. Ἀσσάρια: "Assaria: obols. Numa the first king of Rome appointed after Romulus was the first to present the Romans with (money) of iron and bronze, all his predecessors having paid with (money of) leather and earthenware: these from his own name he named nummia, as stated by Tragkylios" (*i.e.* Suetonius Tranquillus). Conflicting versions where both are doubtful tend to discredit one another. But the whole notice about Numa hardly affects those about Servius. The temptation to equate Numa with nummus must have been great. Yet nobody before Suetonius appears to have succumbed to it, and the claim he makes for Numa is concerned only with a very primitive stage in the history of the currency.

[1] Livy I. 42. [2] Florus I. 6. 3.
[3] Plut. *Num.* 17 (from Varro (?), see Pauly Wissowa s.v. collegium, p. 391); cp. Pliny, *N.H.* XXXIV. 1, XXXV. 46.
[4] Mommsen, *Roem. Staatsr.* III. 287, who connects the Servian organization of the collegia with the Servian centuries of artizans.
[5] For other views see Kornemann *ap.* Pauly Wissowa s.v. collegium; cp. also Mommsen, *de Colleg.* 31.
[6] Mommsen, *Hist. Rome*[2], I. p. 249; Humbert *ap.* Saglio, *Dict. d. Antiq.* s.v. collegium, p. 1292.
[7] *E.g.* Dion. Hal. IV. 4, "seducing the poor citizens by benevolences and gifts." So, *ibid.* 3, 9, 10, 40, and Livy I. 47; Cic. *de Rep.* II. 21 (38), "Servius began to reign…because, when Tarquin was falsely said to be seriously wounded but alive, he assumed the royal insignia, and gave judgments and freed debtors at his own expense."

made of his distributions of corn and land to the plebs¹. In short, king Servius, if he be regarded as a historical personage, appears to have inherited the policy as well as the position of his predecessor, and his violent accession and no less violent end to have been due mainly to feuds within the palace. The same conclusion is the most natural one to draw from his Etruscan name of Mastarna², quite apart from the etymological value of Gardthausen's suggestion³ that the name Mastarna is a prefixed form of Tarquin.

His methods of purchasing the support of the lower classes:

his relations with the Tarquins.

Servius was eventually overthrown by Tarquinius Superbus, who is said to have secured the throne "by buying up the poorest of the common people⁴." It is in the account of his reign that we find the fullest statements as to the Tarquins' relations to labour while they were kings of Rome. Nothing could be more explicit than Livy's statement on that point:

Tarquinius Superbus secures the throne by buying up the poor. When king he employs Etruscans and Roman citizens on a large scale as artizans and quarrymen.

He summoned smiths from every part of Etruria and employed upon it (*i.e.* on the building of the temple of Jove on the Tarpeian Mount) not only public funds, but also *workmen from among the plebeians*⁵.

The statement that Tarquin's employees were largely plebeians (and not slaves) is repeated by Livy later in the same book. In this second passage Brutus, declaiming against the state of things that had existed under the Tarquins, is made to declare that "men of Rome had been changed from soldiers into artizans and quarrymen⁶,"

---

¹ Dion. Hal. IV. 13, "immediately upon securing the throne he (Servius) distributed the public land to the poorer class of Romans (τοῖς θητεύουσι 'Ρωμαίων)": Livy I. 46, "Servius,...having first conciliated the goodwill of the plebeians by dividing among them individually land taken from the enemy, dared to put to the people the question whether they wished and bade him to be king"; cp. Varro *ap.* Non. p. 43, "uiritim: et extra urbem in regiones XXVI. agros uiritim liberis attribuit"; Aur. Vict. *de Vir. Ill.* VII. 7, "he distributed corn to the plebs."

² *C.I.L.* XIII. 1668.

³ Gardthausen, *Mastarna*, p. 27. Professor R. S. Conway tells me that tarna =Tarcna strikes him as *a priori* possible.

⁴ Dion. Hal. IV. 30.

⁵ Livy I. 56. On the building of this temple see also Livy I. 38; Cic. *de Repub.* II. 36 (20); Dion. Hal. III. 69; IV. 59; Tac. *Hist.* III. 72; Plut. *Popl.* 13; Florus I. 1. 7; Aur. Vict. *de Vir. Ill.* 8; Zonaras VII. 11.

⁶ Livy I. 59.

Dionysius is as explicit and more detailed[1]:

> He was not content to offend against the plebeians merely in this way. He enrolled all the plebeians who were loyal to him and suitable for military requirements, and the rest he compelled to find employment on the public works in the city, thinking it a very great danger for monarchs when the worst and poorest of the citizens are unemployed: at the same time he was anxious during his reign to complete the works left half-finished by his grandfather—the channels to drain away the water...and...the hippodrome amphitheatre.... On these works all the poor were employed, receiving from him a moderate provision, some quarrying[2], some hewing wood, some leading the waggons that conveyed this material, others bearing the burdens on their own shoulders; others again digging out the underground cellars and moulding the vaults in them and erecting the corridors: subordinated to the artizans thus engaged there were coppersmiths and carpenters and stonemasons, who were removed from their private shops and kept employed on the public requirements.

So in the same book[3]:

> Tarquin after this achievement (Gabii) gave the people a rest from expeditions and wars, and occupied himself with the building of the temples.... He set all the artizans to work on the undertakings.

And a little later[4] Brutus is made to tell the Romans that Tarquin "compels them like bought slaves to toil at quarrying and wood-cutting and carrying burdens[5]."

---

[1] Dion. Hal. IV. 44.
[2] Reading doubtful.   [3] Dion. Hal. IV. 59.
[4] Dion. Hal. IV. 81.

[5] For other public works ascribed to the Tarquin dynasty see Livy I. 45; Dion. Hal. IV. 26 (Servius, temple of Diana on the Aventine).

Livy I. 44 (agger, fosse, and wall of Servius; cp. Strabo V. 234); Livy I. 36–8 (well begun by Priscus); Dion. Hal. III. 67; Aur. Vict. *de Vir. Ill.* 6 (wall of Tarquinius Priscus); Eutrop. I. 6 (walls and cloacae of Tarquinius Priscus).

Pliny, *N.H.* III. 9 (agger of Tarquinius Superbus on the East side of the city).

It was in the reputed period of the Tarquins that the people of Latium seem to have first learned to make walls of squared stones, Pinza, *Bull. Comm.* 1897, pp. 228 f.

Serv. ad *Aen.* XII. 603 f. (Cass. Hem., second century B.C.), (Superbus, cloaca), Pliny, *N.H.* XXXVI. 24 (Priscus, cloaca), the Chronographer of 354 A.D., Joh. Laur. Lyd. (sixth century), *de Mens.* IV. 24, Joh. Antioch. (seventh century), *F.H.G.* IV. p. 553, Isidore of Seville (seventh century), *Etym.* V. 27. 23, Suid. (tenth century), s.v. Σούπερβος, all say that Tarquinius Superbus introduced into Rome penal labour (see below, p. 226) in mines and quarries. There appear to have been quarries on the slopes of the Capitol which may have been worked in the regal period. Pais argues that they could not have been worked before the fifth century because they were called lautumiae, a name borrowed from

It is nowhere explicitly stated that it was to this control of the free labour of the city that the Tarquins owed their power. On the contrary, according to Livy the populares helped to turn Superbus out for the very reason that he had forced them into this banausic life. "They were indignant that they had been kept by the king so long employed as smiths and doing the work of slaves[1]." This by itself would certainly suggest that the Tarquins had used their kingly power to turn the free men of Rome into artizans and quarrymen, and not their army of employees to turn a capitalist into a king. But the smiths summoned from Etruria, who are associated with the Roman plebeians, recall the "large number of skilled workmen" mentioned by Strabo as working for Demaratus at Tarquinii, and suggest that we have here a continuation of the activities that had made the fortune of the Tarquin family while still in Etruria[2].

There is a further statement in the same chapter of Livy that certainly harmonizes better with this latter alternative. At the time when the plebeians suddenly discovered the degrading nature of their occupations, not apparently without the help of the abler members of the nobility, Livy informs us that the king had run out of money, "exhausted by the magnificence of his public works." Similarly Dionysius makes Brutus urge on his fellow-conspirators that now

He loses the throne when he can no longer pay these employees.

Siceliot Greek: his view is based on the groundless assumptions (i) that a Siceliot word could not reach Rome before the fifth century, and (ii) that the quarries cannot be older than their name. In point of fact the quarries have been inferred from the name being frequently applied by Livy in his third decade to a prison known also as the Tullianum, Varro, *L.L.* v. 151, or Mamertine prison, or more recently as the church of San Pietro in Carcere. The prison is one of the most ancient structures in Rome, and has been compared with the beehive tombs of Greece.

The whole Capitol and Palatine are completely catacombed to a great depth by shafts and passages of most uncertain dates, discussed by Boni, *J.R.S.* III. pp. 247–250, and called by him favissae. Can Boni's favissae, or any part of them, be the lautumiae of the Tarquins? See Dion. Hal. iv. 44.

[1] Livy I. 57.

[2] Cicero probably regarded the wealth of Superbus as military spoil; cp. *de Rep.* II. 46 (25), "deinde uictoriis diuitiisque subnixus exsultabat insolenter," but on a point like this his words are of little weight. Equally valueless as evidence for the state of things in regal Rome are his contemptuous references to artizans, *de Off.* I. 150 (42), "opifices omnes in sordida arte uersantur: neque enim quidquam ingenuum habere potest officina."

is the time to carry out their plot, when the armed citizens are "no longer controlled by (Tarquin's) presents as formerly[1]." That Tarquin's regime was one of sweat and wages but never of blood and iron is borne out by Cicero, who observes that "we never hear of Tarquin's putting Roman citizens to death[2]."

Later writers speak of Superbus as employing penal labour and various forms of torture and intimidation on a large scale[3]. But these statements, which have plainly a common origin, are no less plainly embroideries upon the aristocratic misrepresentations of the Tarquins' labour policy. The truth is expressed by Florus: "in senatum caedibus, in omnes superbia, quae crudelitate grauior est bonis, grassatus[4]." In other words Superbus was a harsh and unpopular employer[5]. This personal unpopularity must have contributed along with the exhaustion of the royal treasury to reconcile the common people to the republican regime, which for them was certainly the beginning of an era of oppression and misery, since they had lost in the king their natural protector[6].

If the Tarquins' power was really commercial in origin, and if the account of it in writers of the age of Livy is in the main outline historical, then the facts ought to be found influencing the history of the early republic and in particular the measures taken by the aristocrats to prevent the restoration of the monarchy. What is in fact the sort of situation represented as most alarming them from this point of view?

Suspected attempts at restoring the kingship:

The first indication of the direction of their fears is to be found in the account of Collatinus' banishment, recorded by Livy as having taken place in the first year of the republic. According to Livy[7] it was simply the hated name of Tarquin that led to his banishment. Collatinus was reluctant to withdraw: he only did so from fear that later, when no longer consul, the same fate might overtake him with

Collatinus and his wealth and "benevolences";

---

[1] Dion. Hal. iv. 71, οὔτε δωρεαῖς ἔτι κατεχόμενοι ὡς πρότερον.

[2] Cic. *Phil.* iii. 10 (4).

[3] Pliny, *N.H.* xxxvi. 24; Dio Cass. ii. fr. xi. 6; the Chronographer of 354 A.D.; Joh. Laur. Lyd. *de Mens.* iv. 24; Joh. Ant. *F.H.G.* iv. p. 553; Isid. *Etym.* v. 27. 23; Suid. s.v. Σούπερβος.

[4] Florus i. 7.

[5] Cic. *pro Rab.* 13 (4) is, however, no evidence for Superbus personally, but only for the severity of ancient law.

[6] Bloch, *Répub. Rom.* p. 57.   [7] Livy ii. 2.

the loss of his property into the bargain—cum bonorum amissione. Livy does not always work over his material sufficiently to make it quite harmonize with his own interpretation of it. It looks as though it was the bona, the wealth of Collatinus, that led to his expulsion. Though plainly not the strongest influence in Rome at the time, it may have been sufficiently strong to be a perpetual menace to the aristocratic government. It is the "primores ciuitatis" who insist on his withdrawal. If in Dionysius[1] on another occasion Collatinus is made to argue "that it was not the tyrants' money that had been harming the city, but their persons," the protestation only shows that there were others who did not share this view, but thought rather, with Dionysius' Marcus Valerius, that there was a danger lest the people, "beguiled by the tyrant's benevolences,...should help to restore Tarquin to the throne[2]." The same view is implied in a speech put by Dionysius[3] into the mouth of one of the popular leaders at the time of the first secession. He reminds his hearers that "the people were never put to any disadvantage by the kings, and least of all by the last ones": he recalls an occasion on which the king had "distributed five minae of silver to every man," and reminds the patricians how the plebeians had rejected the great gifts that the banished Tarquins had offered them as an inducement to break faith with the patrician government.

It may well have been from similar fears that in the following year the remainder of the Tarquins' property was distributed among the people: "(bona regia) deripienda plebi sunt data[4]." A few chapters later Livy states that so long as the banished Tarquin was still alive, the people received from the senate "multa blandimenta[5]." The nobles are described by Dionysius as "taking many measures friendly to the poor, that they might not go over to the tyrants and be won over by considerations of personal gain and betray the commonwealth[6]." The senate seems to have been fighting the Tarquins with their own weapons. The blandimenta that kept Superbus off the throne may well have been synonymous with the benignitas that got Priscus on to it.

After the death of Tarquin at the court of the Greek tyrant at

---

[1] Dion. Hal. v. 5. Note, *ibid.* v. 12, C.'s banishment was ultimately arranged on a financial understanding. He took with him 25 talents into exile.
[2] Dion. Hal. v. 64.   [3] Dion. Hal. vi. 74.
[4] Livy ii. 5; so Dion. Hal. v. 13.   [5] Livy ii. 9.
[6] Dion. Hal. v. 22.

Cumae there were three prominent Romans who rightly or wrongly were suspected of aiming at the kingly power. It may be worth while examining in each of the three cases the circumstances that are said to have given rise to these suspicions.

Spurius Cassius[1] is not described as having been personally very rich, and our authors introduce into their accounts of him nothing to support the charge that he was aiming at overthrowing the existing government.

Cassius and his exceptional financial position;

They leave it possible to conceive of him as a constitutional reformer who when consul sought to relieve a widespread distress by distributions of land[2] and perhaps corn[3] and by taking the state finances into his own hands[4]. The outcry against him is made to come mainly from the landed classes who fear that his proposals may touch their own pockets. As far as they are thinking about the constitution it is the financial position that the consul has created for himself that is the chief ground of their alarms. "By his distributions of money the consul was erecting a power perilous to liberty:...the way was being paved to monarchy." Later on we find Cassius having money dealings with the people. He proposes that the sums that they have paid the government for corn brought from Sicily in time of famine should be refunded to them: "but this was looked on by the plebeians as a cash payment for the throne, and refused." Though there is nothing to show that the Cassius of Livy and Dionysius had either the desire or the real equipment to repeat the career of Tarquinius Priscus, yet the narrative about him is none the less relevant. It depicts the early republican as deeply alarmed at any individual who secures any kind of financial predominance in the state. Very possibly this feeling

---

[1] Diod. xi. 37; Livy ii. 41; Dion. Hal. viii. 69, 77; Cic. *de Rep.* ii. 35 (60), 27 (49), *de Amicit.* 8 (28), 11 (36), *Phil.* ii. 44 (114); Pliny, *N.H.* xxxiv. 9 (4), 14; Val. Max. v. 8. 2 (the above all quoted Mommsen, *Roem. Forsch.* ii. p. 173, n. 37); Florus i. 17. 26. The Greek writers say he aimed at a tyranny.

[2] So specifically Livy, Dion. Hal., Val. Max., Florus, in the passages cited above; cp. Pliny, *N.H.* xxxiv. 14, "eam (statuam) quam apud aedem Telluris statuisset sibi Sp. Cassius qui regnum affectauerat."

[3] Livy. Note the bronze statue of Ceres erected from the proceeds of his property after his fall. See next note.

[4] Cp. Dion. Hal. viii. 78. At his death his peculium (personal fortune) was confiscated and dedicated to Ceres, Val. Max. v. 8. 2, but there is no hint that it was very large. It appears to have only sufficed to make a single bronze statue, Livy ii. 41, Pliny, *N.H.* xxxiv. 9 (4). Dionysius speaks of the great wealth of Cassius' opponents.

may account for the ostentatious exhibition of poverty in which early republican nobles are so often depicted as indulging[1].

In the case of Spurius Maelius there are no such complications.

Maelius and his exceptional wealth and organized body of clients.

If we accept Livy and Dionysius, Maelius' policy did not threaten the property of any of the nobles. The fears that he would restore the kingship may have been mistaken, but they were almost certainly genuine. Is there any resemblance between extant accounts of Maelius' career and the speculations that we have been engaged in as to the early history of the first Tarquin? There is not only a resemblance but a striking one. Maelius was extremely rich: not dives merely but praedives[2]. When he set about relieving Rome from famine, he was able to do so not only at his own expense but through his own clients and connexions: "buying up corn at his own expense through the agency of his friends (hospitum) and clients[3]."

Marcus Manlius, the third to be condemned to death for aiming at the throne, need not detain us. He is essentially a military character, like his contemporary Dionysius of Syracuse[4].

Manlius.

---

[1] *E.g.* Livy II. 16, Publicola (perhaps, however, merely a wrong inference from the statement that the government paid for his funeral (so also Dion. Hal. v. 38); but cp. the way that in fifth century Athens enormously rich men like Nikias avoided anything that might draw attention to their wealth).

[2] Livy IV. 13–16; so Dion. Hal. XII. 1. 1, "most potent in wealth, having recently inherited his father's estate" (whence Mommsen, *Roem. Forsch.* II. p. 211, describes him as "according to Dionysius a rich merchant's son"); Florus, *Epit.* I. 17. 26, "Spurium largitione suspectum regiae dominationis praesenti morte (populus) multauit." Maelius is repeatedly said to have aimed at the kingship, so Cic. *de Rep.* II. 27 (50), *de Senect.* 16 (56), *de Amic.* 11 (36), *Phil.* II. 11, 34, 44 (26 and 27, 87, 114) (cp. also *in Cat.* I. 1. 3); Varro, *L.L.* v. 157; Val. Max. VI. 3. 1 (Rom.); Diod. XII. 37 ($\epsilon\pi\iota\theta\acute{\epsilon}\mu\epsilon\nu o\varsigma$ $\tau\upsilon\rho\alpha\nu\nu\acute{\iota}\delta\iota$); Dion. Hal. XII. 1 ($\epsilon\pi\iota\theta\acute{\epsilon}\sigma\epsilon\iota$ $\tau\upsilon\rho\alpha\nu\nu\acute{\iota}\delta o\varsigma$); Plut. *Brut.* 1.

[3] Livy IV. 13; cp. Dion. Hal. XII. 1. 2, "having many associates and employees ($\epsilon\tau\alpha\acute{\iota}\rho o\upsilon\varsigma$ $\kappa\alpha\grave{\iota}$ $\pi\epsilon\lambda\acute{\alpha}\tau\alpha\varsigma$) he sent them in various directions supplied with money from his own pocket to collect food."

[4] See especially Mommsen, *Roem. Forsch.* II. p. 189, who follows Dion. Hal. and believes the seditio Manliana to have been an armed revolt. Note, however, that Livy says that at Manlius' trial he brought to court 400 individuals whom, at his own expense, he had saved from financial ruin (VI. 20; cp. VI. 14: so also Aur. Vict. *de Vir. Ill.* 24), and that the site of his house became the mint (Livy VI. 20). Aurelius Victor, *loc. cit.*, states further that he was accused by the senate of having secreted Gallic treasures.

But the real bulwark of the republic of the fifth century as it appears in the pages of our authors is not the right arm of Servilius Ahala. It is a fundamental change that came over the lower classes of the free population. In a passage of Livy that has already been quoted, Brutus is made to charge the Tarquins with having converted the men of Rome from soldiers into artizans and quarrymen (opifices ac lapicidas). Brutus had just effected a revolution at Rome. To represent a revolution as a return to antiquity was as natural with the Roman as it is with us[1]. It is possible, though improbable, that the Tarquins had turned the plebeians from soldiers into artizans. The situation clearly indicated by Brutus is that he and his fellow-nobles are turning them from artizans into soldiers. It is not merely in the speeches put by Livy and Dionysius into the mouths of Brutus and his colleagues that we find the establishment of the republic associated with a reorganization of the state upon a military basis. The development of the comitia centuriata as the main organization of the citizens of Rome for political purposes is associated with the beginnings of the republic: the centuries were originally and fundamentally a military organization[2].

The republican government changes Tarquin's artizans into soldiers and makes war a paying (and ultimately a paid) profession:

The agrarian measures that appear so early in the narratives of the historians need not deceive us. As far as they are authentic they must have been either insincere or idealist[3]. The republican nobility is painted from the first as teaching the distressed plebeians to look not for farms and allotments but for wars and prize money. The picture of the transfiguration of the plebeians into soldiers is completed in the narrative of the siege of Veii (406-396 B.C.), when pay for military service is introduced[4] and war becomes a leading means of earning a livelihood[5].

In short it would appear that the nobles ceased to dread a restoration of the monarchy otherwise than by armed force when and only when their government became the principal and most popular employer in the state.

---

[1] It does not for the moment matter whether the misrepresentation goes back to Brutus or only to Livy or somewhere in between.
[2] Mommsen, *Rom. Hist.*³ (English translation), I. p. 328.
[3] Cp. Salvioli (French translation), *Capitalisme dans le Monde Antique*, p. 77.
[4] Livy IV. 59-60; cp. Dion. Hal. IV. 19.
[5] Salvioli, *Capitalisme*, p. 227.

The Alcmaeonidae at Athens put an end to the possibility of a revival of the tyranny (and incidentally to all respect for constructive manual labour) by instituting state payments for services as jurymen, sailors on warships, and the like. Conditions at Rome were in some ways very different from those at Athens. But the Roman nobles appear to have aimed at securing the same result as the Athenian by very similar means. How far this parallel holds, at least as between the extant narratives, may be illustrated from the history of the family that took the leading place in the early Roman republic.

cp. fifth century Athens.

The part played by Brutus in the narrative is politically as insignificant as that of Harmodius in the overthrow of the tyranny at Athens. The political geniuses of the early Roman republic are all to be found in the great house of the Claudii[1]. Our accounts make the family first come to Rome in the sixth year of the republic. The head of the family at that time is described by Dionysius as "of noble birth and influential through his wealth[2]." He arrives, "bringing with him a great establishment and numerous friends and retainers." Mommsen[3] gives strong reasons for thinking that the family cannot have first come to Rome at so late a date. But the arrival may well have been a return from exile like that of the Alcmaeonidae to Athens after the fall of Hippias. The analogies between the Claudii and the Alcmaeonidae deserve consideration, the more so as they seem to be uninfluenced by any ancient recognition of their existence. It looks as though the wealthy Claudii, like the wealthy Alcmaeonidae, "took the commons into partnership[4]." Mommsen has pointed out[5] how many "well known traits of the ancient tyrannus" occur in the picture of the decemvir Appius. His contemporary Pericles was called the new Peisistratus. If there are such strong reasons for equating the early Claudii, whose historical existence can scarcely be seriously questioned, with the contemporary Alcmaeonidae, it becomes increasingly probable that the history of Rome and Athens in the sixth century ran on parallel lines.

The earlier Claudii and their antityrannical policy.

One great difference between fifth century Rome and fifth century Athens was that Athens had had her own coinage from well back into the sixth century, whereas Rome, as already mentioned, struck

---

[1] Mommsen, *Hist. Rome* (English translation[2]), I. p. 495 f.
[2] Dion. Hal. v. 40.   [3] *Ibid.* p. 498.
[4] Hdt. v. 66.   [5] *Ibid.* pp. 500–1.

her first pieces about 338 B.C. No famous name is associated with these earliest pieces. The most prominent man in Rome during the first generation after 338 was another Claudius, the censor Appius Claudius Caecus. His greatest achievement was the epoch-making Via Appia, the first of the great series of roads that knit together the Roman Empire. The city owed to him also its first aqueduct. On these great public works he spent, without the previous sanction of the senate, the money

Appius Claudius Caecus (censor 312 B.C.):

his public works,

Fig. 33. *Aes graue* with wheel.

accumulated in the treasury[1]. The sums thus spent must have represented the first large accumulation of the new Roman currency.

Appius' connexion with the early coinage of Rome was probably not confined to spending it. The second series of Roman *aes graue* was coined in Campania and bears on the reverse a wheel (fig. 33). Numismatists have long associated the appearance of this wheel with the

his probable connexion with Roman coinage,

---

[1] Diod. xx. 36; cp. Livy, ix. 29, uiam muniuit et aquam in urbem duxit eaque unus perfecit.

construction of the Appian way that led from Rome to the Campanian capital¹.

his numerous clients,
One detail only is wanted to complete the picture of a potential tyrant of the early Greek type, such as has been depicted in every section of this volume, and that feature appears in Valerius Maximus. According to that writer², who flourished early in the first century A.D., Appius possessed "plurimas clientelas."

and Mommsen's conjecture that he aimed at a tyranny.
All this gives added significance, in the light of our enquiries, to a brilliant conjecture of Mommsen³ that Appius actually attempted to make himself tyrant. Mommsen relies mainly on a sentence in Suetonius⁴ which runs: "Claudius Drusus, after a crowned statue had been set up to him at Appi Forum, endeavoured by means of his clients (clientelas) to seize Italy." The context dates the event between the decemvirate and the first Punic War. The possible period is further limited by the fact that Appi Forum was only founded by Appius Claudius Caecus. The name of the would-be tyrant as given by Suetonius is Claudius Drusus, but this, Mommsen shows, must be corrupt. The mention of Appi Forum points definitely to Appius Claudius Caecus, the only person whose name is associated with the place. In another passage of his history⁵, Mommsen himself observes how Appius shows the spirit of the Tarquins.

"Secessions."
If we look at the history of the early republic from the plebeian point of view, there is at least one important feature in the extant narratives that supports our main conclusions. The most notable weapon that the fifth century plebeians are represented as employing against the nobles is the "secession." The first is recorded under the year of Spurius Cassius' consulship, when the men whom Tarquin is accused of having made into "artizans and quarrymen" proceeded in a body to the "mons sacer" outside the city, and refused to come back and resume work until their grievances had been dealt with. The resemblance of the secession to the modern strike has already been recognized⁶. It may

¹ Hill, *Historical Roman Coins*, p. 18; see also *ibid.* pp. 10–18, based on Haeberlin's *Systematik*.
² Val. Max. VIII. 13. 5 (Rom.).
³ Mommsen, *Hist. Rome* (English translation²), I. p. 504.
⁴ Suet. *Tiberius*, 2.   ⁵ Mommsen, *op. cit.* II. p. 94.
⁶ *E.g.* Bloch, *Répub. Rom.* p. 58. One of the earliest recorded strikes in England is that of the Wisbech shoemakers who in 1538 left the town and established

be an accident, but if so it is a remarkable one, that the chief weapon of the class on which Tarquin's power appears to have rested should have been one that reappears in history with the organization of the industrial classes in modern times.

Before we proceed to discuss the value of the narratives that we have been quoting, there are a few further notices in them that have a place in this discussion, though they deal not with Rome but with other cities of Central Italy.

The part played at Ardea in 440 B.C. by the working-classes.
In 440 B.C. the plebeians of Ardea, a city about 20 miles S. of Rome, are described by Livy[1] as engaged in a struggle with the optimates, and as getting the worst of it. Thereupon the losing party "quite unlike the Roman plebs,....prepared to besiege the city (*i.e.* Ardea) with a crowd of workmen (opificum), attracted by the prospect of plunder." The Latin leaves it possible that the crowd of workmen (opificum) with which the plebs of Ardea prepared to besiege their city should be understood as a separate body, conceivably metics or slaves. At Veii in 400 B.C. the artifices are said to have been slaves[2]. But though in Etruria in 400 B.C. this may have been normally the case, in Latin Ardea forty years earlier we may well have conditions not unlike those that have been inferred above for sixth century Rome. Even if the opifices of Ardea are to be understood as slaves, the united body of plebeians and opifices acting in opposition to the optimates comes nearer to Brutus' description of the situation at Rome under the Tarquins than does anything that can be found in our historians' pictures of Rome in the fifth century. Livy is thinking of the Roman plebeians of the early republican period, not of the opifices and lapicidae of the age of the Tarquins, when he says that the plebs of Ardea was quite unlike the Roman plebs[3].

themselves on a neighbouring hill from which they summoned their masters to come out and meet them and hear their demands for higher wages. Webb, *Hist. of Trade Unionism*, p. 3.

[1] Livy IV. 9.

[2] Below, p. 235.

[3] The reported attempts at servile insurrections in fifth century Rome (Livy III. 15–16; Dion. Hal. v. 51) seem never to have had plebeian support, and are perhaps to be partly explained as a result of a more complete severance between the free and servile population. The alleged participation of ambitious slaves "seduced by hopes of freedom" (Dion. Hal. v. 53) in a conspiracy to restore Tarquinius Superbus is not the same thing.

In the year 400 B.C. according to Livy the people of Veii, "taedio annuae ambitionis, regem creauere[1]." Nothing is said by Livy about feelings and parties in Veii itself, except this statement that they were bored with annual elections. All that Livy mentions is the way in which the appointment was received elsewhere in Etruria. The event, he says, gave offence to the peoples of Etruria. Their hatred of kingly power was not greater than that which they felt against the king personally. He had previously made himself generally unpopular by his wealth and arrogance (opibus superbiaque). He had once brought a solemn celebration of the games to a violent conclusion: indignant at having been rejected by the votes of the twelve peoples in favour of another candidate for the priesthood, he had suddenly, in the middle of the performance, withdrawn the workmen (artifices), a great part of whom were his own slaves[2].

The rich Veientine employer who became king of his city in 400 B.C.

The result of the Veientine's wealth had been, according to Livy, to make him unpopular. But it is a reasonable inference from Livy's narrative that he was unpopular only with the aristocrats who continued to control the government in the other cities of Etruria. His accession can hardly have been disagreeable to the Veientines who made him king.

As noticed just above before he became king he had also been the employer and actually the owner of a great proportion of the "artifices" of the city. It is nowhere stated that the artifices helped to make him king in Veii as they had helped to make him unpopular in the rest of Etruria: but the important part played by the opifices at Ardea a generation previously suggests that this may well have been the case. If the events took place as recorded it is hard to believe that there was not some connexion between the Veientine's royal power and his previous riches and control of the skilled labour of the city[3].

[1] Livy v. 1.

[2] *Ibid.* This sudden withdrawal of the supply of labour by the subsequent king of Veii should be noted in connexion with the discussion (above, p. 233) of the significance of the Roman "secessions."

[3] The story of his interference in the national games might perhaps be regarded with suspicion. It recalls Pheidon. But the essence of the story, the sudden withdrawal of the supply of labour, is not in the Pheidon story. It rather recalls what happened at Columbus, Ohio, in midwinter, 1891, when the gas kings suddenly cut off the gas. Hy. D. Lloyd, *Wealth against Commonwealth*, p. 365.

So far we have been assuming that the extant accounts of the Tarquins have a historical basis. That assumption, as remarked already, is by no means beyond dispute. Not a statement has been quoted so far in this chapter that has not within the last century been pronounced to be historically worthless. Recently however there has been a movement to treat the narrative with much more respect than it generally received a generation ago. The new attitude is not merely a reaction against the excessive scepticism of the nineteenth century. Largely it is based on fresh evidence, mainly archaeological. Inscriptions show that writing was no extraordinary accomplishment at Rome in those early days. Excavations of cities that have been sacked make it most unlikely that the sack of Rome in 390 B.C. meant the complete destruction of the city records. In the face of facts like these more weight is now given to passages where our authorities for the history of sixth and fifth century Rome allude to more or less contemporary records, whether Roman or Greek. The evidence for falsification and invention is indeed considerable, but it is now for the most part realized that the critics of the nineteenth century greatly overestimated its application. The credibility of early Roman history is too big a subject to deal with at all adequately in a work like this. It is necessary however to examine more in detail those parts of the narrative with which this enquiry is more particularly concerned.

II. The credibility of the narrative.

Some scholars are still to be found who dispute *in toto* the Tarquins' historical existence. Of this ultra-sceptical school the most recent and voluminous exponent is Professor Pais of Naples[1]. Pais accepts nearly all the views of nearly all the sceptics in so far as they are purely destructive. But the main inspiration of his unbelief is not this destructive criticism but the ease with which he finds that he can explain the growth of our narratives on the assumption that they are false[2]. In the case of the Tarquins Pais first points out in the

The historical existence of the Tarquins has been denied, e.g. by Pais.

---

[1] Pais' most recent works are his *Storia Critica* and *Ricerche*; but for English readers I have thought it better to refer mainly to his earlier but equally characteristic *Ancient Legends of Roman History* (1906).

[2] The method is of course much older than Pais; cp. G. C. Lewis, *Credib. Early Rom. Hist.* 1. p. 228, "we have no difficulty in explaining the fictitious character of the events of that early period provided we consider them fictitious." For an early instance see Bachofen, *Tanaquil* (1870), where the Etruscan Tarquin-Tanaquil are equated with the Lydian Heracles (ancestor of Demaratus)-Omphale; cp. Damonno, the wife of Gyges, etc. (above, p. 135). Bachofen's

usual way the inconsistencies and impossibilities and reduplications[1] in the narrative, and the uncertainties that hang over it as a whole. Then, after rejecting it as history, he accounts for it as myth. He equates Tarquinius philologically with Tarpeius[2]. The Tarpeian rock was the slope of the Roman Capitol over which condemned criminals were hurled to meet their doom. There are passages in Varro and elsewhere that make it possible that the whole Capitol was once called the Tarpeian Mount[3]. On the strength of them Tarquinius is explained as Tarpeius, the original guardian deity of the Roman citadel. All the stories told about Tarquin are, according to Pais, attempts to explain customs and buildings and natural features connected with the Tarpeian Mount. Hence his association with the temple on the top of the Capitol and with the quarries on its sides. Hence the stories of his cruelty and of his own violent death. Hence too we hear of Tarquinian laws: they are merely laws passed on the Mons Tarpeius or sanctioned by the god Tarpeius[4].

I do not propose to deal in detail with these criticisms. They do not seem to me to need it. So many unquestionably historical characters would succumb to Pais' treatment.

Pais' arguments tested by applying them to Alfred the Great. Imagine for a moment that the Anglo-Saxon Chronicle had never circulated, and that the original had perished in a Danish raid. Imagine further that Asser's life of Alfred had met with a similar fate. Both calamities might easily have happened, and if they had, king Alfred would be as easily disposed of as king Tarquin himself.

Alfred did none of the things that tradition ascribes to him. He did not institute trial by jury or the division of England into shires. He was not the founder either of University College, Oxford, or of the British navy. The stories of his victories over the Danes are extremely doubtful on the face of them[5]. Alfred does not conquer his enemies: he merely converts them. The legend admits that he

comparison may be not altogether groundless, but it is sufficiently explained by assuming, as these stories perhaps imply, that the political status of women among the Lydo-Etruscans was not quite so backward as it has hitherto been in Europe generally. The traces of impropriety which Bachofen detected in these ladies' behaviour may be merely a reflexion of the European attitude towards the claims of women for any sort of political equality with men.

[1] Tarquin = Tarchon the friend of Aeneas.   [2] Pais, *Legends*, pp. 105, 122.
[3] Varro, *L.L.* v. 41; Dion. Hal. III. 69; Pais, *Legends*, pp. 109–116.
[4] Pais, *Legends*, pp. 116–127.
[5] Cp. G. C. Lewis, *Credib. Early Rom. Hist.* I. p. 472.

had his headquarters in an impassable swamp, and that the conquered Danes ruled the country. Twice in two centuries the Danish invaders sweep over England after the death of a king Aethelred. Both times there is a campaign on the Berkshire Downs. The decisive battle is fought in the first case at Ashdown, in the second at Essendune, which is palpably a mere variation of the same name. In each case the conquest is succeeded by the reign of a Saxon Edward. The second Edward is admitted by tradition to have been less concerned with royalty than with religion[1]. The first will be shown in a moment to have been the son of a god. Elder as applied to the first Edward is neither more nor less suspicious than Priscus as applied to Tarquin. This simple device of duplication probably explains the story of Alfred in Athelney. It is a reflexion backwards of the story, possibly historical, of Hereward's exploits in the similar swampy fastness of Ely.

The one legend that remains inextricably associated with Alfred is that of the cakes. Alfred the fugitive in his Arician grove[2] at Athelney is made known to his followers only after the burning of the cakes. The inference is obvious. Alfred is a vegetation deity of the same order as Demeter, the wandering goddess who was found by the mistress of the house where she sought refuge burning not cakes but Triptolemus the corn god himself[3]. The mistress of

---

[1] Note, too, the curious history of his successor, who, though claimed as a Saxon king, is said to have been of Danish extraction. He bears the name of a son of Knut, and spends his brief reign in disposing of another king Harold, who is admittedly a Scandinavian. All this must surely be a clumsy attempt to anglicize the last of the Danish kings.

[2] Cp. Pais' explanation of Servius Tullius as the fugitive slave god of Aricia, *Legends*, pp. 142 f.

[3] Ovid, *Fasti*, IV. 549 f. Caeculus, the mythical founder of Praeneste, was found as a babe in a hearth, Virg. *Aen.* VII. 681 (cp. X. 544), and Cato *ap.* Schol. Veron. *ad loc.* He was conceived by a spark and manifested by a fire, Serv. ad *Aen.* VII. 681. Servius Tullius himself offers a still closer analogy. He was the issue of the union between a disguised princess (cp. Livy I. 39) and a burning hearth (according to Frazer, *Magic Art*, II. 267–8, the normal form of parentage among the early kings of Rome; cp. Plut. *Romulus*, 2), which made known its passion for her when she was bringing it cakes ($\pi\epsilon\lambda\acute{\alpha}\nu\text{ous}$). Subsequently Servius announced his coming kingship by himself catching fire, Dion. Hal. IV. 2; Pliny, *N.H.* XXXVI. 70; Plut. *Fort. Rom.* 10 (*Moral.* 323); Ovid, *Fasti*, VI. 627–36. These four references have both birth and burning. For birth see also Arnob. *adv. Gent.* V. 18 (quoting Flaccus); for burning Florus I. 1. 6; Serv. ad *Aen.* II. 683; Aur. Vict. *de Vir. Ill.* 7; Laur. Lyd. *de Ostent.* 279 (18 B, C); Cic. *Divin.* I. 53 (121).

the house appears also in the Alfred myth. But in other ways, and especially in the recognition scene, the story has been obviously contaminated by Christian influence[1].

So far therefore from dismissing the cake story from Alfred's history, we find that it is the very essence of the legend. In fact, when we recall such divinities as Dionysus Botrys, Dionysus the Grape, we must be tempted to wonder whether king Alfred and his cakes are not one and the same divinity.

The introduction of the Greek Demaratus into the Tarquin story has sometimes been regarded with extreme suspicion. For the late Professor Pelham it seems to have been a proof that Tarquin was merely Herodotus translated into Latin. He uses it as such in a handbook on Roman history[2]. Even if only the literary records are considered Pelham's inference if not unreasonable is certainly rash. The story of the voyage of Demaratus stands on quite a different footing from the long speech put by Dionysius into the mouth of Brutus, in which the founder of the Roman republic is made to quote the double kingship at Sparta as a precedent for the double consulship[3]. Brutus' speech is palpable fiction. The Demaratus story on the other hand may indeed have been borrowed from that of Philip the son of Butacides, who in the last quarter of the sixth century fled from Croton "with his own trireme and a crew of his own employees[4]" and sailed first to Cyrene and then with Dorieus the Spartan to Sicily, where they tried to establish a settlement but were killed by the Phoenicians and Egestaeans. But if on other and independent grounds we find reason for thinking that the story of Demaratus' voyage in the seventh century[5] is in the main outline historical, then we may reasonably find a confirmation of it in the well attested facts of Philip's adventures in the century following,

The Greek Demaratus has been regarded as a Greek fiction:

but there is nothing improbable about the narrative,

---

[1] Cp. S. Luke xxiv. 30, 31.

[2] Pelham, *Outlines*², p. 7; cp. Niebuhr, *History of Rome* (trans. Walter), I. p. 231.   [3] Dion. Hal. IV. 73.

[4] οἰκηίῃ τε τριήρει καὶ οἰκηίῃ ἀνδρῶν δαπάνῃ, Hdt. v. 46–7; cp. VIII. 62, where Themistocles threatens to sail to the far West with the whole population of Athens.

[5] Pais, *Legends*, p. 312, n. 7, asserts that "that tradition which makes him (Tarquinius Priscus) a contemporary of Romulus was received among the official versions." But Dion. Hal. II. 37, which alone he quotes in support, speaks only of a nameless lucumo from Solonium.

in the statement[1] that Caere, the Southern neighbour of Tarquinii, contained a Greek element at the time of the Tarquins[2], and further in the fact that Demaratus is made to quit Corinth at a time when we have the authority of Herodotus[3] for believing that many prominent Corinthians were being driven to quit their city. The migration of the Tarquins from Tarquinii to Rome corresponds with the Etrusco-Carthaginian alliance against the Greeks of which the best remembered fact is the subsequent disaster that overtook the Phocaeans in Corsica in 536 B.C. When the Tarquins are banished from Rome they flee to the Greek city of Cumae, while the Romans who have banished them proceed to make an alliance with Carthage[4]. All through the Tarquin narrative we may discern a strictly historical background that fully explains their comings and goings. The same may of course be said of countless heroes of modern historical romances. But in these historical romances the fictitious characters seldom play the leading political part that is played by the tyrant kings of the Tarquin dynasty.

The evidence of institutions also tends rather against the sceptics. Cicero notes that the organization which Tarquinius Priscus was said to have introduced for maintaining the Roman cavalry was the same in principle as that which had once prevailed in Corinth[5]. The sceptics may indeed argue that the Corinthian character of the Roman practice was the reason why it was attributed to the son of Demaratus. But this line of argument rests on pure assumption, and leaves with its advocate the onus of explaining this similarity between the institutions of Corinth and Rome.

[1] Strabo v. 220, 226.

[2] There are the same two *a priori* possibilities about the Greek artists Gorgasus and Damophilus, said by Pliny (*N.H.* xxxv. 45) to have adorned the temple of Ceres in the Circus Maximus, which is said to have been dedicated in 494 B.C. In this case there is the further complication that the adornment may have been indefinitely later than the dedication. But there is no evidence that it was. Greek inscriptions on the temple recorded that the right side was the work of Demophilus, the left of Gorgasus. It is begging the question to say that these artists must be later than 390 B.C. because the inscriptions are mentioned by Pliny. Rayet (*Mon. de l'Art Ant.* I. p. 7 of chapter entitled "Louve en Bronze") regards Pliny's statement as confirming the extant archaeological evidence for Greek artistic influence on early republican Rome. This is going too far in the opposite direction: but Rayet's view has no inherent impossibility. Nothing is said about restoration or reconstruction in the account of the work of these Greek artists on the Roman temple.

[3] Hdt. v. 92.   [4] Martha, *l'Art Étrusque*, p. 120, n. 1.   [5] Cic. *de Rep.* II. 20 (36).

CH. VIII ROME 241

There is in fact another source of evidence now available which greatly alters the balance of probabilities. Cicero may after all be right when he says "influxit non tenuis quidam e Graecia riuulus

which is con- in hanc urbem, sed abundantissimus amnis illarum
firmed disciplinarum et artium[1]," and proceeds at once to illustrate his statement from the career of Demaratus.

Fig. 34. Corinthian vase found at Tarquinii.

by the finding at Tarquinii of VII–VI century Corinthian pottery,

At the time when the story makes Demaratus leave Corinth for Etruria Corinth was probably the chief industrial state in Greece. Her chief industry was pottery. Corinthian pottery of this period has

[1] Cic. *de Rep.* II. 19 (34).

been found in many parts of the Greek world, including the chief cities of Etruria[1]. At Corneto (Tarquinii), the town from which Tarquinius Priscus is said to have migrated to Rome, many specimens from the necropolis of the ancient city are to be seen in the museum. An example is shown in fig. 34[2]. Unless the Corinthian pottery found in such distant regions as Etruria has distinct local peculiarities, it is generally assumed to have been imported from Greece. Corinth did unquestionably export pottery

Fig. 35. Corinthian terra cotta tablet depicting the export of vases.

A Corinthian terra cotta tablet has come down to us (see fig. 35)[3] that depicts a ship surmounted by a row of vases that can only represent the cargo. The wide area of its distribution and the very numerous sites on which it has been found point to export from a single centre. On the other hand a large

---

[1] E.g. from Caere, Pottier, *Album*, I. nos. E 629–40; *Roem. Mitt.* II. p. 155, XXII. pp. 133–4, 150–1; *Bullettino dell' Inst.* 1884, pp. 122–3, 1885, p. 211.

[2] Cp. above, fig. 22 from Corinth. The Corinthian pottery from Tarquinii is well illustrated Montelius, *Civ. Prim. Ital.* Sér. B, plates 297, 298.

[3] *Cat. Berl. Vas.* 831 = *Ant. Denk.* I. pl. 8, fig. 3a. In discussing this tablet Wilisch, *Jahresb. Gymn. Zittau*, 1901, p. 20 and fig. 22, associates it with the Demaratus tradition.

export trade from one main centre is quite consistent with branch establishments. If Corinthian potters went to Etruria, it is hard to see how we are to distinguish the vases they made before leaving home from those that they produced afterwards. The question whether the characteristic pale clay of the Corinthian pottery is to be found in Central Italy does not arise. The raw material would be imported quite as easily as the finished product. But there is other archaeological evidence that takes us further, and makes it not only possible but probable that Greek potters as well as Greek pottery found their way to Etruria at the period to which the Demaratus story, if historical, must be assigned, *i.e.* about the middle of the seventh century[1]. I refrain purposely at this point from drawing my own conclusions, and shall confine myself to the views and statements of archaeologists who have devoted special attention to the material in question.

and by the many finds in Central Italy of VII and VI century objects of Greek style but local workmanship.
In the seventh century graves that have been found in so many cities of Etruria there occur, besides objects that may well be imported from Greece, many others that are essentially Greek in character, but show local peculiarities. For instance at Caere, which was so closely connected with Tarquinii and Rome, in the famous tomb excavated in 1836 by General Galassi and the arch-priest Regulini, a quantity of metal work of this description was found. The tomb has been recently reopened and the contents discussed at length by G. Pinza[2]. On some of the vases of a very familiar Greek type found in the same grave Pinza remarks that "the coarse clay allows us to imagine that they are of local fabric[3]."

When we come to Central Italian finds that date from the sixth century Greek objects that there is good reason for regarding as locally produced become positively plentiful. They include vases and bronzes, architectural terra cottas and sepulchral frescoes[4]. Such

[1] For travelling potters cp. Bent, *J.H.S.* VI. (1885), p. 198, on the modern potters of Siphnos: "In springtime they start on their travels far and wide and settle in towns and villages for days and weeks until the place is supplied with large and well made earthenware, amphorae, and cooking utensils."

[2] *Roem. Mitt.* XXII. p. 122; so *Bull. Comm.* 1898, p. 273, n. 3.

[3] *Roem. Mitt.* XXII. p. 162; cp. Furtwaengler, *Ant. Gemm.* III. pp. 174-5; see also *Roem. Mitt.* XXII. p. 156, quoting Furtwaengler, *Olymp.* IV. 114 f.

[4] Vases and bronzes have been attributed to local workshops on stylistic grounds. The frescoes must obviously have been executed *in situ*. As regards

a mass of material points again to a large number of Greek or Greek-trained workmen in Central Italy at the time of its production, and though that time is rather later than Demaratus and the objects are Ionic, not Corinthian, yet it increases the plausibility of the Demaratus story, the more so as the change from Corinthian to Ionic reflects the policy ascribed in our ancient literary authorities to Servius Tullius[1].

Those who deny the historical existence of Demaratus naturally deny also that of his Greek workmen Eucheir and Eugrammus. Even Rizzo, who admits a historical basis for the Demaratus story, declares that these names are "obviously fictitious[2]."

The names of Demaratus' Greek workmen are not (pace Rizzo) "obviously fictitious."

The taint of the ultra-sceptical school still lingers. Else why should a countryman of Tintoretto say that Eucheir and Eugrammus are "obviously fictitious" names? In spite of its obvious fictitiousness the name Eucheiros was actually borne by a Greek potter, several of whose vases have come down to us signed "Eucheiros made me the son of Ergo-

---

the architectural terra cottas, their size and the number required for each building raise the question of local fabric quite apart from their style and technique. Unfortunately hitherto remains of this sort have been inadequately excavated and no less inadequately published. Rizzo, whose valuable article on the Conca finds is referred to more fully below, regards the earliest Conca series as "di manufattura non di arte locale."

[1] See further pp. 245-6, 251-4. The absence in some cases of seventh century Corinthian counterparts to the sixth century Ionic finds is due mainly to the accidents of discovery. The earliest architectural terra cottas from the regions round Rome are for instance all sixth century and Ionic: but the literary tradition ascribes the invention of terra cotta antefixes to Butades, who worked at Corinth (Pliny, *N.H.* xxxv. 43 (12); cp. *ibid.* 45; cp. also *Year's Work Class. Stud.* 1914, p. 2 (D. Lamb on recent finds at Corfu)). We may expect therefore that when more attention has been paid to excavation and publication we shall find that seventh century Italy possessed (which probably means produced) architectural terra cottas, and that these terra cottas were in style Corinthian. A fresco at Tarquinii, *Bull. Comm.* 1911, p. 26, fig. 9, depicts a gable which recalls that of the actual temple recently unearthed in the Corinthian colony of Corcyra. At Conca the votive offerings, which go back further than the architectural terra cottas, include both Proto-Corinthian and Corinthian pottery (Pinza, *Mon. Ant.* xv. p. 494; Barnabei and Cozza, *Notiz.* 1896, pp. 29 f.). That the Conca finds lend plausibility to the Demaratus story is recognized by Rizzo, *Bull. Comm.* 1911, p. 44, who, however, does not appear to recognize the historical significance of the material being Ionian.

[2] Rizzo, *Bull. Comm.* 1911, pp. 43-6.

timos[1]." This Eucheiros the son of Ergotimos (itself a good industrial name) lived not in the seventh century but in the sixth: also, he was not a Corinthian but an Athenian. But even if we refrain from emphasizing the pride of family which his signature shows as compared with that of most potters, who sign with only their own names, and refrain too from recalling the facts that Greeks so very frequently bore the names of their grandfathers and that potters like Amasis almost certainly migrated to Athens about the middle of the sixth century, when Athens was supplanting the rest of Greece and more particularly Corinth in the pottery industry, still the sixth century Athenian Eucheiros completely disposes of the "obvious fictitiousness" of one detail of the Demaratus story. So far from being obviously fictitious the Corinthian Eucheir has every appearance of historical reality. So too has his alleged relationship to the founder of the Tarquin dynasty at Rome. If the first tyrant of Corinth got his name from a pot and very possibly owed his tyranny to the Corinthian potteries, it is not surprising if a Corinthian emigrant to Italy took potters with him and used them to build up the position which enabled him to make himself tyrant in the city of his adoption[2]. In both cases we are dealing with conjectures, but it may be fairly claimed that the two conjectures lend one another mutual support.

There are no traditions connecting Servius with Corinth: such notices as we have of his relations with the Greeks connect him with Ionia. Both Livy[3] and Dionysius[4] and also Aurelius Victor[5] state that Servius built a temple of Artemis and made it the centre of a Latin league, in imitation of the temple of Artemis at Ephesus, which was the meeting-place of the Ionian league. It has

Servius and Greece: the narrative connects him not with Corinth but with Ionia.

---

[1] Klein, *Meistersig.*[2] p. 72, nos. 1–3. For the absurdity of saying that the name Eucheir is obviously fictitious, cp. the fact that one of the greatest composers of early English church music (dominantly vocal) bears the name of Byrd. What too does Rizzo think about the historicity of M. Pottier, the distinguished French archaeologist to whom we owe the catalogue of the Greek vases in the Louvre?

[2] Demaratus is said to have fled from the tyranny of Cypselus (above, p. 216). He may have been an unsuccessful rival of Cypselus for the Corinthian tyranny. Cp. the facts quoted, p. 52, as to Miltiades the rival of Peisistratus tyrant of Athens, and the tyranny that Miltiades secured for himself in the Thracian Chersonese.

[3] Livy I. 45.   [4] Dion. Hal. IV. 25–6.   [5] Aur. Vict. *de Vir. Ill.* 7.

already been suggested that Servius' monetary reforms may have a historical basis, and be due to intercourse with the Phocaeans, who had founded Marseilles in 600 B.C. The city of Phocaea, though in Aeolian territory, was reckoned Ionian[1].

The Ionizing Servius is said to have reigned from 578 to 534 B.C.

Ionian influence in Central Italy at the reputed period of Servius is confirmed by archaeological finds.

In the middle of the sixth century, or in other words at just the same period, a corresponding change occurs in the archaeological finds, in which experts are agreed in recognizing Ionian influence if not Ionian workmanship. Among the objects which display the new style are the vases known as Caeretan hydriae[2] and Pontic amphorae[3] and a group that has been classified as among the latest products of Clazomenae[4], and a group of bronzes from Perugia[5]. Of the sixth century examples of the famous frescoes that adorn or disfigure the chamber tombs of Etruria some have been attributed to Ionian artists[6], as have also architectural terra cottas of the same period found in Latium at Conca (the ancient Satricum)[7] and Velletri[8].

In dealing with the architectural terra cottas from Conca Rizzo suggests[9] that the potters who worked there came from Cumae or some other Greek city in Campania.

Rome and Cumae.

[1] Strabo, IV. 179, 180, remarks on the similarity of the images of Artemis at Ephesus, at Marseilles, and in the Servian temple at Rome; see Seeley, *Livy I.* chap. 45.

[2] E.g. *Brit. Mus. Cat. Vases*, II. fig. 41 and pl. II., Buschor, *Gr. Vasenmal.*[1] p. 94.

[3] Buschor, *Gr. Vasenmal.*[1] pp. 97–9 and figs. 62, 63.

[4] *Ibid.* pp. 87–90 and fig. 56. Clazomenae lay only 20 miles from Phocaea, the city with which we have just seen reasons for associating Servius.

[5] *Roem. Mitt.* IX. (1894), pp. 253 f. and especially 254–5, 269 (where Petersen compares with Ephesian work) and 287–296 (particularly close parallels from Clazomenae).

[6] E.g. Montelius, *Civ. Prim. Ital.* ser. B, pl. 342; Rizzo, *Bull. Comm.* 1910, p. 320, 1911, p. 43, discussing representations of temple gables in some of the frescoes.

[7] Graillot, *Mélanges d'Arch. et d'Hist.* 1896, pp. 148 f.; Barnabei and Cozza, *Notiz. d. Scav.* 1896, pp. 28 f.; Rizzo, *Bull. Comm.* 1910, pp. 307 f.; cp. Walters, *Brit. Mus. Cat. Terracottas*, pp. xvii. and 171–9 (Ionic Greek architectural terra cottas from Lanuvium and Caere), 183 (Etruscan terra cotta sarcophagus under Ionic influence from Caere).

[8] Rizzo, *Bull. Comm.* 1910, p. 318. The Velletri examples show a striking resemblance to finds made in Asia Minor at Larissa near Phocaea.

[9] *Bull. Comm.* 1911, pp. 46–7; cp. 1910, p. 313.

CH. VIII   ROME   247

In this connexion he remarks[1] that so far the traces of intercourse between Rome and Campania during the first two centuries of the city (*i.e.* 750–550 B.C.) seem rather scanty. He attributes this to gaps in excavation. Once more he seems not to notice that the negative archaeological evidence harmonizes with the literary tradition. Cumae must have been powerfully influencing Rome in the very early days when the Romans borrowed the Cumaean alphabet. But then comes a period when Cumae is eclipsed by Corinth[2]. Cumae only begins to recover her influence Romewards when Corinthian influence is on the wane. The Tarquins' story begins at Corinth: it ends at Cumae, where Superbus, when banished from Rome, is said to have sought refuge[3] with Aristodemus who was perhaps the last Greek tyrant of the old commercial type[4].

It has been argued that nobody could have built shops in the Forum in the time of the Tarquins because recent excavations have shown that till a comparatively late date the Forum was used as a cemetery: that, apart from this, arcades and shops must have been impossible in the Forum until it had been drained: and that the building of the main drain, the cloaca maxima, ascribed to Tarquin by Livy, has been shown by excavation to belong to a very much later age.

The earliest Forum shops (from the graves on the site) and the great drain (from its brickwork) have been dated after the regal period: but

As regards the main drain, archaeology has indeed shown that it was bricked and vaulted at a late date; but there is no reason for thinking that it began its existence with the masonry that now encloses it. The London Fleet and Tyburn suggest the opposite. The most recent volume on the subject is emphatic on this point. "The earliest Roman sewer consisted undoubtedly of a natural watercourse, the channel of which was widened and deepened[5]." "There is no doubt that the first attempts at artificial drainage date from the regal

the drain cannot be dated from its brick facing,

---

[1] *Bull. Comm.* 1911, p. 47.
[2] Perhaps after the "Sacred" war of the beginning of the sixth century when the fall of Krisa cut off Cumae from her mother city, see below, pp. 259–260.
[3] Cic. *Tusc. Quaest.* III. 12 (27); Livy II. 21; Dion. Hal. VI. 21; cp. VII. 2, 12.
[4] See below, pp. 278–9.
[5] Platner, *Topography of Rome*[2] (1911), p. 106. Cp. Huelsen, *Forum Romanum*, trans. Carter, 1906, p. 3.

period. The first part of the city to be drained was the Forum valley[1]."

and the Forum graves show only (pace Pais) that the cemetery was secularized not later than late in the regal period.

Those who maintain a post-regal date for the building of the Forum base their arguments on the finds of pottery in the Forum graves. The finds have been numerous and their evidence is valuable, and it is necessary briefly to review it. The latest style of pottery found in these graves is the Proto-Corinthian. This very distinctive and widely distributed pottery[2] has been the subject of much controversy as regards its place of origin, but its chronology is well established. It flourished in the seventh century: during the sixth it persisted in a few stereotyped forms, of which at least two[3] lived on in a degraded form into the fifth. Vases of this style quoted by Boni[4] as coming from two of the latest graves in the Forum are illustrated in the *Notizie degli Scavi*[5] (fig. 36). Both the vases illustrated might well be seventh century. At Rhitsona in Boeotia the types were completely obsolete by the middle of the sixth century, not one example occurring among some 2500 vases excavated from graves of the latter half of the century. This mass of pottery included about 150 Proto-Corinthian vases, but the number is divided about equally between kothons like *J.H.S.* XXXI. p. 75, fig. 4, and small skyphoi such as *J.H.S.* XXIX. p. 319, fig. 7, no. 9, with just two or three pyxides like *J.H.S.* XXIX. p. 312, fig. 2, no. 8.

In the Forum graves there are a certain number of vases of other styles that cannot be dated so accurately as the Proto-Corinthian

---

[1] Platner, *ibid.* p. 105. Pais claims the story of Curtius (445 or 362 B.C.; Varro, *L.L.* v. 148; Livy VII. 6) as an alternative version of the draining of the Forum. The existence of two conflicting versions would not, *pace* Pais, *Legends*, pp. 35–6, prove that neither was true; in this particular case we have not two rival stories, since the Curtius legend refers not to the original draining of the site, but to a sudden flood, such as that which so alarmed the Romans in the days of Horace (*Odes*, I. ii. 12–20). The Forum continues to be seriously flooded from time to time.

[2] On this pottery and its provenance see below, Appendix B, pp. 315–319. Considering the claims of Corinth to have produced ware of this style it is interesting to note that some quantity of it has been found in Rome, *e.g. Mon. Ant.* xv. figs. 88 *a, b*, and 89, pp. 109 f., pl. IX. 9, 10, 14, 15, 18, pl. X. 1, 4, 5, pl. XVII. 9. See also below, nn. 4, 5.

[3] Ure, *Black Glaze Pottery*, pls. X. 3, XI. 1, 2.

[4] *Notiz.* 1903, p. 380; 1911, p. 161.

[5] 1903, p. 388, fig. 17; 1911, p. 160, fig. 3 *d*.

but suggest on stylistic grounds a somewhat later date. None of them however would naturally be put later than towards the end of the sixth century, and very few so late as that[1]. Occasional burials of a later date would be evidence for a later conversion from cemetery to Forum only if intramural burials were unknown in Rome. As a matter of fact there is explicit evidence that they took place[2].

After what has been said about the Tarquins and sixth century Rome generally it is scarcely necessary to discuss in detail the historicity of Servius Tullius. For representative modern views on him see Mueller-Deecke[3] (Servius symbolizes the supremacy of Volsinii, the Tarquins that of Tarquinii); De Sanctis[4] (Servius is the Etruscan invader who drove out the Tarquins); Gardthausen[5] (Servius is the Roman counterpart of the Greek tyrant, the Tarquins the legitimate kings, leaders of the rich and noble). This whole chapter is a refutation of Gardthausen's view about the Tarquins: the other suggestions are compatible with my own. Etruria may well have exercised as strong an influence on a sixth century tyranny at Rome as did Persia on those of sixth century Ionia.

Views on the historicity of Servius Tullius.

Fig. 36. Proto-Corinthian vase found in the Roman Forum.

Pais[6] fancifully explains Servius as the priest god, the *seruus rex*, of Aricia, who was imported to Rome in 338 B.C., well known to English readers as

> The priest who slew the slayer
> And shall himself be slain.

Mastarna is differentiated from Servius[7] and said to have a historical prototype in Mezentius, the enemy of Aeneas. My criticisms of Pais in reference to the Tarquins are equally applicable here.

[1] See Appendix E.　　　[2] See Appendix F.
[3] *Etrusker*, I. p. 114.　　　[4] *Journal des Savants*, 1909, p. 213.
[5] *Mastarna*, p. 43.　　　[6] *Legends*, pp. 142 f.
[7] *Ibid.* p. 134.

In the early period of the Roman republic the chief Greek influence to judge from the narratives was that of Athens and the Alcmaeonidae¹. Once more we

Rome and Athens.

Fig. 37. Ionic terra cotta antefix found in Rome.

find the written documents and the archaeological evidence in agreement. During the second half of the sixth century

---

¹ Above, p. 231. Ceres, Liber, and Libera, whose worship is said to have been introduced into Rome in the seventh year of the republic, are plainly the Attic-Eleusinian triad.

Attic imports had been gaining a great preponderance in Central Italy[1].

Thus from the time when the Greek Demaratus is said to have settled in Tarquinii to that at which the last Roman Tarquin is said to have sought shelter in the Greek Cumae the series of Greek connexions implied in our narrative is found reflected in the results of excavations. We have based our conclusions on a mass of material

Fig. 38. Similar antefix found in Samos.

from various sites scattered all over Central Italy. The evidence from Rome itself could not have been made the basis of the discussion. It is not sufficiently abundant. Its scantiness however need cause no misgivings. It is sufficiently accounted for by the unbroken ages of crowded occupation that differentiate Rome from the surrounding cities. The finds from Rome, as far as they go, confirm the other evidence by showing that first Corinth, then Ionia and finally Athens did actually influence Rome during the period of the last royal dynasty. Corinthian vases have been found in the city from time to time[2], though not, it should be noticed, in the Forum cemetery[3]. The

The finds from Rome itself confirm the narratives by showing first Corinthian influence, then Ionian, and then Attic.

[1] Martha, *L'Art Étrusque*, p. 125, mentions several thousand Attic vases from the single city of Vulci.

[2] *E.g. Mon. Ant.* xv. p. 242 a, b, c, pl. IX. 16, pl. X. 3, pl. XVII. 11.

[3] Except perhaps *Notiz.* 1903, p. 137, fig. 17; cp. Sieveking and Hackl, *Cat. vases Munich*, 613, pl. 30, classified as Italian Corinthian.

influence of Ionia in the sixth century is seen in such objects as a series of cups[1] closely resembling the "later Ionic vases" of the Munich catalogue[2], or again in a bearded antefix (fig. 37) found near the church of S. Antonia and compared by Pinza[3] with examples published by Boehlau in his *Aus ionischen Nekropolen*[4]

Fig. 39. Terra cotta head found on the Roman Capitol.

(fig. 38), or yet again in the archaic terra cotta head (fig. 39) found in 1876 near the church of the Aracoeli on the Capitol[5], which much resembles the stone head (fig. 40) from the Athenian Acropolis described by Dickens as "an undoubtedly early example

[1] *Notiz.* 1903, pp. 407, 412, 424, 425, figs. 36, 42, 55, 57.
[2] Sieveking and Hackl, pl. 18. 481. [3] *Mon. Ant.* xv. fig. 157 and p. 508.
[4] Pl. XIII. 6. [5] *Mon. Ant.* xv. fig. 153 *b*.

of imported Chiot art¹." An amphora in the Attic black figure style (fig. 41) has been found on the Quirinal². "The most exquisite early Attic" is reported by Boni from the Palatine³. Attic Ionic influence has been seen in the Capitoline she-wolf (fig. 42), which is held by Petersen to commemorate the expulsion of the kings,

Fig. 40. Stone head found on the Acropolis at Athens.

and may be compared with the statue of a lioness put up at Athens to commemorate Leaina, the mistress of the tyrannicide Aristogeiton⁴.

---

¹ Dickens, *Cat. Acrop. Mus.* p. 193 on Athens Nat. Mus. no. 654.
² *Mon. Ant.* xv. p. 263, fig. 105.
³ *J.R.S.* III. p. 249. Such vague language is unworthy of its distinguished author, particularly in a paper in which he repeatedly pleads for scientific precision.
⁴ Petersen, *Klio*, 1908, pp. 440 f.; 1909, pp. 29 f.; cp. Michaelis, *Cent. Arch. Discov.* p. 250. Experts have differed to the extent of eighteen centuries in the dating of this fine animal. Early scholars attributed it to a dedication of 296 B.C. recorded by Livy x. 23, when the consuls "simulacria infantium conditorum urbis sub uberibus lupae posuerunt." But 296 B.C. is no time for so archaic a work. This led certain German scholars, including Bode, to regard it as a work of the twelfth or thirteenth century A.D., and the cast of it at Berlin was expelled from the Classical collections. Already, however, in 1867 Bachofen in the

Fig. 41. Vase in Attic black figure style found on the Quirinal.

Fig. 42. The Capitoline wolf.

This completes the evidence for the credibility of our narrative[1].

Conclusions on the question of credibility.
It is not conclusive. The archaeological material on which we have had so largely to rely, though it reflects the various Greek influences that are said to have affected their history, does not for instance establish Demaratus as a historical character. But it does fully establish him as a historical possibility. It disposes us to give much more weight than was customary a generation ago to statements and allusions that tend to confirm the historical basis of our narratives. We no longer pass over the possibility that Demaratus may have been a living prototype of Philip the son of Butacides[2], and not a mere study in fiction based on the career of the adventurous Crotonian. In the light of the extremely rich collection of Greek pottery from Caere[3], the childish story told by Strabo[4] of how Caere got its name from the Greek χαῖρε no longer discounts his other statement in the same passage that in early times the city had a treasury at Delphi, a statement that is confirmed by Herodotus[5], who tells us that the people of Caere consulted the Delphic oracle about the year 540 B.C. In short there is every possibility that Tarquin at Rome may have had consciously before his eyes the career of Cypselus at Corinth. The accounts here offered both of the Tarquins and of the Corinthian tyrants are admittedly conjectural: but when two such conjectures based on independent evidence are found to harmonize so well both with one another and with a broad general explanation of the narratives they deal with, it may be fairly claimed that they render one another mutual support.

Annali dell' Inst. pp. 184–8 had incidentally suggested (as possible though not likely) a date at the end of the sixth century B.C. A reasoned argument for this dating was first put forward by Rayet, *Mon. de l'Art Ant.* I. vii. Rayet shows that the wolf was in existence in the ninth century A.D., that the animals of the twelfth and thirteenth centuries A.D. are stylistically different, and that the Capitoline wolf has close affinities with other representations of animals that are unquestionably archaic Greek. The children are of course much later.

[1] It has not been thought necessary to combat the ultra-sceptical views of Mommsen (*Roem. Forsch.* II. pp. 156 f., 199 f.) and Pais (*Ancient Italy*, pp. 276 f.; *Ancient Legends*, chap. XI.), as to the historical existence of Cassius and Maelius.

[2] Above, p. 239.

[3] Martha, *L'Art Étrusque*, p. 123; *Roem. Mitt.* XXII. pp. 131, 133–4, 150–1, 162; Pottier, *Album*, I. E 629–40.

[4] Strabo v. 220.

[5] Hdt. I. 167.

But let us for the moment adopt the attitude of the sceptics, and assume the whole story of the Tarquins to be false. In that case the numerous Greek elements can be explained only as plagiarisms from the corresponding figures in Greek history, the seventh and sixth century tyrants. But the Greek element includes the story of Demaratus and his Corinthian workmen and his wealth, and the part that these played in the events that led up to his son Tarquinius Priscus becoming king of Rome. In other words, for the hypothetical authors of this hypothetical fiction the typical early Greek tyrant was a great capitalist and a great employer[1].

If Tarquin is a Greek fiction, it preserves an early Greek conception of the typical early tyrant as a great capitalist.

[1] In Chapter I of this book I have tried to show that this conception of the tyrant disappears from Greek literature with the advent of Dionysius of Syracuse. If, therefore, the Tarquin story is only pseudo-history, it must have been concocted in the fifth century.

Chapter IX. *Sicyon, Megara, Miletus, Ephesus, Leontini, Agrigentum, Cumae*

"Ne perdons rien du passé. Ce n'est qu'avec le passé qu'on fait l'avenir."
ANATOLE FRANCE.

Sicyon.

THE tyranny at Sicyon lasted longer than in any other Greek state[1]. It started about the same time as that of Cypselus at Corinth and continued in the same family for about a century. The tyrants rested their power on the support of the pre-Dorian population of their city, and the establishment of the tyranny was probably to a large extent a racial movement representing a rising of the pre-Dorian stratum of the population against their Dorian conquerors.

How the tyrant family secured its power is another question. Until the other day our only information on the subject was to the effect that the founder of the dynasty was a cook or butcher ($\mu\acute{a}\gamma\epsilon\iota\rho\text{o}\varsigma$)[2], who was helped to power by the Delphic oracle[3]. Thanks however to a papyrus recently unearthed by the Oxford scholars Grenfell and Hunt and published by them in 1915 we have now considerable fragments of a detailed account of the founder of the dynasty[4].

The fragment confirms the statement that the tyrants of Sicyon were sprung from a butcher and settles the vexed question of the relationship of Andreas and Orthagoras (the two earliest known members of the family) by showing that Orthagoras was the first tyrant and Andreas was father of Orthagoras. It also shows that Orthagoras himself was bred as a butcher. But it is devoted mainly to the military exploits of the youthful Orthagoras, and though it does not take us down to the day when he made himself tyrant it

---

[1] Aristot. *Pol.* VII. (V.), 1315 b; Strabo (where, however, the reference includes the third century Aratus) VIII. 382.
[2] Diod. VIII. 24; Liban. *Orat. c. Severum*, III. p. 251 Reiske; Hellad. *ap.* Phot. 530 a Bekker. Cp. Foerster, *Phil.* XXXV. p. 710.
[3] Plut. *Ser. Num. Vind.* 7 (*Moral.* 553).
[4] *Oxyrhync. Pap.* XI. no. 1365.

plainly brings us very near it, and as it leaves him in the position of polemarch on active service it seems to illustrate and support the statement of Aristotle that the early tyrants often owed their power to some high magistracy or military position that they had previously secured in the state. But there are several reasons why this military aspect should not be overrated. The account of how Orthagoras actually seized the tyranny is after all wanting. The extant fragment says that he secured the position of polemarch "partly also by reason of the goodwill of the mass of the citizens towards him," and gives this as a separate reason[1] from that of his military successes. More over the author of the fragment was possibly Aristotle himself, who is known to have written a lost *Constitution of the Sicyonians*; and although Grenfell and Hunt regard Ephorus as more probably the author, Ephorus lived at the same time and wrote under the same historical influences as Aristotle and was probably misled in the same way concerning the character of the early tyranny[2]. The outstanding fact in the early career of Orthagoras is still his tradesman origin.

Little is known of the later career of Orthagoras except that he governed mildly, and of his successor Myron (Olympian victor in 648 B.C.[3]) nothing is recorded that throws any direct light on the origin of the tyranny: but the case is different when we come to Cleisthenes, the last and most famous of this family of tyrants, whose reign covered roughly the first third of the sixth century[4]. With Cleisthenes the Sicyonian tyranny entered on a new phase.

Aristotle quotes Sicyon as an instance of a city where the government changed "from tyranny to tyranny....from that of Myron to that of Cleisthenes[5]." The story of how Cleisthenes got his two brothers out of the way is told by Nicolaus Damascenus[6]. But what Nicolaus gives is purely a tale of domestic crime, a change from tyrant to tyrant not from tyranny to tyranny. Perhaps the change referred to by Aristotle is to be connected with the fact that Cleisthenes followed an aggressive foreign policy[7]. He was violently

---

[1] *Pace* De Gubernatis, *Atti R. Accad. Torino*, 1916, p. 293.

[2] See above, pp. 26 f. De Gubernatis, *ibid.* pp. 294–7, suggests as author Menaechmus of Sicyon, who probably flourished about the time of the Diadochoi, see Abel, *Schol. Pind. Nem.* ix. p. 254.   [3] Paus. vi. 19 2.

[4] He took part with Solon in the Sacred War (about 590 B.C.) and was the grandfather of the Athenian Cleisthenes who reformed the Athenian constitution in 508 B.C.

[5] Aristot. *Pol.* vii. (v.), 1316a.   [6] Nic. Dam. *F.H.G.* iii. p. 394.

[7] Aristot. *Pol.* 1315b (διὰ τὸ πολεμικὸς γενέσθαι Κλεισθένης).

hostile to Argos[1], and took a leading part in the "sacred" war that was fought about Delphi at the beginning of the sixth century B.C.[2] He was a contemporary of Periander who appears to have changed the character of the tyranny at Corinth by making the government warlike. It is not unlikely that the change effected by Cleisthenes at Sicyon was in the same direction. In turning to war it does not follow that he forsook trade. He may have held the view that trade follows the flag. The "sacred" war had its secular side. It arose about the refusal of the people of Krisa, who possessed the port of Delphi, to remove their harbour dues.

Krisa was a place of importance in early times[3], so much so that what was later known as the Gulf of Corinth was called the Gulf of Krisa. The territory of the Krisaians lay just opposite Sicyon, and it seems not improbable that the Sicyonians, with their allies the Corinthians[4], aimed at wresting from their rivals across the water their position in the gulf which was the starting-point of trade with the far West[5]. According to a Pindar scholiast the Krisaians had control of the sea at the beginning of the war and

---

[1] Hdt. v. 67 (Κλεισθένης γὰρ Ἀργείοισι πολεμήσας...). Athen. XIII. 560c implies that Argos and Sicyon were on the same side in the Krisaian war, but no conclusions can be based on this romantic passage which ascribes the war (like the Trojan war) to the rape of some Argive women. An Argive (Leokedes, son of the tyrant Pheidon) appears among the suitors of Agariste, Cleisthenes' daughter. He has been suspected by the moderns as being chronologically impossible, as being the only Dorian, and as raising the number from twelve to thirteen (Macan ad Hdt. VI. 127); but his *a priori* improbability is not decisive against his historical reality. Cleisthenes may have changed his policy towards the end of his career, though against this must be set the evidence for rivalry between Sicyon and Argos over the foundation (?) of the Nemean games right at the end of Cleisthenes' reign, Bury, *Nemean Odes*, pp. 250–1.

[2] Paus. II. 9. 6; X. 37. 6 ("so the Amphictyons resolved to make war on the Kirrhaians, and they appointed Cleisthenes, tyrant of Sicyon, to the command"); Polyaen. III. 5 (cp. VI. 13); Frontin. *Strat.* III. 7. 6; Schol. Pind. pref. to *Nem.* IX. (quoted below).

[3] Cp. Hom. *Il.* II. 520; *Hymn. Apoll.* 438; Paus. VII. 19. 7.

[4] Hdt. VI. 129; cp. Nic. Dam. *F.H.G.* III. p. 395.

[5] Strabo IX. 418 εὐτυχήσαντες γὰρ οἱ Κρισαῖοι διὰ τὰ ἐκ τῆς Σικελίας καὶ τῆς Ἰταλίας τέλη πικρῶς ἐτελώνουν τοὺς ἐπὶ τὸ ἱερὸν ἀφικνουμένους. ibid. supra, πόλις ἀρχαία Κίρρα ἐπὶ τῇ θαλάττῃ ἱδρυμένη...ἵδρυται δ' ἀπαντικρὺ Σικυῶνος, πρόκειται δὲ τῆς Κίρρας τὸ Κρισαῖον πεδίον εὔδαιμον. πάλιν γὰρ ἐφεξῆς ἐστιν ἄλλη πόλις Κρῖσα, ἀφ' ἧς ὁ κόλπος Κρισαῖος, cp. Mariéjol, *de Orthagoridis*, pp. 29 f.; Beloch, *Gr. G.*² I. i. p. 337, n. 3. Whether Kirrha is either geographically or etymologically distinct from Krisa is immaterial for our enquiry.

owed their ultimate defeat to the fact that Cleisthenes built a fleet and destroyed their naval supremacy[1]. It looks very much as though Cleisthenes was trying to win for Sicyon the sea-borne trade that had been flowing into Krisa. With the aid of a fleet that must for the time have made Sicyon a really important naval power[2] he crushes the trade rival across the water and wins its place for his own city and himself[3].

Bury assigns to Cleisthenes the leading part in the reorganizing of the Pythian games at Delphi after the Sacred War[4], and pictures the Sicyonian tyrant as doing for the Delphic Pythia much what Periander and Peisistratus are depicted as doing for the Corinthian Isthmia and the Athenian Panathenaia and Pheidon very possibly did for the great games at Olympia. Bury's general picture of the early tyrants as founders or reorganizers of these great Greek games is quite in harmony with the chronological evidence and with all that is known about the various tyrants' activities and characters[5]. Developing these games might well be part of a broad commercial policy, the more so as the games were under divine patronage and

---

[1] Schol. Pind. preface to *Nem.* IX. φησὶ δέ ἐν τῷ πολέμῳ τῶν Κρισαίων κατὰ θάλασσαν ῥᾳδίως τὰ ἐπιτήδεια ποριζομένων καὶ διὰ τοῦτο μακρᾶς γενομένης τῆς πολιορκίας Κλεισθένην τὸν Σικυώνιον ναυτικὸν ἰδίᾳ παρασκευάσαντα κωλῦσαι τὴν σιτοπομπίαν αὐτῶν, καὶ διὰ ταύτην τὴν εὐεργεσίαν τὸ τρίτον τῶν λαφύρων ἔδοσαν τῷ Κλεισθένει καὶ Σικυωνίαν (alii Σικυωνίοις), ἀφ' οὗ καὶ Σικυώνιοι τὰ Πύθια πρῶτον παρ' ἑαυτοῖς ἔθεσαν. The authority here used by the scholiast is uncertain. Possibly it is Menaechmus of Sicyon, on whom see above, p. 258, n. 2.

[2] Sicyon has not much of a harbour (Bursian, *Geog. Gr.* II. i. p. 30), but it managed to raise a respectable squadron of ships for the Persian and Peloponnesian wars (Hdt. VIII. 43; Thuc. II. 9), when its importance was far less than in the age of the tyrants.

[3] According to one reading of the scholium to Pindar, *Nem.* IX. it was to these proceedings that Cleisthenes owed his throne: καὶ διὰ ταύτην τὴν εὐεργασίαν τὸ τρίτον τῶν λαφύρων ἔδοσαν τῷ Κλεισθένει καὶ Σικυωνίαν. (See above, n. 1.) But the name of a country in the objective accusative without the article is unusual, and MS. evidence appears to support the reading Σικυωνίοις.

[4] Bury, *Nemean Odes*, Appendix D. The year 586 B.C. is generally given as the date of the first Pythian games; but our authorities state that the festival was older. What happened after the Sacred War was a change in the character of the festival, which from being purely musical became largely athletic (Strabo IX. 421; Paus. X. 7. 2–5).

[5] To the instances quoted by Bury add perhaps the interferences of Polycrates in the great Delian festival, above, pp. 70, 71.

ensured periodic opportunities for peaceful intercourse in an age of chronic warfare[1]. Under such circumstances gatherings of this kind naturally tend to become the "commercial affair (ἐμπορικὸν πρᾶγμα)" that the Delian festival admittedly grew to be[2]. Everything known about the early Greek tyrants shows how capable they were of turning such a tendency to good account. That Delphi in particular had from early times a commercial character has already been conjectured by Cornford[3]. In the early years of the Sicyonian tyranny the greatness of the Euboean cities Chalcis and Eretria had begun to be steadily on the decline. The time had come to change the course of the Eastern part of this great trade route and instead of Krisa, Delphi, Thebes, Euboea to substitute another line, in which Sicyon and probably Athens should be dominating points. This is probably what Cleisthenes had in view when he so strongly supported Solon in the Sacred War.

It follows that to make him the founder of the Delphic Pythia is a view that cannot be accepted without reservations. The available evidence represents Cleisthenes as rather the rival than the champion of Delphi. A Pindar scholiast already quoted states that he instituted Pythian games in his own Sicyon. There is no other evidence for Pythian games at Sicyon, but Herodotus gives a long account of the way in which Cleisthenes radically reformed the chief existing festival in the city. This festival, like the Delphic Pythia of the days before the Sacred War, was devoted largely to musical and poetical competitions. Its patron was the ancient hero Adrastus, whose connexions were all with Argos, the Dorian city whose influence in Sicyon Cleisthenes was bent on overthrowing. Cleisthenes ejected Adrastus from Sicyon by the curious process of burying beside him the body of his bitterest enemy, the Theban

---

[1] See especially Isocr. *Panegyr.* 43 (49).

[2] Strabo x. 486; cp. Livy 1. 30, "Tullus (*i.e.* Tullus Hostilius, king of Rome) ad Feroniae fanum mercatu frequenti negotiatores Romanos comprehensos querebatur"; S. Matt. xxi. 12, "and Jesus entered into the temple of God, and cast out all them that sold and bought in the temple, and overthrew the tables of the money-changers." From this point of view the Greek games may be compared, too, with some of the great fairs of mediaeval Europe; see, *e.g.*, Dagobert I, diplom. ann. 629; Pipin, diplom. ann. 753, de festo S. Dionysii, cited Barth, *Corinth. Comm.* p. 9, n. 1. Cp. also the fairs held in the neighbourhood of sanctuaries in pre-Mohammedan Arabia, Margoliouth, *Mohammed,* p. 6.

[3] Cornford, *Thucydides Mythistoricus*, p. 35.

Melanippus (which he borrowed for the purpose from Thebes), and then removing the body of Adrastus which was assumed to depart voluntarily from so unpleasant a neighbourhood.

The reformed festival was held in honour of this Theban hero and the Theban wine god Dionysus. The ejected Adrastus had been one of the leaders in the famous expedition of the Seven against Thebes[1]. There can be little doubt that when the festival was instituted Cleisthenes was aiming at an entente with the great inland city that formed the first main stage on the route from Delphi to Euboea and the North. But the attempt was a failure. Thebes was conspicuously unrepresented at the wooing of Cleisthenes' daughter Agariste[2], and the tyrant is furious when one of the suitors performs what has plausibly been suggested to have been a Theban dance[3]. Relations with Delphi may have run a similar course. In the first celebration of the reformed Delphian Pythia Cleisthenes competed; and the way that he approached the Delphic oracle before reorganizing his own Sicyonian festival shows that he wanted an understanding with the authorities there, to whom his family was perhaps largely indebted for its throne[4]. But the oracle would have nothing to do with Cleisthenes' proposals and used abusive language to the tyrant for making them. Relations between the god and the tyrant can hardly have remained cordial after this incident and the Thebans presumably sided with the god.

Whatever the precise outcome of Cleisthenes' policy with Delphi and Thebes the likelihood remains that one main object of that policy had been to give a new direction to the city's trade. We have been assuming that the Sicyon of the tyrants was an important centre of commerce and industry. This has been denied by Eduard Meyer[5]. The evidence is meagre: but as far as it goes it is entirely against Meyer's hypothesis, which makes it hard to explain how

---

[1] Cp. Grote (ed. 1888), II. pp. 65–66, who acutely argues that Cleisthenes aimed mainly at suppressing not our Homer but the lost *Thebais* when he prohibited the recitation of Homer in Sicyon. The *Thebais* glorified the Dorian heroes who overthrew prehistoric Thebes.

[2] Macan ad Hdt. VI. 127.

[3] A. B. Cook, *C.R.* XXI. p. 169, but cp. *ibid.* p. 233.

[4] The oracle had prophesied, and therefore presumably favoured, the establishment of the tyranny by Orthagoras, *Oxyrhync. Pap.* XI. 1365; Diod. VIII. 24; Plut. *Ser. Num. Vind.* 7 (*Moral.* 553), (where the tyranny of Orthagoras is made to result from an outrage committed at the Pythian games).

[5] "Sikyon ist keine Handelstadt," *Ges. d. Alt.* II.¹ p. 628.

the city became so great and prosperous at this time. We have seen already that Cleisthenes possessed a powerful fleet and that his proceedings suggest far-reaching commercial designs. The evidence as to industry points in the same direction. Some distinguished archaeologists have actually assigned to the Sicyon of Andreas and Orthagoras one of the leading industries of the period, the making of the remarkably fine pottery now usually known as Proto-Corinthian. Their are arguments by no means decisive[1], and in any case there is nothing to associate the Sicyonian tyrants personally with Sicyonian potteries; but there are literary notices which point to the Orthagorids as having been, like the other early tyrants, builders and, presumably, employers of local labour. The Olympian "treasury" which Pausanias thought to have been put up by the tyrant Myron[2] has been shown by excavation to have been fifth century work[3]. But in this treasury Pausanias saw two "bronze chambers" (models of buildings?) one of which bore an inscription saying that it was a dedication of Myron and the people of Sicyon. This inscription may have misled Pausanias into ascribing to Myron the building that contained it[4]. The bronze chamber on which the dedication was inscribed was on a large scale. It weighed 500 Aeginetan talents or about 19 tons. From towards the end of the period of the tyranny Sicyon was famous for its school of sculptors, who worked largely in bronze, and though no statement has been preserved as to the workmanship of Myron's dedication, it may not unreasonably be used as evidence that the Sicyonians of his reign were already experts in the working of bronze[5]. As regards buildings,

[1] Below, pp. 316–7 and references, *ibid*. [2] Paus. vi. 19. 2.
[3] Frazer, Paus. *ad loc*. [4] Frazer, *ibid*.
[5] The Cretan sculptors Dipoenus and Scyllis came about 580 B.C. to Sicyon, "which was long the home of all such crafts. The Sicyonians contracted with them for statues of the gods, but before they were completed the artists complained that they were ill used and departed to Aetolia" (Pliny, *N.H.* xxxvi. 4). Gardner suggests that the artists left Sicyon on the death of Cleisthenes (*Gk. Sculp.*² p. 103). The wild and half civilized Aetolia seems an odd refuge for such highly skilled craftsmen. Beyond Aetolia from Sicyon lay the city of Ambracia, which Pliny declares to have been crammed with works of Dipoenus (*N.H.* xxxvi. 4). On the strength presumably of this statement, Gardner (*ibid.*) makes the artists retire to Ambracia from Sicyon. Ambracia was a Corinthian colony and appears to have continued under a tyrant of the house of Cypselus after the fall of the great tyrant houses in the isthmus states. The Sicyonians were ordered by Apollo to recall the artists and let them finish their work, and this was done though it cost the Sicyonians dear (*magnis mercedibus*

Cleisthenes with the spoils that he gained in the Sacred War is known to have erected at Sicyon a magnificent portico[1].

Pollux, the lexicographer of the second century A.D., says that the Sicyonians in the time of the tyrants (as also the Athenians under the Peisistratids) wore a particular kind of rough woollen dress "that they might be ashamed to go down into the city[2]." The statement may be true and the explanation false. If both are accepted, it by no means follows that the policy of the Sicyonian tyrants was dominantly agricultural[3]. We may possibly have here a record of a measure intended to prevent the commercialized city from attracting to itself the agricultural population that was of such vital importance to the normal self-sufficing Greek city-state. There is little doubt that the government of the Sicyonian tyrants was popular with the lower classes. Aristotle declares that it lasted so long because they treated their subjects so well[4]. If Herodotus and Ephorus give a less favourable account of them, the reason is probably that their sources were aristocratic and anti-tyrannical[5].

Megara.

The tyranny at Megara is associated with the single name of Theagenes[6], whose reign is dated by the support that he gave to his son-in-law Cylon, winner of

impetratum est, Pliny, *N.H.* XXXVI. 4). It may be noted that tyranny too was revived at Sicyon. A tyrant Aeschines was expelled by the Spartans, presumably towards the end of the sixth century, Plut. *de Hdt. Malig.* 21 (*Moral.* 859). The wanderings of Dipoenus and Scyllis thus point to a possible connexion between the tyrannical form of government and good conditions for skilled labour.

[1] Paus. II. 9. 6.
[2] Poll. VII. 68; Mariéjol, *de Ortbagoridis*, pp. 11–12, compares the Megareans who

πρόσθ' οὔτε δίκας ᾔδεσαν οὔτε νόμους,
ἀλλ' ἀμφὶ πλευρῆσι δορὰς αἰγῶν κατέτριβον,
ἔξω δ' ὥστ' ἔλαφοι τῆσδε νέμοντο πόλεος
καὶ νῦν εἰσ' ἀγαθοί. THEOGNIS 54–7.

[3] *Pace* Bury, *Hist. Greece*³, p. 155.
[4] Aristot. *Pol.* VII. (v.), 1315 b; cp. *Oxyrhync. Pap.* XI. 1365, ll. 58 f.
[5] Busolt, *Gr. G.*² I. p. 663. Cleisthenes, the last and best remembered of the dynasty, seems to have made himself particularly obnoxious to the upper classes. His marked antipathy to Homer, the poet of aristocracy and divine right, may have had a social as well as a racial basis, as may have been the case also with his treatment of the Argive-Sicyonian hero, king Adrastus, whose festival, which doubtless savoured of aristocratic ancestor worship, he replaced by the cult of the parvenu and plebeian wine-god Dionysus.
[6] Thuc. I. 126; Aristot. *Rhet.* I. 2; Aristot. *Pol.* VII. (v.), 1305 a; Paus. I. 28. 1, 40. 1, 41. 2; Plut. *Qu. Gr.* 18 (*Moral.* 295).

an Olympian victory in 640 B.C.[1] and would-be tyrant of Athens.

According to Aristotle in the *Rhetoric* Theagenes, like Peisistratus and Dionysius, scheming to make himself tyrant asked for the (usual) bodyguard, and having secured it became tyrant. But as pointed out in the first chapter this only shows that winning the tyranny meant possessing an armed force. It says nothing as to how the armed force was acquired. Armed forces are not to be had for the asking. For the way in which Theagenes got his our only evidence is another passage of Aristotle, this time from the *Politics*, which says that Theagenes secured his power "after slaughtering the flocks and herds of the wealthy[2]."

In the latter part of the fifth century "most of the Megareans got their living by making exomides" (the normal dress of the poorer classes)[3]. Meyer assumes this to have been a fourth (*sic*) century development, but altogether against the evidence[4]. Not only is the woollen industry known to have been one of the main occupations of Megara in the fifth century, but the prosperity of the city in the seventh century is only comprehensible if we assume that it was already engaged in the woollen trade. As observed by Busolt[5], Megaris has on the whole a barren stony soil that was mostly suited only for the pasture of its numerous flocks of sheep. The Megareans must have manufactured goods to take to their distant colonies, from which they imported corn and other raw material.

The colonial activities of Megara went back well into the seventh century. Some of her colonies such as Chalcedon and Byzantium and Heraclea Pontica[6] lay on the route of the Argonauts that led to the land of the golden fleece. Other seventh century colonies of Megara lay in the far West in Sicily, where she founded Megara Hyblaea in the latter part of the eighth century and Selinus in the second half of the seventh.

[1] Euseb. *Chron.* I. ch. 33. Theagenes is brought down by Beloch into the sixth century, but on the weakest possible evidence.

[2] Aristot. *Pol.* VII. (v.), 1305 a. Cauer's idea, *Part. u. Polit. in Megara u. Athen*, p. 16, that the rise of Theagenes coincided with a severe blow to the colonial power of Megara in the Black Sea has no evidence to support it.

[3] Xen. *Mem.* II. 7. 6; cp. Aristoph. *Ach.* 519, *Pax* 1002.

[4] *Kleinschr.* pp. 116–17; cp. 119, n. 1. Meyer quotes Isoc. *de Pace*, 117 (183), on the humble beginnings of Megara, but the passage suggests no particular dates.

[5] *Gr. G.*² I. p. 470.   [6] Xen. *Anab.* VI. 2. 1; Arrian, *Perip.* 18.

Thus Megara's colonial activities in the seventh century correspond closely with those of Miletus, the city that colonized most of the ports of the Black Sea and owed so much of her wealth to her trade in wool with the Italian Sybaris[1].

That Megara herself was engaged in the woollen industry at this early date is made not unlikely by several fragments of evidence. Demeter at Megara bore the title Malophoros. "Various statements," says Pausanias, "are made about this title, and in particular that Demeter was named Malophoros by those who first reared sheep in the land[2]." The word Malophoros may mean either "Sheep-bearing" or "Apple-bearing," but the account of the title in Pausanias shows that the Megareans understood it as meaning "Sheep-bearing," and regarded it as of high antiquity and certainly as older than the days when the flocks of the well-to-do were slaughtered by Theagenes.

According to Pliny[3] fulling was invented by a Megarean named Nikias. Buechsenschuetz[4] infers from this passage that fulling or milling was of great importance in the ancient wool industry. Bluemner[5] quotes it to prove the importance of the industry at Megara. The most important inference to be drawn from it both of them seem to have overlooked, namely that the industry at Megara must have been of high antiquity.

The care bestowed by the Megareans on sheep-breeding is alluded to by the sixth century Theognis

$$\kappa\rho\iota o\grave{\upsilon}\varsigma\ \mu\grave{\epsilon}\nu\ \kappa\alpha\grave{\iota}\ \check{o}\nu o\upsilon\varsigma\ \delta\iota\zeta\acute{\eta}\mu\epsilon\theta\alpha,\ K\acute{\upsilon}\rho\nu\epsilon,\ \kappa\alpha\grave{\iota}\ \check{\iota}\pi\pi o\upsilon\varsigma\ \epsilon\grave{\upsilon}\gamma\epsilon\nu\acute{\epsilon}\alpha\varsigma^{6}.$$

Megarean woollen goods at the end of the fifth century were much worn by Athenian slaves who, as Cauer observes[7], came largely from the region of the early Megarean colonies.

It seems therefore not unlikely that when Theagenes slaughtered

---

[1] On the relationships between Megara and Miletus at this period practically nothing is known. They appear to have been friendly, Meyer, *G. d. A.* II. p. 676 (but cp. Cauer, *Part. u. Polit. in Megara u. Athen*, pp. 14 f.). Corinth on the other hand appears to have been friendly to Samos the rival of Miletus, and we hear of an early collision between Corinth and Megara (Meyer, *G. d. A.* II. p. 449). It is therefore not unlikely that the great wool trade of Miletus with the far West passed through Megara rather than through the rival isthmus state of Corinth.

[2] Paus. I. 44. 4.   [3] *N.H.* VII. 57.
[4] *Hauptstätten d. Gewerbfleisses*, p. 89.   [5] *Gewerbliche Tätigkeit*, p. 71.
[6] Theog. 183–4.   [7] *Part. u. Polit. in Megara u. Athen*, p. 24.

the flocks of the wealthy at Megara his blow was aimed at a class of capitalists whose wealth was already based on the woollen trade, as was that of the direct ancestors in Tudor times of our own modern capitalists[1].

This possibility has been recognized by Poehlmann[2] who quotes Xenophon on the Megarean wool industry in reference to Theagenes. Poehlmann imagines the blow as dealt by the discontented masses and inspired by simple hatred. But our one authority attributes it not to the rebellious masses but to Theagenes himself. On a point of definite fact like this Aristotle deserves to be taken precisely as he expresses himself. Can it be that Theagenes' coup was a simple but effective means of securing for himself the monopoly of the Megarean woollen industry?

If this was in fact the aim of Theagenes he was merely anticipating the methods of certain modern monopolists. In December 1888 the Whiskey Combination in the United States is said to have blown up a troublesome independent still in Chicago[3]. There are records of a similar attempt to blow up rival works at Buffalo[4]. For these cases I quote again from a work on the danger of a new tyranny of wealth that the writer, whose book appeared in 1894, thought at the time to be threatening the United States.

The most lasting memorial that Theagenes left behind him was the water conduit that he constructed for the city[5]. The extant remains seem to belong to a later date, but this is no reason for either post-dating the tyrant or not accepting him as its constructor. The remains now to be seen may well be due to a reconstruction, perhaps by the famous Megarean Eupalinus, who constructed the Samian waterworks for Polycrates. Underground conduits like the Megarean were being made half a century before the reign of Theagenes, as is shown by the underground canal constructed by Hezekiah to bring to Jerusalem the waters of Miriam (Gihon)[6]. Tyranny at Megara was short lived. The only tyrant ended his life in exile.

When they had banished Theagenes the Megareans for a short while behaved with moderation...but after that they began behaving outrageously to the rich: in particular the poor entered their houses and demanded to be

---

[1] H. Sieveking, *Viertelj. f. Soc. u. Wirt.* VII. p. 64.
[2] *Sozialismus*², I. p. 195, n. 2.
[3] Hy. D. Lloyd, *Wealth against Commonwealth*, chap. III.
[4] *Ibid.* chap. XVIII.   [5] Paus. I. 40. 1, 41. 2.
[6] Meyer, *Ges. d. Alt.* I.¹ p. 567. Hezekiah came to the throne 714 B.C.

entertained and feasted sumptuously, and treated them all with violence and insult if they did not get what they desired. Finally they passed a decree and recovered from the money-lenders the interest that they happened to have paid.

This passage of Plutarch[1] throws no direct light on either the character or the basis of Theagenes' power. The outbreak that it describes may have been due to the comparative weakness of the new government. It is equally possible that it occurred because the fall of the tyranny had made things much worse for the working classes, on whose support and favour Theagenes had probably based his power[2].

This period of Megarean history is better known than the corresponding phase of any other Greek city, thanks to the verses of Theognis. Their evidence for the character of the early tyrannies has been discussed in Chapter I. If, as there maintained, his exhortations not to be won over by gains to exalt any tyrant and his complaints about tradesmen controlling the state all point to fears of a tyranny of wealth, then it is particularly likely that his alarm may have had a historical basis in the career of Theagenes.

Miletus.

At Miletus during the seventh and sixth centuries[3] there appear to have been several periods of tyranny with intervals of anarchy in between. The most famous and powerful of the Milesian tyrants was Thrasybulus, whose reign must have begun towards the end of the seventh century. While he was tyrant the city enjoyed great material prosperity. Then in the middle of the sixth she was afflicted with two generations of civil war, after which there came a great revival of prosperity under the tyrant Histiaeus. Plutarch records the names of two other tyrants, Thoas and Damasenor, but only to introduce an account of the state of things that followed their overthrow. They may have been joint successors of Thrasybulus[4], much as the Athenians tended to regard Peisistratus as having been succeeded by Hippias and Hipparchus ruling conjointly. Or possibly Plutarch is mentioning two successive rulers of a distinct period of tyranny, the latter of whom only was

---

[1] Plut. *Qu. Gr.* 18 (*Moral.* 295).
[2] So Cauer, *Part. u. Polit. in Megara u. Athen*, p. 31.
[3] Hdt. I. 20–22, v. 28, vi. 46; Aristot. *Pol.* III. 1284a, vii. (v.), 1305a; Plut. *Qu. Gr.* 32 (*Moral.* 298); Suid. s.v. Γέργηθες, Περιβολή, Τύρβη; Athen. XII. 523f–524b; Myres, *J.H.S.* XXVI. 110–115 (on Milesian thalassocracy).
[4] Swoboda *ap.* Pauly Wissowa s.v. Damasenor. This possibility is stated as a fact by A. G. Dunham, *Hist. Miletus*, p. 127.

deposed, in which case they are probably to be put before Thrasybulus[1], somewhere about the middle of the seventh century.

The fall of Thoas and Damasenor was followed by a struggle between two parties called Ploutis(?) and Cheiromache, names which sound remarkably like Capital and Labour.

There is no certainty as to either the etymological or the historical meaning of these names. Plutarch seems to identify the Ploutis (?) faction with a body called Aeinautai (always on shipboard)[2] and the reading Plontis, connected with πλοῖον (ship), has been proposed by Plass[3]. Cheiromache again means not hand-workers but hand-fighters, a name that need not have any industrial implication. Hand-fighters might be just people who did not wear swords, the lower classes generally. But Cheiromache is said by Eustathius to have been a synonym for χειρῶναξ, a common word for artizan[4], and Suidas speaks of rival parties in Miletus composed of the wealthy (πλούσιοι) and the manual labourers (Γέργηθες, s.v., explained as χειρώνακτες), and though the period to which he is referring is quite uncertain, he still lends some support to the Capital and Labour interpretation of Plutarch's Ploutis (?) and Cheiromache[5]. The latter name would have been given to the party by its opponents, much as though enemies of a modern labour party should call them the Strikers or Down-Toolers. The other name for labour (Γέργιθες or Γέργηθες) is said by Heraclides Ponticus[6] to have been given to it by the faction of the wealthy, a statement quite compatible with the explanation of the name as derived from a place and denoting the poor subject Carians, the descendants of the pre-Hellenic population of the Milesian territory[7]. Perhaps we may see a hint that Gergethes and Cheiromache were alternative names both given to labour by its rich opponents in the reply given by the oracle to the party of the rich after they had been brutally massacring the party of the

---

[1] So Beloch *Gr. G.*² I. i. p. 359.

[2] For a quite different interpretation see Wecklein, *Sitzb. Bay. Akad. Muenchen: philos.-philol. Kl.* 1873, p. 45; Wachsmuth, *Stadt Athen*, I. 481.

[3] *Tyrannis*, p. 226.

[4] Eustath. ad *Odyss.* I. 399. He himself so uses it ad *Odyss.* XII. 103 and *Opusc. de emen. vita monach.* 126.

[5] Poehlmann, *Sozialismus*², I. 183, regards Cheiromache as consisting mainly of "the compact masses of journeymen, labourers and tradespeople, whom the great developments of industry, trade, and shipping were concentrating in ever growing numbers in the cities."

[6] *Apud* Athen. XII. 524 a.   [7] How and Wells, ad *Hdt.* v. 28.

poor. "I too" says the god "take heed of the murder of the unwarlike Gergithes[1]." The rebuke gains in point if the Gergithes had been also called Cheiromachoi, the manual *fighters*[2].

Of the early careers of the Milesian tyrants we know practically nothing. Aristotle indeed[3] refers to Miletus as a place where tyranny arose from the great power possessed by the magistrate called prytanis. But as argued already in discussing the office of polemarch held before his tyranny by Cypselus, a position of this kind does not by itself explain a tyrant's rise to supreme power. Moreover in the case of Miletus there is nothing to show which tyrant Aristotle is referring to. When on the throne Thrasybulus pursued the policy of "cutting off the heads of those ears of corn which he saw higher than the rest" or in other words of "putting to death those who were eminent among his subjects[4]." It is fairly certain that a ruler who pursued this policy did not rest his power on the support of the upper classes. One of the few anecdotes about the tyrant tells how he outwitted the king of Lydia by a misleading display of corn in the Milesian market-place[5].

The accession of Histiaeus seems to have synchronized with a revival of the commercial prosperity of Miletus. Histiaeus was the friend and vassal of Darius of Persia, and the basis of his power must therefore not be sought exclusively in the internal conditions of Miletus. But on the other hand the Persians seem to have been remarkably free from any tendency to Persianize the nations they subdued. Their sins were those rather of Abdul Hamid than of the Young Turks. Purely internal conditions continued to operate much as before[6].

In the absence therefore of all evidence as to how Histiaeus came by his power[7] it becomes interesting to see how he sought to

---

[1] Athen. XII. 524 b.

[2] Casaubon *ap.* Schweighaeuser, *Athen.*, *ad loc.* explains "unwarlike" as referring to the children who were tarred and burnt along with their elders; but there is no indication that the oracle is thinking particularly of the children, nor would unwarlike be a very appropriate adjective for them.

[3] *Pol.* VII. (v.), 1305 a. [4] Hdt. v. 92; so Aristot. *Pol.* III. 1284 a.
[5] Hdt. I. 21–22. [6] E. Meyer, *G. d. A.* III. 1, p. 57.

[7] Miletus must have profited enormously by the fall of Polycrates (about 523 B.C.) and the raising of the blockade that he had maintained against all the subjects or allies of the Great King.

Hdt. IV. 137 makes Histiaeus assert that it was thanks to Darius that the Ionian tyrants were on their thrones, and that if the power of Darius was expand it. The chance came to him when he had won Darius' confidence and gratitude in his Scythian campaign and the Great King invited him to choose his reward. "He asked for Myrcinus in Edonia, wishing to found in it a city[1]." Darius granted his request and the foundation was begun. But when the news of this gift reached Megabazus, the able Persian officer who had reduced Edonia and other parts of Thrace and Macedonia, he was much alarmed, and remonstrated with his master:

O King, what manner of thing hast thou done, granting to a clever and cunning Greek to acquire a city in Thrace? Where there is an inexhaustible supply of timber for building ships and oars, and mines of silver, and a large population of Greeks living in the neighbourhood and a large population of barbarians: if they get a patron (προστάτης) they will do what he directs day and night. Now therefore do thou stop him from doing this, that thou be not involved in a war against thine own[2].

As pointed out by Grundy[3] Myrcinus occupied a most important site on great strategic and commercial highways. But there is no reason to suspect Herodotus when he tells us that the town owed its importance first and foremost not to its geographical situation but to its minerals and forests. It is as a great mine-owner and shipbuilder and the employer of hosts of miners and shipbuilders and seamen that Histiaeus threatens to make himself a ruler sufficiently powerful to be a danger to the Great King himself[4].

Ephesus.

The earliest tyrant of Ephesus appears to have been Pythagoras, who overthrew the government of the Basilidae. Baton of Sinope[5], who wrote a history of the tyrants of Ephesus[6], states that Pythagoras lived "before Cyrus the Persian."

destroyed neither would he (Histiaeus) be able to rule the Milesians nor any other tyrant any other people. But the Greek does not say that Darius had put the tyrants on their thrones, and the words of Histiaeus are described as an opinion, not as an assertion of fact. Herodotus therefore neither states nor suggests that the Ionian tyrannies were due to the active interference of Darius. After the Ionian revolt the Persian satrap "established democracies in the Greek cities," or in other words openly proclaimed that they might govern themselves.

[1] Hdt. v. 11.   [2] Hdt. v. 23. Cp. above, p. 62.
[3] Grundy, *Great Persian War*, p. 66.
[4] For this view cp. my remarks in Chapter II on the part played by the Thracian mines in "rooting" and maintaining the tyranny of Peisistratus. Cp. also the later attempt of Histiaeus to secure the Thracian island of Thasos with its great fleet and extremely productive mines, Hdt. vi. 46.
[5] *Ap.* Suid. s.v. Pythagoras.   [6] Athen. vii. 289 c.

This seems to be rather an understatement of the tyrant's antiquity, since we hear of two other tyrants, Melas and Pindaros, of whom the latter was son and successor of the former and was deprived of his throne by Croesus[1], and of yet another pair, by name Athenagoras and Komas, who lived at the same time as the poet Hipponax and must therefore be assigned to about the middle of the sixth century[2], while during part of the reign of Croesus, after the fall of Pindaros, Ephesus appears to have enjoyed a moderate democracy, guided by the aesymnetes Aristarchus[3]. All this leaves little room for Pythagoras in the period just preceding Cyrus, and since too the Basilidae were almost certainly one of the hereditary aristocracies, like the Bacchiadae of Corinth, that overthrew the hereditary monarchy in most Greek cities before the end of the dark ages, it becomes probable that Pythagoras flourished at the beginning of the sixth century or possibly even in the seventh[4].

According to our only authority, Suidas, who quotes Baton on the date of Pythagoras and very possibly used him for the rest of his notice, Pythagoras displayed an insatiable passion for money (ἔρως χρημάτων ἄμετρος) and showed himself a cruel tyrant (τύραννος πικρότατος) but "with the people and the multitude he both was and appeared to be well liked, sometimes making them hopeful by his promises, sometimes secretly distributing small gratuities[5]." "Those however who enjoyed reputation or power he plundered and subjected to confiscations[6]." Suidas deals only with the tyrant on the throne and draws plainly from a most unfriendly source[7]: but as far as he goes he suggests that the power of Pythagoras was based on wealth.

[1] Ael. *V.H.* III. 26; Polyaen. VI. 50; cp. Hdt. I. 26.
[2] Suid. s.v. Hipponax.
[3] Pauly Wissowa s.v. Ephesus, pp. 2788–9, quoting Suid. s.v. Aristarchos. The rope with which the Ephesians bound their city to the temple during the siege by Croesus and the liberal contribution by Croesus to the rebuilding of the temple are no evidence, *pace* E. Curtius, *Ephesus*, pp. 14–15, that the government of the city at this period passed for a time into the hands of the priesthood.
[4] So Buerchner *ap.* Pauly Wissowa s.v. Ephesus, p. 2788. Plass, however, *Tyrannis*, pp. 229–30, regards Melas and Pindaros as Basilids and Pythagoras as later than them.
[5] τῷ δήμῳ καὶ τῇ πλήθυι ἦν τε καὶ ἐδόκει κεχαρισμένος, ἅμα τὰ μὲν αὐτοὺς ἐπελπίζων ὑποσχέσεσιν, τὰ δὲ ὑποσπείρων αὐτοῖς ὀλίγα κέρδη.
[6] τούς γε μὴν ἐν ἀξιώσει τε καὶ δυνάμει περισυλῶν καὶ δημεύων.
[7] Cp. *e.g.* ἀπέχρησε μὲν οὖν καὶ ταῦτα (his behaviour to his subjects) ἂν κάκιστα ἀνθρώπων ἀπολέσαι αὐτόν· ἤδη δὲ καὶ τοῦ θείου κατεφρόνει, κ.τ.λ.

The tyrant Pindarus, who was overthrown by Croesus, was a grandson of Alyattes, Croesus' father and predecessor[1]. Ephesus was one of the chief termini of the great caravan route from the Far East that ran to Sardis and then branched to several places on the coast. In the chapter on Lydia we have had occasion to notice the story of the eighth century Lydian Ardys, who when banished from his native land went into business at Cyme (another of these branch termini) and from there returned as ruler to Sardis. Radet may therefore be right in thinking that the Ephesian tyrants shared with the Lydian the monopoly of the trade that traversed this great road[2]. The overthrow of Pindarus is perhaps to be associated with the story of the financial dealings of Croesus while his father Alyattes was still on the throne[3]. To pave the way to his own succession as against his half brother, the half Greek Pantaleon, Croesus has to borrow large sums of money. He first tries in Sardis, and failing there proceeds to Ephesus, where he succeeds in raising money, not however from the house of Melas, but from a certain Pamphaes the son of Theocharides. It is hardly rash to assume that the tyrant family at Ephesus were putting their money on the half Greek candidate, and that Pindarus fell because his family had taken the wrong side in this great battle of high finance.

Leontini.

Panaitios of Leontini was the first in Sicily to seize the tyranny (Panaitios primus in Sicilia arripuit tyrannidem), which he is stated to have done a few years before the end of the seventh century[4]. The stratagem by which he made himself tyrant is described by Polyaenus[5]. The people of Leontini were at war with Megara, and Panaitios was polemarch. The actual coup was a matter of disarming the rich citizens who served on horseback (τοῖς εὐπόροις καὶ ἱππεῦσι), which he did with the help of their grooms. But before carrying out this *coup d'état* Panaitios had started a conflict between these rich knights and the

[1] Ael. *V.H.* III. 26.

[2] Radet, *Lydie*, p. 172. There is, however, *pace* Radet (pp. 82, 134), no evidence that the Melas, son-in-law of Gyges, described by Nic. Dam. *F.H.G.* III. p. 396 as prince of Daskylion was an ancestor of Melas the father of Pindarus (so also Gelzer, *Rhein. Mus.* XXXV. pp. 520–1) and a predecessor of this later Melas as tyrant of Ephesus. Radet assumes the Daskylion of Nic. Dam. to be a mistake for Ephesus.

[3] Nic. Dam. *F.H.G.* III. p. 397; see above, p. 137.

[4] Euseb. and Hieron. *Chron.*

[5] Polyaen. v. 47.

poor who served on foot (τοὺς πένητας καὶ πεζούς). Aristotle[1] adds little. He classes Panaitios with "Cypselus in Corinth, Peisistratus in Athens, and Dionysius in Syracuse, and others who in the same way (became tyrants) from demagogy," a view that has already been dealt with[2]. His other statement, that the government of Panaitios succeeded an oligarchy, is credible but unilluminating[3].

Agrigentum. Phalaris of Agrigentum, a tax collector, when the citizens wished to erect a temple of Zeus Polieus for two hundred talents on the citadel as being rocky and strong and for the further reason that it would be pious to give the god the highest place, undertook, if he was given charge of the work, to have the best craftsmen and provide the material cheaply and offer sound securities for the money. The people trusted him, thinking that thanks to his life as a tax-collector he had experience of such proceedings. So taking the public money he hired many foreigners and bought many prisoners and carried up to the citadel much material of stone, timber, iron. And when the foundations were already being dug, he sent down his herald to proclaim "whoever gives information against those who stole the stone and iron on the citadel shall receive such and such a reward." The people were annoyed at the report of the material being stolen. "Well then," said he, "allow me to enclose the acropolis." The city allowed him to enclose it and to raise a wall round it. He released the prisoners, armed them with the stones and hatchets and axes, made an attack during the Thesmophoria, killed most of the men, and having established himself as master of women and children, became the tyrant of the city of Agrigentum[4].

For over two centuries the name of Phalaris has been chiefly associated with the famous controversy between the Cambridge Bentley and the Oxford Boyle as to the authenticity of the letters ascribed to him. The spuriousness of these letters was so convincingly established by the Cambridge scholar, that everyone since then seems to have shrunk from attributing historical value to anything whatsoever that Phalaris is reported to have done. It so happens that the best known tradition about Phalaris tells of his extreme

---

[1] *Pol.* VII. (v.), 1310*b* 29, 1316*a* 37 (based perhaps on Antiochus of Syracuse, Endt, *Wien. Stud.* XXIV. p. 53).

[2] Above, Chap. I, pp. 26 f.

[3] Freeman, *History of Sicily*, II. 56, used it to rebut the view that the struggle that ended with the tyranny of Panaitios was "only a strife between the rich and the poor" and to infer that it was probably racial. The significant "only" sufficiently explains the inference.

[4] Polyaen. v. 1. 1.

cruelty[1], and more particularly how he did his victims to death by roasting them alive in a brazen bull[2]. This bull story has no doubt helped further to discredit Phalaris as a strictly historical character.

Yet there can be no dispute that Phalaris did make himself tyrant of Agrigentum and that his cruelty made a lasting impression on the people whom he ruled. His existence and importance is shown by a whole series of references to him that begins with Pindar[3] and includes allusions in Aristotle[4]. Considering that the tyrant probably died only one generation before Pindar was born[5], there is no reason why a trustworthy tradition about him should not have been preserved and more particularly why the account of his early days in Polyaenus should not have a historical basis.

If it has, its significance is important. It means that Phalaris owed his tyranny in the ultimate instance to his skill in finance and more immediately to the control of large sums of money that gave him great influence over the lower classes who earned their living by manual labour[6].

Polyaenus cannot be decisively confirmed. But still less can he be decisively discredited. The story itself suggests that its source

---

[1] Cic. *ad Att.* VII. 12. 2, 20. 2; *de Div.* I. 23; Val. Max. III. iii. extern. 2; Plut. *Ser. Num. Vind.* 7 (*Moral.* 553); Lucian, *Ver. Hist.* II. 23; *bis Acc.* 8; *Phalaris*, A and B *passim* (*ibid.* A 6, Phalaris declares that he punished conspirators savagely, cp. Plut. *Amat.* 16 (*Moral.* 760), simply because they thwarted his intention of governing mildly; *ibid.* A 8, 9, men naturally kindly like himself are more pained by inflicting punishments than by receiving them); Athen. XIII. 602 *a–b*; Ael. *V.H.* II. 4. The last two give an anecdote where Phalaris shows that he can be merciful as well as cruel.

[2] Pind. *Pyth.* I. 95 f., cp. Schol. *ad loc.*; Timaeus *F.H.G.* I. pp. 221–2 (Polyb. XII. 25; Diod. XIII. 90; Schol. Pind. *Pyth.* I. Timaeus appears to have denied the historical existence of the bull); Diod. XIX. 108; Cic. *Verr.* IV. 33; Ovid, *A.A.* I. 653; *Trist.* III. xi. 41 f.; *Ib.* 441; Pliny, *N.H.* XXXIV. 19; Plut. *Parall.* 39 (*Moral.* 315); Lucian, *Phalaris*, A I, 11; B 11.

[3] Pind. *Pyth.* I. 95 f.

[4] Aristot. *Pol.* VII. (v.), 1310 *b*; and (?) *Rhet.* II. 20 (possibly referring to another Phalaris). The fable of the horse and stag is attributed to Stesichorus when Phalaris was στρατηγὸς αὐτοκράτωρ of Himera and asking for the bodyguard with which he intended to make himself tyrant.

[5] Euseb. Ol. 52. 3–56. 3; Suid. s.v.; cp. Schol. Pind. *Ol.* III. 68 (38). For an earlier date see Euseb. Ol. 32. 3–39. 2 and Pliny, *N.H.* VII. 57 (tyrannus primus fuit Phalaris Agrigenti), but these two passages make the tyrant flourish before the foundation of the city that he ruled.

[6] Holm, *Gesch. Sic.* I. 149 (cp. *Hist. of Greece*, I. p. 363), who, however, fails to see the full application of his own words.

was the temple of Zeus Polieus, and a temple founded in the sixth century may well have kept some record, oral or written, of the days of its foundation. There is of course the possibility of forgery, but forgeries generally have some motive, such as gain or glory or love of the sensational. No such motive can easily be imputed to this narrative of Polyaenus, whose picture of Phalaris is borne out by notices in various other writers.

Lucian for instance makes the tyrant a great builder and great financier and a great patron of the common people[1]. Lucian's Phalaris is represented as defending himself at Delphi against the charge of cruelty: he certainly utters many paradoxes in so doing; but the point of the picture is that it is based on the received tradition, and it may fairly be used as evidence on a question such as that which is being here considered.

Aristotle classes Phalaris among the tyrants who owed their position to some high office that they had previously held[2], a statement which is good evidence for Phalaris as a historical personage and as far as it goes accords with Polyaenus.

"When the Agrigentines were rid of Phalaris they decreed that nobody should wear a blue-grey cloak: for the servants of the tyrant wore aprons (περιζώματα) of blue-grey[3]." The prohibition of these blue-grey aprons makes it look as if the men who overthrew the tyranny of Phalaris thought it necessary to disband his army of uniformed employees.

Further the part of the narrative of Polyaenus that most concerns us here can claim a certain probability from what is known of an early namesake and fellow-townsman of the Syracusan tyrant Agathocles. According to Diodorus[4] this earlier Agathocles, who lived while Syracuse was still under a landed aristocracy called γεωμόροι, probably about 700 B.C.,[5]

Being chosen to have charge of the building of the temple of Athena, picked out the finest of the stones that were being quarried and met the expense out of his own pocket (τὴν μὲν δαπάνην ἐκ τῆς ἰδίας οὐσίας ἐποιεῖτο), but misused the stones and built a costly house. At this they say

---

[1] Lucian, *Phalaris*, A 3.

[2] Aristot. *Pol.* VII. (V.), 1310*b*, τύραννοι κατέστησαν...οἱ περὶ τὴν Ἰωνίαν καὶ Φάλαρις ἐκ τῶν τιμῶν.

[3] Plut. *Praec. Ger. Rep.* 28 (*Moral.* 821); on the overthrow of Phalaris see also Plut. *cum Princ. Philosoph.* 3 (*Moral.* 778).

[4] Diod. VIII. 11.

[5] Pauly Wissowa s.v. Agathokles, 14*b* (in Supplement Heft 1).

the divine power gave forth a sign: Agathocles was struck by lightning and consumed by fire along with all his house. The Geomoroi confiscated his property to the state, although the kleronomoi (the financial officials) showed that he had taken nothing of the monies of the temple or of the state. They devoted his house to the gods and forbade those who came there to set foot in it, and to this day it is called the embrontaion (*i.e.* the place struck by lightning).

The positions of Phalaris and Agathocles as described by Polyaenus and Diodorus are very similar. Both are in charge of the building of a great temple, the Greek word in each case being ἐπιστάτης, which means literally superintendent, but is rather a vague term and appears to include the idea of contractor[1]. Both again misuse their position, and in neither case is the offender charged with misappropriation. Phalaris secures himself a tyranny, Agathocles builds himself a house. But the house is a very special sort of house, and though the builder is specifically acquitted of any dishonest dealings about it, it brings down on him the wrath both of the gods and of the government. The gods burn him and his house: the government confiscate his property. What sort of a house was it that had such disastrous consequences for its builder? A close parallel is offered by the history of the Roman Maelius, who is said in the fifth century B.C. to have had his house pulled down and his property confiscated. In the case of Agathocles the gods, when they destroyed his house, are said to send a sign (ἐπισημαίνειν): in that of Maelius the offence that caused his house to be demolished is pronounced to be not a scelus but a monstrum. The charge that brought down on Maelius these extreme penalties was that of aiming at the throne. Maelius was extremely rich, and had a large army of clients, and we may reasonably infer that his house was so severely dealt with because it looked too much like a royal palace. Considering the analogies in the story of Agathocles with that of Maelius on the one hand and that of Phalaris on the other, it looks not unlikely that the exception taken to the house of Agathocles was due to its palatial character. Private dwellings in early Greek cities were notoriously simple and unpretentious[2]. A house in which it was possible to employ stones intended for a great temple was obviously quite the reverse. It would challenge comparison with the govern-

---

[1] Cp. perhaps the use of ἐπίστασις above, p. 81.
[2] Dem. *Olynth.* III. 25–6; *Aristocr.* 207; περὶ Συντάξ. 29 (=III. 35; XXIII. 689; XIII. 174).

ment buildings and might be used as the rallying-place for an armed attack[1] upon the government, and it was this in all probability that brought on it so terrible a fate.

The stories of Agathocles and Maelius lend support to the view that Polyaenus in his account of the rise of Phalaris is describing the normal way in which tyrannies were established at this early period in Sicily and Italy. If so, the normal tyrant in early Sicily and Italy was some very rich man who used his riches to secure financial control of some large section of the labouring classes and this control was sometimes secured by undertaking big building operations which provided not only continuous work for numerous employees but often too a strong and imposing headquarters that could soon be converted into the castle or palace from which he ruled the whole state[2].

Cumae. Aristodemus of Cumae is dated by the fact that he gave shelter to Tarquinius Superbus when banished from Rome[3]. "In those days Cumae was renowned throughout Italy for its wealth and power[4]." Before he became tyrant he is said to have distinguished himself as a soldier[5]. But it was not as

[1] The military stratagems attributed to Phalaris by Polyaenus, v. 1. 3, 4, and Frontinus, III. 4. 6, are not very illuminating, but note that in one of them Phalaris is made to achieve his aim by a fraudulent deal in corn.

[2] Somewhere about the time of Phalaris Sicily was invaded by a Carthaginian army under a commander named Malchus, Justin XVIII. 7. It has been suggested that Phalaris was pre-eminently the leader of the Agrigentines against the Punic peril (Bury, *Hist. Greece*², p. 297), and that he played a similar part to that played during a later invasion by the Syracusan Dionysius. For this suggestion there is no evidence whatsoever. There is no certainty either that the invasion of Malchus occurred in the age of Phalaris or that Agrigentum was endangered by it or even alarmed. On the other hand there are hints that Phalaris was the reverse of anti-Carthaginian. The Semites of Carthage were devoted to the cult of Moloch, in whose worship no small part was played by the molten image of a calf and the offering to it of human sacrifices. Perhaps the most likely origin of the story of the bull of Phalaris is to be sought in this Moloch worship. The tyrant may have had a large Phoenician contingent among his foreign employees and have very much shocked his Greek subjects by allowing these Semites to practise Semitic rites in Agrigentum. Meyer, however, *Ges. d. Alt.* II. p. 682 n., suggests a connexion between the bull of Phalaris and the Cretan bull cult. Note that the story of the bull of Phalaris impressed Grote as having a historical basis: "The reality of the hollow bull appears to be better authenticated than the nature of the story would lead us to presume," *Hist. Greece*, ed. 1888, IV. p. 65; cp. *ibid.* p. 296, n. 1.

[3] Livy II. 21, 34; Dion. Hal. VI. 21. [4] Dion. Hal. VII. 3.
[5] Dion. Hal. VII. 4, 5; Plut. *Mul. Virt.* 26 (*Moral.* 261).

a soldier that he is represented as securing the tyranny. "He won over the people by turning demagogue....relieving many of the poor out of his own purse....distributing money to them man by man, and depositing for the common good the presents he had received from the people of Aricia[1]." At the end of his reign he is represented as employing citizens on a large scale on manual labour: "he chanced about that time to be making a trench round the place, a work neither necessary nor useful, but merely because he wished to weary and exhaust the citizens with toils and labours. For each was ordered to remove a certain extent of earth[2]." The chronology of the tyrant's career is not altogether easy and the narrative not entirely credible[3], but we appear to have a tyrant of the early type, taking a prominent part in war and politics but relying largely at any rate on the control of labour and the power of wealth.

[1] Dion. Hal. VII. 4. 5, 6. 4.   [2] Plut. *Mul. Virt.* 26.
[3] See Niese *ap.* Pauly Wissowa s.v. Aristodemus (8).

Chapter X. (a) *Capitalist Despots of the Age of Aristotle*, (b) *the Money Power of the Rulers of Pergamum*, (c) *Protogenes of Olbia*

STRESS has been laid on the influence that has been exercised by Dionysius of Syracuse upon all who have written about the early tyranny since he came to power. This of course does not mean that the military-demagogue type of tyrant, of which Dionysius is the supreme example, was never at all anticipated in any of its features by any of the rulers of the seventh and sixth centuries. Nor does it mean that the new order of things that culminated in Dionysius completely swamped the old. Aristotle himself was personally connected with a tyrant who appears to illustrate the survival into the fourth century of the seventh and sixth century type. The ruler in question, Hermias tyrant of Assos and Atarneus

(*a*) Capitalist despots of the days of Aristotle.

was a eunuch, the slave of a certain banker: he went to Athens and attended the lectures of Plato and Aristotle, and returning he shared the tyranny of his master who had previously secured (ἐπιθεμένῳ) the places round Atarneus and Assos. Subsequently he succeeded him and sent for Aristotle and married his niece to him[1].

---

[1] Strabo XIII. 610; cp. 614. See further Diod. XVI. 52; Diog. Laert. V. 1. 3–11 (quoting Demetrius Magnes and Theocritus); Dion. Hal. *Ep. ad Amm.* 5; Demetrius, *de Eloc.* 293; Hesych. Miles. *F.H.G.* IV. p. 156; Harpocrat. s.v. Ἑρμίας; Hesych. s.v. Τάρνη; Suid. s.v. Ἀριστοτέλης; Et. Mag. s.v. Ἑρμῆς; Lucian, *Eunuch.* 9; Himerius, VI. 6; Tertull. *Apol. adv. Gent.* 46; Euseb. *Prep. Ev.* XV. 2. Suid. s.v. Ἀριστοτέλης and Hesych. Miles. make Aristotle marry a daughter of Hermias; Diog. Laert. "a daughter or niece"; Euseb., Harpocrat., Suid. s.v. Ἑρμίας and *Et. Mag.* an adopted daughter who was by birth the tyrant's sister (Euseb.).

Plato (?), *Ep.* VI., implies that two of Hermias' companions had attended the Academy, but not Hermias himself. But even so the letter, if genuine, is evidence of intercourse between Hermias and Plato.

The sources for Hermias are collected and discussed by Boeckh, *Klein. Schrift.* VI. 188 f. and Larcher, *Mém. Acad. Insc. et B.-Lettr.* XLVIII. pp. 208 f. Larcher, writing in 1792, is less complete, but extremely interesting from his attitude

In this "slave, banker, philosopher and despot" Leaf sees a tyrant who owed his position to his wealth[1]. He quotes Euaion, the pupil of Plato[2], who not far off to the north at Lampsacus "lent money to the city on the security of the Acropolis, and, when the city defaulted, wanted to become tyrant, until the Lampsacenes gathered against him and after paying him the money cast him out[3]." On the other side of Assos, at Cyme, the public porticoes once passed into the hands of some bankers who had lent money to the city on that security[4]. Leaf might have gone on to quote the case of Timaeus the Cyzicene, who, like Euaion and perhaps Hermias, had been a pupil of Plato:

Timaeus the Cyzicene having granted bonuses (ἐπιδοὺς) of money and corn to the citizens and having on that account won credit among the Cyzicenes as being a worthy man, after a short while made an attempt on the city (ἐπέθετο; cp. ἐπιθεμένῳ above of the predecessor of Hermias) by means of Aridaios[5].

The attempt failed but there can be no doubt that Timaeus like Euaion "wanted to become tyrant" by means of his wealth.

It is curious to notice that the method of securing power practised by the pupils of Plato and Aristotle is precisely that which was prescribed by our own Doctor Johnson: "No, Sir, the way to make sure of power and influence is by lending money confidentially to your neighbours at a small interest or perhaps at no interest at all, and having their bonds in your possession[6]." In Aristotle's own

---

towards Hermias' rebellion from the king of Persia. "Moi-même, j'ai longtemps été persuadé qu'un rebelle qui avoit été justement puni du dernier supplice, n'étoit pas un personnage assez important pour mériter qu'on s'en occupât. Mais en le voyant célébré par Aristote j'ai pensé qu'un homme qui s'étoit attiré les louanges d'un grand philosophe devoit sortir de l'espèce d'obscurité à laquelle il étoit en quelque sort condamné"; p. 208; cp. p. 225, where Larcher explains the Greek conception of the rights of nationality and their refusal to submit to a foreign conqueror. This perverted attitude of the Greeks he attributes to their benighted religion.

[1] *J.H.S.* xxxv. p. 167. Note that Hermias was famed for fair dealing. "If ever he made any purchase and this happened frequently in the case of books, the vendor, being his subject (ἰδιώτης), would demand a price less than their value. But Hermias used to correct the mistake and declare that the book was worth more and pay accordingly" (Suid.).

[2] Diog. Laert. III. 1. 31 (46).   [3] Athen. XI. 508 f.

[4] *J.H.S.* xxxv. p. 167.

[5] Athen. XI. 509 a.

[6] Boswell, ed. Fitzgerald, I. p. 422.

day it appears to have been followed, though without success, in the greatest commercial city of the age:

> After this Anno, a man of Carthage, who in personal wealth was more than a match for the state, was absorbed with a desire to seize supreme power....He stirred up the slaves that with their aid he might suddenly crush the unsuspecting state....This happened in the days of Philip[1].

Thus there is a basis for Leaf's suggestion that Euboulos of Assos, the master and predecessor of Hermias, had made himself tyrant by similar means[2]. But if Aristotle had before him the career of Hanno the Carthaginian, and if a whole group of his own fellow-students made the attempt, and in one case at least successfully, to become financier despots in a corner of the world particularly familiar to the philosopher[3], how are we to explain the fact that his writings take no account of the commercial tyrant? Once more, if I am not mistaken, the cause is largely Dionysius. If, as seems probable, there was this late outcrop of attempts at a commercial tyranny, none the less the type had long ceased to play any great part in history[4]. Hanno was a failure: moreover he tampered with the slaves of Carthage and this enabled Aristotle to classify him with Pausanias the Spartan. For Aristotle the tyrant is a soldier or a demagogue or both. Plutocracy with him means oligarchy[5]. As he himself says, "if one individual possesses more than the rest of the wealthy, on the oligarchic principle it is right that he should rule

---

[1] Orosius IV. 6; cp. Aristot. *Pol.* VII. (V.), 1307a above.

[2] Euboulos (the unnamed banker of Strabo XIII. 610; cp. Diog. Laert. V. 1. 5 (3)) is quoted by Aristotle (*Pol.* II. 1267a) as demonstrating to a Persian satrap that it would not pay for him to besiege Atarneus, on which Boeckh observes that "the idea is worthy of a banker," *Kl. Schr.* VI. p. 188. He seems to have been notoriously accessible to economic arguments. "Anyhow Kallisthenes in his Apophthegms says that the poet Persinos, being neglected by Euboulos of Atarneus went to Mitylene, and when Euboulos expressed surprise wrote to him that it was because he found it more pleasing exchanging in Mitylene than in Atarneus the Phocaean staters he had brought with him," Poll. IX. 93.

[3] Besides his connexions with Hermias Aristotle had been brought up παρά τινι Προξένῳ Ἀταρνεῖ, Ammon. *Vita Arist.*

[4] Boeckh, *Kleine Schriften*, VI. p. 191, says of Hermias, "seine Macht darf man nicht gering anschlagen"; but Atarneus τὸ τοῦ Ἑρμείου τυραννεῖον (Strabo XIII. 614) is described by Himerius (*Or.* VI. 6) as πόλις μέγεθος οὐ μεγάλη. Even on the most liberal estimate it sinks into utter insignificance in the light of the conquests of Alexander, which so shortly followed it.

[5] *Pol.* II. 1273a; III. 1280a.

alone¹." If forced to catalogue the government of a commercial despot he would probably have described it is an oligarchy of one. But it is doubtful whether the government of Hermias was strictly speaking the rule of a single individual.

An inscription now in the British Museum speaks repeatedly of Ἑρμίας καὶ οἱ ἑταῖροι² which Leaf translates and explains into "Hermias and company, Bankers and Despots." The precise nature of these companions is uncertain: but their repeated mention in a treaty suggests that Hermias tried to avoid the appearances of single rule³. Lastly the personal element may have had its influence even with the great philosopher. Not only was he in close personal connexion with Hermias; but his one deviation into poetry, his remarkable ode to Virtue⁴, was written in honour of Hermias after his fall. According to one version of the story the philosopher's devotion to the memory of his friend cost him his life⁵. Plainly for Aristotle the ruler of Atarneus was no tyrant⁶, and it follows that Euaion and Timaeus, even if their efforts had been successful, would not have been so either. Plato on the other hand would have particular

---

¹ *Pol.* VIII. (VI.), 1318 a.

² Hicks, *Manual Gk. Hist. Inscr.* no. 100. The expression occurs four times in the thirty-two extant lines of the inscription. Hermias is mentioned without his partners only once, right at the end.

³ Perhaps also the reality. Plato's sixth letter, which is addressed to Hermias and Erastos and Koriskos (cp. Diog. Laert. III. 1. 31 (46)), urges the three to form a "single bond of friendship" (μίαν φιλίας συμπλοκήν). Boeckh, *Kl. Schr.* VI. p. 191, describes Hermias' tyranny as "eine Hetairie mehrerer, an deren Spitze ein anerkanntes Haupt stand." Hermias was at least primus inter pares; cp. the use made of his seal, Polyaen. VI. 48.

⁴ Diog. Laert. V. 1. 7 (6); Athen. XV. 696; cp. also the epigram ascribed to Aristotle on Hermias' statue at Delphi, Diog. Laert. *ibid.*

⁵ Suid. s.v. Ἀριστοτέλης; cp. Athen. XV. 696 a–b; Diog. Laert. V. 1. 7; Hesych. Miles. *F.H.G.* IV. 156–7.

⁶ *Pace* Endt, *Wien. Stud.* XXIV. pp. 67–68. He is not called tyrant by Aristotle either in the Paean (where he is called Ἀταρνέος ἔντροφος, v.l. ἔντροπος (=ἐπίτροπος, viceroy, steward?), see Larcher, *op. cit.* p. 244), or in the epitaph Diog. Laert. V. 1. 7. The *Oeconomica*, included among the works of Aristotle and probably written by one of his pupils, refers to him without calling him tyrant (II. 28: on authorship see ed. Teubner, introd. p. viii). Nor is Euboulos so called where mentioned in the *Politics* (II. 1267 a). Demetrius may be following the Aristotelian tradition when he calls Hermias simply ὁ τοῦ Ἀταρνέως ἄρξας (but cp. *ibid.* παρὰ τοῖς τυράννοις). So Suid. ὅστις ἦν ἄρχων Ἀταρνέως. In other writers Hermias is generally styled tyrant (so Strabo, Diod., Diog. Laert., Dion. Hal., Lucian).

cause to regard as a tyrant the Syracusan ruler by whom he is said to have been sold into slavery for twenty minae[1]. In short this group of would-be philosopher kings probably did as much as Dionysius himself to blind Aristotle and later writers to the true nature of seventh and sixth century tyranny[2].

If Aristotle had lived another forty years he might have witnessed quite near Atarneus the rise of another and much more notable monarchy, that of the Attalids of Pergamum, which was also based almost exclusively on wealth. Pergamum had become the fortified treasury of Lysimachus when he succeeded to the Thracian dominions of Alexander the Great. The keeping of the fort and the 9000 talents of treasure that it contained was entrusted to a certain Philetairos. He was a eunuch, but well brought up, and he showed himself worthy of the trust. In spite of, or rather perhaps as the result of, the quarrels of the Diadochoi, he continued for twenty years master of the fort and of the money[3]. There seems little doubt that Philetairos was of humble birth[4], and that he owed his rise to this gift of finance which secured him first the management and then the possession of these 9000 talents. He began his independent career by going over from Lysimachus, whose realm lay mainly in Europe, to Seleucus, the most able of the Diadochoi in Asia[5]. Shortly afterwards Seleucus was murdered by Ptolemy

(b) The money power of the rulers of Pergamum (283–133 B.C.).

---

[1] Diod. xv. 7; Plut. *Dio*, 5; Diog. Laert. III. 1. 14 (19). The story may be a fiction (Burnet, *Thales to Plato*, p. 211), but if so it is probably based on the fact of a quarrel between the tyrant and the philosopher.

[2] Dionysius himself had a clearer conception of the danger of a monopolist becoming a political potentate, as appears from a passage of Aristotle himself. "In Sicily a certain person who had had money deposited with him bought up all the iron from the iron works (σιδηρείων), and after that, when the merchants came from the emporia, he was the sole salesman. He did not greatly overcharge; but none the less on fifty talents he made a hundred. When Dionysius perceived this he told him to take off the money, but not to remain any longer in Syracuse, since he had discovered a source of income that was prejudicial to his interests." (Arist. *Pol.* II. 1259 a.) The incident as described hardly, however, suggests that the monopolist was Dionysius' greatest danger.

[3] Strabo XIII. 623.

[4] An inscription published *J.H.S.* XXII. p. 195 gives his father the Greek name of Attalus, but he is described by Athenaeus, XIII. 577b, quoting Carystius, as the son of a courtesan flute girl from Paphlagonia, and by Pausanias, I. 8. 1, as a Paphlagonian eunuch.

[5] Strabo XIII. 623; Paus. I. 10. 4.

Keraunos, the Greek king of Egypt; but Philetairos, who believed firmly in the fortunes of the Seleucids, secured the friendship of Antiochus, the son and successor of Seleucus, by buying the body of the murdered king at a heavy price from Keraunos and sending it to Antiochus[1]. Philetairos was always ready to draw upon his 9000 talents if by doing so he could purchase power. When the people of the neighbouring town of Pitane were in debt to the extent of 380 talents, Philetairos advanced a portion of that sum, and thereby secured influence over that city[2]. Gifts were made to Cyzicus with similar intentions and results[3]. The island of Aegina became a Pergamene possession for the price of 30 talents[4]. These proceedings are typical of the way in which the rulers of Pergamum established and maintained their position. As Holm observes[5] their power was a money power. Like every other political power that has hitherto arisen, that of the Attalids was partly military. Soon after the death of Philetairos and the accession of Attalus, the second ruler of the dynasty, Asia Minor was overrun by the Celtic hordes which finally settled down to a peaceful life in what was known thenceforth as Galatia. The promiscuous maraudings of these barbarians were checked and eventually crushed by Attalus and his successors. But the Attalids were still more notable for their works of peace. Under their government Pergamum became one of the most active centres of art and industry in the whole world. The city, elaborately constructed in terraces on a lofty hillside, offered a remarkably successful example of scientific town-planning, and must have involved a large and highly organized army of architects, builders, masons, and the like. The Pergamene school of sculpture flourished exceedingly. We owe to it Lord Byron's dying gladiator, who has long since been recognized as a copy of a dying Galatian carved at Pergamum to commemorate a victory of Attalus I over the Celtic invader. Much of Pergamene art is exaggerated and ugly, but that does not diminish its economic significance, and Mommsen is justified in describing Attalus I as the Lorenzo de' Medici of antiquity[6]. We have already compared

---

[1] Appian XI. 10 (*Syr.* 63).

[2] Fraenkel, *Inschr. v. Perg.* no. 245, fr. C, l. 44; Bevan, *House of Seleucus*, I. p. 156.

[3] *J.H.S.* XXII. p. 193 f.   [4] Polyb. XXIII. 8.

[5] Holm, *Hist. Greece*, IV. p. 280.

[6] Mommsen, *Hist. Rome* (English trans.), II. p. 403.

the Medici with the early Greek tyrants. But it is not merely that the Pergamene rulers and early tyrants like Gyges have a common resemblance to the Italian merchant princes of the early renaissance. A distinct resemblance between the Attalids and the house of Gyges has been already recognized and developed by Adolph Holm. The two powers are much the same geographically; both are the great connecting link between the Greek Aegean and the Asiatic lands that lie to the east of it; both organize the forces of material prosperity against barbaric invasions from the north; both have money as the basis of their power[1].

The history of Philetairos and his successors at Pergamum increases the probability that Leaf is right in his picture of the banker despots of the days of Plato and Aristotle. The picture is scarcely complete enough to be quite convincing, but it may be supplemented and confirmed from the history of a financial magnate named Protogenes, who flourished at Olbia probably towards the end of the third century B.C.

(c) The rich Protogenes, financial director of Olbia about 200 B.C.

Protogenes is known only from a single inscription put up during his lifetime to record his benefactions to his native city[2]. The date of the inscription is not quite certain. The lettering points to the second century B.C. but does not exclude a rather earlier date, and a reference in the inscription to danger threatening Olbia from certain Galatians rather favours a date before 213 B.C.

Within the space of three years Protogenes made gifts to his city amounting to 12,700 gold pieces and made up of the following items: four times he contributes to help buy off the barbarians who at this period were constantly threatening the city; twice he pays for repairs to the city walls; he built or repaired the public granary, the bazaar gateway, and the barges that brought the stone for these building operations; he redeemed for 100 pieces of gold the city plate, which was about to be put in the melting-pot by one of the city's creditors; he pays down three hundred pieces of gold for wine which the city fathers had purchased and then found that they could not pay for; he contributes directly or indirectly to the purchase of large quantities of corn for the city; he remits to the amount of

---

[1] Holm, *Hist. Greece* (English trans.), IV. pp. 280, 296.

[2] Published in full by Minns, *Greeks and Scythians*, pp. 641–2, and discussed, *ibid.* pp. 460–3 and *passim*.

6000 gold pieces (*i.e.* nearly half his total benefaction) private debts owed to himself or his father.

During the three years covered by these gifts Protogenes was financial director of the city's affairs, a position which he had reached after a wide experience of public business (πλεῖστα δὲ χειρίσας τῶν κοινῶν, τρία δὲ ἔτη συνεχῶς πάντα διῴκησεν ὀρθῶς καὶ δικαίως).

To see in this financial direction of the city's affairs an instance of a commercial tyranny would be a pure hypothesis. It is not even certain that Protogenes made all his gifts quite voluntarily. One of his contributions for the purchase of corn was made after the demos had passed a resolution that the wealthy ought to advance money for this purpose[1]. On one of the occasions when he paid for repairs to the town walls he did so at the invitation of the people[2]. "Advance" and "invitation" may be euphemisms for "tax paying" and "compulsion," and the payments made by Protogenes may have had affinity to the liturgies paid to the state by rich Athenians in the fifth century rather than to the benevolences that Lucius Tarquinius is said to have paid voluntarily for his own ends to the people of Rome. But this latter hypothesis is not better founded than the other. "Advance" and "request" may after all mean what they say. We do not know what became of Protogenes after his three years as financial director. The financial directorship may correspond to the magistracy that is said to have frequently led directly to the tyranny, *e.g.* at Corinth and Miletus. Protogenes is of course much later in date, but the Greek cities of South Russia were the home of many curious survivals. At Olbia itself for instance we find a style of pottery that in Greece proper was typical of the fifth and fourth centuries persisting apparently into the first[3]. There are even hints that Olbia had once at least and perhaps comparatively recently gone through a social and economic revolution something like those that so often convulsed the cities of the seventh and sixth centuries just before they fell under tyrants, *e.g.* Athens before the tyranny of Peisistratus, or Miletus before that of Histiaeus. While the city was being besieged by a certain Zopyrion the Olbiopolitans had "set slaves free, given foreigners citizenship, and cancelled all debts[4]." If this Zopyrion is the governor left by

[1] Minns, p. 641, l. 65. [2] Minns, p. 642, l. 59.
[3] Ure, *Black Glaze Pottery*, p. 35, n. 6.
[4] Macrob. *Sat.* I. xi. 33.

Alexander in Thrace[1] this revolution must be dated at least a century earlier than Protogenes. If, with Grote, we refuse to accept this identification, the revolution is left dateless. In any case it shows that such upheavals did happen in Olbia, and serves to remind us how very incomplete is the material with which we are dealing. But the value for our enquiry of the Protogenes enscription does not depend on any speculations of this kind. What it does is to give us a detailed picture of an exceptionally wealthy man in an ancient Greek city state who for a considerable period largely financed his city. If Protogenes could do this in Olbia there can be nothing inherently improbable in the hypothesis that other great capitalists had done something similar in other cities. If Protogenes did not turn his position into a political tyranny, that would be no proof that others did not do so: and the fact remains that the assumption that Protogenes was not on the way to become a tyrant, or indeed that he did not actually become one, if not precisely wild[2] is purely hypothetical.

The records of Protogenes illustrate the sort of way in which the financial magnate might win the supreme place in his city. The whole group of facts associated with his name and with those of Euboulos, Hermias, Euaion, Timaeus, Philetairos, and Attalus shows once again that at least there is nothing improbable in the theory that the power of the seventh and sixth century tyrants was built up on a similar financial or industrial basis, the more so considering the evidence adduced already for believing that conditions in the earlier period were uniquely favourable for the establishment of a money power. We have seen why the financial despots of the age of Plato and Aristotle should not have helped to preserve the memory of earlier money powers. It is no less easy to see why the same should have been the case with the rulers of Pergamum. An exceptional circumstance saved the house of Philetairos from being reproached with its mercenary basis, and curiously enough that circumstance was one which illustrates how very mercenary that basis was. When Attalus III, the last of his house, died in 133 B.C., he made the Roman people his heirs[3]. His fortune was used by the Gracchan

---

[1] Minns, p. 459. [2] Cp. Minns, p. 462, n. 2.

[3] Strabo XIII. 624. The significance of this proceeding cannot be put better than in the words of Holm, *Hist. Greece*, IV. p. 527: "It is characteristic of the Pergamene dynasty that it concluded its career in the spirit in which it began it. Its rule was of private origin: Philetairos had appropriated treasure and

revolutionaries to equip the impoverished Romans whom they were restoring to the land by their agrarian laws. The dynasty too, with its clear eye for the main chance, had always consistently sought the friendship of Rome[1]. Though most of our authorities for the history of the Attalids are Greek, the Greeks in question were all pro-Roman, with the result that we see the Attalids essentially from the Roman point of view. They stood in much the same relationship to the Romans as the house of Gyges did to the Greeks; and the Romans to whom Attalus III had left all his treasure and possessions were as little inclined to think harshly of their benefactor as were the Greeks whom Croesus had so largely benefited inclined to be critical of his "hospitable virtue[2]." In both cases the man of business was known only as the patron of deserving charities. We have to go to rulers like the Tarquins and Peisistratids, whose history we owe ultimately to their own subjects and employees, to hear the money-power described as it really was and given its true name of tyranny.

treasury. After that the Pergamene rulers had raised themselves to the rank of kings by their money and their clever policy, and as such had achieved much good. The last sovereign of the line, however, reverted to the view that his position was of a private nature and he disposed of everything that he claimed as if it were private property."

[1] Strabo XIII. 624. The friendship dated from at least 211 B.C., Livy XXVI. 24.
[2] οὐ φθίνει Κροίσου φιλόφρων ἀρετά, Pind. *Pyth.* I. 93-94; but cp. what the poet says *ibid.* 95-98, about what was probably a similar government (see above, pp. 274-8), that the Greeks knew from the inside: "Phalaris men tell of everywhere with hate" (ἐχθρὰ Φάλαριν κατέχει παντᾷ φάτις).

Chapter XI. *Conclusion*

ἀγαθὸν δὲ ὄντα διαφερόντως καὶ πλούσιον εἶναι διαφερόντως ἀδύνατον.
PLATO, *Laws*, v. 743 a.

"We adopted a law that if you bought an office you didn't get it. I admit that that is contrary to all commercial principles, but I think it is pretty good political doctrine."—WOODROW WILSON.

THIS final chapter will contain (*a*) a *résumé* of the evidence already adduced; (*b*) a short general discussion of the credibility of the whole mass of extant evidence; and (*c*) an attempt to view in their proper perspective the conclusions that the evidence seems to warrant.

(a) *Résumé of previous chapters*

Introductory chapter.

The age of the first known metal coins is also the age of the first rulers to be called tyrants. Ancient evidence and modern analogy both suggest that the new form of government was based on the new form of capital. The modern analogy is to be found in the financial revolution which has largely replaced metal coins by paper (thereby rendering capital very much more mobile, just as was done by the financial revolution of the age of the tyrants) and has led many people to fear a new tyranny of wealth. The ancient evidence is to be found in the scanty extant writings of the sixth century B.C. (Solon and Theognis), in scattered notices about early tyrants or tyranny in fifth century writers (Thucydides, Herodotus, Pindar), in certain statements of Aristotle, in references to industrial conditions both during and after the age of the tyrants, in the history of the states where there was never a tyranny, and in the steps taken to prevent a recurrence of tyranny.

If the commercial origin of the early tyranny is not explicitly formulated by any ancient writer it should be remembered how meagre are contemporary documents and how little Greek writers say about economic causes. It is true also that my view is at variance with statements of Plato, Aristotle, and subsequent writers: but their picture of the rise of tyranny clashes with known facts about the seventh and sixth centuries and is due to false generalizations from the conditions of their own days and particularly from the career of Dionysius of Syracuse.

Athens. Peisistratus made himself tyrant by organizing the Attic "hill men" (Diakrioi, Epakrioi) against the two previously existing rival factions of the "plain" and the "coast." The accepted explanations of these "hill men" are improbable. They cannot have been farmers or shepherds, who were always very conservative, are not recorded as having subsequently supported Peisistratus, and must have lived principally in the plain and very little in the forest-clad mountains where modern theories generally locate them. Nor were the "hill men" confined to the mountainous district of North Attica, the mistaken identification of which with the "hill country" is due to mistaken views as to the triple division of Attica into "hill," "coast," and "plain," which wrongly assigns all South Attica to the "coast" and limits the "coast" to South Attica. These views on the triple division of Attica in the days of Peisistratus are based on the weakest of evidence and are made improbable by the subsequent topographical arrangements of Cleisthenes (502 B.C.), and by the later uses of the terms Diakria and Epakria. The Epakria contained a village named Semachidai which, as shown by a recently found inscription, lay in the hilly mining district of South Attica. Furthermore the Attic "akron" *par excellence* was Cape Sunium, the Southern apex of the Attic mining district and of the whole Attic peninsula. In view of these facts it becomes probable that the Sunium and Laurium mining district was the "hill country" *par excellence*. The mines were almost certainly in full work at this period, and the miners, unlike those of later ages, free men, good material for a political faction.

That Peisistratus based his power on silver mines is made very likely by what is known of his subsequent career. He finally "rooted his power" on money derived partly from home, partly from the Thracian mining district; he went to the Thracian mining district to prepare for his second restoration; his first restoration is attributed to the dressing up as Athena of a Thracian woman named Phye, who is very possibly to be explained away as the Athena who begins about this time to appear on Attic coins: for this interpretation of the Phye story compare the names "girl," "virgin," "Pallas" colloquially given to the Attic coins, and the jest about Agesilaus being driven out of Asia by the Great King's archers, a colloquial name for Persian gold coins.

The tyranny fell at Athens when the tyrants lost control of the Thracian mining district. Shortly afterwards the ambitious Histiaeus, the Greek friend of the Persian king into whose power the mines had passed, incurred the suspicions of the Persian sovereign through attempting to build up a political power on these very mines and miners.

The history of the Alcmaeonid opposition to the house of Peisistratus likewise suggests that the government of Athens at this period depended first and foremost on the power of the purse.

Samos. Polycrates is perhaps best known for his piracies, but it seems not unlikely that these piracies were in fact an elaborate commercial blockade of Persia that proved almost as unpopular among Greek neutrals as among the subjects of the Great King against whom it was mainly directed. As tyrant Polycrates is found controlling the commercial and industrial activities of his state, building ships, harbour works, and waterworks, and very possibly a great bazaar, and probably employing much free labour on these works. Before he became tyrant he already had an interest in the chief Samian industries, the working of metal and the manufacture of woollen goods. Aiakes the father of Polycrates is probably the Aiakes whom a recently discovered Samian inscription appears to connect with the sea-borne trade of the island. The tyrant is said to have owed his fall to an attempt to get money enough to rule all Greece, a statement of particular value considering the tendency to administer poetic justice that is so frequently displayed by Herodotus, who is our authority for this statement.

Egypt. The great developments of trade and industry that just preceded the age of tyranny in Greece had their parallel if not their origin in Egypt. At the height of this development in Egypt a new and powerful dynasty arises which bases its power on commerce and on the commercial and industrial classes. Already towards the end of the eighth century we find King Bocchoris (somewhat after the manner of the Argive Pheidon) devoting special attention to commercial legislation. His successor Sethon is said by Herodotus to have based his power on "hucksters and artizans and tradespeople." During these reigns the country was always being occupied or threatened by foreign invaders from Ethiopia or Assyria. The first Egyptian king of this period to rule all Egypt in normal conditions of peace and quietness was Psammetichus I, who rose to power about the same time as Cypselus in Corinth and Orthagoras in Sicyon. Psammetichus according to Diodorus converted his position from that of a petty Delta chieftain (one of twelve who shared the rule of the part of the country not in foreign occupation) into that of supreme ruler of the whole country as a result of the wealth and influence that he won by trading with Phoenicians and Greeks.

This last statement if true establishes Psammetichus as a commercial tyrant. It occurs only in Diodorus, and receives no direct confirmation in earlier writers, but it is in entire harmony with all that is known about events and conditions in Egypt at this period, and more particularly with the notices just quoted as to Bocchoris and Sethon, with the history of Amasis and the other later Saites as recorded in Herodotus, and with the conclusions to be drawn from the excavation of Naukratis and the other Greek settlements that played so important a part in Saite Egypt.

Lydia. From the middle of the eighth century B.C. till the early part of the fifth Lydia appears to have been a power in which the ruler based his position on wealth and struggles for the throne were fought with the weapons of trade and finance. This according to the accounts is the case with Spermos and Ardys in the eighth century and with Croesus in the sixth: the story of Gyges and his magic ring may also be explained in the same sense. A similar state of things is indicated in the advice which Croesus is made by Herodotus to give to Cyrus, in the story of the revolt of Pactyes, and in that of Xerxes and the rich Pythes.

At about the time to which we can trace back this state of things in Lydia, two events were taking place that are both attributed to Lydia, namely the striking of the first metal coins and the appearance of the first tyrant. In neither case are the dates very precise. The first coins are more probably to be placed late in the eighth century than early in the seventh, and though Gyges is stated to have been the first tyrant, there are reasons for suspecting that he may have been merely the first ruler of his kind to attract the attention of the Greeks. The magic ring too by which he secured his tyranny is sometimes attributed not to Gyges but to some (not very remote) ancestor of his or to the eighth century plutocrat Midas king of the neighbouring Phrygia. But on any showing the ring falls within the limits of time and place to which may be ascribed the earliest coins and the earliest tyrant. Rings are one common form of early currency and it is not impossible that it was to the ring in this sense that the first tyrant owed his tyranny. This view, which implies that the earliest coins were private issues and that the coinage was only nationalized when the principal coiner became chief of the state, is supported alike by evidence and analogies.

Pheidon, who was probably the first ruler to be called tyrant in European Greece, is described by Herodotus as "the man who created for the Peloponnesians their measures," a description that at once suggests that it was this commercial step that differentiated Pheidon the tyrant from the kings who preceded him. Later writers, of whom the earliest is Ephorus, go further and state that silver was first coined by Pheidon in Aegina. The statement has been called in question, but it is confirmed by the chapters of Herodotus (v. 82 f.) which describe the early relations between Argos, Aegina, and Athens. In the light of recent archaeological enquiries it becomes highly probable that Argos became predominant in Aegina as described in these chapters of Herodotus (which are unfortunately most vague in their chronology) just about the time when Pheidon most probably reigned; and this probability is increased by the tradition that Pheidon recovered the lot of Temenos, the domain of the kings of Argos in early Dorian times, which included the island of Aegina. The occupation of Aegina by Argos which we have seen reason to associate with Pheidon gave rise according to Herodotus to a change in the "measures" (which probably included the weights system) in use on the island, the new measures being half as great again as those previously in use. The Aeginetan standard on which the Aeginetan coins were struck is roughly half as great again as the other and probably earlier standard used in ancient Greece. The statement of Ephorus that silver was first coined by Pheidon in Aegina is thus strikingly confirmed, which means that the first ruler to strike coins in European Greece was also the first to be called tyrant.

The tyranny at Corinth coincides with the great industrial and commercial developments of the city described by Thucydides (1. 13) in words that are a paraphrase of his description of the state of things that led to the rise of tyrannies in Greece generally. Scholars agree that the tyrants had a direct interest in some of these developments, notably shipping, colonizing and coinage. The main industry of Corinth at this period seems to have been pottery, with which she supplied much of the Greek world. Of the early career of the first tyrant, Cypselus, very little is known beyond the story in Herodotus which professes to explain how the infant Cypselus got his curious name. We have examined in some detail the meaning of the words cypselus and cypsele, and found that they probably mean potter and pot, so that the man who established the tyranny at Corinth seems to have borne a name that associates him with the main industry of his city.

Rome.

Both in date and in character the corresponding period at Rome to the age of the tyrants in Greece is that which is occupied by the reigns of the Tarquins. The first king of this dynasty, Tarquinius Priscus, is said to have been the son of a rich Corinthian named Demaratus. Early in life the first of the Tarquins had settled in Rome. It was by means of his wealth that he secured the throne. Both he and his father are said to have been great employers of labour, and the accounts imply that their employees were free men. Servius Tullius, who succeeded Tarquinius Priscus, is said to have been the first at Rome to strike coins, and to have secured the support of the poor by gifts and benevolences. When the last of the Tarquins, Tarquinius Superbus, overthrew Servius Tullius and secured the throne, he did so by buying up the poorest of the common people. After his succession he is described as employing Etruscans and Roman citizens on a large scale as artizans and quarrymen. He loses the throne when he can no longer pay these employees.

During the first century of the republic the established government several times thought itself threatened with attempts to restore the kingship. In each case it is the wealth or the exceptional financial position of the suspected person that causes the alarm. Early republican statesmen are repeatedly reported as charging the Tarquins with having degraded Roman citizens (from their natural position as soldiers and gentlemen) into tradesmen and artizans, a charge which implies the reverse change as having accompanied the change from kingly government to republican. The final blow to the monarchist movement at Rome seems to have been dealt when army pay was instituted, and the government as paymaster of the army became the greatest employer of paid free labour in the state.

One later attempt to establish a tyranny at Rome has been suspected by Mommsen. The man he suspects of it is Appius Claudius Caecus, the censor of 312 B.C. Appius was noted for the number of his clients and the great public works that he conducted, and he probably had a close connexion with the first real coinage struck by Rome. Attention has also been drawn to the accounts of the secessions, with their curious resemblances to modern strikes and their implication of organization on the part of labour. At Ardea in North Latium about the year 440 B.C. the working-classes are described as playing a decisive part in the struggle for supreme power. At Veii in the year 400 B.C. we are told of a rich employer who became king of his city.

The statements just quoted have all been often regarded with extreme scepticism. The reasons for this scepticism have been examined in the chapter on Rome. It is impossible to resume them here. If my conclusions are not entirely wrong, the scepticism of the last century represented an excessive reaction against the undue credulity of earlier ages. Recent archaeological discoveries enormously increase the probability of the narrative in its main outlines. But if after all the sceptics are right on this particular question, and the Tarquin narrative is a fiction, it is none the less of historical value, and confirms the view that the early tyrannis was commercial, since, if fiction, it must be an early Greek fiction, preserving an early Greek conception of the typical early tyrant as a great capitalist.

In Chapter IX we surveyed the evidence for the origin of the early tyrannies at Sicyon, Megara, Miletus, Ephesus, Leontini, Agrigentum, and Cumae. The material is scanty and it is enough here to recall that as far as it goes it supports the theory of a commercial origin. At Sicyon the tyranny is founded by a tradesman the son of a tradesman. At Megara Theagenes rises to power as the result of what looks very like the creation of a corner in the staple product of his city. At Miletus and Leontini we find tyrants arising as the result of something like class war between rich and poor, while a later tyrant of Miletus tries to establish a great political position by getting control of the mines and miners of Thrace. At Ephesus and Cumae the tyrants' power is said to be based on the money that they distributed among the poorer classes, while at Agrigentum the tyrant is definitely stated to have secured the tyranny through his position as a great employer.

Other early tyrannies.

In the times of Aristotle there are several cases in the Pergamene district of rich bankers and the like making attempts, of which one at least was successful, to secure supreme political power in their cities by means of their

Capitalist despots of later ages.

wealth. The close personal relationship in which Aristotle stood to some of them partly explains why they are not classed by him as tyrants.

Not long afterwards the far more important power of the rulers of Pergamum owed its origin entirely to the enormous wealth of the founder of the dynasty.

Later still at Olbia chance has preserved an inscription which records how a very rich Olbiopolitan named Protogenes became "financial director" of his city. Though there is no evidence that Protogenes ever became a tyrant the inscription shows that the sort of position which we have imagined to have been normally built up by the would-be tyrant of the seventh or sixth century was actually secured some three or four centuries later by a wealthy individual in this remote and backward Greek city on the Black Sea.

(b) *The credibility of the evidence as a whole*

The value of the various items of evidence collected and reviewed in the preceding chapters varies very greatly. In some cases we have precise statements bearing closely on the point in question and made by almost contemporary writers. At the other end of the list we have anecdotes of doubtful relevance and doubtful authenticity found in writers who lived centuries after the period to which they refer. It is difficult to sum up the value of so miscellaneous a collection. The estimate is bound to vary greatly according to the temperament and training of the person who makes it. There are however two points which seem in the present state of scholarship to need especial emphasis.

The first of these refers to the generally prevalent attitude towards the question of historical truth as it affects generally the period under consideration. No one who has read at all widely in modern writings on ancient history can have failed to observe that the scepticism or credulity of any given scholar has always depended largely on that of his generation. Up to a point this is inevitable: but we are reaching a stage when it is no longer necessary to follow quite so blindly as has hitherto been done the natural reaction from excessive credulity to excessive scepticism and *vice versa*. The pendulum has now been swinging long enough for its motion to be observed and allowed for. There is no doubt that scholars of a few generations ago were often and perhaps in general unduly credulous. But it is no less certain that the main tendency of the past century has been to react from excessive credulity to no less excessive scepticism. The beginnings of the sceptical reaction were observed by Byron:

> I've stood upon Achilles' tomb
> And heard Troy doubted: Time will doubt of Rome.

The doubts about Troy have been triumphantly dispelled by the spade. So likewise, as we have seen already, have many doubts as to the reality of the Tarquins' Rome. But the wonderful discoveries of the last forty years at Troy, Mycenae, Knossos, Phaistos, and other sites of early Cretan civilization have diverted the attention of scholars from later periods. It need therefore cause no surprise if in the preceding pages there has repeatedly been occasion to criticize prevailing views as excessively and uncritically sceptical.

The second point on the question of historical truth that I wish here to emphasize is concerned more directly with the evidence collected in this book. As already admitted, the collection contains many items of doubtful value: it could not be otherwise if it was to be at all complete. The cumulative effect of so much dubious evidence upon some mental temperaments is to discredit the mass of evidence as a whole. It is important therefore to bear in mind the character of our material. It is a heap, not a chain. Its strength is to be measured by its strongest items rather than by its weakest. Weak or irrelevant items do not invalidate any that are relevant and cogent. On the contrary, points of evidence that are individually unconvincing may have a powerful cumulative effect if they are found all pointing, however dimly, in one definite direction, and all suggesting a single explanation arrived at on independent grounds. When dealing with the dawn of history it is uncritical to reject a whole body of evidence merely because it is made up of details scarcely any of which are capable of proof. The evidence of history, or at any rate of Greek history, in its childhood is like that of many an individual child. The child's idea of truth is often more fluid than that of the adult. It may be harder in any given case to be sure of the exact facts. But it may all the same be certain that facts more or less accurately recorded form a large element of the information.

That, it may be fairly claimed, is how the evidence that has been presented in this volume ought to be regarded. Its cumulative value is really considerable. It should be remembered how independent our witnesses are. Livy on the Tarquins of Rome is corroborated by Diodorus on Psammetichus of Egypt: Herodotus on early tyrants generally is borne out by his critic Thucydides: the later writers who have been quoted so frequently and in such numbers drew upon a great variety of sources: literary evidence is confirmed by archaeological, as for instance when a conjecture as to the "hill men" of Peisistratus that I put forward in 1906 is corroborated by an inscription that was first published just after the publication of my conjecture. When witnesses are so many and they speak on such a variety of topics and under such a variety of circumstances and to all appearances without the possibility of any common cue, the chances of collusion become remote in the extreme.

(c) *Conclusions*

But granted that the various items of evidence that we have so far collected have all a real historical value, and granted too that they lend one another a considerable amount of mutual support, there is a further line of criticism that deserves a careful consideration. The evidence may all be true and yet the inferences that have been drawn from it be false, or at least ill-balanced and misleading. Kings and tyrants have in all ages tended to be extremely rich. In most ages great riches have been indispensable for anyone aiming at great political power, and the greater the power aimed at naturally enough the greater the riches required to secure it. Admittedly the tyrants lived in a commercial age, and the influence of wealth was particularly strong. Does the evidence that has just been presented prove in reality very much more than that? Some of the statements about the men who became tyrants are indeed sufficiently explicit, as for example that about the trading of the young Psammetichus, or the wealth and workmen of the young Lucius Tarquinius, but apart from the question of their trustworthiness they are all so brief and meagre that it is impossible to be sure that we see them in the right perspective. They are not very adequate for forming any picture of the men they refer to or even of their financial position.

In short the early tyrants may have all been rich and all men of business and yet their riches and business activities may have been neither the basis nor the distinguishing feature of their rule. They arose in a many-sided age, and there were many other developments that might have conceivably brought them to the top. The doctrine of the divine right of kings had lost its hold. The struggles between the kings and the nobles had doubtless led both parties to appeal to the people, and from that it might well be no far step to the people's appointing its own rulers. Then again there had been a revolution in the art of war. The Homeric days were over when the heavy-armed chieftain was everything and his followers a more or less useless rabble. In the new kind of warfare large bodies of trained men-at-arms counted for everything[1]. Such a change might easily encourage a whole series of military officers to seize the supreme power. Furthermore in the case at any rate of the outlying Greek cities, and particularly those of Asia Minor[2], the constant danger from barbarian neighbours might readily suggest the appointment of a military dictator. And we do in fact find the early tyrants described as having been previously demagogues or soldiers.

But we find also that these descriptions go back only to Aristotle and have their source in fifth and fourth century conditions. Even if they went further back, the objection just raised against the commercial explanation applies still more strongly here. Kings and rulers who govern in fact as well as in name are generally something of public speakers or soldiers. It is almost an impossibility to find a self-raised ruler who cannot be described as either a demagogue or a polemarch[3].

Similarly with the notices about important offices of state alleged to have been held by various tyrants before they attained to supreme power. They are indeed among the most reliable items of information that we possess about the early tyrants. But their significance can be easily overrated. If ever a merchant who was aiming at the tyranny sought to strengthen his political influence by obtaining office, the record of his magistracy would be much more likely to be preserved than that of his commercial successes. When we come to the detailed evidence as presented in the previous pages the balance in favour of the commercial theory may be claimed as decisive.

If once the commercial origin of the tyrants' power is admitted, the various facts recorded about individual tyrants certainly gain in meaning and coherence. The mercenaries, the monetary reforms and innovations, the public works, the labour legislation, the colonial policy and the commercial alliances with foreign states, which have

---

[1] Beloch, *Gr. G.*² i. i. 348.   [2] Beloch, *Gr. G.*² i. i. 359.

[3] Cp. recent days, when a relapse into some of the conditions of the dark ages turned "business men" into polemarchs or publicists and in some notorious cases into both combined.

been repeatedly found associated with the early tyrants and which give the preserved accounts of them such a distinct stamp, become far more significant if it is granted that the tyrant's power was based on his control of the labour and trade of his city. As has been already observed, the fact that a theory explains the connexions between an obviously connected group of phenomena is no proof of its truth: but on the other hand a theory which fails to explain satisfactorily such a connexion is at an obvious disadvantage as compared with one which does. That is one further reason why the typical tyrant is not to be explained as a successful soldier or demagogue whose riches came to him suddenly at the same moment as his throne. The adventurer of either of these types might indeed further the commercial developments of the city that he had seized. It would be of course to his interest to do so. But as a general rule the man who has secured a fortune at a single stroke does not care to improve it by years of patient and organized effort. If all or any considerable number of the tyrants reviewed above had owed their positions to their sword or their tongue, there would inevitably have been some cases of commercial retrogression under the tyrannis, whereas in fact there are none.

This is a fundamental fact. The tyrants were one and all first-class business men. If they did not deliberately use their wealth to secure their position, there is only one other possible explanation of their history: their financial abilities must have led their fellow-countrymen to put them in the way of seizing the throne, and that is roughly the account of them that is to be found in some modern histories, where they are vaguely pictured as the more or less passive products of blind economic forces. This view seems to me untenable. It cannot be reconciled with the impression made by the early tyrants on writers like Aristotle. More fatal still, we have a series of "lawgivers" like Solon, who was a business man who gained his position precisely in the way just indicated. Some of Solon's friends reproached him with his folly in not making himself tyrant. But the fact remains that no "lawgiver" of the period did so[1], and that the titles of νομοθέτης and αἰσυμνήτης that were given these legally appointed dictators were never applied either by friends or enemies to any of the tyrants at any period of their careers[2].

[1] Except perhaps Pheidon, who is exceptional in other ways as well.
[2] The lawgiver and the tyrant are often sharply contrasted, e.g. Lucian, Phalaris A, 8.

One fact has still to be explained. Different as are the views about tyrants and tyranny expressed by different ancient writers at different times they have this feature in common. All alike express their hatred of tyrannical government. For Plato the man who becomes a tyrant "is changed from a man into a wolf[1]." When Herodotus digresses into a debate on the merits of the chief forms of government, he makes the critic of tyranny declare that there is nothing more unjust than it or more bloodthirsty in the whole world[2]. There is no judgment from heaven on the man who lays low a tyrant. This doctrine of Theognis[3] is perpetually preached all through Greek history. Harmodius and Aristogeiton the Athenian tyrannicides were celebrated in sculpture[4] and in song[5] and their names were constantly on the lips of orators[6].

There are apparent exceptions to this attitude. The Aristotelian *Constitution of Athens*, chapter XVI., records that "the tyranny of Peisistratus was often praised as the life of the days of Kronos," *i.e.* as the Golden Age, and the pseudo-Platonic *Hipparchus*, 229 *b*, speaks of it in similar terms: (under the tyrants) "the Athenians lived much as in the days when Kronos was king." But the Aristotelian version states also what it was that evoked this praise. "Peisistratus always secured peace and maintained quiet. Therefore his tyranny was often praised." The phraseology of the two quotations shows that the praise was given not to the form of government, but to the peaceful life that it procured, a life that might be, and sometimes has been, associated with the most oppressive of governments.

The word tyrant appears to be Lydian, and to have been first applied among the Greeks to the rulers who followed in the steps of the Lydian Gyges, whom some ancient writers describe as the first tyrant[7]. Originally it was used in a colourless sense as a synonym for king or monarch[8]. It is still so used in the tragedians

---

[1] *Rep.* 566 a. [2] v. 92.
[3] 1181–2; cp. 1203–4. [4] E. Gardner, *Greek Sculpture*[2] figs. 44, 45.
[5] *E.g.* the famous drinking-song beginning ἐν μύρτου κλαδί.
[6] For hatred and condemnation of tyranny or praise of tyrannicides see further Aristoph. *Thesm.* 335 f.; Polyb. v. 11; Cic. *de Off.* III. 6; Xenoph. *Hiero*, II. 8; Plut. *Timol.* 5, 37; Ael. *V.H.* XIV. 22. [7] See above, pp. 133–4.
[8] Nordin, *Klio*, v. pp. 402 f., explains the title τύραννος as adopted in the seventh century because kingship was then revived as a reality while king meant a functionary who was essentially powerless. This explanation may well be true, but it throws no light on the character of the revived reality.

and frequently in Herodotus[1]. But wherever the tyrant is spoken of in contradistinction to the king it is always in terms of detestation.

It must have been something in the character of the early tyrants that first gave the word the evil connotation, which it has preserved until this day[2]. What that something was is not easy to determine with certainty. Much of it may be mere misrepresentation. Aristotle[3] makes a statement about the tyrants with whom he was acquainted that is generally true of all monarchies. The tyrant, he says, "supports the people and the masses against the nobles (γνωρίμους)." We must not forget that the extant narratives represent almost exclusively the point of view of the aristocracy. It has often been suggested that this fact may account for the almost unanimous condemnation of the tyranny. But is this explanation altogether adequate? The Greek tyrant and the Roman rex are not the only monarchs who have had a bad press. The Emperors of Rome and the kings of Israel and Judah suffered likewise. Yet Jewish priests and Roman senators were not able to turn the titles of King and Emperor and Caesar into a byword and reproach. There must have been some very special circumstances to account for the universal execration of the name of tyrant. Is it not perhaps to be found in the commercial character of its origin? From the days of the Zeus-born king of Homer and long before, back to the very beginnings of leadership among men, legitimate kingship has always been held to rest upon the personal capacity of the ruler. This is the basis of belief in hereditary monarchy, or any other system that attaches

---

[1] *E.g.* I. 7, 73, 100, 109; II. 147 (the dominions of the twelve rulers who divided Egypt after Sethon are called tyrannies, the rulers themselves are called kings); v. 113 ("Philokypros, whom Solon of Athens, when he came to Cyprus, praised in his poems most of all tyrants" (τυράννων μάλιστα)); VII. 52, 99, 164; VIII. 67, 137, 142.

[2] The term has of course at different periods been applied to governments that differed widely from one another both in the character and in the basis of their power. There is no reason for classing Cypselus and Dionysius together as the same kind of ruler, as Holm (*Gk. Hist.* I. p. 266, n. 15), followed by Bury (*Gk. Hist.*[2] p. 147; cp. Francotte, *Mélanges*, pp. 62 f.), has gone out of his way to do. Holm's points have already been met: they are (1) For Phalaris, Peisistratus and Polycrates brute force was as indispensable as for later tyrants like Dionysius and Agathocles. (2) These latter owed their rise as much as earlier tyrants to the hatred that the lower classes bore the nobles. (3) Herodotus does not distinguish king from tyrant. Bury's dogmatism on this point and his denial of the existence of an "age of tyrants" is responsible for the inception of this book.

[3] *Pol.* VII. (v.), 1310b.

great importance to birth and upbringing. It is no less the basis of much republicanism which from one point of view is merely a denial of the value of heredity and specialized political education. Men have often been ready, and with reason, to endure much from a ruler whose power is based on his personality. But there is one basis of political power that mankind has never tolerated, and that basis is mere riches. They have felt with Plato that the plutocrat as such has no right at all to rule. "He seemed to be one of the city rulers," says Plato[1], of the oligarch whose power is based on his wealth, "but in reality he was neither its ruler nor its servant, but merely a consumer of its stores." Plato was here at one with his countrymen[2]. In the fifth century, as we know from the history of the wealthy Nikias, riches did not exclude an Athenian from the highest position in the state. But neither did they constitute a claim to political power. In his famous funeral oration Pericles twice claims that at Athens poverty is no bar to a political career. Pericles is speaking of course for his own age. If the evidence collected in this book has any value, the state of things during the first four generations or so after the invention of a metal coinage was very different. Money for a while became the measure of a man, and wealth by itself brought political power.

We must beware of expecting simplicity anywhere in history[3]. Even from the purely commercial point of view there were doubtless powerful side-currents that have left no trace in our extant records. The power of the Medici in Florence was based on their commercial supremacy. But it did not rest entirely on their actual trading. In part it was based on their position in the Papal treasury among the mercatores Romanam curiam sequentes, and in part again on the struggle between Emperor and Pope[4]. Similar factors must have influenced the careers of Pheidon and other early tyrants of Greece. In part again these early tyrants seem to have stood for a racial movement. This was certainly the case at Sicyon, where the tyranny marked the ascendancy of the pre-Dorian population; probably also at Corinth, where the first tyrant's father belonged to the Aeolic

---

[1] *Rep.* 552 *b.*

[2] Cp. Isocr. *Paneg.* 62 (105), "thinking it monstrous that the few should be masters of the many and that those who are below them in point of property but in other respects not a whit their inferiors should be excluded from office."

[3] Poehlmann, *Grundriss*[4], p. 73, n. 1 (my theory a "falsche Verallgemeinerung"). [4] Sieveking, *Viertelj. Soc. Wirt.* VII. p. 81.

pre-Dorian element of the population[1]. This racial factor is easily reconciled with the commercial, quite apart from the possibility that the pre-Dorian element that comes to the top at this period may have been closely related to the Levantine race that plays so prominent a part in Aegean commerce of the present day.

Nor must the personal element be left out of account, though so lamentably little is known about it. Cypselus and Pheidon, Peisistratus and Polycrates were certainly great personalities in their way. The leaders in any movement are generally that. On the whole they seem to have ruled well. Their government, except towards opponents and rivals, was by no means oppressive. All the more surprising therefore is their general condemnation. It is indeed scarcely possible to explain it except on the view that they ruled by right not of their personalities but of their riches. The prosperity that they brought to their cities was altogether material. The famous works of Polycrates were altogether the works of men's hands. It is characteristic of the rule of a typical early tyrant like Periander that he encouraged the worship of Dionysus and Aphrodite at the expense of the cults of Poseidon and Apollo[2]. No doubt his object was partly to break down the monopoly of priestly office and religious privilege that had hitherto been enjoyed by the aristocracy[3]: but it is significant that while the tyrants' policy meant a material advance in all directions, it meant also a materialization even of religion. That is why with a clearness of judgment that can be matched outside Greece only in Dante, the united verdict of all the Greeks utterly condemned them.

Two centuries after the expulsion of the tyrants from Athens, the city again fell under a ruler who is said to have made its material welfare his chief care, and "to have prided himself that there was much profitable trade in the city and that all enjoyed in abundance the necessaries of life." Such according to Demochares, a nephew of Demosthenes, was the boast of Demetrius of Phaleron, and for it he is utterly condemned by Demochares as "taking pride in things that might be a source of pride to a tax-collector or an artizan." The condemnation is quoted by Polybius as "no common charge[4]."

[1] How and Wells, *Hdt.* v. 92 β 1, regard an anti-Dorian reaction as a usual feature of early Peloponnesian tyrannies.
[2] Busolt, *Lakedaim.* I. p. 209; cp. Hdt. I. 23; Suid. s.v. Ἀρίων; Strabo VIII. 378.
[3] Busolt, *Lakedaim.* I. p. 210.
[4] Polyb. XII. 13.

Polybius plainly regards it as particularly damning, for he quotes it *à propos* of certain monstrous charges that were current about Demochares to prove that Demetrius must have refrained from supporting them for lack of evidence and not from lack of ill-will. Demochares and Polybius are a long step from the early tyrants: but both in a sense belong to the period that followed the tyrants' fall. Their views about Demetrius and his materialistic policy may well be an inheritance from an earlier age.

The age of the tyrants lasted for little more than five generations, and never so long as that in any one city[1]. This fact may have some consolation for those who fear a modern tyranny of wealth, and offers perhaps an analogy for the observations of H. G. Wells on the transitory character of the modern financial boss[2]. The determination not to be permanently governed by mere wealth is as strong to-day as it was twenty-five centuries ago. "The loathing of capital with which our labouring classes to-day are growing more and more infected" is explained by William James[3] as "largely composed of this sound sentiment of antipathy for lives based on mere having." He contrasts[4] the "military and aristocratic" ideal of the "well-born man without possessions."

It is of course particularly hard to test the scorn of possessions of a class that can always help itself to them at a crisis, and, as William James himself admits, the ideal has always been "hideously corrupted[5]." Certainly at the present day the antipathies between aristocracy and militarism and capitalism are, to say the least of it, not particularly marked. It is the democracy that loathes capitalism. But this may be merely a phase. The anti-capitalist movement may end by labour becoming fatally materialised or fatally impoverished, and in any country where that happens the way will be open for a new Peisistratus.

[1] Except at Sicyon it seldom lasted more than two generations; cp. Hdt. v. 92, where the oracle prophesies that Cypselus and his sons shall be kings of famed Corinth, but not his sons' sons, αὐτὸς καὶ παῖδες, παίδων γε μὲν οὐκέτι παῖδες.

[2] *Anticipations*, pp. 156–7; cp. the North of England saying that it is three generations from clogs to clogs.

[3] *Varieties of Religious Experience*, p. 319.

[4] *Ibid.* p. 318.

[5] Cp. H. G. Wells, *Tono Bungay*[1], p. 486, on the governing classes of Great Britain as seen at Westminster, "the realities are greedy trade, base profit-seeking, bold advertisement—and kingship and chivalry...are dead."

Appendix A (to p. 37). *The supposed Agricultural and Northern Diakria*

THE agricultural or pastoral explanation of the party that supported Peisistratus has no inherent probability[1]. Of course if it was specifically stated on good authority that in his days people of either of these two classes played the decisive part in politics, objections would be silenced. But the ancient evidence points all the other way. Aristotle repeatedly states that of all people farmers and herdsmen are least prone to support revolutions[2], and definitely pictures these two classes as having played an entirely passive part both under the regime of the early tyrants and during its establishment[3]. When on the throne Peisistratus gave financial help to impoverished farmers[4], a fact that is brought by Grundy[5] into connexion with his supposed agricultural Diakrioi. But in doing so Grundy disregards some of the words that he himself quotes, which show that the tyrant is dealing not with his supporters but with a body of men who were not interested in politics but threatened to become so if driven off the land. Geographically there is nothing to connect with the Diakria the men whom Peisistratus thus relieved. In his earlier days the most distressed and discontented part of the agricultural population were the pelatai and hektemoroi[6] who worked the lands of the rich[7] and therefore presumably lived in the Plain.

(A) The farming population took little part in politics,

According to the *Constitution of Athens* the hill men were made up largely of people not of pure race, whose claim to citizenship was more than doubtful[8]. Such a description is singularly inapplicable to the people on the land in Attica, where in the fifth

---

[1] See *e.g.* Mauri, *Citt. Lav. dell' Attica*, p. 30.
[2] Aristot. *Pol.* VIII. (VI.), 1319 a.   [3] *Ibid.* 1318 b.
[4] Aristot. *Ath. Pol.* 16; cp. Ael. *V.H.* IX. 25 and Max. Tyr. XXIII. (Teubner, =Duebner, p. 117).
[5] Grundy, *Thuc. and his Age*, p. 117.
[6] For a full discussion of these people see Gilliard, *Réformes de Solon*, chap. VI.
[7] Aristot. *Ath. Pol.* 2.
[8] οἱ τῷ γένει μὴ καθαροί...ὡς πολλῶν κοινωνούντων τῆς πολιτείας οὐ προσῆκον. Aristot. *Ath. Pol.* 13.

century they still prided themselves on having an undisturbed autochthonous population. Plutarch speaks of the hill men as a "mob of hirelings[1]." In the days just after Solon shepherds and small farmers of the hektemor class may have been hirelings, but they can hardly have ever been a mob.

There is therefore little to be said for the attempt to identify the hill men with the shepherds and hypothetical farmers of Mount Parnes. We cannot even be certain that the latter ever existed.

The soil of Attica was notoriously poor, abounding in stony districts ($\phi\epsilon\lambda\lambda\epsilon\hat{\iota}s$) useful only for pasture[2]. Attica claimed to be the land not of corn but of the olive. Demeter had her seat not in the great plain of Attica, but in the small and much more fertile plain of Eleusis.

None of the champions of an agricultural hill party dwelling on Mount Parnes seems to have seriously enquired into the upper limit of cultivation with wheat on the mountains of Attica. The only ancient writers who talk of agriculture being carried on there are the writer of the Aristotelian *Constitution of Athens* and Statius.

and lived but little on the mountains,

The former[3] tells the story of the man with the farm on Hymettus ($\tau\grave{o}\nu$ $\dot{\epsilon}\nu$ $\tau\hat{\wp}$ $\Upsilon\mu\eta\tau\tau\hat{\wp}$ $\gamma\epsilon\omega\rho\gamma\upsilon\hat{\upsilon}\nu\tau\alpha$). The story says nothing about the frequency of farms on Hymettus or of the height up the hill-

---

[1] $\theta\eta\tau\iota\kappa\grave{o}s$ $\emph{ὄχλος}$, Plut. *Sol.* 29.

[2] Thuc. I. 2. Xenophon indeed, *de Vect.* 1. 3, calls Attica all productive ($\pi\alpha\mu\phi\rho\omega\tau\acute{a}\tau\eta$), and declares that things that could not even grow in many places bear fruit in Attica. But the context shows that this only applies to the most favoured districts, cp. *ibid.* 5, quoted below; the reference, too, is strictly to the variety of Attic crops (doubtless a result of Athenian luxury and enterprise); cp. Plato, *Critias*, 110*e*–111*a*: "(fifth century) Attica can vie with any land in the variety and excellence of its products ($\tau\hat{\wp}$ $\pi\acute{a}\mu\phi\rho\rho o\nu$ $\epsilon\mathring{\upsilon}\kappa\alpha\rho\pi\acute{o}\nu$ $\tau\epsilon$ $\epsilon\mathring{\iota}\nu\alpha\iota$); but in those days" (*i.e.* in the mythical past) "in addition to their quality it produced them in great abundance." Theophrastus, *Hist. Plant.* VIII. 8, says that "at Athens the barley produces more meal than anywhere else, since it is an excellent land for that crop"; but this says nothing as to the amount of land in Attica under barley. Boeckh, *Public Economy*, I. p. 109, calculates that in ancient Attica 955,500 plethra out of a total area of 2,304,000 were under corn; but his calculation is based on a series of conjectures as to the yearly consumption and import which hardly weigh against the considerations adduced below.

[3] Aristot. *Ath. Pol.* 16. So (*ap.* Leutsch, *Paroemiograph. Gr.* II. p. 756) Mantissa, I. 76 (where Peisistratus expresses surprise at anyone farming such land, $\tau\acute{\iota}\nu\alpha s$ $\kappa\alpha\rho\pi o\grave{\upsilon}s$ $\mathring{a}\nu\alpha\iota\rho o\acute{\upsilon}\mu\epsilon\nu o s$ $\tau o\iota\alpha\hat{\upsilon}\tau\alpha$ $\gamma\epsilon\omega\rho\gamma o\acute{\iota}\eta$ $\chi\omega\rho\acute{\iota}\alpha$), and, with no reference to Hymettus, Zenob. IV. 76 (*ap.* eosd. I. p. 105).

side of this particular farm. But it does say something about the soil and the crops. The soil consisted of stones, the crops, so the farmer told Peisistratus, were "troubles and sorrows." This hardly suggests that in the days of the tyranny Hymettus was of any great importance agriculturally. The same conclusion is suggested by the story of the clever Pelasgians who succeeded in cultivating the land at the foot of Hymettus, much to the surprise of the Athenians[1].

Statius[2] speaks of the ploughmen of fragrant Hymettus (olentis arator Hymetti), and the vineyards of Parnes (Parnesque benignus uitibus). The former is almost a contradiction in terms. Fragrant is an allusion to the famous honey of Hymettus, or to the thyme that produced it[3]. Thyme and honey do not go with cornfields. A "Parnes kindly to vines" is not easily reconciled with Pausanias, who makes the mountain a good hunting-place for bears and wild boars[4]. Plato declares that in his days some of the Attic mountains were barren except for their yield of honey[5], whereas once they had been covered with forests[6], some of which had only recently been cut down. The fame of the honey of Hymettus went so far back, that the mountain was claimed as the place where bees were first created[7]. Aristotle divides bees according to whether their haunts are cultivated ($\ddot{\eta}\mu\epsilon\rho\alpha$) or mountainous ($\dot{o}\rho\epsilon\iota\nu\acute{a}$). The latter are described in the next sentence as haunting the forests ($\dot{v}\lambda o\nu\acute{o}\mu o\iota$)[8].

At the present day the Attic mountains are scarcely cultivated at all[9], *which were occupied by forests and wild beasts.* and though in ancient Attica cultivation may have been more intense, yet apart from the difficulties of carrying it up the mountain side, the whole scheme of life presupposes vast supplies of timber for shipbuilding, fuel, and countless other purposes. Bursian is probably right when he says that in antiquity Parnes was "thickly covered with forest in which numerous beasts found shelter, including wild boars and bears[10]." During the period of Athens' greatness, between

---

[1] Hdt. VI. 137.
[2] Stat. *Theb.* XII. 622, 620.   [3] Athen. I. 28 d, θύμον Ὑμήττιον.
[4] Paus. I. 32; cp. Plut. *Sol.* 23 (Solon offered rewards for killing wolves).
[5] Plato, *Critias*, 111 c; cp. references, Bursian, *Geog. Gr.* I. p. 254.
[6] Cp. the "forest clad mountain (ὄρος κατaειμένον ὕλῃ)" of *Odyss.* XIII. 351.
[7] Columella IX. 2.
[8] Aristot. *Hist. Anim.* IX. 624 b.
[9] Zimmern, *Greek Commonwealth*, p. 44, quoting J. L. Myres.
[10] Bursian, *Gr. Geog.* I. p. 252; cp. Cavaignac, *Études Financ.* p. 13; Guiraud, *Prop. Fonc.* p. 505, n. 5. Bursian is based on Paus. I. 32 (quoted above).

550 and 350 B.C., the supply of timber must have been constantly diminishing. Yet towards the end of the fifth century the charcoal-burners had their centre at Acharnae, below the southern slopes of Parnes, only about seven or eight miles from Athens. Thucydides excludes Acharnae from the plain[1], and we must infer that it was not then the land of corn and vines that it is now. If not forest it was waste. If the land round Acharnae had not been claimed for farming, it is hardly likely that farmers abounded higher up[2].

The same inference is suggested by a passage of Xenophon which implies that corn could not be grown in the mining district, which is distinctly hilly but does not reach anything like the height of Pentelicon, Hymettus, or Parnes, "and there is also land which when sown does not bear fruit, but being mined supports a population many times larger than it would if it was producing corn: and its argentiferous character is plainly due to Providence," etc.[3]

Then again frequent mention is made in ancient Attic documents of "boundary estates" and these are explained by the scholiast to Aeschines as "lands on the border of the country, extending either to the mountains or the sea[4]." Such a definition implies that the mountains were almost as unused to cultivation as the sea itself.

---

[1] Thuc. II. 20, 23; cp. Loeper, *Ath. Mitt.* XVII. (1892), p. 394, n. 1.

[2] Another possibility is to equate the Plain of Thucydides with the Parts round the City of Cleisthenes. This is only probable on the assumption that the Cleisthenic triple division followed the lines of the old local parties, and that the old names persisted in unofficial usage. It implies that the Peisistratan Diakria corresponded roughly to the Cleisthenic Mesogeia and extended far south of Brauron (see p. 311). But more probably Thucydides is using "plain" in its natural sense of low-lying level open country.

[3] Xen. *de Vect.* I. 5; cp. Strabo IX. 400, "far the best honey comes from the mining district." The passage from the *de Vect.* is misunderstood by Grundy, *Thuc. and his Age*, p. 151, n. 2, who says, "the reference is certainly to a widespread system of market-gardening and perhaps also to the purchasing power of the product of vine cultivation." Grundy gives no evidence that cabbages or other vegetables or even wine were many times as valuable as corn; he plainly takes ὀρυττομένη as though it were σκαπτομένη, and appears to think that the sentence refers to Attica at large, a view that is rendered most unlikely both by the language (ἔστι δὲ καὶ γῆ ἡ σπειρομένη οὐ φέρει καρπόν, not καὶ σπειρομένη μὲν ἡ γῆ οὐ φέρει καρπόν), and the context (the crops of Attica are finished with in I. 4, and the sentence just quoted follows a statement about the Attic quarries and precedes the declaration that the mines are the gift of God).

[4] Schol. Aesch. *c. Timarch.* 97 (13); cp. Harpocrat. s.v. ἐσχατιά, and *Lex. Seguer. ap.* Bekker, *Anec. Gr.* p. 256. See further Boeckh, *Pub. Econ.* I. p. 86.

In Italy too the limit of cultivation of wheat seems to have been low. Latin writers repeatedly contrast the forest-clad mountains with the arable lowlands, and in some cases the mountains that these writers have in mind are considerably lower than the heights of Parnes[1].

Enough has been said to show how little reason there is for picturing the mountains of North and East Attica in the days of Peisistratus as the home of a large and active agricultural population. It remains for us to examine the evidence for thinking that this district was known as the "Hill Country." We shall find that if possible it is flimsier still. The supporters of the prevailing view base their case mainly on the definition of the Diakria found in the printed editions of Hesychius. This definition is the main source of all existing misconceptions. It is necessary therefore to examine it. The words of Hesychius as generally quoted are these. "Diakrieis: not only certain of the Euboeans but also of the Athenians: also a place ($\tau \acute{o} \pi o \varsigma$) in Attica: the Diakria is the land from Parnes to Brauron." The modern name for the hills at Brauron is Περάτι (End), which seems at first sight to harmonize well with the definition of the Diakria just quoted. But if we examine any good map of Attica, we see that Περάτι does not end the Southern extension of Parnes; it forms the North-east extremity of the hills of South Attica. That is a first difficulty. It is at least unusual to define the limits of a district by places beyond those limits. We do not say that Germany extends from Tilsit to Verviers.

(B) The case for a North-east "Hill Country" rests on misreadings or misinterpretations of ancient authorities.

The second objection is far more serious. It is that the MSS. say nothing of Brauron. The word they give is Balylon (εἰς Βαλυλωνος, sic). This was emended by Aldus to Babylon. Brauron is a conjecture of Palmerius, and by no means a certain one. In Byzantine times the familiar Babylon (pronounced Vavylon) would indeed be a very natural corruption for the then obscure Brauron (pronounced Vrafron). The MS. Balylon is not nearly so likely to be a phonetic corruption of Brauron. It might conceivably be an

---

[1] Lucret. v. 1370–5; Virg. *Aen.* XI. 316–20 and Servius, *ad loc.*; cp. *Aen.* XI. 569; Tac. *Ann.* I. 17. The Latin evidence all shows that when Pliny, *N.H.* XVIII. 12, says that foreign wheat can only be compared with the mountain crops of Italy (montanis Italiae agris), he is using "mons" of anything that is not valley. Caesar, it should be remembered, speaks of the mountains of Kent.

orthographic corruption of Aulon, a place or region in the mining district in the extreme South of Attica[1]. The εἰς with the genitive of the MS. suggests however some more complete corruption[2].

But even if the reading "to Brauron (εἰς Βραυρῶνα)" were certain, Hesychius would still be a doubtful authority on this point. His definition of the "Coast" runs thus: "the Coast: Attica, whence also the ship Paralos (ἡ παραλία· ἡ Ἀττική, ἔνθεν καὶ ἡ ναῦς πάραλος)." This presumably means that the Coast was a synonym for Attica, the coastland *par excellence*. Such a definition might be supported by philological connexions between Ἀττική and ἀκτή[3]. Conceivably with ἡ Ἀττική we should understand not γῆ but παραλία: the Coast means *par excellence* the Attic coast (compare the modern "Riviera"). This interpretation is supported by our author's definition of the men of the coast (οἱ πάραλιοι), which runs "those who occupy the coast of Attica." Neither interpretation vindicates Hesychius as an authority on the triple division of Attica. He makes no mention of the Plain.

Modern writers, it is true, give the word "coast" (παραλία) a conventional meaning and confine it to the Southern apex of the Attic triangle, the district of Attica that has the largest proportion of coast to interior[4]. Their view has one fact in its favour. After the expulsion of the tyrants, when Cleisthenes set himself to break up the old local political parties, the whole of this Southern apex was included among the "coast" trittyes or (th)ridings of his new triple division of the whole country. But there are indications that the inclusion of this whole district in the coast was never anything but an artificial arrangement[5] to prevent either of the other two divisions from overbalancing the coast[6]. The Cleisthenic coast was

---

[1] *C.I.A.* II. 782; Aeschin. *c. Timarch.* 121 (17).

[2] The MS. is much abbreviated and very corrupt, Schow, *Hesych.* p. x.

[3] Cp. Strabo IX. 391.

[4] Cp. the maps of Milchhoefer, *Abh. Berl. Acad.* 1892 after p. 48, and Loeper, *Ath. Mitt.* XVII. pl. XII. Milchhoefer's "coast" goes considerably further North than Loeper's.

[5] Perhaps not altogether so, at least after the Persian peril and Themistocles had given the mining district something of a naval character. See *Ath. Mitt.* x. p. 111.

[6] "It would be tedious to enumerate the demes of the interior owing to their number," Strabo IX. 399, just after a (presumably full) enumeration of the Attic coast demes. The city was probably growing rapidly at the time of Cleisthenes' reforms.

of course not confined to this Southern apex. The moderns who imagine this restricted use base their assumption on a misunderstanding of their authorities. They quote Thucydides II. 55, where in reference to a Peloponnesian raid on Southern Attica he speaks of "the so-called coast land." But the precise words of Thucydides show that the ravages were confined to the coast[1], while inscriptions and passages in other writers prove that the name "coast" was not confined to the Southern apex of Attica but was normally applied to the whole Attic seaboard[2]. When Thucydides uses the expression "what is called the coast land" he need not be taken as meaning that the name "coast" in Attica was used as a synonym for what Herodotus calls the Sunium Heights[3]. Very possibly he is commenting rather on the fact that the Attic coast was called by the poetical name πάραλος γῆ, παραλία (the land of the brine) instead of the good fifth century prose word παραθαλάσσιος, ἐπιθαλάσσιος (the land by the sea). He himself uses ἐπιθαλάσσιος in the very next chapter for the coast land of the Peloponnese[4].

Another text which has been thought[5] to establish a Northern or North-Eastern Diakria and a Southern Paralia is a fragment of Sophocles[6] in which the mythical king Pandion divides Attica between his three sons. Two scholia of Aristophanes[7] and a notice in Suidas[8] equate the North-Eastern of these divisions with the Diakria. But against this equation must be set that of Stephanus Byzantinus[9], who says that the Diakria fell to the son who received according to Sophocles the Southern division.

[1] "First they ravaged the land that looks towards the Peloponnesus, then (ἔπειτα δέ) that which faces Euboea and Andros." "The addition of δέ emphasizes the antithesis," Marchant, *Thuc.* II. ad loc.

[2] Hdt. V. 81; Strabo IX. 395, 400; *C.I.A.* II. 1059 (cp. Strabo IX. 398), 1194, 12c6b, 1195.

[3] γουνὸς Σουνιακός, Hdt. IV. 99. The meaning of γουνός is not certain, but see Liddell and Scott s.v.: Macaulay translates "hill region."

[4] Hesych. and Suid. explain παραλία and πάραλος by παραθαλάσσιος, M. Psellus by ἐπιθαλαττίδιον.

[5] See Loeper, *Ath. Mitt.* XVII. p. 429.
[6] Strabo IX. 392.
[7] *Vesp.* 1223, *Lysis*, 58.
[8] Suid. s.v.
[9] Steph. Byz. s.v.

Appendix B (to p. 168). *The Date of the Argive-Aeginetan Embargo on Attic Pottery*

THE outstanding facts in the history of Attic pottery are these. During the dark ages Attic pottery takes perhaps the foremost place in the whole of Greece Proper. The dominant ware of this period is of a well defined style generally known as Geometric, of which the Attic "Dipylon" ware (fig. 43) is a superior and well

Fig. 43. Dipylon vase.

represented variety[1], that appears to have been in considerable request beyond the borders of Attica[2]. The period of eclipse for Attic pottery is the seventh century and the beginning of the sixth. During this period oriental influences made themselves felt in all Greek arts and crafts. In Greece Proper the dominant pottery of the period is the Corinthian (figs. 22, 34), and another ware that began somewhat earlier but largely overlapped it, generally known as Proto-Corinthian (fig. 44). These two fabrics flooded most of Greece as well as Sicily and Italy, and are found in abundance in many Greek cities of the East. But in Attica Dipylon ware seems to have held the market well into the seventh century[3], and to have been followed by the vases known as Proto-Attic and Phaleron[4], which occupy only a humble place in the ceramic history of the period[5]. Then in the first half of the sixth century Attica developed its famous Black Figure style (fig. 41), that quickly drove all competitors out of the market.

Fig. 44. Proto-Corinthian vase.

From the commercial point of view an embargo on Attic pottery

[1] See *e.g.* Kroker, *Jahrb.* I. pp. 112-13; Buschor, *Gr. Vasenmal.*¹ p. 39; Mueller and Oelmann, *Tiryns*, I. p. 161.
The Geometric of the Argolid is described by Poulsen, *Dipylongräber*, p. 66, as a "featureless variety" (unpersönliche Gattung).

[2] On export of Dipylon ware see Pottier *ap.* Saglio, *Dict. d. Ant.* s.v. vases, p. 634; Prinz, *Funde aus Naukratis*, p. 77 (Cyprus and Thera).

[3] Beloch, *Rhein. Mus.* 1890, p. 590, following Kroker, *Jahrb.* I. pp. 95 f., who however is mistaken (*ibid.* p. 113) in dating Dipylon vases with war ships depicted in action as necessarily later than 664 B.C. See below, pp. 321 f. So also F. Poulsen, *Dipylongräber*, pp. 13 (seventh? century Egyptian objects in Dipylon graves), 27-28 (Proto-Corinthian vases in Attic Geometric graves).

[4] Boehlau, *Jahrb.* II. (1887), pp. 33-66. For the name Phaleron see *Jahrb.* II. p. 44.

[5] Late seventh century Attic ware, style of Netos amphora, has been found at Naukratis, where Prinz, *Funde*, p. 77, argues that it must have been taken by Aeginetans, since Aegina was the only European Greek city with a concession at Naukratis. But for the general poverty of Athens at that period cp. the Acropolis finds, which show some thousand Dipylon sherds, as against only about forty Proto-Attic, 160 Vourva (Attic with zones of animals and rosette fill-ornament, date probably about 600 B.C.), fifteen Proto-Corinthian, and 125 Corinthian; Graef, *Vasen Acrop. Athen*, pp. 23, 34, 41, 44, 51. At least two of the Proto-Corinthian sherds, and a very considerable number of the Corinthian may be sixth century.

between about 670 and 570 B.C. would have been practically pointless. It is only before the earlier date and after the later that Attic pottery was a menace to its rivals. As between these dates all that is known of the history of pottery in the Argolid and Aegina inclines strongly in favour of the earlier period. The most ardent protectionist will admit that protection is useless without something to protect, and from 570 B.C. onwards neither Argos nor Aegina appears to have had any interest in any possible rival to Attic ware. But in the early part of the seventh century Argos and Aegina alike were flooded with both Corinthian[1] and Proto-Corinthian[2] pottery, and, as may be gathered from the traditions about the lot of Temenos[3], it is highly probable that they were much interested in pushing these wares, which are found in large quantities not only in Greece Proper, but also in Italy, Asia Minor, and even further afield[4]. Corinthian pottery is unquestionably a Corinthian product[5]. The place of origin of Proto-Corinthian is, as has been already noticed, much disputed. It has been claimed for Aegina itself[6], and for Argos[7]. Corinth is a possibility[8], as also is Chalcis, for which latter the abundant finds at Cumae are interesting but by no means decisive evidence[9]. Most archaeologists prefer Sicyon[10].

[1] Thiersch *ap.* Furtwaengler, *Aegina*, p. 451.
[2] *Ath. Mitt.* 1897, p. 262 (Aegina); Furtwaengler, *Aegina*, p. 448.
[3] Above, pp. 176 f.
[4] Prinz, *Funde aus Naukratis*, p. 69, following Loeschcke, *Ath. Mitt.* XXII. p. 264.
[5] Above, pp. 185-7, 241-3.
[6] Thiersch, *Aegina*, p. 448; Graef, *Woch. Klass. Phil.* 1893, p. 139.
[7] Hoppin, *Argive Heraeum*, I. p. 59, II. pp. 119 f. (arguing from the unbroken development of the style that can be traced in the Heraeum finds); Dragendorff, *Thera*, II. p. 193; but cp. Furtwaengler, *Aegina*, p. 477; *Berl. Phil. Woch.* 1895, p. 202; Poulsen, *Dipylongräber*, p. 75.
[8] Cp. finds at Corinth itself and at the Corinthian Syracuse. Corinthian is admittedly not a development of Proto-Corinthian; but from this to argue with Prinz, *Funde aus Nauk.* p. 70, that Proto-Corinthian cannot be a Corinthian product is to assume that an industry once in existence makes it impossible for a rival concern, producing a different style of article, to be started in the same city, even in the case of so cosmopolitan a centre as Corinth.
[9] Gabrici, *Mon. Ant.* XXII. p. 362; de Ridder, *de Ectypis*, p. 56, n. 4.
[10] Furtwaengler, *Aegina*, p. 477; Thiersch, *Aegina*, p. 448; Prinz, *Funde aus Nauk.* p. 70; K. F. Johansen, *Sikyoniske Vaser*. The Chigi vase, a Proto-Corinthian masterpiece, has an inscription in an alphabet that is neither Argive, Aeginetan, nor Chalcidian (see especially the lambda), but may well be Sicyonian.

The balance of expert opinion at present is certainly in favour of the North-east Peloponnesus[1]. In Chapter VI evidence is cited to show that the whole of this region was probably under Argive domination previous to the establishment of tyrannies at Corinth and Sicyon about the year 660 B.C. But after that the situation changes. Corinth and Sicyon become strong cities, friendly to one another and hostile to Argos[2]. Corinthian pottery eclipses all its rivals, with Proto-Corinthian as an easy but lagging second. If Argos had wanted protection for her native pottery in the second half of the seventh century, she would have excluded not Attic pottery, but the wares of Corinth, and perhaps Sicyon[3]. Attic pottery revived and began to dominate the Greek market about 570 B.C., and that is the date to which the embargo is assigned by Hoppin, who published the pottery from the Argive Heraeum. But if that was the date, then, as he himself declares, its motive can have been "nothing but simple spite, since no increased activity on the part of the Argive potters is the result[4]." The motive that Hoppin so rightly desiderated can best have been at work when Proto-Corinthian and Corinthian pottery was already on the market, but Corinth and Sicyon were not yet under tyrants.

Thus on *à priori* grounds the early years of the seventh century form far the most likely period for an Aeginetan or Argive embargo on the pottery of Attica[5]. The power that destroyed the Dipylon ships[6] might well have struck a blow at Dipylon pottery, if only to improve its own position in the carrying trade.

It remains to test this general probability by the evidence of the sites more immediately concerned.

In Aegina Attica Black Figure pottery has been found in some abundance[7]. In fact Attic pottery found a ready entrance from the

---

[1] Pottier in Saglio, *Dict. d. Ant.* s.v. Vases, p. 637, sums up for North Peloponnesus not far from Corinth; Frickenhaus, *Tiryns*, I. p. 103, Argolis but not Argos (cp. *ibid.* pp. 145–6, Mueller and Oelmann on a type of geometric Kraterskyphos common in the Argolid that leads up directly to Proto-Corinthian).

[2] Above, pp. 179–180.

[3] For Sicyonian potteries being important at this time see Waldstein, *Arg. Heraeum*, II. p. 166, n. 1, and cp. above, p. 316, n. 10.

[4] *Argive Heraeum*, II. p. 175.

[5] Busolt, *Gr. G.*² II. p. 200, thinks it dates "probably as early as the seventh century."   [6] Below, pp. 321 f.

[7] *B.S.A.* XI. pp. 226–7; Furtwaengler, *Aegina*, p. 478; Thiersch, *ibid.* p. 458; Pallat, *Ath. Mitt.* 1897, p. 324.

latter half of the seventh century onwards[1]. If there is any stage of Attic pottery that is poorly represented on the island, it is the Proto-Attic and Phaleron. Such at any rate is the evidence of the excavations at the temple of Aphaia; and the scarcity of early orientalizing Attic harmonizes with what is known of the Geometric pottery from the site. This latter style, so Thiersch reports[2], is richly represented, and in two groups, which are plainly imports from the neighbouring regions of Attica and the Argolid. The Attic ware predominates at first, the finds at Eleusis and the Athenian Kerameikos offering the closest analogies. Towards the end of the Geometric style, when it begins to connect up with Proto-Corinthian, the second great group of imports begins, with types that are also found in great numbers in the Argolid, at Tiryns and the Argive Heraeum.

Again, in the Aeginetan temple of Aphrodite, where the pottery found by Stais has been published by Pallat[3], Geometric sherds, in clay and technique not to be distinguished from Attic, were fairly numerous, but coming down from the eighth century to the seventh, we are told that the Attic pottery of the period, the so-called Proto-Attic, is represented only by a few types, some of which are perhaps only imitations of the genuine Attic.

Similarly, the excavators of the Argive Heraeum report that "in the Argolid we find the Geometric style ceasing almost abruptly, while the Argive style becomes as it were emancipated[4]." Argive is the Americans' name for Proto-Corinthian[5].

The vast majority of the fragments of this period from the Aphrodite temple are Proto-Corinthian or early Corinthian[6]. Attic pottery reappears among the finds of about the middle of the sixth century, with a few sherds of Kleinmeister kylikes. Pallat indeed[7]

---

[1] Thiersch *ap.* Furtwaengler, *Aegina*, p. 458 (Vourva).

[2] *Aegina*, p. 436; cp. Furtwaengler, *ibid.* p. 474.

[3] *Ath. Mitt.* 1897, pp. 265 f.

[4] *Argive Heraeum*, II. pp. 121-2. Hoppin, *ibid.* p. 102, thinks the Heraeum Geometric probably Argive rather than Attic. As regards the abrupt termination of Geometric on the Heraeum site, it should be remembered that the temple only dates from the eighth to the seventh century, Frickenhaus, *Tiryns*, p. 118, and that a previous secular settlement appears to have come to a violent end.

[5] And for much else as well, including some Argive.

[6] Pallat, *Ath. Mitt.* 1897, pp. 273 f., 315; cp. Studniczka, *Ath. Mitt.* 1899, pp. 361 f.

[7] *Ath. Mitt.* 1897, p. 332; cp. Buschor, *Gr. Vasenmal.*[1] pp. 64, 66.

speaks further on of the Proto-Attic (*i.e.* early seventh century Attic) that is richly represented at Aegina, and Loeschcke too speaks of all stages of Attic ware from Dipylon onwards occurring in the island[1]. Unfortunately, such terms as rare and abundant are still used by archaeologists in the loosest and most misleading way. The only vases Loeschcke quotes are a "Tyrrhenian" amphora, and an Ergotimos cup, *i.e.* two early sixth century vases, both from the Fontana collection, and attributed to Aegina only on the authority of dealers or collectors of the early part of the nineteenth century[2]. The fact remains that in the properly recorded excavations on the island, it is early in the seventh century that Attic pottery occupies its least prominent position, and that in the museum at Aegina[3], which includes the Aphaia finds and specimen pieces from the 1904 excavations at the Aphrodite temple, there is plenty of Mycenaean, Geometric, Proto-Corinthian, and Corinthian pottery, some early Black Figure (about 550 B.C.), and a fair number of late Black Figure vases, but no Proto-Attic at all.

For Argos the evidence is limited mainly to the finds from the Heraeum, the temple some miles from the city, that was excavated by the Americans. As mentioned already, the evidence from this site has been used for dating the embargo in the second half of the sixth century[4]. Unfortunately, the American report is mistaken in the dating of some of its finds. It ascribes to the first half of the sixth century the archaizing Attic potter Nikosthenes, who flourished in the second half[5]. The only two types of Attic fragments that the report states to have been found in considerable numbers[6] both belong to the latter part of the century, and not, as the report states, to the first half of it. The finds therefore can hardly be quoted as indicating an exclusion of Attic pottery that started in the middle of the sixth century. They include only a very few fragments of early seventh century Attic[7].

The indignant Argives and Aeginetans who, at the date that we are trying to determine, had crushed the Athenians in Aegina, did

---

[1] *Ath. Mitt.* 1897, p. 263.
[2] See *Arch.-epig. Mitt. aus Oesterreich*, II. pp. 17 f.
[3] Visited by the writer in the spring of 1914.
[4] How and Wells, *Hdt.* v. 88. 2.
[5] *Argive Heraeum*, II. p. 175; *C.R.* XII. pp. 86–87.
[6] *Argive Heraeum*, II. p. 177, nos. 14, 16.
[7] *Argive Heraeum*, II. p. 173.

not merely exclude Attic pottery from the temple or temples of their outraged deities. They insisted further on the exclusive use of local pottery. It is highly probable that a whole mass of this local pottery, used for this very purpose, has actually come down to us. In the recent excavations of the Heraeum at Tiryns, the vast majority of the dedicated vases are miniature vessels of local fabric. The number reaches nearly a thousand, forming a series that begins in the seventh century and runs right through the sixth century into the fifth[1]. Miniature vases similar in style, and presumably of about the same date, were found in like abundance in the Argive Heraeum[2], where they were dated by the Americans many centuries too early. They form the most characteristic series of vase dedications in the temple. It has been suggested with much plausibility by Frickenhaus in the Tiryns publication[3], that it was just such a mass of similar votive vases that was seen by Herodotus in the temple of Damia and Auxesia in Aegina. If Frickenhaus is right, the exclusion of Attic pottery from certain temples in Aegina and the Argolid is naturally put back at least into the seventh century. Frickenhaus refuses to believe that the use of these "native pots" was due to the reason given by Herodotus. But does the association of these harmless little local vases with an anti-Attic policy really look like an aetiological invention?

In the Aphaia temple on Aegina a quantity of local hand-made ware was found in the form of pots, jugs, plates, hydriae, amphorae, etc., large enough for use. Furtwaengler refers to them as $\chi \acute{v} \tau \rho a\iota$[4], another form of the word used by Herodotus of the native pots dedicated to Damia and Auxesia. Similar plain ware for practical use is found on many sites[5], and is not likely to have attracted the notice of Herodotus, though on the other hand the word that he uses (pots, $\chi v \tau \rho \acute{\iota} \delta \epsilon s$) points to plain coarse ware[6]. If this is the ware he noticed, our dating is not however affected, since the principal shapes find their nearest parallels in Geometric graves.

[1] Frickenhaus, *Tiryns*, I. pp. 97–98.
[2] *Argive Heraeum*, II. pp. 96–97; cp. *Tiryns*, I. pp. 97–98, 117.
[3] *Tiryns*, I. p. 95.
[4] Furtwaengler, *Aegina*, p. 441, quoting "pot dealer" ($\chi v \tau \rho \acute{o} \pi \omega \lambda \iota s$), applied to Aegina by Pollux VII. 197.
[5] *E.g.* Thera, see Dragendorff, *Thera*, II. p. 231.
[6] Cp. Prinz, *Funde aus Naukratis*, p. 69.

Appendix C (to p. 169). *Early Athenian Sea Power*

THE earliest naval battle known to Thucydides was fought between the Corinthians and the Corcyraeans in 664 B.C.[1]. The Dipylon ships are built with rams (fig. 45. *a*), which by itself sufficiently shows their warlike character[2]. Some of them are depicted fighting, or with fallen sailors lying all around (fig. 45. *c*)[3], a fact which led Kroker[4] to date them after 664 B.C. If Kroker's argument was sound, they would have to be dated later still, for it is highly unlikely that Athenian vases would depict for the local market a battle in which Athenians were not concerned[5]. But even 664 B.C. seems too late a date for the vases. Seventh century Greek pottery everywhere shows Oriental influence. This is the case with typical seventh century Attic, which is known as Proto-Attic and Phaleron ware. Dipylon pottery may have lasted on into this century, but it belongs mainly to the eighth and ninth[6]. A Geometric cup with a naval fight found at Eleusis[7] occurred in the lowest stratum of the Geometric graves and is dated by Poulsen fairly early in the style[8].

There is however no necessary discrepancy with Thucydides. Helbig[9] points out that all Dipylon fights seem to be duels between single pairs of ships. Most of these Dipylon war-ships are depicted on huge vases that took the place of tombstones, so that the single

---

[1] Thuc. I. 13.   [2] Torr, *Rev. Arch.*³ xxv. p. 25.

[3] Torr, *ibid.* figs. 3, 6 (probably), 10, 11, 12; Cartault, *Mon. Gr.* 1882-4, p. 53, figs. 2, 3.

[4] *Jahrb.* I. pp. 111-13; cp. Torr, *Rev. Arch.*³ xxv. p. 25. Kroker and Torr are answered by Pernice, *Ath. Mitt.* XVII. (1892), pp. 304-6; Pottier, *Cat. Vases Louvre*, I. pp. 222-3.

[5] On the same psychological grounds, quite apart from the historical evidence for Athenian naval power during the dark ages, we must reject Assmann's suggestion, *Arch. Anz.* 1895, pp. 118-19, that the Dipylon ships are the vessels of "the dreaded Phoenician pirates."

[6] Brueckner and Pernice, *Ath. Mitt.* XVIII. pp. 135-7; Pottier, *Cat. Vases Louvre*, I. pp. 231-3; Helbig, *Mém. Acad. Inscr. et B.-L.* XXXVI. (1898), p. 390.

[7] *Arch. Eph.* 1898, pl. V. 1.

[8] Poulsen, *Dipylongräber*, p. 100.

[9] *Mém. Acad. Inscr. et B.-L.* XXXVI. (1898), p. 400; *pace* Kroker, *Jahrb.* I. p. 111.

322 EARLY ATHENIAN APP. C

Fig. 45. Dipylon ships.

ship, or ship-duel, might be explained by the single sea-captain who lay beneath[1]. But against this explanation must be set the single ships and single ship fights on smaller Dipylon vases and the naval

Fig. 46. Vase painting signed by Aristonothos.

duel on the vase signed by Aristonothos, probably an Argive potter of the first half of the seventh century (fig. 46)[2]. One late Dipylon

[1] Suggested and rejected by Brueckner and Pernice, *Ath. Mitt.* XVIII. p. 153.
[2] *Wiener Vorlegeblätter*, 1888, pl. I. 8; Walters-Birch, *Hist. Anc. Pott.* I. pl. XVI.; Buschor, *Gr. Vasenmal.*[1] pp. 60–61.

fragment (fig. 45. *d*)¹ shows a ship's crew fighting warriors on land, and the vessel's prow, in which Helbig sees the form of a horse's head, is thought by him to indicate that it came from Caria or Phoenicia, where this kind of prow ornament is known to have been used². The horse's head is not very distinct. Its identification is regarded as uncertain by Furtwaengler³. At the best it is not decisive for Helbig's inference. But he is probably right, when he sees in the Athenian ships of the Dipylon period a naval force intended to protect Attica against pirates⁴, which may never have fought a pitched battle at all⁵.

Some such state of things as Helbig outlined is required to explain the behaviour of the naval forces of the combatants in the early Aeginetan war. The war is described as occurring just after the Aeginetans had built ships and become masters of the sea⁶. The fleet may have been the outcome of the shipbuilding recorded in the Hesiodic Eoiai, where it is said of the Aeginetans that they "were the first to fashion ships with oars on either side, and first to set up sails, the wings of the ship that crosses the sea⁷." The thalassocracy must have been local⁸, and may well mean simply that Aegina had outstripped Athens, and become the leading member of the Kalaurian league, though possibly it is to be associated with the early Aeginetan settlement at Naukratis⁹. The Athenians claimed to have sent only a single ship to Aegina. But this appears to have been the version of the official bulletin, with the incapacity apparently inherent in such documents for describing a serious reverse as such. "The Aeginetans said that the Athenians had come not with one ship but with many¹⁰."

¹ *Mém. Acad. Inscr. et B.-L.* xxxvi. (1898), p. 394, fig. *e* = *Arch. Zeit.* XLIII. (1885), pl. VIII. 1. Just after Helbig's publication another Attic Geometric vase was published by Skias from his excavations at Eleusis, which shows a ship's crew attacking men on land, *Arch. Eph.* 1898, p. 110, and pl. V. 1.

² Strabo II. 99.

³ *Arch. Zeit.* 1885, p. 133; so Assmann, *Berl. Phil. Woch.* 1899, p. 18.

⁴ *Op. cit.* pp. 397–400.

⁵ As noticed by Torr, *Rev. Arch.*³ xxv. p. 25, the only naval engagement mentioned in Homer occurs between a fleet and a land force, *Il.* xv. 367 f.; cp. Sallust, "nauigationem inuadendarum terrarum causa ortam."

⁶ Hdt. v. 83. Duris of Samos, Schol. Eurip. *Hec.* 934, attributes the Athenian attack on Aegina to previous Aeginetan raids on Attica.

⁷ Kinkel, *Epic. Frag.* p. 118, fr. 96.

⁸ Cp. Myres, *J.H.S.* xxvi. p. 85.

⁹ See above, p. 109.   ¹⁰ Hdt. v. 86.

That Athens too possessed a fleet is implied when Herodotus says that the Argives crossed to Aegina undetected[1]. Yet there is no hint of a sea battle. Both sides have their explanation[2], but neither is very satisfactory. The state of things implied by Herodotus' narrative of the Aeginetan war is remarkably like that pictured by Helbig for the time of the naval activities of the Dipylon ships.

One further point on this naval question may be noted, though it must not be pressed. Triremes are mentioned in connexion with the crossing of the Athenians to Aegina. This may be a mere anachronism[3]. But there is nothing to prove that it is so. A state of things which includes fleets of triremes, but no naval actions on a large scale, suits admirably the early part of the seventh century, before the naval battle of 664 B.C. and after the invention of the trireme. The first triremes in Greece are said to have been built at Corinth, some time before 704 B.C., when Ameinokles constructed four for the Samians[4]. Some of the Dipylon ships appear already to possess two banks of oars (fig. 45. b)[5]. Ships with two banks of oars appear on monuments of Sennacherib (700 B.C.)[6].

Triremes were used by the Pharaoh Necho (610-594 B.C.)[7]. Both Sennacherib and Necho probably relied largely on Phoenician sailors and shipwrights. "We are told that the Sidonians were the first to construct a trireme[8]." All these statements fall in excellently with the notice of Thucydides. It is true that in the next chapter he says that Aegina and Athens possessed few triremes a little before the death of Darius (486 B.C.), and uses this fact to argue that Greek naval power only developed on a large scale from about that time. His facts are hardly to be questioned; but in his conclusions he appears to be misled by the fallacy (which he shares with so many moderns) that no development of first class importance could possibly be dated much earlier than his own age[9].

The troubles that overtook Aegina about the time of her break

---

[1] Hdt. v. 86.

[2] Athens, Hdt. v. 85; Aegina, Hdt. v. 86. 2.

[3] So Macan, *Hdt.* IV.-VI. ad VI. 82. 2 and vol. II. pp. 105-6.

[4] Thuc. I. 13.

[5] *Ath. Mitt.* XVII. p. 298, figs. 5, 6; p. 303, figs. 9, 10; Pernice, *ibid.* pp. 294, 306; cp. *Mon. Grecs*, 1882-4, pl. IV. 2, 3 and pp. 51-2.

[6] Layard, *Mon. of Nineveh*, series I. pl. 71.

[7] Hdt. II. 159.   [8] Clem. Alex. *Strom.* I. 16.

[9] Against this view see Kroker, *Jahrb.* I. p. 110, n. 39; cp. Beloch, *Gr. G.*² I. i. p. 275, n. 1; Busolt, *Gr. G.*² I. p. 449.

with Epidaurus probably included a war with Samos[1], in which the Samians "sent an expedition against Aegina, and did much harm to the Aeginetans, and received much from them[2]." In such a state of affairs Aegina would be doing her utmost to turn out ships on the up-to-date pattern with which Ameinokles was supplying the enemy.

The Dipylon ships are rightly associated by many modern scholars with the naukraric organization that is found existing at Athens at the end of the dark ages[3]. The presidents of the naukraroi (or perhaps of the naukraries) are said by Herodotus to have been administering (ἔνεμον) Athens at the time of Cylon's attempted tyranny, *i.e.* about 632 B.C.[4] The statement is challenged by Thucydides, who says that "at that time the nine archons conducted most of the business of the state[5]." Herodotus however is at the worst only being inaccurate. The naukraroi were very possibly "the authorities in charge of the siege (οἱ ἐπιτετραμμένοι τὴν φυλακήν)" of Thucydides and were probably responsible for the levy *en masse*, recorded by Thucydides himself (ἐβοήθησαν πανδημεὶ ἐκ τῶν ἀγρῶν), that led to Cylon's discomfiture[6]. Herodotus may have exaggerated the authority of the naukraroi to palliate the guilt of the Alcmaeonid archon who put Cylon's followers to death[7].

Attica in the days of Cylon was divided into forty-eight of these naukraries, each of which had to provide a ship[8]. The business of the naukraroi was however largely financial[9], so much so that later

---

[1] Above, pp. 177–8.   [2] Hdt. III. 59.
[3] Brueckner and Pernice, *Ath. Mitt.* XVIII. p. 153, followed by *e.g.* Helbig, *Mém. Acad. Inscr. et B.-L.* XXXVI. (1898), pp. 387 f. Against this view see Assmann, *Berl. Phil. Woch.* 1899, pp. 16 f., who argues merely (1) that the dead on the ships proves them Phoenician, (2) that if the Athenians depicted their own ships, there would be more ships on Black and Red Figure Attic vases. But against this note (1) that the Dipylon vases are funeral vases, (2) that, in spite of Salamis, fifth century Attic vases do not abound with pictures of enemy ships.   [4] Hdt. v. 71.   [5] Thuc. I. 126.
[6] Forchhammer, *Philol.* 1874, p. 472; Schoemann, *Jahrb. Class. Phil.* CXI. (1875), p. 451; J. W. Headlam, *C.R.* VI. p. 253; Busolt, *Gr. G.*[2] II. p. 190, n. 2.
[7] Wecklein, *Sitz. bayr. Akad., philos.-philol. Kl.* 1873, pp. 33–34; G. Gilbert, *Jahrb. Class. Phil.* CXI. p. 10; Macan, *Hdt.* IV.-VI., and How and Wells, *Comment. Hdt.* ad Hdt. v. 71.   [8] Aristot. *Ath. Pol.* 8; Pollux VIII. 108.
[9] Aristot. *Ath. Pol.* 8, "organized for the collection of taxes and their disbursement (τὰς εἰσφορὰς καὶ τὰς δαπάνας τὰς γιγνομένας)": cp. Pollux VIII. 108; Photius s.v. ναύκραροι; perhaps also s.v. ναύκληρος; Suidas; and *Lex. Seguer.* ap. Bekker, *Anec. Gr.* p. 282.

writers, who may have known them best from references to them in the laws of Solon, seem to have regarded them as exchequer officials[1], the more so as Cleisthenes replaced the naukraric organization by demes[2], which had no naval associations.

Even the etymological connexion of naukrary with ναῦς (navis, ship) has been called in question. Doubt is first cast on it by Pollux, who wrote his *Onomasticon* in the second century A.D.[3]. Modern writers have proposed alternative derivations. Grote derives it from ναίω (I dwell), and explains the naukraroi as the principal householders[4], a reflex of the suffrage basis of the nineteenth century. Others[5] connect it with an obscure word ναύω, said by Hesychius and Photius to mean "I beseech," and connected by Photius with ναός (temple). ναός and ναύω they connect with a dubious gloss of Pollux[6], which explains ναύκληρος (ship's captain) by the rare word ἑστιοπάμων (householder, lit. hearthholder), and which they emend by reading ναύκραρος for ναύκληρος. As further Hesychius defines ναύκληρος (sic) as the president of a community (συνοικία) they connect the origin of the naukraries with the unification (συνοικισμός) of Attica by Theseus, symbolized by a common hearth[7].

These philological doubts have been met by G. Meyer[8], who argues that even assuming that ναός means "hearth," compounds would require not ναυ- but ναο- or ναυο-. Phonetic analogies all point to a derivation from ναῦς (ship)[9]. -κραρος is to be con-

[1] Mitchell and Caspari's edit. of Grote, p. 8, quoting Aristot. *Ath. Pol.* 8. 3; cp. Hesych. s.v. ναύκλαροι (sic, but in error for ναύκραροι; cp. *ibid.* "afterwards they were called demarchs"), who describes naukraroi simply as "the men who collected the taxes from each district."

[2] Aristot. *Ath. Pol.* 21 (quoted Harpocrat. s.v. ναυκραρικά); Schol. Aristoph. *Clouds*, 37; Pollux VIII. 108; Photius s.v. ναυκραρία; Suidas s.v. δήμαρχοι.

[3] Pollux VIII. 108, "ship, from which perhaps naukrary has got its name."

[4] Grote, *Hist.*, edit. 1888, II. p. 426. Cp. Pollux I. 74–5, X. 20, the master of the (whole) house is called ναύκληρος (sic).

[5] Wecklein, *Sitz. bayr. Akad.* 1873, p. 43; Wachsmuth, *Stadt Athen*, I. 481, n. 4; the derivation from ναῦς is denied also by Assmann, *Berl. Phil. Woch.* 1899, p. 19, and Keil, *Solon. Verfass.* p. 94, and doubted by Buechsenschuetz, *Berl. Phil. Woch.* 1907, p. 815. [6] Pollux I. 74. So X. 20.

[7] Hesych. s.v. ναύειν, "to supplicate, from the fact that suppliants flee for refuge to the hearth"; *ib.* s.v. ναύκληρος (sic)· ὁ συνοικίας προεστώς.

[8] G. Meyer in G. Curtius, *Stud.* VII. pp. 176–9.

[9] To the evidence for nau- in naukrary meaning ship add *Lex. Seguer.* in Bekker, *Anecd. Gr.* 283. 20 s.v. naukraroi, "Those who equip the ships, and act as trierarchs, and are subordinate to the polemarch."

nected with κραίνω (make, complete) or perhaps with κραίνω meaning "I rule[1]."

Pollux's uncertainty about the derivation simply reflects the uncertainty about the history of the naukraries that was prevalent in his days. No naval activities of the naukraroi are recorded by any ancient writer[2]. But this proves nothing. Naukraries probably had a long history at Athens, like ship-money in England, and in the course of time lost their dominatingly naval character.

Gilbert indeed[3] doubted the existence of naukraries before the time of Solon, who is suggested as a possible founder by a Scholiast of Aristophanes[4]. He suspects the evidence of the pro-Alcmaeonid Herodotus, and notes that he describes the attempt of Cylon and its suppression by the naukraroi as having happened "before the time" not of Solon but "of Peisistratus." He argues also against the possibility of a pre-Solonian Attic fleet of forty-eight ships, since Solon, when he attacked Salamis, sailed against the island with nothing but a large number of fishing-boats and one thirty-oared vessel[5]. He quotes Photius, who s.v. ναυκραρία says, "Solon having thus called them, as Aristotle states." His views are not tenable. Even if Herodotus is trying to whitewash the Alcmaeonidae, it by no means follows that he is very far from the truth in his account of the naukraries. If he mentions Peisistratus and not Solon, it is simply because Cylon aimed at becoming not a lawgiver but a tyrant. A weak Athenian fleet in Solon's time is no proof that the Athenian fleet had never been stronger. When Photius says "thus called" (ὀνομάσαντος), he may quite as well mean "used this name for" as "gave this name to": if he intended it for the latter, all that follows is that he misunderstood Aristotle, as did also the Scholiast to Aristophanes, *Clouds*, 37.

De Sanctis has gone even further than Gilbert, and brings down the establishment of the naukraries, along with the attempt of

---

[1] Glotz, *Et. Soc. et Jurid.* p. 246; cp. *Odyss.* VIII. 391, ἄρχοι κραίνουσι.

[2] Unless, as maintained by Boeckh, *Public Econ.* II. p. 327, n. 285, one is to be inferred from the comparison made by the Atthidograph Kleidemos between naukraries and the symmories of his own day; Phot. s.v. ναυκραρία; cp. Pollux VIII. 108.

[3] *Jahrb. Cl. Phil.* CXI. (1875), pp. 12 f. (answered by Schoemann, *Jahrb. Cl. Phil.* CXI. (1875), pp. 452 f., and Duncker, *Ges. d. Alt.* VI.⁵ p. 120, n. 2); so also Lenschau ap. Bursian, *Jahresb.* 176 (1918), pp. 194–5.

[4] *Clouds* 37, "whether established by Solon or even earlier."

[5] Plut. *Solon*, 9.

Cylon, to the time of Peisistratus[1]. He argues mainly from the naval developments under the tyrant, which, as seen already, are no evidence whatever against a much earlier date.

There is no reason to doubt the existence of the naukraries in 632 B.C. The question to be settled is how much further they go back, and what was the naval need that they were organized to meet.

A date not much before Cylon is argued for by Schoemann[2], who can find no earlier occasion for their institution than the seventh century struggle with Megara, by Duncker[3], who similarly explains them as instituted out of rivalry to the seventh century navies of Athens' neighbours, by Philippi[4] who dates them 683 B.C. (institution of annual archons), and by Busolt[5], on account of their connexion with the financial classification and organization of the seventh century. As regards Schoemann and Duncker it has been shown above in Chapter VI how very unlikely it is that Athens started an elaborate naval organization in the seventh century. Busolt's connexion of the naukraries with seventh century financial organization shows only that they then existed: it does not follow that they were then created. Whether or no Glotz is right in tracing them back to Homeric times[6], the balance of probabilities indicates that they go back to the period of the Dipylon pottery[7], and were organized for protection or reprisals against the raiders that then infested the Attic coasts, much as in England the Danegeld was instituted to deal with the pirates of a corresponding period in our own history. There may be something in the view that equates the naukraric organization with the council of Theseus[8], if by Theseus is meant the head of the Athenian state who established some sort of order on the waters and coasts of the Saronic Gulf

---

[1] De Sanctis, *Attbis*², pp. 305 f.; so Costanzi, *Riv. Stor. Ant.* v. pp. 514-15.

[2] *Jahrb. Cl. Phil.* cxi. (1875), p. 454.

[3] *Ges. d. Alt.* v.⁵ p. 474.

[4] *Attisch. Bürgerrecht*, p. 152; cp. Wachsmuth, *Stadt Athen*, I. pp. 473-4.

[5] *Gr. G.*² II. p. 189, n. 1; cp. p. 191.

[6] Glotz, *Et. Soc. et Jurid.* pp. 231-43; but cp. Buechsenschuetz, *Berl. Phil. Woch.* 1907, pp. 815-16.

[7] Helbig, *Mém. Acad. Inscr. et B.-L.* xxxvi. p. 405; cp. Wilamowitz, *Aristot. u. Athen*, II. 54; Gilliard, *Réformes de Solon*, p. 108, n. 2.

[8] Wecklein, *Sitz. bayr. Akad., philos.-philol. Kl.* 1873, pp. 30-48; Forchhammer, *Philol.* xxxiv. p. 472, on the meagre evidence of Thuc. II. 15; Plut. *Theseus*, 24.

after the overthrow of the Cretan civilization[1]. To quote the words of two particularly sober writers[2]:

> After the breakdown of the Minoan thalassocracy Athens certainly took her part in policing the Saronic Gulf....Her men of war are frequently depicted on Dipylon vases of the ninth and eighth centuries. In later times need of this protecting squadron may have grown less, when the navies of Megara, Aegina, Chalcis, and Eretria cleared the Aegean of corsairs. We may suppose that the naukraroi of the seventh century seldom saw active naval service[3].

The writers just quoted, following Helbig, imagine the ancient naukraries pursuing their naval activities as members of the Kalaurian league, and the latter, which lasted on as a religious body through classical times, as gradually taking a back place with the development of the other naval states they mention. Their picture however leaves out of account the chief fact known about the history of the league. Its original members were Hermione, Epidaurus, Aegina, Athens, Prasiae, Nauplia, and the Minyan Orchomenos. Then at the end of the list Strabo adds, "Nauplia used to be represented by Argos, and Prasiae by Sparta[4]." Strabo is here referring to a later period. It looks as though Argos and Sparta were intruders into the league, who sought membership to secure influence or a recognized position in the Saronic Gulf, just as in later times Philip of Macedon, for political reasons, set such store on recognition by the Delphic Amphictyony[5]. Is it unreasonable to suppose that the two intruders secured their places in the league each at the time of his aspirations to Peloponnesian hegemony, Sparta in the sixth century, and Argos under Pheidon? All the known circumstances bear out this supposition, at least for Argos which alone at present concerns us. It fits alike the naval power of Athens in the dark

---

[1] Above, p. 169.

[2] Mitchell and Caspari, p. 8 of their edition of Grote.

[3] With this last remark contrast my whole account of the first Aeginetan war. Boeckh, *Public Econ.* I. p. 341, notes that in the time of Cleisthenes the number of ships in the fleet is fifty (Hdt. VI. 89), corresponding to that of the naukraries, which had been raised from the earlier forty-eight, Photius, s.v. ναυκραρία.

[4] Strabo VIII. 374, ὑπὲρ τῶν Ναυπλιέων Ἀργεῖοι συνετέλουν, ὑπὲρ Πρασιέων δὲ Λακεδαιμόνιοι; cp. C. Mueller, *Aeginetica*, I. § 7.

[5] "There was a sort of Amphictyonic council" at Kalauria, Strabo VIII. 374 (Ephorus), who quotes

ἴσον τοι Δῆλόν τε Καλαυρείαν τε νέμεσθαι
Πυθώ τ' ἠγαθέην.

ages, the eclipse of that power in the seventh century, and the expansion of Argos just at this period. Nauplia is said by Pausanias[1] to have fallen to Argos only at the end of the seventh century. But Asine, which lies further from Argos, is said to have been conquered by her a hundred years earlier[2]. Beloch argues with some reason that the nearer city must have been conquered first. But there is no need to follow him in his passion for lowering dates, and bring down the time of the conquest of Asine. There is more reason for putting back the date of the fall of Nauplia, and thus bringing it into the period of Argive expansion under Pheidon[3].

Make this not unlikely modification in the picture just quoted from Mitchell and Caspari, and the early war between Athens and Aegina finds a satisfactory historical setting. Before the war Athens, Epidaurus, and Aegina are the leading states in the Saronic Gulf. As a result of it Athens is crippled at sea, and her place, and even more than her place, is taken by Argos. The evidence is admittedly scanty, but as far as it goes it points to the first Aeginetan war as marking the downfall of the naval power that Athens had enjoyed during the dark ages, or, as the legend puts it, after the fall of Minos, when the Kalaurian league and the navy of the naukraries were potent realities. The power that brings about this downfall is that of the Argive tyrant Pheidon.

Appendix D (to p. 170). *Early Athenian Dress*

THUCYDIDES[4] quotes Athenian dress in the introductory chapters of his first book to illustrate his thesis that civilization and comfort are extremely modern things. He divides Athenian history from this standpoint into three periods, the first that when men went about armed, the second that of luxurious Ionic fashions, and the third that in which they reverted to simple or rational dress ($\mu\epsilon\tau\rho\iota\alpha$

---

[1] Paus. IV. 24. 4, 35. 2.
[2] Paus. III. 7. 4, IV. 14. 3.
[3] So F. Cauer in Pauly Wissowa s.v. Argolis, p. 730, "about the time of the second Messenian war."
[4] Thuc. I. 6.

ἐσθής). It is difficult to date the beginning of Thucydides' second period later than the first half of the seventh century. At the time indeed when Thucydides wrote his remarks it was not very long since elderly men of the wealthy class in Athens had given up the Ionic dress. It has sometimes been maintained that the dress was always confined to old men, and that Thucydides implies that Ionic at Athens had been recently in full fashion. But the tone of the passage suggests rather the old gentleman who clings to the fashions of an earlier age. Already in the seventies of the fifth century B.C. the woman who typifies Greece in Xerxes' dream is dressed by Aeschylus in Doric robes[1] and the monuments confirm the view which regards the Persian Wars as marking the change.

But that does not end Thucydides' evidence. He speaks of fashions in Sparta as well as in Athens. The return to simple dress was started by the Spartans (μετρίᾳ δ' αὖ ἐσθῆτι πρῶτοι Λακεδαιμόνιοι ἐχρήσαντο). This statement has two implications[2]. The Spartans must have reverted to Doric costume before the Persian Wars, and previous to this reversion they must, like the Athenians, have worn some sort of Ionic costume. The importance of these allusions to Sparta seems scarcely to have been realized, no doubt because the controversy took shape before the excavations of the British School at Sparta had challenged many of the received views on the history of archaic Sparta. The very large finds of ivory and lead figurines of the seventh and sixth centuries[3] show that artistically at least the Spartans of that period were by no means the austere devotees of simplicity that they became in the classical age. Spartan simplicity in fact probably dates in large measure from the days of Chilon, the reformer of the middle of the sixth century[4]. It is not improbable that the simple dress at Sparta came in with the simple life at just about this period. It is already implied for Spartan young women by the epithet φαινομηρίδες (showing the thigh) of the poet Ibycus, a contemporary of Chilon. There is nothing in Thucydides to discountenance the assumption of an

---

[1] πέπλοισι Δωρικοῖσιν, *Persae*, 182-3.

[2] As already noted by Studniczka, *Ges. Altgr. Tracht*, p. 18, although (like Helbig, *Hom. Epos*², 163, 164, and Holwerda, *Rhein. Mus.* 1903, p. 520) he overlooks the important word αὖ. Partly perhaps because he wrote before the excavations of Sparta, partly because of his preconceived views on other points, Studniczka has failed to see the full force of his own observations.

[3] *B.S.A.* XIII. pp. 77 f.

[4] G. Dickens, *J.H.S.* XXXII. pp. 17-19.

interval of about fifty years between the beginning of simple dress at Sparta, and its adoption at Athens[1]. The tyranny at Athens roughly covers this period, and standing as it did for material luxury, sufficiently accounts for the interval. Athenian luxury, at least in the matter of dress, is said by Thucydides to have started earlier than Spartan, and Spartan, if it went out in the middle of the sixth century, must plainly have come in considerably before that date.

The Ionic costume is said by Herodotus to be strictly speaking not Ionian but Carian[2]. Eastern influence began to pass over from the Greek cities of Asia Minor and pervade the more progressive parts of Greece Proper early in the seventh century[3]: so that once again this seems to be the most probable period for the assumption of Ionic dress at Athens.

The same date is arrived at by working forward from Thucydides' first period, the age when men habitually went about armed. Thucydides is notoriously sceptical about the existence of the culture so familiar to us now under the names of Mycenaean and Minoan and it does not come into his three periods of Greek dress. The first of these is plainly the dark age that followed the downfall of Crete and Mycenae, the age of the Geometric pottery which about the year 700 B.C. began to make way for orientalizing styles. This is the period *par excellence* of dress-pins and fibulae as shown by archaeological finds[4], and the end of it, *i.e.* the beginning of the seventh century, would be the natural time for regulations curtailing or prohibiting their use.

Much has been made of the fact that Thucydides deals exclusively with male attire and Herodotus with female, and scholars who maintain that the Aeginetan disaster occurred towards the middle

---

[1] Dorian states followed Sparta in this revival earlier than did Athens; see Kalkmann, *Jahrb.* XI. pp. 41–42.

[2] Hdt. v. 88; cp. Studniczka, *Ges. Altgr. Tracht*, pp. 14 f. on the Semitic origin of χιτών, the distinguishing garment of the Ἰάονες ἑλκεχίτωνες (Hom. *Il.* XIII. 685). The discrepancy with Hdt. that some scholars have found in Thuc. I. 6 is only apparent, see Holwerda, *Rhein. Mus.* 1903, p. 520.

[3] See especially the pottery of the period.

[4] Skias, *Arch. Eph.* 1898, p. 103, n. 3 (Eleusis); Furtwaengler, *Aegina*, p. 474. As compared with the Geometric pin the archaic (post-geometric) type is shorter, but thicker, stronger, and the ornamental knobs thicker and closer. This type is particularly well represented at the Argive Heraeum (Thiersch *ap.* Furtwaengler, *ibid.* p. 414): that is to say, the period when dress-pins became heavier in the Argolid is once again the end of the Geometric period.

of the sixth century argue that in early Athens men would take the lead even in matters of dress[1] and that the early date implied by Thucydides for the male Ionic costume in Attica need not hold for the female as well. If the distinct dates were established beyond dispute the difference of sex might serve as an explanation. We have seen however that there is nothing in the words of Herodotus to justify a sixth century date for the adoption of Ionic costume by Athenian women.

Appendix E (to p. 249). *The Dating of the latest Vases from the Forum Cemetery*

AMONG the Forum vases that look late are some skyphoi like the "Later Ionic" of Sieveking and Hackl's Munich Catalogue, *e.g. Notiz.* 1903, p. 137, fig. 17, pp. 407 f., figs. 36, 42, 55, 57 (the last two from the same grave as fig. 53, see *ibid.* fig. 52). These skyphoi are closely related to a series of small, flat, handleless bowls similarly decorated, *Notiz.* 1903, p. 137, fig. 17, p. 388, figs. 14, 15 (grave G), p. 409, fig. 39 (grave I), p. 425, fig. 56 (grave K): for the stylistic connexion cp. *Notiz.* 1903, p. 425, fig. 56 (handleless bowl) with *ibid.* fig. 57 (skyphos). The context in which they were found at Rome points to a date not later than fairly early in the sixth century: *Notiz.* 1903, p. 137, fig. 17, was found acting as a lid (see *ibid.* fig. 16) to the skyphos *ibid.* fig. 17 of the later Ionic style; *Notiz.* 1903, p. 388, figs. 14, 15, were found in a single skeleton grave (*ibid.* p. 385 and fig. 11) along with the Proto-Corinthian lekythos, p. 388, fig. 17, that is probably of the seventh century, and other vases that are probably of the sixth: fig. 39 is from a single skeleton grave that contained also the "later Ionic" skyphoi, figs. 36, 42 (*ibid.* p. 400 and figs. 28, 31); fig. 56 is from a single skeleton grave and had a similar context (*ibid.* p. 418 and fig. 52). All these handleless cups (figs. 14, 15, 39, 56) are pierced near the brim with pairs of small holes. This is a practice known in Greek pottery of the Geometric and Proto-Corinthian period (*J.H.S.* xxx. p. 341, n. 42: add *Notiz.*

---

[1] So Studniczka, *Ges. Altgr. Tracht*, p. 19. The distinction is rightly disregarded in Abrahams, *Gk. Dress*, pp. 42, 58.

1895, p. 238, found in the same grave with two sixth century black figure vases. Two vases apparently somewhat similar in shape, style, and decoration to this flat, handleless series, but without the bored holes, were found at Rhitsona in graves of the end of the sixth century, *Arch. Eph.* 1912, p. 115, fig. 15) but not to black and red figure Attic pottery: it occurs on the probably seventh century cup from grave M, *Notiz.* 1905, pp. 151, 155, figs. 9, 12.

Other late-looking vases are the two figured *Notiz.* 1905, p. 150, fig. 7. Pais, *Ricerche*, I. (1915), p. 382, quoting Helbig dates them later than the sixth century. But Piganiol, *Journ. des Sav.* 1915, p. 552, n. 4, supported by Dugas, argues for the possibility of an earlier date on the ground that, though the shape might belong to the end of the fifth century, the decoration, for which cp. Louvre C 44, figured by Pottier, *Album*, I. pl. 23, points to the seventh. This argument will hardly do as it stands. The vase cannot be older than its shape, which rather recalls the fifth and fourth century festooned cups from Gnathia. But though it so much recalls that period, it does not seem to find an exact parallel in it, and the divergence may be more significant than the similarity. No other vases were found in the same grave with these two, so there is no context to suggest an earlier date: but if I am not mistaken, fifth and fourth century Gnathia ware is similarly recalled with a similar slight difference by another Forum vase, *Notiz.* 1903, p. 408, fig. 37, found in a grave with nine others (including figs. 36, 38, 39, 42, quoted above) which all point to a sixth century date. It must not be assumed that features common to early Greek and Italic wares always began earlier in Greece: a whole series of Etruscan bucchero vases has broad ribbon-shaped vertical handles that in Greek ware are distinctive of the late sixth century potter Nikosthenes: yet one of these bucchero vases comes from the early (seventh century) Regulini Galassi tomb at Caere, see *Roem. Mitt.* XXII. p. 126, fig. 18, p. 207. For Forum examples see *Notiz.* 1903, pp. 408, 422, figs. 38, 53.

Appendix F (to p. 249). *Evidence for Intramural Burials in Rome*

SERVIUS declares that the people of Rome and other cities originally buried all their dead within the city and actually within the house[1]. The latter statement appears to be an inference from the worship of the lares, "people used all to be buried in their own houses, whence has arisen the practice of worshipping the lares within the house," but may be none the less true for that reason[2]. Intramural burials are prohibited in the Twelve Tables, "hominem mortuum in urbe ne sepelito neve urito[3]," a prohibition which implies a practice still to some extent prevalent at the time[4]. In the consulship of Duilius the prohibition was re-enacted[5], showing that even then the practice was not altogether obsolete. Quite a number of

---

[1] Serv. ad *Aen.* XI. 206, v. 64, VI. 152. Burial within the village, near, or more often in the house itself, was usual in Latium in the neolithic period from which the Romans inherited much ritual (*e.g.* the use of stone knives in sacrifice and stone arrow-heads in declaring war), Pinza, *Bull. Comm.* 1898, pp. 77, 84-85, 116 f. Hence possibly the practice of burying vestal virgins within the city.

Intramural burial was practised at Megara (Paus. I. 43, 44; Plut. *Phoc.* 37), Sicyon (Plut. *Arat.* 53; Hdt. v. 67; cp. Becker, *Charicles*, Eng. trans.[8] p. 393), Sparta (Plut. *Lycurg.* 27, *Inst. Lac.* 18 (*Moral.* 238)), and Tarentum (Polyb. VIII. 30; cp. Athen. XII. 522 f. and *Notiz. d. Scav.* 1895, p. 238). For graves of particularly distinguished individuals the market-place was the usual spot (Pindar, *Pyth.* v. 93; Thuc. v. 11, which, however, implies that the market-place was subsequent to the tomb; Paus. II. 13. 6; Plut. *Timol.* 39; Strabo VIII. 371). Cp. also (Plato), *Minos*, 315*d*, and Rohde, *Psyche*, I. p. 228, n. 3, II. p. 340, n. 2.

[2] Cp. Frazer, *Magic Art*, II. p. 232, cases (differently explained by Frazer) of new-born children being brought to the hearth as a mode of introducing them to the ancestral spirits. Pinza, *Bull. Comm.* 1898, pp. 116-17 *à propos* of early burials within the house quotes the lares grundules, explained in the light of the statement of Fulgentius, *Serm. Ant.* 7, that till late times children were buried sub grundo. Unfortunately Fulgentius is a doubtful authority on a point of this sort: see Roscher, *Lex.* s.v. Lares, p. 1886.

[3] *Ap.* Cic. *de Leg.* II. 23 (58).

[4] Marquardt, *Privatleben*[2], p. 360.

[5] Serv. *Aen.* XI. 206. Smith, *Dict. Biog. and Myth.*, states that the Duilius in question is the consul of 260 B.C. The first Duilius to attain the office was K. Duilius in 336 B.C., a sufficiently late date. The prohibition was again re-enacted in the reign of Hadrian, *Dig.* 47, 12, 3, sect. 5.

exceptions were allowed by law. Vestal virgins (both good and bad) and imperatores were as such exempted[1]. To come to concrete instances, the grandfather of King Tullus Hostilius is said to have been buried "at the best spot in the Forum[2]." Tullus is a dubious figure in Roman history, and still more so is his grandfather. There is some uncertainty too about the case of the novem combusti, contemporaries of Spurius Cassius in the early years of the republic[3]. They may have been not cremated but burnt alive[4]. But there are plenty of later instances. Cicero implies that the exceptions were well known when after quoting the prohibition in his *de Legibus* he makes another character in it at once exclaim: "But what of the famous men who have been buried in the city since?," and immediately proceeds to quote the families of Valerius Publicola and Postumius Tubertus, and the individual case of C. Fabricius, buried in the Forum itself in 275 B.C. The exceptions in favour of the Valerii and the Postumii apparently go back to the beginning of the republic, when the consuls P. Valerius Publicola and P. Postumius Q. f. Tubertus were buried within the walls[5]. To the same period went back the concession to the Claudii of a burial-place under the Capitol[6]. The intramural (?) tomb of the Cincii, and that of "quidam Argiuorum illustres uiri" said to have been

[1] Serv. ad *Aen.* XI. 206; Plut. *Qu. Rom.* 79 (*Moral.* 283).

[2] Dion. Hal. III. 1.

[3] Casagrandi, *Nouem Combusti* (appendix to *Minores Gentes*), gives all the restorations of the gloss; his own runs "*nouem combusti* fuerunt legati] T. Sicinii. Volsci [eos interfecerunt cum proelium] inissent aduersus [Romanos. sumptu publi]co combusti feruntur [et sepulti in crepidi]ne quae est proxime Cir[cum, ubi locus est la]pide albo constratus." If the locus lapide albo constratus was proxime Circum, it may have been, technically at least, outside the city at the time of the obsequies.

Mommsen, *Roem. Forsch.* II. p. 168 (Sp. Cassius), speaks of the cremation as having taken place "auf dem roemischen Markt": he gives no evidence for the locality. The nouem combusti were in any case exceptional personages. But even so they are a warning against hasty conclusions from the archaeological evidence.

[4] Val. Max. VI. 3. 2 (Rom.); cp. Dio Cass. V. fr. 22; Zonaras VII. 17.

[5] The Valerii were buried "close to the Forum (σύνεγγυς τῆς ἀγορᾶς) under the Velia," Dion. Hal. V. 48; cp. Plut. *Poplic.* 23. Plutarch *Qu. Rom.* 79 says that the Fabricii as well as the Valerii had the right of burial in the Forum, but made only formal use of it. Cicero and Plutarch are easily reconciled by supposing that some formality in the Forum took place always and the actual burial occasionally.

[6] Suet. *Tib.* 1.

buried within the city, rest on more doubtful evidence[1]. That of the seven military tribunes buried near the Circus in 267 B.C. may have been still without the city.

The archaeological evidence for intramural burials at Rome has been discussed by Graffunder. At least two cases are well attested for the early republican period[2].

[1] Festus s.v. Romanam portam and Argea; cp. Jordan, *Topog. Rom* I. i. p. 176, n. 40; p. 190, n. 64; II. p. 283; but cp. Pinza, *Bull. Comm.* 1898, p. 116.

[2] Graffunder, *Klio*, XI. pp. 116–20, one on the Palatine, the other on the Esquiline. Being nowhere near the Forum they are probably cases of inherited rather than strictly individual merit: cp. Pinza, *Mon. Ant.* XV. p. 778.

INDEX

A.J.A. see *American Journal of Archaeology*
Aahmes, see Amasis, Pharaoh of Egypt
Abdul Hamid, 270
Abel (E.), *Scholia Vetera in Pindari Nemea et Isthmia*, cited 258 n. 2
Abertawe (Swansea), 106 n. 3
Abhandlungen d. bayerisch. Akademie d. Wissenschaften zu Muenchen, cited 199 n. 11, 200 n. 1
Abhandlungen d. hist. phil. Gesellschaft Breslau, see Haase
Abhandlungen d. preussisch. Akademie d. Wissenschaften zu Berlin, cited 39 n. 1; see also Diels, Erman, Lepsius, Milchhoefer, Schweinfurth, Wiegand
Abhandlungen d. saechsischen Gesellschaft d. Wissenschaften, see Overbeck
Abraham, 96
Abrahams (E. B.), *Greek Dress*, cited 166 n. 1
Abu Symbel, 123, 212
Abydos, 92
Academy, see Dennis
Acarnania, 52
Acharnae, 310
Achilles, 48, 298
Acragas, see Agrigentum
Acropolis of Agrigentum, 274; of Athens, 17, 40 n. 6, 53, 63, 252, 253, 315 n. 5; of Lampsacus, 281
Actaeon, favourite of Archias, 181
Adrastus, 179 n. 2, 261, 262, 264 n. 5
Adrianople, 200 n. 1
Aeacus, 176 n. 3
Aegean Sea, 33, 112, 130, 135, 286, 305, 330
Aegeis, 41 n. 3
Aegina, Aeginetans, 34, 57 n. 5, 64 n. 3, 68, 109, 116, 117, 154–157, 160–162, 164–171, 173–178, 212 n. 8, 285, 294, 314–320, 324–326, 330, 331, 333
Aeginetan weight system, 24 n. 1, 133, 156, 161, 164, 171–173, 175, 263, 294

Aegon, 158 n. 6
Aeinautai, 269
Aelian, *Historia Animalium*, cited 95 n. 1; *Varia Historia*, cited 10 n. 6, 17, 126 n. 4, 136 n. 3, 137 n. 1, 145 n. 3, 150 n. 6, 155 n. 2, 193 n. 1, 272 n. 1, 273 n. 1, 275 n. 1, 302 n. 6, 307 n. 4
Aeneas, 237 n. 1, 249
Aenus, 200 n. 1
Aeolic (pre-Dorian) stock, 193, 304; see also pre-Dorian
Aeolis, Aeolians, 69 n. 5, 246
aes formatum, 219
aes graue, 219, 232
aes rude, 219, 220
aes signatum, 219, 220
Aeschines, *contra Timarchum*, cited 12 n. 7, 13, 312 n. 1; Schol. *contra Timarchum*, cited 310
Aeschines, Socratic philosopher, 30
Aeschines, tyrant of Sicyon, 66, 263 n. 5
Aeschines of Semachidai, 39 n. 1
Aeschylus, *Agamemnon*, cited 57 n. 5; *Persae*, cited 47, 69 n. 4, 332; Schol. *Persae*, cited 40 n. 9; Schol. *Prometheus Bound*, cited 134 n. 2
Aesop, 56 n. 3
aesymnetes, αἰσυμνήτης, 8, 272, 301
Aethelred, 238
Aetolia, 196 n. 5, 263 n. 5
Africa, 3, 54, 87
Africanus, cited 93 n. 1, 98–100, 143 n. 2, 159
Agamemnon, 10
Agamemnon, king of Cyme, 147
Agariste, 157, 259 n. 1, 262
Agatharcides of Cnidus, 90 n. 3, 203 n. 4
Agathocles, 208–211, 276–278, 303 n. 2
Agesilaus, 20, 57, 291
ἀγορανόμοι, 12
ἀγοράζω, 80
agrarian laws, 230, 289
agriculture, 16, 24, 34, 264, 307–311; see also farmers
agricultural labourers, 24, 37, 38

INDEX

Agrigentum, Acragas, 10 n. 1, 14, 274–278 *passim*, 296
agroikoi, 48; see also farmers
Ahala, see Servilius Ahala
Aiakes, father of Polycrates, 81, 292
Aiakes, nephew of Polycrates, 75
αἰχμοφόρος, 143
Aipeia, 169 n. 1
Aithalia, 203 n. 4
ἀκήρατος, 68
Akkad, 197
akron, ἄκρον, ἄκρα, ἄκρη, 40, 41, 44, 291
ἀκτή, 312
Ala Shehr, 130 n. 7
alabastron, 119
Aladdin, 127, 148
Albertus (J.), ed. Hesychius, cited 40
Alcibiades, 17
Alciphron, cited 155 n. 1
Alcmaeon, 64, 65
Alcmaeonidae, Alcmaeonids, 14, 64–67, 231, 250, 292, 326, 328
Aldus, 311
Alexander Aetolus, cited 180 n. 2
Alexander Aphrodisiensis, *Problems*, cited 199 n. 9
Alexander the Great, 54 n. 1, 282 n. 4, 284, 288
Alexandria, 160 n. 7
Alexis, cited 21, 74
Alfred the Great, 91 n. 4, 237–239
Alopeke (modern Ampelokipi), 39 n. 1
Alyattes, 59 n. 6, 128, 137–139, 143 n. 1, 145 n. 3, 152 n. 2, 187 n. 8, 273
Amasis, Aahmes, Pharaoh of Egypt, 68, 71, 83, 84, 87, 96 n. 4, 101–105, 107 n. 4, 109, 112, 114, 115 n. 2, 116 n. 3, 117 n. 4, 121–124, 126, 293
Amasis, potter, 245
Ambracia, 189, 213 n. 4, 263 n. 5
Ameinokles, 184, 325, 326
Amelung (W.), *apud* Pauly-Wissowa, cited 166 n. 1
Amen Rud, see Ammeris
America, see United States of America
American Journal of Archaeology, cited 38 n. 2, 81 n. 3
American Journal of Philology, see Smith (K. F.)
American School of Classical Studies, Athens, 163, 187 n. 2, 319
Ammeris, Amen Rud, Rud Amen, Nut Amen, 88 n. 1, 99
Ammianus Marcellinus, cited 208 n. 4

Ammonius, *Vita Aristotelis*, cited 282 n. 3
Amon, god of Thebes, 97
Ampelokipi, see Alopeke
Amphictyons, Amphictyony, 65, 259 n. 2, 330
Amphikrates, king of Samos, 69 n. 5, 177, 178
ἀμφιφορῆες, 201
Amphipolis, 36 n. 1
Amphitrope (modern Metropisi), 39
amphorae, 113, 201, 205, 243 n. 1, 246, 253, 320
Anacreon, 84
Anaktorion, 189
Anaphlystus, 39, 41
Anatolia, 72
Anaxilas of Rhegium, 74, 75
Ancus Martius, 216, 217 n. 1
Andocides, cited 47 n. 7
Andreas, father of Orthagoras, 257, 263
Andros, 313 n. 1
Angel of the Lord, 92
Anglo-Saxons, 89 n. 1, 238
Anglo-Saxon Chronicle, 237
Ἀγκὼν γλυκύς, 76, 77 n. 3
Annali dell' Instituto, see Bachofen
Anno, see Hanno
Annual of the British School at Athens, cited 317 n. 7; see also Burrows, Edgar, Hogarth, Petrie, Ure
antefix, terra cotta, 250–252
Anthologia Lyrica, cited 14; see also Bergk
Anthologia Palatina, cited 201
Antike Denkmäler, cited 242 n. 3
Antiochis, 39, 41 n. 3
Antiochus I, 147 n. 1, 285
Antiochus of Syracuse, 274 n. 1
Antiphilus (*Anth. Pal.*), cited 201
S. Antonia, church of, 252
Anysis, 88 n. 1
Apamea, 147 n. 1, 208
Aphaia, temple of, 318–320
Aphrodite, 107 n. 4, 118, 119, 191 n. 3, 305, 318, 319
Apis stelai, 99 n. 1
ἀπόγονος, 157
Apollo, 65, 70, 107 n. 4, 110, 116, 117, 123, 138 n. 9, 144, 263 n. 5, 305
Apollodorus, cited 180
Apollonius Rhodius, *Argonautica*, 195 n. 2; *Foundation of Naukratis*, cited 117; Schol. *Argonautica*, cited 44 n. 4, 146 n. 7, 180, 181

Appi Forum, 233
Appian, *Bellum Civile*, cited 39 n. 4, 50 n. 1; *Bellum Mithridaticum*, cited 189 n. 8; *Bellum Syriacum*, cited 285 n. 1
Appian Way, see Via Appia
Appius Claudius Caecus, 211, 232, 233, 295
Appius Claudius the decemvir, 231
Apries, Haa ab ra, Hophra, 88 n. 1, 105, 122, 123
Apuleius, *Florida*, cited 69 n. 4
aqueducts, 62 n. 6, 76, 232, 267
Arabia, Arabians, Arabs, 100 n. 8, 116, 261 n. 2
Arabian Nights, 145
Aracoeli, church of, 252
Aratus, 257 n. 1
arbitrators, 11
Arcadia, 211, 212
Arcesilaus II of Cyrene, 74 n. 3
Arcesilaus III of Cyrene, 74, 82 n. 1
Archäologische-epigraphische Mitteilungen aus Oesterreich, cited 319 n. 2
Archäologische Zeitung, see Furtwaengler, Preller
Archäologischer Anzeiger, cited 110 n. 4, n. 7, 115 n. 1; see also Assmann, Fabricius
Archaiologike Ephemeris, cited 15 n. 4, 169 n. 5; see also Doerpfeld, Skias
"archers," Persian coins, 57, 291
Archias of Corinth, 180–182
Archias of Sparta, 84
Archilochus, cited 36 n. 3, 55 n. 4, 129 n. 6, 134, 143 n. 3, 145 n. 4, 152
archons, 326, 329
Ardaillon (E.), *Les Mines de Laurium*, cited 40 n. 9, 46, 48 n. 3; *apud* Saglio, *Dictionnaire des Antiquités*, cited 44 n. 5
Ardea, 234, 235, 296
Ardys, 135, 136, 143, 152, 273, 293
Argeadae, 183
Argolis, the Argolid, 164, 177, 179, 315–318, 320, 333 n. 4
Argonauts, 148 n. 3, 265
Argos, Argive, 24 n. 1, 33, 69 n. 5, 79 n. 2, 82, 149, 152 n. 2, chap. VI *passim*, 184, 185, 259, 261, 264 n. 5, 292, 294, 314, 316–319, 323, 325, 330, 331, 337
Argive pottery, 318; see also Proto-Corinthian

Aricia, 238, 249, 279
Aridaios, 281
Arion, 191 n. 2
Aristagoras, historian, 90 n. 1, 96 n. 4
Aristagoras, tyrant, 59 n. 1, 62 n. 4
Aristarchus of Ephesus, 272
Aristides, Publius Aelius, cited 184 n. 2
Aristippus, 30
Aristodemus of Cumae, 14, 247, 278
Aristodemus, ancestor of Spartan kings, 180
Aristogeiton, 253, 302
Aristokypros, 158
Aristonothos, 323
Aristophanes, *Acharnians*, cited 17, 59 n. 1, 265 n. 3; *Birds*, cited 58, 61; *Clouds*, cited 40, 51 n. 2, 207 n. 6; *Frogs*, cited 17, 187 n. 1; *Lysistrata*, cited 63; *Peace*, cited 265 n. 3; *Plutus*, cited 13 n. 1, 20; *Thesmophoriazusae*, cited 17, 207, 302 n. 6; *Wasps*, cited 51 n. 2, 201 n. 8; Schol. *Birds*, cited 54, 58 n. 1; Schol. *Clouds*, cited 327 n. 2, 328; Schol. *Knights*, cited 51 n. 2, 61; Schol. *Lysistrata*, cited 313; Schol. *Peace*, cited, 199 n. 3, n. 9, 200; Schol. *Thesmophoriazusae*, cited 207 n. 5; Schol. *Wasps*, cited 201 n. 8, 313
Aristotle, 6, 22, 32, 192, 195, 200 n. 2, 212, 258, 267, 280–282, 284, 286, 288, 290, 296, 297, 300, 301, 328
Aristotle, *Constitution of the Athenians*, 19 n. 1; cited 13 n. 6, 16 n. 6, n. 9, 29 n. 1, 31, 35 n. 1, n. 4, 36, 37, 46–48, 49 n. 3, 51 n. 2, 55 n. 1, 59 n. 5, 60, 61, 64, 65, 166 n. 6, 171 n. 2, 302, 307, 308, 326 n. 8, n. 9, 327 n. 1, n. 2; *Constitution of the Sicyonians*, 258; *Historia Animalium*, cited 199, 211, 309; *Meteorologica*, cited 87 n. 9; *Mirabiles Auscultationes*, cited 138, 147, 148; *Ode to Virtue*, 283; *Oeconomica*, cited 63, 189, 283 n. 6; *Politics*, cited 1, 2, 10–12, 14, 18–20, 22 n. 1, 24 n. 3, 25, 27, 28, 31, 35 n. 3, n. 5, 67, 76 n. 4, 77, 154, 182, 189 n. 1, 190 n. 2, 191 n. 2, 194, 196 n. 6, 198, 213, 257 n. 1, 258, 264, 265, 268 n. 3, 270, 274–276, 282–284, 303, 307; *Rhetoric*, cited 18, 134 n. 4, 264 n. 6, 265, 275

INDEX

Arnobius, *adversus Gentes*, cited 238 n. 3
Arrian, *Periplous*, cited 265 n. 6
Artemidorus of Ephesus, 90 n. 3
Artemis, 128, 130 n. 6, 245, 246 n. 1
artifices, 235
artizans, 15–21, 49, 92, 95, 103, 139, 217, 218, 222–225, 230, 233, 269, 292, 295, 305; see also manual labour
aryballi, 112
as, 149
Ashdown, 238
Ashmolean Museum, Oxford, 112 n. 8
Asia, 57, 58, 135, 191 n. 3, 221, 284, 286, 291
Asia Minor, 20, 91, 132, 142, 144, 155, 187, 205, 246 n. 8, 285, 300, 316, 333
Asine, 331
Asser, *Life of Alfred*, 237
Assmann, *Archäologischer Anzeiger*, cited 321 n. 5; *Berliner Philologische Wochenschrift*, cited 324 n. 3, 326 n. 3, 327 n. 5
Assos, 280–282
Assurbanipal, 88, 91, 99 n. 3
Assyria, 86, 88, 89 n. 1, n. 3, 91, 92, 97–99, 101, 102, 121 n. 4, 129, 144, 214, 292
Asylum, Asyla, 39 n. 4, 50
Atarneus, 280–284
ἀτελής, 135
Athelney, 238
Athena, 14, 16, 51–55, 60, 61, 63, 214 n. 4, 276, 291
Athena Ergane, 16 n. 7
Athenaeus, cited 21 n. 4, 22 n. 3, 23 n. 1, 45, 50 n. 2, 51 n. 2, 55 n. 1, 70 n. 5, 73 n. 5, n. 6, 74, 76–80, 100, 101 n. 5, 103 n. 6, 104 n. 4, 117 n. 3, 118 n. 5, 126 n. 4, 139 n. 3, 144 n. 3, 167 n. 1, n. 4, n. 5, 187 n. 1, 191 n. 3, 208 n. 1, n. 4, 211 n. 6, 259 n. 1, 268 n. 3, 269 n. 6, 270 n. 1, 271 n. 6, 275 n. 1, 281 n. 3, n. 5, 283 n. 4, n. 5, 284 n. 4, 309 n. 3, 336 n. 1
Athenagoras, 272
Athenische Mitteilungen, see *Mitteilungen des deutschen archäologischen Instituts in Athen*
Athens, Athenians, 7, 12, 13–17, 19, 21, 25, 28, 30, 31, chap. II *passim*, 69, 72 n. 2, 76 n. 5, 78, 80 n. 5, 83, 86, 92 n. 2, 137, 147, 149, 151 n. 2, 162 n. 3, 163, 165, 166, 168–176, 178 n. 1, 181, 183 n. 6, 196 n. 5, 215, 229 n. 1, 231, 239 n. 4, 245, 250–253, 258 n. 4, 260, 261, 264–266, 268, 274, 280, 287, 291, 292, 294, 302–305, 309–311, 321–334
Athribis, 214 n. 3
Atotes the miner, 48
Attalids, 284–286, 289
Attalus, (?) father of Philetairos, 284 n. 4
Attalus I, 285, 288
Attalus III, 288, 289
Atti d. Reale Accademia d. Torino, see De Gubernatis
Attica, Attic, 16, 21 n. 1, chap. II *passim*, 74, 79, 166, 168–170, 174, 251, 291, 307–313, 315, 327, 329, 334
Attic pottery, 34, 113, 115, 167, 168, 170, 202, 203, 245, 251 n. 1, 253, 254, 314–320, 321, 335; see also Proto-Attic, Black Figure, Red Figure
Atys, 140
Aubert (H.) and Wimmer (F.), ed. Aristotle *Historia Animalium*, cited 211 n. 3
Augustus, 37
Aulon, 312
Aurelius Victor, *de Viris Illustribus*, cited 215–217, 221, 223 n. 1, n. 5, 224 n. 5, 229 n. 4, 238 n. 3, 245
Australia, 164
Auxesia, 167, 170, 175, 320
Avignon, 3

B.C.H. see *Bulletin de Correspondance Hellénique*
B.S.A. see *Annual of the British School at Athens*
Babelon (E.), in *Corolla Numismatica*, cited 56 n. 2, 60 n. 2; *Journal International d'Archéologie Numismatique*, cited 51 n. 3, 52, 53, 56 n. 2, 64; *Les Origines de la Monnaie*, cited 129 n. 1, 130 n. 2, 131 n. 2, 137 n. 2, 141, 142, 148 n. 6, 149, 150, 152 n. 2, 161 n. 1, 162 n. 3, 220 n. 4; *Revue Numismatique*, cited 69 n. 5, 75 n. 1, 128 n. 1, 130 n. 2, 131 n. 2, 132, 133, 143 n. 1
Babylon, 123, 214, 3f1
Babylonian weight standard, 132
Bacchiads, 26 n. 2, 180–183, 187 n. 9, 190, 192–194, 196 n. 3, 197, 272
Bacchis, 193 n. 3

Bacchylides, cited 129 n. 7, 138 n. 9, 144 n. 4, 169
Bachofen, *Tanaquil*, cited 236 n. 2; *Annali dell' Instituto*, cited 253 n. 4
Baedeker, *Greece*, cited 39 n. 6
Baetis (modern Guadalquivir), 177 n. 6
Bakenranf, see Bocchoris
Balylon, 311
βάναυσον, τὸ, 20
Bank of England, 26
bankers, 2, 3, 137 n. 2, 141–143, 152, 280–283, 286, 296
Barnabei and Cozza, *Notizie degli Scavi*, cited 244 n. 1, 246 n. 7
Barth (H.), *Corinthiorum Commercii et Mercaturae Historiae particula*, cited 187 n. 1, 192 n. 5, 261 n. 2
Basilidae, 271, 272
Baton of Sinope, cited 271, 272
Battus of Cyrene, 123
Bauer, *Sitzungsberichte d. Akademie d. Wissenschaften in Wien*, cited 197 n. 6, n. 8, 209
bazaar, 4, 77, 286, 292
Becker (W. A.), *Charicles*, cited 336 n. 1
beehives, 199–201
beehive tombs, 224 n. 5
Bekker (I.), *Lexicon Seguerianum* (in *Anecdota Graeca*), cited 39, 41 n. 3, 57, 310 n. 4, 326 n. 9, 327 n. 9
Beloch (J.), 177 n. 3, 265 n. 1, 331; *Griechische Geschichte*², cited 33 n. 1, 51, 52, 63, 67 n. 1, 158, 161 n. 3, 192 n. 1, 210, 259 n. 5, 269 n. 1, 300 n. 1, n. 2, 325 n. 9; *Rheinisches Museum f. Philologie*, cited 21 n. 1, 34 n. 2, 51 n. 4, 315 n. 3; *Zeitschrift f. Socialwissenschaft*, cited 22 n. 7
benignitas, 227
Bent (J. T.), *Journal of Hellenic Studies*, cited 44 n. 5, 243 n. 1
Bentivoglio, Santo, 2
Bentley (Richard), 274
Bérard (V.), *Bulletin de Correspondance Hellénique*, cited 48 n. 2
Berezan, 110, 114
Bergk (T.), *Anthologia Lyrica*, cited 48 n. 4, 180 n. 2
von Bergmann, *Numismatische Zeitschrift*, cited 148 n. 6
Berkshire Downs, 238
Berlin Museum, 204, 253 n. 4

Berliner Philologische Wochenschrift, see Assmann, Buechsenschuetz, Furtwaengler
Bermion, Mount, 146 n. 7
Bernardini tomb, 93 n. 3
von Bernhardi (F. A. J.), *Germany and the Next War*, cited 5, 6
Bertha, sister of Charlemagne, 193 n. 7
Besa, 39
Bevan (E. R.), *House of Seleucus*, cited 285 n. 2
Binder (J. J.), *Laurion*, cited 44 n. 5
Birch (S.), *History of Ancient Pottery*, cited 187 n. 1
von Bissing (W.), 93
Black Figure pottery, 107 n. 4, 110, 113, 115, 202, 203, 253, 254, 315, 317, 319, 326 n. 3, 335
Black Glaze pottery, 107 n. 4, 108
Black Sea, 112, 114, 265 n. 2, 266, 297
blandimenta, 227
Bloch, *La République Romaine*, cited 226 n. 6, 233 n. 6
Bluemner (H.), *apud* Hermann, *Lehrbuch d. griechischen Antiquitäten*, cited 201 n. 4; *Gewerbliche Tätigkeit*, cited 187 n. 7, 266; *Technologie u. Terminologie der Gewerbe u. Künste*, cited 203 n. 2, n. 4; *Wochenschrift f. klassische Philologie*, cited 199 n. 1; see also Hitzig and Bluemner
Bocchoris, Bakenranf, 88 n. 1, 93–98, 100, 103, 292, 293
Bode (W.), 253 n. 4
Boeckh (A.), *Corpus Inscriptionum Graecarum*, cited 80 n. 4; *Kleine Schriften*, cited 280 n. 1, 282 n. 2, n. 4, 283 n. 3; *Public Economy of Athens*, cited 23 n. 1, 44 n. 2, 56 n. 4, 308 n. 2, 310 n. 4, 328 n. 2, 330 n. 3
Boehlau (J.), *Aus ionischen u. italischen Nekropolen*, cited 110 n. 9, 111 n. 1, n. 2, 112, 252; *Jahrbuch des deutschen archäologischen Instituts*, cited 315 n. 4
Boeotia, 24, 106, 108, 114, 196 n. 5, 198 n. 5, 248
Boeotian Kylix style of pottery, 110
Bolbitine mouth of the Nile, 90, 91
Bollettino di Filologia Classica, see Costanzi
Bologna, 2
bona, 227
Bonacossi, *La Chine et les Chinois*, cited 133, 141 n. 3

Boni (G.), *Journal of Roman Studies*, cited 224 n. 5, 253; *Notizie degli Scavi*, cited 248
Bonnet (A.), see Salvioli
Borrell (H. P.), *Numismatic Chronicle*, cited 131 n. 1
Bosporus, 76
Boston Museum of Fine Arts Report, cited 60 n. 1
Boswell, *Life of Johnson*, cited 281
"boundary estates," 310
Bourlos, 91
Boyle (Charles), 274
Brahami, 39 n. 1
Branchidae, 81, 123
Brandis (J.), *Münz-, Mass-, u. Gewichtswesen*, cited 74 n. 6, 130 n. 3; *Zeitschrift f. Numismatik*, cited 150 n. 1
Brants, *Revue de l'Instruction Publique en Belgique*, cited 21 n. 3
Brasidas, 50 n. 7
Brauron, 310 n. 2, 311, 312
breakwater, 70, 76
Breasted (J. H.), *Ancient Records of Egypt*, cited 44 n. 5, 95 n. 3, 98 n. 6, 99 n. 3, 100 n. 4, 122 n. 5, 123 n. 1, 212 n. 6; *History of Egypt*, cited 87 n. 3, 92 n. 1, 97 n. 3, 100 n. 4, 101 n. 1
Bremer (W.), *Die Haartracht des Mannes in archaisch-griechischer Zeit*, cited 55 n. 5, 56 n. 1
brickmakers, 20
Brilessos, 44
Britain, 89 n. 1, 306 n. 5
British Museum, 81, 101, 109 n. 6, 128, 171 n. 6, 283
British Museum Catalogue of Chinese Coins, cited 141 n. 3
British Museum Catalogue of Greek Coins, Corinth, cited 188 n. 2; Ionia, cited 132, 133; Lydia, cited 130 n. 7, 138 n. 1; Troas, cited 131 n. 1
British Museum Catalogue of Coins of Central Greece, cited 54 n. 5
British Museum Coins of the Roman Republic, cited 220 n. 3, 221 n. 7
British Museum Catalogue of Greek Vases, cited 62 n. 6, 246 n. 2; of *Terracottas*, cited 246 n. 7; of *Jewellery*, cited 171 n. 1; of *Finger Rings*, cited 70 n. 3
British Museum Excavations at Ephesus, cited 128 n. 3, 130 n. 6
British School at Athens, 332

bronze, 80 n. 4, 89–91, 122, 203, 228 n. 3, n. 4, 263; casting, 87; and copper coinage, 142, 218, 219, 221; sculpture, 243, 246, 263
brooches, 168, 170, 171, 173, 174; see also *fibulae*, jewellery
Brueckner and Pernice, *Athenische Mitteilungen*, cited 169 n. 7, 321 n. 6, 323 n. 1, 326 n. 3
Brugsch (H.), cited 96 n. 2, 97 n. 4; *Geschichte Aegyptens*, cited 125 n. 3
Brutus, 223–225, 230, 231, 234, 239
Brygos, potter, 204 n. 1
Bryson, 81
Bubastis, 121 n. 3
bucchero vases, 335
Buda-Pesth, 106 n. 3
Buechsenschuetz (A. B.), *Berliner Philologische Wochenschrift*, cited 327 n. 5, 329 n. 6; *Besitz u. Erwerb im griechischen Altertume*, cited 22; *Die Hauptstätten des Gewerbfleisses im klassischen Altertume*, cited 266
Buerchner (L.), cited 272 n. 4
Buffalo, 267
bull, brazen, 275, 278 n. 2
Bulletin de Correspondance Hellénique, cited 55 n. 3, 108 n. 2; see also Bérard, Gerster, Kampanes
Bullettino della Commissione Archeologica Municipale di Roma, see Pinza, Rizzo
Bullettino dell' Instituto, cited 242 n. 1
Bunbury sale, 55 n. 3
de Burgh (W. G.), 27 n. 4
Burgon (T.), cited 150
burials, intramural, 249, 336–338
Burnet (J.), *Thales to Plato*, cited 30 n. 1, 284 n. 1
Burrows (R. M.), *Recent Discoveries in Crete*, cited 76 n. 7; and Ure (P. N.), *Annual of the British School at Athens*, cited 107 n. 1, 108 n. 1, 110 n. 6, 113 n. 1; *Journal of Hellenic Studies*, cited 108 n. 1, 113 n. 1, 114 n. 5, 248
Bursian (C.), *Geographie von Griechenland*, cited 44, 260 n. 2, 309; *Jahresbericht ü. d. Fortschritte d. klassischen Altertumswissenschaft*, see Lenschau
Bury (J. B.), *History of Greece*, cited 45 n. 5, 159 n. 2, 170, 212 n. 5, 264 n. 3, 278 n. 2, 303 n. 2; *The Nemean Odes of Pindar*, cited 157, 160 n. 5, 259 n. 1, 260

Buschor (E.), *Griechische Vasenmalerei*, cited 114 n. 6, 169 n. 3, 246 n. 2, n. 3, 315 n. 1, 318 n. 7, 323 n. 2
Busolt (G.), cited 159 n. 2; *Griechische Geschichte*², cited 2, 35 n. 2, 48 n. 6, 70 n. 2, 128 n. 1, 156, 157 n. 4, 159 n. 2, 160, 187, 188, 189 n. 3, n. 4, 191 n. 4, 192 n. 1, 193 n. 2, 194, 214, 264 n. 5, 265, 317 n. 5, 325 n. 9, 326 n. 6, 329; *Die Lakedaimonier*, cited 187 n. 9, 192 n. 1, n. 4, n. 5, 305 n. 2, n. 3
Butacides, 239, 255
Butades, sculptor, 186 n. 1, 244 n. 1
butcher, 257
Butler County Democrat, cited 5 n. 8
Byrd (William), 245 n. 1
Byron, Lord, 3, 127, 285, 298; *Don Juan*, cited 148
Byzantium, 265, 311

C.I.A. see *Corpus Inscriptionum Atticarum*
C.I.G. see *Corpus Inscriptionum Graecarum*
C.I.L. see *Corpus Inscriptionum Latinarum*
C.R. see *Classical Review*
Cadys, 135, 136 n. 3
Caeculus, 238 n. 3
Caere, 219, 240, 242 n. 1, 243, 246, 255, 335
Caeretan hydriae, 246, 255
Caesar (title), 4, 303
Caesar, Julius, 32, 311 n. 1; *de Bello Gallico*, cited 162 n. 1
Cairo, 77
cakes, 238, 239
California, 142 n. 5
Caligula, 160
Camarina, 10 n. 2
Cambyses, 72, 80, 102 n. 1
Camirian pottery, 112 n. 1; see also Milesian pottery
Campania, 160, 232, 233, 246, 247
Camps at Daphnae, 112 n. 4, 121
canals, 87, 189, 191, 267
Candaules, 136, 144, 146
Canopus, 96 n. 2
Capitol, Rome, 224 n. 5, 237, 252–254, 337
Capitoline wolf, 253, 254
Capua, 233
caravans, 135, 145, 147, 149, 273
Caria, Carians, 89, 90, 96, 122, 123, 145, 269, 324

Caromemphites, 96 n. 4
carpenters, 14, 17, 20, 134 n. 4, 222, 224
Cartault (A. G. C.), *Monuments Grecs*, cited 321 n. 3
Carter (J. B.), trans. Huelsen, *Forum Romanum*, cited 247 n. 5
Carthage, 30, 72, 240, 278 n. 2, 282; see also Phoenicians
Carthagena, 45
Carystius, 284 n. 4
Casagrandi (V.), *Nouem Combusti* (appendix to *Minores Gentes*), cited 337 n. 3
Casaubon, *apud* Schweighaeuser, ed. Athenaeus, cited 270 n. 2; ed. Athenaeus, cited 77 n. 1; ed. Diogenes Laertius, *Solon*, cited 40 n. 6
Caspari (M. O. B.), see Mitchell
Cassiodorus, *Variae*, cited 218
Cassius Hemina, 224 n. 5
Cassius Iatrosophistes, *Problemata*, cited 199 n. 9
Cassius, Spurius, 32 n. 2, 228, 233, 255 n. 1, 337
caste, 87 n. 3, 122 n. 1
Castelnuovo di Porto, 219
Castor, cited 181
Cato, *apud* Schol. Veron. *ad* Virgil, *Aen.*, cited 238 n. 3
Caucasus, 41, 44
Cauer (F.), *apud* Pauly-Wissowa, cited 161 n. 2, 331 n. 3; *Parteien u. Politiker in Megara u. Athen*, cited 46 n. 5, 265 n. 2, 266, 268 n. 2
Cavaignac (E.), *Études sur l'histoire financière d'Athènes au Ve siècle*, cited 21 n. 1, n. 2, 41 n. 2, 309 n. 10; *Vierteljahrschrift f. Social- u. Wirtschafts-Geschichte*, cited 47 n. 6
cavalry organization, 240
Cecrops, 41 n. 3
Cedrenus, *Synopsis Historiarum*, cited 71 n. 4
Celts, 285
centuries, 230
Ceres, 228 n. 3, n. 4, 240 n. 2, 250 n. 1
χαῖρε, 255
Chalcedon, 265
Chalcis, 261, 316, 330
Chalmers' shillings, 142 n. 5
chamber tombs, 246
chambers of bronze, 263
Chancellor of the Exchequer, 4
χαρακτήρ, 64
Charaxos, 104

INDEX

Charisius, *Ars Grammatica* (ed. Keil), cited 218 n. 5
Charlemagne, 193 n. 7
Charon, 134 n. 4
Cheiromache, Cheiromachoi, 269, 270
χειρώναξ, 269
Chem Peh'-resu, 214 n. 5
Chersias, 195, 196, 197 n. 3
Chersonese, Thracian, 53, 63 n. 7, 199 n. 10, 245 n. 2
Chicago, 267
Chigi vase, 316 n. 10
Chilon, 332
China, 133, 141, 142
Chios, 23 n. 1, 191 n. 3, 253
χλανίς, 79, 80
χρήματα, χρηματίζεσθαι, 25, 36
Chronicles, 2nd *Book of*, cited 92 n. 3
Chronographer of 354 A.D., cited 224 n. 5, 226 n. 3
χρυσοῦ καὶ ἀργύρου, 132
church music, 245 n. 1
χύτραι, χυτρίδες, 320
Ciccotti (E.), *Il Tramonto d. Schiavitù nel Mondo antico*, cited 3 n. 2, 20, 22, 29 n. 3
Cicero, *de Amicitia*, cited 228 n. 1, 229 n. 2; *ad Atticum*, cited 57 n. 2, 275 n. 1; *Brutus*, cited 35 n. 3; *in Catilinam*, cited 229 n. 2; *de Divinatione*, cited 238 n. 3, 275 n. 1; *de Finibus*, cited 70 n. 3; *de Legibus*, cited 336 n. 3, 337; *de Officiis*, cited 15 n. 6, 20 n. 6, 145 n. 6, 151 n. 4, 225 n. 2, 302 n. 6; *de Oratore*, cited 35 n. 3; *Philippics*, cited 226, 228 n. 1, 229 n. 2; *pro Rabirio*, cited 226 n. 5; *de Republica*, cited 215 n. 2, 221 n. 5, 222 n. 7, 223 n. 5, 225 n. 2, 228 n. 1, 229 n. 2, 240, 241; *de Senectute*, cited 229 n. 2; *Tusculanae Quaestiones*, cited 247 n. 3; *in Verrem*, cited 275 n. 1; Schol. Bobiens. *pro Sulla*, cited 215 n. 2
Cimmerians, 137, 141 n. 1, 144, 146, 187
Cimon, 67
Cincii, 337
Cincinnati *Commercial Gazette*, cited 5 n. 8
Circus, Circus Maximus, 240 n. 2, 338
Classical Philology, see Frank
Classical Review, cited 112 n. 8, 319 n. 5; see also Cook, Headlam
Claudii, 231, 337; see also Appius
Claudius Drusus, 233
Claudius (Emperor), 215 n. 2
Clazomenae, pottery of, 114, 115 n. 2, 121 n. 5, 246
Clearchus, cited 76 n. 6, 77, 78 n. 1, 139 n. 3
Cleisthenes of Athens, 17, 28, 29, 39, 45, 65, 66, 67, 258 n. 4, 291, 310 n. 2, 312, 327, 330 n. 3
Cleisthenes of Sicyon, 66, 179 n. 2, 180 n. 3, 215, 258–264
Clement of Alexandria, *Stromata*, cited 93 n. 2, 146 n. 7, 325 n. 8
Cleomenes of Sparta, 79 n. 2
Cleomenes (Cleomis) of Methymna, 191 n. 3
Cleon, 30
Cleonae, 194
Clerc (M.), *Les Métèques Athéniens*, cited 22
clientela, clients, 233, 277, 296
cloaca maxima, 247
Clytus, cited 73, 74
Cnidus, 90 n. 3
coast, party of the coast, 35, 41, 47, 48, 52, 64 (shore), 291, 312, 313
Cobbett (William), *Paper against Gold*, cited 3
cobblers, bootmakers, 17, 139 n. 2
coinage, debasement of, 64 n. 3, 74, 183 n. 6; invention of, 1, 2, 3, 127, 129, 131, 133, 140, 147, 155, 161, 178, 290, 293, 304
coins, 52–58, 60, 61, 63, 64, 74, 75, 84, 127–133, 137, 138, 140–143, 147, 149, 150, 155–157, 160–162, 164, 166 n. 2, 170–173, 175, 176, 178, 188, 199–201, 204, 205, 209, 213 n. 4, 218–221, 231, 232, 246, 290, 293–296, 304
Collatinus, 226, 227
collegia opificum, 222
colonies, colonization, 189, 190, 265, 266, 294, 300
Colophon, 133
colossus, 189, 192 n. 5
"colts" (coins), 188
Columbus, Ohio, 235 n. 3
Columella, cited 201 n. 5, n. 8, 309 n. 7
Comitia centuriata, 230
Commons, House of, 4
Companion to Greek Studies, cited 179 n. 3
Companion to Latin Studies, cited 221 n. 6

INDEX

Conca (Satricum), 219 n. 4, 243 n. 4, 244 n. 1, 246
Constantinople, 77
Constitution of the Athenians, see Aristotle
contracts, 93
Conway (R. S.), quoted 76 n. 7, 134 n. 5, 223 n. 3
Conze (A.), *Jahrbuch*, cited 205 n. 2, n. 3, n. 4, 206 n. 3
cook, 257
Cook (A. B.), *Classical Review*, cited 262 n. 3
copper, 82, 203 n. 1, n. 4
copper coinage, see bronze coinage
copper mines, 37 n. 1
coppersmiths, 14, 222, 224
Coptic, 126
Corcyra (Corfu), 63 n. 5, 184, 187 n. 9, 188, 213, 214, 244 n. 1, 321
Corinth, 14, 21, 22, 28 n. 7, 30, 31, 33, 34, 62 n. 6, 63, 68, 76 n. 5, 123, 124, 167, 178–180, 182, 183, chap. VII *passim*, 215–217, 240–242, 244, 245, 247, 248 n. 2, 251, 255–257, 259, 260, 263 n. 5, 266 n. 1, 272, 274, 287, 293–295, 304, 306 n. 1, 316, 317, 321, 325
Corinthian drachma, 57; helmet, 54 n. 6; pottery, 1, 21, 34, 46, 109 n. 5, 112, 117 n. 4, 186, 187, 208 n. 1, 212 n. 8, 241–245, 251, 295, 315–319
corner (in oil), 2, 12
Corneto, 93, 187, 215; see also Tarquinii
Cornford (F. M.), *Thucydides Mythistoricus*, cited 25, 261
Corolla Numismatica: Numismatic Essays in Honour of Barclay V. Head; see Babelon, Evans, Fox
Corpus Inscriptionum Atticarum, cited 14, 15, 39, 40 n. 9, 41 n. 3, 50 n. 3, n. 5, 56 n. 4, 312 n. 1, 313 n. 2
Corpus Inscriptionum Graecarum, 80 n. 4, 208 n. 2
Corpus Inscriptionum Latinarum, cited 215 n. 2, 223 n. 2
Corsica, 221 n. 2, 240
Costanzi (V.), *Bollettino di Filologia Classica*, cited 51 n. 4; *Rivista di Storia Antica*, cited 34 n. 2, 51 n. 4, 177 n. 3, 329 n. 1
Cozza, see Barnabei
Crassus, 23
Cratinus, 13 n. 3

Crete, Cretan, 128, 156 n. 2, 169, 263 n. 5, 298, 330, 333; Cretan bull cult, 278 n. 2
criers, 17
Crimea, 1
Croeseids, 130, 137
Croesus, 104 n. 3, 123, 127, 128, 130–133, 136 n. 3, 137–140, 143 n. 1, n. 3, 144, 145 n. 2, n. 3, n. 4, 148 n. 3, 152, 176, 215, 272, 273, 289, 293
Cromwell, 194
Croton, Crotonian, 239, 255
Cruchon (G.), *Banques dans l'Antiquité*, cited 141 n. 1, 143 n. 1, 221 n. 4
crucifixion of followers of Spartacus, 23
Cumae, 14, 228, 240, 246, 247, 251, 278–279, 296, 316
Curtius (E.), *Ephesus*, cited 272 n. 3; *Griechische Geschichte*, cited 36 n. 3, 159 n. 2, 198 n. 9; *Peloponnesos*, cited 191 n. 6; *Stadtgeschichte v. Athen*, cited 63 n. 2
Curtius (G.), *Studien z. griech. u. latein. Grammatik*, cited 327 n. 8
Curtius (L.), *Athenische Mitteilungen*, cited 81, 82
Curtius, Marcus, 248 n. 1
Cyaxares, 90, 91
Cyclades, 169 n. 1
cylinders, inscribed Assyrian, 91, 98, 99 n. 3
Cylon, 34, 69, 264, 326, 328, 329
Cyme, 130 n. 6, 131, 135, 136, 147, 155 n. 2, 273, 281
Cynosura, 40
Cyprus, Cypriote, 46, 108 n. 7, 119, 128, 156 n. 2, 160, 169 n. 1, 303 n. 1, 315 n. 2
Cypsela in Thrace, 199, 200, 204–206
cypsele, 197–209, 211, 295
Cypselids, 14, 76 n. 5, 189, 192, 196, 213, 263 n. 5
Cypselus of Arcadia, 211, 212
Cypselus I of Corinth, 9, 26 n. 2, 28 n. 7, 31, 95 n. 1, 180, 187–190, 192 n. 5, 193–200, 207–211, 216, 245 n. 2, 255, 257, 270, 274, 292, 295, 303 n. 2, 305, 306 n. 1
Cypselus II of Corinth, 213, 214
Cypselus, father of Miltiades, 199 n. 10
cypselus bird, 211
Cyrene, 74, 82 n. 1, 123, 239
Cyrnus, 8

INDEX

Cyrus, 8 n. 3, 71–73, 123, 138, 139, 145 n. 2, 152, 197, 209, 271, 272, 293
Cythera, 176, 177
Cyzicus, 281, 285

Dactyls of Ida, 44
Dagobert I diploma, cited 261 n. 2
δακτύλιοι, δακτυλιογλύφοι, 149
Dale, Sir D., 11 n. 2
Damasenor, tyrant of Miletus, 268, 269
Damia and Auxesia, 167, 170, 175, 320
Damocratidas, 158 n. 6
Damonno, 135, 136, 143, 236 n. 2
Damophilus, 240 n. 2
Danegeld, 329
Danes, 237, 238
Dante, 305; *Paradiso*, cited 57 n. 4
Daphnae (Defenneh), 109 n. 5, 112, 113, 115 n. 2, 121, 122
Daphnae pottery, 115 n. 2, 121 n. 5
daric, 57, 130, 132, 140, 172 n. 4, 291
Darius, 29, 58, 59, 61, 62, 72, 76, 79, 80, 87 n. 9, 140, 142, 152 n. 2, 270, 271, 325
Daskalio, 42
Daskylion, 273 n. 2
Decelea, 45
decemvirate, 233
De Cou (H. F.), *Argive Heraeum*, cited 164 n. 1
dedications, votive offerings, 14, 82, 107 n. 4, 108, 116–118, 124, 144 n. 3, 162, 163, 170, 175, 189, 192 n. 5, 198, 244 n. 1, 263
Deecke, see Mueller
Defenneh, see Daphnae
Deinomenidae, 30
Deiokes, 146 n. 4
Deiophontes, 176
Delos, 49, 70, 71, 162 n. 3, 166 n. 2, 171 n. 5, 260 n. 5, 261
Delphi, 65, 66, 123, 130, 137, 140, 144, 147, 162 n. 3, 194, 198 n. 5, 207 n. 3, 208, 255, 257, 259–262, 276, 283 n. 4, 330
Delta, 88, 95, 96, 98, 99, 121 n. 3, 293
demagogues, 11, 26–32, 35, 190 n. 2, 217, 274, 279, 280, 282, 300, 301
Demaratus, 182, 187 n. 6, 215–218, 225, 236 n. 2, 239–245, 251, 255, 256, 295

Demeter, 238, 266, 308; Malophoros, 266; hymn to, 22
Demetrius, *de Elocutione*, cited 280 n. 1, 283 n. 6
Demetrius Magnes, cited 280 n. 1
Demetrius of Phaleron, 305, 306
demiourgoi, δημιουργοί, δημιουργίαι, 16, 48
Demochares, 305, 306
Demodike of Cyme, 147, 155 n. 2
Demosthenes, 49, 305
Demosthenes, *c. Aphobum*, cited 12; *c. Aristocratem*, cited 277 n. 2; *c. Eubulidem*, cited 19, 20 n. 1; *c. Midiam*, cited 65; *c. Olympiodorum*, cited 13; *Olynthiac Orations*, cited 277 n. 2; *c. Phaenippum*, cited 48 n. 1; περὶ Συντάξεως, cited 277 n. 2; Schol. *c. Aristocratem*, cited 51 n. 2
Demoteles, 69 n. 5
Dennis (G.), *Academy*, cited 76 n. 2
Derbyshire, 40
Diadochoi, 258 n. 2, 284
Diakria, Diakrieis, διακριεῖς, Diakrioi, διάκριοι, 37, 39–41, 44, 48 n. 6, 49, 291, 307–313
Diakrioi, Euboean, 41 n. 2; Rhodian, 41 n. 2
Diamantaras, *Athenische Mitteilungen*, cited 57 n. 3
Diana, 224 n. 5
Dickens (G.), *Catalogue of the Acropolis Museum, Athens*, cited 252, 253; *Journal of Hellenic Studies*, cited 332 n. 4
didrachm, 64, 171 n. 6, n. 8, 172
Didymus, cited 33 n. 1
Diels (H.), *Abhandlungen d. preussisch. Akademie d. Wissenschaften zu Berlin*, cited 35 n. 2
Digest, cited 336 n. 5
Dindorf (L.), ed. Diodorus, cited 48 n. 6
Dio Cassius, cited 226 n. 3, 337 n. 4
Dio Chrysostom, *Orations*, cited 35 n. 3, 148 n. 3, 189 n. 8, 198
Diodorus Siculus, cited 10 n. 6, 23 n. 1, 48 n. 6, 59 n. 1, 78 n. 2, 87 n. 7, n. 9, 89–93, 95, 97, 99 n. 1, 100 n. 4, n. 8, 103, 105, 117, 121 n. 4, 122 n. 1, n. 4, 123 n. 1, n. 10, n. 11, 138 n. 8, 146 n. 7, 156 n. 3, 176 n. 2, 180 n. 2, 203 n. 4, 208, 209, 210 n. 4, 211 n. 1, 215 n. 2, 216, 217 n. 1, 228 n. 1, 229 n. 2, 232 n. 1, 257 n. 2, 262 n. 4,

275 n. 2, 276, 277, 280 n. 1, 283 n. 6, 284 n. 1, 293, 298
Diogenes Laertius, cited 30 n. 2, 69 n. 1, 150 n. 3, 167 n. 1, n. 2, 190 n. 1, n. 2, 191 n. 3, n. 6, n. 7, 192, 195, 196, 212 n. 2, n. 8, 280 n. 1, 281 n. 2, 282 n. 2, 283 n. 3, n. 4, n. 5, n. 6, 284 n. 1
Diogenianus, cited 71 n. 1
Dion of Syracuse, 30
Dionysius of Halicarnassus, *Antiquitates Romanae*, cited 32 n. 2, 37 n. 4, 48 n. 6, 191 n. 2, 215 n. 2, 216–218, 221 n. 2, 222 n. 7, 223 n. 1, n. 4, n. 5, 224–231, 234 n. 3, 237 n. 3, 238 n. 3, 239, 245, 247 n. 3, 278 n. 3, n 4, n. 5, 279 n. 1, 283 n. 6, 337 n. 2, n. 5; *Epistola ad Ammaeum*, cited 280 n. 1; *Isocrates*, cited 13 n. 1
Dionysius of Syracuse, 24, 27, 30–32, 72, 196, 210, 221, 229, 256 n. 1, 265, 274, 278 n. 2, 280, 282, 284, 291, 303 n. 2
Dionysus, 262, 264 n. 5, 305; Botrys, 239
Diphilus, cited 208 n. 1
Dipoenus, 263 n. 5
Dipylon pottery, 169, 314, 315, 317, 319, 321–326, 329, 330
Dives, 102
dives, 229
Doerpfeld (W.), *Archaiologike Ephemeris*, cited 62 n. 6; *Athenische Mitteilungen*, cited 63 n. 2
Dorians, 157 n. 7, 158, 176, 179, 180, 257, 259 n. 1, 261, 262 n. 1, 294, 305 n. 1, 333 n. 1; pre-Dorian stock, 257, 304, 305; see also Aeolic stock
Doric dress, 169, 332
Doriche, 104
Dorieus, 239
δορυφόρος, 143
drachma, δραχμαί, 57, 58, 64, 149, 162, 171–173, 175
δραχμαὶ τοῦ Στεφανηφόρου, 56
Draco, 53 n. 2
Dragendorff (H.), *Thera*, cited 316 n. 7, 320 n. 5
drains, 224, 247
dress, 164, 167–170, 174, 331–334
drivers, 14
Drumann (W.), *Arbeiter u. Communisten in Griechenland u. Rom*, cited 19

Duemmler (F.), *Jahrbuch des deutschen archäologischen Instituts*, cited 112 n. 4
Dugas (Ch.), *apud* Piganiol, *Journal d. Savants*, 335
Duilius, 336
Dumont (A.), *Revue Archéologique*, cited 205 n. 4, 206
dumps, 128, 156 n. 2; see also ingots
Duncker (M. W.), *Geschichte des Alterthums*, cited 145 n. 4, 159 n. 5, 166 n. 1, n. 3, 192 n. 1, 198 n. 9, 214 n. 7, 328 n. 3, 329
Dunham (A. G.), *History of Miletus*, cited 117 n. 1, 268 n. 4
Durazzo, 190 n. 3
Duris of Samos, cited 78, 178, 324 n. 6
dyeing, dyers, 14, 139 n. 2, 187, 222
Dying Gladiator, 285
Dymaean War, 159

ecclesia, 17
Edessa, 183
Edgar (C. C.), *Catalogue of the Greek Vases in Cairo Museum*, cited 112 n. 5; *Annual of the British School at Athens* and *Journal of Hellenic Studies*; see Hogarth and others
Edonia, 271
Edward the Confessor, 238
Edward the Elder, 238
Edward VII, 102 n. 1
Eetion, 193
ἐγείρω, 35
Egestaeans, 239; see also Segesta
Egypt, 1, 44 n. 5, 48 n. 6, 68, 71–73, 80, 83, chap. IV *passim*, 145 n. 4, 148 n. 3, 149, 191, 203 n. 4, 212–214, 285, 292, 293, 298, 303 n. 1, 315 n. 3
Eion, 59 n. 1
Eldorado, 41, 177 n. 7
electrum, electrum currency, 44 n. 5, 74 n. 6, 127–133, 142, 147, 150, 152
Elephantine, 123
Eleusis, Eleusinians, 15, 41 n. 3, 169 n. 5, 250 n. 1, 308, 318, 321, 324 n. 1, 333 n. 4
Elis, 123, 134 n. 2, 154, 159, 160
Ely, 238
embroiderers, 14
embrontaion, 277
Emperor, Holy Roman Empire, 304
employees, 14, 15, 21, 62, 77, 223, 225, 239, 278, 289, 295

ἐμπορίη, 80
ἐμπορικὸν πρᾶγμα, 261
Encyclopaedia Britannica, cited 77 n. 3; see also Griffith
Endt (J.), *Beiträge zur ionischen Vasenmalerei*, cited 120 n. 4; *Wiener Studien*, cited 10 n. 6, 14 n. 6, 31 n. 2, 274 n. 1, 283 n. 6
ἐνεργαζόμεναι παιδίσκαι, 139
England, English, 15 n. 6, 126 n. 5, 233 n. 6, 237, 238, 249, 306 n. 2, 328, 329
engravers, 14
Enkomi, 128, 141
Ennea Hodoi, 59 n. 1
Enneakrounos, 62
ἐνύπνιον, 81
Epakria, Epakrioi, ἔπακροι, 37, 39, 41, 45, 291
Epaminondas, 179 n. 3
Ephesus, 90 n. 3, 128, 130 n. 6, 132, 136, 137, 141, 143 n. 1, 144 n. 3, 145 n. 3, 147 n. 3, 156 n. 2, 191 n. 3, 221 n. 2, 245, 246 n. 1, 271–273 *passim*, 296
Ephorus, cited 26 n. 2, 155, 157, 161, 163, 164, 173, 175, 176, 192–194, 196 n. 4, 258, 264, 294, 330 n. 5
Epidamnus, 190 n. 3
Epidaurus, 165–167, 174–176, 178, 326, 330, 331
ἐπιδιδόναι, 281
Epiphanius, *de Mensuris et Ponderibus*, cited 120 n. 3
ἐπισημαίνειν, 277
ἐπίστασις, ἐπιστάτης, 81, 277
ἐπιτετραμμένοι τὴν φυλακήν, 326
ἐπιθαλάσσιος, 313
ἐπιτίθεσθαι, 280, 281
ἔπρησεν, 81
Erastos, 283 n. 3
Erechtheum, 14 n. 9, 20 n. 7
Eretria, 36, 37, 72 n. 2, 261, 330
ἐργασία, ἐργαζόμενοι, 17, 19
ἐργαστήρια, 218
Ergotimos, 245, 319
Erichthonios, 155 n. 2
Erman (J. P. A.) und Schweinfurth (G.), *Abhandlungen d. preussischen Akademie d. Wissenschaften zu Berlin*, cited 87 n. 6
ἔρως χρημάτων ἄμετρος, 272
Erotici Scriptores (ed. Didot), cited 93 n. 2
Erythrae, 133
Esquiline, 338 n. 2

Essendune, 238
ἔστρωται, 79
Ethiopia, Ethiopian, 95–102, 122, 125 n. 3, 292
Ethiopian dynasty in Egypt, 86, 88 n. 1, 93, 95, 97
Etruria, Etruscans, 10, 30, 93, 187, 203 n. 4, 215–217, 219, 220, 223, 225, 234, 235, 241–243, 246, 249, 295, 335
Etruscan language, 134 n. 5
Etrusco-Carthaginian alliance, 240
Etymologicum Gudianum, cited 134 n. 1, n. 5
Etymologicum Magnum, 41 n. 3, 76 n. 7, 134 n. 1, n. 5, 155 n. 2, 156 n. 1, 162, 163, 193 n. 3, 201 n. 2, 280 n. 1
Euaion, 281, 283, 288
Euboea, 37, 60, 156 n. 1, 261, 262, 311, 313 n. 1
Euboeic standard, 171, 172
Euboulos, 282, 283 n. 6, 288
Eubulus Comicus, cited 54 n. 2
Eucheir, workman of Demaratus, 207, 217, 244, 245
Eucheiros, potter, 244, 245
Eugrammus, 208, 217, 244
Eumelos, 195
eunuch, 280, 284
Eupalinus, 76, 267
Eupatridai, 48
Euphorion, cited 133, 143 n. 2
Euphronios, 169
εὐπορία, εὔποροι, 89, 273
Euripides, 17, 54 n. 2; *Bacchae*, cited 148 n. 1; *Cyclops*, cited 40 n. 9; *Hecuba*, cited 174 n. 3; *Iphigenia in Tauris*, cited 182 n. 4; *Sciron*, cited 57; Schol. *Hecuba*, cited 178 n. 1, 324 n. 6
Europe, 23, 236 n. 2, 284
Eurystheus, 207
Eusebius, *Chronicon*, cited 52, 70 n. 3, 93 n. 1, 95, 96 n. 1, n. 3, 99, 143 n. 2, 146 n. 6, 159 n. 6, 160, 172 n. 5, 190 n. 3, 265 n. 1, 273 n. 4, 275 n. 5
Eusebius, *Praeparatio Evangelica*, cited 280 n. 1
Eustathius, *Commentary on the Iliad*, cited 155 n. 2; *Commentary on the Odyssey*, cited 77 n. 2, 269; *Commentary on Dionysius Periegetes*, cited 37 n. 1, 70 n. 3, 79 n. 2, 90 n. 5; *Opusculum de emendenda vita monachica*, cited 269 n. 4

Eutropius, cited 224 n. 5
Evans (Sir Arthur), *Corolla Numismatica*, cited 128
Evans, Lady, *Greek Dress*, cited 170 n. 1
Exchequer, Chancellor of, 4
exomides, 265

Fabricii, 337 n. 5
Fabricius, Gaius, 337
Fabricius (E.), *Athenische Mitteilungen*, cited 76 n. 2; *Archäologischer Anzeiger*, cited 76 n. 2
factories, 12, 20, 22
faience, 93, 94, 109, 124
fairs, 261 n. 2
Falconer (T.), ed. Strabo, cited 159 n. 2
Falerii, 219
farmers, 18, 37, 44, 48, 49, 307, 308, 310; see also agriculture
Faustulus, 197
favissae, 224 n. 5
Feronia, 261 n. 2
Ferrari, *Agathokles*, cited 209 n. 3
Festus, cited 134 n. 5, 221 n. 5, 338 n. 1
fibulae, 333
figurines, 118, 119, 332
Fikellura ware, 112–114, 116, 121 n. 5
flatum, 218
flax workers, 14
Fleet (London), 247
Florence, 2, 3, 56 n. 3, 304
Florentinus, *Geoponica*, cited 201 n. 8
Florus, *Epitome Liui*, cited 215 n. 2, 222 n. 2, 223 n. 5, 226, 228 n. 1, n. 2, 229 n. 2, 238 n. 3
flower girls, 55–57
flute players, 222
Foerster (R.), *Philologus*, cited 257 n. 2
Fontana Collection of Greek Vases, 319
Forchhammer (P.), *Philologus*, cited 326 n. 6, 329 n. 8
Forum at Rome, 218, 247–249, 251, 334, 335, 337, 338 n. 2
Fotheringham (J. K.), *Journal of Hellenic Studies*, cited 96 n. 3
fountains, 62, 76 n. 5
Fowler, W. Warde, 211 n. 4
Fox (Earle), *Corolla Numismatica*, cited 53 n. 2, 56 n. 2, 156 n. 2, 161 n. 1
Fraenkel (M.), *Inschriften von Pergamon*, cited 285 n. 2

Fragmenta Historicorum Graecorum, cited 26 n. 2, 36 n. 3, 39 n. 2, n. 3, 59 n. 6, 65 n. 4, 66 n. 3, 79 n. 2, 93 n. 1, 95 n. 2, 98 n. 9, 99 n. 2, 102 n. 2, 130 n. 2, 134 n. 1, n. 2, 135 n. 1, n. 3, n. 4, n. 8, 136 n. 2, n. 3, 137 n. 1, 138 n. 5, 144 n. 1, 145 n. 1, n. 4, n. 5, 146 n. 1, 147 n. 3, 151 n. 1, 156 n. 3, 166 n. 1, 178 n. 1, 180 n. 3, 183 n. 4, 189 n. 1, 190 n. 1, n. 3, n. 4, 191 n. 3, 192 n. 1, n. 2, 194 n. 1, 211 n. 6, 213 n. 3, n. 4, 214 n. 7, 224 n. 5, 226 n. 3, 259 n. 4, 273 n. 2, n. 3, 275 n. 2, 280 n. 1, 283 n. 5
France, 5, 50, 142, 162
France, Anatole, cited 5, 257
François vase, 113
Francotte (H.), *Mélanges* (Liège, 1910, *Bib. Fac. Phil.*), cited 303 n. 2
Frank (T.), *Classical Philology*, cited 219 n. 1
Frazer (J.), *Magic Art*, cited 238 n. 3, 336 n. 2; ed. Pausanias, cited 80 n. 6, 179 n. 10, 263 n. 4
Frederic, father of George III, 157 n. 4
Freeman (E. A.), *History of Sicily*, cited 274 n. 3
frescoes, 243, 244 n. 1, 246
Frickenhaus (A.), *Tiryns*, cited 114 n. 5, 163, 164, 317 n. 1, 318 n. 4, 320
von Fritze (H.), *Zeitschrift f. Numismatik*, cited 36 n. 3, 53 n. 2, 56 n. 2
Frohberger, *de opificum apud veteres Graecos conditione*, cited 15 n. 7
Frontinus, *Stratagems*, cited 259 n. 2, 278 n. 1
Frye, Senator, quoted 5 n. 8
Fulgentius, *Sermones Antiqui*, cited 336 n. 2
fulling, 266
furnace, 199, 202, 203, 205, 207, 208 n. 1
Furtwaengler (A.), *Antike Gemmen*, cited 243 n. 3; *Archäologische Zeitung*, cited 324; *Berliner Philologische Wochenschrift*, cited 170 n. 6; *Beschreibung der Vasensammlung im Antiquarium, Berlin*, cited 46 n. 7, 203 n. 3, n. 4, 204 n. 1, 207 n. 2, 242 n. 1; *Olympia*, cited 243 n. 3; *Winckelmannsfeste Program*, cited 171 n. 1; Thiersch and others, *Aegina*, cited 316 n. 1, n. 2, n. 6, n. 7, n. 10, 317 n. 7, 318, 320 n. 4, 333 n. 4

Gabii, 224
Gabrici (E.), *Monumenti Antichi*, cited 316 n. 9
Galassi, General, 93 n. 3, 243, 335
Galatia, Galatians, 285, 286
Galen, *Protrepticus*, cited 13 n. 5, 70 n. 3
Gallipoli, 52
Gambacorti, 2
games, 71, 123, 154, 159, 160, 178, 235, 258–262, 265
Gardner (Ernest), *Naukratis*, see Petrie and Gardner; *Handbook of Greek Sculpture*, cited 63 n. 1, 81 n. 4, 263 n. 5, 302 n. 4
Gardner (Percy), *History of Ancient Coinage*, cited 130 n. 3, 171; *Earliest Coins of Greece Proper*, cited 53 n. 2, 159 n. 5, 161 n. 2, 188; *Gold Coinage of Asia before Alexander the Great*, cited 130 n. 3, 143 n. 1; *Samos and Samian Coins*, cited 75 n. 1; *Numismatic Chronicle*, cited 57 n. 5
Gardthausen (V.), *Mastarna oder Servius*, cited 223, 249
garlands, 55–57, 60
Garrucci (R.), *Le monete dell' Italia antica*, cited 220 n. 4
Gellius, Aulus, cited 17 n. 3, 221 n. 5
Gelo of Syracuse, 10 n. 6, 30
Gelzer, *Rheinisches Museum*, cited 136 n. 1, n. 3, 137 n. 3, 138 n. 7, 140 n. 4, 141 n. 1, 145 n. 4, 146 n. 1, n. 6, 273 n. 2
genealogies, 156–159, 176, 212
Genesis, cited 149
Geographi Graeci Minores, cited 90 n. 5, 91 n. 1
Geometric pottery, 163, 169, 314, 315, 318–321, 333, 334; see also Dipylon pottery
Geomoroi, γεωμόροι, 69, 276, 277
George II, 157 n. 4
George III, 157 n. 4
George, King of Greece, 143 n. 1
Gercke und Norden, *Einleitung i. d. Altertumswissenschaft*, cited 157 n. 8
Gergethes (Γέργηθες), Gergithes (Γέργιθες), 269, 270
Gerhard (E.), *Trinkschalen u. Gefässe*, cited 203 n. 3, n. 4
Germany, Germans, 163, 197 n. 6, 253 n. 4, 311
Gerster, *Bulletin de Correspondance Hellénique*, cited 191 n. 6

Gibraltar, 177
Gihon (Miriam), 267
Gilbert, *Jahrbücher f. Classische Philologie (Neue Jahrbücher f. Philologie und Paedagogik)*, cited 53 n. 2, 63 n. 9, 326 n. 7, 328
Gilliard (C.), *Quelques Réformes de Solon*, cited 48 n. 6, 307 n. 6, 329 n. 7
Glotz (G.), *Études sociales et juridiques sur l'Antiquité grecque*, cited 328 n. 1, 329
γλυκὺς ἄγκων, 76, 77 n. 3
Gnathia ware, 335
γνώριμοι, 303
Goettingsche Gelehrte Anzeigen, see Wilisch
gold, 44 n. 5, 54 n. 1, 80 n. 4, 84, 139, 143, 144 n. 3, n. 4, 145, 147, 148, 152, 171 n. 1, 189, 192 n. 5, 198
gold currency, 3, 4, 18, 57, 128, 130–133, 140, 142 n. 5, 152, 156 n. 1, 172, 286, 287, 291; see also daric
gold mines, 39 n. 4, 44 n. 5, 50, 54 n. 1, 58 n. 1, 59 n. 1, 87, 138, 148, 203 n. 4
Golden age, 302
Golden Fleece, 41, 265
goldsmiths, 222
Gonussa, 193
Gorgasus, 240 n. 2
Gorgos, Gorgias, Gordios, 213
γουνὸς Σουνιακός, 41, 44
Government-owned industry, 22 n. 7
Gracchi, 32
Gracchan revolutionaries, 288, 289
Graef (B.), *Die antiken Vasen v. d. Akropolis zu Athen*, cited 315 n. 5; *Wochenschrift f. klassische Philologie*, cited 316 n. 6
Graffunder (P.), *Klio*, cited 338
Graillot, *Mélanges d'Archéologie et d'Histoire*, cited 246 n. 7
Great King (= King of Persia), 20, 57, 61, 69 n. 5, 72, 130, 140, 270 n. 7, 271, 291, 292
greengrocer, 17
Gregorius Cyprius, cited 190 n. 1
Grenfell (B. P.) and Hunt (A. S.), *Oxyrhynchus Papyri*, cited 104, 257, 258, 262 n. 4, 264 n. 4
Griffith (F. Ll.), *Encyclopaedia Britannica*, cited 87 n. 5; *Catalogue of the Demotic Papyri in the Rylands Library at Manchester*, cited 87 n. 4,

INDEX

93 n. 2, 98 n. 5, 100 n. 4, 125, 126; *High Priests of Memphis*, cited 97, 98 n. 6, 101
Groddech, 195 n. 4
Grote (G.), *History of Greece*, cited 36 n. 1, 66 n. 1, 70 n. 1, 80, 180 n. 3, 262 n. 1, 278 n. 2, 288, 327
Grueber (H. A.), *Coins of the Roman Republic in the British Museum*, cited 221 n. 7
Grundy (G. B.), *Great Persian War*, cited 271; *Thucydides and the History of his Age*, cited 37 n. 7, 307, 310 n. 3
Guadalquivir (Baetis), 177 n. 6
De Gubernatis, *Atti d. Reale Accademia d. Torino*, cited 66, 258 n. 1, n. 2
Guérin (V.), *Patmos et Samos*, cited 76 n. 2
guilds, 87
Guiraud (P.), *La Main-d'Oeuvre dans l'Ancienne Grèce*, cited 36; *La Propriété Foncière en Grèce*, cited 309 n. 10
Gutschmid, cited 104 n. 6; *Neue Beiträge z. Geschichte d. alten Orients*, cited 92 n. 1; *Philologus*, cited 90 n. 1, 99 n. 6, 214 n. 6
Gyges, 9, 26, 91, 92, 99 n. 3, 127, 130 n. 2, 134, 136, 137, 139 n. 3, 141, 143–149, 151, 152, 187 n. 8, 221, 236 n. 2, 273 n. 2, 286, 289, 293, 302
Gylippus, 58

Haa ab ra, see Apries
Haase, *Abhandlungen d. historisch. philologisch. Gesellschaft Breslau*, cited 37 n. 7, 38 n. 2
Habron, 181
Hackl (R.), see Sieveking (J.)
Hadrian, 63, 336 n. 5
Haeberlin (E. J.), *Aes Grave*, cited 219, 221 n. 7; *Die Systematik des ältesten roemischen Münzwesens*, cited 233 n. 1
ἁμαξοπηγῶν, 135
Hammer, *Zeitschrift f. Numismatik*, cited 146 n. 7, 148 n. 3
Hanno, 30 n. 3, 282
Hanover, House of, 157 n. 4
hare, 74, 75
Harmodius, 231, 302
Harold, King of England, 238 n. 1
Harpocration, cited 16 n. 7, 56 n. 4, 171 n. 4, 280 n. 1, 310 n. 4, 327 n. 2

Head (B. V.), *Historia Numorum*[2], cited 56 n. 2, 63 n. 7, 75 n. 1, 128 n. 1, 132 n. 3, 143 n. 1, 147 n. 1, 156 n. 2, 159 n. 5, 161 n. 1, 171 n. 6, 172 n. 3, 188, 208 n. 3, 209 n. 6; *Numismatic Chronicle*, cited 53 n. 2, 55, 63 n. 9; see also *British Museum Excavations at Ephesus; Catalogue of Greek Coins, Corinth, Ionia*
Headlam (J. W.), *Classical Review*, cited 326 n. 6
Hebrew, 126
Hebrus, 200 n. 1
hektemoroi, 13, 307, 308
Helbig (W.), cited 335; *Das homerische Epos*[2], cited 166 n. 1, 170 n. 1, 332 n. 2; *Mémoires de l'Académie des Inscriptions et Belles Lettres*, cited 169, 321, 324, 325, 326 n. 3, 329 n. 7, 330
Helladius, cited 257 n. 2
Hellanicus, cited 102 n. 2
pre-Hellenic population, 269
Hellenium at Naukratis, 104–106, 107 n. 4, 110, 116, 118
Hellenomemphites, 96 n. 4
Hellespont, 63, 92
helots, 24
ἡμέρα, 309
Hephaestus, 14, 16, 92, 97
Hera of Argos, 162
Hera of Samos, 69 n. 5, 76, 116
Hera, temple of, see Heraeum
Heraclea Ioniae, 131
Heraclea Pontica, 265
Heraclean tables, 208
Heracles, 146, 176, 178, 207, 236 n. 2
Heraclid royal family, 158 n. 6, 196, 211 n. 6
Heraclides, cited 79 n. 2, 135 n. 8, 147 n. 3, 167 n. 1, 190 n. 1, n. 2, n. 4, 191 n. 3, 192 n. 1, n. 2, 193 n. 3, 269
Heraeum at Argos, 161–164, 175, 316 n. 7, 318–320, 333 n. 4; at Samos, 76, 82; at Tiryns, 320
Hereward, 91 n. 4, 238
Hermann (C. F.), *Lehrbuch der griechischen Antiquitäten*, vol. I (*Staatsaltertümer*), cited 28 n. 5, vol. IV (*Privataltertümer*), cited 201 n. 4
Hermes, shrine of, 135
Hermes, cited 171 n. 6; see also Lehmann-Haupt, Niese
Hermias, 280–283, 288
Hermione, 330

Hermocapelia, 135 n. 4
Hermogenes (ed. Spengel), cited 51 n. 2
Hermotybies, 90 n. 1
Herodotus, 6, 9, 18, 25, 26, 33, 194 n. 6, 196, 212 n. 3, 215, 290, 292, 293, 295, 298, 320, 328; cited 8 n. 3, n. 13, 17, 22 n. 2, 26 n. 2, 27–29, 31, 35–37, 40 n. 8, 41, 46 n. 1, n. 6, 47, 50 n. 6, 51 n. 2, n. 3, 52, 54, 55, 58, 59 n. 1, n. 2, n. 3, n. 4, n. 5, 60–62, 63 n. 5, n. 7, 64, 65, 67, 68 n. 2, n. 3, n. 4, n. 5, n. 6, n. 7, n. 8, 69 n. 5, 70 n. 3, n. 4, 72, 73 n. 1, n. 4, n. 6, 74, 75 n. 1, 76, 77 n. 8, 78 n. 4, n. 5, n. 6, n. 8, 79–81, 82 n. 1, 83–85, 87 n. 1, n. 2, n. 8, n. 9, n. 10, n. 11, 88–92, 96 n. 4, 97 n. 1, n. 6, 99–101, 102 n. 1, n. 2, 103–105, 112 n. 4, 116, 117, 121 n. 4, 122 n. 1, n. 4, 123, 124, 126 n. 3, n. 4, 129–131, 133, 136 n. 2, 137 n. 1, n. 3, n. 5, 138, 139, 140 n. 1, n. 2, n. 3, 143, 144 n. 1, n. 3, n. 4, n. 6, 145 n. 1, n. 2, n. 3, n. 4, 146 n. 1, n. 4, 147 n. 4, 154, 155, 156 n. 3, 157, 158, 161–167, 169–176, 177 n. 4, n. 7, 178 n. 1, 179 n. 2, 180 n. 3, 187 n. 8, 189 n. 2, 190 n. 1, 191 n. 2, n. 3, 193 n. 4, n. 6, 197, 198, 207, 209 n. 5, 210 n. 1, 211, 214 n. 7, 231 n. 4, 239, 240, 255, 259 n. 1, n. 4, 260 n. 2, 261, 264, 268 n. 3, 270 n. 4, n. 5, n. 7, 271, 272 n. 1, 294, 302, 303, 305 n. 2, 306 n. 1, 309 n. 1, 313, 324 n. 6, n. 10, 325, 326, 330 n. 3, 333, 334, 336 n. 1
Herostratos, 103, 118, 119
Hesiod, 24
Hesiod, *Eoiai*, cited 324
Hesychius, cited 39 n. 5, 41 n. 2, 51 n. 2, 54 n. 2, 70 n. 5, 122 n. 4, 129 n. 7, 199 n. 3, n. 4, n. 5, n. 8, n. 9, 200–202, 280 n. 1, 311, 312, 313 n. 4, 327
Hesychius Milesius, cited 280 n. 1, 283 n. 5
hetaerae, 68, 93, 104, 139 n. 3
Heuzey (L.), *Catalogue des Figurines antiques de terre cuite du Musée du Louvre*, cited 123 n. 12
Hezekiah, 267
Hicks (E. L.), *Manual of Greek Historical Inscriptions*, cited 283 n. 2

Hicks (R. D.), *Companion to Greek Studies*, cited 179 n. 3
Hiero, 10, 30, 138 n. 9
Hierocles, cited 135 n. 4
Hieronymus, see Jerome
Hill (G. F.), *Handbook of Greek and Roman Coins*, cited 24 n. 1; *Historical Greek Coins*, cited 53 n. 2, 54 n. 5, 156 n. 2, 161 n. 1; *Historical Roman Coins*, cited 233 n. 1; *Sources for Greek History between the Persian and Peloponnesian Wars*, cited 59 n. 1
hill, party of the, hillmen, hill country, 29, 31, 37, 38, 39, 44, 45, 48, 291, 299, 307–313
Himera, 275 n. 4
Himerius, cited 280 n. 1, 282 n. 4
Hipparchus, 51 n. 2, 268
hippeis, 16, 49
Hippias, tyrant of Athens, 33 n. 1, 50, 51 n. 2, 56 n. 2, 59–61, 63 n. 4, 64, 66, 74, 231, 268
Hippias of Elis, cited 134 n. 2, 160
Hipponax, cited 139 n. 1, 272
Hipponikos, 12
Hirschensohn, *Philolog. Obozrenie*, cited 51 n. 4
Hirschfeld (O.), *Rheinisches Museum*, cited 91, 106, 117 n. 3, n. 5, 120 n. 4, 123 n. 8; *apud* Pauly Wissowa, cited 166 n. 1
Histiaeus, 61, 62, 268, 270, 271, 287, 292
Hittites, 149
Hitzig and Bluemner, *Pausanias*, cited 158 n. 3, 198 n. 9
Hoar, Senator, quoted 5 n. 8
Hogarth (D. G.), *Excavations at Ephesus*, see British Museum Excavations at Ephesus
Hogarth (D.G.) and others, *Annual of the British School at Athens*, cited 106–110, 115 n. 2, 116 n. 3, n. 6, 118 n. 1, n. 2, n. 3, 119 n. 5, 120 n. 2; *Journal of Hellenic Studies*, cited 106, 110, 118 n. 2, n. 4
Holm (A.), *History of Greece*, cited 23 n. 1, 159 n. 5, 198 n. 9, 275 n. 6, 285, 286, 288 n. 3, 303 n. 2; *Geschichte Siciliens im Alterthum*, cited 275 n. 6
Holwerda (A. E. J.), *Album Herwerden*, cited 53 n. 2, 56 n. 2; *Rheinisches Museum*, cited 332 n. 2, 333 n. 2

Homer, 27 n. 4, 40 n. 2, 134, 180, 262 n. 1, 264 n. 5, 303; *Iliad*, cited 16 n. 1, 179, 259 n. 3, 324 n. 5, 333 n. 2; *Odyssey*, cited 16 n. 1, 36 n. 3, 40, 201, 309 n. 6, 328 n. 1; *Hymns*, cited 259 n. 3
Homeric age, 16, 300, 329; talent, 172 n. 4
Homolle (Th.), *apud* Saglio, *Dictionnaire des Antiquités*, cited 162 n. 3
honey, 309, 310 n. 3
Hophra, see Apries
hoplite, 90, 121
Hoppin (J. C.), *Argive Heraeum*, cited 167 n. 6, 316 n. 7, 317
Horace, *Epist.*, cited 201 n. 1; *Odes*, cited, 248 n. 1
horse rearing, 187
Horus, 91 n. 4
house martin, 211
How and Wells, *Herodotus*, cited 87 n. 9, n. 10, 90 n. 1, 125 n. 3, 140 n. 5, 144 n. 4, 156 n. 5, 161 n. 2, 165 n. 5, 166 n. 1, n. 4, 168 n. 1, 190 n. 3, 193, 269 n. 7, 305 n. 1, 319 n. 4, 326 n. 7
Howorth (H. H.), *Numismatic Chronicle*, cited 53 n. 2, 56 n. 2
hubris, ὕβρις, 8, 181
Huelsen (Ch.) (trans. Carter), *Forum Romanum*, cited 247 n. 5
ὑλονόμοι, 309
Humbert (G.), *apud* Saglio, *Dictionnaire des Antiquités*, cited 222 n. 6
Hunt (A. S.), see Grenfell
hydriae, 246, 255, 320
Hyginus, cited 147 n. 2
Hymettus, 39 n. 6, 44, 308–310
Hyperakria, Hyperakrioi, Ὑπεράκριοι (Athenian), 37, 39–41; (Milesian), 40 n. 8, 41 n. 2
Hyperbolus, 207
Hyperboreans, 138 n. 9
Hyperides, cited 47 n. 7, 54 n. 2
Hysiae, 177

Iamblichus, cited 69 n. 1, 93 n. 2
Iasos, vase from, 204–206
Ibycus, 332
Ida, 44
Imbros, 134 n. 5
Imhoof-Blumer (F.), *Monnaies Grecques*, cited 200 n. 1
imperatores, 337
impressisse monetam, 218
Inaros, 104, 118

India, Indian, 142, 197 n. 6
ingots of metal, 141, 142 n. 4, 150, 152 n. 2; see also dumps
inscriptions, 14, 15, 20 n. 7, 38–41, 44, 48, 50, 56 n. 4, 75, 81, 87, 106–109, 113, 116–118, 123, 128 n. 4, 174 n. 5, 198 n. 2, 208, 212, 221 n. 2, 236, 240 n. 2, 263, 283, 284 n. 4, 286, 288, 291, 292, 297, 299, 313, 316 n. 10; see also cylinders
Ionia, 4, 27 n. 2, 83, 89, 90–92, 108, 123, 133, 245, 246, 249, 251–253
Ionian art, 244, 246; dress, 169, 170, 331–334; league, 245; mercenaries, 122, 123; philosophers, 1; pottery, 118, 120 n. 1, 334; revolt, 72 n. 2, 158, 270 n. 7; terra cottas, 252; tyrants, 270 n. 7
iron, 203, 274; currency, 23, 163 n. 1, 164 n. 1, 221 n. 7; mines, 37 n. 1
Isaiah, cited 92 n. 3, 98 n. 2
Isidore of Seville, *Etymologiae*, cited 224 n. 5, 226 n. 3
Isis, tomb of, 119 n. 3
Ismenias, 24 n. 5
Isocrates, 12; *Antidosis*, cited 65; *Areopagiticus*, cited 17; *de Biga*, cited 64 n. 4, n. 5; *Busiris*, cited 122 n. 1; *de Pace*, cited 265 n. 4; *Panathenaicus*, cited 10, 35 n. 3; *Panegyricus*, cited 261 n. 1, 304 n. 2
Israel, 303
Isthmus, 215
Isthmian games, 260
Italy, Italian, 1, 2, 3, 50, 56, 112, 187, 189, 194, 216, 233, 234, 243–245, 251, 266, 278, 286, 311, 315, 316
Italian pottery, 335

J.H.S. see *Journal of Hellenic Studies*
J.I.d'A.N. see *Journal International d'Archéologie Numismatique*
Jacoby (F.), *Marmor Parium*, cited 155 n. 2, 160 n. 4, 181
Jahrb. = *Jahrbuch des deutschen archäologischen Instituts*, cited 187 n. 4; see also Boehlau, Conze, Duemmler, Kalkmann, Kroker, Winter
Jahrbücher f. Nationalökonomie u. Statistik, see E. Meyer
Jahrbücher f. Classische Philologie, see Gilbert, Schoemann, Wilisch
Jahresbericht des Gymnas. Zittau, see Wilisch
James of Hereford, Lord, 11 n. 2

James (W.), *Varieties of Religious Experience*, cited 306
Janus, 219
Japan, 142
Java, 142
Jebb, *Attic Orators*, cited 10 n. 5; ed. Sophocles, cited 16 n. 7, 134 n. 5
Jerome, cited 52, 95, 96 n. 1, 103, 172 n. 5, 273 n. 4
Jerusalem, 267
Jevons (W. S.), *Money*, cited 3 n. 6, 142 n. 6, 162 n. 2
Jew, 194
jewellery, 164, 167, 170, 171, 175
Job, Book of, cited 149 n. 2
Johansen (K. F.), *Sikyoniske Vaser*, cited 316 n. 10
John of Antioch, cited 93 n. 1, 224 n. 5, 226 n. 3
Johnson, Dr, 281
Jones (Stuart), *Journal of Hellenic Studies*, cited 198 n. 2
Jordan, *Topographie der Stadt Rom*, cited 338 n. 1
Josephus, cited 97 n. 5
Josiah, 116, 123
Journal des Savants, see Piganiol, Reinach (A. J.), De Sanctis
Journal International d'Archéologie Numismatique, cited 171 n. 6, n. 8; see also Babelon, Svoronos
Journal of Hellenic Studies, cited 112 n. 8, 114 n. 1, 155 n. 1, 284 n. 4, 285 n. 3; see also Bent, Burrows, Dickens, Edgar, Fotheringham, Hogarth, Stuart Jones, Leaf, Macan, Mahaffy, Munro, Myres, Ramsay, Ridgeway, Ure
Journal of Roman Studies, cited, see Boni
Jove, temple of, 223
Juba, king of Libya, 201 n. 8
Judah, 123, 303
jurymen, payment of, 19, 25, 231
Justin, cited 29 n. 2, 31, 54 n. 1, 73 n. 1, 129 n. 6, 136 n. 2, 138 n. 3, 156 n. 5, 183 n. 1, 208 n. 4, 211 n. 1, 221, 278 n. 2

Kabeirion, 108 n. 2
Kahrstedt, *apud* Pauly Wissowa, cited 120 n. 4
kalasiries, 90 n. 1
Kalaurian league, 324, 330, 331
Kalkmann (A.), *Jahrbuch*, cited 333 n. 1
Kallikrates, 13 n. 3
Kallirrhoe, 62
Kallisthenes, *Apophthegms*, cited 282 n. 2
Kamaresa, 43, 44 n. 3
Kaminia, 44 n. 5
Kampanes, *Bulletin de Correspondance Hellénique*, cited 56 n. 2
κάπηλος, καπηλεῖον, καπηλεύειν, 73, 135
Kapsala, 44 n. 5
Karanos, 156, 183
Kavalla, 37
Keil (B.), *Die Solonische Verfassung*, cited 168 n. 3, 327 n. 5
Kelainai, 140, 147 n. 1
Kent, 311 n. 1
Kephisia, 38
κεραμεαί, κεραμευτική τέχνη, 200, 209
Kerameikos (Athens), 318
Keraunos, see Ptolemy Keraunos
κεροπλάστης, 55
Khamois, Satni, 97, 100–102
κιβωτός, κιβώτιον, 198, 208
Kibotos, 147 n. 1
Kieff, 142 n. 4
Kinch (K. F.), *Vroulia*, cited 93 n. 4, 109, 110 n. 4, 112 n. 1, 114
Kings, Second Book of, cited 92 n. 3, 98 n. 2
Kinkel (G.), *Epicorum Graecorum Fragmenta*, cited 324 n. 7
Kirchhoff (A.), *Studien z. Geschichte d. griechischen Alphabets*[4], cited 104 n. 7, 106
Kirrha, Kirrhaians, 259 n. 2, n. 5
κιστοφόρος, 57
κιθαρηφόρος, 57
Kitsovouno, 43
Kleidemos, Atthidograph, 328 n. 2
Klein (W.), *Die griechischen Vasen mit Meistersignaturen*, cited 245 n. 1; *Sitzungsberichte d. Akademie d. Wissenschaften in Wien*, cited 198 n. 9
kleinmeister kylikes, 115, 318
kleronomos, 277
Klio, see Graffunder, Nordin, Perdrizet, Petersen, Seeck
Knapp (P.), *Korrespondenz-Blatt f. die Gelehrten- u. Real-Schulen Wuerttembergs*, cited 189 n. 7, 192 n. 1, 193 n. 3, n. 7, 194 n. 5, 196 n. 4, n. 5, 197 n. 7, 214 n. 2
Knossos, 128, 141, 298
Knut, 238 n. 1
Kodros, 169 n. 1

INDEX

Koehler (U.), *Athenische Mitteilungen*, cited 50 n. 3, 163 n. 1; *Rheinisches Museum f. Philologie*, cited 173 n. 1, 174 n. 5; *Sitzungsberichte d. preuss. Akademie d. Wissenschaften zu Berlin*, cited 31 n. 2
Kolaios, 68, 177
Kollytos, 55
Komas, 272
κομίζειν, 139
κόψας (μέτρον), 182
κόραι, 54
Κορινθία συγγραφή, Κορινθιακά, 195
Koriskos, 283 n. 3
Kornemann (E.), apud Pauly Wissowa, 222 n. 3, n. 5
Korrespondenz-Blatt f. die Gelehrten- u. Real-Schulen Wuerttembergs, see Knapp
kothons, 248
κραίνω, 328
Kreon, 9
Kresphontes, 180
κρητῆρες, 201
Krisa, Krisaians, 66, 247 n. 2, 259–261
Kroker (E.), *Jahrbuch*, cited 315 n. 1, n. 3, 321, 325 n. 9
Kronos, 302
Ktesias, 157
kylikes, 74 n. 3, 115, 318

Labda, 193
labyrinth, 76, 89 n. 3
Lacedaemon, Lacedaemonia, 144 n. 4; see also Sparta
Lade, battle of, 75, 84
Lakedes, 158
Lakydes, 158 n. 4
Lamb (D.), *Year's Work in Classical Studies*, cited 244 n. 1
Lampsacus, 53, 63, 281
Lancastrians, 101
Landwehr, *Philologus*, cited 35 n. 2, 48 n. 6
Lanuvium, 246 n. 7
lapicidae, 230, 234
Lapithae, 193
Larcher (P. H.), *Mémoires de l'Académie des Inscriptions et Belles Lettres*, cited 280 n. 1, 283 n. 6
lares, 336
lares grundules, 336 n. 2
Larissa, near Phocaea, 246 n. 8
larnax, λάρναξ, 198, 199, 209
Latium, 219 n. 4, 224 n. 5, 234, 246, 296, 336 n. 1

de Launay (L.), apud Saglio, *Dictionnaire des Antiquités*, cited 44 n. 5, 203
laundrymen, 20
laura, 76, 77
Laurentius Lydus (Johannes), *de Magistratibus*, cited 48 n. 6; *de Mensuris et Ponderibus*, cited 224 n. 5, 226 n. 3; *de Ostentatione*, cited 238 n. 3
Laurium, 21, 23 n. 1, 36, 38, 39, 41–46, 49, 50, 58, 61
Lauth (F. J.), *Aus Aegyptens Vorzeit*, cited 97 n. 4
lautumiae, 224 n. 5
lawgivers, 8, 11, 16, 35, 93 n. 2, 182, 183, 301
Lawson (Thos. W.), *Frenzied Finance*, cited 4 n. 1, 5 n. 8
Layard (A. H.), *Monuments of Nineveh*, cited 325 n. 6
Layton (W. T.), *Capital and Labour*, cited 11 n. 2
Lazarus, 102
leaden coins, 74
Leaf, *Journal of Hellenic Studies*, cited 281–283, 286
Leaina, 253
leather currency, 221 n. 7
leather workers, 14, 17, 222
Lebadea, 162 n. 3
Lebedos, 131
Ledl (A.), *Studien zur älteren athen. Verfassungsgeschichte*, 34 n. 2
Lehmann-Haupt (C. F.), cited 157; *Hermes*, cited 161 n. 3
Lelantine war, 68 n. 2, 117 n. 1
Lemnos, 134 n. 5
Lenormant, 24 n. 1, 89 n. 3, 150; *La Monnaie dans l'Antiquité*, cited 74 n. 6, 141; *Monnaies Royales de la Lydie*, cited 130 n. 7; *Monnaies et Médailles*, cited 56 n. 4
Lenschau (T.), apud Bursian, *Jahresbericht*, 34 n. 2, 328 n. 3
Leokedes, 154, 157, 158, 259 n. 1
Leontini, 273–4 *passim*, 296
Leontis, 50 n. 3
Lepsius (K. R.), *Abhandlungen d. preussisch. Akademie d. Wissenschaften zu Berlin*, cited 148 n. 3; *Denkmäler*, cited 123 n. 9; *Königsbuch*, cited 98
Lermann (W.), *Athenatypen*, cited 53 n. 2, 56 n. 2, 63 n. 7
Lesbians, Lesbos, 96 n. 1, 104, 120

Letters of Phalaris, 274
Leukas, 189, 191
λευκὸς χρυσός, 133
Leutsch und Schneidewin, *Paroemiographi Graeci*, cited 71 n. 1, 73 n. 2, 76 n. 6, 77 n. 4, 78 n. 7, 79 n. 2, 190 n. 1, 308 n. 3
Levantine race, 305
Lewis (Geo. Cornewall), *On the Credibility of Early Roman History*, cited 215, 236 n. 2, 237 n. 5
Lexicon Seguerianum, ed. Bekker, cited 39, 41 n. 3, 57, 310 n. 4, 326 n. 9, 327 n. 9
Libanius, *Oratio c. Severum*, cited 257 n. 2
Liber and Libera, 250 n. 1
Libya, 68, 74, 86, 89 n. 1, 92 n. 2, 122, 124, 125 n. 3, 201 n. 8
Liddell and Scott, *Lexicon*, cited 80, 313 n. 3
Limir-Patesi-Assur, 214 n. 3
Liopesi, 58 n. 3
liturgies, 67, 79, 287
Livy, cited 54 n. 1, 57 n. 2, 184 n. 2, 215 n 2, 216–218, 221 n. 2, 222 n. 1, n. 7, 223, 224 n. 5, 225–230, 232 n. 1, 234, 235, 238 n. 3, 245, 247, 248 n. 1, 253 n. 4, 261 n. 2, 278 n. 3, 289 n. 1, 298
Lloyd (Hy D.), *Wealth against Commonwealth*, cited 4, 5, 6, 14, 235, 267
Locrians, 22
Lodi, 2
Loeper (R.), *Athenische Mitteilungen*, cited 38 n. 5, 41 n. 3, 44 n. 3, 45, 50, 310 n. 1, 312 n. 4, 313 n. 5
Loeschcke (G.), *Athenische Mitteilungen*, cited 316 n. 4, 319
London, 3, 247
Long Walls, 13 n. 3
λόφος, 39, 44
Lophos Loutrou, 42
Lords, House of, 3
Louvre, 74 n. 3, 245 n. 1
λύχνων, οὐκ τῶν, 207
Lucian, *Bis Accusatus*, cited 151 n. 4, 275 n. 1; *Charon*, cited 144 n. 4; *Eunuchus*, cited 280 n. 1, 283 n. 6; *Lexiphanes*, cited 199 n. 9; *Navigium*, cited 151 n. 4; *Phalaris*, cited 275 n. 1, n. 2, 276, 301 n. 2; *Prometheus*, cited 203 n. 4; *Vera Historia*, cited 275 n. 1; Schol. *Cataplus*, cited 134 n. 5; Schol. *Lexiphanes*, cited 199 n. 3, n. 9, 200

Lucius Tarquinius, 216; see also Tarquinius Priscus
Lucretius, cited 311 n. 1
lucumo, 239 n. 5
Lucumo, 216; see also Tarquinius Priscus
Luke, cited 239 n. 1
Lycian language, 134 n. 5
Lycophron, son of Periander, 214 n. 7
Lycophron, *Cassandra*, cited 59 n. 1
Lydia and Lydians, 1, 4, 46, 59 n. 6, 64, 72, 73, 86, 90 n. 4, 91, 92, 104 n. 3, 123, chap. v *passim*, 155 n. 2, 187, 188, 191, 236 n. 2, 270, 273, 293, 302
Lydian stone, 129
Lygdamis, 70 n. 2
Lykos, 155 n. 2
Lynkestai, 183, 190 n. 3
Lyons, 215 n. 2
Lysias, *c. Eratosthenem*, cited 12; *c. Frumentarios*, cited 12
Lysimachus, 284

Macan (R.), *Herodotus*, cited 54 n. 6, 59 n. 4, n. 6, 68 n. 4, 156 n. 2, 157 n. 7, 159 n. 2, 161 n. 2, 165, 166, 168, 174, 175 n. 1, 259 n. 1, 262 n. 2, 325 n. 3, 326 n. 7; *Journal of Hellenic Studies*, cited 31 n. 2
Macarius, cited 77 n. 4
Macaulay (G. C.), translation of Herodotus, cited 313 n. 3
Macdonald (G.), *Coin Types*, cited 128 n. 1, 133 n. 4, 143 n. 1, 150
MacDonald (J. Ramsay), *Unemployment and the Wage Fund*, cited 5 n. 8
Macedonia, 59, 61, 147, 156, 157, 158 n. 6, 159, 183, 271, 330
Macfie (J. W. Scott), *Revue d'Ethnologie et de Sociologie*, cited 171 n. 1
μάχιμοι, 122
Macrobius, *Saturnalia*, cited 287 n. 4
Maeander, 131, 147 n. 1
Maeandrius, 84
Maelius, Spurius, 229, 255 n. 1, 277, 278
Maeonian dynasty, 144
μάγειρος, 257
Magians, 209
magic, 101
Magnesia, 131
Mahaffy (J. P.), *Journal of Hellenic Studies*, cited 160
Malalas, cited 71 n. 4, 72 n. 5
Malchus, 278 n. 2

Malcolm (J.), *Memoir of Central India*, cited 142 n. 3
Mallet (D.), *Les Premiers Établissements des Grecs en Égypte*, cited 56 n. 3, 87 n. 6, n. 8, 89 n. 3, 90 n. 1, n. 4, 91 n. 3, n. 4, n. 9, 92 n. 2, 103 n. 1, 105 n. 1, 107, 120 n. 4, 121 n. 2, 122, 123 n. 12, 124 n. 2
Mamertine prison, 224 n. 5
Manetho, cited 95 n. 2, 99, 100
Manlius, Marcus, 229
Mantineans, 212 n. 1
Mantissa, cited 308 n. 3
Mantyes, 58, 59, 62
Manu, laws of, 221 n. 4
manual labour, 13–22, 231, 269, 275, 279
Marathon, 38, 66
Marcellinus, *Vita Thucydidis*, cited 33 n. 1, 50 n. 7
Marchant (E. C.), *Thucydides Book II*, cited 313 n. 1
Marcopoulo, 39 n. 6
Margoliouth (D. S.), *Mohammed*, cited 261 n. 2
Mariéjol (J. H.), *de Orthagoridis*, 259 n. 5, 264 n. 2
Mariette (A.), cited 100 n. 4
Marius, 32
Marmor Parium, cited 155 n. 2, 156 n. 3, 157 n. 1, 160 n. 4, 181, 210 n. 1
Maronea, 36 n. 3, 44 n. 3, 46, 47, 50
Marquardt (J.), *Privatleben d. Roemer*, cited 336 n. 4
Marseilles, 246
Marshall (F. H.), see *British Museum Catalogue of Rings*
Martha (J.), *L'Art Étrusque*, cited 240 n. 4, 251 n. 1, 255 n. 3
Marx (Karl), 6 n. 3, 21
masons, 95, 285; see also stone-masons
Maspero (G.), cited 93, 100 n. 4; *Bibliothèque Égyptologique*, cited 96 n. 2, 99 n. 3, n. 4; *Histoire Ancienne*[5], cited 87 n. 9, 99 n. 4, 103, 197 n. 5; *Passing of the Empires*, cited 123 n. 5; *Popular Stories of Ancient Egypt*, cited 101 n. 3, 102 n. 1, n. 3
Mastarna, 223, 249
Matthew, cited 261 n. 2
Mau (A.), *apud* Pauly Wissowa, cited 203 n. 4
Mauri (A.), *I Cittadini Lavoratori dell' Attica*, cited 15 n. 2, 17, 37 n. 7, 307 n. 1
Maximus Tyrius, cited 70 n. 3, 180 n. 2, 307 n. 4
Medes, Media, 90, 91 n. 1, 123, 146 n. 4, 157
Medici, the, 2, 285, 286, 304
Mediterranean, 72, 87
Medon, 158
Megabazus, 62, 271
Megacles' daughter, 52
Megara, 8, 14, 16 n. 2, 29, 31, 76, 166 n. 2, 168, 187 n. 9, 264–268, 296, 329, 330, 336 n. 1
Megara Hyblaea, 265, 273
Megaris, 265
Megiddo, 116
Mela, cited 87 n. 1
Mélanges d'Archéologie et d'Histoire, see Graillot
Melanippus, 262
Melas, 136, 272, 273
Melissa, 212
Meltas, K. of Argos, 158
Mémoires de l'Académie des Inscriptions et Belles Lettres, see Helbig, Larcher
Memphis 80, 88, 95, 96 n. 4, 97, 98, 100
Menaechmus of Sicyon, 258 n. 2, 260 n. 1
Menander, *Twins*, cited 50 n. 2
Mendes, 121 n. 3
mercatores Romanam curiam sequentes, 304
mercenaries, 36, 78, 89, 90, 92, 102 n. 1, 121–124, 140, 145, 165 n. 5, 166, 212, 300
Mermnadae, Mermnads, 1, 139 n. 1, 144 n. 3, 147 n. 3
Meroe, 98
Merovingians, 142
Mesogeia, Mesogeioi, 39 n. 6, 310 n. 2
Messana, 75
Messene, 179 n. 3, 180
Messenian War, 68 n. 2, 158 n. 6, 167 n. 2, 177, 179, 182, 331 n. 3
metal industry, 21, 69, 73, 74, 80, 81, 146 n. 7, 187, 203 n. 4, 243, 292
Methymna, 191 n. 3
metics, 67, 234
μετρία ἐσθής, 331, 332
μέτρον, μέτρα, 170–172, 182
μετρονόμοι, 171
Metropisi, see Amphitrope
Meyer (E.), *Geschichte d. alten Aegyptens*, cited 102 n. 1, 117 n. 5, .

125 n. 3; *Geschichte d. Altertums*, cited 6 n. 3, 29 n. 2, 37 n. 7, 47 n. 2, 54 n. 1, 59 n. 4, 64, 69 n. 5, 70 n. 1, 83 n. 5, 90 n. 4, 105 n. 1, 122, 145 n. 4, 148 n. 5, 168 n. 3, n. 4, 173 n. 2, 180 n. 4, 192 n. 1, 262, 266 n. 1, 267 n. 6, 270 n. 6, 278 n. 2; *Jahrbücher f. Nationalökonomie u. Statistik*, cited 3 n. 3; *Kleinschriften*, cited 21 n. 2, 265; *Rheinisches Museum*, cited 193 n. 2

Meyer (G.), *apud* G. Curtius, *Studien zur griech. u. latein. Grammatik*, cited 327

Mezentius, 249

Michaelis (A.), *Century of Archaeological Discoveries*, cited 63 n. 2, 74 n. 3, 253 n. 4

Midas, 146, 147, 151, 152 n. 2, 155 n. 2, 213 n. 4, 293

middlemen, 1, 129 n. 3

Migne, *Bibliotheca Patrum Graecorum*, cited 71 n. 4

Milchhoefer, *Abhandlungen d. preussisch. Akademie d. Wissenschaften zu Berlin*, cited 38, 45, 58 n. 3, 312 n. 4; *Athenische Mitteilungen*, cited 50 n. 4; *apud* Pauly Wissowa, cited 41 n. 3

Miletus, Milesians, 21, 33, 59 n. 1, 61, 62, 63 n. 7, 72–74, 79, 90, 92, 96, 103, 104, 110–112, 116, 117, 121 n. 5, 123, 124, 132, 133, 135 n. 7, 145 n. 3, 191, 212, 266, 268–271 *passim*, 287, 296; Milesian hyperakria, 40 n. 8; Milesian pottery, 1, 107 n. 4, 110–112, 114, 116, 118, 212 n. 8; Milesians' Fort, 90, 91, 104, 117, 118, 120, 121, 123 n. 8

military despotism, 24, 27–32, 35, 144, 190 n. 2, 196, 258, 280, 282, 300, 301

millionaires, 13 n. 4, 35

Milo, 193 n. 7

Miltiades, 52, 199 n. 10, 245 n. 2

Miluhha, Miluhhi, 98, 99 n. 3

miners, 12–14, 20, 38, 44, 45, 47–49, 152, 271, 291, 292, 296

mines, mining districts, 15, 21, 36–39, 41, 44–47, 49–51, 58 n. 1, 59–62, 64, 68, 87, 137, 140, 146 n. 7, 147, 148, 183 n. 6, 224 n. 5, 271, 291, 292, 296, 310, 312 n. 5

Minns (E. H.), *Greeks and Scythians*, cited 286, 287, 288

Minoan culture, 333; thalassocracy, 330

Minos, 169, 331

Miriam (Gihon), 267

μισθός, 21

Mitchell (J. M.) and Caspari (M. O. B.), ed. Grote, cited 327 n. 1, 330, 331

Mitteilungen des deutschen archäologischen Instituts in Athen, cited 108 n. 2, 210 n. 1, 312 n. 5, 316 n. 2; see also Brueckner, L. Curtius, Diamantaras, Doerpfeld, Fabricius, Koehler, Loeper, Loeschcke, Milchhoefer, Oikonomos, Pallat, Pernice, Studniczka

Mitteilungen des deutschen archäologischen Instituts in Rom, cited 215 n. 2, 242 n. 1, 255 n. 3, 335; see also Petersen, Pinza

Mitylene, 168, 282 n. 2

mixing bowls (craters), 82, 125, 126, 201, 205, 213

Mnason, 22

Mnesarchus, 69 n. 1

Mohammed, 261 n. 2

Moloch, 278 n. 2

Mommsen (A.), *Heortologie*, cited 16 n. 7

Mommsen (Th.), *de Collegiis*, cited 222 n. 5; *History of Rome*, cited 32 n. 1, 222 n. 6, 230 n. 2, 231, 233, 285, 295; *Roemische Forschung*, cited 228 n. 1, 229 n. 2, n. 4, 255 n. 1, 337 n. 3; *Roemisches Staatsrecht*, cited 222 n. 4

mons sacer, 233

monstrum, 277

Montelius (O.), *Civilisation Primitive en Italie*, cited 119 n. 3, 242 n. 2, 246 n. 6

Monumenti Antichi, cited 248 n. 2, 251 n. 2, 253 n. 2; see also Gabrici, Pinza, Schiaparelli

Monumenti Inediti pubblicati dall' Instituto di Corrispondenza archeologica, cited 213 n. 4

Monuments Grecs, cited 325 n. 5

Moret (A.), *de Bocchori rege*, cited 93 n. 2, n. 4, 100 n. 4

Moses, 197

moulders of gold and ivory, 14

μούναρχος, 27

Movers (F. C.), *Die Phoenizier*, cited 191 n. 3

mtk, 125, 126

INDEX

Mueller (C.), *Aeginetica*, cited 160, 166 n. 1, 167, 176 n. 3, 177, 330 n. 4
Mueller (K.) and Oelmann (F.), *Tiryns*, cited 315 n. 1, 317 n. 1
Mueller and Deecke, *Die Etrusker*, cited 221 n. 1, 249
Muenzer und Strack, *Die antiken Münzen Nord-Griechenlands*, cited 37 n. 3, 60 n. 2
Mullach (F. W. A.), *Fragmenta Philosophorum Graecorum*, cited 19 n. 4
Mundella, Mr, 11 n. 2
Munich, 251 n. 3, 252
Munro (J. A. R.), *Journal of Hellenic Studies*, cited 40 n. 1
Muretus, *Variae Lectiones*, cited 31 n. 2
Muses, 27 n. 4
music, 73, 260 n. 4, 261
Mycenae, 162, 298, 333
Mycenaean culture, 169, 333; period, 163, 164; pottery, 319
Mykalessos, 106, 108; see also Rhitsona
Mylonpolis, 214 n. 6
Myrcinus, 59 n. 1, 61, 62, 271
Myres (J. L.), *Journal of Hellenic Studies*, cited 96, 191 n. 2, 268 n. 3, 324 n. 8; *apud* Zimmern, 309 n. 9
Myrina, 131
Myron, tyrant of Sicyon, 258, 263
Myrrina, 51 n. 2
ἐν μύρτου κλαδί, 302 n. 5

nails as money, 162
ναίω, 327
Nakauba, see Nechepsus
ναός, 327
Naples, 23
National Baptist of Philadelphia, cited 5
ναύκληρος, 327
naukraries, naukraroi, ναυκραρία, ναύκραρος, 326–331
Naukratis, 53, 56 n. 3, 68, 92 n. 2, 103–118, 120–122, 124, 172 n. 1, 212 n. 8, 293, 315 n. 5, 324
Naukratite pottery, 107 n. 4, 114–116, 117 n. 4, 118
ναύω, 327
Nauplia, 330, 331
ναῦς, 327
nauis, 327
Naxos, 70 n. 2, 155 n. 2
Neboshazban, 214; see also Psammetichus I
Nechepsus (Nakauba), 88 n. 1, 98
Necho I (Nekau), 88, 98, 101 n. 1, n. 2

Necho II (Nekau), 87, 88, 116, 123, 124, 325
negroes, 101
Neilos, 169 n. 1
Neith, 102 n. 1, 214 n. 4
Nemean games, 259 n. 1
Nemesis, 83, 84
Neochabis (Nekauba), 100
neolithic age, 336 n. 1
Netos amphora, 113, 315 n. 5
Neue Jahrbücher; see *Jahrbücher f. Classische Philologie*
New York Daily Commercial Bulletin, cited 5; *State Investigation Report*, cited 5 n. 8; *Sun*, cited 5
Nicolaus Damascenus, cited 59 n. 6, 130 n. 2, 135, 136, 137 n. 1, n. 2, n. 3, 138 n. 5, n. 7, 144 n. 1, 145 n. 1, n. 4, n. 5, 146 n. 1, 180 n. 3, 183, 189 n. 1, n. 8, 190 n. 1, n. 2, n. 3, 191 n. 1, n. 3, 192–194, 196, 197, 211 n. 6, 213, 214 n. 7, 258, 259 n. 4, 273 n. 2, n. 3
Niebuhr (G. B.), *History of Rome*, tr. Walter, cited 239 n. 2
Niese (B.), *Hermes*, cited 212 n. 3; *apud* Pauly Wissowa, cited 279 n. 3
Nigeria, 171 n. 1
Nikias, 12, 13, 49, 51, 229 n. 1, 304
Nikias, a Megarian, 266
Nikolaos, son of Periander, 214 n. 7
Nikosthenes, potter, 319, 335
Nile, 87, 91, 103, 121, 197
Niloxenos, 104 n. 3
Nilsson (M. P.), *Timbres Amphoriques de Lindos*, cited 151
Nisaea, 29
Nitokris, 99 n. 3
νόμισμα, 149
νόμος, 167
νομοθέτης, 301
Nonius Marcellus, cited 223 n. 1
Norden, see Gercke
Nordin (R.), *Klio*, cited 302 n. 8
Notizie degli Scavi, cited 219 n. 4, 251 n. 3, 252 n. 1, 334, 335, 336 n. 1; see also Barnabei, Boni, Cozza, Pasqui
nouem combusti, 337
Novgorod, 142 n. 4
Numa, 221 n. 7, 222
Numismatic Chronicle, cited 60 n. 2; see also Borrell, Gardner (P.), Head, Howorth, Ridgeway, Six

Numismatische Zeitschrift, see v. Bergmann
Nut Amen, see Ammeris
nymph, 117
Nymphi, 130 n. 7

ὀβελοί, ὀβελίσκοι, 149, 162–164
obols, 172 n. 2, 221 n. 7
Oedipus, 9
Oelmann (F.), see Mueller (K.)
Ohio, 235 n. 3
οἰκέται, 22
Oikonomos, *Athenische Mitteilungen*, cited 38, 39, 40 n. 9, 44 n. 1
οἰκονόμος, 10
oil presses, 2
Oil, Standard, 5
ointments, manufacture of, 187
Olbia, 286–288, 297
olentis arator Hymetti, 309
olive oil and yards, 34, 69, 308
Olympia, 192 n. 5, 194, 198, 199, 263
Olympian games, 123, 154, 159, 160, 175, 178, 258, 260, 265
ὀλυμπιονίκης, 34
Omphale, 236 n. 2
κατ' ὄναρ, 81
ὀνομάσαντος, 328
opibus superbiaque, 235
opifices, 222, 230, 234, 235
Oppert (J.), *Mémoire sur les Rapports de l'Égypte et de l'Assyrie*, cited 97 n. 4, 98 n. 4
optimates, 234
oracle, 158 n. 6, 209, 269, 270; see also Delphi
Orchomenos, Minyan, 330
ὀρεινά, ὀρεινή, 40, 309
Oriental influence, 321
Orientalische Litteraturzeitung, see Spiegelberg
Oroetes, 84
Orosius, cited 30 n. 3, 45 n. 4, 54 n. 1, 187 n. 1, 282 n. 1
Orthagoras, 9, 28, 179, 180, 257, 258, 262 n. 4, 263, 293
Orthagorids, 179, 263
ostracism, 67
Ouinin (=Ionians), 123
Overbeck, *Abhandlungen d. saechsischen Gesellschaft d. Wissenschaften*, cited 198 n. 9
Ovid, *Ars Amatoria*, cited 275 n. 2; *Fasti*, cited 238 n. 3; *Ibis*, cited 275 n. 2; *Metamorphoses*, cited 147 n. 2; *Tristia*, cited 275 n. 2
"owls" (coin), 53, 54, 58, 61
"ox" (? coin), 57 n. 5
Oxford, 3 n. 2, 112 n. 8, 237, 257
Oxyrhynchus papyri, 104, 257, 258, 262 n. 4, 264 n. 4

Pactolus, 129, 147, 148
Pactyes, 139, 152, 293
Paestum, 221 n. 2
παιάν, παιανίζω, παιωνίζω, 61
Paianians, 55, 58, 59 n. 5, 61
painters, 14
Paionia, Paionians, 59–62, 147, 183 n. 6
παῖς, 157
Pais (Ettore), 194 n. 6, 224 n. 5, 236; *Ancient Italy*, cited 255 n. 1; *Ancient Legends of Roman History*, cited 236 n. 1, 237, 238 n. 2, 239 n. 5, 248 n. 1, 249, 255 n. 1; *Ricerche sulla Storia e sul Diritto pubblico di Roma*, 236 n. 1, cited 335; *Storia Critica di Roma*, 236 n. 1
Palatine, 224 n. 5, 253, 338 n. 2
Palazzo di Giustizia (Rome), 65 n. 3
Palestine, 92
Palladius, cited 201 n. 5, n. 6
"Pallas," παλλάδες (coins), 54, 291
Pallas (goddess), 16, 54; see also Athena
Pallat, *Athenische Mitteilungen*, cited 317 n. 7, 318
Palmerius (Le Paulmier), *Exerc.*, cited 40
Pamphaes, 273
Pamphilus, 39 n. 1
Panaitios, 273, 274
Panathenaic amphorae, 113; games, 260
Panciatighi, 3
Pandion, 313
πανδοκεύων, 135
Pangaion, Mt, 36, 54 n. 1, 56, 59, 148
Panionios, 191 n. 3
Panofka (T.), *Res Samiorum*, cited 68 n. 1
Pantagnotos, 82
Pantaleon, 137, 273
Papal treasury, 304
Pape (W.), *Griechische Eigennamen*, cited 199 n. 10
paper currency, 3, 4
Paphlagonia, 48, 50, 284 n. 4
Paphos, 118, 119
papyri, 48 n. 6, 104, 257
Paralia, παραλία, πάραλος γῆ, παράλιοι, 41, 312, 313

INDEX

Paralos (ship), 312
παραθαλάσσιος, 313
Parian Marble, see Marmor Parium
Parnes, Mt, 40, 41, 44, 308–311
παρθένοι (coins), 54
Pasqui, *Notizie d. Scavi*, cited 219 n. 3
παστάδες, 218
patricians, 216, 227
Patrokleides, 194, 197
Pauly Wissowa, cited 41 n. 3, 56 n. 1, 120 n. 4, 148 n. 5, 156 n. 2, 161 n. 2, 162 n. 3, 166 n. 1, 201 n. 8, 203 n. 4, 207 n. 4, 222 n. 3, n. 5, 268 n. 4, 272 n. 3, n. 4, 276 n. 5, 279 n. 3, 331 n. 3
Pausanias, *Description of Greece*, 160, cited 46 n. 6, 62 n. 5, n. 6, 65 n. 5, 70 n. 3, 145 n. 1, 157 n. 2, 158, 159, 162 n. 3, 165 n. 2, 167 n. 1, n. 2, 169 n. 2, n. 4, 176 n. 3, 177 n. 1, n. 3, 179, 183 n. 3, 193 n. 5, 195, 198, 211, 212 n. 2, 258 n. 3, 259 n. 2, n. 3, 260 n. 4, 263, 264 n. 1, n. 6, 266, 267 n. 5, 284 n. 4, n. 5, 309, 331, 336 n. 1
Pausanias the Spartan, 24, 30, 282
Payne (Henry B.), 5
Peak of Derbyshire, 40
Pearson, ed. Sophocles, cited 16 n. 7
Pegasus, 57, 188, 209
Peile, cited 134 n. 5
Peiraeans, trittys of, 41 n. 3
Peirene, 62 n. 6
Peisistratids, 14, 15, 25, 31, 264, 289, 292
Peisistratus, 7, 10, 13, 15, 16 n. 7, 28–32, chap. II *passim*, 76 n. 5, 137, 166, 167, 215, 221, 231, 245 n. 2, 260, 265, 268, 271 n. 4, 274, 287, 291, 299, 302, 303 n. 2, 305–307, 308 n. 3, 309, 310 n. 2, 311, 328
Pelasgians, 309
pelatai, 13, 307
Pelham (H.), *Outlines of Roman History*, cited 239
Peloponnese, Peloponnesians, 66, 72, 154, 155, 156 n. 1, 173, 175, 176, 178, 180, 294, 305 n. 1, 313, 317, 330
Peloponnesian brooches, 168; war, 19, 23 n. 1, 26, 33 n. 1, 45, 260 n. 2; weights and measures, 161, 172
Pelusium, 124
Pelusian mouth of Nile, 121
πενέσται, 24
πένητες καὶ πεζοί, 274

pentekosiomedimnoi, 16, 49
Pentelicon, 39 n. 6, 310
Penteskuphia, 207 n. 2, 208 n. 1
Pepoli, Roméo, 2
Περάτι, 311
Perdiccas, 24 n. 5
Perdrizet (P.), *Klio*, cited 36 n. 2, 46 n. 6, 47 n. 3, 50 n. 1, 59 n. 4
perfume vase, 119
Pergamum, Pergamus, Pergamene, 135 n. 4, 148, 284–286, 296, 297
Periander, 21, 24 n. 5, 31, 63, 104 n. 3, 124, 166, 167, 187 n. 8, 189–192, 195–197, 212–215, 259, 260, 305
Pericles, 13 n. 3, 14, 15, 17, 49, 67, 231, 304
Periklytos of Tenedos, 162 n. 3
περιζώματα, 276
Pernice, *Athenische Mitteilungen*, 321 n. 4, 325 n. 5; see also Brueckner
περόναι, 170, 333
Perrot (G.), *Histoire de l'Art dans l'Antiquité*, cited 112, 116 n. 5, 169 n. 3
Perseus, 198, 214 n. 5
Persia, Persians, 20, 24, 31, 33, 47, 50, 53, 57, 61, 62, 66, 69–73, 75, 77 n. 3, 79, 80, 83, 84, 92 n. 2, 102 n. 1, 123, 124, 130, 132, 133, 138–140, 144, 145 n. 2, 172 n. 4, 249, 270, 271, 280 n. 1, 282 n. 2, 291, 292, 312 n. 5
Persian wars, 19, 25, 26, 32, 96, 260 n. 2, 332
Persinos, 282 n. 2
Peru, 44 n. 5
Perugia, 246
Petersen (E.), *Klio*, cited 253; *Roemische Mitteilungen*, cited 246 n. 5
Petra, 193 n. 7
Petrie (Flinders), *apud* Hogarth, *Annual of the British School at Athens*, 119 n. 5; *History of Egypt*, cited 87 n. 9, 88 n. 1, n. 2, 97 n. 5, 98 n. 5, 100, 101 n. 4, 121, 123 n. 1, 125 n. 3; *Tanis*, cited 109 n. 5, 112 n. 3, n. 4, 121
Petrie and Gardner, *Naukratis*, cited 103, 104 n. 7, 105–107, 109, 110 n. 3, 113 n. 2, 114 n. 1, n. 2, 116, 118 n. 1, n. 2, 119, 172 n. 1
Phacussa, 214 n. 6
φαινομηρίδες, 332
Phaistos, 298
Phalaris, 14, 27 n. 2, 274–278, 289 n. 2, 303 n. 2

Phaleas, 22 n. 1
Phaleron, 305
Phaleron ware, 315, 318, 321
Phalkes, 179
Phanes, 102 n. 1, 124
Phanias of Ephesus, cited 144 n. 3
Pharaoh, 88 n. 1 and chap. IV *passim*, 212
Pharaoh's daughter, 197
Phasis, 148 n. 3
Pheidias (= Pheidon), 155 n. 2
Pheidon of Argos, 9, 26, 27 n. 2, 64 n. 3, 69 n. 5, 149, 152 n. 2, 154–162, 164, 170, 171 n. 3, 172–186, 221, 235 n. 3, 259 n. 1, 260, 292, 294, 301 n. 1, 304, 305, 330, 331
Pheidon of Corinth, 182
φελλεῖς, 308
Pherecrates, *Metalleis*, cited 51 n. 2
Pheron, 97 n. 1
Philadelphia, 130 n. 7
Philaidae, Philaids, 33, 63
Philemonides, 12
Philetairos, 284–286, 288
Philip of Macedon, 36, 54 n. 1, 282, 330
Philip, son of Butacides, 239, 255
Philippi (Macedonia), 39 n. 4, 50
Philippi (A.), *Beiträge zu einer Geschichte d. Attischen Bürgerrechtes*, cited 329
Philistus, 30
Philochorus, cited 36 n. 3, 39, 65, 66 n. 3, 134 n. 5
Philokypros, tyrant of Soli, 158, 303 n. 1
Philolog. Obozrenie, see Hirschensohn
Philologus, see Foerster, Forchhammer, Gutschmid, Landwehr, Unger
φιλοπότης, 126
Philostratus, *Vita Apollonii*, cited 151 n. 4
Phocaea, 130 n. 6, 221, 240, 246, 282 n. 2
Phocians, 22
Phoenicia, Phoenicians, 87, 89, 90 n. 4, 93 n. 4, 106, 120, 239, 278 n. 2, 293, 321 n. 5, 324, 325, 326 n. 3
Phoenician standard, 132
Phoronid, 44 n. 4
φορτία, 68, 89
Photius, cited 19 n. 3, 54 n. 2, n. 4, 56 n. 4, 70 n. 5, 71 n. 1, 79 n. 2, 151 n. 1, 257 n. 2, 326 n. 9, 327, 328, 330 n. 3

Phrygia, 49, 62 n. 4, 140, 146, 147, 155 n. 2, 208, 213 n. 4, 293
Phye, 51, 52, 54, 55, 58–60, 291
φυλή τε καὶ φρατρία, 217
Pianchi, 88 n. 1, 95, 98, 99 n. 3, 100 n. 4
piece work, 20
Pi-emro, 106 n. 3
Pieria, 147
S. Pietro in Carcere, church of, 224 n. 5
Piganiol (A.), *Journal d. Savants*, cited 335
Pigres, 58, 59, 62
Pillars of Herakles, 68
πίμπρημι, 81
Pindar, 9–10, 290; *Isthmians*, cited 156 n. 1; *Nemeans*, cited 177 n. 7; *Olympians*, cited 10 n. 1, n. 2; *Pythians*, cited 10 n. 3, 275, 289 n. 2, 336 n. 1; Schol. *Nemeans*, cited 258 n. 2, 259–261; Schol. *Olympians*, cited 157 n. 6, 176 n. 3, 182, 186 n. 2, 195 n. 3, 275 n. 5; Schol. *Pythians*, cited 275 n. 2
Pindaros, tyrant of Ephesus, 272, 273
Pinza (G.), *Bullettino della Commissione Archeologica Municipale di Roma*, cited 221 n. 2, 224 n. 5, 243, 336 n. 1, n. 2, 338 n. 1; *Monumenti Antichi*, cited 244 n. 1, 252, 338 n. 2; *Roemische Mitteilungen*, cited 243
Pipin, diploma, cited, 261 n. 2
piracy, 70, 71, 129, 292, 321 n. 5, 324, 329, 330
Pisa (Italian), 2; (Peloponnesian), 159, 160
Pisamiilki, see Psammetichus (Assyrian form)
Pitane, 285
πίθος, 207
plague, 92
plain, party of the, 35, 47, 48, 291, 307, 312
Plaka, 42
Plass (H. G.), *Die Tyrannis*, cited 70 n. 2, 71 n. 5, 198 n. 9, 269, 272 n. 4
Plataea, 26; in Libya, 68
Platner (S. B.), *Topography of Rome*², cited 247 n. 5, 248 n. 1
Plato, 6, 28 n. 1, 29, 280, 281, 283, 286, 288, 290; *Alcibiades*, cited 18; *Amator*, cited 18; *Apology*, cited 18; *Critias*, cited 16, 40, 308 n. 2, 309; *Gorgias*, cited 18, 208 n. 1; *Hippar-*

chus, cited 302; *Laws*, cited 16, 18, 176 n. 2, 181 n. 3, 290; *Letters*, cited 30 n. 1, 189 n. 8, 280 n. 1, 283 n. 3; *Meno*, cited 24 n. 5, 85 n. 1; *Minos*, cited 336 n. 1; *Phaedo*, cited 26 n. 2; *Phaedrus*, cited 198; *Protagoras*, cited 16 n. 7, 189 n. 8; *Republic*, cited 18, 20 n. 6, 24 n. 5, 26, 27, 28 n. 4, n. 5, 29 n. 6, 30, 129 n. 3, 145, 149, 151, 189 n. 8, 302, 304; *Timaeus*, cited 122 n. 1, 214 n. 4; Schol. *Hippias Major*, cited 190 n. 1; Schol. *Phaedrus*, cited 198 n. 3

Plautus, *Captivi*, cited 12 n. 3

plebeians, 216, 217 n. 2, 223–225, 227, 228, 230, 233, 234

πλεκταί, 200

Pliny, *Natural History*, cited 17 n. 3, 40 n. 9, 44 n. 1, 68 n. 1, 70 n. 3, 71 n. 2, 80 n. 6, 87 n. 1, 122 n. 4, 129 n. 7, 135 n. 4, 146, 171 n. 3, 172 n. 5, 186 n. 1, n. 2, 211 n. 7, 215 n. 2, 217, 218, 220, 222 n. 3, 224 n. 5, 226 n. 3, 228 n. 1, n. 2, n. 4, 238 n. 3, 240 n. 2, 244 n. 1, 263 n. 5, 266, 275 n. 2, n. 5, 311 n. 1

πλοῖον, 269

Plotheia, 38, 41 n. 3, 45

ploughmen, 20

πλούσιοι, 269

Ploutis, Plontis (?), 269

Plutarch, 22, 39, 181, 183, 196, 269; Lives: *Agesilaus*, cited 20; *Aratus*, cited 336 n. 1; *Brutus*, cited 229 n. 2; *Cato Major*, cited 166 n. 6; *Cimon*, cited 50 n. 7, 59 n. 1; *Demetrius*, cited 93; *Demosthenes*, cited 12 n. 6; *Dio*, cited 284 n. 1; *Fabius Maximus*, cited 162 n. 1, 164 n. 1; *Lycurgus*, cited 336 n. 1; *Lysander*, cited 23, 58, 162 n. 1, 164 n. 1; *Nikias*, cited 12 n. 4, 151 n. 2; *Numa*, cited 160, 222; *Pericles*, cited 13 n. 3, 14, 15, 17, 49 n. 2, 70 n. 5; *Phocion*, cited 336 n. 1; *Poplicola*, cited 223 n. 5, 337 n. 5; *Romulus*, cited 238 n. 3; *Solon*, cited 12 n. 1, 13, 16 n. 5, 34 n. 4, 35 n. 1, n. 2, n. 5, 37 n. 6, 49 n. 3, 63 n. 3, 65 n. 6, 169 n. 1, 170 n. 4, 308, 309 n. 4, 328 n. 5; *Themistocles*, cited 46; *Theseus*, cited 16 n. 4, 329 n. 8; *Timoleon*, cited 302 n. 6, 336 n. 1; Moralia: *de Alexandri Magni Fortuna aut Virtute*, cited 158 n. 6; *Amatoriae Narrationes*, cited 180; *Amatorius*, cited 35 n. 2, 37 n. 6, 275 n. 1; *Apophthegmata Laconica*, cited 57 n. 5, 130 n. 4; *de Ei apud Delphos*, cited 189 n. 8; *de Exilio*, cited 168, 199 n. 5; *de Fortuna Romanorum*, cited 238 n. 3; *Instituta Laconica*, cited 336 n. 1; *de Iside et Osiride*, cited 100 n. 4, n. 8; *de Malignitate Herodoti*, cited 191 n. 3, 195 n. 1, 263 n. 5; *de Mulierum Virtutibus*, cited 49 n. 1, 123 n. 5, 140 n. 3, 278 n. 5, 279 n. 2; *Parallela*, cited 275 n. 2; *Paroemia*, cited 76 n. 6, 77 n. 2, n. 4; *Praecepta Gerendae Reipublicae*, cited 35 n. 2, 37 n. 6, 276 n. 3; *cum Principibus Philosophandum*, cited 276 n. 3; *de Pythio Oraculo*, cited 136 n. 3, 137 n. 1, 167; *Quaestiones Graecae*, cited 69 n. 3, n. 5, 144 n. 6, 145 n. 4, 264 n. 6, 268; *Quaestiones Romanae*, cited 337 n. 1, n. 5; *Regum et Imperatorum Apophthegmata*, cited 179 n. 1, 208 n. 4; *Septem Sapientum Conuiuium*, cited 104 n. 3, 124 n. 1, 191 n. 2, 195, 197, 198, 207 n. 3, 213 n. 4; *de Sera Numinis Vindicta*, cited 257 n. 3, 262 n. 4, 275 n. 1; *de Tranquillitate Animi*, cited 134 n. 4; *de Vita et Poesi Homeri*, cited 134 n. 2; *de Vitioso Pudore*, cited 95 n. 1

Poehlmann (R.), *Geschichte d. socialen Fragen u. des Socialismus i. d. antik. Welt*, cited 4 n. 2, 267, 269 n. 5; *Grundriss der griechischen Geschichte*, cited 37 n. 7, 192 n. 1, 304 n. 3

polemarch, 194, 196, 197, 258, 270, 273, 300, 327 n. 9

Polledrara, 119 n. 3

Pollux, cited 13 n. 5, 19, 54 n. 2, 57 n. 5, 129 n. 2, n. 7, 138 n. 1, 143 n. 3, 147 n. 3, 152 n. 1, 155 n. 2, 156 n. 1, 162 n. 1, 172 n. 2, n. 6, 175 n. 2, 199 n. 6, n. 7, n. 8, n. 9, 200 n. 2, 264, 282 n. 2, 320 n. 4, 326 n. 8, n. 9, 327, 328

πῶλος (coin), 57

Polyaenus, cited 10 n. 6, 20 n. 4, 51 n. 2, 52, 69 n. 5, 70 n. 2, 90 n. 1, 96 n. 4, 140 n. 3, 145 n. 3, 147 n. 5, 211 n. 6, 259 n. 2, 272 n. 1, 273, 274 n. 4, 275–278, 283 n. 3

Polybius, cited 45 n. 3, 189 n. 4, 196 n. 5, 209, 210, 215 n. 2, 216, 275 n. 2, 285 n. 4, 302 n. 6, 305, 306, 336 n. 1
Polycharmus, cited 103, 118, 119
Polycrates, 10, 14, 21, 24 n. 5, 31, 49, 62, chap. III *passim*, 123, 124, 169, 177, 215, 260 n. 5, 267, 270 n. 7, 292, 303 n. 2, 305
Pompey, 23, 32
Pontic amphorae, 246
"pony" (coin), 57
Pope, 304; see also papal
populares, 225
πόρνη, 139
Porphyrius, *de Antro Nympharum*, cited 201 n. 3
Porzio (G.), *I Cipselidi*, cited 27 n. 5, 31 n. 2, 192 n. 1, 194 n. 6, 196, 197 n. 4
Poseidon, 169 n. 2, 305
Postumius Tubertus, Postumii, 337
Potamos, Potamioi, 44 n. 3, 50
ποτήρια, 80
Potidaea, 190 n. 3
potteries, 21, 115, 207, 210, 214, 263
potters, 20, 139 n. 2, 186, 207–211, 217, 222, 243–246, 295, 323
potter's wheel, 186, 210
pottery, 34, 53, 87, 105–119, 121 n. 5, 139 n. 1, 163, 164, 167–170, 174, 175, 185–187, 200–203, 205–208, 210, 212 n. 8, 214, 241–245, 248, 251, 252, 255, 263, 287, 295, 314–325, 333–335
Pottier (E.), 245 n. 1; *Musée du Louvre, Catalogue des Vases Antiques*, cited 321 n. 4, n. 6; *Vases Antiques du Louvre* (Album), 242 n. 1, 255 n. 3, 335; *apud* Saglio, *Dict. d. Antiq.*, cited 201, 315 n. 2, 317 n. 1
Poulsen (F.), *Dipylongräber*, cited 315 n. 1, n. 3, 316 n. 7, 321; *Der Orient u. die frühgriechische Kunst*, cited 93 n. 3, n. 4, 112 n. 1, 119
praedives, 229
Praeneste, 219 n. 3, 238 n. 3
Prasiai, 330
Preller, *Archäologische Zeitung*, cited 198 n. 9
priest, 92, 272 n. 3, 303, 305
primores ciuitatis, 227
Prinz (H.), *Funde aus Naukratis*, cited 92 n. 2, 109, 110, 111 n. 2, 112 n. 2, n. 7, 113, 114 n. 2, 116 n. 4, n. 6, 117 n. 4, n. 5, 120 n. 1, n. 2, 123 n. 12, 212 n. 8, 315 n. 2, n. 5, 316 n. 4, n. 8, n. 10, 320 n. 6
private coinage, 141, 142, 143, 150, 152, 294
Procles of Epidaurus, 167
Proclus, *Comment. in Platonis Rempublicam*, cited 151 n. 4; *in Timaeum*, cited 16 n. 7
Prodicus, cited 19 n. 4
προστὰς τοῦ δήμου, προστάτης, 27, 271
Proto-Attic pottery, 92 n. 2, 113, 315, 318, 319, 321
Proto-Corinthian pottery, 109, 117, 163, 185, 186, 244 n. 1, 248, 249, 263, 315–319, 334
Protogenes, 286–288, 297
prytanis, 270
Psammetichus of Corinth, 212–214
Psammetichus (Psamtek) I of Egypt, chap. IV *passim*, 212, 214, 292, 293, 298, 299
Psammetichus II of Egypt, 88 n. 1, 90
Psammetichus III of Egypt, 88 n. 1
Psammetichus the Libyan, 92 n. 2
Psammetichus, priest, 212 n. 6
Psammetichus son of Theocles, 212
Psammouthis, see Psammetichus II
Psaumis, 10 n. 2
Psellus (M.), cited 313 n. 4
Ptah, 97, 98
Ptolemaic story, 102 n. 1
Ptolemies, 160, 203 n. 4
Ptolemy Keraunos, 284, 285
Ptolemy, *Geographike Syntaxis*, cited 122 n. 4, 179
Ptoon, Mt, 108 n. 2
Publicola (Valerius), 229 n. 1, 337
Punic Wars, 32, 233
Pylaimenes, 48
Pyrrhic War, 32
Pythaenetus, cited 167 n. 4
Pythagoras of Ephesus, 271, 272
Pythagoras of Samos, 69 n. 1
Pythes, 49, 140, 147 n. 1, 152, 293
Pytheus, 140; see also Pythes
Pythia, 144 n. 3
Pythian games, 260–262
Pytho, 137; see also Delphi
pyxides, 248

quarries, quarrying, 21, 224, 225, 230, 233, 237, 276, 295
Quirinal, 253, 254

INDEX

Radet (G.), *La Lydie et le Monde grec*, cited 2, 77 n. 3, 130 n. 1, n. 2, n. 3, 131, 132 n. 3, 133 n. 4, 134 n. 5, 135, 136, 138, 139 n. 2, 140, 141, 143 n. 3, 144, 145 n. 2, n. 3, n. 4, 146, 147 n. 3, 148, 273; *Revue des Universités du Midi*, cited 128 n. 1, 135, 143 n. 3, 159 n. 5
Ramsay (W. M.), *Journal of Hellenic Studies*, cited 147 n. 3
Ramses II, 87 n. 9, 101
Ramses III, 44 n. 5
Rayet (O.), *Monuments de l'Art Antique*, cited 240 n. 2, 253 n. 4
Red Figure pottery, 107 n. 4, 108, 204, 326 n. 3, 335
Red Sea, 87
Regling (K.), *apud* Pauly Wissowa, 148 n. 5, 156 n. 2, 162 n. 3
Regulini-Galassi tomb, 93 n. 3, 243, 335
Reinach (A. J.), *Journal des Savants*, cited 110 n. 8
Reinach (S.), *Chroniques d'Orient*, cited 147 n. 3; *Cultes, Mythes, et Religions*, cited 169; *Revue Archéologique*, cited 70 n. 3
Reinach (Th.), *L'Histoire par les Monnaies*, cited 128 n. 1, 129 n. 3, 130 n. 2, 159 n. 5, 172 n. 4; *Revue Numismatique*, cited 161 n. 2, 162 n. 3
Renaissance, 3, 32, 286
Revillout (E.), *Précis du droit égyptien*, cited 93 n. 2; *Les Rapports historiques et légaux des Quirites et des Égyptiens*, cited 93 n. 4; *Revue Égyptologique*, cited 102 n. 1, n. 2, 123 n. 7; *Society of Biblical Archaeology Proceedings*, cited 123 n. 7
Revue Archéologique, see Dumont, Reinach (S.), Torr
Revue de l'Instruction Publique en Belgique, see Brants
Revue des Universités du Midi, see Radet
Revue Égyptologique, see Revillout
Revue d'Ethnologie et de Sociologie, see Macfie
Revue Historique, see Waltz
Revue Numismatique, see Babelon, Reinach (Th.)
rex, 303
Rhagon, 38
Rhegium, 74, 75, 210
Rheinisches Museum f. Philologie, see Beloch, Gelzer, Hirschfeld, Holwerda, Koehler, Meyer (E.), Ruehl
Rheneia, 70, 71, 112
Rhitsona (Mykalessos), 106-108, 109 n. 4, 110, 113 n. 1, 114, 248, 335
Rhodes, 109, 112, 114, 119 n. 3, 171 n. 1, 187 n. 4
Rhodian pottery, see Milesian pottery
Rhodopis, 56 n. 3, 68
Rhoecus, 69 n. 1, 76, 80 n. 6
de Ridder (E.), *de Ectypis quibusdam aeneis quae falso uocantur Argiuo-Corinthiaca*, cited 316 n. 9
Ridgeway (W.), *Origin of Metallic Currency and Weight Standards*, cited 132 n. 3, 148 n. 6, 150, 160, 170-172; *Companion to Greek Studies*, cited 128 n. 2, 150 n. 5; *Journal of Hellenic Studies*, cited 172; *Numismatic Chronicle*, cited 129 n. 7
ring of Gyges, 145-152, 293; of Midas, 146, 151; of Minos, 169; of Polycrates, 70 n. 3, 83, 169; of Venetian doge, 169; rings as money, 148, 149, 171 n. 1, 293; rings (seal), 150
Riviera, 312
Rivista di Storia Antica, see Costanzi
Rizzo (G. E.), 245 n. 1; *Bullettino della Commissione Archeologica Municipale di Roma*, cited 243 n. 4, 244, 246, 247
road makers, 14
roads, 130, 136, 190 n. 3, 232, 233, 273
Roberts (E. S.), *Introduction to Greek Epigraphy*, cited 106 n. 7, 123 n. 9
Rockefellers, 12
Roemische Mitteilungen, see *Mitteilungen des deutschen archäologischen Instituts in Rom*
Rohde (E.), *Psyche*, cited 336 n. 1
Roland, 193 n. 7
Rome, Romans, 12 n. 3, 14, 15 n. 6, 20 n. 2, 22 n. 2, 23, 25, 32, 63 n. 4, 65 n. 3, 149, 160, 162 n. 3, 183 n. 6, 207, 211, chap. VIII *passim*, 261 n. 2, 277, 278, 287-289, 295, 296, 298, 303, 336-338
Roman Empire, 139 n. 2, 232; Emperors, 60, 303
Romulus, 197, 198, 209, 221 n. 7, 239 n. 5
rope makers, 14
Roscher (W. H.), *Lexikon*, cited 336 n. 2
de Rougé (E.), *Inscription Historique du roi Pianchi Mériamoun*, cited

96 n. 2; *Notice de quelques textes hiéroglyphiques récemment publiés par M. Greene*, cited 99 n. 3, n. 4; (ed. J. de Rougé) *Chrestomathie Égyptienne*, cited 95 n. 3
de Rougé (J.), *Étude sur les textes géographiques du temple d'Edfou*, cited 99 n. 3
royal road, great road, 130, 136, 273
Rud Amen, see Ammeris
Ruehl, *Rheinisches Museum*, cited 56 n. 2
Rufous (or Eastern) Swallow, 211 n. 4
Russia, 1, 110, 112 n. 1, 114, 142, 287
Rylands Library, Manchester, *Catalogue of Greek Papyri*, cited 66 n. 2; *Catalogue of the Demotic Papyri*, see Griffith

Sabacon (Shabaka), 88 n. 1, 93, 96, 97
Sacred War, 65, 66, 247 n. 2, 258 n. 4, 259–261, 264
Sadyattes, King, 145 n. 3
Sadyattes, merchant, 137, 138, 152
Saglio (E.), *Dictionnaire des Antiquités grecques et romaines*, cited 44 n. 5, 46 n. 7, 56 n. 4, 142 n. 4, 162 n. 3, 201 n. 2, 203, 222 n. 6, 315 n. 2, 317 n. 1
sailors, 14
Sais, 87–89, 96, 98, 100, 102 n. 1, 104, 120 n. 3, 123, 124
Saite dynasty, 88, 95, 97, 99–103, 105, 121–124, 125 n. 3, 212, 214, 293
Salamis, 26, 29 n. 1, 166 n. 2, 168, 326 n. 3, 328
von Sallet (A.), *Zeitschrift f. Numismatik*, cited 75 n. 1
Sallust, cited 324 n. 5
Salonika, 190 n. 3
Salvioli (G.) (French translation by Bonnet (A.)), *Le Capitalisme dans le Monde Antique*, cited 5, 230 n. 3, n. 5
Samaina, 70, 74, 75, 84
Samnite War, 32
Samos, Samians, 14, 21, 33, 49, chap. III *passim*, 86, 110, 112, 116, 117, 124, 150 n. 6, 151, 177, 178, 215, 251, 266 n. 1, 267, 292, 324 n. 6, 325, 326
Samian pottery, see Fikellura
Samtavi Tafnekht, 100
Samwer (C.), *Geschichte des älteren roemischen Münzwesens*, cited 219 n. 1

De Sanctis (G.), *Atthis*[3], cited 34 n. 2, 51 n. 4, 328, 329; *Journal des Savants*, cited 249
Sandys (J.), ed. 'Αθηναίων Πολιτεία[2], cited 35 n. 2, 37 n. 7
Sappho, 56 n. 3, 104, 120
sarcophagus, 246 n. 7
Sardis, 1, 33, 58, 76, 83, 129–131, 135, 138 n. 9, 139, 140, 152, 187, 191 n. 3, 273
Sargon of Akkad, 197
Saronic Gulf, 169 n. 4, 182, 329–331
satni (title), 97
Satni Khamois, 97, 100–102
Satni Tafnekhte, 102
Satrai, 59 n. 1
satrap, satrapy, 83, 132, 270 n. 7
Satricum (Conca), 219 n. 4, 246
Satyrus, cited 156
Saulmugina, 99 n. 3
Saxon, see Anglo-Saxon
Sayce (A. H.), ed. Herodotus, cited 87 n. 11, 89 n. 3, 90 n. 1, 91 n. 4; *Encyclopaedia Britannica*, cited 197 n. 5
Scandinavian, 238 n. 1
scarabs, 105, 106, 109, 118 n. 2, 119 n. 3, 124
Schiaparelli, *Monumenti Antichi*, cited 93 n. 3, n. 4
Schoemann (G. F.), *de Comitiis Atheniensium*, cited 40 n. 5; *Jahrbücher f. Classische Philologie*, cited 326 n. 6, 328 n. 3, 329
Scholia, see under authors concerned
Schow (N.), ed. Hesychius, cited 312 n. 2
Schrader (E.), *Cuneiform Inscriptions and the Old Testament*, cited 98 n. 3
Schubert (R.), *Geschichte der Könige von Lydien*, cited 135 n. 4, 138 n. 7, 144, 145 n. 4; *Geschichte des Agathokles*, cited 209 n. 3, n. 4, 210 n. 2, n. 4
Schubring (J.), *de Cypselo Corinthiorum tyranno*, cited 194 n. 3, 196 n. 5, 197, 198 n. 9, 199 n. 10, 211
Schweighaeuser (J.), ed. Athenaeus, cited 270 n. 2
Schweinfurth (G.), see Erman
Scotland, 162
sculptors, sculpture, 14, 53 n. 2, 81, 101, 128, 206, 228 n. 3, n. 4, 252, 253, 263, 285, 302
Scyllis, 263 n. 5
(Pseudo-) Scymnus, cited 91 n. 1

INDEX

Scythia, 72, 271
sea power, 68, 70–73, 81–83, 87, 95–97, 103, 165, 168, 169, 177, 184, 321–331; see also thalassocracy
seals, 149–151
secessions, 227, 233, 235 n. 2, 296
Seeck (O.), *Klio*, cited 34 n. 2, 53 n. 2, 56 n. 2
Seeley (J.), ed. Livy I, cited 246 n. 1
Segesta, 80 n. 5; see also Egestaeans
Seleucus, Seleucids, 284, 285
Selinus, 265
Sem of Ptah, 98, 100
Semachos, Semacheion, Semachidai, 38, 39, 41 n. 3, 50, 291
σήμαντρον, 150
Semites, 278 n. 2
Semitic origin of χιτών, 333 n. 2
Sennacherib, 92, 97, 100, 325
serfs, 13, 24
Servilius Ahala, 230
Servius, *ad Vergil. Aeneid.*, cited 224 n. 5, 238 n. 3, 311 n. 1, 336, 337 n. 1
Servius Tullius, 218–223, 224 n. 5, 238 n. 2, n. 3, 245, 246, 249, 295
seruus rex, 249
Sethon, Sethos, 88 n. 1, 92, 93, 97–103, 105 n. 2, 292, 293, 303 n. 1
Seti I, 87 n. 9
setmi, 97
Seven against Thebes, 262
seven sages, 189
Sevenoaks, 125 n. 3
Shabaka, see Sabacon
Shabataka, 88 n. 1, 97, 98 n. 3, n. 4, 125 n. 3
Sharpe (S.), *History of Egypt*⁶, cited 121 n. 3
sheep breeding, 266
shekel, 132, 133
Shelley (P. B.), trans. Euripides, *Cyclops*, cited 40 n. 9
Shepnepet, 99 n. 3
shipbuilders, shipbuilding, 20, 62, 68, 70, 75, 184, 271, 292, 309, 324, 325, 326
ships, 164, 169, 242, 315 n. 3, 317
shires, 237
shoemakers, 20, 233 n. 6
shops, 135, 218, 224, 247
Sicily, Sicilian, 10, 30, 45, 75, 80 n. 5, 112, 180 n. 4, 181, 182, 187, 189, 209, 220, 228, 239, 265, 273–278, 284 n. 2, 315
Siceliot Greek, 224 n. 5

Sicyon, 28, 66, 157, 178–180, 186 n. 1, 193, 215, 257–264 *passim*, 293, 296, 304, 306 n. 1, 316, 317, 336 n. 1
Sidonians, 325
Sieveking (H.), *Vierteljahrschrift f. Social- u. Wirtschafts-Geschichte*, cited 3, 26 n. 2, 267 n. 1, 304 n. 4
Sieveking (J.) and Hackl (R.), *Die königliche Vasensammlung zu Muenchen*, cited 251 n. 3, 252 n. 2, 334
Sigeium, 63
Sigismund, Emperor, 3
signauit, 218
silphium, 74 n. 3
silver, 80 n. 4, 81, 144 n. 3, 177, 227; currency, 4, 18, 57, 58, 61, 127, 128, 131–133, 140, 152, 155, 164 n. 1, 172, 218, 219, 220 n. 4, 221, 294; mines, 38–40, 47, 54 n. 1, 59 n. 1, 62, 68, 271, 291; see also Laurium
Sinope, 50, 135 n. 7, 271
Siphnos, 243 n. 1
Siphnian mines, 44 n. 5, 46, 47
Sipylus, Mt, 129
σιτοφύλακες, 12
Sitzungsberichte d. preussischen Akademie d. Wissenschaften zu Berlin, see Koehler, Wiegand
Sitzungsberichte d. bayerischen Akademie d. Wissenschaften zu Muenchen, see Wecklein
Sitzungsberichte d. Akademie d. Wissenschaften in Wien, see Bauer, Klein
Six (J.), *Numismatic Chronicle*, cited 53 n. 1, 56 n. 2, 64, 128 n. 4, 131
Skabala (? Kavalla), 37
Skapte Hyle, 50 n. 7
Skias (A.), *Archaiologike Ephemeris*, cited 324 n. 1, 333 n. 4
Skiddaw, 40
skyphoi, 248, 334
slaves, slavery, slave labour, 12, 13, 15, 18–23, 30 n. 3, 45, 47 n. 7, 48, 51, 67, 79, 150 n. 6, 151 n. 2, 187 n. 8, 191, 192, 218, 222–225, 234, 235, 266, 280–282, 284, 287; see also helots, πενέσται, serfs, thetes
slave revolts, 23, 45, 234 n. 3
smelting, 44, 48
Smith (G.), *Assurbanipal*, cited 88 n. 2, 91 n. 7, 99 n. 3, 101 n. 2, 143 n. 2, 144 n. 5, 214 n. 3
Smith (K. F.), *American Journal of Philology*, cited 147 n. 6, 148 n. 4

U. T.   24

Smith (W.), *Dictionary of Greek and Roman Biography and Mythology*, cited 336 n. 5
smiths, 14, 17, 20, 223, 225
Smyrna, 77, 130, 131
Snooks, Mrs, 125 n. 3
Snowdon, 40
Society of Biblical Archaeology Proceedings, see Revillout
Sociological Review, see Zimmern
Socrates, 17, 18, 19 n. 4
Soli, 158
Solon, 7, 8, 9, 12, 13, 16, 17, 28, 33–35, 49, 53 n. 2, 63 n. 3, 65, 95 n. 1, 150 n. 3, 158, 166, 170–172, 258 n. 4, 261, 290, 301, 303 n. 1, 308, 309 n. 4, 327, 328; cited 7, 8, 9 n. 3, 14, 28 n. 1, 48, 55
Solonium, 239 n. 5
Sophanes, 174
Sophocles, *Antigone*, cited 129; *Oedipus Tyrannus*, cited 9, 174 n. 3; fragments cited 16 n. 7, 313
Sosias, 51
Sostratos, 68, 177
Σουνιικὸς γουνός, 41, 44
Sourdille (C.), *Hérodote et la Religion d'Égypte*, cited 98 n. 3
σῴζω, 82
Spain, 1, 46, 68, 117, 177
Sparta, Spartans, 20, 23–25, 45, 53, 57, 63 n. 4, 74 n. 5, 84, 144 n. 4, 164 n. 1, 175–177, 178 n. 4, 180, 196 n. 5, 239, 263 n. 5, 282, 330, 332, 333, 336 n. 1
Spartacus, 23
Spermos, 135, 136, 152, 293
σφραγίς, 149
Spiegelberg, *Orientalische Litteraturzeitung*, cited 125 n. 3
spits as coins, 149, 162–164
Spurius Cassius, see Cassius
Spurius Maelius, see Maelius
Staffordshire, 80 n. 6
Stais (V.), 318
Stallbaum (G.), *Platonis Meno*, cited 85 n. 1
Standard Oil Company, 5, 26
stater, 57, 130, 132 n. 3, 137; see also daric, Croeseids
σταθμός, 171
Statius, *Thebais*, cited 308, 309
statuettes (figurines), 118, 119
Stein (H.), ed. Herodotus, cited 51 n. 3
στέφανος, στεφανόπωλις, στεφανηφόρος ἥρως, 55–57

Stephanus Byzantinus, cited 37, 38 n. 4, 40 n. 2, 41 n. 3, 68 n. 7, 96 n. 4, 103, 104, 135 n. 3, 212 n. 1, 313
Stephinates, 88 n. 1, 98, 99, 100
von Stern (E.), *Zeitschrift f. aegyptische Sprache*, cited 125 n. 3
Stesichorus, 275 n. 4; cited 177 n. 6
stm, stne, 97
stone masons, 14, 224
stove, 204, 205
Strabo, cited 40, 41 n. 3, n. 4, 54 n. 1, 59 n. 2, 63 n. 7, 65 n. 5, 70 n. 3, 71 n. 2, 79 n. 2, 80, 84 n. 2, 87 n. 9, 90, 91, 92 n. 2, 103, 104 n. 4, 122 n. 1, n. 4, 129 n. 6, 138 n. 3, n. 4, 139, 146 n. 7, 148, 149 n. 1, 155 n. 2, 157 n. 2, 158, 159, 167 n. 2, 175 n. 3, 176, 177 n. 3, 178, 179, 180 n. 4, 183 n. 2, 184, 187 n. 1, 189 n. 4, 190 n. 3, 191 n. 3, 192 n. 5, 195 n. 1, 198, 215 n. 2, 217, 224 n. 5, 225, 240 n. 1, 246 n. 1, 255, 257 n. 1, 259 n. 5, 260 n. 4, 261 n. 2, 280 n. 1, 282 n. 2, 283 n. 6, 284 n. 3, n. 5, 288, 289 n. 1, 305 n. 2, 310 n. 3, 312 n. 3, n. 6, 313 n. 2, n. 6, 324 n. 2, 330, 336 n. 1
Strack (M. L.), see Muenzer
Strattis, 50 n. 2
στρωμναί, 79
Strymodorus, 59 n. 1
Strymon (Struma), 36, 37, 50, 54, 58, 59, 62, 148
Studniczka (F.), *Athenische Mitteilungen*, cited 318 n. 6; *Beiträge zur Geschichte der altgriech. Tracht*, cited 166 n. 1, n. 7, 170 n. 1, 332 n. 2, 333 n. 2
Suetonius, cited 221 n. 7; *Caligula*, cited 76 n. 4; *Tiberius*, cited 233, 337 n. 6
Suez Canal, 87
Suidas, cited 16 n. 7, 41 n. 3, 50 n. 2, 58 n. 1, 59 n. 1, 70 n. 5, 71 n. 1, 74, 75, 79 n. 1, n. 2, 95 n. 1, 104 n. 4, 137 n. 3, 145 n. 1, n. 6, 171 n. 4, 189, 195 n. 5, 199 n. 2, n. 3, n. 5, n. 8, 200 n. 3, 201 n. 2, 221 n. 7, 224 n. 5, 226 n. 3, 268 n. 3, 269, 271 n. 5, 272, 275 n. 5, 280 n. 1, 281 n. 1, 283 n. 5, n. 6, 305 n. 2, 313, 326 n. 9, 327 n. 2
σύλη, συλον, 81, 82
Sunium, 40, 41, 44, 291, 313
Superbus, see Tarquinius Superbus
Susemihl (F.), 213 n. 4
Svoronos, *Journal International d'Ar-*

chéologie Numismatique, cited 37, 53 n. 2, 60 n. 1, 62 n. 2, 64 n. 3, 156 n. 2, 160, 163, 171 n. 1, 183 n. 6
swallow, 211 n. 4, n. 7
Swansea, 106 n. 3
Swoboda (H.), *apud* Pauly Wissowa, 268 n. 4
Sybaris, 112, 266
Syloson, 69 n. 5, 79, 80, 82, 84
symmories, 328 n. 2
Symonds (J. A.), *Renaissance in Italy, Age of the Despots*, cited 3
Syncellus, cited 95, 156 n. 3
Syracuse, 10, 24, 27, 30, 58, 72, 138 n. 9, 151, 180, 182, 208–210, 221, 274 n. 1, 276, 278 n. 2, 280, 284, 291, 316 n. 8
Syria, 99 n. 3, 123, 131

Tabalos, 139
Tacitus, *Annals*, cited 311 n. 1; *Histories*, cited 223 n. 5
Tafnekht, see Tnefachthus
Taharqa (Tirhakah), 88 n. 1, 97, 98, 99 n. 3, n. 5
tailors, 20
Tanaquil, 236 n. 2
Tanis, 121 n. 3
tanners, 20, 222
Tarbell (I. M.), *History of the Standard Oil Company*, cited 5 n. 8
Tarchon, 237 n. 1
Tarentum, 336 n. 1
Tarpeian Mount, Tarpeius, 223, 237
Tarquinii (Corneto), 93, 94, 182, 187, 215–219, 225, 240–243, 244 n. 1, 249, 251
Tarquinius (name), 237
Tarquinius Priscus, Lucius, 215–218, 221, 222 n. 7, 224 n. 5, 227–229, 238, 239 n. 5, 240, 242, 256, 287, 295, 299
Tarquinius Superbus, 183 n. 6, 218, 223–227, 233, 234 n. 3, 247, 251, 278, 295
Tarquins, 14, 207, 215, 218, 223, 224 n. 5, 225–227, 230, 233, 234, 236, 237, 239, 240, 245, 247, 249, 255, 256, 289, 295, 296, 298
Tartessus (Tarshish), 68, 69, 81, 82, 177
taxation, taxes, 189, 190, 192 n. 1, 259, 287
tax-collector, 274, 305, 326 n. 9, 327 n. 1
τέχνη, 49
τεχνῖται, 21

Tefnakhte, see Tnefachthus
Tegea, 24 n. 1
Τειχιούσης, 81
Teisias, 106
Tellus, 228 n. 2
Temenos, 154, 156–159, 176, 178–180, 183 n. 3, 294, 316
temple, 162, 224, 277; in Aegina (Aphaia), 318–320; (Aphrodite), 318, 319; (Damia and Auxesia), 167, 170, 174, 175, 320; Agrigentum (Zeus Polieus), 274, 276; Argos (Hera), 161–164, 175, 316 n. 7, 318–320, 333 n. 4; Athens (Athena), 63; (Olympian Zeus), 14, 63, 76 n. 5; Corcyra, 244 n. 1; Corinth (Aphrodite), 191 n. 3; (Apollo), 76 n. 5; Delphi (Apollo), 65; Eleusis, 15; Ephesus (Artemis), 128, 130 n. 6, 245, 272 n. 3; Naukratis, 108; (Aphrodite), 118, 119; (Apollo), 110; Olympia, 159; Pallene in Attica (Athena), 52; Rome (Artemis, Diana), 224 n. 5, 245, 246 n. 1; (Ceres), 240 n. 2; (Jupiter Tarpeius), 223, 237; (Tellus), 228 n. 2; Sabine (Feronia), 261 n. 2; in Samos (Hera), 76, 82; Syracuse (Athena), 276; Tiryns (Hera), 320
Tenedos, 162 n. 3
tent-makers, 17
terra cottas, architectural, 243, 244 n. 1, 246, 250–252; see also antefix
terra cotta tablets, 46, 186, 187, 207 n. 2, 242
Terrien de la Couperie (A.), see *British Museum Catalogue of Chinese Coins*
Tertullian, *Apologia adversus Gentes*, cited 280 n. 1
tetradrachm, 131
Tetrapolis, 41 n. 3
Thackeray (W. M.), *Virginians*, cited 157 n. 4
thalassocracy, 76, 83, 95, 96, 165 n. 3, 174, 191 n. 2, 268 n. 3, 324, 330; see also sea power
Thales, 1, 2, 12
Thasos, Thasians, 36 n. 3, 47, 271 n. 4
Theagenes, 9, 14, 30, 62 n. 6, 76 n. 5, 264–268, 296
Thebais (Homeric), 262 n. 1
Thebes, Boeotian, 24 n. 5, 108 n. 2, 164 n. 1, 261, 262
Thebes, Egyptian, 90 n. 1, 97, 99 n. 3
Themistius, *Orations*, cited 65 n. 5

Themistocles, 46, 47, 239 n. 4, 312 n. 5
Theocharides, 273
Theocles, 212
Theocritus, cited 69 n. 2, 79, 201 n. 8, 280 n. 1
Theodorus, 69 n. 1, 73, 76, 80, 83
Theognis, 7–9, 16 n. 2, 195 n. 5, 268, 290; cited 8, 9, 47 n. 2, 57 n. 5, 266, 302
Theomestor, 84
Theophrastus, 189; *Historia Plantarum*, cited 56 n. 2, 308 n. 2; *de Lapidibus*, cited 129 n. 7
Theopompus, cited 144 n. 3, 156, 158 n 6, 195 n. 2
Thera, Theraeans, 82 n. 1, 315 n. 2, 320 n. 5
θεράπαιναι, 22
Thero, 10 n. 1
Thersites, 28 n. 1
Theseus, 16, 169, 327, 329
Thesmophoria, 274
Thessalos, 56 n. 2
Thessaly, 24, 193
thetes, θῆτες, θητικὸς ὄχλος, 14, 16, 19, 49
Thiersch (H.), see Furtwaengler
Thirlwall (C.), *History of Greece*, cited 51 n. 3
Thoas of Miletus, 268, 269
Thomas (E.), *Ancient Indian Weights*, cited 142 n. 3; *Chronicles of the Pathan Kings of Delhi*, cited 142 n. 3
Thonis, 93
Thoricus, 40 n. 9, 41, 44 n. 1
Thrace, 36 n. 1, n. 3, 37, 50–52, 54–56, 58–62, 64, 72, 199–201, 271, 284, 288, 291, 292, 296
Thracian Chersonese, 53, 63 n. 7, 199 n. 10, 245 n. 2
Thrasybulus, 124, 191, 268–270
Thucydides, 25, 26, 33, 290, 299; cited 9, 15 n. 2, 23 n. 1, n. 2, 24 n. 2, n. 4, 28 n. 5, 30 n. 3, 31 n. 1, 34 n. 3, 36 n. 1, 45 n. 5, 50, 51 n. 2, 62 n. 5, 63 n. 6, 68 n. 1, 70, 80 n. 5, 170, 174, 177, 178 n. 1, 180 n. 4, 184, 185, 190 n. 3, 193 n. 7, 212 n. 1, 260 n. 2, 264 n. 6, 294, 308 n. 2, 310, 313, 321, 325, 326, 329 n. 8, 331–334, 336 n. 1
Thyessos, 135
Tiber, 197, 221
Tilden (Mr), 5
Tillyard (H. J. W.), *Agathocles*, cited 209 n. 2, n. 3, 210 n. 1, n. 4
Tilsit, 311

Timaeus of Cyzicus, 281, 283, 288
Timaeus of Sicily, 210; cited 22, 209, 220, 275 n. 2
Timarchus, 12
timber, 62, 271
Times, cited 5
Timoleon, 209
Tintoretto, 244
Tirhakah, see Taharqa
Tiryns, 163, 318
Tmolus, Mount, 129, 148
Tnefachthus I (Tafnekht), 88 n. 1, 95, 96, 98, 100, 101 n. 1
Tnefachthus II, 88 n. 1
Torr, *Revue Archéologique*, cited 169, 321 n. 2, n. 3, n. 4, 324 n. 5
"tortoises" (coins), 57 n. 5, 64 n. 3, 143 n. 1, 154, 156, 183 n. 6
touch-stone, 129
trade unions, 3
treasuries at Delphi (Corinthian, Caeretan), 187 n. 8, 255
treasury at Olympia (Sicyonian), 263
Triakon, 176 n. 3
trial by jury, 237
tribunes, military, 338
Trinakria, 44
Triptolemus, 238
triremes, 68, 165, 177, 191, 239, 325
Tritonis (Lake), 54, 55
Troezen, 169 n. 4
Trojan wars, 180 n. 4, 259 n. 1
Troy, 149, 298
trusts, 3, 5
Truth's Investigator, *The Great Oil Octopus*, cited 5 n. 8
Tudors, 101, 267
Tullianum, see Mamertine prison
Tullus Hostilius, 261 n. 2, 337
τυραννὶς τελευταία, 29
τύραννος, 134, 302 n. 8
Turkey, 50, 270
Twelve Tables, 221, 336
Tyburn, 247
Tyrrhenians, 134 n. 5
Tyrrhenian amphora, 319
Tzetzes, *Chiliades*, cited 70 n. 3, 79 n. 4, 87 n. 9, 134 n. 5, 176 n. 3; *ad Lycophronem*, cited 59 n. 1, 195 n. 2, n. 3

unemployment, 13 n. 5
Unger, *Philologus*, cited 159, 160, 183 n. 5
United States of America, 4, 5, 142, 267
University College, Oxford, 237

INDEX

Ure (P. N.), *Black Glaze Pottery from Rhitsona in Boeotia*, cited 108 n. 1, n. 6, 248 n. 3, 287 n. 3; *Journal of Hellenic Studies*, cited 38, 81, 155; see also Burrows (R. M.)
Usimares, pharaoh of Egypt, 101
usurers, 2

Valerii, 337; see also Publicola
Valerius (Marcus), 227
Valerius Maximus, cited 17 n. 3, 35 n. 3, 51 n. 2, 70 n. 3, 184 n. 2, 217 n. 5, 228 n. 1, n. 2, n. 4, 229 n. 2, 233, 275 n. 1, 337 n. 4
Varro, *de Lingua Latina*, cited 218 n. 3, 224 n. 5, 229 n. 2, 237, 248 n. 1; *de Re Rustica*, cited 201 n. 5, n. 6, n. 8; *apud* Charisium, cited 218; *apud* Nonium Marcellum, cited 223 n. 1; (?) *apud* Plutarchum, cited 222 n. 3
Vasco da Gama, 87
Vedic, 134 n. 5
Veii, 230, 234, 235, 296
Velabrum, 12 n. 3
Velia, near Paestum, 221 n. 2; in Rome, 221 n. 2, 337 n. 5
Velletri, 246
Venice, 56 n. 3, 70 n. 3
Verrius Flaccus, cited 134 n. 5
Verviers, 311
Vestal virgins, 336 n. 1, 337
Vetterfeld, 171 n. 1
Via Appia, 232, 233
Victoria, Queen, 157 n. 4
Victorian age, 194
Vicus Tuscus, 221 n. 2
Vierteljahrschrift f. Social- u. Wirtschafts-Geschichte, see Cavaignac, Sieveking (H.)
Vignate, Giovanni, 3
Virgil, *Aeneid*, cited 238 n. 3, 311 n. 1; Schol. Veron. 238 n. 3
"Virgin" (coin), 54–57, 291
Vitruvius, cited 13 n. 5
Vittorio Emanuele monument, 65 n. 3
Volsinii, 249
Vourva pottery, 315 n. 5, 318 n. 1
Vroulia, 109, 114
Vulci, 119 n. 3, 251 n. 1

Wachsmuth (C.), *Die Stadt Athen*, cited 269 n. 2, 327 n. 5, 329 n. 4
wages, 14, 15, 18, 20, 21, 48, 49, 77, 226, 230, 295
waggoners, 14

Waldstein (C.), *Argive Heraeum*, cited 317 n. 3, 318, 319 n. 5, n. 6, n. 7, 320 n. 2
Walker (A.), 187 n. 2
Wallon (H.), *Histoire de l'Esclavage dans l'Antiquité*, cited 16 n. 8, 23 n. 1, 47 n. 7
Walter (F. A.), trans. Niebuhr, *History of Rome*, cited 239 n. 2
Walters (H. B.), see *British Museum Catalogue of Terracottas*
Walters (H. B.) and Birch (S.), *History of Ancient Pottery*, cited 323 n. 2
Waltz (P.), *Revue Historique*, cited 22 n. 6
Walzius, *Rhetores Graeci*, cited 51 n. 2
Watson (Mr), 11 n. 2
weaving, 187
Webb (S.), *History of Trade Unionism*, cited 233 n. 6
Wecklein, *Sitzungsberichte d. bayerisch. Akad. d. Wissenschaften zu Muenchen*, cited 269 n. 2, 326 n. 7, 327 n. 5, 329 n. 8
Wedgwood, 80 n. 6
Weissenborn (H.), *Hellen*, cited 159 n. 2
Welldon (J. E. C.), trans. Aristotle, *Politics*, quoted 35 n. 5
Wells (H. G.), 125 n. 3; *Anticipations*, cited 306; *Tono Bungay*, cited 306 n. 5
Westminster, 306 n. 5
wheel-wrights, 14, 20
Whiskey Combination, 267
Wiedemann (A.), *Aegyptische Geschichte*, cited 91 n. 4, 95 n. 1, 97 n. 4, 99 n. 5, 125 n. 3, 212 n. 6; *Geschichte Aegyptens*, 122 n. 4; *Herodotus II*, cited 87 n. 9, 89 n. 3, 90 n. 4, 91 n. 9, 102 n. 1, 104 n. 6, 106 n. 8, 122 n. 1, n. 4, n. 5, 214 n. 5
Wiegand (Th.), *Abhandlungen* and *Sitzungsberichte d. preussisch. Akademie d. Wissenschaften zu Berlin*, cited 76 n. 2, 110 n. 4, 111 n. 3
Wiener Studien, see Endt
Wiener Vorlegeblätter, cited 323 n. 2
von Wilamowitz-Moellendorf (U.), *Aristotel u. Athen*, cited 173 n. 2, 329 n. 7
Wilisch (E.), *Eumelus*, cited 195 n. 2, n. 4; *Goettingsche Gelehrte Anzeigen*, cited 180 n. 3, 191 n. 3, 194, 195 n. 1, 196 n. 4; *Jahresbericht d. Gymnas. Zittau*, cited 46 n. 7, 187 n. 7, 188 n. 1, 191 n. 3, 192 n. 1,

n. 4, 242 n. 3; *Jahrbücher f. Classische Philologie*, cited 180 n. 2, 183 n. 5
Willers (H.), *Geschichte der roemischen Kupferprägung*, cited 156 n. 2, 171 n. 6, 219
Wilson, President Woodrow, cited 5, 290
Wimmer (F.), see Aubert
Winckelmannsfeste Program, see Furtwaengler
Winckler (H.), *Altorientalische Forschungen*, cited 143 n. 2
wine trade, 104, 120, 125, 126, 143 n. 1, 286
Winter (F.), *Jahrbuch d. deutsch. archäologischen Instituts*, cited 205 n. 1
Wisbech, 233 n. 6
Wochenschrift f. klassische Philologie, see Bluemner, Graef
wolf, Capitoline, 253, 254
women in industry, 20 n. 1; political status of, 236 n. 2
woollen industry, 2, 3, 21, 69, 74, 79, 265–267, 292
"working girls," 139
Wyttenbach, 158 n. 3

Xanthias, 68
Xanthus, cited 130 n. 2, 144 n. 1
Xenophanes, cited 129, 131, 133
Xenophon, *Anabasis*, cited 265 n. 6; *Cyropaedia*, cited 123 n. 3, 144 n. 4; *Hellenica*, cited 20 n. 4, 27 n. 5, 148 n. 2; *Hiero*, cited 302 n. 6; *Memorabilia*, cited 13 n. 3, 17, 18 n. 1, 20 n. 1, 265 n. 3, 267; *Oeconomicus*, cited 17, 19 n. 4; *de Republica Lacedaemoniorum*, cited 17; *de Vectigalibus*, cited 12 n. 4, 18, 44 n. 1, 46, 47, 51 n. 1, 150 n. 6, 308 n. 2, 310
Xerxes, 24 n. 5, 140, 152, 293, 332
ξυλίνη κιβωτός, 198

Year's Work in Classical Studies, see Lamb (D.)
Young Turks, 270

Zeitschrift f. aegyptische Sprache, see v. Stern
Zeitschrift f. Numismatik, see Brandis, v. Fritze, Hammer, v. Sallet
Zeitschrift f. Socialwissenschaft, see Beloch
Zenobius, cited 71 n. 1, 73, 78 n. 7, 79 n. 2, 95 n. 1, 308 n. 3
zeugitai, 16, 49
Zeus, 138 n. 9, 198, 303; Olympios, temple of, 14, 63, 76 n. 5; Patroos, altars of, 180; Polieus, temple of, 274, 276
Zimmern (A. E.), *Greek Commonwealth*, cited 309 n. 9; *Sociological Review*, cited 15 n. 5, 20 n. 6
Zonaras, cited 215 n. 2, 223 n. 5, 337 n 4.
Zopyrion, 287

LaVergne, TN USA
14 April 2010
179274LV00004B/6/A